THE
WEBSTER'S
DICTIONARY

1994 EDITION

Published by PSI & Associates, Inc.
13322 SW 128th Street, Miami, FL 33186
(305) 255-7959

INCLUDES
NEW
COMPUTER
SECTION

"The Webster's Dictionary is not associated with, or published by, the original publishers of Webster's Dictionary or their successors."

Copyright © **MCMLXXIX** Ottenhiemer Publishers, Inc.;
Updated 1994 PSI & Associates, Inc.

Cover design by; 1994 Barbara Baron.

Published by; PSI & Associates, Inc.

ISBN# 1-22993-294-5

How to Use This Dictionary

example: **ăd-mīre',** v., regard highly; **-r; ration**
     A   B   C   D

A. Each entry word is shown in bold-face type.
1. (-) shows the division between each syllable.
2. (′) indicates the accented syllable.
3. Pronunciation marks are shown only for vowels and are found above the vowel. Vowels without marks have no sound.
4. Irregular pronunciation is indicated in parentheses following the word.

    example: **cham-pāgne' (shăm)**

5. If there is more than one pronunciation for a word, only the most common is generally given. In situations where different parts of speech of the same word are pronounced differently, each pronunciation is given.

    example: **äl'têr-nāte,** v., do by turns; a. **(nȧte),** every other; **tion**

B. The part of speech for each word is abbreviated (see Abbreviation Key) and is printed in italics.
1. Some words have one meaning for different parts of speech.

    example: **ăn'swêr,** n., v., reply

2. Some words have different meanings for each part of speech.

    example: **ȧ-lêrt',** n., alarm; v., warn; a., quick

3. Some words have similar meanings for different parts of speech.

    example: **gī'ȧnt,** n., a., (one) of great size

4. Some words are commonly used in the plural form and are indicated by pl.

    example: **băc-tē'rĭ-ȧ,** n. pl.

C. The definition is in a short, concise form.
1. For most nouns, a, an, and the have been omitted before the definition.
2. For all verbs, to has been omitted before the definition.
3. Words often have many meanings; only the more common are given.

D. Endings of words derived from the entry word are printed in bold-face type following the definition.
1. Their parts of speech are not indicated unless they are different from those listed in the Suffix Key or not listed at all.

    example: **Ȧ-mĕr'ĭ-cȧ,** n., Western Hemisphere, United States; **-n,** n.

The new word becomes **American.**

2. If there is a hyphen (-) before the ending, it is added directly to the entry word to make a new form.

   example: **ăd-mīre′,** *v.*, regard highly; **-r**

   The new word becomes **admirer.**
3. If there is no hyphen (-) before the ending, then the ending replaces the last few letters or syllable so that the ending is comprised of a complete syllable or syllables.

   example: **ăd-mīre′,** *v.*, regard highly; **ration**

   The new word becomes **admiration.**

Pronunciation Key

Symbol	Key Word
ă	ăt
ā	āce
â	bâr
ȧ	sofȧ
ä	äll
a͡u	a͡uto
ĕ	bĕd
ē	bē
ê	hêr
ė	mėchanic
e͡w	fe͡w
ĭ	ĭn
ī	īce
î	sîr
ï (ē)	alïen
ŏ	ŏx
ō	gō
ô	ôr
ö	wörd
ȯ	gallȯp
o͡i	o͡il
o͝o	bo͝ok
o͞o	bo͞ot
o͡u	o͡ut
o͡w	co͡w
ŭ	ŭp
ū	ūse
û	ûrn
ȳ (ī)	bȳ
ÿ (ē)	berrÿ
ẏ (ĭ)	mẏth

The following combinations are always pronounced as shown below unless otherwise noted.

Symbol		Key Word
ch		chain
ck	(k)	back
dg	(j)	edge
gh	(silent)	night
gn	(n)	gnat
ism	(ĭz-ėm)	egotism
kn	(n)	knot
ph	(f)	graph
pn	(n)	pneumonia
ps	(s)	psalm
qu	(k)	quit
rh	(r)	rhyme
wh	(w)	what
wr	(r)	write

Abbreviation Key

a.	adjective
adv.	adverb
art.	article
coll.	colloquial
conj.	conjunction
cont.	contraction
etc.	et cetera
ex.	example
int.	interjection
n.	noun
pl.	plural
prep.	preposition
pro.	pronoun
sing.	singular
v.	verb

Suffix Key

These suffixes or word endings are used throughout this dictionary. Each will always have the same pronunciation and be the same part of speech unless otherwise indicated in the entry word itself.

-àge	n.
-àl	a.
-āte	v.
-bĭl-ĭ-tÿ	n.
-ble (b'l)	a.
-blÿ	adv.
-cial, -tial (shil)	a.
-cious, -tious (shis)	a.
-dȯm	n.
-ėd	a.
-ēe	n.
-ēer	n.
-ėn	v.
-êr	n.

-ĕss	n.
-fŭl	a.
-hōŏd	n.
-ĭc	a.
-ĭcs	n.
-ĭ-fȳ	v.
-ĭng	a.
-iȯn (yȯn)	n.
-ĭsh	a.
-ĭsm (ĭz-ėm)	n.
-ĭst	n.
-ĭ-tĭs	n.
-ĭ-ŭm	n.
-īze	v.
-lĕss	a.
-līke	a.
-lȳ	adv.
-mĕnt, -mėnt	n.
-nce	n.
-ncȳ	n.
-nĕss	n.
-nt	a.
-ôr, -ör	n.
-oŭs	a.
-shĭp	n.
-sion, -tion (shĭn)	n.
-sĭve	a.
-stêr	n.
-tĭve	a.
-tûre (chêr)	n.
-tûre (chŭr)	n.
-ȳ	n.

A

ă, *a.*, one, each　　[eater
âard'vârk, *n.*, African ant-
à-băck', *adv.*, backwards
ăb'ácŭs, *n.*, counting
　frame with beads
à-băft', *adv.*, *prep.*, behind
ăb-à-lō'nē, *n.*, mollusk
　yielding mother-of-pearl
à-băn'dŏn, *v.*, give up;
　-ment; -er; -ed; -edly
à-bāse', *v.*, degrade, hu-
　miliate; **-ment**
à-băsh', *v.*, embarrass,
　shame; **-ment**
à-bāte', *v.*, lessen; **-r;**
　-ment; table　　[house
ăb-ăt-tŏir', *n.*, slaughter-
ăb'bĕss, *n.*, head nun
ăb'bēy, *n.*, monastery
ăb'bŏt, *n.*, head monk
ăb-brē'vĭ-āte, *v.*, shorten;
　tor; tion; tory
ăb'dĭ-cāte, *v.*, resign office
　or power; **tor; tion**
ăb'dŏ-mĕn, *n.*, body be-
　tween chest and pelvis;
　minal
ăb-dŭct', *v.*, kidnap; **-or;**
　-ion
ăb'êr-rāte, *v.*, deviate;
　tion
à-bĕt', *v.*, aid in doing
　wrong; **-ter; -tor; -ment**
ăb-hôr', *v.*, hate, detest;
　-rer; -rence; -rent
à-bīde', *v.*, await, endure;
　-r
à-bĭl'ĭ-tў, *n.*, skill, talent
ăb'jĕct, *a.*, wretched,
　base; **-ion; -ness; -ly**
àb-jūre', *v.*, renounce; **ra-**
　tion; -r; ratory
ăb-lāte', *v.*, remove by sur-
　gery; **tion**
à-blāze', *a.*, on fire
ăb-lū'tion, *n.*, washing the
　body; **tary**
ăb'nĕ-gāte, *v.*, re-
　nounce; **tor; tion**
ăb-nôr'mál, *a.*, not usual;
　-ity; -iy　[conveyance
à-bôard', *adv.*, on or in a
à-bōde', *n.*, residence

à-bŏl'ĭsh, *v.*, do away with
à-bŏm'ĭ-nāte, *v.*, loathe,
　hate; **tor; tion; nable**
ăb-ō-rĭg'ĭ-nē, *n.*, earliest
　inhabitant; **nal**
à-bôrt', *v.*, miscarry; **-ion;**
　-ionist; -ive
à-boŭnd', *v.*, be plentiful
à-brāde', *v.*, rub off; **-r;**
　dant
à-brā'sion, *n.*, scrape;
　sive　　　　　　[side
à-brĕast', *adv.*, side by
à-brĭdge', *v.*, shorten;
　-ment
à-broäd', *adv.*, outside
ăb'rȯ-gāte, *v.*, abolish;
　tor; tion; tive
à-brŭpt', *a.*, sudden; **-ion;**
　-ness; -ly [sue in body
ăb'scĕss, *n.*, pus-filled tis-
àb-scĭnd', *v.*, cut off
àb-scŏnd', *v.*, secretly run
　away; **-er**
ăb'sĕnt, *a.*, away; **-ee;**
　sence; -eeism
ab'sĕnt–mĭnd'ĕd, *a.*, for-
　getful; **-ly; -ness**
ăb'sȯ-lūte, *a.*, uncondi-
　tional; **-ness; -ly**
ăb-sŏlve', *v.*, forgive
ăb-sôrb', *v.*, suck up, take
　in; **-er; -ability; -ency;**
　-ent; -able
àb-stāin', *v.*, refrain; **-er**
àb-stē'mi-oŭs, *a.*, moder-
　ate; **-ness**
ăb-străct', *n.*, summary; *v.*,
　remove; *a.*, theoretical;
　-er; -ion; -ness; -ive; -ly
ăb-strūse', *a.*, obscure;
　-ness; -ly
ăb-sûrd', *a.*, ridiculous;
　-ity; -ness; -ly
à-bŭn'dȧnt, *a.*, plentiful;
　dance; -ly
à-būse', *v.*, mistreat; **sive;**
　siveness
à-bўss', *n.*, deep pit
ăc-à-dĕm'ĭc, *a.*, scholas-
　tic; **-ai; -aily**
ä-cȧp-pĕl'lȧ, *a.*, without
　accompaniment

ăc-cēde', v., consent; -r; -nce

àc-cĕl'êr-āte, v., go faster; tor; tion [stress

ăc'cĕnt, n., emphasis; v.; -uation; -uate; -ual

àc-cĕpt', v., receive; -er; -or; -ance; -ant; -able; -ably; -ableness; -ability

àc-cĕs'sô-rў, n., extra; rial

ăc'cĭ-dĕnt, n., chance, mishap; -al

àc-clāim', v., applaud

àc-clà-mā'tion, n., applause; tory

àc-clīv'ĭ-tў, n., upward slope

ăc'cò-lāde, n., honor, award

àc-cŏm'mò-dāte, v., make fit, lodge; tor; tion; tive

àc-cŏm'pà-nў, v., go with; niment; nist

àc-cŏm'plĭce, n., partner in crime

àc-cŏrd', v., agree; -ance; -ant; -antly; -ingly

àc-cŏr'dĭ-òn, n., musical instrument; adj., folding

àc-cŏst', v., approach, greet

àc-coù'têr, v., equip; -ment

àc-crĕd'ĭt, v., authorize; -ation

àc-crūe', v., increase

àc-cū'mū-lāte, v., collect; tor; tion; tive; tively

ăc'cû-rà-cў, n., exactness

àc-cūse', v., blame; -r; singly [ate

àc-cŭs'tòm, v., habitu-

à-cêrb', a., bitter, sour; -ity; -ate [acid

ăc'è-tāte, n., salt of acetic

ăc'è-tōne, n., liquid paint remover [blowtorch

à-cĕt'ў-lēne, n., gas for

ăch-rò-măt'ĭc (ăk), a., colorless; -ly

ăc'ĭd, a., sour; -ity; -ify; -ic

àc-knŏwl'èdge, v., admit; gment; -able

ăc'mē, n., summit

ăc'nē, n., skin disease with pimples [helper

ăc'ò-lўte, n., altar boy,

à-coūs'tĭc, a., of hearing; -al; -ally; -s

àc-quāint', v., make aware; -ance

ăc'quĭ-ĕsce, v., consent; -nce; -nt

àc-quire', v., get; -ment

àc-quĭt', v., absolve; -ter; -tal; -tance

ā'cre, n., land measure; -age

ăc'rĭ-mō-nў, n., harsh manner; nious

ăc'rò-băt, n., skilled gymnast; -ic

ăc'rò-nўm, n., word formed from initials; -ic

ăct, n., deed; v., do, perform; -or; -ress; -ion

ăc'tĭve, a., busy, moving; vity

ăc'tū-àl, a., real; -ity; -ize; -ly [statistician

ăc'tū-ār-ў, n., insurance

à-cū'ĭ-tў, n., keenness

à-cū'mĕn, n., sharpness

ăc'-ū-pŭnc-tûre, n., Chinese pain-relieving practice of inserting needles into body

à-cūte', a., sharp; -ness; -ly

ăd'àge, n., old saying

ăd'à-mànt, a., inflexible

ădd, v., sum up, total; -er; -ition; -itional; -itionally; -able; -ible; -ibility; -itive [added

àd-dĕn'dŭm, n., thing

ăd'dêr, n., snake

àd-dĭct', v., give to habit; -ion; -ive

ăd'dle, v., confuse

àd-drĕss', n., speech, place of residence; v., speak or write to; -ee; -er

àd-dūce', v., cite, quote; -r; -nt

ăd'e-nōĭds, n., lymph tissue behind nose

àd-ĕpt', a., very skilled; -ness; -ly [ciency

ăd'è-quà-cў, n., suffi-

ăd-hēre', v., stick; -r; -nce;

A
B

-nt
ăd′ĭt, *n.*, mine entrance
ăd-jā′cĕnt, *a.*, near; **ncy**
ăd′jĕc-tĭve, *n.*, word quali-
fying a noun; **val**
ăd-jŏin′, *v.*, next to
ăd-joûrn′, *v.*, suspend,
postpone; **-ment**
ăd′jŭnct, *n.*, addition; **-ly;**
-ive; -ively
ăd-jūre′, *v.*, charge under
oath; **-r; ration; ratory**
ăd-jŭst′, *v.*, conform; **-er;**
-or; -ment; -able
ăd-lĭb′, *v.*, improvise
ăd-mĭn′ĭs-tĕr, *v.*, govern
ăd-mīre′, *v.*, regard highly;
-r; ration; rable; rably;
rability; ringly
ăd-mĭt′, *v.*, let in, acknowledge; **-tance; -tedly**
ăd-mŏn′ĭsh, *v.*, advise;
nitor; -ment; nition; ni-
tory
à-do′ (dū), *n.*, fuss [brick
à-dō′bē, *n.*, sun-dried
ăd-ò-lĕs′cĕnce, *n.*, teen-
age years; **scent**
à-dŏpt′, *v.*, take as one's
own; **-er; -ion; -ive;**
-ively; -able
à-dôrn′, *v.*, add beauty;
-ment
Ăd-rĕn′ăl-ĭn, *n.*, hormone
that stimulates heart
ăd′ŭ-lāte, *v.*, highly flatter;
tor; tion; tory
à-dŭlt′, *a., n.*, mature (person); **-hood; -ness**
à-dŭl′tĕr-ў, *n.*, extramarital
sexual relations; **rer**
ăd-vănce′, *v.*, go forward;
-r; -ment
ăd-văn′tàge, *n.*, benefit;
geous; geously
ăd-vĕn′tŭre, *n.*, exciting
happening; *v.*, risk; **-r;**
-ss; -some; turism; tur-
ist; turous; turously;
turousness
ăd′vĕrb, *n.*, word modify-
ing verb, adjective, or
adverb; **-ial; -ially**
ăd′vĕr-sàr-ў, *n.*, oppo-
nent; **sative**
ăd-vĕrt′, *v.*, refer, call attention to; **-ence; -ency;**

-ent; -ently
ăd-vĕr-tīse′, *v.*, make
known; **-r; -ment**
ăd-vīce′, *n.*, opinion
ăd-vīse′, *v.*, counsel; **-r;**
sor; -ment; sory; -d;
-dly; sable; sably; sa-
bility; sableness
ăd′vo-cāte, *v.*, support;
tor; cacy; tion; tory
āer′āte, *v.*, expose to air;
tor; tion
āer′ĭ-àl, *n.*, antenna; *a.*,
like air, high up; **-ist**
āer′ĭē, *n.*, eagle's nest
āer-ō-dў-năm′ĭcs, *n.*,
study of air movement
āer-ŏm′ė-tĕr, *n.*, air meas-
urer [aircraft
āer-ò-nāu′tĭcs, *n.*, study of
aĕs-thĕt′ĭc, *a.*, of artistic
beauty; **-ism; -al; -ally**
ăf′fà-ble, *a.*, friendly; **bil-**
ity; bly
àf-fáir′, *n.*, business, event
àf-fĕct′, *v.*, influence; **-ive;**
-ively; -ed; -edness
àf-fĕc′tion, *n.*, fondness;
-ate; -al; tive; tèr
ăf-fī-dā′vĭt, *n.*, sworn written statement
àf-fĭn′ĭ-tў, *n.*, connection,
attraction; **tive**
àf-firm′, *v.*, assert as true;
-er; -ation; -ance; -ant;
-ative; -atively; -able
àf-flā′tŭs, *n.*, inspiration
àf-flĭct′, *v.*, cause pain;
-ion; -ive; -ively
ăf′flū-ĕnce, *n.*, wealth; **nt;**
ntly
ăf fôrd′, *v.*, bear the cost
àf-frāy′, *n.*, public fight
àf-frŏnt′, *v.*, offend
à-fiēld′, *adv.*, astray
à-fôre-mĕn′tioned, *adj.*,
mentioned before
à-frāid′, *a.*, fearful
à-frĕsh′, *adv.*, again
ăft, *adv.*, toward stern
ăf′tĕr-ĕf-fĕct, *n.*, later
result [quence
ăf′tĕr-măth, *n.*, conse-
ăf′tĕr-tāste, *n.*, lingering
taste [reflection
ăf′tĕr-thôught, *n.*, later
ăf′tĕr-wàrd, *adv.*, later

à-gain' (gĕn), *adv.*, once more [contrary to
à-gainst' (gĕnst), *prep.*,
à-gāpe', *a.*, *adv.*, surprised [precious stone
ăg'ate (īt), *n.*, hard, semi-
āge, *n.*, period of time; *v.*, grow old; **-less**
ā'gĕn-cў, *n.*, means, bureau acting for another
à-gĕn'dä, *n.*, list of things to do
ā-gent, *n.*, one acting for another, active force; **-ial**
ăg-glŏm'ĕr-āte, *v.*, collect into a heap; **tion; tive**
ăg-grăn'dīze, *v.*, increase power; **-r; -ment**
ăg'grà-vāte, *v.*, make worse, annoy; **tion**
ăg-grĕs'sion, *n.*, attack; **sor; sive**
ăg-grieve', *v.*, injure
à-ghăst', *a.*, horrified
ăg'īle, *a.*, quick, light movement; **lity**
ăg'ī-tāte, *v.*, disturb, excite; **tor; tion**
ăg-nŏs'tĭc, *n.*, one who doubts God's existence; **-ism; -ally**
ăg'ō-nў, *n.*, great pain, distress; **nize**
à-grăr'ĭ-àn, *a.*, of land, rural; **-ism**
ăg'rĭ-cŭl-tûre, *n.*, science of farming; **rist; ral; rally**
à-grŏn'ō-mў, *n.*, science of farm production; **mist; mic; mical** [shore
à-grŏund', *a.*, *adv.*, on
ā'gūe, *n.*, fever with chills; **guish**
à-hĕad', *a.*, *adv.*, forward
à-hoy'(ŏi), *inter.*, sailor's
āid, *n.*, *v.*, help [call
āil, *v.*, be in ill health; **-ment**
āim, *n.*, intention; *v.*, point; **-less; -lessness; -lessly**
āir, *n.*, gases surrounding earth; *v.*, ventilate; **-iness; -y; -ily**
āir'crăft, *n.*, flying machine [for aircraft
āir'fiĕld, *n.*, landing field

āir fôrce, *n.*, military branch using airplanes
āir'līne, *n.*, aircraft transport company; **-r**
āir'māil, *n.*, mail sent by aircraft [flying machine
āir'plāne, *n.*, power-driven
āir'pôrt, *n.*, landing place for aircraft
āir rāid, *n.*, airplane attack
aīsle (il), *n.*, passageway along rows of seats
à-kĭn', *a.*, related, similar
ăl'à-băs-têr, *n.*, white stone
à-lârm', *n.*, warning signal, fear; *v.*, frighten; **-ist**
à-lăs', *int.*, cry of sorrow
ălb, *n.*, priest's white robe
ăl'bà-trŏss, *n.*, large seabird of the South Seas
ăl-bē'īt, *conj.*, although
ăl-bi'nō, *n.*, animal lacking coloration of hair, eyes, skin; **nism**
ăl'bŭm, *n.*, book with blank pages for collecting
ăl-bū'mĕn, *n.*, egg white, complex protein; **minoid; minous**
ăl'chĕ-mў, *n.*, medieval chemistry; **mist; mize; mic; mical; mically**
ăl'cò-hôl, *n.*, intoxicating liquid
ăl'cōve, *n.*, recess of a room [cilman
ăl'dêr-măn, *n.*, local coun-
āle, *n.*, kind of beer
à-lêrt', *n.*, alarm; *v.*, warn; *a.*, quick [for fodder
ăl-făl'fà, *n.*, legume used
ăl'gĕ-brà, *n.*, mathematics of equations; **-ist; -ic; -ical; -ically**
ā'lĭ-às, *n.*, assumed name
ăl'ī-bī, *n.*, excuse
à-līght', *v.*, dismount; *a.*, burning
à-līgn', *v.*, line up; **-ment**
ăl'ī-mĕnt, *n.*, food; *v.* (mĕnt), nourish; **-ation; -ary; -al; -ally**
ăl'ī-mō-nў, *n.*, support money in divorce
à-līve', *a.*, living, alert
ăl'kà-lī, *n.*, acid neutral-

izer; **loid; -ze; -c; -ne, -nity**

äll,a., n., adv., entire, every

àl-lāy', v., calm

àl-lĕge', v., declare without proof; **gation**

àl-lē'giànce, n., loyalty

ăl'lè-gô-rÿ, n., symbolic story; **rist; rize; rical; rically** [cally fast

àl-lĕ'grō, a., adv., musi-

ăl'lêr-gÿ, n., sensitivity of body to things; **gist; gic**

àl-lē'vï-āte,v., relieve; **tor; tion; tive; tory**

ăl'lêy, n., narrow lane

àl-lī'ànce, n., union, league

àl-līt'ĕr-ā-tion, v., repetition of initial word sounds; **rate; tive; tively**

ăl'lò-cāte,v., allot, distribute; **tion; cable**

àl-lŏt', v., assign shares; **-ment**

àl-lōw', v., let; **-ance; -able; -ably** [ture

ăl-loy' (lŏi), n., metal mix-

àl-lūde',v., refer

àl-lūre',v., entice; **-ment**

àl-lü'sion,n., casual mention; **sive; sively**

ăl'lÿ,n., helper, associate; v. **(àl-lÿ'),** unite

ăl'mà mát'êr, n., school attended

ăl'mà-năc, n., calendar with extra data

ăl-might'ÿ,a., all-powerful

ăl'mònd, n., edible nut

ălms,n., money, food, etc., for poor

à-lōne',a., adv., by oneself

à-lông', prep., beside; adv., forward, together

à-lōof', a., adv., distant

ălp, n., high mountain

ăl-păc'à,n., llama domesticated for its wool

ăl'phà-bĕt,n., ordered letters of a language; **-ize; -ical; -ically**

àl-rĕad'ÿ, adv., previously

àl-right',a., adequate; int., yes

ăl'tàr, n., holy platform or table

ăl'têr, v., change; **-ation; -able; -ative**

ăl'têr-cāte, v., quarrel; **tion**

ăl'têr-nāte,v., do by turns; a. **(nàte),** every other; **tion**

ăl-têr'nà-tïve, n., choice; **-ly**

ăl-thōugh', conj., even if

ăl'tïm'è-têr, n., instrument measuring height

ăl'tï-tūde,n., height; **dinal**

ăl'tō, n., lowest female voice

ăl-tò-gĕth'êr, adv., wholly

ăl'trū-ïsm, n., selflessness; **ruist; ruistic; ruistically**

à-lü'mĭ-nŭm, n., light metal; **nize; nous**

à-lŭm'nŭs, n. (pl. **nī**), graduate

ăl-vē'ò-lŭs, n. (pl. **-lï**), small cavity

ăl'wāys, adv., forever

à-măl'gà-māte, v., unite; **tor, tion; tive**

à-măss', v., collect; **-er; -ment**

ăm'à-têur, n., nonprofessional; **-ism; -ish; -ishly; -ishness**

à-māze', v., surprise; **-ment; zingly** [woman

ăm'à-zŏn, n., strong

ăm-băs'sà-dôr, n., topranking diplomat; **-ship; dress** [brown

ăm'bêr, a., yellowish-

ăm-bĭ-dĕx'troŭs,a., using both hands equally

ăm-bĭg'ū-oŭs, a., vague; **guity**

ăm-bĭ'tion, n., drive to succeed; **tious**

ăm-bĭv'à-lénce, n., conflicting feelings; **nt; ntly**

ăm'ble, v., walk leisurely

ăm'bū-lànce, n., vehicle to carry sick [tack

ăm'bŭsh, n., surprise at-

à-mēl'ĭò-rāte,v., improve; **tor; tion, tive; able**

ā-mĕn', int., so be it

ă-mē'nà-ble,a., easily led

à-mĕnd', v., change; -er;
-ment; -able   [sation
à-mĕnds', n. pl., compen-
à-mĕn'ĭ-tў, n., pleasant-
ness
À-mĕr'ĭ-cà, n., western
hemisphere,   United
States; -n
à-mĕrse', v., punish by
fine; -ment
ăm'ĕ-thŷst, n., purple gem
ā'mĭ-à-ble, a., good na-
tured; bility
à-mĭd', prep., among
à-mĭss', a., adv., wrong
ăm'ĭ-tў,   n.,   friendly
relations   [gas
àm-mō'nĭ-à, n., pungent
ăm-nē'sĭà, n., memory
loss; sic
ăm'nĕs-tў, n., pardon
à-moē'bà, n., one-celled
animal; bic   .
ā-môr'ăl, a., without moral
sense; -ity; -ly
ăm'ô-roŭs, a., full of love;
-ness; -ly
à-môr'phoŭs, a., shape-
less; hism; -ly; -ness
ăm'ôr-tīze, v., pay gradually; zation; zable
à-moŭnt', n., sum; v.,
equal
ăm'pēre, n., unit of electrical current; rage
ăm-phĭb'ĭ-àn,   n.,   one
adapted to land and
water; bious
ăm'ple, a., plentiful; -ness
ăm'plĭ-fŷ, v., increase;
fier; fication   [dance
ăm'plĭ-tūde, n., abun-
ăm'pū-tāte, v., surgically
cut off; tor; tee; tion
à-mūse', v., entertain; -r;
-ment, sable
ăn, art., one
ăn-à-cŏn'dà, n., large
snake that crushes its
prey
ăn'à-grăm, n., new words
from letters of another
word; -matize; -matic;
-matical; -matically
à-năl'ô-gў, n., likeness;
gist; gize; gous; gical;
gically

à-năl'ŷ-sĭs, n., examina-
tion of parts of whole;
lyst; lyze; lytic; lytical;
lytically   [ness
ăn'âr-chў (kў), n., lawless-
hist; hism; histic; hic
à-năth'ĕ-mà,   n.,   religious curse; mize
à-năt'ô-mў, n., study of
body structure;   mist;
mize; mical; mically
ăn'cĕs-trў, n., family lineage; tor; ral; rally
ăn'chôr (kôr), n., iron object to secure ship; -age
ăn'chô-rīte (kô), n., hermit
ăn'chô-vў, n., small her-
ăn'cient, a., old   [ring
ăn-dàn'tē, a., adv., slow
ănd'īrón, n., fireplace support for wood
ăn'ĕc-dōte, n., brief story;
tal; tic; tical
à-nē'mĭ-à, n., low count of
red blood cells; mic
ăn-ĕs-thĕt'ĭc,   n.,   drug
causing   feeling   loss;
tist; tize
à-new' (nū), adv., again
ăn'gĕl, n., God's messen-
ger; -ic
ăn'gêr, n., fury, rage; gry
ăn'gle, n., shape of two
lines meeting at a point,
corner
ăn'glêr, n., fisherman
ăn-gôr'à, n., kind of wool
ăn'guĭsh, n., v., distress
ăn'gū-làr, a., having an-
gles; -ity; -ly; -ness
ăn-hў'droŭs, a., without
water
ăn'īle, a., old-womanish
ăn'ĭ-măl, n., living be-
ing; -ist; -ism; -istic;
-istically; -ity; -ize
ăn-ĭ-mŏs'ĭ-tў, n., hostility
ăn'ĭ-mŭs, n., ill will
ăn'kle, n., joint connecting
leg and foot
ăn'klĕt, n., ankle orna-
ment, sock   [ords
ăn'nàls, n., pl., yearly rec-
àn-nī'hĭ-lāte, v., destroy;
tor; tion; tive
ăn-nĭ-vêr'sà-rў, n., event
recurring yearly

ăn'nō-tāte, v., make notes about; **tor; tion; tive**

ăn-nōunce', v., declare; **-r; -ment**

ăn-noy' (nŏi), v., bother; **-er; -ance**

ăn'nū-ăl, a., yearly; **-ly**

ăn-nŭl', v., do away with

ăn'ōde, n., positive electrode; **dic**

ā-nŏint', v., consecrate with oil; **-er; -ment**

ă-nŏm'ă-lÿ, n., deviation from norm; **lism; listic; lous; lously; lousness**

ā-nŏn', adv., soon

ā-nŏn'ÿ-moŭs, a., nameless; **mity; -ly** [more

ăn-ŏth'êr, adj., prep., one

ăn'swêr, n., v., reply; **-able**

ănt, n., tiny wingless insect

ănt-ăc'ĭd, n., acid neutralizer

ăn'tē, n., poker stake

ăn-tē-bĕl'lŭm, a., before Civil War

ăn'tē-lōpe, n., deer

ăn-tĕn'nă, n., aerial

ăn-tē'rĭ-ôr, adj., at front

ăn'tē-rōōm, n., waiting room

ăn'thĕm, n., national hymn

ăn-thŏl'ō-gÿ, n., literary collection; **gist; gize; gical**

ăn'thră-cīte, n., hard coal

ăn'thrăx, n., cattle disease

ăn-thrō-pŏl'ō-gÿ, n., study of man; **gist; gical; gically**

ăn'tĭ-bŏd-ÿ, n., body substance that fights toxins

ăn-tĭc'ĭ-pāte, v., expect; **tor; tion; pant; tive; tory**

ăn-tĭ-clī'măx, n., descent from important to trivial; **mactic**

ăn'tĭ-dōte, n., remedy to counteract poison; **tal**

ăn'tĭ-gĕn, n., substance causing body to make antibodies

ăn-tĭ-hĭs'tă-mĭne, n., drug to treat allergies

ăn'tĭ-mō-nÿ, n., metal; **nic; nous; nial**

ăn-tĭ-păs'tō, n., appetizer

ăn-tĭp'ă-thÿ, n., dislike; **thetic; thetical, thetically** [posite

ăn'tĭ-pōde, n., exact op-

ăn-tīque', n., old relic

ăn-tĭ-Sĕ-mĭt'ĭc, a., against Jews; **tism; mite**

ăn-tĭ-sĕp'tĭc, n., a., (substance) inhibiting infection; **sepsis -ize; -ally**

ăn-tĭ-sō'cĭăl, a., unfriendly

ăn-tĭth'ē-sĭs, n., contrast; **thetical**

ăn-tĭ-tŏx'ĭn, n., serum to prevent disease; **xic**

ăn'tō-nÿm, n., opposite meaning to word

ā'nŭs, n., bowel opening; **nal** [metal on

ăn'vĭl, n., block to hammer

ănx-ī'ē-tÿ, n., uneasiness; **xious; xiously, xiousness**

an'ÿ (ĕn), a., one or some of several

an'ÿ-how (ĕn), adv., in any case

an-ÿ-môre' (ĕn), adv., now

ā-ôr'tă, n., main artery from heart

ā-pāce', adv., swiftly

ā-pârt'heid (hād), n., policy of racial segregation

ă-pârt'mĕnt, n., room(s) to live in

ăp'ă-thÿ, n., lack of interest; **hetic, hetically**

ăp'êr-tûre, n., opening

ā'pĕx, n., highest point

ā-phā'sĭ-ă, n., loss of use or understanding of speech [plant juice

ā'phĭd, n., bug that sucks

ăph'ō-rĭsm, n., saying

āp'ī-âr-ÿ, n., bee-keeping place; **rist**

ā-pīēce', adv., each [dant

ā-plĕn'tÿ, a., adv., abun-

ā-pŏl'ō-gÿ, n., expression of regret; **gize; gizer**

ā-pŏs'tle, n., missionary

ā-pŏs'trō-phē, n., punctuation mark [gist

ā-pŏth'ē-cār-ÿ, n., drug-

ăp-pâll', v., shock; **-ing**

ăp-pă-rā'tŭs, n., equipment

ăp-păr'ĕl, *n.*, clothing

ăp-pȧ-rĭ'tion, *n.*, ghost; **-al**

ȧp-pēal', *v.*, make a request

ȧp-pēar', *v.*, seem; **-ance**

ăp-pĕl-lā'tion, *n.*, name; **tive**

ȧp-pĕn'dĭx, *n.*, additional part　　　　[sire

ăp'pė-tīte, *n.*, strong de-

ȧp-plaud', *v.*, approve,

ăp'ple, *n.*, fruit　　　[clap

ȧp-plī'ȧnce, *n.*, useful device

ăp'plĭ-cȧ-ble, *a.*, relevant; **bility**

ȧp-point', *v.*, assign; **-or;** **-ee; -ment**

ȧp-pôr'tion, *n.*, allot; **-ment**

ăp'pṓ-sĭte, *a.*, suitable; **tion; tional; tionally;** **-ly; -ness**

ȧp-prē'cĭ-āte, *v.*, value; **tor; tion, tory, tive;** **tively; tiveness; ciable;** **ciably**

ȧp-prĕn'tĭce, *n.*, helper learning a trade; **-ship**

ȧp-prīse', *v.*, notify

ȧp-prōach', *v.*, come near; **-able; -ability**　[proval

ăp-prṓ-bā'tion, *n.*, ap-

ȧp-prŏx'ĭ-māte, *v.*, come near; *a.* (**āte**) nearly; **tion; -ly**

ā'prĭ-cŏt, *n.*, fruit　[ment

ā'prŏn, *n.*, protective gar-

ăp-rṓ-pōs' (pō) *a.*, *adv.*, relevant

ăpt, *a.*, suitable; **-ly; -ness**

ăp'tĭ-tūde, *n.*, fitness

ăq'uȧ, *n.*, water; **queous**

ȧ-quȧr'ĭ-ŭm, *n.*, a water tank for fish

ā'quė-dŭct, *n.*, channel for supplying water

ăr'ȧ-ble, *a.*, fit for farming

ȧ-răch'nĭd, *n.*, eight-legged insects

âr'bĭ-têr, *n.*, umpire

âr'bĭ-trāte, *v.*, settle a dispute; **tor; tion; tive;** **tional**

âr'bôr, *n.*, shaded place

ârc, *n.*, circle segment

ârch, *n.*, curved structure;

a., main

âr-chaē-ŏl'ṓ-gÿ (kē), *n.*, study of ancient times; **gist; gical; gically**

âr-chā'ĭc (kā), *a.*, old; **-ly**

ârch'êr, *n.*, shooter of arrows with bow; **-y**

âr-chĭ-pĕl'ȧ-gō (kĭ), *n.*, group of islands

âr'chīves, *n. pl.*, public records; **vist; val**

âr'dör, *n.*, passion; **dent;** **dently**

âr'dū-oŭs, *a.*, hard; **-ly;** **-ness**

âr'ē-ȧ, *n.*, surface; **-l**

ȧ-rē'nȧ, *n.*, fighting area

är'gūe, *v.*, quarrel, dispute; **gument; gumentation; gumentative;** **gumentatively; guable; guably**

â'rĭ-ȧ, *n.*, melody of opera

är'ĭd, *a.*, dry

ȧ-rīse', *v.*, get up

ȧ-rĭth'mė-tĭc, *n.*, science of numbers; **-ian, -al;** **-ally**

ârk, *n.*, boat, chest

ârm, *n.*, body's upper limb; *v.*, furnish weapons; **-ful**

âr-mȧ-dĭl'lō, *n.*, animal with armorlike covering

âr'mĭ-stĭce, *n.*, truce

âr'mör, *n.*, protective covering

âr'mör-ÿ, *n.*, arsenal

âr'mÿ, *n.*, unit of soldiers

ȧ-rō'mȧ, *n.*, smell; **-tic;** **-tically**

ȧ-roūse', *v.*, awaken, stir

âr-rāign', *n.*, accuse; **-ment**

âr-rānge', *v.*, put in order; **-ment**

âr-rēar', *n.*, overdue debt

âr-rĕst', *v.*, stop, seize

âr-rīve', *v.*, come to a place; **-val**

är'rōw, *n.*, pointed rod to shoot with bow

âr'sė-nȧl, *n.*, storehouse of weapons　　[element

âr'sė-nĭc, *n.*, poisonous

ârt, *n.*, skill, creative work; **-ist; -istry; -y; -istic;** **-istically; -ful**

âr'tēr-ȳ, *n.*, blood vessel

âr-thrī'tĭs, *n.*, joint inflammation; **tic**

âr'tĭ-cle, *n.*, item

âr-tĭc'ū-lāte, *v.*, say clearly; *a.* **(lāte)**, able to speak; **tor; tion; -ly; -ness**

âr'tĭ-făct, *n.*, simple man-made object

âr'tĭ-fĭce, *n.*, clever trick

âr-tĭ-fĭ'ciȧl, *a.*, not real; **-ity; -ly**

âr-tĭl'lêr-ȳ, *n.*, mounted guns; **rist**

âr'tĭ-sȧn, *n.*, craftsman

ăs, *adv.*, *prep.*, like; *conj.*, while [material

ăs-bĕs'tŏs, *n.*, fireproof

ȧs-cĕnt', *n.*, a way up

ȧs-cĕt'ĭc, *a.*, *n.*, self-denying (person); **-ism; -ally**

ăs'cŏt, *n.*, neck scarf

ȧs-crībe', *v.*, credit; **bable**

ā-sĕx'ū-ȧl, *a.*, sexless

ăsh, *n.*, fire residue, tree

ăsh'ĕn, *a.*, pale

ȧ-shôre', *a.*, *adv.*, on land

ăs'ĭ-nīne, *a.*, silly

ȧ-skănce', *adv.*, sideways

ăsp, *n.*, poisonous snake

ȧ-spăr'ȧ-gŭs, *n.*, stalky green vegetable

ăs'pĕct, *n.*, phase

ăs-pêr'ĭ-tȳ, *n.*, harshness

ȧs-pêr'sion, *n.*, slander

ăs'phȧlt, *n.*, tarlike mixture

ăs-phȳx'ĭ-āte, *v.*, suffocate; **tor; tion; xiant**

ăs'pĭc, *n.*, gelatin mold

ăs'pĭ-rā-tôr, *n.*, suction apparatus

ăs'pīre', *v.*, be ambitious; **-r; ration**

ăs'pĭ-rĭn, *n.*, pain-reducing pill or powder

ăss, *n.*, donkey, fool

ȧs-sāil', *v.*, attack; **-er; -ment; -ant; -able**

ȧs-săs'sĭn, *n.*, killer; **-ation; -ate**

ȧs-săult', *n.*, *v.*, attack

ȧs-sĕnt', *n.*, *v.*, consent; **-er; -ation**

ȧs-sêrt', *v.*, declare; **-er; -or; -ion; -ive; -ively;**

-iveness

ȧs-sĕss', *v.*, set tax value on; **-or; -ment**

ăs'sĕt, *n.*, valuable thing

ȧs-sīgn', *v.*, allot; **-er; -or; -ee; -ation; -ment; -able**

ȧs-sĭm'ĭ-lāte, *v.*, resemble, absorb; **tion; tionism; tionist; tive**

ȧs-sō'cĭ-āte, *v.*, join; *n.* **(āte)**, friend, partner; **tion; tive**

ȧs-sôrt', *v.*, classify; **-ment**

ȧs-suāge', *v.*, lessen; **-ment**

ȧs-sūme', *v.*, take on; **-r; mable**

ȧs-sūre', *v.*, make certain; **-r; rance**

ȧs-sûr'gĕnt, *a.*, upward

ăs'tēr, *n.*, flower

ăs'têr-ĭsk, *n.*, starlike sign

ăs'têr-oĭd, *n.*, small planet; *a.*, starlike

ăsth'mȧ, *n.*, breathing disorder; **-tic**

ȧ-stĭg'mȧ-tĭsm, *n.*, eye defect causing blurriness

ȧ-stîr', *a.*, *adv.*, in motion

ȧs-tŏn'ĭsh, *v.*, surprise; **-ment**

ȧ-strāy', *adv.*, in error

ȧ-strīde', *adv.*, legs apart

ȧs-trĭn'gĕnt, *a.*, contracting; **ncy; -ly**

ȧs-trŏl'ō-gȳ, *n.*, science of human prediction by stars; **ger; gist; gical; gically**

ȧs-trŏn'ō-mȳ, *n.*, science of stars; **mer; mical; mically**

ȧs-tūte', *a.*, clever

ȧ-sŭn'dêr, *adv.*, apart

ȧ-sȳ'lŭm, *n.*, refuge

ā'thē-ĭsm, *n.*, belief that God does not exist; **st; stic; stical; stically**

ăth'lēte, *n.*, skilled sport participant; **tics; tic; tically** [crosswise

ȧ-thwart' (ôrt), *adv.*, *prep.*,

ăt'lȧs, *n.*, book of maps

ăt'mȯs-phēre, *n.*, air surrounding earth; **ric**

ăt'ôll, *n.*, coral island

ăt'ôm, *n.*, basic component of matter; **-ize; -ic; -icity; -ics** [device

ăt'ôm-ĭz-êr, *n.*, spraying

à-tōne', *v.*, make amends; **-ment**

ăt'ö-nÿ, *n.*, lacking body tone; **tonic; tonicity**

ā'trĭ-ŭm, *n.*, central court

à-trŏc'ĭ-tÿ, *n.*, cruelty; **cious; ciousness; ciously**

ăt'rŏ-phÿ, *n.*, waste away; **hic**

àt-tăch', *v.*, fasten; **-ment; -able**

ăt-tà-che' (shā), *n.*, diplomatic staff member

àt-tăck', *n.*, *v.*, assault; **-er**

àt-tāin', *v.*, reach; **-ment; -able; -ability**

àt-tāin'dêr, *n.*, forfeiture of civil rights

àt-tāint', *v.*, dishonor

àt-tĕnd', *v.*, be present; **-ance; -ant**

àt-tĕn'tion, *n.*, notice, care; **tive; tiveness; tively**

àt-tĕst', *v.*, certify; **-er; -or; -ation** [roof

ăt'tĭc, *n.*, space just under

àt-tīre', *n.*, *v.*, dress

ăt'tĭ-tūde, *n.*, manner; **dinal; dinize**

àt-tör'nēy, *n.*, lawyer

àt-trăct', *v.*, draw toward; **-er; tion; tive; -able**

ăt'trĭ-būte, *n.*, quality

àt-trĭ'tion, *n.*, gradual wearing away

ā-tÿp'ĭ-càl, *a.*, abnormal; **-ly**

au'bûrn, *a.*, reddish-brown

auc'tion, *n.*, public sale; **-eer**

äu-dăc'ĭ-tÿ, *n.*, bold courage; **cious; ciousness; ciously**

äu'dĭ-ble, *a.*, can be heard; **bility; bly**

äu'dĭ-ènce, *n.*, assembly of listeners

äu-dĭ-ō-vĭs'ū-àl, *a.*, about both hearing and seeing

äu'dĭt, *n.*, formal financial examination; **-or**

äu-dĭ'tion, *n.*, tryout

äu'gêr, *n.*, drill

äug-mĕnt', *v.*, increase; **-er; -ation; -ative; -able**

äu'gŭr, *v.*, foretell

äu-gŭst', *a.*, grand

äuk, *n.*, diving bird

au'rà (ô), *n.*, sensation about

äu'rĭ-cle, *n.*, heart chamber

äus-pĭ'cioŭs, *a.*, favorable; **-ness; -ly**

äu-thĕn'tic, *a.*, genuine; **-ity; -ate; -ator; -ation; -ally**

äu'thŏr, *n.*, creator, writer; **-ship; -less**

äu'thŏr-ize, *v.*, empower; **-r; zation**

äu-tō-bī-ŏg'rà-phÿ, *n.*, story by and about oneself; **her; hic; hically**

äu-tŏc'rà-cÿ, *n.*, dictatorship; **tocrat; tocratic**

äu'tŏ-grăph, *n.*, one's signature; **-y; -ic; -ically**

äu-tŏ-măt'ĭc, *a.*, spontaneous; **-ally**

äu-tŏn'ö-mÿ, *n.*, independence; **mist; mous**

äu'tŏp-sÿ, *n.*, examination of dead body

äu'tŭmn, *n.*, fall season

äux-ĭl'ia-rÿ, *a.*, additional, assisting

à-vāil', *v.*, be helpful; **-able; -ably; -ability**

ăv'à-rĭce, *n.*, greed for wealth; **cious; ciousness; ciously**

à-vĕnge', *v.*, take revenge; **-r**

à-vêr', *v.*, declare true

ăv'êr-àge, *n.*, sum divided by its parts; *a.*, normal

à-vêrt', *v.*, turn away

ā'vĭ-ār-ÿ, *n.*, birds' cage

ā-vĭ-ā'tion, *n.*, science of airplanes; **tor; viate**

ăv-ö-cā'tion, *n.*, hobby; **-al**

à-vŏĭd', *v.*, escape; **-able; -ably**

à-vow', *v.*, declare; **-er; -al**

à-wāre', *a.*, conscious

**A
B**

äwe, *n.,* reverence; *v.,* inspire; **-some**

äw'fŭl, *a.,* terrible; **-ly**

äwk'wård, *a.,* ungraceful; **-ness; -ly** [dow shade

äwn'ĭng, *n.,* outside wina-wrȳ', *a.,* twisted, wrong

ăx, ăxe, *n.,* chopping tool

ăx'ĭ-ŏm, *n.,* obvious truth; **-atic; -atically**

ăx'le, *n.,* rod on which wheel turns

ăx'ŏn, *n.,* nerve cell

aȳe, *adv.,* yes [shrub

a-zăl'eà, *n.,* flowering

äz'ûre, *a.,* sky-blue

B

băa,*n.,* sheep cry; *v.,* bleat

băb'ble, *n.,* meaningless talk; *v.,* make sounds

bābe, *n.,* baby

bă-bōōn',*n.,* large monkey

bā'bȳ,*n.,* very young child

bā'by-sĭt, *v.,* watch over children; **-ter**

băc-cà-läu'rē-àte, *n.,* college bachelor's degree

băc-cà-rat' (râ), *n.,* gambling card game

băc-cĭv'ŏr-oŭs, *a.,* berryfeeding

băch'-è-lŏr, *n.,* unmarried man; **-hood**

băck, *n.,* rear part of; *v.,* support; *a., adv.,* at the rear; **-er**

băck'bĭte, *v.,* slander

băck'bŏne,*n.,* spine, main support, courage

băck'fire, *n.,* unexpected result; *v.,* go awry

băck'găm-mòn, *n.,* board game

băck'groŭnd, *n.,* past events, less important place [rect, insincere

băck'hănd-ĕd, *a.,* indi-

băck'ĭng, *n.,* endorsement

băck'lăsh, *n.,* sudden reaction [reserve

băck'lŏg, *n.,* something in

băck'sĭde, *n.,* rump, buttocks

băck'slăp-pêr, *n.,* overly friendly person [virtue

băck'slīde, *v.,* slip from

băck'stāge, *a., adv.,* behind the stage, wings, etc. [withdraw

băck'trăck,*v.,* revisit path,

băck'ŭp,*a.,* alternate, supportive

băck'wård, *a., adv.,* behind, reversed

băck'wā-têr, *n.,* stagnant water [pork meat

bā'còn,*n.,* salted, smoked

băc-tē'rĭ-à, *n. pl.,* onecelled microorganisms; **-l; -lly**

băd, *a.,* not good, evil; **-ly**

bădge, *n.,* membership pin [bother

bădg'êr, *n.,* animal; *v.,*

băd-ĭ-nàge', *n.,* playful talk

băd'mĭn-tòn, *n.,* game played hitting feather ball

băf'fle, *v.,* confuse; **-r; -ment**

băg, *n.,* soft container; *v.,* enclose in bag, hang loosely; **-ful**

băg-à-tĕlle', *n.,* trifle

bā'gĕl, *n.,* hard roll

băg'gàge, *n.,* traveler's equipment

băg'pīpe,*n.,* Scottish reed instrument [diamond

bà-guĕtte', *n.,* narrow-cut

bāil, *n.,* deposit to ensure prisoner's appearance; *v.,* dip out water

bāi'lĭff, *n.,* deputy sheriff

bāi'lĭ-wĭck, *n.,* one's area of interest

bâirn, *n.,* child

bāit, *n.,* food to catch fish or animals; *v.,* entice

băl'ánce, *n.,* weighing device, equality; *v.,* weigh, equalize

băl'cò-nȳ, *n.,* projecting platform with rail

băld, *a.,* hairless on head

băl'dêr-dăsh, *n.,* nonsense

bāle, *n.,* large bundle

bâlk, *n.,* hinder, stop; **-y**

bâll, *n.,* round object for games, social dance

băl′làd, *n.,* story-telling song; **-eer; -ry**

băl′làst, *n.,* heavy matter to balance ship

băl-lė-rĭ′nà, *n.,* woman ballet dancer

băl′let (lā), *n.,* artistic group dance

bál lĭs′tĭcs, *n.,* study of bullets

bàl-loͦon′, *n.,* air-filled bag; *v.,* expand   [vote

băl′lŏt, *n.,* paper for voting,

băl′lẏ-hoͦo, *n.,* loud talk

bălm, *n.,* healing ointment

bà-lō′nėẏ, *n.,* nonsense

bâl′sà, *n.,* light wood

bâl′sàm, *n.,* aromatic resins, oils   [for railing

băl′ŭs têr, *n.,* support post

băm-bĭ′nō, *n.,* baby

băm-boͦo′, *n.,* tall, hollow, woody grass stems

băm-boͦo′zle, *v.,* trick, confuse; **-r; -ment**

băn, *n.,* public edict; *v.,* forbid

bà-năn′à, *n.,* oblong yellow-skinned fruit

bănd, *n.,* strip that binds, group of musicians; *v.,* join together   [injury

bănd′àge, *n.,* strip to bind

băn-dăn′nà, *n.,* large print handkerchief

băn-deau′(ō), *n.,* headband   [fighter

băn-dė-rĭl-lė′rō, *n.,* bull-

băn′dė-rōle, *n.,* pennant

băn′dĭt, *n.,* robber   [tor

bănd′màs-têr, *n.,* conduc-

bănd′wăg-òn, *n.* (coll.), winning side   [forth

băn′dẏ, *v.,* hit back and

bāne, *n.,* ruin; **-ful**

băn′gle, *n.,* bracelet

băng′ŭp, *a.* (coll.), excellent

băn′ĭsh, *v.,* send away; **-ment**

băn′is-têr, *n.,* railing

băn′jō, *n.,* guitar-like instrument; **-ist**

bănk, *n.,* financial institution, shore, row of objects

bănk′rŭpt, *n.,* inability to pay debts; **-cy**

băn′nêr, *n.,* flag·with slogan or motto

băn′quĕt, *n.,* elegant feast

băn′tàm, *n.,* small fowl

băn′tàm-weight (wāt), *n.,* 113–118-pound boxer

băn′têr. *v.,* joke; **-er; -ingly**

băp′tĭsm, *n.,* rite with water to join church; **st; tize**

bâr, *n.,* oblong solid piece, musical measure, legal profession, counter serving liquor; *v.,* close, exclude

bârb, *n.,* sharp point, biting remark; **-ed**

bâr′bė-cūe, *n.,* meat roasted over open fire; *v.,* roast, broil

bâr′bêr, *n.,* hair-cutter

bâr′bêr-rẏ, *n.,* spiny shrub with red berries

bâr-bĭ′tu-ràte, *n.,* drug used as sedative

bârd, *n.,* poet   [uncover

bāre, *a.,* naked, mere; *v.,*

bāre′băck, *a.,* *adv.,* on horse with no saddle

bāre′fâced, *a.,* shameless; **-ness**

bāre′lẏ, *adv.,* scarcely

bâr′gaĭn, *n.,* agreement; *v.,* barter; **-er**

bârge, *n.,* flat-bottomed freight boat; *v.,* enter rudely

bâr′ĭ-tōne, *n.,* male voice between tenor and bass

bâr′ĭ-ŭm, *n.,* chemical element

bârk, *n.,* tree-covering, dog's cry; *v.,* snap; **-er**

bâr′lėẏ, *n.,* cereal grain

bâr′mâid, *n.,* woman serving drinks

bârm′ẏ, *a.,* foamy

bâr′nà-clė, *n.,* ship-clinging shellfish

bârn′stôrm, *v.,* perform in rural areas; **-er**

băr′òn, *n.,* nobleman; **-ess; -age**

bà-rō′ni-àl, *a.,* grand

bà-rōque′, *a.,* overdecorated   [mitory

băr′ràck, *n.,* soldiers' dor-

băr-rà-cū′dà, *n.,* fierce fish
bár-räge′, *n.,* heavy attack
băr′rà-trÿ, *n.,* encouragement of causing lawsuits; **tor; trous**
băr′rĕl, *n.,* large wooden cylindrical container
băr′rĕn, *a.,* sterile
bár-rĕtte′, *n.,* hair clasp
băr′rĭ-êr, *n.,* obstacle
băr′rĭs-têr, *n.,* lawyer
băr′rōw, *n.,* pushcart, hill
bâr′tĕnd-êr, *n.,* one serving liquor
bâr′têr, *v.,* trade [turret
bâr′tĭ-zàn, *n.,* overhanging
bà-sălt′, *n.,* volcanic rock; **-ic**
bāse, *n.,* foundation, principle, goal; *a.,* low, dishonest; **-sic; -sal**
bāse′bâll, *n.,* team game with bat and ball, ball used
bāse′bôard, *n.,* wall molding next to floor
bāse′mĕnt, *n.,* lowest floor of building, cellar
băsh, *v.,* smash; *n.,* party
băsh′fŭl, *a.,* shy; **-ly; -ness**
băs′ĭl, *n.,* herb
bà-sĭl′ĭ-cà, *n.,* ancient Roman building, church
bā′sĭn, *n.,* washbowl, bay
băsk, *v.,* warm oneself
băs′kĕt, *n.,* woven wood container; **-ry**
băs′kĕt-bâll, *n.* team game with basket, ball
băss, *n.,* fish, low, deep tone or voice
băs′sĕt, *n.,* dog
băs-sĭ-nĕt′, *n.,* basketlike baby bed
bás-soon′, *n.,* bass wind instrument; **-ist**
băss′wood, *n.,* tree
bāste, *v.,* moisten roasting meat; sew loose stitches
băs′tion, *n.,* fortified place
băt, *n.,* stout club, flying mammal; *v.,* strike, flutter; **-ter; -tery**
bătch, *n.,* quantity done
bà-teau′(tō), *n.,* flat-bottomed boat [washing
băth, *n.,* washing, water for

bà-thŏm′ė-têr, *n.,* apparatus measuring water depth
bā′thŏs, *n.,* sentimentality
băth′rōbe, *n.,* lounging garment
bà-thÿm′ė-trÿ, *n.,* science of water depth; **ric; rical; rically** [method
bà-tĭk′, *n.,* cloth-dyeing
bà-tĭste′, *n.,* fine thin cloth
bà-tŏn′, *n.,* slender stick for leading music
băt-tăl′iòn, *n.,* large group of soldiers
băt′tĕn, *n.,* wood strip
băt′têr-ÿ, *n.,* sĕt, power source, beating
băt′tle, *n., v.,* fight
băt′tle-mĕnt, *n.,* low wall on tower
bāu′ble, *n.,* trinket
bāux′īte, *n.,* mineral having aluminum
bäwd′ÿ, *a.,* obscene; **ily; iness**
bäwl, *v.,* cry; **-er**
bāy, *n.* water inlet, alcove; *v.,* bark; *a.,* reddish-brown
bāy′bĕr-rÿ, *n.,* shrub
bāy′ȯ-nĕt, *n.,* blade on end of rifle [let
baÿ′oū, *n.,* marshy river inlet
bà-zâar′, *n.,* street of shops; charity sale
bà-zōō′kà, *n.,* weapon
bēach, *n.,* sandy shore
bēa′còn, *n.,* warning light
bēad, *n.,* small round object for stringing, drop; **-y**
bēa′dle, *n.,* parish officer
bēa′gle, *n.,* hunting dog
bēak′êr, *n.,* glass container
bēam, *n.,* long thick piece of wood, ray, smile
bēan, *n.,* vegetable, edible seed, its pod; *v.* (coll.), hit on head
beār, *n.,* animal; *v.,* carry, give birth, endure, produce; **-er**
bēard, *n.,* hair on face, whiskers; **-ed; -less**
bēar′ĭng, *n.,* one's manner,

posture; relationship

bēast, *n.*, animal, gross person; **-ly; -liness**

bēat, *n.*, throb, route, musical unit; *v.*, hit repeatedly, mix, flap, win; *a.*, tired; **-er**

beau (bō) *n.*, sweetheart

beaū'tĭ-fŭl, *a.*, eye-pleasing; **-ly**

beaū'tў, *n.*, pleasing quality; **teous** [animal

bēa'vêr, *n.*, dam-building

bĕck'ŏn, *v.*, summon

bė-clŏud', *v.*, darken, confuse

bė-còme', *v.*, change into, suit; **coming** [base

bĕd, *n.*, thing to sleep on,

bė-däub', *v.*, smear

bė-däz'zle, *v.*, confuse

bĕd'bŭg, *n.*, wingless bug

bė-dĕck', *v.*, adorn

bė-dĕv'ĭl, *v.*, torment; **-ment**

bĕd'fĕl-lōw, *n.*, friend

bė-dĭz'ĕn, *v.*, cheaply decorate

bĕd'lȧm, *n.*, insane asylum; confusion

bēe, *n.*, insect that makes honey, group meeting

bēech, *n.*, tree

bēef, *n.*, cow or bull meat; **-y**

bēe'līne, *n.*, direct route

bēep, *n.*, high-pitched sound; **-er**

bēer, *n.*, alcoholic drink brewed from malt; **-y**

bēet, *n.*, root vegetable

bēe'tle, *n.*, insect, mallet; *v.*, jut

bė-fäll', *v.*, happen

bė-fĭt', *v.*, be suitable; **-ting; -tingly**

bė-fŏg', *v.*, confuse

bė-fôre', *adv., prep., conj.*, earlier

bė-fŏul', *v.*, make dirty

bė-friĕnd', *v.*, help

bė-fŭd'dle, *v.*, confuse

bĕg, *v.*, ask for; **-gar; -garly** [cause

bė-gĕt', *v.*, give birth to,

bė-gĭn'nĭng, *n.*, origin

bė-gŏne', *v., inter.*, go away

bė-gō'nĭ-ȧ, *n.*, plant

bė-grŭdge', *v.*, envy

bė-guile', *v.*, deceive, amuse

bė-hāve', *v.*, act, conduct oneself

bė-hĕst', *n.*, order [back

bė-hīnd', *a., adv., prep.*, in

bė-hŏld', *v., int.*, look

bė-hŏld'ĕn, *a.*, grateful

bė-hōove', *v.*, be morally necessary [tan

beige (bāzh) *a.*, grayish-

bė-jew'ĕl, *v.*, decorate with jewels [cize

bė-lā'bôr, *v.*, beat, criti-

bė-lāy', *v.*, secure

bĕlch, *v.*, expel gas from mouth

bė-lēa'guêr, *v.*, besiege

bĕl'frў, *n.*, bell tower

bė-līe', *v.*, falsify; **-r**

bė-liĕf', *n.*, faith, trust, opinion

bė-liĕve', *v.*, take as true, think; **-r; lievable; lievability; lievably**

bė-lĭt'tle, *v.*, make seem unimportant; **-r; -ment**

bĕll, *n.*, cuplike object that can ring

bĕlle, *n.*, pretty girl

bĕll'hŏp, *n.*, hotel porter

bĕl'lĭ-cōse, *a.*, quarrelsome

bĕl'lōw, *v.*, roar

bĕl'lōws, *n., sing. & pl.*, device that makes air

bĕll'wĕth-êr, *n.*, male sheep that leads flock

bĕl'lў, *n.*, abdomen, stomach

bė-lōw', *a., adv., prep.*, lower, beneath

bĕlt, *n.*, strap around waist, area; *v.*, hit; **-ed**

bė-mīre', *v.*, make dirty

bė-mōan', *v.*, mourn

bĕnch, *n.*, long hard seat; **-er**

bĕnd, *n., v.*, curve; **-er; -able** [lower, under

bė-nēath', *a., adv., prep.*,

bĕn'ė-dĭct, *n.*, newly married ex-bachelor

bĕn-ė-dĭc'tion, *n.*, blessing; **tory**

ben'e-fit, *n.,* charitable act, help; **ficial; ficially**

be-nign', *a.,* kind, not harmful; **-ity; -ant; -ly**

ben'i-son, *n.,* blessing

ben'zene, *n.,* clear liquid from coal tar

ben'zine, *n.,* liquid used in gasoline and for dry cleaning

ben'zo-caine, *n.,* anesthetic ointment

be-queath', *v.,* give by will; **-al** [will

be-quest', *n.,* that left by

be-rate', *v.,* scold

be-reave', *v.,* deprive, leave lonely; **-ment; -d**

be-ret' (rā), *n.,* flat round cap

ber-i-ber'i, *n.,* disease of vitamin B deficiency

ber'ry, *n.,* small juicy fleshy fruit

ber-serk', *a., adv.,* violent rage; **-er** [anchor, job

berth, *n.,* bed, place to

ber'tha, *n.,* woman's wide

ber'yl, *n.,* mineral [collar

be-ryl'li-um, *n.,* metallic element

be-seech', *v.,* beg for; **-ingly**

be-set', *v.,* attack; **-ting**

be-siege', *v.,* attack, overwhelm; **-r**

be-smear', *v.,* soil

be'som, *n.,* broom

be-sot', *v.,* make drunk; **-ted** [with spangles

be-span'gle, *v.,* decorate

be-spat'ter, *v.,* spread dirt, slander

be-speak', *v.,* order, engage beforehand

bes'tial, *a.,* beastlike, savage; **-ity; -ize; tiary**

be-stir', *v.,* exert

be-stow', *v.,* give; **-al**

be-strew', *v.,* cover over

be-stride', *v.,* straddle

bet, *n.,* wager; *v.,* pledge a thing as result of con-

be-take', *v.,* go [text

be'tel, *n.,* climbing plant

be-tide', *v.,* happen

be-to'ken, *v.,* indicate, show

be-tray', *v.,* deceive; **-er; -al**

be-tween', *adv., prep.,* in the middle of, connecting [measure angles

bev'el, *n.,* tool to draw or

bev'er-age, *n.,* any drink

bev'y, *n.,* group

be-ware', *v.,* be careful

be-witch', *v.,* cast a spell, enchant; **-ment; -ery**

be-yond', *adv., prep.,* farther on

bez'el, *n.,* metal holding ring's jewel; tool's cutting edge

bi-an'nu-al, *a.,* twice a year; **-ly** [prejudice

bi'as, *n.,* diagonal line,

bib, *n.,* under-chin apron

Bi'ble, *n.,* sacred book, Old and New Testament; **licist**

bib-li-og'ra-phy, *n.,* list of writings; **pher; phic; phical; phically**

bib-li-op'e-gy, *n.,* art of bookbinding

bib'li-o-phile, *n.,* book collector; **list; lism; listic**

bib'u-lous, *a.,* spongy; fond of liquor; **-ly; -ness**

bi-cam'er-al, *a.,* having two legislative bodies

bi-cen-ten'ni-al, *n., a.,* (period of) two hundred years; **tenary** [cle

bi'ceps, *n.,* large arm mus-

bick'er, *v., n.,* squabble; **-er** [tooth

bi-cus'pid, *n.,* two-pointed

bid, *n., v.,* command, offer; **-der; -ding; -able**

bid'dy, *n.,* chicken, gossipy woman

bide, *v.,* stay, reside

bi-en'ni-al, *a.,* every two years; **-ly** [coffin

bier, *n.,* framework to hold

biff, *n., v.* (coll.), strike, hit

bi'flex, *a.,* two-curved

bi-fo'cal, *n.,* two-part lens for near, far vision

big'a-my, *n.,* having two spouses at once; **mist;**

mous
bĭg′heärt-ėd, a., generous
bĭg′hôrn, n., wild sheep
bĭght, n., bend, curve
bĭ-kï′nĭ, n., woman's very brief two-piece bathing suit
bïle, n., fluid of liver; **lious** [barrel, ship)
bĭlge, n., broadest part (of
bĭlk, v., swindle; **-er**
bĭll, n., list of charges owed, proposed law, paper money, bird's beak; v., present charges; **-er; -able**
bĭl′lėt, n., soldiers' housing, job
bĭll′fôld, n., wallet
bĭll′liárds, n., table game with balls and cue
bĭl′lĭng, n., actor's listing on playbill
bĭl′lĭön, n., thousand millions; **-aire; -th**
bĭl′lōw, n., large wave; **-y**
bĭl′lў, n., policeman's stick
bĭ-mŏnth′lў, a., adv., every two months
bĭn, n., storage container
bï′nä-rў, a., double, two-
bĭ′nāte, a., in pairs [fold
bĭnd, v., tie, bandage, obligate; **-er; -ing**
bĭnd′ėr-ў, n., place for binding books
bĭnd′ĭng, n., book cover
bĭnge, n., spree
bĭn′gō, n., game
bĭn-ŏc′ū-lárs, n. pl., field glasses   [terms
bĭ-nō′mĭ-ál, a., having two
bĭ-ō-chĕm′ĭs-trў, n., study of chemistry of living matter
bĭ-ō-dė-grād′á-ble, a., naturally decomposable
bĭ-ŏl′ŏ-gў, n., study of life; **gist; gic; gical; gically**
bĭ-ŏm′ė-trў, n., measurement of life; **rics; ric; rically**
bĭ-ō-phўs′ĭcs, n., physics of living things; **cist; cal**   [of living tissue
bĭ′ŏp-sў, n., examination
bĭ-pâr′tĭ-sàn, a., repre-

senting two groups; **-ship; tition**   [mal
bĭ′pĕd, n., two-footed ani
bĭ-rä′cĭál, a., involving two
bïrch, n., tree   [races
bîrd, n., feathered animal with wings   [person
bîrd′brāin, n., silly, stupid
bîrd′s′-eӯe, a., seen from above, overall
bĭ-rĕt′tà, n., priest's cap
bîrl, v., spin, revolve
bîrth, n., being born, beginning, origin
bîrth′rāte, n., number of births per year   [bread
bĭs′cuĭt, n., small, soft
bi-sĕx′ū-ál, a., of both sexes; **-ity; -ism; -ly**
bĭsh′ŏp, n., high-ranking Christian clergyman
bĭs′mŭth, n., metallic element; **-ic, -ous**
bĭ′sŏn, n., buffalo   [soup
bĭsque, n., thick creamy
bĭt, n., bridle's mouthpiece, small piece
bĭtch, n., female dog; v., complain
bïte, n., mouthful, sting, wound; v., cut with teeth
bĭt′ĭng, a., cutting, sharp; **-ly**
bĭt′têr, a., sharp, sorrowful; **-ness; -ly**
bĭt′têrn, n., marsh bird
bĭt′têr-sweēt, n., plant; a., pleasant and sad
bĭ-tū′mĕn, n., mineral substance; **minize; minization; minous**
bĭv′oū-ăc, n., temporary camp   [two weeks
bĭ-weēk′lў, a., adv., every
bĭ-zârre′, a., odd, fantastic
blăb, v., chatter; **-ber**
blăck, a., color of coal, dark, evil   [against
blăck′băll, n., v., vote
blăck′bĕr-rў, n., fruit
blăck′bôard, n., chalkboard   [fame
blăck′ĕn, v., darken, de-
blăck′guärd, n., scoundrel; v., abuse with words; **-ly**   [skin pore
blăck′hĕad, n., clogged

blăck'jăck, *n.,* steel-filled club, card game

blăck'lĭst, *n.,* list of undesirables [threat

blăck'mäil, *n.,* coercion by

blăck'smĭth, *n.,* iron-worker, one who shoes horses [face

blăck'tŏp, *n.,* asphalt sur-

blăd'dêr, *n.,* body sac for urine

blāde, *n.,* broad, flat surface, cutting edge

blāme, *v.,* accuse, criticize; **mable; -ful; -less; -lessness**

blănch, *v.,* make white; **-er**

blănd, *a.,* soft, mild

blănk, *n.,* empty space

blăn'kėt, *n.,* bed cover; *v.,* cover

blāre, *n., v.,* loud sound

blär'nēy, *n.,* smooth talk of flattery

blă-sé (sā), *a.,* bored

blăs'phė-mȳ, *n.,* irreverent talk; **eme; mous**

blăst, *n.,* sudden air gust, explosion

blā'tănt, *a.,* loud, obvious; **-ly; ncy**

blăth'êr, *n.,* foolish talk; **-er** [light; *v.,* mark

blāze, *n.,* bright flame,

blā'zêr, *n.,* sports jacket

blā'zŏn, *n.,* coat of arms; *v.,* adorn; **-ry**

blēach, *n., v.,* (chemical) to whiten

blēach'êrs, *n. pl.,* cheap stadium seats

blēak, *a.,* bare, harsh; **-ness; -ly**

blēar, *v.,* dim by tears; **-y -iness; -ily**

blēat, *n.,* sheep's cry

blēed, *v.,* lose blood; **-er**

blēep, *n.,* short, sharp sound [mar

blĕm'ĭsh, *n.,* defect, *v.,*

blĕnch, *v.,* become pale

blĕnd, *v.,* mix; **-er**

blĕss, *v.,* make holy, happy; **-ing; -ed**

blīght, *n.,* destruction, plant disease; **-er**

blīnd, *n.,* window shade; *a.,* unable to see; **-ness; -ly**

blĭnk, *v.,* open and close eyes, flash on and off; **-er**

blĭss, *n.,* happiness

blĭs'têr, *n.,* skin swelling

blĭtz, *n.,* destructive attack

blĭz'zárd, *n.,* bad snow

blōat, *v.,* swell [storm

blŏb, *n.,* drop, lump of

blŏc, *n.,* alliance [mass

blŏck, *n.,* large solid piece, city square; *v.,* obstruct, hinder; **-er, -age**

blŏck'āde, *v.,* shut off a place

blōke, *n.* (coll.), chap

blŏod, *n.,* red liquid in body; **-y; -iness; -ily; -less; -lessness; -lessly**

blŏod'cûr-dlĭng, *a.,* horrible

blŏod'hŏund, *n.,* tracking dog

blŏod'shĕd, *n.,* killing

blŏod'shŏt, *a.,* red, inflamed [kill

blŏod'thîrst-ȳ, *a.,* eager to

blŏom, *n., v.,* flower; **-er; -y**

blŏop'êr, *n.,* mistake

blŏs'sŏm, *n.,* flower; *v.,* bloom, develop

blŏt, *n., v.,* stain, disgrace, destroy; **-ter**

blŏuse, *n.,* woman's shirt

blŏus'ŏn, *n.,* long full blouse

blōw, *n.,* wind, hit, shock; *v.,* move air by mouth, wind; **-er; -y** [gun

blōw'gŭn, *n.,* dart or pellet

blōw'hârd, *n.,* boastful person

blōw'tôrch, *n.,* torch shooting hot flame

blŭb'bêr, *n.,* fat; *v.,* cry

blŭdg'eŏn, *n.,* short heavy club

blūe, *a.,* color of sky, sad

blūe'bĕll, *n.,* flower

blūe'bĕrrȳ, *n.,* fruit

blūe'bîrd, *n.,* blue

songbird   [tocrat
blūe'blŏod, *n.* (coll.), aris-
blūe chĭp, *a.,* of stable
  stock
blūe-cŏl'làr, *a.,* industrial
blūe'grăss, *n.,* Kentucky
  grass, southern folk music
blūe'jāy, *n.,* bird   [plan
blūe'prĭnt, *n.,* detailed
blŭff, *n.,* steep bank, cliff;
  v., mislead; **-ness; -ly**
blū'ĭng, *n.,* blue substance
  to whiten fabric
blŭn'dêr, *n.,* error; *v.,*
  stumble, err; **-er; -ingly**
blŭnt, *a.,* dull, abrupt;
  -ness; -ly
blûr, *n., v.,* smear,
  smudge; **-ry; -riness**
blûrt, *v.,* say suddenly
blŭsh, *v.,* redden, be embarrassed; **-er**
blŭs'têr, *v.,* blow stormily,
  speak noisily; **-er; -y;
  -ous; -ingly**
bō'à, *n.,* snake
bōar, *n.,* wild hog
bōard, *n.,* flat piece of
  wood, council, meals for
  pay; *v.,* close with
  boards, get on, house;
  -er
bôard'ĭng-house, *n.,*
  place where meals, food
  are paid for   [walkway
bôard'wălk, *n.,* wood
bōast, *v.,* brag; **-ful; -ful-
  ness; -fully**
bōat, *n.,* small watercraft;
  -ing
bŏb, *n.,* girl's short haircut;
  v., move up and down;
  -ber
bŏb'bêr-ÿ, *n.,* commotion
bŏb'bĭn, *n.,* reel for thread
bŏb'bÿ, *n.,* English police-
bŏb'căt, *n.,* lynx   [man
bŏb'ò-lĭnk, *n.,* songbird
bŏb'slĕd, *n.,* racing sled
bŏb-whīte', *n.,* small quail
bŏck, *n.,* dark beer
bōde, *v.,* be omen of
bŏd'īce, *n.,* upper part of
bōd'ĭng, *n.,* omen   [dress
bŏd'ÿ, *n.,* whole physical
  structure, main part,

group; **Ily**   [guard
bŏd'ÿ-guârd, *n.,* person's
bŏg, *n.,* small marsh; *v.,*
  sink; **-gy**   [tate
bŏg'gle, *v.,* startle, hesi-
bō'gŭs, *a.,* false
bō'gÿ, *n.,* evil spirit
bŏil, *n.,* skin swelling; *v.,*
  bubble, heat, seethe
bŏil'êr, *n.,* tank for heating
  water
bŏis'têr-oŭs, *a.,* rowdy; **-ly**
bōld, *a.,* fearless, shameless, striking; **-ness; -ly**
bò-lĕr'ō, *n.,* short vest
bōll, *n.,* cotton seed pod
bōll'wēe-vĭl, *n.,* insect
bō'lō, *n.,* single-edged
  knife   [sage
bò-lō'gnà, *n.,* smoked sau-
bōl'stêr, *n.,* long narrow
  pillow; *v.,* strengthen
bōlt, *n.,* flash, bar for lock-
  ing, roll of cloth; *v.,* fasten, rush out
bŏmb, *n.,* explosive device; *v.,* attack
bŏm'bāst, *n.,* pompous
  talk; **-ic; -ically**
bŏm'bĭ-nāte, *v.,* buzz;
  tation   [wealth
bò-năn'zà, *n.,* source of
bŏn'bŏn, *n.,* candy
bŏnd, *n.,* anything binding,
  surety against theft
bŏnd'àge, *n.,* slavery
bōne, *n.,* hard tissue of
  skeleton; *v.,* remove
  bones, study hard
bŏn'êr, *n.,* error
bŏn'fīre, *n.,* large outdoor
  fire   [sound
bŏng, *n.,* deep ringing
bŏn'gō, *n.,* antelope, pair
  of small drums
bŏn'nĕt, *n.,* hat
bŏn'nÿ, *a.,* handsome,
  pretty; **niness; nily**
bŏn-saī', *n.,* dwarfed tree
bō'nŭs, *n.,* something extra
bōo'bōo, *n.,* (coll.) mistake
bōo'bÿ, *n.,* stupid person
bōo-gĭe-wōo'gĭe, *n.,* jazz
  music
bōo-hōo, *v.,* weep loudly
bōok, *n.,* bound printed

work; v., list, engage ahead

book'end, n., device to keep book upright

book'ing, n., engagement

book'keep-ing, n., record of business transactions; **keeper**

book'māk-êr,n., bet taker; **making**

book'mō-bīle, n., travelling lending library

book'plāte,n., label to tell owner

book'stôre, n., place to buy books   [reader

book'wörm, n., avid

boom,n., prosperous time, beam, deep hollow sound; v., increase

boon,n., benefit

boon'docks, n., pl., wilderness

bôor,n., rude person; **-ish** a.; **-ishly; -ishness**

boost, n., v., push up; **-er;** **-erism**   [v., kick

boot,n., shoe above ankle,

booth,n., small enclosure, stall   [**-ger; -ged**

boot'lĕg, v., sell illegally;

boot'ÿ, n., spoils of war

bô'rȧ-cīte, n., mineral

bôr'ăx, n., white salt

bôr-dĕl'lō,n., brothel

bôr'dêr, n., edge, boundary

bôre,n., hole, dull person; v., drill a hole

bôre'dȯm,n., uninterested state

bôrn, a., brought into life

bör'ōugh, n., self-governing district

bör'rōw, v., temporarily take

bôrsch,n., beet soup

bŏs'cȧge, n., wooded place

bŏsh,n., int., nonsense

bŏs'ȯm, n., woman's breast; **-y** a.

bŏss, n., supervisor; v., order; **-ism; -y**

bŏ'tăn-ÿ,n., study of plant life; **nist; nize; nizer;** **tanical; ically**

bŏtch, v., do poor work; **-er; -y** a.

bōth,a., pro., the two;adv., conj., equally

bōth'êr,v., annoy; **-some**

bŏt'tle, n., container; **-er;** **-ful** n.

bŏt'tle-nĕck, n., retardation of progress

bŏt'tȯm, n., lowest part; **-less; -most** a.

bŏt'ŭ-līsm, n., food poisoning

boū-cle' (klā), n., small curly yarn

boū'doir (âr), n., lady's private room

boū-gàin-vĭl'lē-ȧ, n., flowering vine

bough, n., tree branch

boūil-lȧ-bāisse', v., fish stew

boūil'lŏn, n., clear broth

boūl'ė-vârd, n., broad street   [**-r**

bŏunce, v., spring back;

bŏund, n., v., leap, limit; a., tied, headed

bŏund'ȧ-rÿ, n., limit, border

bŏund'êr,n., cad

bŏun'tÿ, n., bonus, generosity; **teous; tiful; ti-** **fulness; tifully**

boū-quet' (kā), n., bunch of flowers, scent

boûr'bȯn, n., whiskey

bôur-geois' (zhwȧ),n., a., middle class; **sie**

bŏut, n., contest, spell

boū-tīque',n., fashionable shop   [**vine**

bō'vĭd, a., of ox family;

bow, n., ship's front; v., bend body, submit

bōw, n., curve, arrow shooter, looped knot

bōwd'lêr-īze, v., remove offensive parts; **ism;** **ization**   [part

bow'ĕl,n., intestine, inner

bōwl, n., deep rounded container; v., roll ball

bōw'lĕg, n., curved leg; **-ged**

bōwl'êr,n., derby hat

bōwl'ĭng, n., game with

ball and pins; **bowler**
bŏw'mǎn, *n.*, archer
bŏx, *n.*, container, group of seats, evergreen shrubs; *v.*, fight
bŏx'câr, *n.*, enclosed railroad car
bŏx'ĭng, *n.*, sport of fighting; **boxer**
boy (bŏĭ), *n.*, male child; **-hood; -ish; -ishness; -ishly** [deal with
boy'cŏtt (bŏĭ), *v.*, refuse to
bō'zō, *n.*, uncouth fellow
brăb'ble, *v.*, squabble
brāce, *n.*, pair, clamp; *v.*, tighten, support
brāce'lĕt, *n.*, wrist or arm ornament
brāc'ĭng, *a.*, refreshing
brăck'ĕn, *n.*, fern
brăck'ĕt, *n.*, wall support
brăck'ĭsh, *a.*, salty; **-ness**
brăct, *n.*, modified leaf
brăd, *n.*, fastener, nail
brāid, *v.*, interweave strands; **-er**
brāin, *n.*, nerve tissue in skull; intelligence; *v.*, (coll.) hit head
brāin'chĭld, *n.*, idea
brāin'stôrm, *n.*, (coll.) sudden idea; **-ing** *n.*
brāin'wǎsh, *v.*, indoctrinate
brāise, *v.*, cook, brown and simmer
brāke, *n.*, *v.*, (device to) stop motion; **-age; -less**
brāke'mǎn, *n.*, conductor's assistant
brăm'ble, *n.*, prickly shrub
brăn, *n.*, wheat grain's skin or husk [tree limb
brănch, *n.*, part or division,
brănd, *n.*, mark burned on, label; **-er**
brăn'dĭsh, *v.*, wave
brăn'dў, *n.*, liquor from wine; **-died**
brăsh, *a.*, hasty
brăss, *n.*, metal of copper and zinc, (coll.) high official; **-y** *a.*
brăs-sârd', *n.*, armor
brăs-siēre', *n.*, undergarment for breasts

brăt'tle, *n.*, clatter
brȧ-vȧ'dō, *n.*, pretended courage
brāve, *a.*, bold, courageous; **-ry; -ly**
brȧ'vō, *int.*, well done!
brāwl, *n.*, *v.*, quarrel, fight; **-er**
brāwn, *n.*, muscular strength; **-y; -iness**
brāy, *n.*, donkey's cry
brāze, *v.*, make of brass; **-er** [**-ly**
brăz'ĕn, *a.*, bold; **-ness;**
brȧ'zĭl, *n.*, tree, nut
brēach, *n.*, violation
brĕad, *n.*, leavened flour mixture baked, (coll.) money
brĕadth, *n.*, width
brĕad'wĭn-nêr, *n.*, money earner
breāk, *v.*, split apart, ruin, interrupt; **-er; -age; -able** [work
breāk'down, *n.*, failure to
breāk'êr, *n.*, wave
breāk'fȧst, *n.*, morning meal
breāk'throūgh, *n.*, important advance
breāk'ŭp, *n.*, ending
breāk'wȧ-têr, *n.*, barrier against waves
brĕast, *n.*, milk secreting gland, bosom, bust
brĕast'plāte, *n.*, chest armor
brĕath, *n.*, inhaling and exhaling air; **-less; -lessness; -lessly**
brēathe, *v.*, inhale and exhale air, live; **-r**
brĕath'tāk-ĭng, *a.*, thrilling
brēech, *n.*, lower part
brēed, *n.*, similar type; *v.*, produce, raise; **-er; -ing**
brēeze, *n.*, gentle wind
brēeze'wāy, *n.*, covered passageway
brĕth'rĕn, *n.*, *pl.*, spiritual brothers
brē'vĭ-ār-ў, *n.*, prayer book
brĕv'ĭ-tў, *n.*, briefness
brew, *v.*, prepare beer, boil, plot; **-er; -age**
brībe, *n.*, inducement to do

something wrong; **-r; -ry**

brĭc′à-brăc, *n.*, small objects of art

brĭck, *n.*, baked clay building block

brĭck′lè, *n.*, *a.*, brittle

brīde, *n.*, woman getting married

brīde′grŏŏm, *n.*, man getting married

brīdes′māid, *n.*, bride's wedding attendant

brĭdge, *n.*, connection, structure spanning water or road, card game

brĭdge′wŏrk, *n.*, mounting of false teeth

brī′dle, *n.*, head harness for horse; *v.*, restrain

brĭĕf′cāse, *n.*, carrying case for papers

brī′êr, *n.*, thorny bush

brĭg, *n.*, boat, navy jail

brĭ-gāde′, *n.*, unit of soldiers

brĭg′ànd, *n.*, bandit; **-age**

brīght, *n.*, shining; cheerful; **-en,** *v.*, **-ness; -ly**

brĭl′liànt, *a.*, bright, intelligent; **liance; liancy; -ly**

brĭm, *n.*, edge; **-ful**

brīne, *n.*, salt water; **-y,** *a.*

brĭnk, *n.*, edge, verge

brĭsk, *a.*, quick, cool, active; **-ness; -ly**

brĭs′kĕt, *n.*, animal's breast

brĭs′tle, *n.*, stiff prickly hair; **tly; tliness**

brĭt′tle, *a.*, stiff, fragile; **-ness; -ly** [**-er**

brōach, *v.*, bring up, utter;

brŏad, *a.*, wide; **-ness; -ly**

brŏad′clŏth, *n.*, fine woolen cloth

brŏad-mīnd′ĕd, *a.*, tolerant; **-ness; -ly**

brō-cāde′, *n.*, rich cloth with metallic thread

brŏc′cò-lī, *n.*, edible plant

brō-chĕtte′, *n.*, skewer

brō′gàn, *n.*, heavy work shoe [shoe

brŏgue, *n.*, accent, coarse

broĭl, *v.*, cook by direct heat, become angry; **-er**

brŏk′ĕn, *a.*, out of order, cracked

brŏk-ĕn-heärt′ĕd, *a.*, crushed by grief; **-ly**

brō′kêr, *n.*, hired agent; **-age**

brō′mīde, *n.*, sedative, platitude; **midic**

brŏn′chĭ-ål, *a.*, of windpipe; **chitis; chitic**

brŏn′cō, *n.*, wild horse

brŏnze, *n.*, metal alloy of copper and tin

brōoch, *n.*, ornamental pin

brōod, *n.*, family offspring; *v.*, worry; **-er, -y,** *a.*

brōok, *n.*, stream; *v.*, endure

brōom, *n.*, long-handled brush for sweeping, shrub

brŏth, *n.*, clear thin soup

brŏth′ĕl, *n.*, house of prostitution

brŏth′êr-lў, *a.*, friendly

brŏw, *n.*, forehead

brŏw′bēat, *v.*, bully

brŏwn, *n.*, color of chocolate; **-ish**

brŏwn′iĕ, *n.*, elf, rich chocolate cookie

brŏwse, *v.*, glance through, feed on leaves; **-er**

brūise, *v.*, hurt

brūme, *n.*, fog

brŭnch, *n.*, one meal for both breakfast and lunch

brŭnt, *n.*, main impact

brŭsh, *n.*, utensil with bristles for hair, paint; thicket; *v.*, use brush, touch [missal

brŭsh′-ŏff, *n.* (coll.) dis-

brŭsque, *a.*, curt, blunt

brūte, *n.*, *a.*, animal, cruel person; **brutish**

bŭb′ble, *n.*, film holding air and gas; *v.*, boil foam, belch; **bly**

bŭc′cà-nēer, *n.*, pirate

bŭck, *n.*, male deer, (coll.) dollar; *v.*, rear upward

bŭck′bôard, *n.*, wagon with seating

bŭck′ĕt, *n.*, pail; **-ful**

bŭck′le, *n.*, clasp for belt

and shoes; v., join, bend

bŭck′shŏt, n., large lead bullet [front tooth

bŭck′tōoth, n., protruding

bŭck′whēat, n., grain

bū-cŏl′ĭc, a., rural; **-ally**

bŭd, n., developing flower; v., start to grow; **-der**

bŭdge, v., move

bŭdg′ĕr-ĭ-gâr, n., bird

bŭdg′ĕt, n., v., plan for expenses; **-er; -ary**

bŭff, v., polish; **-er**

bŭf′fȧ-lō, n., wild oxen

bŭf′fet (fā), n., counter for serving food

bŭf-fōon′, n., clown

bŭg′gȳ, n., horse-drawn carriage; a., insane

bŭ′gle, n., small trumpet

buĭld, v., put together, construct; **-er**

bŭlb, n., underground bud; **bulbous**

bŭlge, n., v., swell; **-y,** a.

bŭlk, n., mass; **-y; -iness; -ily**

bŭll, n., male bovine, elephant, seal, etc., Papal edict, nonsense; **-ish**

bŭll′dōze, v., bully, dig out; **-er** [gun

bŭl′lĕt, n., metal shot from

bŭl′lĕ-tĭn, n., brief statement

bŭll′finch, n., songbird

bŭll′frŏg, n., large frog

bŭll′hĕad-ĕd, a., stubborn

bŭll′hôrn, n., voice amplifier [ingot

bŭl′lĭon, n., gold or silver

bŭl′lȳ, n., v., (one who) frighten(s)

bŭl′rŭsh, n., marsh plant

bŭl′wàrk, n., fortification

bŭm′ble-bēe, n., large bee

bŭmp, n., v., knock against; **-y** [guard

bŭmp′ĕr, n., metal car

bŭmp′tioŭs, a., arrogant; **-ness; -ly** [knot

bŭn, n., small roll, hair in

bŭnch, n., cluster, group of things; **-y; -iness**

bŭnd, n., league; **-ist**

bŭn′dle, n., things held together

bŭng, n., barrel stopper

bŭn′gȧ-lōw, n., one story house, cottage [-r

bŭn′gle, v., botch, spoil;

bŭn′ĭon, n., foot swelling

bŭnk, n., shelflike bed

bŭnk′ĕr, n., storage bin, sand pit in golf

bŭn′nȳ, n., rabbit

bŭnt, n., v., butt, push

bŭn′tĭng, n., decorative cloth [marker

būoȳ, n., floating warning

bûr, n., prickly seed case

bûr′dĕn, n., load; **-some; -somely**

bu′reau (rö), n., chest of drawers, agency

bûrg, n., town; **-er**

bûr′gĕon, v., sprout, grow

bûr′ĭ-ȧl, n., burying a body

bûrke, v., get rid of

bûrl, n., knot in wood

bûr′lȧp, n., coarse hemp cloth

bûr-lĕsque′, n., comic satire, sexy entertainment

bûr′lȳ, a., big and strong; **iness**

bûrn′ĭsh, n., v., polish

bûrr, n., rough edge

bûr′rō, n., donkey

bûr′rōw, n., animal dug hole or ground tunnel

bûr′sȧr, n., college treasurer; **-y; -ial**

bûr-sĭ′tĭs, n., inflammation of sac in joints

bûrst, v., explode; **-er**

bur′ȳ (bĕr), v., put in grave, hide

bŭs′boy (bŏi), n., waiter's assistant

bŭsh, n., shrub, low thickly grown plant; **-y,** a.

bŭshed, a., bewildered, (coll.) tired

busi′nĕss (bĭz), n., one's work, commerce, concern; **-man; -woman**

bŭst, n., sculpture from chest up, breast; v., break, become bankrupt

bŭs′tle, n., commotion, skirt padding in back; v., busily hurry

bus′ȳ (bĭz), a., active, in-

dustrious; **-ness**
bū'tāne, *n.,* flammable gas
bŭtch'êr, *n.,* meat slaugh-
terer and cutter; **-er; -y;**
-ly
bŭt'lêr, *n.,* male house
servant   [ram
bŭtt, *n.,* thick end, stub; *v.,*
bŭtte, *n.,* lone steep hill
bŭt'têr, *n.,* yellowish fat
churned from cream; *v.,*
spread butter; **-y** *a.*
bŭt'têr-fĭn-gêrs, *n.,* one
who drops things
bŭt'têr-flȳ, *n.,* insect with
4 large colored wings
bŭt'têr-scŏtch, *n.,* hard,
sticky candy
bŭt'tŏck, *n.,* half of rump
bŭt'tŏn, *n.,* small disk or
knob for fastening gar-
ments
bŭt'trĕss, *n.,* wall support
bŭx'ŏm, *a.,* plump, jolly
buȳ, *v.,* get by paying
money, purchase; **-er**
bŭz'zàrd, *n.,* bird of prey
bȳ'-ănd-bȳ', *adv.,* before
long
bȳe'-bȳe', *n.,* int. goodbye
bȳ'gŏne, *a.,* past
bȳ'-prŏd-ŭct, *n.,* secondary result
bȳ'-stănd-êr, *n.,* onlooker
bȳ'wāy, *n.,* side road
bȳ'wŏrd, *n.,* saying, proverb

C

căb, *n.,* taxi, train, truck
operator's compartment
cà-băl', *n.,* plot (ter)
căb'à-là, *n.,* secret belief;
list; lism; listic;
listically   [house
cà-bă'nà, *n.,* private bath-
căb-à-ret' (rā), *n.,* café
with entertainment
căb'băge, *n.,* leafy
vegetable [story house
căb'ĭn, *n.,* simple one-
căb'ĭ-nĕt, *n.,* furniture with
shelves and/or drawers;
advisory council; **-ry**
cā'ble, *n.,* thick wire or
rope; *v.,* send message

overseas
cà-bōose', *n.,* trainmen's
car at rear
căb'rĭ-ōle, *n.,* graceful
curved furniture leg
căb-rĭ-ò-let' (lā), *n.,* two-
wheeled carriage
căche (căsh), *n.,* hidden
storage
cà-chet' (shā), *n.,* official
seal   [hen
căck'le, *n., v.,* shrill like
căc'tŭs, *n.,* desert plant
căd, *n.,* ill-bred man
cà-dăv'êr, *n.,* dead body;
-ic; -ous; -ousness;
-ously   [ant
căd'diē, *n.,* golfer's attend-
cā'dence, *n.,* rhythmic
flow of sound; **dency;**
dent
cà-dĕt', *n.,* student of military school
cădge, *v.,* beg; **-r**
căd'mĭ-ŭm, *n.,* metallic
element   [symbol
cà-dū'cē-ŭs, *n.,* medical
căf-ė-tē'rĭ-à, *n.,* self-serv-
ice restaurant
căf'fēine, *n.,* stimulant in
coffee and tea
căf'tàn, *n.,* long full robe
cāge, *n.,* barred enclosure
for animals
cā'gēy, *a.,* (coll.) sly
cāis'sŏn, *n.,* ammunition
wagon   **[-ment**
cà-jōle', *v.,* coax; **-r; -ry;**
cāke, *n.,* sweet baked
dough; *v.,* solidify
cāke'wălk, *n.,* dance
căl'à-mīne, *n.,* mineral for
lotions and ointments
cà-lăm'ĭ-tȳ, *n.,* disaster;
tous; tousness; tously
căl'cĭ-ŭm, *n.,* chemical
element in bone, lime-
stone
căl'cŭ-lāte, *v.,* compute;
lation; -d; -dly; lable;
lably; lability
căl'cŭ-lāt-ĭng, *a.,* shrewd
căl'cŭ-lŭs, *n.,* kind of
higher mathematics
căl'drŏn, *n.,* large kettle
căl'ĕn-dàr, *n.,* list of
months and days

căl'ĭbêr, *n.*, degree of worth, gun measurement; **brator; bration; brate**

căl'ĭ-cō, *n.*, cotton cloth

căl'ĭ-pêr, *n.*, measuring tool

ca'lĭph, *n.*, Moslem ruler

căl-ĭs-thĕn'ĭcs, *n.*, exercises [watertight

călk, *v.*, fill cracks to make

căll, *n.*, *v.*, summon, shout, order; telephone

căll'êr, *n.*, visitor

căl-lĭg'rȧ-phȳ, *n.*, penmanship; **pher; phist; graphic**

căl'loŭs, *a.*, insensitive; **losity; -ness; -ly**

căl'lōw, *a.*, inexperienced; **-ness** [skin

căl'lŭs, *n.*, hard place on

călm, *n.*, stillness; *a.*, quiet, tranquil; **-ness; -ative; -ly**

căl'ȯ-rĭē, *n.*, unit of food energy; **loric**

căl'ŭ-mĕt, *n.*, Indian peace pipe

căl'ŭm-nȳ, *n.*, slander; **niator; niation; niate; nious; niously**

cȧ-lȳp'sō, *n.*, West Indian music

cā'lȳx, *n.*, flower's protective leaves

căm, *n.*, rotating machine part [curve

căm'bêr, *n.*, slight convex

căm'brĭc, *n.*, fine linen or cotton cloth [hump

căm'ĕl, *n.*, animal with

căm'ė-ō, *n.*, gem with carved figure

căm'êr-ȧ, *n.*, picture-taking device

căm'ĭ-sōle, *n.*, woman's undergarment

căm'ȯu-flăge, *n.*, disguise; **-r**

cămp, *n.*, temporary lodging, for vacations, the military; **-er**

căm-pāign', *n.*, planned actions, military battle

căm-pȧ-nĭ'lē, *n.*, bell tower

căm'phȯr, *n.*, substance for protecting clothes; **-ate; -ic**

căn, *n.*, metal container; *v.*, to be able to, may

cȧ-năl', *n.*, artificial waterway; **-ize; -ization**

cȧ-nârd', *n.*, false story

cȧ-năs'tȧ, *n.*, card game

căn'-căn, *n.*, high kicking dance

căn'cĕl, *v.*, make void, do away with; **-er; -ler; -lation**

căn'cêr, *n.*, malignant growth; **-ous**

căn-dė-lá'brŭm, *n.*, branched candlestick; **-bra** *pl.* [cence

căn-dĕs'cĕnt, *a.*, glowing;

căn'dĭd, *a.*, frank, informal

căn'dĭ-dāte, *n.*, office seeker; **dacy**

căn'dle, *n.*, wax stick for burning

căn'dȯr, *n.*, frankness

căn'dȳ, *n.*, sweet food made with sugar; **died**

cāne, *n.*, walking stick

cā'nīne, *a.*, *n.*, (of) dog

căn'ĭs-têr, *n.*, small can or box [-ous

căn'kêr, *n.*, ulcerous sore;

căn'nĭ-bȧl, *n.*, eater of human flesh; **-ism; -istic; -istically**

căn'nĭng, *n.*, preservation of food

căn'nȯn, *n.*, large, mounted gun

căn'nȳ, *a.*, shrewd, cautious

cȧ-noe' (nū), *n.*, small boat moved by paddle(s)

căn'ȯn, *n.*, church law, clergyman; **-ical**

căn'ȯn-īze, *v.*, declare a saint; **zation**

căn'ȯ-pȳ, *n.*, awning, rooflike covering

cănt, *n.*, insincere talk, dialect, tilt, slant

căn'tȧ-lōupe, *n.*, orange melon

căn-tȧ'tȧ, *n.*, choral composition

căn-tēen', *n.*, water container, military store

căn'têr, *n.,* horse's easy gallop [chant

căn'tĭ-cle, *n.,* religious

căn'tĭ-lē-vêr, *n.,* beam supported at one end

căn'tŏn, *n.,* small district

căn'tŏr, *n.,* synagogue's lead singer [cloth

căn'vås, *n.,* heavy hemp

căn'våss, *v.,* examine, solicit; **-er**

căn'yŏn, *n.,* deep, narrow valley

căp, *n.,* brimless hat, bottle top; *v.,* cover, do better

cā'på-ble, *a.,* able, skilled; **-ness; bly; bility**

cå-pā'cioŭs, *a.,* roomy; **-ness; -ly**

cāpe, *n.,* sleeveless loose outer garment; land jutting into water

cā'pêr, *n.,* prank; *v.,* leap about

căp'ĭl-lār-ў, *n.,* tiny blood vessel; *a.,* hairlike; **larity**

căp'ĭ-tål, *n.,* large letter, place of government, wealth; *a.,* punishable by death, chief

căp'ĭ-tål-ĭsm, *n.,* economic system of private investment; **ist; istic; istically**

căp'ĭ-tŏl, *n.,* chief government building

cå-pĭt'ū-lāte, *v.,* surrender; **lation** [rooster

cā'pŏn, *n.,* castrated

cå-prīce', *n.,* whim; **pricious**

căp'sīze, *v.,* overturn

căp'sŭle, *n.,* small case, ex. for dose of medicine; **lar; late** *a.*

căp'taĭn, *n.,* leader; **-cy; -ship**

căp'tĭon, *n.,* headline, title

căp'tioŭs, *a.,* critical; **-ness; -ly**

căp'tĭve, *n.,* prisoner *a.,* forced; **tivity**

căp'tûre, *v.,* seize, catch; **tor** [key

căp'ū-chĭn (shĭn), *n.,* moncår, *n.,* wheeled vehicle,

automobile [falo

cå-rå-bäo', *n.,* water buffalo

cår'å-měl, *n.,* chewy candy; **-ize**

cår'åt, *n.,* unit of weight for precious stones

căr'å-văn, *n.,* group of travellers

căr'å-wāy, *n.,* seed for flavoring

câr'bīne, *n.,* short rifle; **-er**

câr-bŏ-hў'drāte, *n.,* organic compound, energy food, ex. starch, sugar

câr'bŏn, *n.,* chemical element, **-ation; -ate; -ize; -aceous; ic**

câr'bŭn-cle, *n.,* garnet, pus-bearing skin sore

câr'bŭ-re-tôr (rā), *n.,* device to mix air and gasoline [dead body

câr'cåss, *n.,* animal's

câr-cĭ-nŏ'må, *n.,* cancer

cârd, *n.,* stiff piece of paper, usually printed

câr'dĭ-ăc, *a.,* of heart

câr'dĭ-nål, *n.,* Catholic high official, red songbird; *a.,* chief, red; **-ship; -ly**

câre, *n.,* concern, worry; *v.,* be interested in, wish

cå-rēen', *v.,* lean

cå-rēer', *n.,* occupation in life; **-ist**

cå-rĕss', *n., v.* touch with love; **-er; -ive; -ively**

câre'tăk-êr, *n.,* custodian, one who cares for building

câr'fåre, *n.,* price to ride bus

câr'gō, *n.,* ship's freight

căr'ĭ-boū, *n.,* reindeer

căr'ĭ-cå-tûre, *n.,* exaggerated portrait or description [ious

căr'ĭěs, *n.,* tooth decay;

căr'ĭl-lŏn, *n.,* set of bells

căr'ĭ-ōle, *n.,* horse carriage

cå'rĭ-ŏn, *n.,* dead flesh

câr'līne, *n.,* witch

câr'någe, *n.,* killing of

many people

câr′nál, *a.*, of flesh, sexual; **-ity; -ly**

câr-nā′tion, *n.*, flower

câr′nĭ-vàl, *n.*, merrymaking, travelling show

câr′ŏl, *n.*, joyful song

câr′ŏ-tēne, *n.*, red or orange vegetable pigment

cà-rouse′, *v.*, drink at a party

câr′pél, *n.*, flower part

câr′pén-têr, *n.*, skilled worker in wood; **try**

câr′pét, *n.*, heavy cloth floor covering

câr′pŭs, *n.*, wrist and its bone; **pal**

câr′rĭage, *n.*, wheeled vehicle for people, posture

câr′rÿ, *v.*, take to another place, support, hold; **rier**

cârt, *n.*, two-wheeled vehicle; *v.*, carry; **-er; -age**

câr-tĕl′, *n.*, industrial monopoly

câr′tĭ-làge, *n.*, elastic-like body tissue, gristle; **laginous**

câr-tŏg′rà-phÿ, *n.*, map making; **pher; graphic**

câr′tŏn, *n.*, large cardboard box

câr-tōōn′, *n.*, humorous drawing

câr′trĭdge, *n.*, metal case for bullet or gunpowder

câr-ÿ-ăt′ĭd, *n.*, female statue used as column

căs-càde′, *n.*, waterfall

cāse, *n.*, instance, lawsuit, holder

cā′sė-ĭn, *n.*, milk protein

cāse′mént, *n.*, window frame

cā′sė-oŭs, *a.*, of cheese

căsh′ew, *n.*, nut

căsh-iêr′, *n.*, one who deals with money

căsh′mēre, *n.*, soft wool fabric

cà-sī′nō, *n.*, gambling hall

căsk, *n.*, barrel

căs′kĕt, *n.*, coffin, chest

căs-sĕtte′, *n.*, film or tape holder   [game

căs-sī′nō, *n.*, simple card

căs′sòck, *n.*, clerical garment   [bird

căs′sò-wār-ÿ, *n.*, flightless

căst, *n., v.*, throw, mold; *n.*, actors in a play

căst′à-wāy, *n.*, shipwrecked person

căste, *n.*, social class

căst′êr, *n.*, wheel used as furniture leg

căs′tĭ-gāte, *v.*, punish; **tor; tion; tory**   [dence

căs′tle, *n.*, fortified resi-

căs′trāte, *v.*, remove testicles; **tion**

căs′ū-ál, *a.*, by chance, informal; **-ty; -ness; -ly**

căs′ū-ĭst-rÿ, *n.*, oversubtle reasoning; **istic; istical; istically**

căt′à-clÿsm, *n.*, disaster; **mic; mal**

căt′à-cōmb, *n.*, underground burial place

căt′à-lĕp-sÿ, *n.*, loss of consciousness; **leptic**

căt′à-lŏg, *n., v.*, list; **-er; -ist**

căt′à-lÿst, *n.*, agent causing chemical reaction; **lyze; lytic; lytically**

căt-à-mà-răn′, *n.*, sailboat

căt′à-pŭlt, *v.*, hurl, launch

căt′à-răct, *n.*, waterfall, eye disease

cà-târrh′, *n.*, nose and throat disease; **-al; -ous**

cà-tăs′trò-phē, *n.*, sudden disaster; **strophic; strophically**

căt′càll, *n.*, shrill noise of disapproval

cătch, *v.*, capture, get; **-er**

cătch′ÿ, *a.*, arousing interest; **catchiness**

căt′ė-chĭsm, *n.*, religious doctrine; **chist; chize; mal; chistic; chistical**

căt′ė-gôr′ÿ, *n.*, grouping; class; **rization; rize**

cā′têr, *v.*, provide food, serve; **-er**

căt′êr-pĭl-làr, *n.*, moth or butterfly larva

căt′êr-wäul, *n., v.*, howl like a cat

cȧ-thȧr'sĭs, *n.,* release of emotion; **thartic**

cȧ-thē'drȧl, *n.,* imposing church [bladder

cȧth'ė-tȇr, *n.,* tube to drain

cȧth'ōde, *n.,* negative electrode

cȧth'ŏ-lic, *a.,* universal; **-ity; -ize**

cȧt'sŭp, *n.,* tomato sauce

cȧt'tÿ, *a.,* spiteful

cȧt'wȧlk, *n.,* narrow bridge

cȧu'cŭs, *n.,* political meeting

cȧu'dȧl, *a.,* taillike

cȧuse, *n.,* reason, motive; *v.,* bring about; **sation; -ity; causal**

cȧuse'wȧy, *n.,* raised road

cȧus'tic, *a.,* burning, sarcastic; **-ity; -ally**

cȧu'tȇr-ize, *n.,* burn with hot iron; **zation** [ing

cȧu'tion, *n.,* danger warn-

cȧv'ȧ-liȇr, *n.,* gentleman; *a.,* gay, arrogant

cȧv'ȧl-rÿ, *n.,* military troops on horseback

cȧve, *n.,* hollow place in earth

cȧve'-ĭn, *n.,* collapse

cȧve'mȧn, *n.,* prehistoric man

cȧv'ĭ-ȧr, *n.,* fish eggs as appetizer

cȧv'ĭl, *v.,* find fault; **-er**

cȧv'ĭ-tÿ, *n.,* hole

cȧ-vôrt', *v.,* prance, frolic

cȧw, *n.,* crow's cry [per

cȧÿ-ĕnne', *n.,* hot red pep-

cėase, *n., v.,* stop; **-less**

cė'dȧr, *n.,* tree

cėde, *v.,* give up, surrender [room

cėil'ĭng, *n.,* covering of a

cĕl'ė-brȧte, *v.,* honor with festivity, perform ritual; **tor; tion; tory**

cĕl'ė-rÿ, *n.,* stalked vegetable [-ly

cė-lĕs'tiȧl, *a.,* heavenly;

cĕll, *n.,* small room, unit of living matter; **-ular** *a.*

cĕl'lȧr, *n.,* room(s) under a building

cĕl'lō, *n.,* stringed musical instrument

cĕl'lȯ-phāne, *n.,* transparent plastic sheeting

cĕl'lū-lōse, *n.,* substance in plant cell walls

cė-mĕnt', *n.* substance of mortar or concrete; *s.* stick

cĕm'ė-tȇr-ÿ, *n.,* graveyard

cĕnse, *v.,* burn incense

cĕn'sȯr, *n.,* official judge of media for acceptability **-ship**

cĕn'sŭs, *n.,* official population count

cĕnt, *n.,* 0.01 of a dollar

cĕn'tȧur, *n.,* mythical horseman

cĕn-tĕn'nĭ-ȧl, *a.,* of 100 years; **-ly**

cĕn'tȇr, *n.,* middle point

cĕn'tĭ-grāde, *a.,* of thermometer based on 100 degrees

cĕn'tĭ-pēde, *n.,* insect with many legs

cĕn-trĭf'ŭ-gȧl, *a.,* away from center; **-ly**

cĕn-trĭp'ė-tȧl, *a.,* toward a center; **-ly**

cĕn-tŭ'rĭ-ȧn, *n.,* ancient Roman military officer

cė-phȧl'ĭc, *a.,* of the head; **lous; -ally**

cė-rȧm'ĭcs, *n. pl.,* are of pottery; **ist; ic**

cė'rė-ȧl, *n., a.,* grain for food

cȇr-ė-bĕl'lŭm, *n.,* lower part of brain

cȇr'ė-brŭm, *n.,* main part of brain; **bral**

cȇr'ė-mō-nÿ, *n.,* formal act; **nial; nialist; nialism; nious; niousness; niously**

cȇr-tĭf'ĭ-cȧte, *n.,* document of true facts; **tor, tory**

cȇr'vĭx, *n.,* necklike part

cĕs-sā'tion, *n.,* stopping

cĕss'pōōl, *n.,* sewage pit

cė-tŏl'ȯ-gÿ, *n.,* study of whales; **gist; logical**

chāfe, *n.,* irritation from rubbing; *v.,* rub against

chȧf'êr, *n.,* beetle

chȧ-grĭn' (shȧ), *n.,* embarrassment

chāin, *n.,* series as links, (*pl.*) bondage; *v.,* restrain

chāir'măn, *n.,* presiding officer; **woman; -ship**

chāise, *n.,* horse-drawn carriage, couch-like chair

chă-let' (shă-lā), *n.,* country house

chăl'īce, *n.,* cup, goblet

chăl'lĕnge, *n., v.,* dare, question, contest; **-r -able**

chăm'bêr, *n.,* room, hall

chăm'bêr-lain, *n.,* manager, supervisor

chă-mē'lê-ŏn (kă), *n.,* lizard who can change color

chăm-pāgne' (shăm-pān), *n.,* sparkling white wine

chăm-pāign' (shăm-pān), *n.,* plain

chăm'pī-ŏn, *n.,* winner, *v.,* defend; *a.,* best; **-ship**

chăn'cĕl, *n.,* space near church altar

chăn'cĕl-lŏr, *n.,* high official; **lery; -ship**

chăn-dĕ-liĕr' (shăn), *n.,* hanging lighting fixture

chăn'dlêr, *n.,* supplier; **-y**

chănge'lĭng, *n.,* child substituted for another

chăn'nĕl, *n.,* passage, waterway, television frequency; *v.,* direct; **-ize; -ization**

chănt, *n.,* song, *v.,* speak in singsong; **-er**

chăn'tĭ-clēer (shăn), *n.,* rooster

chā'ŏs (kă), *n.,* confusion; **otic; otically**

chăp'ĕl, *n.,* room of worship

chăp'êr-ŏn (shăp), *n.,* older person in charge of young one

chăp'lain, *n.,* clergyman

chăp'têr, *n.,* part, book division, branch

chăr, *v.,* burn

chăr'ăc-têr (kăr), *n.,* sym-

bol, role, personality, quality

chă-rāde' (shă), *n.,* pantomime game

chăr'cōal, *n.,* partly burned wood

chărge, *n., v.,* load, command, blame, bill, attack; **-r; -able**

chăr'ĭ-ŏt, *n.,* ancient horse-drawn cart; **-eer**

chă-rĭs'mă (kă), *n.,* personal magnetism; **matic**

chăr'ĭ-tў, *n.,* good will, giving to the needy; **table; tableness, tably**

chăr'lă-tăn, *n.,* quack; **-ism**

chărm, *n.,* trinket, spell; *v.* attract, fascinate; **-er; -ing**

chărt, *n., v.,* map, diagram; **-ist; -less**

chărt'êr, *n.,* license; *v.,* hire; **-er**

chăr-treūse' (shâr), *n.,* yellowish-green

chăr'wŏm-ăn, *n.,* cleaning lady

chăr'ў, *n.,* careful

chāse, *n.,* hunt, pursuit; *v.,* run after; **-r**

chăsm, *n.,* deep crack in earth

chăs'sis (ē), *n.,* framework

chāste, *a.,* virtuous, pure; **-ness; -ly**

chăs'tĕn, *v.,* punish; **-er**

chă-teau' (shă-tō), *n.,* house [erty

chăt'tĕl, *n.,* movable prop-

chăt'têr-bŏx, *n.,* incessant talker

chau'vĭn-ĭsm (shō), *n.,* fanatical prejudice, **ist; istic, istically**

chēap, *a.,* low in price; **-ness; -en;** *v.,* **-ly**

chēat, *v.,* swindle, trick; **-er; -ingly**

chĕck, *n., v.,* halt, bill, test control, mark; *n.,* written order to one's bank

chĕck'êr, *n.,* square on chessboard, cashier, (*pl.*) game

chĕck'êred, *a.,* varied

check'māte, *n.*, defeat

chēek, *n.*, face below eye, impudence; -y *a.*

chēer, *n.*, joy, glad shout; *v.*, comfort, encourage; -ful; -fulness; -fully; -less; -y; *a.*, -ly

chēese, *n.*, food made from milk curd

chēese' clöth, *n.*, thin cotton cloth   [cat

chēe'tåh, *n.*, leopard-like

chēf, *n.*, cook

chĕm'ĭs-trÿ, *n.*, science of substances and elements

chĕm-ō-thĕr'å-pÿ (kĕm), *n.*, treatment of infection by chemical drugs; pist; peutic; peutics; peutically

chĕr'ĭsh, *v.*, hold dear

chė-rōot' (shå), *n.*, cigar

chĕr'rÿ, *n.*, small red fruit

chĕr'ŭb, *n.*, angel, sweet child; -ic; -ically

chĕss, *n.*, checkerboard game of skill

chĕst, *n.*, box with lid, cabinet, front part of body above abdomen

chĕv'rŏn (shĕv), *n.*, bar on sleeve for rank

chēw, *v.*, grind with teeth, think; -er, -y *a.*

chĭc (shĭk), *a.*, stylish, smart   [ception

chĭ-cān'êr-ÿ (shĭ), *n.*, de-

chĭck'ĕn, *n.*, edible farm bird; *a.* (coll.) timid

chĭc'ò-rÿ, *n.*, plant for either salad or coffee

chīde, *v.*, scold   [-ly

chiĕf, *n.*, leader; *a.*, main;

chĭf-fŏn' (shĭf), *n.*, sheer fabric

chĭg'gêr, *n.*, larva of a mite

chĭ'gnŏn (shĭ), *n.*, hair knot or roll

chīld, *n.*, young person, offspring; -hood; -less; -ish

chĭl'ĭ, *n.*, hot seasoning

chĭl'ĭ-ăd, *n.*, thousand

chĭll, *n.*, cold feeling, shiver; *v.*, make cool; -y *a.*; -iness; -ily

chīme, *n.*, set of bells; *v.*, ring   [smoke

chĭm'nēy, *n.*, passage for

chĭn, *n.*, face below lips; *v.*, pull up by hands

chĭ'nå, *n.*, porcelain, dishes

chĭn-chĭl'lå, *n.*, rodent bred for its fur

chĭ'nō (shĭ), *n.*, strong cotton cloth

chĭntz, *n.*, shiny cotton cloth; -y *a.*

chĭp, *n.*, small piece, gambling disc; *v.*, break off bits; -per

chĭp'pêr, *a.*, lively

chĭ-rŏg'rå-phÿ (kĭ), *n.*, handwriting; pher; graphic, graphically

chĭ-rŏp'ò-dÿ (kĭ), *n.*, treatment of hands and feet; dist

chĭ-rò-prăc'tĭc (kĭ), *n.*, body treatment by massage; tor

chĭrp, *n.*, *v.*, shrill like a bird

chĭs'ėl, *n.*, cutting tool

chĭt, *n.*, child, voucher

chĭt'ter-lings (chĭt lĭngz), *n.*, pig's intestine as food

chĭv'ål-rÿ (shĭv), *n.*, knight's qualities; ric; rous; rousness; rously

chīve, *n.*, onionlike plant

chlō'rĭne (klō), *n.*, gaseous element; ric; rous

chlō'rò-fôrm (klō), *n.*, liquid anesthetic

chlō'rò-phÿll (klō), *n.*, green pigment of plant cells; -ous

chòc'ò-låte, *n.*, flavor from cacao beans, candy, drink

choĭce, *n.*, selection; *a.*, superior   [singers

choĭr (kwīr), *n.*, group of

chōke, *v.*, unable to breathe; -r; -y *a.*

chŏl'êr-å (kŏl), *n.*, intestinal disease

chò-lĕs'têr-ōl (kó), *n.*, substance in animal fat

chŏmp, *v.*, bite down

chōōse, *v.*, pick, select

chŏp, v., cut; n., sharp blow, slice of meat; **-per**

chôrd, n., combination of musical notes

chôre, n., task, odd job

chôr'ē-ȯ-grăph (kôr), v., design a dance; **-er; -y; -ic; -ically**

chôr'tle, n., v., chuckle

chōs'ėn, a., selected

chŏw, n., dog, (coll.) food

chŏw'dėr, n., thick soup

chrō-măt'ĭc (krō), a., of color, **-ism; -ity; -s; -ally**

chrō'mĭ-ŭm (krō), n., metallic element

chrō'mȯ-sōme (krō), n., carrier of genes in every human cell; **mal**

chrŏn'ĭc (krŏn), a., constant, recurring; **-ity; -ally**

chrȯ-nŏl'ȯ-gÿ (krȯ), n., arrangement of things in order; **gist; ger; logic; logical; logically**

chrȯ-nŏm'ė-têr (krō), n., very accurate clock

chŭb'bÿ, a., plump; **bi-ness**

chŭck, n., cut of meat; v., toss

chŭm, n., close friend; **-my; -miness; -mily**

chŭmp, n., (coll.) fool

chŭnk, n., short thick piece; **-y** a.

chûrch, n., place for worship, religion; **-less; -ly**

chûrl, n., boor; **-ish**

chûrn,, v., make milk into butter, agitate

chūte (shŭt), n., sloping passage for sliding

cĭ-cā'dȧ, n., insect family

cĭc'ȧ-trĭx, n., scar; **trize**

cĭ-gâr', n., roll of tobacco leaves

cĭg-ȧ-rĕtte', n., cut tobacco rolled in paper

cĭl'ĭ-ȧ, n. pl., hairlike growths; **-ry** a.

cĭnch, n., saddle, (coll.) easy thing

cĭnc'tûre, n., belt

cĭn'dėr, n., burned wood, ash

cĭn-ė-mȧ-tŏg'rȧ-phÿ, n., art of photographing movies; **pher; graphic; graphical; graphically**

cĭn'nȧ-mȯn, n., spice

cī'phêr, n., zero, code

cîr'cȧ, adv., prep., about

cîr'cle, n., closed curved line where all points lie equally from center, group

cîr'cuĭt, n., boundary, path (of current)

cîr'cū-lāte, v., move around; **tor; tion; tive; tory**

cîr'cŭm-cīse, v., remove foreskin of penis; **sion**

cîr-cŭm'fêr-ėnce, n., distance around a circle; **ential; entially**

cîr'cŭm-spĕct, a., careful; **-ion; -ly**

cîr'cŭm-stănce, n., happening; **stantial; stantially; stantiality**

cîr-cŭm-vĕnt', v., surround, outwit; **-ion; -ive**

cîr'cŭs, n., arena, show with animals, clowns, etc.   [ease

cîr-rhō'sĭs, n., liver dis-

cîr'rŭs, n., cloud formation

cĭs'têrn, n., tank for water

cĭt'ȧ-dėl, n., fortress

cīte, v., summon by law, quote, mention; **citation**

cĭt'ĭ-zėn, n., inhabitant; **-ry; -ship**

cĭt'rŭs, n., fruit as lemon, orange, etc; **ric; rous**

cĭt'têrn, n., guitarlike instrument

cĭv'ĭcs, n., study of citizenship

cĭv'ĭl, a., of citizens, polite, not military; **-ize; -iza-tion; -ly**   [person

cĭ-vĭl'ȧn, n., non-military

clăd, a., clothed

clāim, n., v., demand; **-er; -ant** n.; **-able**

clăm, n., edible mollusk

clăm'bêr, v., climb clumsily; **-er**

clăm'mÿ, a., moist and cold; **miness; mily**

clăm′ŏr, *n.,* loud noise; **-er; -ous; -ousness; -ously**

clăn, *n.,* group of relatives; **-nish**

clăn-dĕs′tĭne, *a.,* secret; **-ness; -ly**

clăp′bôard, *n.,* tapered board as house siding

clăp′trăp, *n.,* insincere talk

clăr′ĕt, *n.,* dry red wine

clăr′ĭ-fȳ, *v.,* make clear; **fier; fication**

clăr-ĭ-nĕt′, *n.,* woodwind instrument

clăr′ĭ-òn, *a.,* clear, sharp

clăsh, *n., v.,* crash, conflict

clăsp, *n., v.,* grip, embrace; **-er**

clăss, *n.,* like group, status

clăs′sĭc, *a.,* standard, ancient Greek or Roman, excellent; **-ism; -ist; -ity; -ize; -al; -ally**

clăuse, *n.,* sentence part

clăus-trò-phō′bĭ-à, *n.,* fear of being enclosed; **bic**

clā′vêr, *n., v.,* gossip

clăv′ĭ-chôrd, *n.,* pianolike instrument

clăv′ĭ-cle, *n.,* collarbone

clăw, *n.,* sharp nail on animal's foot; *v.,* scratch

clăy, *n.,* sticky earth used to make pottery

clēan, *a.,* free from dirt, pure, entire; *adv.,* completely; **-er; -ness; -able; -ly; -liness**

clēan′-cŭt, *a.,* trim, neat

clēar, *v.,* make bright, prove, remove; *a.,* sunny, easy to see, transparent; **-er; -ness; -ance; -able; -ly**

clēar′ĭng-house, *n.,* place for clearing bank checks

clēat, *n.,* extra piece to make thing secure, spike

clēav′àge, *n.,* division

clēav′êr, *n.,* thick bladed butcher knife

clĕf, *n.,* musical sign

clĕft, *n.,* split, crack

clĕm′ĕnt, *a.,* mild, merciful; **ency; -ly**

clĕnch, *v.,* close firmly

clêr′gÿ, *n.,* religious ministers; **-man** *n.*

clêrk, *n.,* office worker; salesperson; **-ship; -ly**

clĕv′êr, *a.,* skillful, smart; **-ness, -ly**

clĭ-che′ (chā), *n.,* trite idea

clī′ĕnt, *n.,* customer; **-al**

clĭff, *n.,* steep rock

clĭff′hăng-êr, *n.,* suspenseful story

clī′màte, *n.,* weather conditions; **matic**

clī′măx, *n.,* highest point, summit; **mactic; matically**

clĭnch, *v.,* fix firmly, settle; **-er**

clĭng, *v.,* stick; **-er; -y** *a.*

clĭn′ĭc, *n.,* place for medical practice and treatment; **-al; -ally**

clĭp, *n.,* fastening device; *v.,* cut short; **-per**

clĭp′pêr, *n.,* cutting tool, sailing ship

clĭque, *n.,* snobbish group

clōak, *n.,* loose outer garment; *v.,* disguise

clŏck, *n., v.,* (device to) measure time

clŏck′wīse, *a., adv.,* in direction of clock's hands

clŏd, *n.,* earth, dull person; **-dish; -dishness; -dishly**

clŏg, *n.,* shoe; *v.,* hinder, stop up; **-gy, -giness**

clois′têr, *n.,* monastery; *v.,* seclude; **tral**

clōse (ōz), *v.,* shut, stop, end

clōse, *a.,* near, shut in, stuffy; **-ness; -ly**

clŏt, *n.,* lump; *v.,* thicken

clŏth, *n.,* fabric

clōthes, *n., pl.,* garments to wear [bate

clō′tûre, *n.,* stopping debate

cloud, *n.,* visible mass of vapor in air; **-y** *a.;* **-iness; -less**

clōve, *n.,* spice, bulb segment

clō′vĕn, *a.,* split

clō′vêr, *n.,* herb

cloy (ŏi), *v.,* make weary

club, *n.,* heavy stick, social group, card suit; *v.,* hit with club

club'foot, *n.,* deformed foot

cluck, *n.,* sound of a hen

clue, *n.,* fact to help solve mystery [**-y** *a.*

clump, *n.,* mass, cluster;

clum'sy, *a.,* awkward

clutch, *n., v.,* hold tightly

clut'ter, *n.,* mess

coach, *n.,* passenger car or carriage, trainer, *v.,* instruct, train

co-ăd'ju-tánt, *n.,* assistant

cō-ăg'ū-lāte, *v.,* curdle, clot; **tor; tion; tive; lable; lability**

cōal, *n.,* carbon mineral, fuel; **-y** *a.*

cō-á-lĕsce', *v.,* mix; **cence; cent**

cō-á-lǐ'tion, *n.,* alliance; **-ist**

cōarse, *a.,* rough, vulgar, **-en; -ness; -ly**

cōast, *n.,* shore, slide down; **-er; -al**

cōax, *v.,* persuade; **-er**

cŏb, *n.,* corn center, horse

cō'bält, *n.,* metallic element; **-ic; -ous**

cŏb'ble, *v.,* mend

cŏb'ble-stōne, *n.,* stone for paving streets

cŏb'blêr, *n.,* shoe repairman, drink, deep-dish fruit pie

cō'ble, *n.,* small fishing boat [snake

cō'brä, *n.,* poisonous

cō-cāine', *n.,* narcotic drug. anesthetic

cŏc'cŭs, *n.,* bacterium

cŏck, *n.,* rooster, male bird; *v.,* tilt, set

cŏck'chāf-êr, *n.,* beetle

cŏck'eÿed, *a.,* crooked, foolish

cŏck'le, *n.,* shellfish

cŏck'nĕy, *n.,* East Londoner's dialect; **-ish**

cŏck'pǐt, *n.,* pilot's room

cŏck'rōach, *n.,* insect

cŏck'tāil, *n.,* alcoholic drink

cŏck'ÿ, *a.,* self confident; **iness; ily** [der

cō'cōa, *n.,* chocolate pow-

cō'cò-nŭt, *n.,* large hard edible fruit

cŏd, *n.,* fish

cŏd'dle, *v.,* treat tenderly

cōde, *n.,* set of rules, secret message; **-r**

cō'dēine, *n.,* drug for pain

cŏd'ǐ-cǐl, *n.,* addition to a will; **-lary** *a.*

cō-ĕf-fǐ'cĭent, *n.,* that which unites with another

cō-êrce', *v.,* force; **cible; cibly; cion; cive; cively**

cŏf'fēe, *n.,* dark drink made from beans

cŏf'fêr, *n.,* strongbox, funds

cŏf'fǐn, *n.,* box to bury dead body in

cŏg, *n.,* tooth of wheel

cō'gĕnt, *a.,* valid; **gency**

cŏg'ǐ-tāte, *v.,* think; **tor; tion; tive**

cŏ'gnăc, *n.,* brandy

cŏg'nǐ-zănt, *a.,* aware; **zance, nition; zable**

cō'hôrt, *n.,* supporter

cŏif-fūre', *n.,* hair style

coil, *n.,* spiral; *v.,* wind around

coin, *n.,* metal piece of money; **-age**

cō-ǐn-cīde', *v.,* happen together, agree; **dence; dent; dental; dently**

cō'ǐ-tŭs, *n.,* sexual intercourse; **tion**

cōke, *n.,* coal after heating

cō'lä, *n.,* tree whose nuts have caffeine, soft drink

cò-lăn'dêr, *n.,* pan with holes for drainage

cōld, *n., a.,* low temperature, no heat, lack of feeling; **-ness; -ly**

cō'lē-ŭs, *n.,* plant

cŏl'ǐc, *n.,* abdominal pains, baby's fretfulness

cŏl-ǐ-se'ŭm, *n.,* stadium

cŏl-lăb'ò-rāte, *v.,* work together; **tor; tion; tive**

cŏl-lāge', *n.,* art form

cŏl-lăpse', *v.,* fall apart,

fail

cŏl′lår, *n.*, garment for neck

cŏl′lår-bōne,*n.*, long bone joining breast and shoulder bones

cŏl′lård, *n.*, leafy vegetable [tion

cŏl-lāte′,*v.*, compare; **tor;**

cŏl′lēague, *n.*, associate

cŏl-lĕct′, *v.*, gather; **-or; -ion; -ive; -able**

cŏl′lége, *n.*, school of higher learning; **gian** *n.;* **giate** *a.*

cŏl-līde′, *v.*, crash; **lision**

cŏl′liĕr, *n.*, coal miner; **-y**

cŏl-lō′quĭ-ål, *a.*, of informal speech; **-ism; -ly**

cŏl-lū′sion, *n.*, conspiracy; **sive; sively**

cō′lŏn, *n.*, punctuation mark (:), large intestine; **litis** [officer

colo′nėl (kêr), *n.*, military

cŏ-lō′nĭ-ål-ĭsm, *n.*, policy of maintaining colonies; **ist** [columns

cŏl-ŏn-nāde′,*n.*, series of

cŏl′o-nў, *n.*, land settled by outsiders; **nist; nize; nizer; nization; nial**

cŏl′ŏr,*n.*, pigment, shade, hue, red blue etc.; *v.*, paint, alter; **-ful; -fulness; -fully; -ation; -less**

cŏl′ŏr-blīnd, *a.*, unable to see color; **-ness**

cōlt, *n.*, young horse

cŏl′ŭm-bīne, *n.*, flowering plant [row

cŏl′ŭmn,*n.*, pillar, vertical

cŏl′ŭm-nĭst, *n.*, newspaper writer [state

cō′må, *n.*, unconscious

cŏmb, *n., v.*, (device to) smooth hair

cŏm′băt, *n.*, battle; *v.*, (cŏm-băt′) fight; **-ant; -ive; -iveness; -ively**

cŏm′bīne, *n.*, harvesting machine, association

cŏm-bīne′,*v.*, join; **-r; nation; native**

cŏm-bŭs′tion,*n.*, burning; **tive; tible; tibility; tibly**

cŏm′é-dў, *n.*, humorous entertainment [tor

cŏ-mē′dĭ-ån,*n.*, comic actor

cóme′lў, *a.*, beautiful

cŏm′ėt, *n.*, heavenly body with glowing tail

cŏm′fŏrt, *n.*, ease, relief; *v.*, soothe; **-able; -ableness; -ably**

cŏm′fŏrt-êr,*n.*, quilt

cŏm′ĭ-tў, *n.*, politeness

cŏm-mănd′, *n., v.*, order; **-er, -ment**

cŏm′mån-dånt, *n.*, head officer [property

cŏm-măn·deer′, *v.*, seize

cŏm-mĕm′ŏ-rāte, *v.*, celebrate; **tor; tion; tive; tory**

cŏm-mĕnce′, *v.*, begin; **-er; -ment**

cŏm-mĕnd′, *v.*, praise **-able; -ably; -ation; -atory**

cŏm-mĕn′sû-rāte, *a.*, equal in measure; **tion; rable; rability; rably**

cŏm′mĕnt, *n., v.*, remark

cŏm-mêr′ciál, *n.*, T.V. or radio advertisement; *a.*, of trade; **-ism; -ize; ization; -ly**

cŏm′mêrce, *n.*, business

cŏm-mĭn′gle, *v.*, blend

cŏm′mĭ-nŭte, *v.*, pulverize; **tion**

cŏm′mĭs-sār-ў, *n.*, retail store on military base; **sarial**

cŏm-mĭs′sion, *n.*, authority, monetary percentage of sales, military certificate; **-er**

cŏm-mĭt′, *v.*, entrust, do, pledge; **-ment; -tal**

cŏm-mĭt′tēe, *n.*, group working for purpose

cŏm-mōde′, *n.*, small dresser, toilet

cŏm-mō′dĭ-oŭs,*a.*, roomy; **-ness; -ly**

cŏm′mŏ-dòre,*n.*, officer

cŏm′mŏn, *a.*, public, usual, vulgar; **-ness; -able**

cŏm′mon-wĕalth, *n.*, nation [ance

cŏm-mō′tion, *n.,* disturb-
cŏm′müne, *n.,* group living and sharing to-
gether; **nal; nally; nal-
ism; nalize; nalization**
cŏm-mün′ĭ-cāte, *v.,* transmit, make known; **tor;
tion; tive; tiveness;
tively; cable; cabil-
ity; cably**
cŏm-mün′ĭon, *n.,* sharing,
Christian ritual
cŏm′mü-nĭsm, *n.,* economic system of com-
mon ownership; **nist;
nistic; nistically; nize**
cŏm-mü′nĭtỹ, *n.,* people
living together
cŏm-mūte′, *v.,* change,
substitute; **tation; ta-
tive; mutable; mutabil-
ity**
cŏm-mūt′êr, *n.,* one who
travels daily to job
cŏm-păct′, *v.,* pack; *a.,*
close; **-ness; -ly**
cŏm-păn′ĭon, *n.,* friend,
associate; **-able; -abil-
ity; -ably; -ship**
cŏm′pà-nỹ, *n.,* group of
people, business, guest
cŏm-pāre′, *v.,* examine for
likenesses and differ-
ences; **parison** *n.;* **parative; paratively; ra-
ble; rably; rability**
cŏm-pärt′mĕnt, *n.,* division; **-al; -alize; -aliza-
tion**
cŏm′pass, *n.,* range, device for making circles,
device for showing di-
rection; *v.,* go around
cŏm-păt′ĭ-blė, *a.,* getting
along together; **ibility;
-ness; bly**
cŏm-pā′trĭ-ŏt, *n.,* fellow
citizen; **-ism**
cŏm-pĕl′, *v.,* force; **-ler;
-lable**
cŏm-pĕn′dĭ-ŭm, *n.,* summary; **dious**
cŏm′pĕn-sāte, *v.,* make
up for, pay; **tor; tion;
tive; tory**
cŏm-pēte′, *v.,* enter into
rivalry, vie; **petitor, ti-**

tion; **petitive; petitory;
petively**
cŏm′pė-tėnt, *a.,* able,
tence; **tency; -ly**
cŏm-plā′cėnt, *a.,* satisfied; **cency; cence; -ly**
cŏm-plāin′, *v.,* find fault;
-er
cŏm-plāi′sànt, *a.,* agreeable; **sance; -ly**
cŏm′plė-mėnt, *n.,* that
which completes; **-ary;
-al; -arity**
cŏm-plēte′, *v.,* finish; *a.,*
whole; **pletion; -ness;
-ly**
cŏm-plĕxĭon, *n.,* nature,
facial texture
cŏm′plĭ-cāte, *v.,* make involved; **tion; cacy; -d;
-dly**
cŏm′plĭ-mĕnt, *n.,* praise;
-ary; -arily
cŏm-plỹ′, *n.,* conform,
yield; **plier, pliance;
pliancy; pliant; pliantly**
cŏm-pôrt′, *v.,* behave;
-ment
cŏm-pōse′, *v.,* make up,
create, calm; **-r; sition;
-d**
cŏm′pōte, *n.,* dish
cŏm′pound, *n., a.,* combination of parts *v.* (**cŏm-
pound′**) combine, in-
crease
cŏm-prė-hĕnd′, *v.,* understand; **-hension; hen-
sive; -ible; hensible;
hensibility; hensibly**
cŏm-prĕss′, *v.,* press together; *n.* (**cŏm′prĕss**)
wet pad; **-or; -ion; -ibil-
ity; -ible; -ive**
cŏm-prīse′, *v.,* include;
prisal; prisable
cŏm′prŏ-mĭse, *n.,* settlement; *v.,* settle, adjust;
-r [of finance
cŏmp-trōl′lêr, *n.,* director
cŏm-pŭl′sion, *n.,* driving
force; **sive; sively; siveness; sory; sorily**
cŏm-pŭnc′tion, *n.,* remorse
cŏm-pūte′, *v.,* calculate;
-r; tation; putable; put-

ably

cŏm'răde, *n.*, friend;
-ship; -ly

cŏn-cāve', *a.*, curved inward; -ness; -ity; -ly

cŏn-cēal', *v.*, hide; -ment

cŏn-cēde', *v.*, yield, agree
to; -r

cŏn-cēive', *v.*, become
pregnant; think; **ceiva-
ble; ceivably; ceivabili-
ity**   [-er

cŏn-cĕnt', *n.*, agreement;

cŏn'cĕn-trāte, *v.*, ·focus
one's mind; **tor; tion;
tive**

cŏn'cĕpt, *n.*, idea; -ual;
-ually; -ualize; -ualiza-
tion

cŏn-cêrn', *n.*, business,
worry, care; *v.*, deal with;
-ment; -ed

cŏn'cêrt, *n.*, musical program, agreement

cŏn-cĕs'sion, *n.*, yielding,
-sive

cŏnch, *n.*, spiral shell

cŏn-cĭl'ĭ-āte, *v.*, win over,
pacify; **tor; tion; able;
tory; tive**

cŏn-cīse', *a.*, short and
clear; -ness; -ly; sion

cŏn-clāve', *n.*, meeting

cŏn-clūde', *v.*, end, decide; clusion; clusive;
clusively

cŏn-cŏct', *v.*, make, invent; -er; -ion; -ive

cŏn'cŏrd, *n.*, peace, harmony; -ance; -ant;
-antly

cŏn-crēte', *n.*, cement
mixture, *a.* real; -ness;
-ly

cŏn'cŭ-bīne, *n.*, secondary wife; **nage**

cŏn-cûr', *v.*, agree;
-rence; -rency; -rent;
-rently

cŏn-cŭs'sion, *n.*, shock,
brain injury; **sive**

cŏn-dĕmn', *v.*, disap-
prove, declare unfit,
convict; -er; -ation;
-atory; -able

cŏn-dĕ-scĕnd', *v.*, lower
onself; -ence; scen-

sion; -ing

cŏn'dĭ-mĕnt, *n.*, relish

cŏn-dĭ'tion, *n.*, state, requirement; *v.*, make fit;
-al; -ality; -ally

cŏn-dō'lĕnce, *n.*, sympathy

cŏn-dò-mĭn'ĭŭm, *n.*, building jointly owned by ten-
ants

cŏn-dōne', *v.*, forgive; -r;
nation; -able

cŏn'dör, *n.*, large vulture

cŏn'dŭct, *n.*, behavior; *v.*
(cŏn-dŭct') lead, direct;
-or; -ible, -ibility

cŏn'duĭt, *n.*, pipe, tube

cōne, *n.*, solid with round
base and pointed top;
conical

cŏn-fĕc'tion, *n.*, sweet
food; -er; -ery; -ary

cŏn-fĕd'êr-àte, *n.*, ally; *a.*,
united; *v.* (āte) unite;
acy; tion; tive

cŏn-fêr', *v.*, give, discuss;
-rer; -ee; -ment; -ence;
-rable; -ential; -ral

cŏn-fĕss', *v.*, admit; -or;
-ion; -ional

cŏn'fĭ-dĕnce, *n.*, trust, secret; **dent**

cŏn-fĭg-ŭ-rā'tion, *n.*, form

cŏn-fīne', *n.*, *v.*, limit;
-ment

cŏn-fĭrm', *v.*, prove, make
valid, become church
member; -and *n.*; -ation;
-atory; -able

cŏn'fĭs-cāte, *v.*, seize; **tor;
tion; tory**

cŏn-flä-grā'tion, *n.*, big
fire; **grant**

cŏn-fôrm', *v.*, agree,
adapt; -er; -ism; -ist;
-ity; -able; -ability;
-ably

cŏn-found', *v.*, puzzle; -ed

cŏn-frŏnt', *v.*, face; -ation;
-al

cŏn-fūse', *v.*, mix up; sion;
-d; -dly; fusing; fus-
ingly

cŏn-fūte', *v.*, disprove; tation; tative

cŏn-gēal', *v.*, jell; -ment;
-able

còn-gēn'iàl, *a.*, friendly;
-ity; -ly

còn-gěn'ĭ-tàl, *a.*, since
birth; -ly

còn-glŏm'êr-ate (ĭt),*n.*, *a.*,
cluster (ed); *v.* (āte) form
mass; **tion**

còn-grăt'ù-lāte, *v.*, wish
joy; **tor; tion; tory**

cón-grê-gāte, *v.*, assemble; **tor; gant** *n.*; **tive**

cŏn'grèss, *n.*, meeting,
legislature; **-ional; -ion-
ally**

cŏn'grŭ-ènt, *a.*, in agreement, corresponding;
**-ly; ence; ency; gruity;
gruous; gruously**

còn-jěc'tũre, *n.*, guess;
tural; turable; turally

cŏn'jŭ-gàl, *a.*, marital; **-ly**

cŏn-jŭnc-tĭ'và, *n.*, eyelid
part; **vitis**

cón-jŭnc'tion, *n.*, union,
connecting word; **tive;
tively; -al; -ally**

cón-něct', *v.*, join; **-or; -er;
-ion; -ive; -ional**

cón-nĭp'tion, *n.*, fit of
anger   [**nivance**

cón-nīve', *v.*, conspire; **-r;**

cón-nōte', *v.*, suggest;
tation   [**-able**

cŏn'quêr, *v.*, defeat; **-er;**

cŏn-săn'gŭĭne, *a.*, of
same blood; **-ous;
guinity**

cŏn'scīence, *n.*, one's
moral judgment

cŏn'scioùs, *a.*, aware;
-ness; -ly

cŏn'sê-crāte, *v.*, make
holy, devote; **tor; tion;
tory**

cón-sē'cŭ-tĭve, *a.*, in logical order; **tion; -ly;
-ness**

cŏn'sê-quěnce, *n.* result,
importance; **quent;
quently; quential;
quentially; quentiality**

cŏn-sêr'và-tôr-ỹ, *n.*, music school

cón-sêrve', *v.*, save; **-r;
vation; vational; va-
tionalist; vancy**

cón-sĭgn', *v.*, commit; **-or;**

-er; -ee; -ment; -ation

cón-sĭst', *v.*, contain

cŏn'sōle, *n.*, cabinet

cón-sōle', *v.*, comfort; **lation; solatory**

cŏn-sóm-me' (mā),*n.*, hot
or cold broth

cŏn'só-nànce, *n.*, agreement; **cy; nant; nantly**

cŏn'sôrt, *n.*, spouse; *v.*,
(cón-sôrt') associate

cón-spĭc'ū-oùs,*a.*, noticeable; **-ness; -ly**

cón-spīre', *v.*, join in a
plot; **spirator; spiracy;
spiratorial; spiratori-
ally**   [**ficer**

cŏn-stà-ble, *n.*, peace of-

cŏn'stànt, *a.*, continual;
-ly

cŏn-stèl-lā'tion, *n.*, group
of stars; **tory**

cŏn-stêr-nā'tion,*n.*, terror

cŏn-stĭ-pā'tion, *n.*, inability to empty bowels;
pated

cŏn'stĭ-tūte, *v.*, establish,
form; **tive; tively**

cŏn-stĭ-tū'tion, *n.*, structure, fundamental laws
of state, club, etc.; **-al;
-alism; -alist; -ality;
-ally**

cón-strāin', *v.*, hold in;
straint *n.*

cón-strĭct', *v.*, bind, limit;
-or; -ion

cón-strŭct', *v.*, build, devise; **-or; -er; -ion;
-ional; -ionally; -ive;
-ively; -iveness**

cón-strŭe', *v.*, interpret;
struable

cón-sŭlt', *v.*, ask advise;
-er; -ant *n.*; **-ation;
-ative; -atory**

cón-sūme', *v.*, destroy,
use up, waste, eat; **-r**
sumable

cŏn'tăct, *n.*, touching; *v.*,
get in touch with

cón-tā'gioùs, *a.*, spread
by contact; **gion; -ly;
-ness**

cón-tāin', *v.*, hold; **-er;
-ment**

cón-tăm'ĭ-nāte, *v.*, pollute; **tor; tion; tive**

còn-těm'pò-rär-ÿ, *n.*, one of same period; *a.*, modern; **porize; raneous**

còn-těmpt', *n.*, disrespect; **-uous; -uously; -ible; -ibility; -ibleness; -ibly**

còn-těnd', *v.*, fight, compete; **-er; tention; tentious; tentiously**

còn'těnt, *n.*, all that is contained; *a.* **(còn-těnt')** satisfied

còn'těxt, *n.*, meaning; **-ure; -ual; ually**

còn-tǐg'ū-oǔs, *a.*, near; **guity**

còn'tǐ-něnt, *n.*, land mass; **-al; -ally**

còn-tǐn'ūe, *v.*, go on, last; **-r; uance; uation; nuity; uative; uous**

còn-tôrt', *v.*, twist; **-ion**

còn'tôur, *n., v.*, outline

còn'trà-bánd, *n.*, illegal goods; **-ist**

còn'trăct, *n.*, agreement, *v.*, agree formally; **(còn-trăct')** get, shrink; **-or; -ion; -ible; -ibility; -ual**

còn-trǎl'tō, *n.*, lowest female voice

còn'trǎst, *n.*, difference; *v.* **(còn-trǎst')** compare; **-able; -ive**

còn-trǐb'ūte, *v.*, give to; **tor; tion; tive; tory**

còn-trīte', *a.*, sorry for; **tion; -ly; -ness**

còn-trīve', *v.*, scheme, plan; **-r; trivance; trivable**

còn-trōl', *n.*, power; *v.*, restraint direct; **-ler; -able; -ability**

còn-tù-mē'lì-oǔs, *a.*, insulting; **-ly**

còn-tū'sion, *n.*, bruise

còn-và-lěsce', *v.*, gradually recover; **cence; cent** [**-r**

còn-vēne', *v.*, meet, call;

còn-věn'ìént, *a.*, handy; **ience; -ly** [nuns of

còn'věnt, *n.*, community of

còn-věn'tion, *n.*, assem-

bly, custom; **-al; -ally; -ality**

còn-věrse', *v.*, talk; **-r; sation; sationalist; sationally**

còn-vêrt', *v.*, change; **-er; -ible; -ibility; version; versional; versionally**

cŏn-věx', *a.*, curving outward; **-ness; -ity; -ly**

còn-vey' (vā), *v.*, carry; **-or; -er; -ance; -able**

cŏn'vǐct, *n.*, prisoner; *v.* **(còn-vǐct')** find guilty; **-ion**

còn-vǐnce', *v.*, persuade; **-r; cing; cible**

còn-vōke', *v.*, convene

cŏn'voy (voi), *n., v.*, escort

còn-vǔlse', *v.*, have a spasm; **sion; sive; sively; siveness**

cōok'iē, *n.*, small sweet cake [calm

cōol, *a.*, moderately cold,

cōop, *n.*, small cage

cōop'êr, *n.*, barrel maker

cōpe, *v.*, deal with

cō'pǐ-oǔs, *a.*, plentiful, **-ness; -ly**

cŏp'pêr, *n.*, reddish-brown metal [ous snake

cŏp'pêr-hèad, *n.*, poison-

cŏpse, *n.*, thicket

cŏp'ū-lāte, *v.*, have sexual intercourse; **tion; tive; tory**

cŏp'ÿ, *n.*, thing made like another, one of many like books, etc; *v.*, imitate; **copier**

cŏp'ÿ-rīght, *n.*, exclusive legal right to book, song, etc., **-er; -able**

côr'ál, *n.*, stony mass of sea animal skeleton

côrd, *n.*, thick string, wood measurement; **-age; -less**

côr'dial (jǐl), *a.*, friendly; **-ness; -ity; -ly**

côrd'īte, *n.*, gunpowder

côr'dò-vàn, *n.*, leather

côr'dù-roy (rŏi), *n.*, ribbed cotton fabric

côrk, *n.*, bark of oak tree, stopper; *v.*, stop; **-er; -y**

a.

côr′nē-à, n., eyeball's covering

côr′nêr, n., angle where lines or planes meet, v., put in tight position

côr-nĕt′, n., trumpetlike horn

côr′nĭce, n., wall molding

côr-nŭ-cō′pĭ-à, n., horn of plenty

cor-rŏl′là, n., flower's petals; **-ceous**

côr′òl-lār-ÿ, n., deduction

cò-rō′nà, n., crown; **-tion**

côr′ò-nār-ÿ, a., of the heart

côr′ò-nêr, n., official investigator of deaths

côr′pò-ràl, n., noncommissioned military officer; a., of the body

côr-pò-rā′tion, n., chartered organization to act as one; **ràte** a.; **tive**

côrps, n., organized group

côrpse, n., dead body

côr′pū-lènt, a., fat; **lence**

côr-ràl′, n., fenced area for animals

cor-rĕct′, v., a. (make) right; **-or; -ion; -ness; -able; -ive; -ively; -ly; -ness**

côr′rĭ-dòr, n., hall

cór-rŏb′ò-rāte, v., confirm; **tor; tion; tive; rant**

cór-rōde′, v., wear away; **rodible; rosion; rosive; rosively; rosiveness**

côr′rū-gāte, v., make ridged; **tion; -d**

cór-rŭpt′, v., a. (make) dishonest; **-er; -or; -ion; -ness; -ly; -ionist; -ive; -ively; -ible; -ibility; -ibly**

côr-ságe′ (sàz), n., flowers worn by a woman

côr′sèt, n., tight undergarment for torso; **-ry**

côr-tĕge′, n., funeral procession [cal

côr′tĕx, n., outer layer; **ti-**

côr′tĭ-sōne, n., drug

cŏs-mĕt′ĭc, n., a. (preparation) to improve appearance; **tology; tolo-**

gist

cŏs′mòs, n., universe; **mic; mically; mology**

cŏst, n. price, loss

cŏs′tūme, n., style of dress

cŏt, n., folding bed

cō-tĭl′lion, n., formal ball

cŏt′tòn, n., natural fiber, fabric

cŏt′tòn-tāil, n., rabbit

coū′gàr, n., wild cat

cough (cāuf), n., loud air burst from lungs

coūn′cĭl, n., advisory or legislative group; **-lor; -lorship**

coūn′sèl, n., advice, lawyer; v., advise; **-or; -lor; -orship; -lorship**

coūnt, n., total number; nobleman; v., name numbers in order, have value; **-er; -able**

coūn′têr, n., long table or cabinet top; a., adv. opposite

coūn′têr-feĭt, a., false

coūnt′èss, n., noblewoman

coūn′trÿ, n., nation, rural area; **trified**

coūn′tÿ, n., administrative unit of a state [move

coūp, n., blow, brilliant

coūpe, n., two-door car

coū′ple, n., two things, pair; v., join

coū′pòn, n., paper to redeem cash or merchandise

coûr′àge, n., bravery; **-ous; -ousness; -ously**

coû′rĭ-êr, n., messenger

côurse, n., path, series, part of meal, study program

côurt, n., enclosed yard, king's family, etc., judicial assembly; v., seek, woo

côur′tè-sàn, n., court lady

côurt′lÿ, a., elegant

coūth, a., civilized

coū-tūre′ (tôr), n., work of designing fashion; **rier**

cōve, n., small bay

cŏv′è-nànt, n., agreement;

-or; -er; -ee; -al

cŏv'êr, v., place something over; hide, protect; **-er; -age**

cóv'êrt, a., secret; **-ness; -ly**

cŏv'êt, v., envy; **-er; -ous; -ousness; -ously**

cŏw, n., female animal—cattle, whale, etc; v., frighten

cŏw'ârd, n., who lacks courage; **-ice; -ly**

cŏwl, n., monk's hood

cŏw'lĭck, n., unruly piece of hair

cŏx'â, n., hip; **-l**

cŏx'swâin, n., one who steers a boat

coy (coï), a., seemingly shy; **-ness; -ly**

cō'zў, a., comfortable, snug; **ziness; zily**

crăb, n., shellfish, complainer

crăb'bў, a., cross

crăck, n., v., break, split; n., sharp noise, (coll.) try; **-er** [cuit

crăck'êr, n., thin crisp biscuit

crā'dle, n., rocking baby bed

crăft, n., skill, art, boat

crăft'ў, a., sly, artful; **iness; ily**

crăm, v., pack full; **-mer**

crămp, n., painful spasm

crāne, n., large wading bird, lifting machine

crā'nǐ-ǔm, n., skull; **nial; nially; niology**

crănk, n., machine arm for turning, irritable person

crăps, n. pl., dice game

crăss, a., coarse; **-iness; -ly**

crāte, n., large shipping case [pit

crā'têr, n., bowl-shaped

crà-văt', n., necktie

crāve, v., long for; **-r**

crăwl, v., go on hands and knees, move slowly n., swimming stroke

crāy'fĭsh, n., freshwater shellfish

crāy'ŏn, n., colored wax

drawing stick

crāze, n., fad

crēam, n., fatty part of milk, cosmetic paste; **-y** a.

crēase, n., v., fold

crē-āte', v., originate, cause; **tor; tion**

crēa'tûre, n., living being

crē'dênce, n., belief; **dent**

crē-dĕn'zà, n., buffet

crĕd'ĭt, n., trust, honor, financial reputation, college study unit; **-or; -able; -ably; -ableness; -ability**

crēed, n., statement of belief; **-al**

crēek, n., small stream

crēel, n., basket for fish

crēep, n., v., crawl; **-er; -age**

crē'māte, v., burn dead body; **tor; tion**

crepe (crāp), n., thin wrinkled cloth

crē-pŭs'cūle, n., twilight; **lar**

crē-scĕn'dō, a., adv., musically increasing in loudness

crĕs'cênt, n., shape of quarter moon; **-ic**

crĕst, n., top, tuft on animal's head

crē'tĭn, n., idiot; **-ism**

crĕv'ĭce, n., crack, split

crēw, n., group of workers

crēw'êl, n., embroidery

crĭb, n., baby's bed; v., cheat at school work

crĭck'êt, n., insect, ball game

crīme, n., act violating law

crĭmp, v., pleat, make wavy; **-y** a.

crĭm'sŏn, n., a., deep red

crĭn'ŏ-līne, n., stiff petticoat

crĭp'ple, n., lame person; v., make lame or unable; **-r** [emergency

crī'sĭs, n., turning point,

crĭsp, n., brittle, fresh; **-ness; -y** a.; **-ly**

crī-tēr'ĭ-ŏn, n., standard

crĭt'ĭc, n., judge of arts, fault finder

cro-chet' (shā), n., kind of needle work; **-er**

crock, n., earthenware pot

croc'o-dile, n., large reptile

cro'cus, n., flowering plant

crook, n., v., bend; n. (coll.) dishonest person

croon, v., sing softly; **-er**

crop, n., farm product, group; v., cut off ends; **-per**

cro-quet'(kā), n., outdoor game with ball and mallet [ball

cro-quette', n., fried food

cross, n., X mark, Christian symbol; v., oppose, intersect; a., cranky

crotch, n., place where legs fork

crouch, v., stoop

croup, n., respiratory disease

crow, n., black bird, rooster's cry; v., boast

crow'bar, n., long metal bar for prying

crowd, n., large group of people; v., push together

crown, n., jeweled headdress, top, head; v., honor, enthrone

cru'cial, a., very important; **-ly**

cru'ci-fix, n., figure of Christ on cross

cru'ci-fy, v., kill by nailing on a cross; **fier**

crude, a., raw, unrefined; **-ly; -ness; dity**

cru'el, a., causing pain; **-ness; -ly; -ty**

cruise, n., boat trip; v., travel; **-er**

crumb, n., small bit, bad person; **-y** a.

cru-sade', n., church expedition, campaign

crush, v., press into bits, subdue [**-y** a.

crust, n., outer covering;

crus-ta'cean, n., shellfish

crutch, n., cripple's staff, support

crux, n., essense

crypt, n., underground burial place

crys'tal, n., mineral formation, watch face, glassware; **-line** a.; **-lize; -lization; -lography**

cub, n., young bear, lion, etc.

cube, n., solid with six equal square sides; **bic; bical**

cub'ism, n., form of abstract art; **cubist; bistic**

cud, n., food chewed again

cud'dle, v., hold lovingly; **dly**

cudg'el, n., short thick club

cue, n., signal, billiard stick [pants end

cuff, n., band at sleeve or

cui-sine', n., cooking style

cu-lotte', n., women's knee length full pants

cul'prit, n., villain, guilty person

cult, n., system of religious worship, sect

cul'ti-vate, v., raise, grow, develop, refine; **tor; tion; vable; -d**

cul'ture, n., development, way of life; **ral; rally**

cul'vert, n., drain

cum'ber-some, a., hard to handle

cu'mu-late, v., gather together; **tion; tive; tively**

cu'mu-lus, n., cloud type

cun'ning, a., sly, clever; **-ness; -ly**

cup'board, n., storage place

cu'po-la, n., small dome

cur, n., mongrel, mean person; **-rish; -rishly**

cu-ra'tor, n., museum manager

curb, n., street's edge; v., restrain

curd, n., soured milk; **-y** a.

cure, v., make well, heal; **-r; curable; curability**

cu'ri-o, n., rare article

cu'ri-ous, a., eager to learn; **riosity; -ly; -ness**

curl, n., coil (of hair); v., roll up; **-er; -y** a.

curl'i-cue, n., fancy curve

cûr′rȧnt, *n.*, small berry

cûr′rėn-cÿ, *n.*, money, general use

cûr′rėnt, *n.*, flow; *a.*, now happening; -ly

cŭr-rĭc′ū-lŭm, *n.*, course of study; lar

cûr′rÿ, *n.*, seasoning; *v.*, clean animal's coat

cûrse, *v.*, make evil oath, swear [writing

cûr′sĭve, *n.*, flowing hand-

cûr′sȯ-rÿ, *a.*, hastily done

cûrt, *a.*, blunt

cûr′taĭn, *n.*, cloth window covering

cûrt′sÿ, *n.*, respectful bend of body, bow

cûrve, *n.*, bending line; *v.*, bend, twist; vature; vy *a.* [ease shock

cŭsh′ĭon, *n.*, pillow; *v.*,

cŭsp, *n.*, pointed end

cŭss, *n.*, *v.*, curse, swear

cŭs′tȧrd, *n.*, pudding of milk, eggs and sugar

cŭs′tȯ-dÿ, *n.*, in care of; dial

cŭs′tȯm, *n.*, usual practice; -ary; -arily

cŭs′tȯm-êr, *n.*, buyer

cŭs′tȯms, *n. pl.*, import tax

cūte, *a.*, clever, pretty; -ness; -ly

cŭt′ĭ-cle, *n.*, skin around fingernail

cŭt′lȧss, *n.*, curved sword

cŭt-lêr-ÿ, *n.*, cutting tools

cŭt′têr, *n.*, small fast ship

cŭt′thrōat, *n.*, murderer; *a.*, ruthless

cŭt′tle-fĭsh, *n.*, sea animal

cŭt′wŏrm, *n.*, caterpillar feeding on farm crop

cÿ′ȧ-nĭde, *n.*, poisonous substance

cÿ-bêr-nĕt′ics, *n. pl.*, science of brain and computers; ic

cÿ′cle, *n.*, recurring time period; clic; clical; clically [storm

cÿ′clōne, *n.*, violent wind

cÿ-clȯ-rä′mȧ, *n.*, series of pictures on large round wall

cÿl′ĭn-dêr, *n.*, tubelike

solid with flat ends; dri-cal; dricality; drically

cÿm′bȧl, *n.*, brass plate struck for musical sound

cÿn′ic, *n.*, sarcastic person; -al; -ally; -ism

cÿ′prėss, *n.*, tree

cÿst, *n.*, sac in animal tissue; -ic

cÿ-tŏl′ȯ-gÿ, *n.*, study of cells; gist; logic; logical; logically

czâr, *n.*, Russian emperor; -dom; -ism

D

dăb, *v.*, light tap on

dăb′ble, *v.*, do superficially; -r [dog

dăchs′hŭnd, *n.*, long short

dä′crŏn, *n.*, synthetic fiber

dăf′fȯ-dĭl, *n.*, flower

dăft, *a.*, silly, crazy; -ness; -ly [stabbing

dăg′gêr, *n.*, short knife for

dähl′iȧ, *n.*, flower

dāi′lÿ, *a.*, *adv.*, every day

dāin′tÿ, *a.*, delicate; ti-ness; tily

dāir′ÿ, *n.*, place to make milk, butter, etc.

dā′ĭs, *n.*, raised platform

dāi′sÿ, *n.*, flower

dăl′lÿ, *v.*, flirt, loiter; lier; liance [dog

dăl-mā′tiȧn, *n.*, spotted

dăm, *n.*, water barrier

dăm′ȧge, *n.*, injury; *v.*, injure; -able

dăm′ȧsk, *n.*, printed fabric of linen or silk

dămn, *v.*, condemn, curse; -ation; -atory; -ed; -able; -ably

dămp, *n.*, moisture; -en *v.*; -ness; -ish; -ly

dăm′sėl, *n.*, maiden

dăm′sȯn, *n.*, type of plum

dăn′dė-lĭon, *n.*, lawn weed

dăn′dêr, *n.*, temper

dăn′drŭff, *n.*, flaking skin of scalp

dăn′dÿ, *n.*, vain man; *a.*, (coll.) good; -ism; dify; dification; -ish

dăn′gêr, *n.*, possible

harm; **-ous; -ousness;
-ously** [-r
dăn'gle, v., hang loosely;
dăp'pêr, a., smart, trim;
-ness; -ly
dăp'ple, a., spotted
dăre, v., challenge, risk;
-r; ing
dârk, a., without light,
shaded, gloomy; **-ness;
-en** v.; **-ish; -ly**
dâr'lĭng, n., loved one; a.,
beloved, cute
dârn, v., mend by sewing;
-er
dârt, n., small pointed missile; v., throw or move
quickly; **-er**
dăsh, n., little bit, sprint,
mark (—); v., spatter,
rush; **-er**
dăsh'bôard, n., car panel
dăs'tàrd, n., sneaky person; **-ly; -liness**
dā'tà, n. pl., facts, information
dāte, n., time period, appointment, fruit; v., set a
time; **-r; -able; -less**
dāte'line, n., newspaper's
date
dăv'ĕn-pôrt, n., sofa
daw'dle (dău), v., waste
time; **-r** [gin
dăwn, n., daybreak; v., be-
dāy, n., 24 hour period,
hours of sunlight, era
dāy'drĕam, v., imagine
while awake
dāy'tīme, n., time from
sunrise to sunset
dāze, n., bewilderment;
-dly
dăz'zle, v., overpower with
brilliance; **-ment; -ingly**
dēa'còn, n., church officer; **-ess**
dĕad, a., not living, lifeless, dull, complete; **-en**
v.; **-ly**
dĕad'bĕat, n., lazy person
dĕad-lĭne, n., time limit
dĕad'lŏck, n., stalemate
dĕaf-mūte, n., one who
cannot hear or speak
dĕal, v., distribute, is concerned with; **-er; -ing** n.;

-ership
dēan, n., church or college
officer, oldest member;
-ship; -ery
dēar, a., adv., loved, esteemed; costly; **-ness;
-ly**
dĕarth, n., scarcity
dĕath, n., end of life; **-ful;
-ly**
dĕath'trăp, n., dangerous
place
dē-bă'cle, n., defeat
dē-bâr', v., exclude; **-ment**
dē-bârk', v., land; **-ation**
dē-bāse', v., lower; **-r;
-ment**
dē-bāte', v., argue formally; **-r; batable**
dē-bäuch', n., orgy; v.,
corrupt; **-er; -ee; -ment;
-ery; -edly**
dē-bĭl'ĭ-tў, n., weakness;
tate; tation
dĕb'ĭt, n., account entry of
money owed
dĕb-ò-nâir', a., charming
dē-bris' (brē), n., rubble,
litter [-or
dĕbt, n., something owed;
dē-but' (bū), n., first public
appearance, introduc-
tion to society
dĕc'āde, n., ten years
dē-cănt'êr, n., fancy glass
wine bottle
dē-căp'ĭ-tāte, v., cut off
head; **tor; tion**
dē-căth'lŏn, n., athletic
contest with ten events
dē-cāy', v., rot, waste away
dē-cēive', v., fool; **-r; ceivable; ceivingly**
dē-cĕl'êr-āte, v., reduce
speed; **tor; tion**
dē'cĕnt, n., proper;
cency; -ly
dē-cĕp'tion, n., fraud, misleading; **tive; tiveness;
tively**
dē-cīde', v., make up one's
mind; **-r; cidable; -d**
dĕc'ĭ-màl, n., a., (fraction)
of or based on ten; **-ly**
dĕc'ĭ-māte, v., destroy;
tor; tion
dē-cī'phêr, v., decode;

-ment; -able

dė-cī'sion, n., judgment; -al; sive; siveness; sively

deck, n., ship's floor, pack of playing cards; v., adorn

dė-clāre', v., state openly; -r; ration; claratory; clarative

dė-clĕn'sion, n., descent, grammatical case

dė-clīne', v., slope downward, refuse; -r; nation

dē-cŏm-pōse', v., decay; sition; posable

dĕc'ȯ-rāte, v., make attractive, adorn; tor; tion; tive; tiveness; tively

dė-cô'rŭm, n., dignity; rous; rousness; rously

dė-crēase', v., lesson

dė-crēe', n., v., order

dĕc'rė-mėnt, n., loss

dė-crĕp'ĭt, a., worn out; -ly; -ude n.

dĕd'ī-cāte, v., give oneself, inscribe; tor; tion; tory; tive

dė-dūce', v., draw conclusion; ducible

dė-dŭct', v., subtract; -ion; -ive; -ively; -ible; ibility

dēed, n., act, title of ownership

dēem, v., think, regard

dēep, a., adv., far down, intense, of low pitch; -en; -ly; -ness

dēer, n., antlered animal

dė-fāce', v., mar; -r; -ment

dė-făl'cāte, v., embezzle; tor; tion

dė-fāme', v., slander; -r; mation; famatory

dė-fäult', n., failure to do; -er

dė-fēat', v., conquer, win

dĕf'ė-cāte, v., excrete waste; tor; tion

dė-fĕnd', v., protect; -er; -able; -ant n., a.

dė-fĕnse', n., protection; -less; -lessness; -lessly; sible; sibility; sibly; sive; siveness; sively

dė-fêr', v., put off; -rer; -ment; -red

dė-fī'ciėnt, a., lacking; -ly; ciency

dė-fīle', v., make dirty

dė-fīne', v., explain, state meaning; -r; nition; nitional; finable

dĕf'ĭ-nīte, a., exact; -ly

dė-flāte', v., let out air, make less important; tor; tion; tionary

dė-flĕct', v., turn aside; -or; -ion; -ive

dė-fôrm', v., disfigure; -ation; -ity; -ed

dė-fräud', v., cheat; -er; -ation   [-al

dė-frāy', v., pay; -ment;

dĕft, a., quick, skillful; -ness; -ly

dė-fŭnct', a., dead

dė-fȳ', v., oppose; fier; fiance; fiant; fiantly

dė-gĕn'êr-āte, v., rot, decline; a., (āte) depraved; tion; tive; -ness; -ly

dė-grāde', v., lower in rank or value; -r; -able

dė-grēe', n., stage, amount, rank, unit of measure for temperature

dē-hȳ'drāte, v., remove water from; tor; tion

dē'ī-fȳ, v., make a god, idolize; fication; fic

deign (dān), v., condescend, grant

dē'īsm, n., belief in God's existence; deist; deistic

dė-jĕct', v., depress; -ion; -ed

dē-lăm'ī-nāte, v., separate into layers; tion

dė-lāy', v., postpone; -er

dė-lĕc'tȧ-ble, a., very pleasing; bility; bly

dĕl'ė-gȧte, n., representative; v., (gāt) appoint, entrust; gacy; gation

dė-lēte', v., erase; tion

dĕl-ė-tē'rĭ-oŭs, a., harmful; -ness; -ly

dė-lĭb'êr-āte, v., think; tion; tive; tively

dė-lĭb'êr-ȧte, a., done on

purpose; **-ness; -ly**

dĕl'ĭ-cȧte, *a.*, fine, frail, proper; **cacy; -ness; -ly**

dė-lĭ'cioŭs, *a.*, pleasing; **-ly; -ness**

dė-lĭght', *n.*, pleasure; *v.*, rejoice; **-ed; -ful; -fully; -ness** [**-ative**

dė-lĭm'ĭt, *v.*, define; **-ation;**

dė-lĭn'ē-ȧte, *v.*, draw, describe; **tor; tion; tive**

dė-lĭn'quĕnt, *a.*, neglecting duty; overdue; **-ly; quency**

dė-lĭr'ĭ-ŭm, *n.*, wild excitement; **ious; iously; iousness**

dĕll, *n.*, small valley

dĕl'tȧ, *n.*, Greek letter, soil deposit at river's mouth

dė-lŭde', *v.*, fool, mislead; **lusion; lusive; lusively; siveness**

dĕl'ŭge, *n.*, *v.*, flood

dė-lŭxe', *a.*, elegant

dĕlve, *v.*, search; **-r**

dĕm'ȧ-gŏgue, *n.*, leader who stirs up emotion; **gogy; gogism; gogic; gogical**

dė-mȧr-cā'tion, *n.*, limit

dė-mēan', *v.*, degrade, behave

dė-mĕnt'ėd, *a.*, insane

dĕm'ĭ-gŏd, *n.*, minor god

dė-mīse', *n.*, death

dė-mĭt', *v.*, resign; **mission** [fee cup

dĕm'ĭ-tȧsse, *n.*, small cof-

dė-mŏc'rȧ-cÿ, *n.*, government of, by and for the people

dė-mŏl'ĭsh, *v.*, destroy; **-er; -ment; lition**

dē'mŏn, *n.*, devil; **-ic; -ically**

dė-mŏr'ȧl-īze, *v.*, corrupt, weaken morals; **-r; zation** [tion

dė-mōte', *v.*, lower rank;

dė-mŭr', *v.*, object; **-ral**

dė-mŭre', *a.*, shy; **-ly**

dė-nī'ȧl, *n.*, refusal

dĕn'ĭ-grāte, *v.*, blacken; **tor; tion; tory**

dĕn'ĭm, *n.*, coarse cotton cloth

dĕn'ĭ-zėn, *n.*, inhabitant

dė-nŏm-ĭ-nā'tion, *n.*, name, kind, religious sect; **tive**

dė-nŏm'ĭ-nā-tor, *n.*, bottom number of fraction

dė-nōte', *v.*, refer to, mean; **tation; tative; tatively; notable**

dė-nŏŭnce', *v.*, condemn; **-r; -ment**

dĕnse, *a.*, crowded together; **sity; -ness; -ly**

dĕnt, *n.*, hollow in surface

dĕn'tȧl, *a.*, of teeth; **-ly**

dĕn'tĭst, *n.*, tooth doctor; **-ry**

dĕn'tûre, *n.*, false teeth

dė-nūde', *v.*, strip

dė-nŭn'ci-ȧte, *v.*, condemn; **tor; tion; tive; tory** [nier

dė-nÿ', *v.* declare untrue;

dė-ō'dȯr-ȧnt, *n.*, odor destroyer; **dorize; dorizer; dorization**

dė-pȧrt', *v.*, leave, go; **-ed; -ure** *n.*

dė-pȧrt'mĕnt, *n.*, division; **-al; -alize; -alization**

dė-pĕnd', *v.*, rely; **-ence; -ency; -ent; -ently; -able; -ably; -ability; -ableness**

dė-pĭct', *v.*, represent; **-or; -ion**

dė-pĭl'ȧ-tô-rÿ, *n.*, hair removing cosmetic

dė-plēte', *v.*, use up, empty; **tion; tive**

dė-plôre', *v.*, be sorry about; **-r; plorable; plorably**

dė-plŏy' (plŏi), *v.*, extend out; **-ment**

dė-pôrt', *v.*, send away; **-ation; -able**

dė-pôrt'mĕnt, *n.*, behavior

dė-pōse', *v.*, remove from office; **sition; posal** *n.*; **posable**

dė-pŏs'ĭt, *n.*, *v.* (thing) set down, store; **-or; -ory** *n.*

dē'pot (pō), *n.*, storehouse, train station

dė-prȧve', *v.*, corrupt; **-r; pravity; -d; -dly**

dĕp′rĕ-cāte, v., ~ disapprove; **tor; tion; cat-ingly**

dė-prē′cĭ-āte, v., lessen; **tor; tion; tory; tive**

dĕp-rė-dā′tion, n., looting

dė-prĕss′, v., push down, lower, sadden; **-or; -ion; -ible; -ive; -ively; -ive-ness**

dė-prive′, v., take or keep from; **vation; prival; privable; -d**

dĕpth, n., deepness

dė-pūte′, v., appoint

dĕp′ŭ-tỹ, n., assistant; **tize**

dė-rāil′, v., go off the track; **-ment**

dė-rānge′, v., upset; make insane; **-ment; -d**

dĕr′ė-lĭct, a., deserted, neglectful; **-ion**

dė-rīde′, v., make fun of; **-r; rision; risive; ri-sively; risiveness**

dė-rīve′, v., originate; **-r; vation; vational; riva-tive**

dêr′má, n., skin; **-l; -tol-ogy; -tologist; -tologi-cal**

dė-rŏg′à-tô-rỹ, a., insulting; **tive; rily**

dĕr′rĭck, n., lifting machine

dĕs′cănt, n., varied melody

dė-scĕnd′, v., come down, lower; **-er; -ible; scent** n.

dė-scrībe′, v., tell or write about; **-r; scribable; scribably**

dė-scrỹ′, v., see

dĕs′ė-crāte, v., make unholy; **-r; tor; tion**

dĕs′ĕrt, n., dry sandy area, waste

dė-sêrt′, v., abandon, leave; **-er; -ion**

dė-sêrve′, v., merit; **-d; -dly; serving**

dĕs′ĭc-cāte, v., dry completely; **tion; tive**

dė-sīgn′, n., v., plan, pattern; **-er; -ee; -edly**

dĕs′ĭg-nāte, v., point out; **tor; tion; tive**

dė-sîre′, n., v., wish, want; **sirable; sirability; sir-ableness; sirably; sir-ous**

dė-sĭst′, v., stop; **-ance**

dĕsk, n., writing table

dĕs′ó-lāte, v., lay waste; a. **(lĭt)** deserted; **-r; tor; tion; -ly; -ness**

dĕs-pêr-à′dō, n., outlaw

dĕs′pêr-àte, a., hopeless, serious, reckless; **tion; -ly; -ness**

dė-spīse′, v., hate; **pica-ble; picableness; picably [-fully**

dė-spīte′, n., malice; **-ful;**

dė-spīte′, prep., even so

dė-spŏnd′, v., lose hope **-ency; -ence; -ent; -ently**

dĕs′pŏt, n., absolute ruler; **-ism; -ic; -ical; -ically**

dĕs-sêrt′, n., sweet dish ending meal

dĕs′tīne, v., intend; **-d**

dĕs′tĭ-nỹ, n., fate

dĕs′tĭ-tūte, a., very poor; tion [molish

dė-strŏy′ (ŏi), v., ruin, de-

dĕs′uė-tūde, n., disuse

dĕs′ŭl-tô-rỹ, a., random; **riness; rily**

dė-tăch′, v., separate; **-able; -ability; -ment**

dė-tăch′mĕnt, n., group for special service

dė-tāil′, n., item; tell each part; **-ed [-ment**

dė-tāin′, v., hold back; **-er;**

dė-tĕct′, v., discover; **-or; -ion; -ive; -able; -ible**

dė-tĕc′tĭve, n., crime investigator

de-tente′ (dā-tŏnt), n., lessening of international hostility

dė-tĕn′tion, n., holding in custody

dė-têr′, v., try to stop; **-ment; -rence; -rent**

dė-têr′gĕnt, n., cleaning substance

dė-têr′mĭne, v., decide; **-r; -d; nation; native; nate** a.; **nately; nable; nability; nably**

C
D

dė-tĕst′, v., hate; **-er;
-ation; -able; -ability;
-ableness; -ably**

dĕt′ȯ-nāte, v., explode;
tor; tion

dē-tôur′, n., alternate way

dė-trăct′, v., take away
from; **-or; -ion; -ive**

dĕt′rĭ-mėnt, n., harm, disadvantage; **-al; -ally**

deŭce, n., playing card of
two, tennis score, devil

dĕv′ȧs-tāte, v., destroy;
tor; tion; tatingly

dė-vĕl′ŏp, v., grow, ex-
pand; **-er; -ment; -men-
tal; -mentally; -able**

dē′vĭ-āte, v., turn from; **tor;
tion; ant** n., a.; **ance;
ancy; vious; viously,
viousness**

dė-vīce, n., scheme, me-
chanical invention

dĕv′ĭl, n., evil spirit or person; **-ment; -ry; -ish;
ĭshly**

dė-vīse′, v., plan

dė-vŏlve′, v., pass on to;
-ment

dė-vōte′, v., dedicate; **-ee;
tion; -ment; -d; -dness;
-dly**

dė-voŭr′, v., eat; **-er**

dė-voŭt′, a., pious, sin-
cere; **-ness; -ly**

dėw, n., atmospheric
moisture; **-y** a.; **-iness;
-ily**

dĕx-tĕr′ĭ-tў, n., skill; **ter-
ous; terousness; ter-
ously**

dĕx′trōse, n., sugar

dī-ȧ-bē′tĕs, n., disease of
excess sugar in urine;
betic   [**-ally**

dī-ȧ-bŏl′ĭc, a., wicked; **-al;**

dī-ȧ-crĭt′ĭ-cȧl, a., distinguishing; **-ly**

dī′ȧ-dĕm, n., crown

dī′ȧg-nōse, v., find the
cause; **sis** n.; **nostician;**
n.; **nostic; nostically**

dī-ăg′ȯ-nȧl, a., slanting
between corners; **-ly**

dī′ȧ-grăm, n., drawing,
chart; **-matic; -matical;
-matically**

dī′ȧl, n., face of device indicating measurement,
ex. watchface, compass;
v., call on telephone

dī′ȧ-lĕct, n., speech of a
certain region; **-al; -ally;
-ology; -ologist; -olog-
ical**

dī-ȧ-lĕc′tĭc, n., logical ar-
gumentation; **-al**

dī′ȧ-lŏgue, n., conversa-
tion   [circle

dī-ăm′ė-tĕr, n., width of

dī-ȧ-mĕt′rĭ-cȧl, a., op-
posed; **-ly**

dī′a-mȯnd, n., carbon
crystal, gem, rectangu-
lar shape

dī′ȧ-phrăgm (frăm), n.,
muscles between chest
and abdomen

dī-ȧr-rhē′ȧ, n., looseness
of bowel movements; **-l**

dīce, n. pl., spotted cubes
used in games, v., cut
into cubes

dī-chŏt′ȯ-mў (kŏt), n., division of two opposing
parts; **mize; mization;
mous; mously**

dī-chrō-măt′ĭc (krō), a.,
having two colors

dĭck′êr, v., bargain, hag-
gle

dĭck′ēy, n., false shirt front

dĭc′tāte, v., say for another
to write, order; **tion**

dĭc′tā-tȯr, n., ruler with total power; **-ship; -ial;
-ially**   [manner

dĭc′tion, n., speaking

dĭc′tŭm, n., pronounce-
ment

dĭd′dle, v. (coll.) cheat,
waste time

dīe, n., tool for molding,
stamping, etc.; v., stop
living

die′hȧrd, a., very stubborn

dī′ĕt, n., food eaten; v., to
eat to lose weight; **-etic;
-ary**

dĭf′fêr, v., be unlike, disagree; **-ent; -ence; -ent-
ness; -ently**

dĭf-fêr-ĕn′tĭ-āte, v., distinguish between; **tion; al;**

ally; able; ability

dĭf'fĭ-cŭlt, *a.*, hard; **-y; -ly**

dĭf'fĭ-dĕnce, *n.*, shyness; **dent; dently**

dĭf-frăct', *v.*, break into parts; **-ion; -ive; -ively**

dĭf-fūse' (fūz), *v.*, spread-out; **-r; sor; sion; sive; sively; siveness**

dĭg, *v.*, turn up as soil; **-ger**

dĭ'gest, *v.*, absorb as food into body, summarize; **-er; -ion; -ive; -ible; -ibility; -ibly**

dĭg'ĭt, *n.*, finger or toe, numerals 0 to 9; **-al; -ally**

dĭg'nĭ-tār-ў, *n.*, person in high office

dĭ'grăph, *n.*, two letters with one simple sound

dĭke, *n.*, embankment to hold back flood

dĭ-lăp'ĭ-dāt-ĕd, *a.*, broken down

dĭ-lāte', *v.*, expand; **tor; tion; tive; latability; lat-able**

dĭl'ȧ-tô-rў, *a.*, delaying

dĭ-lĕm'mȧ, *n.*, difficult choice

dĭl-ĕt-tănte', *n.*, follower of arts; **-ism; tantish**

dĭll, *n.*, herb

dĭ-lūte', *v.*, weaken, thin down; **-r; tor; tion; -ness**

dĭm, *v.*, darken; *a.*, not bright or clear; **-mer; -ness; -ly**

dĭme, *n.*, coin for ten cents

dĭ-mĕn'sion, *n.*, measurement- **-al; -ally**

dĭ-mĭn'ĭsh, *v.*, decrease; **-able**

dĭm'ple, *n.*, small hollow on body

dĭn, *n.*, steady noise

dĭne, *v.*, eat dinner; **-r**

dĭn'êr, *n.*, small restaurant

dĭnğhў (gў), *n.*, small boat

dĭn'gō, *n.*, Australian dog

dĭn'gў (jў), *a.*, shabby, dirty   [meal

dĭn'nêr, *n.*, main daily

dĭ'nò-saur (sôr), *n.*, large extinct reptile

dĭ'ò-cèse, *n.*, religious district

dĭ-ò-rä'mȧ, *n.*, miniature three dimensional scene

dĭp, *n.*, slope, plunge; *v.*, put quickly into liquid; **-per**

dĭph-thĕ'rĭȧ, *n.*, infectious disease; **ritic**

dĭph'thŏng, *n.*, sound of two joined vowels

dĭ-plō'mȧ, *n.*, certificate of college degree or honor

dĭ-plō'mȧ-cў, *n.*, relations between nations, tact; **mat** *n.*; **matic; matically**

dĭp'pêr, *n.*, ladle

dĭre, *a.*, extreme; **-ness; -ly**

dĭ-rĕct', *v.*, command, guide; **-or; -ion; -ive; -ional**

dĭ-rĕc'tô-rў, *n.*, book of names, addresses, etc.

dĭrge, *n.*, funeral hymn

dîr'ĭ-gĭ-ble, *n.*, manned balloon

dĭrk, *n.*, dagger

dîrn'dl, *n.*, full skirt with gathered waist

dĭrt, *n.*, soil, gossip; **-y** *a.*; **-iness; -ily**

dĭs-ā'ble, *v.*, be handicapped; incapable; **bil-ity; -ment; -d**

dĭs-ȧf-fĭl'ĭ-āte, *v.*, end association; **tion**

dĭs-ȧl-lŏw, *v.*, reject; **-ance**   [**-ance**

dĭs-ȧp-pēar', *v.*, vanish;

dĭs-ȧp-pŏĭnt', *v.*, spoil the hopes of; **-ment; -ed**

dĭs-ȧp-prove' (prōov), *v.*, consider wrong; **proval** *n.*; **provingly**

dĭs-ȧr-rānge', *v.*, undo order of; **-ment**

dĭs-ȧs-sō'cĭ-āte, *v.*, sever relations with; **tion**

dĭs-ăs'têr, *n.*, serious misfortune; **trous; trously**

dĭs-bănd', *v.*, break up; **-ment**

dĭs-bâr', *v.*, exclude from law practice; **-ment**

dĭs-bûrse', *v.*, pay out; **-r; -ment; bursable**

dĭsc, *n.*, disk, phonograph record

C
D

dĭs-cârd', v., throw away

dĭs-cêrn', v., distinguish;
-er; -ment; -ible; -ibly;
-ing; -ingly

dĭs-chârge', v., release,
shoot; -r; -able

dĭs-cī'ple, n., follower

dĭs'cĭ-plĭne, n., training,
conduct; v., punish; -r;
plinable; plinal

dĭs-cŏl'ŏr, v., change
color, fade; -ation

dĭs-cŏm-bŏb'ū-lāte, v.,
confuse   [-ure

dĭs-cŏm'fĭt, v., frustrate;

dĭs-cŏn-tĕnt', a., restless;
-ment; -ed; -edness;
-edly

dĭs-cŏn-tĭn'ūe, v., stop;
uation; uance

dĭs'cŏ-phĭle, n., expert of
phonograph records

dĭs'côrd, n., conflict; v.,
clash; -ant; -ance;
-ancy; -antly

dĭs'cŏ-thēque (tĕk), n.,
nightclub for dancing

dĭs'cŏŭnt, n., price reduction; v., (**dĭs-cŏŭnt'**) take
for less value

dĭs-cŏŭr'âge, v., try to prevent; -ment

dĭs'côurse, n., speech,
talk

dĭs-cŏv'êr, v., find out; -er;
-y; -able

dĭs-crĕd'ĭt, v., disbelieve

dĭs-crēet', a., careful;
-ness; -ly

dĭs-crĕp'ăn-cў, n., inconsistency, mistake; **ant;**
antly

dĭs-crē'tion, n., tactful
judgment; -ary; -al

dĭs-crĭm'ĭ-nāte, v., see a
difference; **tion; tory;**
nable

dĭs'cŭs, n., metal disk
thrown as track event

dĭs-cŭss', v., talk about;
-ion; -able; -ible

dĭs-dāin', n., v., scorn; -ful;
-fulness; -fully

dĭs-ēase', n., illness

dĭs-ĕn-chănt', v., free from
magic; -ment

dĭs-ĕn-cŭm'bêr, v., relieve

a burden

dĭs-ĕn-gāge', v., unfasten;
-ment; -d

dĭs-fā'vŏr, n., dislike

dĭs-fĭg'ûre, v., ruin appearance; -ment; **ration**

dĭs-frăn'chĭse, v., deprive
of rights; -ment

dĭs-grāce', n., v., dishonor; -ful; -fulness;
-fully

dĭs-grŭn'tle, v., displease;
-ment

dĭs-guīse', v., hide the real
nature; -ment

dĭs-gŭst', n., distaste, v.,
sicken; -ing; -ingly; -ed;
-edly

dĭs-heárt'ĕn, v., discourage; -ing; -ingly; -ment

di-shĕv'ĕl, v., become untidy; -ed; -led; -ment

dĭs-ĭl-lū'sion, v., disappoint; -ment

dĭs-ĭn-fĕst', v., remove
pest; -ation

dĭs-ĭn'tĕ-grāte, v., break
up; **tor; tion; tive**

disk, n., flat, circular thing

dĭs'lŏ-cāte, v., displace;
tion

dĭs'măl, a., gloomy; -ly

dĭs-măn'tle, v., strip, take
apart; -ment

dĭs-māy', n., loss of courage; v., appall

dĭs-mĕm'bêr, v., cut into
pieces; -ment

dĭs-ŏwn', v., deny ownership

dĭs-păr'âge, v., belittle;
-ment; aging; agingly

dĭs-păs'sion-âte, a., fair,
unemotional; **ly**

dĭs-pătch', n., message;
v., send; -er

dĭs-pĕl', v., drive away

dĭs-pĕn'sà-rў, n., place for
medical treatment

dĭs-pĕnse', v., give out,
exempt; -r; **sation; sa-
tional; sable; sability**

dĭs-pêrse', v., scatter; -r;
sion; sal n.; **persible;**
sive

dĭs-plāce', v., remove
from; -ment

dĭs-plăy′, v., show

dĭs-pōse′, v., arrange, settle; **-r**

dĭs-pō-sĭ′tion, n., frame of mind, arrangement

dĭs-pós-sĕss′, v., expel, oust; **-or; -ion**

dĭs-prōve′, v., show to be false

dĭs-pūte′, n., argument; v., discuss; **tation; tatious; tative; table; tably; tant** n.

dĭs-qual′ĭ-fȳ (kwal), v., make ineligible; **fication**

dĭs-quĭ′ĕt (kwi), v., disturb, worry; **-ude** n.

dĭs-rė-gârd′, v., neglect; **-ful**

dĭs-rōbe′, v., undress

dĭs-rŭpt′, v., break up; **-er; -or; -ion; -ive; -ively**

dĭs-săt′ĭs-fȳ, v., displease; **faction; factory; fied**

dĭs-sĕct′, v., cut apart, examine; **-or; -ion**

dĭs-sĕnt′, v., disagree; **-er; sension; -ient; -ious; -ing**

dĭs-sėr-tā′tion, n., written thesis

dĭs-sĭm′ŭ-lāte, v., pretend; **tor; tion**

dĭs′sĭ-pāte, v., scatter, waste; **-r; tor; tion; tive; -d**

dĭs′só-lūte, a., immoral; **-ness; -ly**

dĭs-sōlve′, v., melt, end; **lution, solvable; solvent**

dĭs′só-nánce, n., lack of harmony or agreement; **nant; nantly**

dĭs′tăff, n., a., female

dĭs-tāste′, n., v., dislike; **-ful** [disease

dĭs-tĕm′pêr, n., animal

dĭs-tĕnd′, v., expand; **tention; tension; tensible**

dĭs-tĭll′, v., purify by condensing vapor; **-er; -ery; -ation**

dĭs-tĭn′guĭsh, v., see or show a difference; **-able; -ably**

dĭs-tĭn′guĭshed, a., famous

dĭs-tôrt′, v., make out of shape, pervert; **-er; -ion**

dĭs-trăct′, v., draw away from, confuse; **-ion; -ible**

dĭs-trĕss′, n., v., pain, worry; **-ing; -ed; -ful**

dĭs-trĭ′būte, v., give out for; **tion; tive; tively; table**

dĭs-tûrb′, v., upset, interrupt; **-er; -ance**

dĭs-ūse′, v., stop using

dĭtch, n., channel dug in earth

dĭth′êr, n., confused state

dĭt′tō, n., v., copy

dĭt′tȳ, n., simple song

dĭ-ûr′năl, a., every day; **-ly**

dĭ′vá, n., leading woman singer

dīve, v., plunge head first; **-r**

dĭ-vêrge′, v., branch off, differ; **-nce; -ncy; -nt; -ntly**

dĭ-vêr′sĭ-fȳ, v., vary; **sity**

dĭ-vêr′sion, n., distraction; **-ist; -ary** a.

di-vĕst′, v., strip; **-itûre**

dĭ-vīde′, v., split into parts; **-r; vision; visible**

dĭ-vīne′, a., holy, great; **nize; -ly**

dĭ-vĭn′ĭ-tȳ, n., god, study of religion

dĭ-vôrce′, n., legal end of marriage; v., separate

dĭ-vŭlge′, v., make known; **-nce; -ment**

dĭz′zȳ, a., unsteady, confused; **ziness; zily**

dŏc′īle, a., tame, easy to handle; **cility; -ly**

dŏck, n., place to unload ship, truck, etc. v., deduct part

dŏck′ĕt, n., court agenda

dŏc′tŏr, n., physician, one with college's highest degree

dŏc′trĭne, n., belief, teachings; **nal; nally**

dŏc′ŭ-mėnt, n., written record; v., **(mėnt)** prove; **-ation; -ary**

dŏdge, v., move aside quickly, avoid; **-r**

dōe, n., female deer

dŏff, v., take off

dŏg'ĕar, v., turn down page's corner

dŏg'gĕd, a., stubborn; **-ness; -ly**

dŏg'gêr-ĕl, n., jingle

dŏg-măt'ĭc, a., dictorial; **-ally** [tree

dŏg'wōod, n., flowering

dŏi'lÿ, n., small lace mat

dŏl'drŭm, n., low spirit

dōle, n., relief to needy; v., give out [**-ly**

dōle'fŭl, a., sad; **-ness;**

dŏll, n., toy like human

dŏl'lăr, n., U.S. money system, 100 cents

dŏl'lÿ, n., doll; cart for moving heavy objects

dō'lŏ-mīte, n., kind of rock

dō'lŏr-oŭs, a., sad; **-ly**

dŏl'phĭn, n., sea mammal

dōlt, n., stupid person; **-ish; -ishness; -ishly**

dō-māin', n., area of control

dōme, n., large rounded roof; **domical**

dŏ-mĕs'tĭc, n., house servant; a., of the home, tame; **-ity; -ate; -ation; -ly**

dŏm'ĭ-nāte, v., control; **tor; tion; nance; nant; nantly**

dŏ-mĭn'ion, n., power controlled region

dŏm'ĭ-nō, n., mask; tile; **oes** n., pl., game of matching dotted tiles

dŏn, n., dress

dō'nāte, v., give as to charity; **tor; tion**

dŏn'kēy, n., horselike animal

dō'nŏr, n., one who gives

dōom, n., tragic fate; v., condemn

dôor, n., movable panel at entrance

dōpe, n., stupid person, drug; **-y; piness**

dŏr'mănt, a., asleep, still; **mancy**

dôr'mêr, n., window on sloped roof

dôr'mĭ-tô-ry, n., building to sleep many

dôr'săl, a., of the back

dōse, n., medicine taken at one time; **dosage**

dŏs'sĭ-er (ā), n., data on one subject

dŏt'áge, n., senility

dōte, v., be fond; **-r; doting; dotingly**

doŭ'ble, a., adv., twofold, twice as much; v., duplicate, fold; **-y** a.

doŭ-ble-crŏss', v., betray

doubt (dōut), n., uncertainty; v., question: **-er; -ful; -fulness; -fully; -able; -less**

doūche (dŭsh), n., water jet to cleanse body

dŏugh, n., flour mixture for baking; (coll.) money; **-y** a.

doŭr, a., gloomy; **-ness; -ly**

doūse, v., pour liquid over

dŏve, n., kind of pigeon

dŏve'tāil, v., fit together

doŵ'á-gêr, n., wealthy widow

doŵ'ĕl, n., peg

dŏwn, n., descent, soft hair; adv., to lower place or state; a., lower, sad

dŏwn'căst, a., sad

dŏwn'fäll, n., sudden fall, ruin [spirits

dŏwn-heârt'ĕd, a., in low

dŏwn'pôur, n., heavy rain

dŏwn'rīght, a., plain; adv., utterly [tic

dŏwn-tŏ-êarth', a., realis-

doŵ'rÿ, n., property bride brings to husband

doŵse, v., search for water

dōze, n., v., nap; **dozy**

dŏz'ĕn, n., set of twelve

drăb, a., dull; **-ness; -ly**

drăft, n., drink, air current, outline, bank check; compulsory service; v., take into service

drăfts'măn, n., one who draws plans

drăg, n., hindrance; v., pull

along; pass slowly

dråg'nět, *n.*, system for criminal investigations

dråg'ȯn,*n.*, mythical beast

dråg'ȯn-flÿ, *n.*, insect

drāin, *n.*, pipe *v.*, let out liquid slowly, empty; **-age**

drāke,*n.*, male duck

dråm, *n.*,⅛ ounce, small amount

drà'mà, *n.*, play, art of theater; **-tics; -tist; -tize; -tization**

dråpe, *v.*, hang loosely

drås'tĭc, *a.*, extreme; **-ally**

dräw,*n.*, stalemate, attraction; *v.*, pull, attract, inhale, get, make pictures

dräw'båck, *n.*, disadvantage

dräw'brĭdge, *n.*, bridge that can be raised

drawer (drôr), *n.*, sliding box in chest; *pl.*, underpants

dråwl, *v.*, speak slowly

dräwn, *a.*, haggard

dråy, *n.*, cart; **-age**

drĕad,*n.*, *v.*, fear; **-ful; -fulness; -fully**

drĕar'ÿ,*a.*, gloomy; **iness; ily**

drĕdge, *n.*, *v.*, (boat, device to) scoop from water's bottom

drĕgs, *n.*, *pl.*, particles at bottom of liquid

drĕnch,*v.*, soak with liquid

drĕss, *n.*, clothing, woman's garment with skirt; *v.*, put on clothes, prepare

drĕss'êr, *n.*, one who dresses, chest of drawers

drĕss'īng, *n.*, bandage, sauce for food, meat stuffing ⟨ [stress

drĕss'måk-êr, *n.*, seamdrĭft,*n.*, tendency, general meaning, pile of sand, etc.; *v.*, move along by current

drĭll, *n.*, *v.*, (tool to) bore holes, practice

drĭp, *v.*, fall in drops; **-py**

a. [fee pot

drĭp'ȯ-lā-tŏr, *n.*, drip coffee

drĭve, *n.*, motor trip, road campaign; *v.*, force to go, operate a vehicle; **-r**

drĭv'ėl,*n.*, silly talk; **-er**

drĭv'ėn, *a.*, forced

drĭz'zle,*n.*, fine misty rain; **-zly** *a.*

drŏĭt,*n.*, legal right

drŏll, *a.*, funny; **-ery**

drōne, *n.*, male bee; *v.*, hum, talk monotonously

drōōl, *v.*, drip saliva

drōōp, *v.*, hand down, weaken; **-y** *a.*; **-iness; -ily**

drŏp, *n.*, tiny liquid mass, bit, descent; *v.*, let fall, utter; **-per**

drŏp'ȯŭt, *n.*, student who does not finish school

drŏp'sÿ, *n.*, excess body fluid

drŏss,*n.*, rubbish

drōŭght, *n.*, very dry weather, no rain

drōve, *n.*, animal herd

drōwn, *v.*, die in water

drōwse, *v.*, sleep lightly; **-y** *a.*

drŭdge,*n.*, one who works hard; **-ry** [cotic

drŭg, *n.*, medicine, nar-

drŭg'gĭst,*n.*, filler of medical prescriptions

drŭg'stȯre, *n.*, store selling medicine

drŭm, *n.*, *v.*, hollow musical instrument that is beaten; **-mer**

drŭnk,*a.*, intoxicated; **-ard** *n.*; **-en** *a.*

drÿ, *a.*, not wet, not sweet; **-er; -ness**

drÿ'-clēan, *v.*, clean with waterless substance; **-er**

dū'åd,*n.*, couple

dū'ål, *a.*, of two, double; **-ity; -ly; -ize**

dŭb,*v.*, give nickname

dū'bĭ- oŭs,*a.*, doubtful, uncertain; **-ness; -ly; os-ity; bitable; bitably**

dŭch'ĕss,*n.*, duke's wife

dŭck, *n.*, small swimming

C D

bird, cloth; v., dip under water, avoid

dŭct, n., tube, channel

dŭc'tĭle, a., easily molded; **tility**

dŭde, n., dandy, fob

dŭds, n., clothes

dŭe, a., owed, proper, expected; adv., exactly

dŭ'ėl, n., fight between two persons [fee

dŭes, n., pl., membership

dŭ'ĕt, n., music for two performers

dŭg'out, n., shelter

dŭke, n., nobleman; **-dom**

dŭl'cĕt, a., melodious; **-ly**

dŭll, a., mentally slow, sluggish, boring, blunt; **-ish; -ness; -y** adv.

dŭmb, a., unable to talk, (coll.) stupid; **-ness; -ly**

dŭmb'bĕll, n., weight lifted as exercise

dŭm'mÿ, n., imitation, unreal model, stupid one

dŭmp, n., rubbish pile; v., unload, throw away

dŭmp'lĭng, n., ball of dough

dŭn, n., demand for payment

dŭnce, n., dull person

dŭne, n., hill of sand

dŭng, n., animal excrement

dŭn-gȧ-rēes', n., pl., denim work pants

dŭn'geȯn, n., underground prison

dŭnk, v., dip in liquid

dŭ'ō, n., pair, two

dŭpe, v., cheat

dŭ'plĕx, n., two-family house

dŭ'plĭ-cāte, v., copy; a. (cĭt) double; **tion; cable; catable**

dû-rā'tion, n., time of existence

dû-rĕss', n., pressure

dŭsk, n., start of evening darkness, dim; **-y** a.; **-iness; -ily**

dŭst, n., powdery dirt; v., sprinkle powder, clean; **-er; -y** a.; **-less**

dū'tÿ, n., obligation, task; **tiful; tifully**

dū'tÿ, n., tax; **tiable**

dwärf, n., being smaller than normal; **-ish; -ish-ness**

dwĭn'dle, v., decrease

dÿ'äd, n., pair; **-ic**

dÿe, n., v., (substance to) change color; **-r**

dÿ'nȧ-mīte, n., powerful explosive; **-r**

dÿ'nȧs-tÿ, n., family of successive rulers; **tic; tical; tically**

dÿs'ėn-tēr-ÿ, n., intestinal disease; **teric**

dÿs-fŭnc'tion, n., incomplete functioning; **-al**

dÿs-lĕx'ĭ-ȧ, n., reading impairment; **lexic**

dÿs-pĕp'sĭ-ȧ, n., impaired digestion; **peptic**

dÿs'trȯ-phÿ, n., faulty development

E

ēa'gêr, a., keenly desiring; **-ness; -ly**

ēa'gle, n., bird of prey

ēa'gle-eÿed, a., sharp in vision

ēar'drŭm, n., thin membrane in ear

êarl, n., nobleman

êar'mȧrk, v., identify

êarn, v., work for wages or profit, deserve

êar'nėst, a., serious, sincere; **-ness; -ly**

êar'shŏt, n., hearing range

êarth, n., planet we live on, land, soil; **-ly; -liness**

êarth'ėn-wāre, n., baked clay dishes

êarth'quāke, n., trembling of earth's crust

êarth'shāk-ĭng, a., very important [soil

êarth'wŏrm, n., worm in

ēar'wĭg, n., insect

ēase, n., comfort, natural manner v., lessen, move carefully; **-ful; -fully**

ēa'sėl, n., artist's stand for picture

ēast, *n.,* direction of sunrise; *a.,* of the east; **-erly; -ern** *a.;* **-erner**

ēas'ÿ-gō-īng, *a.,* relaxed

ēaves, *n., pl.,* roof's edge

ēaves'drŏp, *v.,* listen secretly

ĕbb, *n.,* fallen tide *v.,* recede, lessen

ĕb'ŏn-ÿ, *n.,* tree; *a.,* dark, black

ē-bŭl'liĕnt, *a.,* bubbling, exuberant; **lience; liition; liency; -ly**

ĕc-cĕn'trĭc, *a.,* strange; **-ity; -ally**

ĕc-clē'sĭ-ȧs-tĭ-cȧl, *a.,* of church and clergy; **-ly; cism** [mation

ĕch'ĕ-lŏn, *n.,* steplike for-

ĕch'ō (ĕk), *n.,* repeated sound [pastry

ē-clâir' (ā-), *n.,* long filled

ĕc-lĕc'tĭc, *a.,* selective from many ideas; **-ally; -ism**

ē-clīpse', *n.,* obscuring of sun by moon or moon by earth's shadow

ē-cŏl'ȯ-gÿ, *n.,* science of man's environment; **gist; logical; logically**

ē-cŏn'ȯ-mÿ, *n.,* money and wealth management, thrift, country's prosperity; **nomics; mist; nomic** [beige

ĕc'rū, *n., a.,* light tan.

ĕc'stȧ-sÿ, *n.,* great delight; **static; statically**

ĕc'ū-mĕn-ĭsm, *n.,* interreligious cooperation, **menic, menical; menically**

ĕc'zė-mȧ, *n.,* skin disease

ĕd'dÿ, *n.,* little whirlpool

ė-dē'mȧ, *n.,* excess body fluid; **-tous**

ē-dĕn'tȧte, *a.,* toothless

ĕdge, *n.,* border, verge

ĕd'ĭ-ble, *a.,* eatable; **bility; -ness**

ē'dĭct, *n.,* public order

ĕd'ĭ-fĭce, *n.,* building

ĕd'ĭ-fÿ, *v.,* instruct or improve morally; **fication**

ė-dī'tion, *n.,* published form of book, issue of newspaper

ĕd'ŭ-cāte, *v.,* teach; **tor; tion; tional; tionally; cable; tive**

ė-dūce', *v.,* extract, draw out; **duct** *n.;* **duction; ducible**

ēel, *n.,* snakelike fish

ēe'riĕ, *a.,* weird; **riness, rily**

ĕf-fĕct', *n., v.,* result, influence; *n., pl.,* belongings; **-er; -ive; -iveness; -ively; -ual; -uate**

ĕf-fĕm'ĭ-nȧte, *a.,* of female traits; **nacy; -ly**

ĕf'fêr-ĕnt, *a.,* carrying away

ĕf-fêr-vĕsce', *v.,* bubble; **cent; cense; cently**

ĕf-fēte', *a.,* exhausted; **-ness; -ly**

ĕf-fĭ'ciĕnt, *a.,* competent; **ciency; -ly**

ĕf'fĭ-gÿ, *n.,* statue or crude image of person

ĕf'flŭ-ĕnt, *n., a.,* (thing) flowing out; **ence**

ĕf-frŏn'têr-ÿ, *n.,* unashamed boldness

ĕf-fŭl'gĕnce, *n.,* great brightness; **ent**

ĕgg, *n.,* female reproductive cell, oval body laid by bird, fish, etc

ĕgg'hĕad, *n.,* intellectual

ĕgg'nŏg, *n.,* thick drink of eggs and milk

ē'gō, *n.,* self, conceit; **-ism, -ist; -istic**

ē'gȯ-tĭsm, *n.,* selfishness; conceitedness; **tist; tistic; tistical; tistically**

ė-grē'giŏŭs, *a.,* very bad; **-ness; -ly**

ē'grĕss, *n.,* exit

ė-jăc'ū-lāte, *v.,* discharge, exclaim; **tor; tion; tory**

ė-jĕct', *v.,* throw out; **-or; -ion; -ive; -able**

ēke, *v.,* barely make do

ė-lăb'ȯ-rāte, *v.,* develop in detail; *a.,* (ĭt) complicated; **tor; tion; tive; -ness; -ly**

e-lăn', *n.,* **(ā)** dash

è-lăpse', v., pass by

è-lāte', v., make happy; tion; -ness; -ly

ĕl'bōw, n., joint between lower and upper arm

ĕld'ẽr, n., older person; a., senior; -ly; -liness

è-lĕct', v., vote, choose; tor; tion; tive; tively

è-lĕc'tör-àte, n., all qualified voters

è-lĕc-trĭ'ciàn, n., workman for electric apparatus

è-lĕc-trĭc'ĭ-tў, n., form of energy

è-lĕc-trō-câr'dĭ-ò-grăph, n., instrument to record heartbeat; -ic

è-lĕc'trò-cūte, v., kill with electricity; tion

è-lĕc'trōde, n., conductor of electricity

è-lĕc'trŏn, n., atom's negatively charged particle; -ic; -ics; -ically

ĕl'è-gànt, n., refined, luxurious; gance; gancy; -ly

ĕl'è-gў, n., mournful poem; giac; gist

ĕl'è-mĕnt, n., basic part, environment, basic chemical substance; -al; -ally

ĕl'è-vā-tör, n., lifting machine

ĕlf, n., tiny fairy, small child; -ish; -ishness; -ishly   [-ation

è-lĭc'ĭt, v., bring forth; -or;

ĕl'ĭ-gĭ-ble, a., qualified; bility; bly

è-lĭm'ĭ-nāte, v., remove, excrete; tor; tion; tive

è-lĭte', n., best group, typewriter type

è-lĭx'ĭr, n., medicine

ĕll, n., right angle wing of building

ĕl-lĭpse', n., oval figure; liptic; liptical; liptically

ĕl-ò-cū'tion, n., manner of speaking; -ist; -ary

è-lŏn'gāte, v., make longer, extend; tion

è-lōpe', v., run away to marry; -ment

ĕl'ò-quĕnt, a., expressive; quence; -ly

è-lū'cĭ-dāte, v., explain; tor; tion; tive

è-lūde', v., avoid, escape; lusion; lusive

è-lū'vĭ-ŭm, n., rock and soil debris; vial

ĕm, n., printer's measure

è-mā'cĭ-āte, v., become too thin; tion

è-măn'cĭ-pāte, v., free; tor; tion; tive; tory

è-măs'cŭ-lāte, v., deprive, castrate; tion; tory; tive

ĕm-bălm', v., preserve a dead body; -er; -ment

ĕm-bănk'mĕnt, n., protective wall or mound

ĕm-bâr'gō, n., legal restriction on trade

ĕm-bârk', v., go aboard, begin; -ment; -ation

ĕm-băr'ràss, v., feel self-conscious; -ment

ĕm'bàs-sў, n., ambassador's official residence

ĕm-băt'tle, v., prepare to fight

ĕm-bĕl'lĭsh, v., decorate, elaborate; -ment

ĕm'bêr, n., glowing coal or wood from fire

ĕm-bĕz'zle, v., steal money entrusted; -r; -ment

ĕm-bĭt'têr, v., make angry; -ment

ĕm-blā'zòn, v., decorate celebrate; -ment

ĕm'blĕm, n., symbol, sign; -atic; -atical; -atically

ĕm-bŏd'ў, v., give form to, include; bodiment

ĕm'bò-lĭsm, n., obstruction of a blood vessel

ĕm-bŏss', v., make raised design; -er; -ment

ĕm'brò-cāte, v., rub with salve, oil, etc

ĕm-brŏĭ'dêr, v., decorate with needlework, embellish; -er; -y

ĕm-brŏĭl', v., involve in fight; -ment

ĕm'brў-ō, n., organism in early stage; -nic; -logy;

-logist

ĕm'ĕr-ȧld, *n.*, green jewel

ė-mêrge', *v.*, come forth;
gency; gent

ė-mêr'gĕn-cӯ, *n.*, sudden
actior. needing action

ė-mĕr'ĭ-tŭs, *a.*, retired with
honorary title

ĕm'ĕr-ӯ, *n.*, an abrasive

ė-mĕt'ĭc, *a.*, causing vom-
iting

ĕm'ĭ-grāte, *v.*, leave one's
country for another; **tion;
grant** *n.*, *a.*

ĕm'ĭ-nėnt, *a.*, high, famous; **nence; nency;
-ly** [on mission

ĕm'ĭs-sȧr-ӯ, *n.*, agent sent

ė-mĭt', *v.*, discharge, transmit; **-ter; mission; missive**

ė-mŏl'li-ėnt, *a.*, softening

ė-mŏl'ū-mėnt, *n.*, salary

ė-mō'tion, *n.*, feeling; **-al;
-ality**

ėm-pă'thӯ, *n.*, understanding of another's situation; **thize; thetic**

ĕm'pêr-ör, *n.*, ruler; **press**

ĕm'phȧ-sĭs, *n.*, stress, importance; **size; phatic**

ĕm-ploy' (plŏĭ), *v.*, use,
hire; **-er; -ee; -ment;
-able**

ĕm-pō'rĭ-ŭm, *n.*, trading
center, department store

ĕm-pӯr'ē-ȧl, *a.*, heavenly

ē'mū, *n.*, flightless Australian bird

ĕm'ū-lāte, *v.*, imitate to
equal or surpass; **tor;
tion; tive; tively; lous**

ė-mŭl'sion, *n.*, oil suspended in watery liquid;
**sive; sify; sification;
sifiable**

ėn-ăm'ėl, *n.*, glossy coating or paint; **-er**

ėn-ăm'ör, *v.*, charm

ėn-cāge', *v.*, confine

ėn-cắp'sů-lāte, *v.*, put in
capsule, condense; **tion**

ĕn-cĕph-ȧ-lī'tĭs, *n.*, brain
inflammation; **tic**

ėn-chănt', *v.*, bewitch, delight; **-er; -ment; -ing**

ėn-clōse', *v.*, fence in, in-

sert; **sure**

ėn-cō'mĭ-ŭm, *n.*, tribute,
praise; **miast** *n.;* **miastic**

en'côre (ăn), audience's
demand for more; *int.*,
more!

ėn-coun'têr, *n.*, battle,
chance meeting; *v.*,
meet

ėn-crōach', *v.*, intrude,
trespass; **-ment**

ėn-cŭm'bêr, *v.*, burden,
hinder; **brance**

ėn-cӯ-clȯ-pē'dĭ-ȧ, *n.*,
book or books with in-
formation; **dic; dically**

ėn-dēar', *v.*, cause to like;
-ment; -ing

ėn-dĕav'ŏr, *n.*, *v.*, try

ėn-dĕm'ĭc, *a.*, native to region; **-al; -ity; demism**

ĕn'dīve, *n.*, leafy salad
green

ĕnd'lĕss, *a.*, eternal, continual; **-ly; -ness**

ĕn'dȯ-crīne, *n.*, any body
gland producing internal
secretion; **nology**

ėn-dôrse', *v.*, sign a
check, approve; **-r;
-ment; dorsable**

ėn-dŏw', *v.*, give money or
gift, provide with; **-ment**

ėn-dūre', *v.*, last, continue;
**durance, durable; dur-
ably; during**

ĕn'ė-mȧ, *n.*, fluid injected
into rectum

ĕn'ė-mӯ, *n.*, one against
another, opponent, foe

ĕn'êr-gӯ, *n.*, vigor, power
to do work; **getic; getically; gize; getics**

ĕn'êr-vāte, *v.*, weaken;
tion

ėn-fôrce', *v.*, urge, make
obey law; **-r; -ment;
-able**

ėn-frăn'chīse, *v.*, free,
give right to vote; **-ment**

ėn-gāge', *v.*, pledge to
marry, hire, involve, en-
ter in battle; **-d; -ment**

ėn-gĕn'dêr, *v.*, cause

ĕn'gĭne, *n.*, machine using
energy, locomotive; **-er**

ĕn-gĭ-nēer'ĭng, *n.*, use of

science in industry

ĕn-gôrge', v., eat greedily; -ment

ĕn-grāve', v., etch letters or design in metal, impress; -r; ing n.

ĕn-hănce', v., make greater; -er; -ment

ĕ-nĭg'má, n., mystery; -tic; -tical; -tically [bid

ĕn-jōĭn', v., command, for-

ĕn-lârge', v., increase size; -r; -ment

ĕn-līst', v., join the military, get; -ment

ĕn-līv'ĕn, v., make active

ĕn'mĭ-tỹ, n., hostility

ĕn-nō'ble, v., dignify

en'nui (ăn'wē), n., boredom [mity

ĕ-nôr'moŭs, a., huge;

ĕ-nough' (nŭf), a., adv., as much as necessary

ĕn-râge', v., anger

ĕn-răp'tŭre, v., enchant

ĕn-rĭch', v., make rich, add vitamins; -ment

ĕn-rōll', v., sign up for; -ment [snugly

ĕn-scŏnce', v., place

en-sem'ble (ăn-săm), n., whole costume, company of actors, musical band

ĕn-shrīne', v., hold sacred

ĕn-sīgn', n., flag, badge, U.S. naval officer

ĕn-snāre', v., trap

ĕn-snârl', v., tangle

ĕn-sūe', v., follow

ĕn-tāil', v., require; -ment

ĕn-tăn'gle, v., confuse, trap; -ment

en-tente' (ăn-tänt), n., agreement between nations

ĕn'têr-prīse, n., project, venture

ĕn-thrăll', v., fascinate

ĕn-tīce', v., attract

ĕn-tīre', a., whole; -ness; -ty; -ly

ĕn'tĭ-tỹ, n., anything real

ĕn-tŏ-mŏl'ŏ-gỹ, n., study of insects; gist

ĕn'trāils, n., intestines

ĕn'trânce, n., place for en-

tering

ĕn-trănce', v., put into trance, entrapture; -ment

ĕn-trēat', v., beg, request; -ment; -y; -ingly

en'tree (än-trā), n., freedom to enter, meal's main course

ĕn-trĕnch', v., establish

en-trĕ-prĕ-neûr' (än), n., one running own business

ĕn-twīne', v., wrap around

ĕ-nŭ'mêr-āte, v., count, list; tor; tion; tive

ĕ-nŭn'cĭ-āte, v., state, speak clearly; tor, tion; tive; ciable

ĕn-vĕl'ŏp, v., cover; -ment

ĕn'vĕ-lōpe, n., paper container for letters

ĕn-vī'rŏn-mĕnt, n., surroundings; -al; -ally

ĕn-vī'sion, v., imagine

ĕn'voy (vŏĭ), n., diplomatic agent

ĕn'vỹ, n., jealousy; v., begrudge; vious; viously; viable; viably

ĕn'zỹme, n., substance causing chemical reactions in body; mology

ē'ŏn, n., long period

ĕp'áu-lĕt, n., shoulder decoration

ĕ-phĕm'êr-ál, a., short lived; -ly

ĕp'ĭc, n. long poem; a., grand, heroic; -al; -ally

ĕp'ĭ-cūre, n., one who enjoys fine foods, wines, etc., gourmet; rean a.; curism

ĕp-ĭ-dĕm'ĭc, n., widespread disease; -ally; miology

ĕp-ĭ-dêr'mĭs, n., outer layer of skin; mal; mic

ĕp'ĭ-grăm, n., witty saying; -matic; -matical; -matically

ĕp'ĭ-grăph, n., building inscription, motto; -ic; -ical; -ically

ĕp'ĭlĕp-sỹ, n., disease marked by convulsive

fits; **leptic** *n.*, *a.*; **leptic-**
ally [part
ep'i-logue, *n.*, concluding
é-pǐs'cō-pàl, *a.*, of or by
bishops; **-ly**
ěp'ĭ-sōde, *n.*, incident;
sodic; sodical; sodic-
ally [lary
é-pǐs'tle, *n.*, letter, **-r; to-**
ěp'ĭ-tăph, *n.*, tombstone
inscription; **-ic; -ial**
ěp'ĭ-thět, *n.*, descriptive
name ex. Philip the Fair;
-ic; -ical
é-pǐt'ò-mē, *n.*, typical example, summary; **mize**
ěp'óch (ók), *n.*, period; **-al;**
-ally [bility
ěq'uà-ble, *a.*, steady; **bly;**
ē'quàl, *a.*, same, alike; **-ly;**
-ity; -ize; quate
é-quā'tion, *n.*, mathematic
expression of equal
quantities; **-al**
é-quā'tŏr, *n.*, imaginary
circle dividing earth
equally in half; **-ial**
é-quěs'trǐ-àn, *n.*, *a.*, (one)
horseback riding; **-ism**
ē-quǐ-lǐb'rǐ-ŭm, *n.*, balance
ē'quine, *n.*, horse
ē'quǐ-nŏx, *n.*, time when
sun crosses the equator;
noctial
ěq'uǐ-tà-ble, *a.*, fair, just;
-ness; bly
é-quǐv'ò-cāte, *v.*, mislead,
lie; **tor; tion; cal; cally;**
calness; cality
ê'rà, *n.*, period of time
é-răd'ĭ-cāte, *v.*, get rid of;
tor; tion; tive; cable
é-rāse', *v.*, rub out; **-r; sure**
é-rěct', *v.*, build; *a.*, upright; **-or; -ion**
ěr'è-mīte, *n.*, hermit;
mitical [work
êrg, *n.*, unit of energy or
êr'mǐne, *n.*, weasel with
expensive white fur
é-rōde', *v.*, wear away; **ro-**
sion; rosive
é-rŏt'ĭc, *a.*, arousing sexual feelings and desires;
êrr, *v.*, be wrong [**-ly**
ěr'rànd, *n.*, trip for a purpose
êr'rànt, *a.*, wandering; **-ly**
êr-rǎt'ĭc, *a.*, irregular; **-ally**
êr'sätz, *a.*, artificial
êr'ü-dīte, *a.*, learned; **-ly**
é-rŭpt', *v.*, burst forth; **-ion;**
-ive; -ible
ěs'cà-lāte, *v.*, increase, go
up [stairs
ěs'cà-lā-tŏr, *n.*, moving
ěs'cà-pāde, *n.*, reckless
adventure
ěs-câr-gōt' (gō), *n.*, edible
snail
ěs'cà-rōle, *n.*, endive
ěs-chew', *v.*, avoid; **-al** *n.*
ěs'côrt, *n.*, one who goes
with another; *v.*,
(ěs-côrt) accompany
ěs'crŏw, *n.*, legal agreement held until condi-
tions are met
ěs'cū-lěnt, *a.*, fit for food
é-sŏph'à-gŭs, *n.*, food
tube to stomach
ěs'pī-ò-nàge, *n.*, spying
ěs-pŏuse', *v.*, marry;
pousal *n.*
ěs-pȳ', *v.*, see
ěs-quire', *n.*, courtesy title
ěs'sāy, *n.*, short written
article; *v.*, **(ěs-sāy)** try
ěs'sènce, *n.*, basic nature
ěs-tăb'lǐsh, *v.*, settle, set
up, prove; **-er; -ment**
ěs-tāte', *n.*, one's possessions, property
ěs-tēem', *n.*, *v.*, regard
highly
ěs'tǐ-màte, *n.*, approximate calculation; *v.*
(māt) judge, guess; **tor;**
tion; tive
ěs-trānge', *v.*, make unfriendly; **-ment**
ěs'trò-gèn, *n.*, female sex
hormone; **-ic**
ěs'tū-ār-ў, *n.*, river mouth;
arial
ětch, *v.*, put design on with
acid; **-er**
é-têr'nàl, *a.*, everlasting,
continual; **nity; -ly;**
-ness
é-thē'rē-àl, *a.*, heavenly;
-ity; -ness; -ly
ěth'ĭcs, *n.*, *pl.*, study of

conduct and moral judgment; **ical, cist**

ĕth'nĭc, *a.*, of a particular group of people, cultural; **-ity; -al; -ally; nology**

ē-tĭ-ŏl'ō-gў, *n.*, study of causes; **logic; logical; logically**

ĕt'ĭ-quĕtte, *n.*, manners, proper behavior

e'tūde (ā), *n.*, music for one instrument

ĕt-ў-mŏl'ō-gў, *n.*, study of word origins; **gist; logical; logically**

eū-gĕn'ĭcs, *n.*, study of improving human qualities; **ic; cist**

eū'lō-gў, *n.*, praise (a dead person); **gize; gizer**

eū'nŭch (nŭk), *n.*, castrated man

eū'phĕ-mĭsm, *n.*, nice word replacing offensive one; **mist; mize; mistic; mistically**

eū'phō-nў, *n.*, pleasant sound

eū-thĕn'ĭcs, *n.*, *pl.*, science of improving man through environmental changes

ē-văc'ū-āte, *v.*, remove; **tor; tion; tive; ant**

ē-vāde', *v.*, avoid, escape; **-r; vasion; vasive; vasiveness; vasively**

ē-văl'ū-āte, *v.*, find value of; **tion; tive**

ē-văn'gĕl-ĭsm, *n.*, preaching of New Testament; **gelist; gelical; gelistic; gelistically**

ē'vĕn, *v.*, equalize; *a.*, level, uniform, calm, divisible by two; *adv.*, exactly, while

ē-vĕnt', *n.*, happening, contest

ĕv'ĕr-grēen, *n., a.*, (plant that) having green leaves all year [**-ly**

ĕv-ĕr-lăst'ĭng, *a.*, forever;

ē-vĕrt', *v.*, turn inside out; **-or; version**

ĕv'ĕr-ў-bŏd-ў, *pro.*, every person [things

ĕv'ĕr-ў-thĭng, *pro.*, all

ĕv'ĕr-ў-whĕre, *adv.*, all places

ē-vĭct', *v.*, put out; **-ion**

ĕv'ĭ-dĕnt, *a.*, easy to see, clear; **-ly**

ē-vĭnce', *v.*, show plainly; **vincible**

ē-vĭs'cĕ-rāte, *v.*, remove, insides, deprive; **tion**

ē-vōke', *v.*, call forth; **ocator; ocation; vocative**

ĕv-ō-lū'tion, *n.*, gradual development, process; **-al; -ally; -ary**

ewe, *n.*, female sheep

ew'ĕr, *n.*, water pitcher

ĕx-ăct', *v.*, demand; **-er; -ion; -able**

ĕx-ăct', *a.*, correct, perfect; **-ness; -ly; -itude** *n.*

ĕx-ăg'gĕ-rāte, *v.*, overstate; **tor; tion; tive**

ĕx-ālt', *v.*, raise, praise, fill with joy; **-er; -ation**

ĕx-ăm'ĭne, *v.*, look at or into, investigate; **-r; nation; nable**

ĕx-ăm'ple, *n.*, sample, typical instance, model

ĕx-ăs'pĕr-āte, *v.*, anger, irritate; **tion**

ĕx'că-vāte, *v.*, dig out, unearth; **tor; tion**

ĕx-cĕl', *v.*, do greater than, surpass; **-lence; -lent; -lently**

ĕx'cĕl-lĕn-cў, *n.*, title of honor [shavings

ĕx-cĕl'sĭ-ōr, *n.*, wood

ĕx-cĕpt', *v.*, leave out; *prep., conj.*, other than, but

ĕx-cĕss', *n.*, lack of moderation; *a.*, (**ĕx'cĕss**) extra; **-ive; -iveness; -ively**

ĕx-chānge', *n., v.*, trade; **-r; -able; -ability**

ĕx-cīte', *v.*, stir up, provoke; **-r; -ment; citable; -d**

ĕx-clāim', *v.*, suddenly cry out; **-er; clamation; clamatory**

ĕx-clūde', *v.*, keep or shut

out; -r; -able; clusion;
clusionary

ĕx-cóm-mū'nĭ-cāte, *v.*,
exclude from church;
tor; tion; tive; tory

ĕx-crēte', *v.*, eliminate
from body; tion; tory

ĕx-crū'cĭ-āt-ĭng, *a.*, very
painful; -ly

ĕx'cŭl-pāte, *v.*, prove
guiltless; tion; tory; pa-
ble

ĕx-cûr'sion, *n.*, short trip

ĕx-cūse', *n.*, explanation;
v., (c'uz) apologize, forgive, let leave; cusable;
cusatory

ĕx'ė-crāte, *v.*, hate, curse;
tor; tive; tory; crable;
crably

ĕx'ė-cūte, *v.*, carry out, do,
kill legally; tion

ĕx-ĕc'ū-tĭve, *n.*, administrator; tory

ĕx-ĕc'ū-tŏr, *n.*, one who
carries out a will

ĕx-ė-gē'sĭs, *n.*, biblical interpretation; getic; get-
ics; getical; getically

ĕx-ĕm'plår, *n.*, model,
sample; -y *a.*, -iness;
-ily

ĕx-ĕmpt', *v.*, free from, excuse; -ion; -ible

ĕx'êr-cīse, *n.*, active use,
bodily exertion, (pl.) formal program; *v.*, use,
drill; -r

ĕx-êrt', *v.*, use actively;
-ion; -ive

ĕx-hāle', *v.*, breathe out;
lation [fumes

ĕx-häust', *n.*, engine

ĕx-häust', *v.*, use up, tire;
-ion; -ive; -ible; -ibility;
-less

ĕx-hĭb'ĭt, *n.*, *v.*, show; -or;
-ion; -ive; -ory

ĕx-hĭl'à-rāte, *v.*, make
lively; tion; tive

ĕx-hôrt', *v.*, urge; -ation;
-atory; -ative

ĕx-hūme', *v.*, remove from
ground; mation

ĕx'ĭ-gĕn-cў, *n.*, emer-
gency, need; gent;
gently

ĕx'īle, *n.*, one forced to
leave country; *v.*, banish

ĕx'ó-dŭs, *n.*, departure

ĕx-ŏn'ė-rāte, *v.*, free from
blame; tor; tion; tive

ĕx-ôr'bĭ-tànt, *a.*, extreme;
tance; tancy; -ly

ĕx'ôr-cīse, *v.*, drive out
evil spirit; cism; cist

ĕx-pănd', *v.*, spread out,
enlarge; pansion; pan-
sive; -able

ĕx-pā'trĭ-āte, *v.*, exile;
tion

ĕx-pĕc'tó-rāte, *v.*, spit;
tion

ĕx-pē'dĭ-ėnt, *a.*, useful,
convenient; ency; ence;
-ly

ĕx-pé-dī'tion, *n.*, journey
for a purpose; -ary;
tious; tiously

ĕx-pĕl', *v.*, force out; -ler;
-lee; -lable; -lant

ĕx-pĕnse', *n.*, cost

ĕx-pē'rĭ-ėnce, *n.*, anything
lived through, knowl-
edge gained; *v.*, meet
with; -d; ential; entially

ĕx-pĕr'ĭ-mĕnt, *n.*, *v.*, test
to prove something;
-ation; -al; -ally

ĕx'pĭ-āte, *v.*, be sorry for;
tor; tion; able

ĕx-pīre', *v.*, end, die, to
breathe out; ration

ĕx'plė-tĭve, *n.*, unneeded
word or phrase; tory

ĕx-plĭc'ĭt, *a.*, clearly
stated; -ly; -ness

ĕx-plōde', *v.*, burst noisily;
-r; plodable; plosion;
plosive

ĕx-plôre', *v.*, look into, discover; -r; ration; plora-
tory; plorative

ĕx-pôrt', *v.*, send goods to
other countries; -er;
-able; -ation

ĕx-pōse', *v.*, show. make
known; sûre

ĕx-pŏs'tŭ-lāte, *v.*, object;
tor; tion; tory

ĕx-prĕss', *n.*, direct
method for transporting

ĕx-prĕss', *v.*, squeeze,
symbolize, say; -ion;

E
F

-ive

ĕx-prō'prĭ-āte, v., take from; tor; tion

ĕx-pŭl'sion, n., forcing out; sive

ĕx-pŭnge', v., erase

ĕx'pûr-gāte, v., delete; -ion

ĕx'quĭ-sĭte, a., delicately beautiful; -ness; -ly

ĕx-tĕm-pŏ-rā'nē-oŭs, a., unplanned; -ly

ĕx-tĕnd', v., expand, offer; -er; -ible; tension; tensive; tensible

ĕx-tĕn'ū-āte, v., give excuse; tor; ting

ĕx-tē'rĭ-ör, n., outside; -ity

ĕx-tê'rmĭ-nāte, v., kill, destroy; tor; tion; tory

ĕx-tê'rnàl, a., outer; -ity; -ize; -ization; -ly

ĕx-tĭn'guĭsh, v., put out; -ment; -able

ĕx'tĭr-pāte, v., root out, destroy; tor; tion; tive

ĕx-tōl', v., praise; -ler; -ment

ĕx-tôrt', v., get money by threats; -er; -ion; -ive

ex-tract, v., pull out, select; -or; -ion; -able

ĕx'trà-dĭte, v., turn over prisoner to another state; tion

ĕx-trā'nē-oŭs, a., not belonging; -ness; -ly

ĕx-trăv'à-gànt, a., excessive, wasteful; gance; gancy; -ly

ĕx'trĭ-cāte, v., release; tion; cable; cability

ĕx-trĭn'sĭc, a., unessential; -ally

ĕx-trŭde', v., push out, -r; trusion; trusive

ĕx-ū'bêr-ànt, a., healthy, high spirited; ance; ancy; -ly

ĕx-ūde', v., ooze in drops

ĕx-ŭlt', v., rejoice; -ation; -ancy; -ant; -antly

eȳe'sõre, n., thing unpleasant to look at

eȳe'tōōth, n., pointed upper tooth

eȳe-wĭt'nĕss, n., person who saw the incident

F

fā'ble, n., story teaching a moral lesson

făb'rĭc, n., cloth, material

făb'rĭ-cāte, v., make, lie; tor; tion   [-ly

făb'ū-loŭs, a., imaginary, hard to believe; -ness;

fà-cāde', n., building front, appearance

fāce, n., front of head, surface; v., meet; facial

făc'ĕt, n., surface of cut gem; aspect

fà-cē'tioŭs, a., witty; -ness; -ly   [cility

fàc'īle, a., easy; -ness; -ly;

făc-sĭm'ĭ-lē, n., copy

făct, n., truth, real happening; -ual; -ually

făc'tion, n., group with similar beliefs; -al; -ally; tious; tiousness; tiously

făc-tĭ'tioŭs, a., not natural; -ness; -ly

făc'tör, n., agent, causal element, multiplier; -ial

făc'ŭl-tȳ, n., ability to do, talent, teaching staff

făd, n., passing fashion; -dish; -dishly; -dishness; -dism

fāde, v., lose color, die out

făg, n., become tired

făg'ŏt, n., bundle of sticks

fāil, v., fall short, unable to do, neglect; -ūre; -ing n.

fāint, v., loose consiousness; a., weak; -ness; -ly

fāir, n., carnival, exhibition; a., blond, just, average, clear and sunny

fāir'lȳ, adv., justly, moderately, clearly

fāith, n., unquestioning belief; -ful; -fully; -less

fāke, n., a., (anything) not genuine, false; v., deceive; -r; -ry

făl'cŏn, n., hunting hawk

făl'dĕ-räl, n., nonsense

fäll, n., descending, capture; v., come down, lower, lose power; -en a.

făl′là-cў, *n.,* misleading idea; **cious; ciousness; ciously**

făl′lĭ-ble, *a.,* liable to error; **-ness; bly; bility**

făll′out, *n.,* radioactive particles after nuclear explosion [active

făl′lŏw, *a.,* unplanted, in-

fălse, *a.,* not true, dishonest; **-ness; -ly; -hood**

făl′tèr, *v.,* stumble, hesitate [utation; **-d**

fāme, *n.,* well-known rep-

făm′′ĭ-lў, *n.,* parents and children, relatives; **milial** [shortage

făm′ĭne, *n.,* acute food

făm′ĭsh, *v.,* be hungry; **-ment**

făn, *n.,* device to circulate air, supporter

făn′cў, *n.,* imagination, notion; *v.,* imagine, like; *a.,* elaborate, decorated; **ciness; cily; ciless; ciful**

făn′fāre, *n.,* trumpet blast, showy display

făng, *n.,* long pointed tooth

făn′tà-sў, *n.* illusion, dream; **size**

fârce, *n.,* exaggerated comedy; **cical, cicality, cically**

fāre, *n.,* fee to travel, food; *v.,* go

fāre′wĕll, *n.,* going away, *int.,* goodbye [ated

fâr′fĕtched, *a.,* exagger-

fà-rī′nà, *n.,* cooked cereal

fârm, *n.,* land for raising crops or animals; *v.,* raise crops, rent out; **-er**

fâr-rēach′ĭng, *a.,* wide effort

fâr′thèr, *a.,* *adv.,* more distant than [distant

fâr′thĕst, *a.,* *adv.,* most

făs′cĭ-nāte, *v.,* attract, charm; **tor; tion; nating**

făs′cĭsm, *n.,* government by dictatorship; **cist**

făsh′ĭòn, *n.,* current style, manner; *v.,* form; **-able; -ably** [ing

făst, *v.,* abstain from eat-

făst, *a.,* quick, firm, loyal; *adv.,* firmly, quickly; **-ness**

făs′tĕn, *v.,* connect, fix in place, tie; **-er; -ing** *n.*

făs-tĭd′ĭ-oŭs, *a.,* very particular; **-ness; -ly**

făt, *n.,* *a.,* (animal tissue that is) oily and greasy; *a.,* plump, fleshy; **-ness; -ten; -ty** *a.*

fāte, *n.,* one's lot, destiny; **-ful; -d**

făth′ŏm, *n.,* six feet deep; *v.,* understand; **-able**

fà-tĭgues′, *n.,* *pl.,* military work clothes

făt′ū-oŭs, *a.,* silly; **tuity; -ness; -ly**

fäu′cĕt, *n.,* device to adjust water flow

fäult, *n.,* defect, error, blame; **-less; -y** *a.*

fäu′nà, *n.,* animals of an area; **-l**

fā′vŏr, *n.,* kind act, small gift; *v.,* like, resemble; **-able; -ably; -ed**

fā′vŏr-ĭte, *n.,* *a.,* (one) highly preferred; **itism**

fäwn, *n.,* young deer; *v.,* show friendliness

fāze, *v.,* bother

fēar, *n.,* feeling of danger; *v.,* be afraid of; **-ful; -fulness; -fully; -less**

fēa′sĭ-ble, *a.,* possible; **bility; bly; -ness**

fēast, *n.,* rich elaborate meal, celebration

fēat, *n.,* remarkable deed

fēath′ĕr, *n.,* outgrowth of a bird's body; **-y** *a.*

fēath′ĕr-weight (wāt), *n.,* boxing weight less than 126 pounds

fēa′tūre, *n.,* facial part, special item; *v.,* give prominence

fē′brĭle, *a.,* feverish

fē′cĕs, *n.,* *pl.,* excrement; **-cal** [-ness; -ly

fĕck′lĕss, *a.,* careless;

fē′cŭnd, *a.,* productive; **-ity; -ate**

fĕd′ĕr-àl, *a.,* of central government; **-ly; -ism;**

-ist
fė-dô'rȧ, n., felt hat
fēe, n., charge for service, payment   [bly
fēe'ble, a., weak; -ness;
fēed, v., give food to, supply; -er
fēel, n., instinctive ability; v., touch, be aware of, believe; -er; -ing n.
feign (fān), v., pretend
feint (fānt), n., false attempt   [relsome
feist'ỹ, a., excited, quar-
fė-lĭc'ĭ-toŭs, a., fitting; -ly
fė-lĭc'ĭ-tỹ, n., happiness; cific   [cat family
fē'līne, n., a., (any cat) of
fĕll, v., cut down
fĕl'lōw, n., a male, companion; -ship
fĕl'ȯn, n., criminal; -y
fē'māle, n., a., (one) of sex that bears children
fĕm'ĭ-nĭsm, n., belief that women need equal rights; nist
fĕnce, n., barrier, enclosure, one who deals in stolen goods; v., fight with swords
fĕnc'ing, n., art of sword fighting
fĕnd, v., resist; -er
fêr-mĕnt', v., change chemically, excite; -ation; -ative; -able
fêrn, n., nonflowering plant
fė-rō'cioŭs, a., wild; city; -ly; -ness
fĕr'rĕt, v., search
fĕr'rĭc, a., of iron; rous
fĕr'rỹ, n., v., (boat to) cross a river
fêr'tĭle, a., productive, able to produce young; -ly; -ness; tility; lize
fêr'vör, n., intensely warm feeling, zeal; vent; vency; vid a.
fĕs'cūe, n., type of grass
fĕs'têr, v., become infected
fĕs'tĭ-vȧl, n., celebration
fĕt'ȧ, n., soft white cheese
fĕtch, v., get, bring
fete (fāt), n., celebration

fĕt'ĭd, a., bad smelling; -ness; -ly
fĕt'ĭsh, n., symbol of magical power
fĕt'têr, n., angle chain; v., restrain, hamper
fĕt'tle, n., condition
fē'tŭs, n., unborn young; tal
feūd, n., bitter argument; v., quarrel; -al; -ality
fē'vêr, n., high body temperature; -ish
fĭ-ȧn-ce' (cā), n., engaged man   [gaged woman
fĭ-ȧn-cee' (cā), n., en-
fĭ-äs'cō, n., failure
fĭ'ȧt, n., decree
fĭ'bêr, n., fabric thread, muscle tissue, quality; brous
fĭck'le, a., changeable
fĭc'tion, n., imaginary happening, story; -al; -ally; titious, titiously
fĭ-dĕl'ĭ-tỹ, n., faithfulness
fĭdg'ĕt, v., more about restlessly; -y a.
fiēf, n., lord's land under feudalism
fiēld, n., piece of land, area of knowledge
fiēnd, n., cruel person, addict; -ish   [-ly; -ness
fiêrce, a., violent, intense;
fĭ-ĕs'tȧ, n., holiday
fife, n., flutelike instrument
fĭg, n., fruit   [-er
fĭght, n., v., battle, conflict;
fĭg'mĕnt, n., thing imagined   [-ly
fĭg'ūr-ȧ-tĭve, a., not exact;
fĭg'ūre, n., form, person drawing, design, number: v., consider, form, compute
fĭg-ū-rine', n., small statue
fĭl'bêrt, n., nut of hazel tree
file, n., line of people, container, tool for smoothing and grinding; v., arrange in order, register
fĭl'ĭ-bŭs-têr, n., excessive talk to delay legislation
fĭl'ĭ-grēe, n., ornamental lace work in metal
fĭl'let (lā), n., boneless

piece of meat, fish, etc.
fĭl'lў, *n.,* young female horse
fĭlm, *n.,* thin coating; **-y** *a.*
fĭlm, *n.,* plasticlike material used in photography; *v.,* make a motion picture; **-ic**
fĭl'têr, *n., v.,* (device to) strain or purify; **-able**
fĭlth, *n.,* dirt, garbage; **-y** *a.* 　　[**-ization; -ly**
fi'nål, *a.,* last; **-ity; -ize;**
fi-nănce', *n.,* study of money management; *v.,* supply money; **cial; cially; ciēr**
fĭnch, *n.,* small songbird
find, *v.,* come upon, discover, learn, locate; **-er; -ing** *n.*
fine, *n.,* money paid as penalty; *a.,* excellent, delicate, sharp
fi-něsse', *n.,* subtle skill
fĭn'gêr-prĭnt, *n.,* impression skin markings on finger tip
fĭn'ĭck-ў, *a.,* too particular; fussy; **ical; icality; ically**
fi'nĭte, *a.,* limited; **tude** *n.*
fĭr, *n.,* evergreen tree
fire'ârm, *n.,* gun, rifle
fire'bîrd, *n.,* brightly colored bird
fire'flў, *n.,* winged beetle with glowing abdomen
fire'trăp, *n.,* unsafe building in case of fire
fire'wörks, *n., pl.,* explosive devices that display light
firm, *n.,* business; *a.,* hard, stable, steady; **-ness; -ly**
fîr'må-mėnt, *n.,* sky
first-āid, *a.,* of temporary medical care
first-clăss', *a.,* of best kind
fĭs'cål, *a.,* financial; **-ly**
fĭsh'mŏn-gêr, *n.,* one who sells fish
fĭs'sion, *n.,* division into parts; **-able**
fĭs'sûre, *n.,* crack, cleft
fĭst, *n.,* clenched hand
fĭt, *n.,* sudden outburst,

convulsion; *v.,* suit, be or make to right size, equip 　　[**-ly**
fĭt'fŭl, *a.,* restless; **-ness;**
fĭx, *n.,* (coll.) predicament
fĭx, *v.,* set firmly, repair, cook; **-er**
fĭx-ā'tion, *n.,* obsession
fĭx'tûre, *n.,* thing firmly in place ex. furniture
fĭzz, *v.,* hiss and bubble; **-y** *a.*
flăb, *n.,* (coll.) sagging flesh; **-by** *a.;* **-biness**
flăb'bêr-găst, *v.,* surprise
flăc'cĭd, *a.,* soft and limp
flăg, *n.,* cloth symbol, banner
flăg'ėl-lāte, *v.,* beat, whip; **tor; tion; tory**
flå-gĭ'tioŭs, *a.,* shamefully wicked; **-ness; -ly**
flăg'ŏn, *n.,* kind of pitcher
flā'grånt, *a.,* evil, notorious; **grancy; -ly**
flăg'stōne, *n.,* paving stone
flāil, *n.,* tool to thresh grain, *v.,* use a flail, beat
flâir, *n.,* natural talent
flāke, *n.,* thin slice; **flaky** *a.*
flăm, *n.,* trick, lie
flăm-boy'ånt (bŏĭ), *a.,* showy; **ance; ancy; -ly**
flāme, *n.,* light of fire, blaze; **flaming**
flăm'må-ble, *a.,* easily set on fire; **bility**
flănk, *n.,* side; *v.,* be at or put to side
flăn'nėl, *n.,* soft wool cloth
flăp, *n.,* flat loose piece; *v.,* wave up and down; **-py** *a.*
flāre, *n.,* sudden burst of fire, signal light; *v.,* blaze
flāre'-ŭp, *n.,* outburst
flăsh, *n.,* sudden light, moment, sudden news report; *v.,* sparkle, move quickly 　　[**isode**
flăsh'băck, *n.,* earlier episode
flăsh'lĭght, *n.,* battery powered hand lantern
flăsk, *n.,* small bottle

flăt, *a.,* level, spread out smoothly, broad and thin, dull; **-ten; -ly; -ness**

flăt'tēr, *v.,* praise too much; please; **-er; -y**

flăt'ŭ-lĕnt, *a.,* having stomach gas, boastful; **ence; ency; -ly**

flăunt, *v.,* show off

flā'vŏr, *n.,* taste; *v.,* add seasoning; **-ing** *n.;* **-ful**

flăx, *n.,* linen plant and its fiber [sect

flēa, *n.,* small wingless in-

flĕck, *n.,* spot, particle

flĕdg'lĭng, *n.,* young bird

flēe, *v.,* run away, escape

flēece, *n.,* sheep's wool; **-y** *a.*

flēece, *v.,* swindle; **-r**

flēet, *n.,* group of ships

flēet, *v.,* move quickly; *a.,* swift; **-ing; -ness; -ly**

flĕsh, *n.,* body tissue, meat, fruit or vegetable pulp; **-y** *a.*

flĕx, *v.,* bend, contract muscle; **-ŭre; -ible; -ibility; -ibly**

flĭck'ēr, *v.,* flutter, burn unsteadily [of stairs

flĭght, *n.,* flying, fleeing, set

flĭm'sў, *a.,* weak, made poorly; **sily; siness**

flĭnch, *v.,* draw back from

flĭp, *n.,* somersault; *v.,* move or turn with a jerk

flĭp, *a.,* disrespectful; **-pant; -pantly; -pancy**

flĭp'pēr, *n.,* broad flat limp of seal, whale, etc. for swimming

flĭt, *v.,* flutter, dart

flōat, *n.,* decorated vehicle for parade; *v.,* stay on top of liquid

flŏck, *n.,* group; *v.,* gather together

flŏg, *v.,* beat with whip

flŏod, *n.,* overflowing of water; *v.,* overflow, fill

flŏod'lĭght, *n.,* very bright light

flŏor, *n.,* bottom surface of room, ocean, etc., building level, (coll.) surprise

flŏp, *n.,* (coll.) failure; *v.,* drop noisily

flôr'ăl, *a.,* of flowers, **-ly; -lst; -istic**

flôr'ĭd, *a.,* rosy, showy; **-ity; -ness; -ly** [**-y** *a.*

flŏss, *n.,* soft silky fibers;

flō-tā'tion, *n.,* floating

flŏunce, *n.,* ruffle; *v.,* jerk

flŏun'dēr, *n.,* flatfish; *v.,* struggle awkwardly

flŏur, *n.,* fine powdery substance ground from grain; **-y** *a.*

flŏur'ĭsh, *v.,* succeed, thrive; **-er; -ing**

flōw, *v.,* move smoothly, as water; **-age; -ingly**

flōw'ēr, *n.,* plant's reproductive organ, blossom; *v.,* bloom; **-y** *a.;* **-ing**

flŭc'tŭ-āte, *v.,* change irregularly; **ant; tion**

flūe, *n.,* chimney shaft

flŭ'ĭd, *n.,* liquid; *a.,* able to flow; **-ity; -ness; -ly**

flŭke, *n.,* stroke of luck; **-y** *a.* [school

flŭnk, *v.,* (coll.) fail in

flŭ-ŏ-rĕs'cĕnce, *n.,* emission of reflected light when exposed to radiation; **cent**

flŭ'ŏrīne, *n.,* gaseous chemical element

flŭr'rў, *n.,* gust, sudden confusion; *v.,* confuse

flŭsh, *n.,* sudden feeling of heat; *v.,* blush, wash out with water; *a.,* wealthy

flŭs'tēr, *v.,* confuse

flūte, *n.,* woodwind instrument

flŭt'tēr, *v.,* flap or vibrate rapidly, tremble; **-er; -y** *a.*

flŭx, *n.,* constant change

flў, *n.,* insect, opening of pants

fly, *v.,* move through air, move swiftly, flee; **fller; -able**

fly'whēel, *n.,* wheel regulating machine's speed

fōal, *n.,* very young horse

fōam, *n.,* white bubbly mass; **-y** *a.;* **-less**

fŏb, *n.,* pocket watch chain

fō′cŭs, *n.,* point where light rays meet, adjustment for clear image, central point; **cal; cally; calize**

fŏd′dêr, *n.,* food for horses, cattle, etc.

fŏg, *n.,* thick mist, confusion; **-gy** *a.;* **-giness**

fŏi′ble, *n.,* small weakness

fŏil, *n.,* thin metal sheet, fencing sword; *v.,* frustrate

fŏist, *v.,* deceive by fraud

fōld, *n.,* sheep pen, group; *v.,* bend over itself

fō′lĭ-âge, *n.,* mass of leaves; **aceous**

fō′lĭ-ō, *n.,* large book

fŏlk (fōk), *n.,* ethnic group; (*pl.*), family; *a.,* of the common people

fŏl′lĭ-cle, *n.,* small body sac, cavity or gland

fŏl′lōw, *v.,* come or go after, happen, support; **-er**

fŏl′lÿ, *n.,* foolishness

fō′mĕnt, *v.,* incite; **-ation**

fŏn′dle, *v.,* caress; **-r**

fŏn-tá-nĕl′, *n.,* soft boneless area of baby's skull

fōod, *n.,* substance eaten, nourishment

fōol, *n.,* silly person; *v.,* joke, trick; **-ery**

fōot′hōld, *n.,* secure place for foot when climbing

fōot′lĭghts, *n., pl.,* lights on floor of stage front

fōot′nōte, *n.,* extra comment at bottom of page

fŏp, *n.,* vain man, dandy; **-pish; -pishness; -pishly**

fôr′âge, *n.,* fodder; *v.,* search for food; **-r**

fôr′āy, *n., v.,* raid, attack

fôr′beăr, *v.,* restrain; **-er; -ance; -ingly**

fôr′bĭd, *v.,* not permit; **-dance; -den** *a.;* **-ding**

fôrce, *n.,* power, violence, united group; *v.,* use power, compel; **-d; -ful; -fully; -fulness; cible; cibly** [pinchers

fôr′cĕps, *n.,* surgical

fôrd, *n.,* shallow place in river; *v.,* cross water; **-able**

fôre-bōde′, *v.,* predict something bad; **boding; bodingly**

fôre′căst, *v.,* estimate in advance, ex. weather; **-er**

fôre-clōse′, *v.,* deny the right to redeem mortgage; **sure; closable**

fôre′hĕad, *n.,* part of face above eyebrows

fŏr′eĭgn, *a.,* of or from another country, strange; **-ness; -er**

fôre′măn, *n.,* man in charge of workers, jury chairman; **-ship**

fŏ-rĕn′sĭc, *a.,* of law courts or debate; **-ally**

fôre′rŭn-nêr, *n.,* person or thing foretelling another

fôre-sēe′, *v.,* know in advance; **-r; -able**

fôre′skĭn, *n.,* skin over end of penis

fôr′ĕst, *n.,* land with thick growth of trees; **-er; -ry**

fôre-stăll′, *v.,* anticipate; **-er; -ment**

fôre′thought, *n.,* previous consideration; **-ful; -fully** [always

fôr-ĕv′êr, *adv.,* for all time,

fôre′wörd, *n.,* introduction

fôr′feĭt, *n.,* penalty; *v.,* give up; **-er; -ûre; -able**

fôrge, *n.,* furnace to heat metal; *v.,* counterfeit, move ahead slowly; **-r**

fôr-gĕt′, *v.,* be unable to remember, neglect, overlook; **-ful; -fulness; -fully**

fôr-gĭve′, *v.,* stop being angry with, pardon; **-er; -ness; givable; giving**

fôrk, *n.,* pronged eating utensil; place of branching; **-ed** [sad

fôr-lôrn′, *a.,* miserable,

fôrm, *n.,* shape, outline, style, type; *v.,* make, develop; **-ation; -ative**

fôr′măl, *a.,* according to

custom, elaborate; **-ity;**
-ize; -ly

fôr'mĭ-dà-ble, a., causing
fear, powerful; **bility;**
-ness; bly

fôr'mū-là, n., fixed rule,
prescription; **-te; -tor;**
-tion

fôr'nĭ-cāte, v., commit il-
licite sexual intercourse;
tion

fôrt, n., military place of
defense; **-ress**

fôrth, adv., onward

fôr'tĭ-fȳ, v., strengthen;
fier; fication; fiable

fôr'tĭ-tūde, n., courage;
tudinous [**-ly**

fôrt'nĭght, n., two weeks;

fôr'tŭne (chun), n., luck,
chance; **-less; nàte** a.;
nately

fô'rŭm, n., place for public
discussion

fŏs'sĭl, n., rocklike remains
of previous animal and
plant life; **-ize; -ization**

fôs'têr, v., help, cherish,
rear; a., sharing in the
care

fŏul, v., dishonor; break
game rules; a., disgust-
ing, filthy, unfair, stormy,
obscene; **-ness**

fŏund, v., base, establish;
-er; -ation; -ational

fŏund'êr, v., stumble, fall,
sink [metal

fŏund'rȳ, n., place to cast

fŏun'taĭn, n., spring or jet
of water

fŏwl, n., bird, domestic
bird

fŏx, n., wild doglike animal; v., trick craftily

frā'càs, n., brawl

frăc'tion, n., part of a
whole; small portion; **-al;**
-ally

frăc'tŭre, n., break in a
bone; v., break; **tural**

frăg'īle, a., easily broken,
delicate; **gility**

frăg'mént, n., broken part;
-ary; -ate; -ation

frail, a., weak; **-ly; -ness;**
-ty n.

frāme, n., basic structure
border; v., make, build,
enclose in border, fal-
sify; **-r**

frăn'chise, n., right to vote
or operate

frănk, a., honest and open;
-ness; -ly

frăn'tĭc, a., wild with worry;
-ally

frà-têr'nàl, a., brotherly;
-ism; -ly; nity; nize; ni-
zation

fräught, a., filled

frāy, n., battle; v., become
ragged

frăz'zle, v., become tired

frēak, a., abnormal, odd;
-y a.; **-ish; -ishly; -ish-**
ness

frĕck'le, n., small brown
spot on skin; **ly**

frēe, v., release; a., not
restricted, open, no cost;
-ly; -dom

frēe-thĭnk'êr, n., one with
unorthodox views

frēeze, v., form into ice,
harden; **-r; freezable**

freight (frāt), n., good
transported; **-er; -age**

frĕn'zȳ, n., wild excitement

frĕs'cō, n., painting on wet
plaster

frĕsh, a., new, clean;
-ness; -ly; -en

frĕt, n., v., worry; **-ful;**
-fully; -fulness

frĭc'tion, n., a rubbing together, conflict; **-less;**
-al

friĕnd, n., person one
knows and likes; **-ship;**
-ly; -liness

fright, n., sudden fear; **-en;**
-eningly; -ful; -fully

frĭg'īd, a., very cold, stiff;
-ness; -ly

frĭll, n., ruffle, unnecessary
ornament; **-y** a.

frĭnge, n., decorative
edge, border; **-y** a.

frĭsk, v., search quickly

frĭt'têr, n., small cake of
fried batter; v., waste

frĭv'ò-loŭs, a., trivial, silly;
-ness; -ly; volity

fröck, *n.,* monk's robe, garment

frönd, *n.,* fern or palm leaf

frönt, *n.,* forward or first part; *v.,* face; **-al**

frön'tiër, *n.,* nation's border, undeveloped region; **-sman** *n.*

fröst, *n.,* frozen dew; **-y** *a.*

fröst'ing, *n.,* sugar mixture for covering cake

frȫwn, *v.,* wrinkle eye brows, look with disapproval

frö'zĕn, *a.,* turned into ice

frü'gàl, *a.,* thrifty; **-ity; -ly**

früit, *n.,* edible plant product, result; **-ful; -fully; -fulness; -less; -y** *a.*

frü-i'tion, *n.,* fulfillment

frŭs'trāte, *v.,* block, disappoint; **tration**

frȳ, *n.,* child; *v.,* cook in hot fat or oil; **-er**

fūch'siá, *n.,* flowering plant

fŭdge, *n.,* soft chocolate candy; *v.,* cheat

fü'ĕl, *n.,* material burned for heat or power

fūgue, *n.,* musical form

fŭll, *a.,* all that can be held, ample, complete; **-ness; -y** *adv.*

fŭl'mĭ-nāte, *v.,* explode with violence; **tor, tion; tory**

fŭm'ble, *v.,* handle clumsily; **-r; blingly**

fūme, *n.,* offensive smoke or vapor; *v.,* give off fumes, show anger

fūm'ĭ-gāte, *v.,* disinfect; **tor; tion**

fŭnc'tion, *n.,* purpose, duty; **-al**

fŭnd, *n.,* pool of money; *v.,* give money to [**-ly**

fŭn-dà-mĕn'tàl, *a.,* basic;

fū'nêr-àl, *n.,* burial rites

fŭn'gŭs, *n.,* a parasitic plant, ex. mold, mushroom

fŭn'nĕl, *n.,* inverted hollow cone with hole at neck

fŭr, *n.,* animal's soft thick hair; **-ry** *a.;* **-riness**

fûr'lōugh, *n.,* military vacation [ing chamber

fûr'náce, *n.,* heat producing

fûr'nĭ-tûre, *n.,* tables, chairs, beds etc. in room

fū'rôr, *n.,* rage

fûr'rōw, *n.,* groove made by plow

fûr'thêr, *v.,* promote; *a.,* additional; *adv.,* moreover [**-ness**

fûr'tĭve, *a.,* secretive; **-ly;**

fū'rȳ, *n.,* violent anger

fūse, *n.,* wick of an explosive; safety device in an electrical circuit

fūse, *v.,* melt together; **fusion; fusible; fusibility**

fū'sĕ-làge, *n.,* body of airplane [**-y** *a.*

fŭss, *n., v.,* bother, worry;

fū'tĭle, *a.,* hopeless; **-ly; -ness; tility**

fū'tûre, *n.,* time to come

G

găb, *n., v.,* chatter; **-ber; -by** *a.*

gā-ble, *n.,* triangular wall under roof's edge

găd, *v.,* wander; **-der**

gădg'ĕt, *n.,* small device

găff, *n.,* large hook

gāi'ĕ-tȳ, *n.,* cheerfulness

gāin, *n.,* increase; *v.,* get, earn, reach; **-er; -ful; -less**

gāit, *n.,* way of walking

gā'là, *n.,* festive occasion

găl'àx-ȳ, *n.,* huge group of stars

gāle, *n.,* strong wind

găll, *n.* bile, boldness; *v.,* annoy

găl'lànt, *a.,* brave and noble, polite; **-ly; -ry**

găl'lêr-ȳ, *n.,* balcony, place for art exhibits

găl'lĭ-vănt, *v.,* search for amusement

găl'lŏn, *n.,* liquid measure, four quarts

găl'lŏp, *n.,* horse's fast gait; *v.,* hurry; **-er**

găl'lōws, *n.,* structure for hanging people

gȧ-lŏsh', *n.*, overshoe

găl'vȧ-nīze, *v.*, shock electrically, coat metal with zinc; **zation; nism; ic; ical; ically**

găm'bĭt, *n.*, chess move

găm'ble, *n., v.*, risk, bet; **-r**

gāme, *n.*, competitive sport, amusement, hunted animals; *a.*, ready, courageous

găm'ŭt, *n.*, whole range

găn'dẽr, *n.*, male goose

găn'glĭng, *a.*, tall and awkward; **gly**

găn'glĭ-ŏn, *n.*, group of nerve cells

găn'grēne, *n.*, decay of body tissue

găng'stẽr, *n.*, member of a criminal gang; **-ism**

găp, *n.*, opening, separation

gāpe, *v.*, look, stare

gȧ'râge, *n.*, automobile shelter or repair shop

gârb, *n.*, style of dress

gâr'ble, *v.*, confuse

gâr'dẽn, *n.*, ground for growing plants; **-er**

gâr'gle, *v.*, rinse the throat with liquid

gâr'goyle (gŏĭl), *n.*, carved creature projecting from gutter of building

gâr'ĭsh, *a.*, gaudy; **-ness; -ly**   [flowers

gâr'lȧnd, *n.*, wreath of

gâr'lĭc, *n.*, plant bulb used as strong seasoning; **-ky** *a.*

gâr'nĭsh, *v.*, decorate. trim; **-er; -ment**

gâr'rĕt, *n.*, attic

gâr'rŭ-loŭs, *a.*, talking much; **lity; -ness; -ly**

gâr'tẽr, *n.*, stocking supporter

găs, *n.*, vapor, substance like air; **-eous**

găsh, *n.*, long deep cut

găs-ȯ-līne', *n.*, liquid fuel for engines

găsp, *v.*, catch one's breath   [stomach

găs'trĭc, *a.*, relating to

găs-trŏn'ȯ-mÿ, *n.*, art of eating; **mist; mer; nomic; nomical; nomically**

găth'ẽr, *v.*, bring together, collect, meet; **-er; -ing** *n.*

gauche (gōsh), *a.*, lacking social grace; **-ness; -ly**

gäud'y, *a.*, showy in bad taste, flashy

gäuge, *n.*, measurement

gäunt, *a.*, very thin; **-ness; -ly**

gäuze, *n.*, loosely woven fabric; **gauzy** *a.*

găv'ĕl, *n.*, mallet for presiding officer

gäwk, *v.*, stare stupidly

gāy, *a.*, happy, lively, bright; **-ness**

gȧ-zē'bō, *n.*, free-standing covered porch

gȧ-zĕlle', *n.*, small antelope

gȧ-zĕtte', *n.*, newspaper

găz-ĕt-tēer', *n.*, dictionary of geographical names

gēar, *n.*, equipment, toothed wheel; *v.*, connect by gears

gĕl, *n.*, jellylike substance

gĕld'ĭng, *n.*, castrated male horse

gĕm, *n.*, precious stone

gĕn'dẽr, *n.*, classification of word by sex

gēne, *n.*, unit of heredity on chromosome

gē-nē-ȧl'ȯ-gÿ, *n.*, study of one's ancestry; **gist; logical; logically**

gĕn'ẽr-ȧl, *a.*, for or of all, common, usual; **-ly**

gĕn-ẽr-ăl'ĭ-tÿ, *n.*, vague statement; **alize; alization**   [tor; tion

gĕn'ẽr-āte, *v.*, produce;

gĕn-ẽr-ā'tion, *n.*, people of same era; **tive**

gē-nẽr'ĭc, *a.*, common; **-ally**

gĕn'ẽr-oŭs, *a.*, giving freely, ample; **osity; -ly**

gĕn'ė-sĭs, *n.*, origin

gē'nĭȧl, *a.*, friendly, kind; **-ity; -ly**

gĕn'ĭ-tàl, *n.*, sex organ

gĕn'lŭs, *n.*, one with great mental talent

gĕn'ò-cīde, *n.*, killing of whole ethnic group; **dal**

gĕn-tēel', *a.*, polite, refined; **-ness; -ly**

gĕn'tīle, *n.*, *a.*, (one) not a Jew　　　**[-ness; tly**

gĕn'tle, *a.*, soft, kind;

gĕn'ū-īne, *a.*, real; **-ly**

gē'nŭs, *n.*, class, type

gē-ŏg'rà-phў, *n.*, science of earth's surface; **pher; graphic; graphical**

gē-ŏl'ò-gў, *n.*, study of earth structure; **gist; gize; logic; logical; logically**

gē-ŏm'ė-trў, *n.*, mathematics of points, lines, surfaces; **ric; rical; rically; trize**

gĕr-ĭ-ăt'rĭcs, *n.*, study of human old age; **ric**

gêrm, *n.*, microscopic organism, seed

gêr-māne', *n.*, related to

gêr'mĭ-nàte, *v.*, start growing; **tion; tive**

gĕs'tāte, *v.*, carry in uterus; **tion**

gĕs'tûre, *n.*, body movement of expression; **-r; ral**

geў'sêr, *n.*, spouting hot spring

ghăst'lў (găst), *a.*, horrible

ghêr'kĭn (gêr), *n.*, immature cucumber

ghĕt'tō (gĕt), *n.*, section of city restricted to a minority group; **-ize**

ghōst (gōst), *n.*, spirit; **-like** *a.*; **-ly**

gĭ'ànt, *n.*, *a.*, (one) of great size

gĭb'bòn, *n.*, small ape

gībe, *v.*, mock, taunt

gĭb'lĕt, *n.*, fowl's edible internal part

gĭft, *n.*, something given

gĭft'ĕd, *a.*, talented

gĭg'gle, *v.*, laugh foolishly; **-r; gly** *a.*　　**[-ing** *n.*

gĭld, *v.*, coat with gold; **-er;**

gĭll, *n.*, fish's breathing organ

gĭm'mĭck, *n.*, clever gadget, trick; **-y** *a.*

gĭn, *n.*, alcoholic liquor, device to separate cotton from its seeds, card game

gĭn'gêr, *n.*, spice

gĭng'hàm, *n.*, cotton cloth woven in checks or stripes

gîrd, *v.*, encircle, prepare

gîr'dle, *n.*, undergarment for abdominal support; *v.*, surround

gîrth, *n.*, horse's saddle band around belly; *v.* encircle

gĭst, *n.*, main point

gĭz'zàrd, *n.*, bird's second stomach

glā'cîêr, *n.*, large mass of ice; **ciate; cial; cially**

glāde, *n.*, forest clearing

glăm'oûr, *n.*, bewitching charm; **orize; orous**

glănce, *n.*, quick look; *v.*, flash

glănd, *n.*, secreting body organ; **-ular** *a.*

glāre, *n.*, angry stare, brilliant light; *v.*, look, shine

glăss, *n.*, hard brittle transparent substance, drinking cup; **-y** *a.*

glâu-cō'mà, *n.*, eye disease; **-tous**

glēam, *n.*, beam of light

glēan, *v.*, collect bit by bit as grain

glēe, *n.*, lively joy; **-ful**

glĕn, *n.*, secluded valley

glĭb, *a.*, in easy manner; **-ness; -ly**

glīde, *v.*, move smoothly

glĭm'mêr, *n.*, faint light

glĭmpse, *n.*, brief view

glĭs'tĕn, *n.*, *v.*, sparkle

glōat, *v.*, show malicious pleasure

glōbe, *n.*, round model of the world, ball; **global; globular** *a.*

glŏss, *n.*, shiny polished surface; **-y** *a.*

glŏs'sà-rў, *n.*, alphabetical list of terms

G
H

glóve, *n.,* hand covering
glōw, *n.,* brightness; *v.,* shine warmly; **-ingly**
glow'êr, *v.,* frown; **-ingly**
glū'cōse, *n.,* type of sugar
glūe, *n.,* sticky liquid; *v.* stick or join with glue; **-y** *a.* [**-ness**
glŭm, *a.,* unhappy; **-ly;**
glŭt, *n.,* excess; *v.,* feed or supply too much
glŭt'tŏn, *n.,* one who does things in excess; **-ous; -y; -ously**
glýc'êr-ĭn, *n.,* colorless syrupy liquid [**-ed**
gnârl, *n.,* knot; *v.,* twist;
gnăsh, *v.,* grind the teeth
gnăt, *n.,* insect
gnōme, *n.,* dwarf
gnū, *n.,* large antelope
gōal, *n.,* end, aim, purpose
gōat'ēe, *n.,* pointed beard
gŏb'ble, *n.,* turkey sound; *v.,* eat greedily, snatch
gŏb'lĕt, *n.,* stemmed glass
gŏb'lĭn, *n.,* evil spirit
gŏd, *n.,* deity, thing or person worshipped, idol; **-hood; -like; -ly**
Gŏd, *n.,* divine being, creator of universe
gŏd'sĕnd, *n.,* something unexpected and needed
gŏg'gles, *n., pl.,* large protective glasses
gōld, *n.,* yellow metal, money; *a.,* deep yellow; **-en** *a.*
gŏlf, *n.,* outdoor sport with ball and clubs
gŏn-ŏr-rhē'à, *n.,* venereal disease; **-l**
gŏŏd, *a.,* favorable, real, pleasant, able, honest, correct, considerable; **-ness**
gŏŏds, *n., pl.,* merchandise, fabric
gŏŏd'ў, *n.,* (coll.) something good to eat; *int.* Yea! [silly person
gōose, *n.,* large water bird,
gō'phêr, *n.,* burrowing rodent
gôre, *n.,* clotted blood; *v.,* pierce with horn; **gory** *a.*

gôrge, *n.,* deep narrow pass; *v.* eat greedily
gôr'geoŭs, *a.,* splendid, beautiful; **-ly; -ness**
gŏs'pĕl, *n.,* Jesus's teaching
gŏs'sà-mêr, *a.,* filmy, thin
gŏs'sĭp, *n.,* idle talk; *v.,* spread rumors; **-y** *a.*
gouge, *n.,* chisel, groove; *v.,* make grooves, cheat
gôur'met (mā), *n.,* excellent judge of food and wine
gout, *n.,* painful swelling of the joints; **-y** *a.*
gŏv'êrn, *v.,* rule, guide, regulate; **-or; -ment; -mental; -mentally; -able; -orship** [dress
gown, *n.,* woman's elegant
grāce, *n.,* beauty, favor, decency; prayer before eating; **-ful; -less**
grāde, *n.,* step, degree, slope, division in school system, test rating; *v.,* classify, rate; **-r; dation**
grā'dĭ-ĕnt, *n.,* slope
grăft, *n.,* skin or plant transplant, political dishonesty; **-er; -age**
grāin, *n.,* seed or fruit of cereal plant, particle
grăm, *n.,* unit of weight
grăm'màr, *n.,* structure and usage of language; **matical; matically**
grănd, *a.,* splendid, great; **-ly; -ness**
grăn'dĭ-ōse, *a.,* impressive, important; **osity; -ly**
grănd'stănd, *n.,* seating structure in stadium
grăn'īte, *n.,* very hard rock
grănt, *v.,* give, bestow an honor, admit; **-er; -able**
grăn'ūle, *n.,* small grain; **late; lator; lation; lative; lar** *a.;* **larity; larly**
grăph, *n.,* drawing showing change in value; **-ic; -ics** [**-al; -ally**
grăph'ĭc, *a.,* vivid; written;
grăph'īte, *n.,* soft, black carbon for pencils

grăsp, *v.,* take hold, understand; **-er; -able**

grăss, *n.,* green lawn plant; **-y** *a.;* **-iness**

grāte, *n.,* framework of bars; *v.,* grind, rub, irritate

grāte'fŭl, *a.,* thankful; **-ly; -ness**

gră'tĭs, *a., adv.,* free

grăt'ĭ-tŭde, *n.,* thankfulness

grȧ-tū'ĭ-tў, *n.,* tip, gift

grāve, *n.,* burial place

grāve, *a.,* serious; **-ness; -ly; gravity**

grăv'ĕl, *n.,* bits of rocks

grăv'ĭ-tў, *n.,* force causing thing toward another

grā'vў, *n.,* meat sauce

grāy, *n.,* color of black and white mixture; *a.,* dull, old, of gray [lightly

grāze, *v.,* eat grass, touch

grēase, *n.,* melted animal fat, oily substance; **greasy**

greăt, *a.,* large, above average, wonderful; **-en; -ness; -ly**

grēed, *n.,* great desire; **-y** *a.,* **-ily; -iness**

grēen, *n.,* color of grass, yellow and blue mixture; *a.,* of green

grēet, *v.,* welcome, meet; **-er; -ing** *n.*

grė-gār'ĭ-oŭs, *a.,* fond of people; **-ness; -ly**

grė-nāde', *n.,* hand bomb

grĭd'dle, *n.,* flat metal pan

grĭd'ĭ-rŏn, *n.,* grill, football field

grĭēv'ȧnce, *n.,* complaint

grĭēve, *v.,* feel sad; **-r; grievous; grievously**

grĭll, *n.,* framework of metal bars; *v.,* broil on grill

grĭm, *a.,* harsh, fierce; **-ly; -ness** [face

grĭm-āce', *n.,* distorted

grĭme, *n.,* dirt; **grimy** *a.*

grĭn, *n., v.,* smile

grĭnd, *n.,* hard work; *v.,* crush by rubbing

grĭp, *v.,* hold tightly; **-per**

grĭs'lў, *a.,* horrible; **liness**

grĭs'tle, *n.,* meat cartilage

grĭt, *n.,* sand particles, courage; *v.,* grind teeth; **-ty** *a.;* **-tily; -tiness**

grĭz'zlў, *a.,* grayish

grō'cĕr, *n.,* food dealer; **-y**

grŏŏm, *n.,* man tending horses, bridegroom; *v.,* make neat, train

grŏŏve, *n.,* long narrow slit, routine [blindly

grōpe, *v.,* feel, search

grōss, *n.,* total, twelve dozen; *a.,* large, vulgar; **-ly; -ness**

grŏŭch, *n.,* complainer; **-y** *a.;* **-ily; -iness**

grŏŭnd, *n.,* land, basis

grŏŭp, *n.,* people or things together [complain

grŏŭse, *n.,* game bird; *v.,*

grōve, *n.,* group of trees

grŏv'ĕl, *v.,* crawl, beg; **-er**

grōw, *v.,* enlarge, mature, raise crops; **-er**

grŏwl, *n.,* rumbling throat sound

grōwth, *n.,* process of growing, development

grŭb, *n.,* wormlike insect larva; *v.,* dig

grŭdge, *n.,* ill will

grŭ'ĕl-ĭng, *a.,* exhausting

grŭe'sȯme, *a.,* horrible; **-ly; -ness** [**-ness**

grŭff, *a.,* rough, rude; **-ly; grŭm'ble,** *v.,* complain, mumble; **bler; bly**

grŭnt, *n.,* deep sound from throat; **-er**

guârd, *n.,* protector; *v.,* keep from harm, defend

gū-bĕr-nȧ-tô'rĭ-ȧl, *a.,* of a governor

guȇr-rĭl'lȧ, *n.,* irregular soldier usually undercover

guĕss, *n., v.,* estimate, judge by chance

guĕst, *n.,* visitor

guīde, *v.,* lead, train, direct; **guidance**

guīld, *n.,* association

guīle, *n.,* deceit; **-ful; -fully; -less; -lessness**

guĭlt, *n.,* feeling of shame

G
H

or remorse; **-y** a.; **-less;
-ily; -iness**

guise, n., appearance

gui-târ', n., stringed musical instrument; **-ist**

gŭlf, n., large arm of ocean, gap

gŭl'lĕt, n., esophagus

gŭl'lў, n., deep ditch

gŭlp, v., swallow deeply

gŭm, n., flesh around teeth, sticky substance; **-my** a.

gŭn, n., device for shooting, firearm; **-ner; -nery**

gûr'gle, n., bubbling sound [in Hinduism

gŭ'rŭ, n., spiritual advisor

gŭsh, v., pour out; **-er; -y** a.

gŭst, n., burst of air; **-y** a.

gŭs'tō, n., taste, zest

gŭt, n., cord from intestine; v., destroy

gŭt'têr, n., channel to run water off roof [throat

gŭt'tûr-ál, a., deep in the

gŭz'zle, v., drink greedily

gўm-nā'sĭ-ŭm, n., place for physical training and sports

gўm-năs'tĭcs, n., exercises for body development; **tic; tically**

gўn-ė-cŏl'ŏ-gў, n., medical science of women; **gist**

gўp, n., v., cheat; **-ster**

gўp'sŭm, n., chalky mineral [group

gўp'sў, n., wanderer of a

gў'rāte, v., spin, rotate; **tor; tion; tory; ral**

H

hăb'êr-dăsh-êr, n., dealer in men's clothing; **-y**

hăb'ĭt, n., automatic practice, costume; **-ual; -ually**

hăb'ĭ-tăt, n., one's natural environment; **-ion**

hăck, n., cutting tool; v., chop, cough

hăck'nĕyed, a., trite

hăft, n., tool handle

hăg, n., ugly old woman;

-gish; -gishly

hăg'gárd, a., worn out; **-ly; -ness** [price; **-r**

hăg'gle, v., argue over

hāil, n., frozen raindrops; v., greet, pour down hail

hāir, n., threadlike outgrowths from skin; **-y** a.; **-less**

hāir'brĕadth, n., a., (space that is) very narrow

hāir'splĭt-tĭng, a., quibbling [peaceful

hăl'cў-ŏn, a., calm,

hāle, a., healthy; v., drag

hălf, n., a. (one) of two equal parts

hălf-heârt'ĕd, a., with little interest or enthusiasm

hălf'-wĭt, n., fool; **-ted**

hăll, n., large public room, passageway

hăl-lė-lŭ'jáh (yá), int., praise the Lord!

hăll'mârk, n., mark of genuineness [**-ed**

hăl'lōw, v., honor as holy;

hál-lŭ'cĭ-nāte, v., imagine unreal thing; **tion; tory**

hā'lō, n., ring of light

hălt, n., v., stop, pause

hăm, n., meat from pig's thigh [beef patty

hăm'bûrg-êr, n., ground

hăm'lĕt, n., small village

hăm'mêr, n., tool for pounding

hăm'mŏck, n., swinging canvas or rope bed

hăm'pêr, n., large covered basket; v., hinder

hănd'băg, n., woman's purse [structions

hănd'bōok, n., book of in-

hănd'cŭff, n., locked bracelet to restrain

hănd'ĭ-căp, n., difficulty, disadvantage; **-ped**

hănd'kêr-chĭef, n., cloth for wiping nose, etc.

hăn'dle, n., part of tool to be held; v., touch, use, manage; **-r**

hănd'ў, a., convenient, clever with hands; **handily; handiness**

hăng, v., suspend, let swing at one end; **-er; -ing**

hăng'ăr, n., aircraft shelter

hăng'ō-vêr, n., after effects of too much liquor

hănk'êr, v., crave

hăn'sóm, n., two-wheeled covered carriage

hăp, n., luck; **-less; -lessly; -lessness**

hăp'pén, v., take place; **-ing** [**pily; piness**

hăp'pў, a., joyous, glad;

há-răngue', n., noisy, scolding speech; **-r**

hàr-ăss', v., constantly bother, worry; **-er; -ment**

hâr'bĭn-gêr, n., one who announces another

hârd, a., solid, difficult, unfeeling; adv., with strength, fully, firmly; **-ness; -en; -ened; -ener; -ening**

hărd'lў, adv., barely

hârd'wāre, n., metal tools equipment and devices

hăre, n., rabbit

hā'rêm, n., place for women in Moslem household

hârk, v., listen

hâr'lé-quĭn, n., clown

hăr'lót, n., prostitute

hârm, n., v., hurt, injure; **-er; -ful; -fulness; -fully; -less; -lessly; -lessness** [organ

hâr-mŏn'ĭ-cà, n., mouth

hâr'mô-nў, n., friendly relations, pleasing arrangement (of music); **nize; nic; nically; nious; niously**

hâr'něss, n., straps to hitch horse to vehicle

hârp, n., stringed musical instrument; v., persist

hâr-pōon', n., spear

hârp'sĭ-chôrd, n., piano-like musical instrument; **-ist**

hăr'rōw, n., machine to break up plowed ground; v., torment; **-ing**

hăr'rў, v., torment, harass

hârsh, a., unpleasant, cruel; **-ly; -ness**

hâr'věst, n., gathering of matured crop; v., reap; **-er**

hăsh, n., mixture, chopped vegetables and meat dish

hăsp, n., hinged fastener

hăs'sóck, n., padded footstool [**hasty** a.

hăste, n., hurry, speed; **-n;**

hătch, n., door, opening on ship's deck; v., bring forth from egg, plan

hătch'ét, n., small ax

hāte, v., dislike greatly; **hatred** n.; **-able; -ful; -fully; -fulness**

hăugh'tў, a., arrogant; **tily; tiness**

hăul, v., pull; **-er; -age**

hăunch, n., rump and upper thigh of body

hăunt, v., visit often

hā'vèn, n., safe place

hăv'óc, n., v., ruin

hăwk, n., bird of prey, advocate of war

hăwk'êr, n., peddler

hăw'thôrn, n., thorny shrub [for animal feed

hāy, n., grass cut and dried

hăz'ảrd, n., danger, chance; **-ous; -ously**

hăze, n., mist, slight confusion; **hazy** a.

hĕad'ĭng, n., title, caption

hĕad'līne, n., newspaper title [rashly

hĕad'lŏng, adv., headfirst,

hĕad'quar-têrs (quôr), n. pl., main office

hĕad'strŏng, a., stubborn

hĕad'wāy, n., progress

hĕad'ў, a., intoxicating; **headily; headiness**

hĕal, v., cure; **-er**

hĕalth, n., physical and mental condition

hĕap, n., v., pile

hĕar, v., receive sounds through ear, listen; **-ing** n. [sip

hĕar'sāy, n., rumor, gos-

hĕarse, n., funeral vehicle for corpse

heârt, *n.,* blood-pumping body organ, main part, humane feeling

heârt'āche, *n.,* grief

heârt'ĕn, *v.,* encourage

heârth, *n.,* fireplace floor

heârt'lĕss, *a.,* unkind

heârt'ў, *a.,* friendly, strong, plentiful; **heart-ily**

hēat, *n.,* hotness, strong feeling, excitement; *v.,* make warm; **-edly**

hēath, *n.,* wasteland

hēa'thĕn, *n.,* irreligious person, pagan

hēave, *v.,* lift and throw with effort, rise and fall rhythmically

hĕav'ĕn, *n.,* sky, place of God, happy state; **-ly**

hĕav'ў, *a.,* weighing much, difficult, intense; **heavily**

hĕck'le, *v.,* annoy; **-r**

hĕc'tĭc, *a.,* confusing, wild; **-ally** [*v.,* avoid

hĕdge, *n.,* row of shrubs;

hē'dŏn-ĭsm, *n.,* devotion to pleasure

hēed, *n.,* close attention; *v.,* notice, **-ful; -fully; -less; -lessly; -lessness**

hēel, *n.,* back part of foot, shoe part, (coll.) cad; *v.,* follow closely, lean

hĕif'êr, *n.,* young cow

height, *n.,* highest point, tallness; **-en**

hei'noŭs (hā) *a.,* outrageous; **-ly; -ness**

hĕir, *n.,* one who inherits; **-ess**

hĕir'lŏŏm, *n.,* inherited personal property

hĕl'ĭ-cŏp-têr, *n.,* aircraft that can hover [ment

hē'lĭ-ŭm, *n.,* gaseous ele-

hĕll, *n.,* place of the damned, torment; **-ish**

hĕl'mĕt, *n.,* hard protective head covering

hĕlp, *n.,* aid, remedy, hired helper; *v.,* assist, aid, remedy, avoid; **-er; -ful; -fully; -fulness; -less;**

-lessly; -lessness

hĕm, *n.,* garment's border; *v.,* surround

hē-mà-tŏl'ò-gў, *n.,* study of blood; **gist; logic; logical**

hĕm'ī-sphēre, *n.,* half a globe; **spheric; spherical**

hĕm'lŏck, *n.,* poisonous plant, evergreen tree

hē'mò-glō-bĭn, *n.,* red pigment of blood; **-ic; -ous**

hē-mò-phĭl'ĭ-à, *n.,* disease of prolonged bleeding

hĕm'ŏr-rhàge, *n.,* heavy bleeding

hĕmp, *n.,* fibrous plant used to make rope

hĕn, *n.,* female fowl

hĕnch'màn, *n.,* trusted helper

hĕn'pĕck, *v.,* nag; **-ed**

hĕp-à-tī'tĭs, *n.,* inflammation of liver

hêr'àld, *n.,* messenger; *v.,* announce

hêrb, *n.,* plant used for seasoning; **-al; -age; -y** *a.*

hêrd, *n.,* group of animals; *v.,* group together

hēre-àf'têr, *n.,* life after death; *adv.,* from now on

hē-rĕd'ĭ-tў, *n.,* passing on of traits to offspring; **tary** *a.;* **tarily; tariness**

hêr'ė-sў, *n.,* belief opposed to church doctrine; **etic** *n.;* **etical**

hêr'mĭt, *n.,* one who lives secluded life; **-age**

hêr'nĭ-à, *n.,* protrusion or rupture of body organ **-te; -tion**

hē'rō, *n.,* brave noble man, central man in story; **-ic; -ism**

hĕr'ò-in, *n.,* narcotic

hĕr'òn, *n.,* large wading bird [fish

hĕr'rĭng, *n.,* small edible

hĕs'ĭ-tāte, *v.,* pause, feel unsure; **ter; tor; tion; tive; tively; tancy; tant; tantly**

hĕt-êr-ò-gē'nē-oŭs, *a.,*

varied, dissimilar; **neity; -ly; -ness**

hĕx'à-gŏn, *n.*, six-sided figure; **-al; -ally**

hī'bêr-nāte, *v.*, sleep all winter; **tor; tion**

hĭc'cŭp, *n.*, throat spasm causing sound

hīde, *n.*, animal skin; *v.*, keep out of sight

hĭd'ē-oùs, *a.*, very ugly; **-ly; -ness**

hīe, *v.*, hurry

hī'ér-ârch-ÿ (ârk), *n.*, system of rank; **chism; chical; chically**

high, *a.*, tall, far up, superior, costly, shrill, excited; **-ly; -ness**

high'båll, *n.*, liquor and mixer

high'boy (bŏĭ), *n.*, tall chest of drawers

high'brow, *n., a.*, intellectual

high-hănd'ĕd, *a.*, arbitrary

high-mĭnd'ĕd, *a.*, proud, moral; **-ly; -ness**

high-strŭng', *a.*, nervous, tense

hī'jăck, *v.*, steal by force; ex. airplane; **-er**

hīke, *n.*, long vigorous walk; *v.*, pull up; **-r**

hĭ-lār'ĭ-oùs, *a.*, funny, merry; **ity; -ly; -ness**

hĭll, *n.*, raised, rounded land; **-y** *a.* [mountains

hĭll'bĭl-lÿ, *n.*, person from

hĭll'ŏck, *n.*, small hill

hĭlt, *n.*, handle, entirety

hĭnd, *a.*, back, rear

hĭn'dêr, *v.*, keep from doing, stop; **drance**

hind'sĭght, *n.*, judgment after event

hĭnge, *n.*, moving metal joint for door

hĭnt, *n.*, suggestion, trace; *v.*, suggest; **-er**

hĭp, *n.*, body part between waist and upper thigh

hīre, *v.*, pay for service, give job to; **-r; -able**

hîr'sūte, *a.*, hairy; **-ness**

hĭs-tŏl'ò-gÿ, *n.*, study of plant and animal tissues

hĭs'tò-rÿ, *n.*, study or record of past events; **rian** *n.*; **toric; torical; torically** [**-ally; -s**

hĭs-trĭ-ŏn'ĭc, *a.*, theatrical;

hĭt, *n.*, blow, something successful; *v.*, strike; **-ter** [fasten

hĭtch, *n.*, obstacle; *v.*, jerk,

hĭtch'hīke, *v.*, travel by asking for auto rides

hīve, *n.*, shelter for bees

hôard, *n.*, hidden supply; *v.*, collect and store away

hôarse, *a.*, sounding husky and rough; **-ly; -ness; -n**

hôar'ÿ, *a.*, grayish-white, old; **hoariness**

hōax, *n.*, trick; *v.*, cheat

hŏb'ble, *v.*, limp; **-r**

hŏb'nŏb, *v.*, associate with

hō'bō, *n.*, tramp

hŏck, *n.*, animal leg joint; *v.*, pawn

hŏck'ēy, *n.*, team sport played on field or ice

hŏdge'pŏdge, *n.*, jumble

hōe, *n.*, garden tool

hōld, *n.*, grip; *v.*, keep in hand or place, have, grasp, contain; **-er**

hōle, *n.*, hollow place, opening

hŏl'ĭ-dāy, *n.*, religious festival, work-free day

hŏl'lêr, *n., v.*, shout, yell

hŏl'lōw, *a.*, empty within, worthless; **-ness; -ly**

hŏl'lÿ, *n.*, evergreen shrub

hŏl'stêr, *n.*, pistol case

hō'lÿ, *a.*, sacred, saintly, of religion; **liness; lily**

hŏm'àge, *n.*, respect, honor [hat

hŏm'bûrg, *n.*, man's felt

hōme, *n.*, place where one lives, family life; **-less**

hōme'lÿ, *a.*, of home, of family, plain

hōme'māk-êr, *n.*, one who manages household

hōme'ÿ, *a.*, cozy, familiar; **-ness**

hŏm'ĭ-cīde, *n.*, killing of a person; **dal; dally**

G
H

hŏm'ĭ-lў, *n.,* sermon; **list**

hŏm'ĭ-nў, *n.,* ground dry corn

hŏ-mŏg'ė-nīze, *v.,* blend (milk); **tion**

hŏm'ȯ-nўm, *n.,* word pronounced as another but defined and spelled differently

hō-mȯ-sĕx'ū-ȧl, *n., a.,* (one) desiring person of same sex; **-ity; -ly**

hōne, *v.,* sharpen

hŏn'ėst, *a.,* truthful, sincere; **-y; -ly**

hŏn'ēy, *n.,* sweet substance made by bees, sweet one

hŏn'ēy-dew, *n.,* melon

hŏn'ēy-sŭck-le, *n.,* vine with fragrant flowers

hŏn'ŏr, *n.,* high regard, dignity, high moral ideals; *v.,* respect greatly; **-able; -ably; -ability; -ableness**

hōōd'lŭm, *n.,* gangster, lawless person

hōōd'wĭnk, *v.,* cheat, trick

hŏŏf, *n.,* horny bottom on feet of cattle, deer, etc.

hŏŏk, *n.,* curved pointed device; *v.,* catch or fasten with hook

hŏŏp, *n.,* large band or ring

hōpe, *n.,* expected desire; *v.,* want and expect; **-ful; -fully; -fulness; -less; -lessly; -lessness**

hôrde, *n.,* crowd

hȯ-rī'zȯn, *n.,* line where sky seems to meet earth; **-tal; -tally**

hôr'mōne, *n.,* stimulating chemical made by gland; **monal; monic**

hôrn, *n.,* bony growth on animal's head, blown musical instrument

hôrn'ў, *a.,* hard; **horniness**

hȯ-rŏľ'ȯ-gў, *n.,* science of measuring time; **gist; logical**

hôr'ȯ-scōpe, *n.,* pattern of heavens used to predict future; **scopic**

hôr'rȯr, *n.,* strong fear, terrible dislike; **rible; ribly; rific; rify; rification**

hôrse, *n.,* large domesticated animal

hôrse-läugh, *n.,* loud laugh

hôrse-pow-êr, *n.,* unit of power for motors

hôrse'răd-ĭsh, *n.,* pungent-tasting white fleshy root

hōse, *n.,* garment for foot, ankle and leg, water tube

hŏs'pĭ-tȧl, *n.,* place for medical treatment; **-ize; -ization**

hōst, *n.,* one who entertains guests, crowd; **-ess**

hōs'tȧge, *n.,* one held as a pledge

hŏs'tėl, *n.,* inn; **-er; -ry**

hŏs'tīle, *n.,* unfriendly; **til-ity; -ly**

hō-tĕl', *n.,* large place with rooms for travellers

hŏt'hĕad, *n.,* rash person; **-ed; -edness; -edly**

hŏŭnd, *n.,* hunting dog; *v.,* continue pursuing

hŏŭse, *n.,* place to live in, family, building, business, legislative body; *v.,* **(hŏŭz)** reside, lodge; **-ful** [ter

hŏv'ėl, *n.,* small poor shel-

hŏv'êr, *v.,* linger anxiously

hŏw-ĕv'êr, *adv.,* in whatever way, yet; *conj.,* although [non

hŏw'ĭtz-êr, *n.,* small can-

hŏwl, *n.,* long mournful cry; **-er; -ing**

hŭb, *n.,* center

hŭb'bŭb, *n.,* noise

hŭck'stêr, *n.,* peddler

hŭd'dle, *v.,* crowd together, hunch oneself up

hŭff, *n.,* fit of anger; *v.,* puff up; **-y** *a.;* **-ish; -iness**

hŭg, *n.,* embrace; *v.,* put arms around, hold closely [**-ness; -ly**

hūge, *a.,* very large;

hŭlk, *n.,* big clumsy person or thing; **-ing**

hŭll, *n.*, seed covering, ship's frame

hū'mån, *n.*, person; *a.*, of mankind; **-ness; -ity; -ism; -ize**

hū-māne', *a.*, kind; **-ness; -ly**

hū-măn-ĭ-tār'ĭ-ån, *n.*, one who thinks of others; **-ism** [**-ness; -r**

hŭm'ble, *a.*, modest; **bly;**

hŭm'bŭg, *n.*, fraud, impostor

hŭm'drŭm, *a.*, dull

hū'mĭd, *a.*, damp; **-ity; -ify; -ification; -ifier; -ly**

hū-mĭl'ĭ-tў, *n.*, modesty, humbleness [bird

hŭm'mĭng-bîrd, *n.*, tiny

hū'mör, *n.*, mood, quality of seeming funny; *v.*, indulge

hŭmp, *n.*, mound, bump; *v.*, arch; **-y** *a.*

hū-'mŭs, *n.*, dark soil from partially decayed matter

hŭnch, *n.*, suspicion; *v.*, arch into hump

hŭn'gêr, *n.*, need for food, desire; *v.*, crave; **gry** *a.*; **grily; griness**

hŭnt, *n.*, *v.*, search; **-er; -ing** *n.*

hûr'dle, *n.*, obstacle; *v.*, jump over; **-r** [**-er**

hŭrl, *v.*, throw with force;

hûr-räh', *int.*, *n.*, shout of joy [storm

hŭr'rĭ-cāne, *n.*, violent

hûr'rў, *n.*, rush; *v.*, move quickly; **ried; riedly**

hûrt, *n.*, *v.*, harm, wound; **-ful; -fully; -fulness**

hûr'tle, *v.*, move swiftly

hŭs'bånd-rў, *n.*, farming

hŭsh, *n.*, *v.*, *a.*, quiet

hŭsk, *n.*, dry covering of fruit

hŭsk'ў, *a.*, dry in throat, big and strong; **huskiness; huskily**

hŭs'tle, *v.*, move roughly, work with energy; **-r**

hŭt, *n.*, crude little house

hŭtch, *n.*, china cabinet, animal cage

hў'brĭd, *n.*, mixed breed;

-ize; -ization; -ity; -ism

hў-dräu'lĭc, *a.*, of moving liquid; **-s; -ally**

hў-drò-ė-lĕc'trĭc, *a.*, of electricity by water power; **-ity**

hў'drò-gėn, *n.*, gaseous chemical element; **-ous; dric; -ate**

hў-ē'nå, *n.*, wolflike animal

hў'giēne, *n.*, science of health, cleanliness; **enic; enically; enist**

hўmn, *n.*, song of praise, religious song; **-ist; -ology**

hў-pêr-ăc'tĭve, *a.*, very active; **tivity**

hў-pêr'bò-lē, *n.*, exaggeration; **bolic; bolical; bolically**

hў-pêr-tĕn'sion, *n.*, abnormally high blood pressure; **sive**

hў'phėn, *n.*, punctuation mark (-); **-ate**

hўp-nō'sĭs, *n.*, sleeplike state when one can respond to suggestion; **notic; notically; notism; notist; notize; nology**

hў-pò-chŏn'drĭ-å, *n.*, abnormal fear of illness; **-c** *n.*

hўp'ò-crīte, *n.*, one who pretends to be what he is not; **critical; critically; risy** *n.*

hў-pò-dêr'mĭc, *n.*, *a.*, (injection) under skin

hў-pŏt'ė-nūse, *n.*, side of triangle opposite right angle

hў-pŏth'ė-sĭs, *n.*, theory; **size; thetical; thetically**

hўs-têr-ĕc'tò-mў, *n.*, surgical removal of uterus

hўs-tē'rĭ-å, *n.*, uncontrolled emotional outburst; **rical**

I

I, *pro.*, person speaking or writing

ī'bĕx, *n.*, wild goat

i'bĭs, n., large wading bird

ice, n., frozen water, coldness; v., freeze, cool, frost a cake; **icy** a.

ice'bêrg, n., great ice mass afloat in sea

ice crĕam, n., creamy frozen dessert

ĭch-thÿ-ŏl'ò-gÿ, n., science of fish; **gist; logical**

i'cĭ-cle, n., hanging stick of ice

ic'ĭng, n., frosting [-ic

i'cŏn, n., sacred image;

ĭ-cŏn'ò-clăst, n., attacker of conventional ideas; **clasm** [psyche

ĭd, n., unconscious part of

i-dē'à, n., thought, belief, plan, notion; **-l**

i-dē'àl, n., perfect model; imaginary concept; **-ism; -ist; -istic; -istically; -ity; -ize; -ization; -izer**

i-dĕn'tĭ-càl, a., same; **-ly**

i-dĕn'tĭ-fÿ, v., recognize as similar, associate; **fication; fier; fiable**

i-dĕn'tĭ-tÿ, n., sameness, individuality

i-dē-ŏl'ò-gÿ, n., system of beliefs; **gist; gize; logical; logically**

ĭd'ĭ-òm, n., accepted phrase or expression; **-atic; -atically**

ĭd-ĭ-ò-sÿn'crà-sÿ, n., personal peculiarity; **cratic; cratically**

ĭd'ĭ-òt, n., mentally retarded person; **ocy; -ic; -ically**

i'dle, a., useless, not busy, lazy; **dly; -ness; -r**

i'dòl, n., worshipped object; **-ater; -atry; -atrize; -atrous; -atrously**

i'dòl-īze, v., worship, adore; **zation**

i'dÿll, n., short poem; **-ic; -ically; -ist** [whether

ĭf, conj., in case that,

ĭf'fÿ, a., (coll.) doubtful

ĭg'lōo, n., Eskimo house of ice

ĭg'nē-oŭs, a., fiery

ĭg-nīte', v., set fire to; **ter; tor; tion; nitable**

ĭg-nō'ble, a., not noble, low; **bly; -ness**

ĭg'nó-mĭ-nÿ, n., disgrace, shame; **minous; minously; minousness**

ĭg-nò-rā'mŭs, n., stupid person

ĭg'nò-rànt, a., lacking knowledge, unaware; **-ly; rance** [tion to; -r

ĭg-nôre', v., pay no atten-

ĭ-guā'nà, n., lizard

ĭlk, n., a., same, type

ĭll, a., bad, sick; **-ness**

ĭl-lē'gàl, a., against the law; **-ity; -ly**

ĭl-lĕg'ĭ-ble, a., impossible to read; **bility; bly**

ĭl-lē-gĭt'ĭ-màte, a., born of unwed parents, unlawful; **macy; -ly** [-ness

ĭl-lĭc'ĭt, a., improper; **-ly**

ĭl-lĭt'êr-àte, a., unable to read or write; **acy; -ly**

ĭl-lŏg'ĭ-càl, a., not logical; **-ity; -ly**

ĭl-lū'mĭ-nàte, v., light up, explain; **tor; tion; tive; nant**

ĭl-lū'sion, n., false idea or look; **-al; -ary; -ist; sive; sively; siveness; sory**

ĭl'lŭs-trāte, v., explain, make picture; **tor; tion; tive; tively**

ĭl-lŭs'trĭ-oŭs, a., bright, famous; **-ly; -ness**

ĭm'àge, n., mental picture, likeness, reflection

ĭ-măg'ĭn-ār-ÿ, a., unreal; **narily; nariness**

ĭ-măg'ĭne, v., conceive in the mind, think; **nation; native; natively; nativeness; inable**

ĭm'bè-cĭle, n., mentally retarded person, fool; **cility** [sorb;-r

ĭm-bībe', v., drink, ab-

ĭm-būe', v., inspire

ĭm'ĭ-tāte, v., act like, copy; **tor; tion; tive; table**

ĭm-măc'ū-làte, a., perfectly clean, sinless;

lacy; -ness; -ly

ĭm-mē′dĭ-āte, a., closest, at once; -ly; acy

ĭm-mė-mô′rĭ-ăl, a., ancient; -ly

ĭm-mĕnse′, a., enormous; sity; -ly; -ness

ĭm-mĕrse′, v., dip into liquid; sion; -d; mersible

ĭm′mĭ-grāte, v., come to live in new country; tion; grant

ĭm′mĭ-nėnt, a., about to happen; nence; -ly

ĭm-mūne′, a., free from disease, exempt from; munity; nize; nization

ĭm-mūre′, v., confine to prison; -ment

ĭm-mū′tȧ-ble, a., unchangeable; bility; -ness; bly

Ĭmp, n., mischievous child; -ish; -ishly; -ishness

ĭm′păct, n., collision, shock; v., (ĭm-păct′) press together; -ed; -ion

ĭm-pāir′, v., injure; -ment

ĭm-pāle′, v., fix on something pointed; -ment

ĭm-păl′pȧ-ble, a., not to be felt or understood; bility; bly

ĭm-pârt′, v., give, tell; -er; -ation; -able

ĭm-pâr′tial, a., fair; -ity; -ly

ĭm-păsse′, n., deadlock

ĭm-păs′sion, v., arouse emotionally; -ed; -edly

ĭm-păs′sĭve, a., unemotional, calm; sivity; -ly

ĭm-pēach′, v., accuse public official of wrong doing; -ment; -able; -ability

ĭm-pĕc′cȧ-ble, a., flawless; bility; bly

ĭm-pė-cū′nĭ-oŭs, a., poor; osity; -ness; -ly

ĭm-pēde′, v., hinder; -r

ĭm-pĕd′ĭ-mėnt, n., obstacle [-ler; -lent

ĭm-pĕl′, v., drive, push;

ĭm-pĕnd′, v., occur soon; -ent; -ence; -ency

ĭm-pĕr′ȧ-tĭve, a., urgent; -ly; -ness

ĭm-pē′rĭ-ăl, a., of an empire; -ism; -istic; -istically; -ly [-ment

ĭm-pĕr′ĭl, v., put in danger;

ĭm-pē′rĭ-oŭs, a., domineering; -ly; -ness

ĭm-pĕr′sŏn-āte, v., imitate, pretend; tor; tion

ĭm-pĕr′tĭ-nėnt, a., irrelevant, rude; nence; nency; -ly

ĭm-pĕr′vĭ-oŭs, a., impenetrable; -ly; -ness

ĭm-pĕt′ū-oŭs, a., impulsive, sudden; -ly; -ness

ĭm′pė-tŭs, n., force of movement, stimulus

ĭm-pĭnge′, v., touch, encroach; -r; -ment

ĭm-plănt′, v., plant firmly; -ation

ĭm′plė-mėnt, n., tool; v., (ĭm-plė-mėnt′) fulfill, do; -ation; -al

ĭm′plĭ-cāte, v., infer, involve; tion; tive; tively

ĭm-plĭc′ĭt, a., suggested; absolute; -ly; -ness

ĭm-plōde′, v., burst inward; plosion; plosive; plosively [plied

ĭm-plȳ′, v., hint, suggest;

ĭm′pôrt, n., imported good, meaning; v., (ĭm-pôrt′) bring goods into country; -er; -ation; -able

ĭm-pôr′tȧnt, a., having value; tance; -ly

ĭm-pôr-tūne′, v., urge, beg; nity; tunȧte a.; -ly; -ness

ĭm-pōse′, v., force on another; position

ĭm-pŏs′tŏr, n., pretender; tûre

ĭm′pȯ-tėnt, a., ineffective, sterile; ence; ency; -ly

ĭm-pound′, v., seize by law; -ment

ĭm-prĕg′nȧ-ble, a., unyielding; bility; bly

ĭm-prĕg′nāte, v., fertilize, make pregnant; tor; tion

ĭm-prĕss′, v., stamp, affect strongly; -ion; -ional; -ionable; -ible; -ibly

ĭm-prĕs′sion-ĭsm, n.,

school of art; **ist; istic; istically** [ing; **-ing** n.

ĭm-prĭnt', v., mark by print-

ĭm-prĭs'ŏn, v., put in jail; **-ment**

ĭm-prŏmp'tū, a., adv., without preparation

ĭm-prove' (prūv), v., make better; **-r; -ment; provable**

ĭm'prŏ-vīse, v., do without preparation; **-r; sor; sation; sational**

ĭm'pū-dĕnt, a., disrespectful; **ence; ency; -ly**

ĭm-pūgn', v., oppose verbally; **-er; -ation; -able**

ĭm'pŭlse, n., sudden force; **sion; sive; sively; siveness**

ĭm-pū'nĭ-tȳ, n., freedom from punishment

ĭm-pūte', v., attribute, charge; **tation; tative; putable; putability; putably**

ĭn, prep., contained by, during, having, concerning, using; adv., to inside

ĭn-āl'iĕn-à-ble, a., that cannot be taken away; **bility; bly**

ĭn-āne', a., foolish; **-ly**

ĭn-às-mŭch', conj., since

ĭn-āu-gu-rate, v., begin, install in public office; **tor; tion; ral**

ĭn'bôrn, a., natural

ĭn'brĕd, a., innate

ĭn-càn-dĕs'cĕnt, a., glowing with heat, bright; **cence; -ly**

ĭn-càn-tā'tion, n., magical spell; **-al; tory**

ĭn-câr'cĕr-āte, v., imprison; **tor; tion**

ĭn-câr'nàte, v., make real; a., **(nàte)** in human form; **tion**

ĭn'cĕnse, n., substance burned for pleasant odor; v., **(ĭn-cĕnse')** make angry

ĭn-cĕn'tĭve, n., motive; a., encouraging

ĭn-cĕp'tion, n., beginning; **tive; tively**

ĭn-cĕs'sànt, a., continual; **sancy; -ness; -ly**

ĭn'cĕst, n., sexual relations with close relatives; **-uous; -uously; -uousness**

ĭn-chō'àte (kō), a., just begun, incomplete; **tion; -ness; -ly**

ĭn'cĭ-dĕnce, n., range of occurrence

ĭn'cĭ-dĕnt, n., occurrence

ĭn-cĭ-dĕn'tàl, a., liable to happen; casual; **-ly**

ĭn-cĭn'êr-āte, v., burn; **tor; tion**

ĭn-cĭp'ĭ-ĕnt, a., beginning; **ence; ency; -ly**

ĭn-cĭ'sion, n., cut

ĭn-cĭ'sĭve, a., sharp, keen; **-ly; -ness**

ĭn-cĭ'sŏr, n., cutting tooth

ĭn-cīte', v., urge to act; **-ment; tation**

ĭn'clīne, n., slope; v., **(ĭn-clīne')** slope, have a tendency; **-r; nation; national; clinable**

ĭn-clūde', v., contain; **cludable; clusion; clusive; clusively**

ĭn-cŏg-nĭ'tō, a., adv., hidden, disguised

ĭn'come (cŭm), n., money one earns

ĭn-côr'pŏ-rāte, v., combine, merge, form into corporation; **tor; tion; tive; -d**

ĭn-côr'rĭ-gĭ-ble, a., unable to change; **bility; bly; -ness**

ĭn'crēase, n., growth; v., **(ĭn-crēase')** become greater; **-r; creasable; creasingly**

ĭn-crĕd'ĭ-ble, a., too unusual, unbelievable; **bility; bly**

ĭn-crĕd'ū-loŭs, a., doubting; **lity; -ly** [gain; **-al**

ĭn'crĕ-mĕnt, n., increase.

ĭn-crĭm'ĭ-nāte, v., accuse, involve in crime; **tion; tory**

ĭn-crŭst', v., cover with crust or hard coat; **-ation**

ĭn'cŭ-bāte, v., hatch eggs, develop; **tor; tion; tional; tive**

ĭn-cŭl'cāte, v., teach by drill; **tor; tion**

ĭn-cŭm'bĕnt, a., currently in office; **bency**

ĭn-cûr', v., bring upon oneself; **-rence** [**-ness**

ĭn-dĕbt'ĕd, a., owing;

ĭn-dēed', adv., truly; int., exclamation of surprise

ĭn-dĕl'ĭ-ble, a., permanent; **bility; bly**

ĭn-dĕm'nĭ-fȳ, v., protect, repay for loss; **fier; nity; nification**

ĭn-dĕnt', v., notch, cut into, make dent; **-ation**

ĭn-dĕn'tûre, n., contract (of service)

ĭn-dē-pĕnd'ĕnt, a., not controlled by another, free; **ence; ency; -ly**

ĭn'dĕx, n., pointer, indication, alphabetical list of topics in book; **-er**

ĭn'dĭ-cāte, v., show, point out; **tor; tion; tive; tively; cant**

ĭn-dict' (dīt), v., accuse of crime; **-er; -or; -ment; -able**

ĭn-dĭf'fĕr-ĕnt, a., neutral, unconcerned; **ence; -ly**

ĭn-dĭg'ĕ-noŭs, a., native inherent; **-ly; -ness**

ĭn'dĭ-gĕnt, a., poor, in poverty; **ence; ency; -ly**

ĭn-dĭ-gĕs'tion, n., difficulty in digesting food; **tive**

ĭn-dĭg'nănt, a., angry; **nation; -ly**

ĭn-dĭg'nĭ-tȳ, n., insult

ĭn-dĭs-pōsed', a., sick; **sition**

ĭn-dĭ-vĭd'ū-ăl, n., single being or thing; a., characteristic, distinct; **-ity; -ize; -ization; -ly**

ĭn-dŏc'trĭ-nāte, v., teach beliefs, drill into; **tor; tion** [**lence; -ly**

ĭn'dŏ-lĕnt, a., lazy, idle;

ĭn-dŏm'ĭ-tă-ble, a., unconquerable; **bility; bly; -ness** [building

ĭn'dôor, a., of inside of a

ĭn-dū'bĭ-tă-ble, a., unquestionable; **bly**

ĭn-dūce', v., persuade, cause; **-r; -ment; ducible** [**-ee; -ion**

ĭn-dŭct', v., install, initiate;

ŭn-dŭc'tĭve, a., conclusive from facts; **tion**

ĭn-dŭlge', v., yield; **-r; -nce; -nt; -ntly**

ĭn-dŭs'trĭ-oŭs, a., busy; **-ly; -ness**

ĭn'dŭs-trȳ, n., business, manufacturing, hard work; **trial; trialist; trialism; trialize; trialization**

ĭn-ē'brĭ-āte, n., a., drunk; v., (āte) make drunk; **tion; -d**

ĭn-ĕf'fă-ble, a., too awesome to be spoken; **bility; bly; -ness**

ĭn-ĕpt', a., unfit, awkward; **-itude; -ly; -ness**

ĭn-êrt', a., inactive; **-ly; -ness**

ĭn-êr'tĭă, n., tendency of matter to stay in rest or motion

ĭn-ĕv'ĭ-tă-ble, a., sure to happen; **bility; bly**

ĭn-ĕx'ō-ră-ble, a., inflexible; **bility; bly**

ĭn-ĕx'plĭ-că-ble, a., mysterious; **bility; bly**

ĭn'fă-mȳ, n., bad reputation, disgrace; **mous; mously**

ĭn'fănt, n., very young child; **fancy**

ĭn'făn-tile, a., babyish immature; **lism**

ĭn'făn-trȳ, n., foot soldiers; **-man,** n.

ĭn-făt-ū-ā'tion, n., foolish love; **ated**

ĭn-fĕct', v., make diseased; **-or; -ion; -ious; -iously; -iousness**

ĭn-fêr', v., conclude by reasoning; **-rer; -ence; -able**

ĭn-fē'rĭ-ŏr, a., lower, poor

in quality; **-ity**

ĭn-fẽr′năl, a., of hell; **-ly**

ĭn-fẽst′, v., overrun; **-er; -ation**

ĭn′fĭ-dĕl, n., disbeliever

ĭn-fĭl′trāte, v., join secretly, penetrate; **tor; tion; tive**

ĭn′fĭ-nĭte, a., endless, vast; **nity; -ly; -ness**

ĭn-fĭrm′, a., weak, feeble; **-ity; -ly; -ness**

ĭn-fĭr′mȧ-rў, n., hospital

ĭn-flāme′, v., set on fire, excite, become red and sore; **flammation; flammable**

ĭn-flāte′, v., blow up, swell; **-r; flatable; -d**

ĭn-flā′tion, n., fall in money value with rise in prices; **-ary**

ĭn-flĕct′, v., change tone in voice; **-ion; -ive**

ĭn-flĭct′, v., cause pain, impose; **-er; -or; -ion; -ive**

ĭn′flū-ĕnce, n., power, authority, prestige; v., have an effect on; **ential; entially** [disease

ĭn-flū-ĕn′zȧ, n., infectious

in′flŭx, n., flowing in

ĭn-fôrm′, v., give knowledge; **-er** [-ly

ĭn-fôr′măl, a., casual; **-ity;**

ĭn-fôr-mā′tion, n., facts; **tive; tively**

ĭn-frăc′tion, n., violation

ĭn-frȧ-rĕd′, a., of invisible rays outside spectrum

ĭn-frĭnge′, v., violate; **-ment** [tion; atingly

ĭn-fū′rĭ-āte, v., enrage;

ĭn-fūse′, v., pour into, instill; **sion; sible; sive**

ĭn-gĕn′ioŭs, a., clever; **ity; -ly; -ness**

ĭn-gĕn′ū-oŭs, a., frank, naive; **-ly; -ness**

ĭn-gĕst′, v., take food into body; **-ion; -ive**

ĭn′gŏt, n., metal bar

ĭn′grāined′, a., firmly fixed

ĭn′grāte, n., thankless person

ĭn-grā′tĭ-āte (shĭ), v., seek one's favor; **tion; ating; atingly** [of mixture

ĭn-grē′dĭ-ĕnt, n., element

ĭn-hăb′ĭt, v., live in; **-er; -ation; -able; -ancy; -ant** n. [halation

ĭn-hāle′, v., breathe in; **-r;**

ĭn-hĕr′ĕnt, a., natural, inborn; **ence; ency**

ĭn-hĕr′ĭt, v., receive (traits, possessions, etc.) from ancestor; **-or; -ress; -ance; -able**

ĭn-hĭb′ĭt, v., keep from doing, restrain; **-or; -ion; -ive; -ory**

ĭn-ĭm′ĭ-căl, a., hostile, unfriendly; **-ly**

ĭn-ĭq′uĭ-tў, n., wickedness; **tous; tously; tousness**

ĭn-ĭ′tial, n., capital letter; a., first; **-ly**

ĭn-ĭ′tĭ-āte (shĭ), v., begin; **tor; tion** •

ĭn-ĭ′tĭ-ȧ-tĭve (shĭ), n., first step, ability to take lead

ĭn-jĕct′, v., push fluid into, insert; **-or; -ion; -able**

ĭn-jŭnc′tion, n., court order; **tive**

ĭn′jûre, v., harm physically; **-r; jury; jurious; juriously; juriousness**

ĭnk, n., colored liquid for writing; **-y** a.

ĭnk′lĭng, n., notion, hint

ĭn′lănd, a., adv., away from sea; **-er**

ĭn-lăw, n., relative by marriage [laid a.

ĭn′lāy, v., set into surface;

ĭn′lĕt, n., narrow strip of water

ĭn-′māte, n., prisoner

ĭnn, n., place providing food and/or bed for travellers

ĭn′nȧrds, n., pl., (coll.) inner organs of body

ĭn-nāte′, a., existing from birth, inborn; **-ly; -ness**

ĭn′nẽr, a., interior

ĭn′nȯ-cĕnt, a., without evil, naive; **cence; -ly**

ĭn-nŏc′ū-oŭs, a., harmless, dull; **-ly; -ness**

ĭn′nȯ-vāte, v., start something new; **tor; tion; tive**

ĭn-nū-ĕn′dō, n., hint, sly

remark

ĭn-nū'mêr-à-ble, *a.*, very many; **bility; bly; -ness**

ĭn-ŏc'ū-lāte, *v.*, inject serum to prevent disease; **tor; tion; tive**

ĭn-ôr'dĭ-nàte, *a.*, too great; **-ly; -ness** [tigation

ĭn'quĕst, *n.*, judicial inves-

ĭn-quīre', *v.*, ask; **-r; quiry; quisition**

ĭn-quĭs'ĭ-tĭve, *a.*, asking many questions, curious; **-ly; -ness**

ĭn-scrībe', *v.*, write words; **scription; scriptive**

ĭn-scrū'tà-ble, *a.*, mysterious; **bility; bly**

ĭn'sĕct, *n.*, tiny animal with six legs

ĭn-sĕm'ĭ-nāte, *v.*, sow seeds, implant; **tion**

ĭn-sêrt', *n.*, *v.*, (something) put in; **-ion**

ĭn-sīde', *n.*, *a.*, interior; *adv.*, indoors; *prep.*, within [**-ness**

ĭn-sĭd'ĭ-oŭs, *a.*, sly; **-ly;**

ĭn'sīght, *n.*, understanding

ĭn-sĭg'nĭ-à, *n.*, badge or mark of rank, office, etc.

ĭn-sĭn'ū-āte, *v.*, imply, hint; **tor; tion; tive**

ĭn-sĭp'ĭd, *a.*, tasteless, dull; **-ity; -ly**

ĭn-sĭst', *v.*, demand strongly; **-ence; -ent; -ently**

ĭn'sò-lént, *a.*, insulting, disrespectful; **ence; -ly**

ĭn-sŏm'nĭ-à, *n.*, inability to sleep; **-c**

ĭn-sō-mŭch', *adv.*, to such an extent

ĭn-soŭ'cĭ-ánt, *a.*, calm, carefree; **ance; -ly**

ĭn-spĕct', *v.*, look at carefully; **-tor; -tion**

ĭn-spīre', *v.*, stimulate, arouse thought or emotion; **-r; spiration; spirational; spirable**

ĭn-stăll', *v.*, put in (office formally); **-er; -ation**

ĭn-stăll'mént, *n.*, one of several parts

ĭn'stànce, *n.*, example

ĭn'stànt, *n.*, moment; *a.*, immediate; **stancy; -ly**

ĭn-stăntā'nē-oŭs, *a.*, immediate; **-ly; -ness**

ĭn-stĕad', *adv.*, as an alternative

ĭn'stĕp, *n.*, arched part of top of foot

ĭn'stĭ-gāte, *v.*, incite; **tor; tion; tive**

ĭn-stĭll', *v.*, teach gradually; **-er; -ation; -ment**

ĭn'stĭnct, *n.*, natural tendency; **-ive; -ively; -ual**

ĭn'stĭ-tūte, *n.*, organization to promote art, science, etc.; *v.*, establish, start; **-r; tor; tion; tional; tionally; tionalize; tive**

ĭn-strŭct', *v.*, teach, command; **-or; -ion; -ional; -ive; -ively**

ĭn'strŭ-mént, *n.*, tool, device producing music; **-al; -ally; -ality**

ĭn-sŭb-ôr'dĭ-nāte, *n.*, *a.*, (one who is) disobedient; **-ly; tion**

ĭn'sŭ-lár, *a.*, of an island

ĭn'sŭ-lāte, *v.*, set apart, protect from heat loss; **tor; tion**

ĭn'sŭ-lĭn, *n.*, hormone regulating use of sugar

ĭn'sŭlt, *n.*, indignity; *v.*, (ĭn-sŭlt') hurt one's pride; **-er; -ing; -ingly**

ĭn-sūr'ànce, *n.*, contract to pay for loss.

ĭn-sūre', *v.*, make sure, protect; **-r; surable; surability**

ĭn-sûr'gént, *a.*, rebellious; **gence; gency; -ly**

ĭn-sûr-rĕc'tion, *n.*, rebellion; **-ist; -al; -ary**

ĭn-tăct', *a.*, kept whole

ĭn-tăn'gĭ-ble, *a.*, vague, not material; **bility; bly**

ĭn'tè-gêr, *n.*, whole number [entire

ĭn'tè-gràl, *a.*, essentially,

ĭn'tè-grāte, *v.*, join together, end racial segregation; **tion; tive; tional; tionist**

ĭn-tĕg'rĭ-tў, *n.*, wholeness,

honesty

ĭn′tĕl-lĕct, n., ability to reason, superior mind; **-ual;** **-uality; -ually; -ive**

ĭn-tĕl′lĭ-gĕnce, n., ability to learn, information

ĭn-tĕl′lĭ-gĕnt, a., having an alert mind; **-ly**

ĭn-tĕl′lĭ-gĭ-ble, a., clear, understandable; **bly;** **bility**

ĭn-tĕnd′, v., have in mind, plan; **tention; -ed**

ĭn-tĕnse′, a., very strong, strenuous; **sity;** **-ly;** **-ness; sive; sively**

ĭn-tĕn′sĭ-fŷ, v., strengthen

ĭn-tĕnt′, n., purpose; a., firmly fixed; **-ly; -ness**

ĭn-tĕr′, v., bury; **-ment**

ĭn-tĕr-ăct′, v., act on each other; **-ion; -ive**

ĭn-tĕr-cēde′, v., plead for another; **cessor; cession**

ĭn-tĕr-cĕpt′, v., stop, interrupt; **-or; -ion; -ive**

ĭn-tĕr-chānge′, v., exchange; **-able; -ably**

ĭn′tĕr-côurse, n., dealings between others, sexual union

ĭn-tĕr-dĕ-pĕnd′ence, n., mutual dependence; **ency; ent; ently**

ĭn-tĕr-dict′, v., prohibit; **tor; tion; tive; tory**

ĭn′tĕr-ĕst, n., concern, fee paid to use one's money; v., show concern; **-ed; -ing**

ĭn-tĕr-fēre′, v., come between, meddle; **-nce**

ĭn-tĕr,fūse′, v., combine; **sion** [a., temporary

ĭn′tĕr-ĭm, n., time between;

ĭn-tē′rĭ-ör, n., inside; a., situated within

ĭn-tĕr-jĕct′, v., insert; **-or; -ion; -ional** [gether

ĭn-tĕr-lŏck′, v., lock to-

ĭn-tĕr-lō-cū′tion, n., conversation; **tor; tory**

ĭn-tĕr-lōpe′, v., intrude; **-r**

ĭn′tĕr-lūde, n., period between

ĭn-tĕr-măr′rŷ, v., marry one of different race; **riage**

ĭn-tĕr-mē′dĭ-āte, n., a go-between; a., in the middle

ĭn-tĕr′mĭ-nà-ble, a., without, end; **bly**

ĭn-tĕr-mĭs′sion, n., period between acts

ĭn-tĕr-mĭt′tĕnt, a., periodic, from time to time; **-ly**

ĭn′tĕrn, n., doctor training in hospital; v., **(ĭn-tĕrn′)** confine; **-ship**

ĭn-tĕr′nàl, a., inside; **-ize; -ization; -ity; -ly**

ĭn-tĕr-nă′tion-àl, a., among nations; **-ize; -ization; -ity; -ly**

ĭn′tĕr-nĭst, n., doctor of internal medicine

ĭn-tĕr-pêr′sŏn-àl, a., between persons; **-ly**

ĭn′tĕr-plāy, n., interaction

ĭn-tĕr′pȯ-lāte, v., alter by inserting new words; **-r; tor; tion; tive**

ĭn-tĕr-pōse′, v., place between; **-r; sition; posal**

ĭn-tĕr′prĕt, v., explain meaning, translate; **-er; -ation; -ive; -able**

ĭn-tĕr′rȯ-gāte, v., question formally; **tor; tion; tive; tively; tory**

ĭn-tĕr-rŭpt′, v., break into the continuity; **-er; -ion; -ive**

ĭn-tĕr-sĕct′, v., divide, cross; **-ion; -ional**

ĭn-tĕr-spêrse′, v., scatter

ĭn′tĕr-stāte, a., among states [between

ĭn′tĕr-vàl, n., space or time

ĭn-tĕr-vēne′, v., come or be between; **vention**

ĭn′tĕr-vieᵂ, n., v. (meeting to) ask questions; **-er; -ee** [will; **tacy**

ĭn-tĕs′tāte, a., having no

ĭn-tĕs′tĭne, n., tube extending from stomach to anus; **tinal; tinally**

ĭn′tĭ-māte, v., hint; **tion**

ĭn′tĭ-màte, a., personal, private; **macy;** **-ly; -ness**

ĭn-tĭm′ĭ-dāte, v., make afraid; **tor; tion**

ĭn′to (tū), prep., inside, to the form of, toward

ĭn-tṓ-nā′tion, n., voice pitch

ĭn-tōne′, v., chant

ĭn-tŏx′ĭ-cāte, v., make drunk; **tion; cant** n., a.

ĭn-trȧ-mū′rȧl, a., among school's members; **-ly**

ĭn-trăn′sĭ-gént, a., refusing to compromise; **gence; gency; -ly**

ĭn-trȧ-stāte′, a., within the state [vein; **-ly**

ĭn-trȧ-vē′noŭs, a., in a

ĭn-trĕp′ĭd, a., brave; **-ity; -ness; -ly**

ĭn′trĭ-cȧte, a., very complex; **cacy; -ly; -ness**

ĭn-trigue′, n., secret plot or love affair

ĭn-trĭn′sĭc, a., innate, essential; **-ally; -ness**

ĭn-trȯ-dūce′, v., bring into, present, begin; **-r; duction; ductory**

ĭn′trȯ-vêrt, n., shy person; **version; versive**

ĭn-trūde′, v., force oneself when not welcome; **-r; trusion; trusive**

ĭn-tū-ĭ′tion, n., instinctive understanding; **-al; -ally; tive; tively**

ĭn′ŭn-dāte, v., flood, overwhelm; **tor; tion**

ĭn-ūre′, v., become used to, accustom; **-ment**

ĭn-vāde′, v., enter forcibly; **-r; vasion; vasive**

ĭn′vȧ-lĭd, n., chronically ill person [tack

ĭn-vĕc′tĭve, n., verbal at-

ĭn-vēi′gle, v., deceive, lure; **-r; -ment**

ĭn-vĕnt′, v., create, make new thing; **-or; -ion; -ive**

ĭn′vén-tȯ-ry, n., itemized list; **rial; rially** [site

ĭn-vêrse′, n., direct oppo-

ĭn-vêrt′, v., turn upside down, reverse; **version**

ĭn-vĕst′, v., put money into, install; **-ment**

ĭn-vĕs′tĭ-gāte, v., examine

in detail; **tor; tion; tive**

ĭn-vĕt′êr-ȧte, a., habitual; **acy; -ly**

ĭn-vĭd′ĭ-oŭs, a., offensive, harmful; **-ly; -ness**

ĭn-vĭg′ȯr-āte, v., fill with vigor; **tor; tion; tive**

ĭn-vĭn′cĭ-ble, a., unconquerable; **bility; bly; -ness**

ĭn-vīte′, v., ask one to attend, tempt; **tation**

ĭn′vȯice, n., list of shipped merchandise

ĭn-vōke′, v., call on God in prayer; **-r; vocation**

ĭn′vȯ-lūte, a., complicated, curled in spiral; **tion**

ĭn-vŏlve′, v., include, complicate, occupy, draw into; **-ment; -d**

ĭn′wȧrd, adj., inside; **-ly; -ness**

ī′ȯ-dīne, n., chemical element, antiseptic; **dize; dous**

ī′ȯn, n., electrically charged atom; **-ize; -ic**

ī-ō′tȧ, n., Greek letter, small quantity

ī-rāte′, a., angry; **-ly; -ness**

īre, n., anger; **-ful; -fully; -fulness**

ĭr-ĭ-dĕs′cént, a., showing shining colors; **cence; -ly** [part of eye

ī′rĭs, n., flower, colored

îrk, v., annoy, **-some**

ī′ron (êrn), n., strong metal, pressing device, strength; v., press cloths

ī′ron-clăd (êrn), a., fixed

ī-rȯ-nȳ, n., the opposite of what is said, done or expected; **ronical; ronically**

ĭr-rā′dĭ-āte, v., light up, make clear; **tor; tion; tive**

ĭr′rĭ-gāte, v., supply with water by ditches; **tor; tion; tive; gable**

ĭr′rĭ-tȧ-ble, a., easily annoyed; **bly; -ness; bility**

ĭr′rĭ-tāte, v., annoy, anger, make sore; **tion; tive**

I
K

ĭr-rŭpt′, v., burst violently **-ion; -ive**

is′lånd (ī), n., land mass surrounded by water; **-er**

isle (īl), n., small island

is′lĕt (ī), n., very small island [theory, system

ism (ĭzĕm), n., doctrine,

ĭ′sò-lāte, v., keep apart; **tor; tion; lable**

ĭ-sò-môr′phĭsm, n., similarity of different things or beings; **phic**

ĭs′sūe (ĭsh), n., result, offspring, disputed point; v., emerge, give out, publish; **suance; suable; suably**

ĭsth′mŭs, n., narrow land strip joining two land masses

ĭt, pro., animal or thing being referred to

ĭ-tăl′ĭc, a., of slanted type; **-s; -ize; -ization**

ĭtch, n., skin irritation, restless desire; **-y** a.; **-iness; -ily**

ĭ′tĕm, n., specific thing; **-ize; -ization**

ĭt′ĕr-āte, v., repeat; **tion; tive; ant** [ancy; **-ly**

ĭ-tĭn′ĕr-ånt, a., travelling;

ĭ-tĭn′ĕr-ār-ÿ, n., trip route

ī′vö-rÿ, n., elephant tusk, creamy white

ī′vÿ, n., climbing vine

J

jăb, v. poke, punch

jăb′bêr, n., v., chatter; **-er**

jăck, n., lifting device, playing card of page boy, electrical plug; v., raise

jăck′ăss, n., male donkey, fool

jăck′ĕt, n., short coat

jăck′knīfe, n., large pocket knife [sional

jăck′lĕg, a., unprofes-

jăck′-ò′-lăn-têrn, n., hollow pumpkin with face cut out [stakes

jăck′pŏt, n., cumulative

jāde, n., green stone; v.,

tire; a., green

jăg, n., spree

jăg′uår, n., large spotted cat

jăl′òu-siē, n., window or door with movable slats

jăm, n., fruit spread, (coll.) predicament, crowding; v., squeeze, crush

jămb, n., side frame of doorway [tion

jăm-bò-rēe′, n., celebration

jăn′gle, n., harsh sound, quarrel [taken

jăn′ĭ-tör, n., building care-

jår, n., cylindrical container, jolt, grating sound; v., shock, shake

jår′gòn, n., incoherent speech, dialect; **-ize**

jăun′dĭce, n., liver disease, yellowing of skin

jăunt, n., short trip

jăv′e-līn, n., light spear

jăzz, n., strong rhythmic music; **-y** a.

jĕal′oŭs, a., resentfully suspicious, envy; **-y; -ly; -ness** [twilled cotton

jēans, n., pl., pants of

jēep, n., small, rugged automotive vehicle

jēer, n., v., mock, ridicule

jė-jūne′, a., dull; **-ly; -ness**

jĕl′lÿ, n., coagulated fruit syrup [creature

jĕl′lÿ-fĭsh, n., jellylike sea

jĕop′ård-īze, v., risk; **ardy** a.

jêrk, n., abrupt movement; v., pull suddenly; **-y** a.

jêr′sēy, n., soft, knitted cloth

jĕt, n., powerful spray, jet-propelled airplane; a., black

jĕt′tĭ-sòn, v., lighten load

jĕt′tÿ, n., wall or pier in water

jew′ĕl, n., gem, precious thing or person; **-er; -ry**

jībe, v., shift course, agree

jĭg′gle, v., shake slightly; **gly**

jĭlt, v., reject a lover

jĭnx, n., (coll.) bad luck

jĭt′têr, v., be nervous; **-y** a.;

teriness
jŏb′bêr, *n.,* distributor of goods, middleman

jŏck′ēy, *n.,* race horse rider; *v.,* maneuver

jŏc′ū-lår, *a.,* joking; **-ity; -ly**

jŏc′ŭnd, *a.,* merry; **-ity; -ly**

jŏdh′pûr, *n., pl.,* riding pants

jŏg, *n.,* notched part; *v.,* nudge, go at slow steady pace; **-ger**

jŏin, *v.,* connect, unite, become a part of; **-er**

jŏint, *n.,* place where two parts connect; *a.,* shared; **-ly**

jŏist, *n.,* beams holding up floor planks

jōke, *n.,* funny thing; *v.,* make fun; **-r**

jŏl′lÿ, *a.,* gay; **lity; lify; liness; lily**

jŏlt, *n., v.,* jerk, shake; **-er; -y** *a.;* **-ingly**

jŏs′tle, *v.,* shove; **-r**

jŏŭnce, *v.,* shake; **jouncy** *a.*

joûr′nål, *n.,* diary, record of happenings, periodical; **-ize**

joûr′nål-ĭsm, *n.,* occupation of news media; **nalist; nalistic; nalistically**

joûr′nēy, *n.,* trip; *v.,* travel

jŏŭst, *n., v.,* fight with lances on horseback

joy (jŏi), *n.,* happiness; **-ful; -fully; -fulness; -ous; -ously; -ousness; -less; -lessly; -lessness**

jū′bĭ-lånt, *a.,* elated; **lance; late; lation; -ly**

jŭdge, *n., v.,* (one who is designated to) hear and decide law cases; **-ship**

jū-dĭ′ciål, *a.,* of judge or law court; **-ly**

jŭg, *n.,* liquid container

jŭg′gle, *v.,* perform skillful tricks; **-r; -ry**

jŭg′ū-lår, *a.,* of neck

jūice, *n.,* liquid of fruit or vegetable; **juicy** *a.*

jŭm′ble, *v.,* mix. confuse

jŭmp, *v.,* leap, move suddenly; **-er; -y** *a.*

jŭmp′êr, *n.,* sleeveless dress [ing

jŭnc′tion, *n.,* place of join-

jŭn′gle, *n.,* tropical forest

jŭnk, *n.,* worthless stuff, trash, Chinese boat; *v.,* throw away

jŭn′kėt, *n.,* pleasure trip, milky dessert

jŭn′tå, *n.,* council

jû-rĭs-dĭc′tion, *n.,* authority; **-al; -ally**

jû-rĭs-prŭ′dênce, *n.,* science of law; **dential; dentially**

jŭst, *a.,* upright, fair, correct; *adv.,* exactly, only, nearly; **-ly; -ness**

jŭs′tĭ-fÿ, *v.,* show to be fair, make excuse for; **fier; fication; fiable; fiability; fiably**

jŭt, *v.,* stick out

jūte, *n.,* strong fiber

jū′vėn-ĭle, *n.,* child; *a.,* young, of youth; **nility**

jŭx-tå-pōse′, *v.,* put side by side; **position**

K

kaī′sêr, *n.,* emperor

kāle, *n.,* cabbagelike vegetable

kå-leī′dò-scōpe, *n.,* tube showing changing designs of colored glass

kăn-gå-rōo, *n.,* leaping animal [like insect

kā′tÿ-dĭd, *n.,* grasshopper-

kaÿ′åk, *n.,* Eskimo canoe

kē′å, *n.,* parrot

kēēn, *a.,* sharp, eager, strong; **-ly; -ness**

kēēp, *n.,* food and shelter; *v.,* adhere to, protect, mantain, hold, continue; **-er; -ing** *n.*

kēēp′såke, *n.,* memento

kĕg, *n.,* small barrel

kĕlp, *n.,* seaweed

kĕn, *n.,* knowledge

kêr′chĭef, *n.,* scarf

kêr′nėl, *n.,* a grain, core

kĕr'ò-sēne, n., oil from petroleum

kĕtch'ŭp, n., tomato sauce

kĕt'tle, n., cooking pot

kĕt'tle-drŭm, n., large copper drum

kēy, n., device to work a lock, lever, explanation, low island, musical tone; a., essential

kēy'nōte, n., basic note of musical scale; a., main

kēy'stōne, n., top stone of arch, main part

khă'kĭ, n., a., dull yellowish-brown, tan

kĭck, n., v., strike with foot, recoil; **-er**

kĭck'băck, n., sudden reaction, illegal return of money

kĭd'năp, v., seize and hold person for ransom; **-per**

kĭd'nĕy, n., organ that excretes urine

kĭll, v., make die, destroy; **-er; -ing** n.

kĭln, n., pottery oven

kĭl'ò-grăm, n., 1000 grams, 2.2 pounds

kĭ-lŏ'mė-têr, n., 1000 meters, ⅝ mile

kĭl'ò-wätt, n., 1000 watts

kĭlt, n., pleated skirt

kĭl'têr, n., (coll.) proper order

kĭ-mō'nò, n., loose robe

kĭn, n., relatives, family; **-ship**

kind, n., sort, type, class

kind, a., gentle, good; **-ly; -ness; -less**

kĭn'dêr-gâr-tĕn, n., class for preschool children

kĭn'dlĭng, n., bits of wood to start fire

kĭn-ĕs-thĕt'ĭc, a., of muscular activity

kĭng, n., male ruler; **-dom; -ly**

kĭng'lĕt, n., songbird

kĭnk, n., curl, twist; **-y** a.

kĭ'ŏsk, n., small open building [imal hide

kĭp, n., small untanned an-

kĭp'pêr, n., smoked herring

kĭss, n., v., caress with lips; **-er**

kĭt, n., carrying case, set of tools, equipment

kĭtch'ėn, n., room for cooking; **-er**

kite, n., paper-covered frame flown in wind

kĭt'tÿ, n., kitten, pooled money, poker stakes

kĭ'wĭ, n., flightless bird

klätch, n., (coll.) informal gathering

klĕp-tò-mā'nĭ-à, n., impulse to steal; **-c** n.

knăck, n., ability

knăp'săck, n., bag carried on back [**knavish**

knāve, n., rascal; **-ry;**

knēad, v., squeeze and press

knēel, v., bend on knee

knĭck'êrs, n., pants ending and gathered below knee

knife, n., cutting or stabbing blade with handle

knīght, n., medieval soldier, honorary rank; **-hood; -ly**

knit, v., loop yarn with needles, unit; **-ter; -ting** n. [a.

knŏb, n., round handle, **-by**

knŏck, n., v., hit, rap, (make) pounding noise

knŏck'à-bout, n., sailboat; a., boisterous

knŏt, n., tangled thread: v., intertwine, tie, unite; **-ter; -ted**

knōw, v., be sure of, aware of or acquainted with; **-er; -ing** a.; **-able**

knōw'hŏw, n., skill

knŏwl'ėdge, n., information, awareness; **-able; -ability; -ably; -able-ness**

knŭck'le, n., finger joint

knûrl, n., v., knot; **-ed; -y** a.

kō-à'là, n., small bear

kō'dĭ-ăk, n., very large brown bear

kō'shêr, a., edible by Jewish dietary laws

kŏw'tŏw', v., show submissive respect

krўp'tŏn, *n.,* gaseous element [citrus fruit

kŭm'quăt, *n.,* small orange

L

lā'bĕl, *n.,* descriptive tag, or word, title; *v.,* mark, tag, call; **-er**

lā'bĭ-ŭm, *n.,* lip; **bial**

lā'bŏr, *n.,* job, all worker, childbirth; *v.,* work; **-er**

lăb'o-rȧ-tô-rў, *n.,* place for scientific work

lăb'ў-rĭnth, *n.,* maze

lāce, *n.,* string to tie shoe, fancy open work fabric; **lacing** *n.;* **lacy** *a.*

lăc'ĕr-āte, *v.,* tear jaggedly, hurt; **tion; erable**

lāce'wĭng, *n.,* insect

lăch'rў-mōse, *a.,* tearful, sad; **mal**

lăck-ȧ-dāi'sĭ-cȧl, *a.,* lacking vigor; **-ly**

lăck'ēy, *n.,* low servant, follower

lȧ-cŏn'ĭc, *a.,* brief; **-ally**

lăc'quêr, *n.,* varnish, polished finish

lȧ-crôsse', *n.,* sport with webbed sticks and ball

lăc'tĭc, *a.,* of milk

lăd'dĕr, *n.,* climbing device with rungs for stepping

lād'ĭng, *n.,* cargo

lā'dle, *n.,* cuplike spoon

lā'dў, *n.,* woman, polite woman; **-like** *a.* [tle

lā'dў-bŭg, *n.,* spotted beetle

lăg, *v.,* fall behind

lăg'gȧrd, *n.,* slow person

lȧ-gōon', *n.,* shallow lake or pond, water inside atoll

lāir, *n.,* animal's den

lā'ĭ-tў, *n.,* laymen as a group [water

lāke, *n.,* enclosed body of

lȧ'mȧ, *n.,* Buddhist monk

lāme, *a.,* crippled, weak; **-ly; -ness**

lȧ-mĕnt', *v.,* mourn, grieve; **-ed; -ation; -able; -ably**

lăm'ĭ-nāte, *v.,* form into or cover with thin layers; **tor; tion; -d**

lămp, *n.,* device for producing light

lăm'poon, *n.,* satire; *v.,* mock [mal

lăm'prēy, *n.,* eellike animal

lănce, *n.,* long spear; **-r**

lănd, *n.,* solid part of earth, soil, ground; *v.,* go on shore, catch; **-ed**

lăn'dău, *n.,* carriage

lănd'lôrd, *n.,* property leaser

lănd'scāpe, *n.,* natural scenery; *v.,* plant lawns and gardens

lănd'slīde, *n.,* sliding down of land, great victory [road

lāne, *n.,* narrow path or

lăn'guȧge, *n.,* means of communication, speech

lăn'guĭsh, *v.,* become weak, suffer; **-er; -ment**

lănk, *a.,* tall and lean; **-y** *a.;* **-ly; -ness**

lăn'o-lĭn, *n.,* oil from wool as ointment base

lăn'têrn, *n.,* portable case for light

lăn'yȧrd, *n.,* rope, cord

lȧ-pĕl', *n.,* folded part of coat's front

lăp'ĭ-dār-ў, *n.,* gem expert

lăpse, *n.,* fault, passing of time; *v.,* backslide, fall end; **-r; lapsable**

lâr'cĕ-nў, *n.,* theft

lârch, *n.,* pine tree

lârd, *n.,* melted hog fat

lârd'êr, *n.,* pantry, food supplies

lârge-mĭnd-ĕd, *a.,* tolerant

lâr-gĕss', *n.,* generous giving [at end

lăr'ĭ-ȧt, *n.,* rope with loop

lârk, *n.,* songbird, fun

lâr'vȧ, *n.,* immature insect

lâr'ўnx, *n.,* voice organ at top of windpipe; **yngeal; yngitis**

lȧs-cĭv'ĭ-oŭs, *a.,* lustful; **-ly; -ness**

lā'sêr, *n.,* device emitting intense light

L
M

lăsh, *n.,* whip, whip stroke; *v.,* strike, tie with rope; **-ing** *n.*

lăs'sĭ-tŭde, *n.,* tiredness

lăst, *n.,* end; *v.,* continue; *a.,* most recent, final; **-ly**

lătch, *n.,* door fastener of bar fitting into notch

lā'tĕnt, *a.,* undeveloped, hidden; **tency; -ly**

lăt'ĕr-ăl, *a.,* sideways; **-ly**

lā'tĕx, *n.,* milky plant or tree liquid

lāthe, *n.,* machine for shaping wood, metal, etc.

lăth'ĕr, *n., v.,* foam; **-y** *a.*

lăt'ĭ-tŭde, *n.,* distance in degrees from equator, scope, freedom; **dinal; dinally**

lăt-ĭ-tū-dĭ-nār'ĭ-ăn, *a.,* very tolerant; **-ism**

lȧ-trīne', *n.,* toilet

lăt'tĭce, *n.,* criss-crossed wooden bars

lăud, *n., v.,* praise; **-ation; -atory; -able; -ability; -ably**

lăugh, *v.,* express merriment orally; **-able; -ably**

lăunch, *v.,* send off, start; **-er**

lăun'dĕr, *v.,* wash and iron (clothes); **-er; dress; dry**

lău'rē-āte, *n.,* one honored

lău'rĕl, *n.,* flowering evergreen, (*pl.*) fame

lăv'ȧ-tô-ry, *n.,* wash room

lăv'ĭsh, *v.,* spend freely; *a.,* more than enough; **-ly; -ness**

lăw, *n.,* rules of conduct, obedience, legal profession; **-ful; -fully; -fulness; -less, -lessly; -lessness**

lăwn, *n.,* grass-covered land

lăx'ȧ-tĭve, *n.,* substance to loosen bowels

lāy, *v.,* put down, place, produce eggs

lāy, *a.,* not professional; **laic; -man**

lāy'ĕr, *n.,* single thickness

lāy-ĕtte', *n.,* infant's full outfit

lāy'ŏff, *n.,* temporary discharge of workers

lā'zȳ, *a.* not eager to work, sluggish; **lazily; laziness**

lēa, *n.,* meadow

lēad, *n.,* first place, clue, main role; *v.,* guide, be first, spend; **-er; -ership; -ing** *n., a.*

lĕad, *n.,* metallic element, bullets, graphite

lēaf, *n.,* flat, green outgrowth of plant stem, page; **-age; -y** *a.*

lēague, *n.,* association, three miles

lēan, *v.,* incline, slant, rely, tend; **-er; -ing** *n.*

lēan, *a.,* with little fat, meager; **-ness; -ly**

lēap, *v.,* spring through air, jump; **-er**

lêarn, *v.,* get knowledge of; **-er; -ing** *n.;* **-ed; -able**

lēase, *n.,* rental contract; *v.,* rent, hire

lēash, *n.,* line to hold animal, ex. dog

lĕath'ĕr, *n.,* tanned animal skin; **-y** *a.*

lēave, *n.,* permission; *v.,* remain, entrust, go

lĕav'ĕn, *n.,* fermented dough, yeast; **-ing** *n.*

lĕch'ĕr, *n.,* lewd man; **-y; -ous; -ously; -ousness**

lĕc'tĕrn, *n.,* reading stand

lĕc'tûre, *n.,* informative talk, speech, scolding; **-r** [shelf

lĕdge, *n.,* narrow edge,

lĕdg'ĕr, *n.,* account book

lēe, *n.,* shelter from wind

lēech, *n.,* bloodsucking worm, parasite [ble

lēek, *n.,* onionlike vegeta-

lēer, *n.,* malicious look

lēe'wāy, *n.,* additional time or space

lĕg'ȧ-cȳ, *n.,* inheritance

lē'găl, *a.,* of law or lawyers, permitted; **-ity; -ize; -ization; -ly**

lė-gā'tion, *n.,* envoy and

staff and residence

lĕg′ĕnd,n., traditional tale, map key; **-ary**

lĕg′ĭ-ble, a., that can be read; **bility; bly**

lē′gĭon, n., military division, large number; **-ary**

lĕg′ĭs-lāte, v., make laws; **tor; tion; tive; tively**

lė-gĭt′ĭ-mȧte, a., lawful, born of a married couple; **macy; tion; mize; -ly** [pods; **minous**

lĕg′ūme, n., plant with

lēi′sûre, n., free time; a., idle; **-ly** [rus fruit

lĕm′ȯn,n., sour yellow cit-

lĕngth, n., measure from end to end, distance, duration; **-en; -y** a.

lē′nĭ-ĕnt, a., kind, merciful; **ency; ence; -ly**

lĕns, n., curved glass for adjusting light rays, focusing part of eye

lĕop′ȧrd,n., large spotted wild cat

lē′ȯ-târd, n., one-piece, tight garment

lĕp′rė-chaun (kŏn), n., elf in form of old man

lĕp′rȯ-sy, n., disease of skin and nerves; **leper; rous**

lē′sion, n., bodily injury

lĕs′sȯn, n., something learned, instruction

lĕst, conj., in case

lĕt, v., allow, rent, cause, leave [ment

lĕt′dŏwn, n., disappoint-

lē′thȧl, a., deadly; **-ity; -ly**

lĕth′ȧr-gy, n., lack of energy; **gic; gize**

lĕt′tėr, n., written message, character of alphabet

leū-kē′mĭ-ȧ, n., cancer of the blood; **mic** [bank

lĕv′ēe, n., built-up river

lĕv′ĕl,n., device for determining plane's evenness, horizontal plane, rank; a., even, flat; **-ness; -ly**

lĕv′êr, n., bar on support used to lift, **-age** [huge

lė-vī′ȧ-thȧn, n., anything

lĕv′ĭ-tāte, v., rise or float in air; **tor; tion**

lĕv′ĭ-ty,n., improper gaiety

lĕv′ÿ, n., tax; v., impose and collect (tax); **leviable** [-ly

lēwd, a., obscene; **-ness;**

lĕx′ĭ-cȯn, n., dictionary

lī′ȧ-ble, a., legally responsible, likely; **bility**

lī′ȧi-sȯn,n., connection for coordination

lī′ȧr, n., one who tells lies

lī′bĕl, n., malicious statement written to harm one's reputation; **-er; -ee; -ous; -ously**

lĭb′êr-ȧl, a., generous, large, tolerant, for reform; **-ity; -ly; -ness; -ism; -ize; -izer; -ization**

lĭb′êr-āte, v., set free; **tor; tion** [person

lĭb′êr-tĭne, n., immoral

lĭb′êr-ty, n., freedom, particular right, familiarity

lī′brȧr-ÿ, n., book collection; **brarian** [era; **tist**

lĭ-brĕt′tō, n., words of op-

lī′cĕnse, n., legal permit, freedom from rules; **-r; -e**

lī′chen (kĕn), n., mosslike plant; **-ous**

lĭc′ĭt, a., legal; **-ly; -ness**

lĭck, v., pass tongue over, (coll.) defeat; **-ing** n.

lĭc′ȯ-rĭce (rĭsh), n., black, sweet flavoring

lĭd, n., movable top

lie, n., false statement; v., tell falsehood, rest in flat position

lieū-tĕn′ȧnt, n., officer

life, n., existence, vigor, activity [ship

life′bōat,n., small boat on

life′guȧrd, n., swimming supervisor

lĭft, v., raise, (coll.) steal; **-er** [necting bones

lĭg′ȧ-mĕnt, n., tissue con-

light, n., energy that stimulates sight, brightness, light source, knowledge; v., brighten, set fire; a.,

bright, fair; **-er; -en;
-ness**

light, *a.,* not heavy, mild,
gay, dizzy; **-en; -ly;
-ness**

light-heârt'ėd, *a.,* gay; **-ly;
-ness** [to guide ships

light'hoŭse, *n.,* light tower

light'nĭng, *n.,* flash of electricity in sky

lĭg'nē-oŭs, *a.,* woody

lĭke, *a.,* similar; *prep.,* similar to, for example; *con.,*
as; **-n; -ness**

lĭke, *v.,* be fond of, wish

lĭke'lў, *a.,* probable; *adv.,*
probably

li'lăc, *n.,* flowering shrub,
pale purple

lĭlt, *n.,* light, swingy rhythm

lĭm'bêr, *a.,* easy to bend

lĭm'bō, *n.,* place of oblivion

lĭme, *n.,* sour green citrus
fruit, substance from
limestone [position

lĭme'lĭght, *n.,* prominent

lĭm'êr-ĭck, *n.,* nonsense
poem of five lines

lĭme'stŏne, *n.,* rock of cal-
cium carbonate

lĭm'ĭt, *n.,* end place or
point; *v.,* restrict; **-er;
-ation; -ative; -ary; -ed;
-less**

lĭm'ou-sĭne, *n.,* large luxury automobile

lĭmp, *v.,* walk lamely; **-er**

lĭmp'ėt, *n.,* mollusk

lĭm'pĭd, *a.,* clear; **-ity;
-ness; -ly**

lĭne, *n.,* rope, wire, etc.,
long thin mark, border,
series, path, stock of
goods; **-ar** *a.*

lĭn'ē-àge, *n.,* ancestry;
eal; eality; eally

lĭn'ėn, *n.,* fabric of flax

lĭn'gêr, *v.,* stay; **-er; -ing;
-ingly**

lin-ge-rie' (lăn-zė-rā'), *n.,*
lady's underwear

lĭn'gō, *n.,* jargon

lĭn-guĭs'tĭc, *a.,* of language; **guist; -s; -ally**

lĭn'ĭ-mėnt, *n.,* medicated
liquid for skin

lĭn'ĭng, *n.,* inside covering

lĭnk, *n.,* loop of chain, connection; *v.,* join; **-age**

lĭn'nėt, *n.,* songbird

lĭ-nō'lē-ŭm. *n.,* floor covering

lĭn'sēed, *n.,* seed of flax

lĭnt, *n.,* cotton fiber, thread
bits [brave

lĭ'ŏn-heârt-ėd, *a.,* very

lĭp'stĭck, *n.,* small stick of
paste to color lips

lĭq'uė-fў, *v.,* change to liquid; **fier; fiable**

lĭ-queûr', *n.,* sweet alcoholic beverage

lĭq'uĭd (wĭd), *n., a.,* (substance) that flows easily

lĭq'uĭ-dāte, *v.,* settle debt,
convert to cash; **tor; tion**

lĭq'uŏr, *n.,* alcoholic drink

lĭst, *n.,* series of items; *v.,*
set forth list, tilt, lean

lĭs'tėn, *v.,* hear, pay attention; **-er** [-ness

lĭst'lĕss, *a.,* spiritless; **-ly;**

lĭ'têr, *n.,* metric measure of
volume · [-ity; -ly

lĭt'êr-ál, *a.,* exact, factual;

lĭt'êr-à-tûre, *n.,* writings,
books; **ary**

lithe, *a.,* limber; **-ness; -ly**

lĭth'ĭ-ŭm, *n.,* metallic element

lĭ-thŏg'rà-phў, *n.,* printing
process; **graph** *n., v.;*
**pher; graphic; graphi-
cally**

lĭ-thŏl'ŏ-gў, *n.,* study of
rocks; **logic; logical;
logically**

lĭt-ĭ-gā'tĭon, *n.,* lawsuit;
gable; gious; giously

lĭt'ûr-gў, *n.,* religious ritual
for worship; **gist; gical;
gically**

lĭve, *v.,* have life, endure,
reside; **livable**

lĭve'lĭ-hŏŏd, *n.,* way of
supporting life, work

lĭve'lў, *a.,* full of life, energetic, gay, vivid

lĭv'êr, *n.,* glandular organ
secreting bile

lĭv'êr-ў, *n.,* care of horses
for a fee. [animals

lĭve'stŏck, *n.,* domestic

lĭv'ĭd, *a.,* bruised, pale,

(coll.) furious; **-ity; -ness**

lōad, *n.,* amount carried, burden; *v.,* fill, add to; **-er; -ing** *n.;* **-ed**

lōaf, *n.,* mass of baked bread

lōaf, *v.,* waste time; **-er**

lōaf'êr, *n.,* moccasinlike shoe

lōam, *n.,* rich soil

lōan, *n.,* something lent; *v.,* lend

lōathe, *v.,* hate; **-r; ing** *n.*

lŏb'bÿ, *n.,* entrance hall

lŏb'bÿ, *n.,* group influencing legislator; **-ist**

lōbe, *n.,* rounded projection

lŏb'stêr, *n.,* sea animal with large claws

lō'cál, *n.,* organization chapter; *a.,* of a particular place; **-ity; -ize; -ization; -ly**

lō'cāte, *v.,* find, establish, place; **-r; tion**

lŏck, *n.,* fastening device, canal section, hair curl *v.,* fasten, jam

lŏck'jäw, *n.,* tetanus

lō-cŏ-mō'tion, *n.,* movement; **tive** [gine

lō-cŏ-mō'tĭve, *n.,* train en-

lō'cŭst, *n.,* grasshopper-like insect, tree

lŏdge, *n.,* small house or hotel, local chapter; *v.,* house, be placed; **-r**

lŏft, *n.,* atticlike space

lŏg, *n.,* tree section, record of journey

lōge, *n.,* theater box

lŏg'ĭc, *n.,* reasoning, science of reasoning; **-al; -ally**

lŏĭn, *n.,* back from ribs to hips [**-er**

lŏĭ'têr, *v.,* spend time idly;

lŏll, *v.,* lounge, hang down

lōne, *a.,* by oneself; **-ly** *a.*

lŏng, *v.,* wish; **-ing** *n.*

lŏng, *a.,* having great length, too much time

lŏn'gĭ-tūde, *n.,* east or west distance across earth; **dinal; dinally**

lŏng'shôre-mán, *n.,* dock

worker

lŏŏk'ŏut, *n.,* careful watching, sentry

lŏŏm, *n.,* weaving machine *v.,* come into sight

lŏŏp, *n.,* line, string, etc. that curves back over itself

lŏŏp'hōle, *n.,* means of evasion or escape

lŏŏt, *n.,* stolen goods; *v.,* steal; **-er**

lŏp, *v.,* cut off; **-per** [**-r**

lōpe, *n.,* long easy stride;

lŏp'sĭd-éd, *a.,* unbalanced; **-ly; -ness**

lō-quā'cioŭs, *a.,* talkative; **city; -ness; -ly**

lôrd, *n.,* master, nobleman, (Lord) God; **-ly; -ship**

lôre, *n.,* knowledge

lose (lūs), *v.,* become unable to find, fail to keep or win; **-r; losable**

lŏss, *n.,* defeat, ruin, failure to keep, waste

lŏt, *n.,* fate, chance decision, share, piece of land, great number

lō'tion, *n.,* liquid for skin

lŏt'têr-ÿ, *n.,* game of selling chances on prizes

lō'tŭs, *n.,* water lily

lŏŭd'spēak-êr, *n.,* device to amplify sound

lŏŭnge, *n., v.,* (place to) rest or relax

lŏŭs'ÿ, *a.,* having lice, (coll.) dirty, poor; **lousily lousiness**

lou'vêr, *n.,* slanted boards in opening for air

lŏve, *n.,* great fondness for, devotion; *v.,* show love, delight in; **-r; lovable; lovably; loving; lovingly**

lōw'êr, *v.,* put down, make less; *a.,* below another, inferior, less

lōw'lÿ, *a.,* of low rank, humble, softly; **liness**

loy'ál (lŏĭ), *a.,* faithful; **-ty; -ly**

lū'brĭ-cāte, *v.,* make smooth, apply oil or grease; **tor; tion; tive;**

L
M

cant *n.*   [**-ness; -ly**
lū'cĭd, *a.*, sane, clear; **-ity;**
lŭck, *n.*, good fortune; **-y**
a.; **-ity; -iness; -less**
lū'crá-tĭve, *a.*, profitable;
-ly; -ness
lū'cŭ-brāte, *v.*, write or
study laboriously; **tion**
lū'dĭ-croŭs, *a.*, absurd; **-ly;**
-ness
lŭg'gáge, *n.*, suitcases,
trunks, etc.
lū-gū'brĭ-oŭs, *a.*, mournful; **-ly; -ness**
lŭll, *n.*, short quiet period;
v., soothe, calm
lŭm'bêr, *n.*, building
wood; *v.*, move heavily
lŭ-mĭ-nĕs'cénce, *n.*, giving off light; **cent**
lŭmp, *n.*, solid mass,
swelling; *v.*, group to-
gether; **-y** *a.;* **-iness**
lū'nár, *a.*, of the moon
lū'ná-tĭc, *n., a.*, (person
who is) insane; **nacy**
lŭng, *n.*, body organ for
breathing
lŭnge, *n.*, sudden thrust
lûrch, *n.*, danger; *v.*, sway
suddenly
lū'rĭd, *a.*, shocking, horrible **-ly; -ness**
lûrk, *v.*, stay hidden ready
to attack   [**-ly; -ness**
lŭs'cioŭs, *a.*, delicious;
lŭst, *n.*, strong craving,
sexual desire; **-ful;**
-fully; -fulness; -y *a.;*
-ily -iness
lŭs'têr, *n.*, brightness,
frame; **trous; trously;**
trousness   [ment
lūte, *n.*, guitarlike instru-
lŭx'ū-rÿ, *n.*, costly comfort
or pleasure; **rious;**
riously; riousness
lÿe, *n.*, strong alkali
lÿmph, *n.*, clear, yellowish
body fluid; **-atic**
lÿnch, *v.*, kill by mob; **-er;**
-ing *n.*
lÿnx, *n.*, wildcat
lÿre, *n.*, small harplike instrument
lÿr'ĭ-cĭst, *n.*, writer of words
in song

M

má-cà'brė, *a.*, gruesome
mác-ăd'ám, *n.*, road made
of crushed stone; **-ize**
măc-á-rō'nĭ, *n.*, tubular
noodles
má-căw', *n.*, large parrot
māce, *n.*, official staff,
spice
măc'êr-āte, *v.*, soften and
break down; **tor; tion**
măch-ĭ-nā'tion (măk), *n.*,
evil scheme
má-chīne', *n.*, device with
moving parts to do work;
chinist; -ry
măck'êr-ėl, *n.*, edible fish
măc'rá-me (mā), *n.*, art of
knotting   thread   into
designs   [verse; **-ic**
măc'rò-cŏsm, *n.*, uni-
măc-rò-scŏp'ĭc, *a.*, visible
to naked eye
măd, *a.*, insane, frantic,
foolish, angry; **-ness;**
-den; -ly   [woman
măd'ám, *n.*, polite title for
măd'căp, *n.*, reckless
person   [cloth
măd'rás, *n.*, fine cotton
măd'rĭ-gál, *n.*, song with
many singing parts
maes'trō (mīs), *n.*, com-
poser, orchestra con-
ductor
măg-á-zīne', *n.*, periodical
publication,   storage
place   [plish-red
má-gĕn'tá, *n., a.*, pur-
măg'gót, *n.*, wormlike insect larva
măg'ĭc, *n.*, use of charms,
spells, tricks of illusion;
-ian *n.;* **-al; -ally**
măg'ĭs-trāte, *n.*, judge;
tracy; tratical
măg'má, *n.*, liquid or mol-
ten rock
măg-năn'ĭ-moŭs, *a.*, generous; **nimity; -ly**
măg'nāte, *n.*, influential
person   [very metal
măg-nē'sĭ-ŭm, *n.*, light sil-
măg'nét, *n.*, iron or steel
that attracts iron or steel;
-ism; -ize; -ic; -ically

măg-nĭf'ĭ-cĕnt, a., splendid; **cence; -ly**

măg'nĭ-fÿ, v., make larger; **fier; fication**

măg'nĭ-tūde, n., greatness of size or influence

măg-nō'lĭ-à, n., flowering tree

măg'pīe, n., kind of crow

mà-hŏg'à-nÿ, n., tree, dark, heavy wood

māid, n., young woman, female servant

māil, n., letters, packages, etc., postal system; v., send by mail; **-man; -er; -ing** n.; **-able; -ability**

māil, n., metal mesh armor

māim, v., cripple, disable; **-er** [portant; **-ly**

māin, a., chief, most im-

māin-tāin', v., continue, keep in repair, support; **tenance**

māize, n., corn, yellow

măj'ĕs-tÿ, n., dignity, grandeur, ruler's title; **tic; tical, tically**

mā'jŏr, n., military officer, main subject; a., main, greater [half

mà-jôr'ĭ-tÿ, n., more than

māke, n., brand; style; v., bring into being, cause to be, amount to, earn, perform, force; **-r; ing** n.

māke'shĭft, a., temporary

māke'-ŭp, n., construction, nature, cosmetics

măl-à-drŏit', a., awkward; **-ly; -ness**

măl'à-dÿ, n., disease

măl'à-prŏp, n., ludicrous misuse of words; **-ism**

mà-lār'ĭ-à, n., infectious disease; **-l; ious**

măl'cŏn-tĕnt, a., dissatisfied

mà-lĕf'ĭ-cĕnt, a., harmful; **cence**

mà-lĕv'ŏ-lĕnt, a., wishing evil; **lence; -ly**

măl-fēa'sànce, n., wrongdoing; **sant**

măl'īce, n., desire to harm; **cious; ciously; ciousness**

mà-līgn', v., speak evil of; a., evil; **-er**

mà-līg'nànt, a., harmful; likely to cause death; **nancy; -ly**

mà-līn'gêr, v., fake illness to escape work; **-er**

māll, n., shaded public walk, shopping center

măl'lärd, n., duck

măl'lē-à-ble, a., can be reshaped; **bility; -ness**

măl'lĕt, n., wooden hammer

măl-nū-trĭ'tion, n., faulty diet [improper practice

măl-prăc'tĭce, n., doctor's

mălt, n., barley used in brewing; **-y; -iness**

măm'măl, n., class of animals who feed on milk from breast

măm'mā-rÿ, a., of breast

măm'mòn, n., riches

măm'mŏth, n., extinct elephant; a., huge

măn, n., human being, adult male, human race; v., supply people; **-hood; -ly**

măn'à-cle, n., handcuff

măn'āge, v., control, conduct, operate; **-r; -ment; -able; -ability; -ableness; -ably**

măn'dāte, n., order, people's will; **tory; tary**

măn'dŏ-lĭn, n., stringed instrument [hair

māne, n., animal long neck

mà-neū'vêr, n., planned military movement; v., scheme; **-ability; -able**

măn'gà-nēse, n., grayish metallic element

măn'gêr, n., trough to hold hay

măn'gle, v., disfigure; **-r**

măn'gō, n., tropical fruit

măn'gÿ, a., shabby; **gily; giness**

măn'ĭ-cūre, n., care of fingernails; **curist**

măn'ĭ-fĕst, n., cargo list; v., make clear; a., obvious; **-ation; -able; -ly**

măn-ĭ-fĕs'tō, n., public

declaration

măn'ĭ-fōld, v., multiply; a., many; **-er; -ness; -ly**

mà-nĭp'ū-lāte, v., handle, control; **tor; tion; lable; tive; tory**

măn'nė-quĭn, n., model of human body

măn'nêr, n., way, style, behavior, (pl.) social customs; **-less; -ly**

măn'ŏr, n., large estate

măn'pŏw-êr, n., human strength [dence

măn'sion, n., large resi-

măn'slăugh-têr, n., accidental killing of person

măn'tėl, n., shelf above fireplace

măn'tĭs, n., insect

măn'tle, n., cloak, cover

măn'ū-ȧl, n., handbook; a., of or by hand; **-ly**

măn-ū-făc'tûre, v., make by machinery; **-r**

mà-nūre', n., animal waste as fertilizer

măn'ū-scrĭpt, n., author's written composition; a., written by hand

măp, n., drawing of earth's surface or sky; v., make a map, plan

mā'ple, n., tree for wood, sap and shade

măr, v., damage, spoil

măr'à-boū, n., large stork

măr'à-thŏn, n., foot race, endurance contest

mà-räud'êr, n., raider

măr'ble, n., hard ornamental limestone

mârch, n., steady advance, progress; v., walk at steady pace; **-er**

māre, n., female horse, sea

măr'gà-rĭne, n., butter substitute

măr'gĭn, n., edge, limit, amount in reserve; **-al; -ality; -ally**

mă-rĭ-jua'nȧ (wȧ), n., plant, drug

mà-rĭ'nȧ, n., yacht harbor

măr-ĭ-nāde', n., tasty solution to soak food in before cooking; **nate**

mà-rīne', n., member of Marine Corps; a., of sea, ships, etc.

măr-ĭ-ȯ-nĕtte', n., puppet operated by strings

măr'ĭ-tȧl, a., of marriage; **-ly**

mâr'jȯ-ràm, n., spice

mârk, n., visible impression, sign, grade, target; v., make a mark, rate; **-er**

măr'kėt, n., place to buy and sell goods; v., sell; **-ing** n.; **-able; -ability**

mărks'màn, n., one who shoots well; **-ship**

mâr'lĭn, n., deep-sea fish

mà-rōōn', n., a., brownish red; v., abandon, leave

măr'rōw, n., soft core inside bones

măr'rÿ, v., join a man and woman legally; **riage; ried; riageable**

mârsh, n., low, wet, soft land; **-y** a. [official

mâr'shȧl, n., high ranking

mâr-sū'pĭ-ȧl, n., mammal with pouch for young

mârt, n., market

mâr'tėn, n., weasellike animal with valuable fur

mâr'tiȧl, a., of war, military; **-ist; -ism; -ly**

mâr'tÿr, n., one who suffers for beliefs; **-dom; -ize; -ization**

mâr'vėl, n., wonderful thing; v., be amazed; **-ous; -ously; -ousness**

măs-că'rȧ, n., cosmetic to color eyelashes

măs'cŏt, n., thing or animal kept for good luck

măs'cū-lĭne, a., male; **linity; -ly**

măsk, n., covering for face

măs'ŏch-ĭsm, n., pleasure from suffering; **ochist; ochistic; ochistically**

mā'sȯn, n., worker in stone or brick; **-ry**

măs-quêr-āde', n., costume party; **-r**

măss, n., large quantity, lump of matter

măs'sà-cre (kêr), n.,

slaughter of many people

măs-sāge′, *n.*, rubbing or kneading body; **seur** *n.*; **seuse** *n.*

măst, *n.*, pole for ship's sail

măs-tĕc′tȯ-mȳ, *n.*, surgical removal of breast

măs′têr, *n.*, man who rules others, owner, expert; **-ful; -fully; -fulness**

măs′têr-pīēce, *n.*, great work of art

măs′tĭ-cāte, *v.*, chew; **tor; tion; tory**

măs′tŭr-bā-tion, *n.*, sexual self-stimulation; **bate; tor**

măt, *n.* small rug, pad, border around picture

măt′ȧ-dôr, *n.*, bullfighter

mătch, *n.*, small stick that ignites, like thing, contest, marriage; *v.*, mate, be equal

māte, *n.*, one of pair, spouse, ship's officer

mȧ-tē′rĭ-ȧl, *n.*, what thing is made of, fabric; *a.*, of matter, physical, essential; **-ity; -ize; -ization; -ly**

mȧ-têr′nȧl, *a.*, of or like mother; **nity; -ly**

măt-ĭ-nee′ (nā), *n.*, afternoon performance

mā′trĭ-ârch, *n.*, woman as head of family; **-y; -al; -ic** [college; **tion**

mȧ-trĭc′ū-lāte, *v.*, enroll in

măt′rĭ-mō-nȳ, *n.*, marriage; **nial; nially**

mā′trĭx, *n.*, mold

mā′trȯn, *n.*, married woman, woman supervisor; **-ly; -liness**

măt′têr, *n.*, physical substance of thing, importance, trouble

măt′tȯck, *n.*, garden tool

măt′trėss, *n.*, cloth case used on bed

mȧ-tūre′, *v.*, develop fully; *a.*, full grown, ripe; **ration; rity; -ly; -ness**

māud′lĭn, *a.*, sentimental

māul, *n.*, large hammer; *v.*, beat; **-er** [tomb

māu-sȯ-lē′ŭm, *n.*, large

māuve, *n.*, *a.*, pale purple

măx′ĭm, *n.*, concise principle

măx′ĭ-mŭm, *n.*, upper limit, greatest amount; **mize; mal**

māy-ȯn-nāise′, *n.*, creamy salad dressing [**-al**

māy′ȯr, *n.*, head of city;

māze, *n.*, intricate network of paths

mĕad′ōw, *n.*, field of grass

mēa′gêr, *a.*, thin, of poor quality; **-ly; -ness**

mēal, *n.*, time for eating, coarsely ground grain

mēan, *v.*, have in mind, intend; **-ing** *n.*; **-ingful; -ingfully; -ingless; -inglessly; -inglessness**

mēan, *a.*, poor, low, cruel, difficult; **-ness; -ly**

mēan, *n.*, average (*pl.* wealth, resources

mē′ăn-dêr, *v.*, roam; **drous**

mēa′slės, *n.*, contagious disease with red spots; **sly**

mĕas′ûre, *n.*, size, amount, system of dimensions, step, law; *v.*, determine extent of, judge; **-ment; -d**

mĕat, *n.*, animal flesh as food, meaning; **-y** *a.*; **-iness; -less**

mė-chăn′ĭ-cȧl (kăn), *a.*, of machines; **-ly; nize; nizer; nization**

mĕd′ȧl, *n.*, metal piece as an award; **-ist**

mĕd′dle, *v.*, interfere; **-r**

mē′dĭ-ȧn, *n.*, midpoint; **al; ally**

mē′dĭ-āte, *v.*, settle a dispute; **tor; tion; tive; tory**

mĕd′ĭ-cīne, *n.*, science of disease and health, drug for treatment; **cate; cation; cal; cally; nal; nally**

mĕ-di-ē′vȧl, *a.*, of period (700–1400 A.D.)

mē-dĭ-ō'cre (cêr), a., ordinary, average; **rity**

mĕd'ĭ-tāte, v., think about;
tor; tion; tive

mē'dĭ-ŭm, n., middle state,
culture, agency; a.,
average [things

mĕd'lĕy, n., mixture of

mēek, a., mild, humble;
-ly; -ness

mēet, v., come together
with, see arrival of, deal
with; **-ing** n.

mĕg-ȧ-lō-mā'nĭ-ȧ, n., passion for grandeur

mĕg-ȧ-lŏp'ȯ-lĭs, n., large
dense urban area

mĕl'ȧn-chŏl-ў (kŏl), n.,
sadness; **cholic; choli-
cally**

mĕl'ĭȯ-rāte, v., improve;
tor; tion; tive; rable

mĕl'lōw, a., ripe, full, rich

mĕl'ȯ-drȧ-mȧ, n., sensa-
tional stage play; **-tist;
-tic; -tics; -tically**

mĕl'ȯ-dў, n., tune, song;
**dize; lodic; lodically;
dious; diously; dious-
ness**

mĕl'ȯn, n., large, juicy,
thick-skinned fruit

mĕlt, v., change from solid
to liquid, heat, soften;
-age

mĕm'bêr, n., part of whole,
one who officially be-
longs; **-ship**

mĕm'brāne, n., thin, soft
skin layer; **nous; nously**

mē-mĕn'tō, n., souvenir

mĕm-ȯ-rȧ-bĭl'ĭ-ȧ, n.,
things worth remember-
ing [to remind

mĕm-ȯ-răn'dŭm, n., note

mē-mô'rĭ-ȧl, n., thing to
help one remember; **-ize**

mĕm'ȯ-rў, n., mental
power to retain past
things

mē-năg'êr-iē, n., collec-
tion of animals

mĕnd, v., repair, improve;
-er; -able

mĕn-dā'ciŏŭs, a., not
truthful; **dacity; -ly;
-ness**

mĕn'dĭ-cȧnt, n., beggar

mē'nĭ-ȧl, a., servile, low;
-ly

mĕn-ĭn-gī'tĭs, n., inflammation of brain tissue

mĕn-strŭ-ā'tion, n.,
monthly blood dis-
charge from uterus;
strate; strual

mĕn-sŭ-rā'tion, n., act of
measuring; **able; abil-
ity; ral; tive**

mĕn'tȧl, a., of the mind,
mentally ill; **-ity; -ly**

mĕn'thōl, n., mint derivative

mĕn'tion, n., brief reference; v., speak about;
-able

mêr'cȧn-tĭle, a., of mer-
chant or trade

mêr'cė-nār-ў, a., inter-
ested in money only,
greedy

mêr'chȧn-dīse, n., goods
bought and sold; **-r**

mêr'cŭ-rў, n., heavy me-
tallic element; **rial; rially; rialness; ric; rous**

mêr'cў, n., kindness, forgiveness; **ciful; cifully;
cifulness; ciless; ci-
lessly; cilessness**

mēre, a., only; **-ly**

mêrge, v., combine, mix;
-nce

mė-rĭd'ĭ-ȧn, n., highest
point, circle through
earth's poles

mė-ringue' (răng'), n.,
beaten eggs and sugar
baked

mĕr'ĭt, n., worth, honor; v.,
deserve; **-orious; -or-
iously; -oriousness;
-less**

mêr'māid, n., imaginary
creature of half woman
and fish

mĕsh, n., net; v., entangle,
interlock; **-y** a.

mĕs'mêr-ize, v., hypno-
tize; **-r; zation; ism**

mĕss, n., communal meal,
jumble, untidy state; v.,
make dirty, meddle; **-y**
a. [cation, idea

měs'såge, *n.*, communi-

mė-tăb'ò-lĭsm, *n.*, conversion of food to energy; **lize; bolic**

mět'ål, *n.*, shiny, solid malleable chemical element; **-ist; -ize; -lic; -lically**

mět'ål-lûr-gÿ, *n.*, science of metals; **gist; gic; gical; gically**

mět-à-môr'phò-sǐs, *n.*, change in form

mět'à-phôr, *n.*, term or phrase of one meaning applied to another; **-ic; -ical; -ically**

mět-à-phŷs'ĭcs, *n.*, philosophy of abstract principles; **ical; ically**

mēte, *v.*, apportion

mē'tē-ör, *n.*, flash of heavenly body entering earth's atmosphere

mē-tē-ör-ŏl'ò-gÿ, *n.*, study of weather and climate; **gist; logical; logically**

mē'têr, *n.*, verse or musical rhythm, unit of length, measuring device; **tric; trical; trically**

měth'āne, *n.*, gas

měth'ŏd, *n.*, orderly procedure; **-ology; ologist; -ical; -ically**

mė-tĭc'ū-loŭs, *a.*, very careful; **losity; -ly; -ness** [city; **itan** *a.*

mė-trŏp'ò-lĭs, *n.*, large

mět'tle, *n.*, courage

měz'zà-nīne, *n.*, floor between two main floors

mez'zō (met), *a.*, musical middle [layer

mi'cà, *n.*, mineral of thin

mi'crò-cŏsm, *n.*, world in miniature; **-ic; -ically**

mi'crò-fĭlm, *n.*, film that copies records in reduced size

mi-crŏm'è-têr, *n.*, device for measuring tiny distances

mi'crò-phōne, *n.*, device that transmits sounds; **phonic**

mi'crò-scōpe, *n.*, device

that enlarges tiny objects

mǐd'dle, *a.*, halfway between two things

mǐd'dle-măn, *n.*, trader who buys from producer and sells to retailer

mǐdge, *n.*, gnatlike insect

mǐdg'ėt, *n.*, very small person; *a.*, miniature

mǐd'rǐff, *n.*, body part between chest and abdomen

mǐd'shǐp-màn, *n.*, student at U.S. Naval Academy

mǐd'wīfe, *n.*, woman who helps another in childbirth; **-ry**

miēn, *n.*, one's manner

mīght, *n.*, strength; **-y** *a.*; **-ily; -iness**

mi'grāine, *n.*, intense headache

mi'grāte, *v.*, move from one place to another; **tion; tory; ant**

mǐl, *n.*, one thousandth of an inch

mild, *a.*, soft, gentle, moderate; **-ly; -ness**

mǐl'dew, *n.*, fungus on things caused by dampness

mile, *n.*, unit of length, 5,280 feet [event

mile'stōne, *n.*, important

mǐ-lieŭ', *n.*, environment

mǐl'ǐ-tànt, *a.*, aggressive; **tancy; -ly**

mǐl'ǐ-tär-ÿ, *a.*, of or by soldiers or war; **tarily; rism; rist; rize**

mǐlk, *n.*, white liquid from female mammals; **-y** *a.*

mǐll, *n.*, grinding machine, factory; *v.*, process in mill, move aimlessly

mǐl-lěn'nǐ-ŭm, *n.*, 1,000 years, period of peace; **nial**

mǐl'lėt, *n.*, cereal grain

mǐl'lǐ-mē-têr, *n.*, one thousandth of a meter

mǐl'lǐ-něr-ÿ, *n.*, women's hats [chanic

mǐll'wrǐght, *n.*, mill me-

mǐm'ē-ò-grăph, *n.*, *v.*,

(machine to) stencil many copies

mĭm′ĭc, *n.,* one who copies; *v.,* imitate; **-ry; -ker**

mĭnce, *v.,* chop up, weaken; **-r**

mĭnd, *n.,* organ that thinks, intelligence; *v.,* obey, care for, object

mĭne, *n.,* excavation to get minerals, gems, etc., large supply, explosive hidden under enemy; *v.,* dig in mine; **-r; mining**

mĭn′êr-ål, *n.,* substance found in earth; **-ize; -izer; -ization; -ogy**

mĭn′gle, *v.,* mix; **-r**

mĭn′ĭ-mŭm, *a.,* smallest possible; **mize; mizer; mization; mal; mally**

mĭn′ĭs-têr, *n.,* person acting for another, diplomat, clergyman; **try; tration; trative; -ial; -ially**

mĭnk, *n.,* brown weasel with valuable fur

mĭn′nōw, *n.,* small fish

mĭ′nôr, *a.,* lesser, under legal age; **-ity**

mĭn′strĕl, *n.,* performer

mĭnt, *n.,* government place where money is made, **-age**

mĭnt, *n.,* aromatic plant

mĭ′nŭs, *a.,* negative; *prep.,* less

mĭ-nūte′, *a.,* tiny; **-ly; -ness**

mĭr′å-cle, *n.,* event that seems to go against scientific fact; **raculous; raculously; raculousness** [sion

mĭ-râge′, *n.,* optical illusion

mĭr′rör, *n.,* glass that reflects image

mĭrth, *n.,* gaiety with laughter; **-ful; -fully; -fulness; -less; -lessly; -lessness**

mĭs′ån-thrōpe, *n.,* hater of all people; **thropy; thropic; thropical; thropically**

mĭs-căr′rȳ, *v.,* go wrong, lose a fetus before full term; **riage**

mĭs-cêl-lā′nē-oŭs, *a.,* varied, mixed; **ny; -ly; -ness**

mĭs′chĭef, *n.,* harm, prank, teasing; **chievous; chievously; chievousness** [ancy

mĭs′crē-ånt, *n.,* villain;

mĭs-dė-mēan′ör, *n.,* minor legal offense [-ly

mĭ′sêr, *n.,* stingy person;

mĭs′êr-ȳ, *n.,* suffering, wretchedness; **erable; erably; erableness**

mĭs-nō′mêr, *n.,* name wrongly applied

mĭs′sĭle, *n.,* object thrown or shot

mĭs′sion, *n.,* special task, delegation, religious errand

mĭs′sión-ār-ȳ, *n.,* church person sent to make converts

mĭs′sĭve, *n.,* letter

mĭst, *n.,* water vapor, thin fog; **-y** *a.;* **-ily; -iness**

mĭs′tle-tōe, *n.,* evergreen plant with white berries

mĭs′trĕss, *n.,* female in control, unmarried woman living with man

mīte, *n.,* tiny parasite

mĭ′têr, *n.,* angled joint, bishop's hat

mĭt′ĭ-gāte, *v.,* lessen; **tor; tion; tive, tory; gable**

mĭ-tō′sĭs, *n.,* simple cell division; **totic totically**

mĭtt, *n.,* baseball glove

mĭx′-ŭp, *n.,* confusion

mōan, *n.,* low, mournful sound; *v.,* bewail, complain

mōat, *n.,* deep ditch around castle

mōb, *n.,* disorderly crowd; *v.,* crowd around

mō′bĭ-līze, *v.,* put into use; **-r; zation; lizable**

mŏc′cå-sĭn, *n.,* soft heelless leather shoe

mŏck, *v.,* ridicule, mimic; *a.,* false; **-er; -ery; -ingly**

mōde, *n.,* fashion, method

mŏd′él, *n.,* small copy, one

to imitate, style, artist's subject; *v.*, form, display clothing; **-er**

mŏd′êr-āte, *v.*, preside make calm; **tor**

mŏd′ĕr-ȧte, *n.*, *a.* (person) avoiding excesses; **tion**

mŏd′ĕrn, *a.*, of present times, new; **-ly; -ness**

mŏd′ĕst, *a.*, shy, humble, decent; **-y; -ly**

mŏd′ūle, *n.*, architectural unit of measurement; **lar** *a.*

mō′hāir, *n.*, goat hair cloth

moĭst, *a.*, slightly wet, damp; **-en; -ener; -ure; -ly; -ness**

mō′lȧr, *n.*, large back tooth

mȯ-lăs′sės, *n.*, thick dark syrup

mōld, *n.*, *v.*, pattern, shape, influence; **-er; -able**

mōld, *n.*, fungus growth on organic matter; **-y** *a.*

mōld′ĭng, *n.*, decorative strip of wood

mōle, *n.*, dark spot on skin, small burrowing mammal

mŏl′ė-cūle, *n.*, smallest whole part of an element; **lar** [**-er; -ion**

mȯ-lĕst′, *v.*, annoy, harm;

mŏl′lĭ-fȳ, *v.*, pacify, soothe; **fier; fication**

mŏl′lŭsk, *n.*, soft-bodied animal enclosed in shell

mōlt, *v.*, shed hair, skin, etc. before getting new growth

mō′mėnt, *n.*, very brief time, importance; **-ary; -arily; -ly**

mō-mĕn′tŭm, *n.*, force of moving object

mŏn′ȧrch, *n.*, sole ruler; **-y; -al; -ally; -ical; -ically; -ism; -ist**

mŏn′ȧs-tĕr-ȳ, *n.*, monks' residence; **tic; tical; tically**

mŏn′ė-tär-ȳ, *a.*, of money, financial; **tarily**

mŏn′ēy, *n.*, medium of exchange or value, wealth; **-ed; -less**

mŏn′gêr, *n.*, dealer, trader

mŏn′grėl, *n.*, *a.* (animal or plant) of mixed breed

mŏn′ĭ-tōr, *n.*, *v.* (person or thing that can) watch, check, warn

mŏnk, *n.*, male religious recluse

mŏn-ȯ-chrō-măt′ĭc, *a.*, of one color; **-ally**

mŏn′ȯ-cle, *n.*, single eyeglass

mȯ-nŏg′ȧ-mȳ, *n.*, marriage to one person at a time; **mist; mous; gamic**

mŏn′ȯ-grăm, *n.*, initials of one's name in design

mŏn′ȯ-grăph, *n.*, scholarly writing on one subject; **-ic** [block; **-ic**

mŏn′ȯ-lĭth, *n.*, single stone

mŏn′ȯ-lŏgue, *n.*, dramatic act for one; **loguist**

mȯ-nŏp′ȯ-lȳ, *n.*, exclusive control of commodity; **list; lize; lizer; lization**

mŏn′ȯ-thē-ĭsm, *n.*, belief in one god; **ist; istic; istical; istically**

mȯ-nŏt′ȯ-nȳ, *n.*, lack of variety, boredom; **nous; nously; nousness**

mŏn-soōn′, *n.*, seasonal wind; **-al**

mŏn′stêr, *n.*, abnormal thing, imaginary creature

mŏn′ū-mėnt, *n.*, memorial structure; **-al; -ally; -alize**

moōd, *n.*, state of mind

moōn, *n.*, planet's satellite

moōn′shīne, *n.*, moon's light, nonsense, unlawful whiskey

moôr, *n.*, open wasteland; *v.*, hold in place

moōt, *a.*, debatable

mŏp, *n.*, bunch of yarn on handle to wash floors, thick mass; *v.*, wipe clean

mōpe, *v.*, be gloomy; **-y** *a.*; **mopish; mopishly**

môr′ȧl, *n.*, *a.*, (standard) of right and wrong; *a.*, vir-

L
M

tuous, good; **-ity; -ist;
-ize; -ly**

mó-răle', *n.*, mental condition, ex. courage, zeal

mò-răss', *n.*, swamp

môr'bĭd, *a.*, diseased,
gruesome; **-ity; -ly;
-ness**

môre-ō'vêr, *adv.*, besides

mô'rēs, *n.*, customs

môrgue, *n.*, place for uni-
dentified bodies

mô'rŏn, *n.*, person with low
intelligence; **-ic**

mó-rōse', *a.*, gloomy; **-ly;
-ness**   [pain

môr'phĭne, *n.*, drug for

mor'rōw (mâr), *n.*, next
day   [food

môr'sėl, *n.*, small bit, as

môr'tăl, *a.*, that must die,
deadly, fatal; **-ity; -ly**

môr'tăr, *n.*, bowl with pes-
tle, cannon, plaster be-
tween bricks

mort'gage (môr), *n.*,
pledge of property for
security on debt; **-e; -r**

môr-tĭ'cĭán, *n.*, undertaker

môr'tĭ-fў, *v.*, humiliate,
shame; **fier; fication**

môr'tū-ār-ў, *n.*, place to
hold dead bodies

mō-sā'ĭc, *n.*, inlaid design
of stone, glass, etc.

mós-quĭ'tō, *n.*, small
blood-sucking insect

môss, *n.*, tiny green plant
on rock; **-y** *a.;* **-iness**

mō-tėl', *n.*, hotel for
motorists   [sect

môth, *n.*, four-winged in-

mō-tĭf', *n.*, main theme

mō'tion, *n.*, movement,
gesture, proposal; **-al;
-less; -lessly; -less-
ness**

mō'tĭve, *n.*, reason for action; **vate; vator; va-
tion; vational; vative**

mŏt'lėy, *a.*, varied

mō'tŏr, *n.*, engine that pro-
duces motion; *v.*, go by
auto; **-ist; -ize**

mŏt'tle, *v.*, blotch

mŏt'tō, *n.*, saying

mŏund, *n.*, small hill

mŏun'taĭn, *n.*, very high
land rise; **-ous; -ously**

môurn, *v.*, grieve; **-er; -ing**
n.; **-ful; -fully; -fulness**

move (mōov), *v.*, change
place, set in motion,
arouse, propose; **-r;
-ment**   [**-er**

mōw, *v.*, cut down (grass);

mū'cĭ-láge, *n.*, glue;
laginous   [**-y** *a.*

mŭck, *n.*, filth, black dirt;

mū'cŭs, *n.*, slimy body secretion; **cous**   [**-dy** *a.*

mŭd, *n.*, wet sticky earth;

mŭd'dle, *v.*, confuse

mŭff, *n.*, cylindrical fur
covering for hand

mŭf'fĭn, *n.*, small round
bread

mŭf'flêr, *n.*, warm neck
scarf, device to silence
noise

mŭg, *n.*, drinking cup; *v.*,
assault; **-ger**

mŭg'gў, *a.*, hot and damp;
giness

mŭlch, *n.*, rotted matter to
protect plants

mūle, *n.*, offspring of donkey and horse, stubborn
person; **mulish**

mŭll, *v.*, ponder

mŭl'lėt, *n.*, edible fish

mŭl'tĭ-ple, *a.*, of many
parts

mŭl'tĭ-plў, *v.*, increase,
add a number so many
times; **plier; plication;
plicative; pliable**

mŭl'tĭ-tūde, *n.*, large number, crowd; **tudinous;
tudinously**

mŭm'ble, *v.*, say indistinctly; **-r; blingly**

mŭm'mў, *n.*, ancient em-
balmed body

mŭmps, *n.*, disease of
glandular swelling

mŭn-dāne', *a.*, of the
world, ordinary; **-ly**

mū-nĭc'ĭ-pál, *a.*, of local
government; **-ity**

mū-nĭf'ĭ-cént, *a.*, very generous; **cence; -ly**

mū-nĭ'tions, *n. pl.*, war
supplies

mū′rål,n., a. (large picture painted) on wall
mûrk′ÿ, a., dark, gloomy
mûr′mür, n., soft steady sound; **-er; -ous**
mŭs′cle, n., fibrous tissue that moves body, strength; **cular** a.; **cularly**
mūse, v., ponder
mū-sē′ŭm, n., place for showing art
mŭsh, n., boiled corn meal; **-y** a.
mū′sĭc, n., rhythmic vocal and/or instrumental sounds; **-al; -ally; -ology**
mŭs′kĕt, n., long gun
mŭs′lĭn, n., sheer simple cotton cloth
mŭs′sėl, n., mollusk
mŭst, n., necessity; v., have to, be sure to
mŭs′têr, v., gather
mŭs′tÿ, a., stale, smelly **tily; tiness**
mū′tāte, v., undergo change; **tion; tional; tionally; table; tability; tably; tableness**
mūte, n., silent person; a., voiceless; **-ly; -ness**
mū′tĭ-lāte, v., maim, cut off, damage; **tor; tion; tive**
mū′tĭ-nÿ, n., revolt against authority; **nous; nously; nousness**
mŭt′tȯn, n., sheep meat
mū′tū-ål, a., interchangeable, shared jointly; **-ity; -ly**
mŭz′zle, n., snout, straps to keep mouth closed, gun's front end
mÿ-ō′pĭ-å, n., nearsightedness; **opic; opically**
mÿr′ĭ-åd,n., great number; a., countless
myr′tle (mîr),n., evergreen
mÿs′têr-ÿ, n., unexplained matter, secret; **rious; riously; riousness**
mÿs′tĭc, n., a. (believer) of magic power; **-al; -ally; -alness; -ism**

mÿth, n., traditional story explaining phenomena; **-ical, -ically; -ology**

N

nåb, v., catch
nå-cĕlle′,n., enclosed part of airplane
nā′dĭr, n., lowest point
någ, n., inferior horse; v., urge or scold constantly
nāil, n., thin horny end of fingers and toes, pointed metal piece to hold wood
nå-īve′, a., innocent, unsophisticated; **-té** n.; **-ly**
nā′kėd,a., without clothes, uncovered; **-ly; -ness**
nāme, n., word for person, place or thing, reputation; **-less** [say
nāme′lÿ, adv., that is to
nāme′sāke, n., person named for another
nåp, n., short sleep, hairy surface of cloth; v., doze
nā′pålm, n., substance in bomb
nāpe, n., back of neck
nåph′thå, n., oily liquid used as solvent, fuel
nåp′kĭn, n., cloth used on lap at mealtimes
nå-pō′lē-ȯn,n., old French coin, pastry
när′cĭs-sĭsm, n., self-love
när-cĭs′sŭs, n., bulbous plant
när-cŏt′ĭc,n., drug for pain or sleep [tion
năr′rāte, v., tell story; **tor;**
năr′rå-tĭve, n., story
năr′rȯw, a., thin in width, limited, biased
nā′sål, a., of nose; **-ity; -ly**
năs′cėnt, a., beginning; **cence; cency**
nå-stûr′tĭŭm, n., flower
năs′tÿ, a., filthy, offensive; **tily; tiness**
nā′tål, a., of birth
nā′tion, n., people organized as state; **-al; -ally**
nā′tion-ål-ĭsm, n., devotion to nation; **ist; istic;**

N O

istically [quality
nă-tion-ăl'ĭ-tў, n., national
nă'tĭve, a., inborn, of place
of origin, natural; -ly;
-ness
nă-tĭv'ĭ-tў, n., birth
năt'ŭ-răl, a., of nature, innate, normal. at ease; -ly
năt'ŭ-răl-īze, v., make a
citizen of; **ization**
nā'tûre, n., basic quality,
type, sort, physical uni-
verse; **turalist**
năught, n., zero, nothing
năugh-tў, a., mischievous;
bad; **tily; tiness**
nău'sē-ȧ, n., sick feeling
in stomach; -te; -nt;
**seous; seously;
seousness; -tinely**
nău'tĭ-căl, a., of sailors,
ships, navigation; -ly
nāve, n., main long part of
church
nā'věl, n., small depres-
sion in abdomen
năv'ĭ-gāte, v., steer ship
or plane, travel; **tor;
tion; tional; tionally;
gable; gability; gably**
nā'vў, n., nation's war-
ships, dark blue; **val**
nāy, n., vote of "no"
nēap, a., low as tide
nēar, v., approach; a.,
adv., close, almost;
prep., at short distance
nēar'bў', a., adv., close at
hand
nēar'lў, adv., almost
nēar-sight'ěd, a., seeing
items nearby well; -ly;
-ness
nēat, a., clean and orderly;
-en; -ly; -ness
něb'ŭ-lȧ, n., star cluster
něb'ŭ-loŭs, a., vague; **losity; -ly; -ness**
něc'és-săr-ў, a., needed,
required, essential; **sity;
sitate; sitation; sarily**
nė-cĕs'sĭ-toŭs, a., in great
need, urgent; -ly; -ness
něck, n., part joining head
to body, narrow part; v.,
caress [scarf
něck'êr-chĭef, n., neck

něck'lȧce, n., ornament
worn around neck
něck'wēar, n., articles
worn around neck
nė-crŏl'ȯ-gў, n., death notice
něc'tȧr, n., delicious beverage, liquid of flowers
něc-tȧr-ĭne', n., fruit
nēē, a., indicating
woman's maiden name,
born
nēed, n., thing required,
want, poverty; v., re-
quire; -er; -y a.; -ness;
-ful; -fully; -fulness;
-less; -lessly; -less-
ness
nēe'dle, n., slender
pointed metal piece for
sewing, injections,
phonograph, etc.
nēe'dle-wŏrk, n., fancy
sewing, embroidery
nė-fār'ĭ-oŭs, a., very
wicked; -ly; -ness
nė-gāte', v., deny; **tor;
tion**
něg'ȧ-tĭve, n., denial, a.,
saying "no," denying,
less than zero; **tivity; -ly;
-ness; tivism**
něg-lěct', n., lack of proper
care; v., fail to do or care
for; -er; -ful; -fully;
-fulness
něg-lĭ-gee' (gā), n.,
woman's dressing gown
něg'lĭ-gent, a., habitually
careless; **gence; -ly**
něg'lĭ-gĭ-ble, a., trifle;
gibility; gibly
nė-gō'tĭ-āte, v., discuss to
reach agreement, sell or
transfer; **tor; tion; able;
ability**
neigh (nā), n., horse's cry
neigh'bŏr (nā), n., person
living near another;
-hood; -ing; -ly; -liness
nēï'thêr, a., pro., conj., not
either
něm'ė-sĭs, n., retribution
nē-ȯ-lĭth'ĭc, a., of late
stone age
nē'ŏn, n., inert gaseous
element [fant

nē'ȯ-nāte, *n.*, newborn in-
nē'ȯ-phȳte, *n.*, new convert, amateur
nē-ȯ-tĕr'ĭc, *n.*, modern
person; *a.*, new; **-ally**
nė-phŏl'ȯ-gȳ, *n.*, study of
clouds; **gist; logical**
nė-phrī'tĭs, *n.*, kidney disease; **phritic**
nĕp'ȯ-tĭsm, *n.*, favoring
relatives in politics; **tist;
tistic**
nêrve, *n.*, cordlike fiber
sending impulse to and
from brain, courage
nêrve'lĕss, *a.*, without
courage, weak; **-ly;
-ness**
nêrv'oüs, *a.*, of nerves,
restless, tense; **vosity;
-ness**
nĕs'ci'ênt, *a.*, ignorant;
ence
nĕst, *n.*, place for birds,
fish to raise young; **-er;
-able** [snug; **-r**
nĕs'tle, *v.*, lie close and
nĕt, *n.*, meshed fabric; *v.*,
snare, clear as profit; *a.*,
final
nĕth'êr, *a.*, lower
nĕt'tle, *n.*, weed; *v.*, irritate, **-r; -some** *a.*
nĕt'wŏrk, *n.*, group of connected things
neü'rȧl, *a.*, of a nerve
neü-rȧl'giȧ, *n.*, pain along
nerve; **gic**
neü-rī'tĭs, *n.*, inflammation
of nerves; **ritic**
neü-rŏl'ȯ-gȳ, *n.*, study of
nervous system; **gist;
logical, logically**
neü-rō'sĭs, *n.*, emotional
disorder; **rotic; roti-
cally; roticism**
neü'têr, *a.*, neither male
nor female
neü'trȧl, *a.*, of neither side,
impartial; **-ity; -ism;
-ize; -izer; -ization; -ly**
neü'trŏn, *n.*, uncharged
particle of atom
nĕv'êr, *adv.*, at no time
nĕv-êr-môre', *adv.*, never
again [however
nĕv-êr-thė-lĕss', *adv.*,

nēw, *a.*, of first time, unfamiliar, recent; **-ly;
-ness** [rival
nēw'cȯm-êr, *n.*, recent ar-
nēw'făn-glėd, *a.*, new,
novel
nēw'lȳ-wĕd, *n.*, recently
married person
nēws, *n.*, new information,
report of recent events;
-y *a.*
nēws'cǎst, *n.*, news
broadcast; **-er; -ing** *n.*
nēws'lĕt-têr, *n.*, regularly
issued bulletin
nēws'pā-pêr, *n.*, news
publication
nēws'rēel, *n.*, short motion
picture of news
nēwt, *n.*, small salamander
nĕxt, *a.*, *adv.*, nearest;
prep., beside
nĕxt'dôor', *a.*, in or at
nearest building or
house
nĕx'ŭs, *n.*, connection
nĭb, *n.*, point, as pen
nĭb'ble, *v.*, take small bites
nīce, *a.*, pleasant, agreeable, good, delicate, re-
fined; **-ty; -ly; -ness**
nīche, *n.*, wall recess
nĭck, *n.*, small cut
nĭck'ĕl, *n.*, hard metallic
element, five cent coin;
-ic; -ous [piano
nĭck-ĕl-ō'dē-ȯn, *n.*, player
nĭck'nāme, *n.*, short substitute name
nĭc'ȯ-tīne, *n.*, poisonous
liquid in tobacco; **tinic**
nĭc'ti-tāte, *v.*, wink rapidly;
tion
nĭg'gȧrd, *a.*, stingy; **-ly;
-liness** [near
nīgh, *v.*, *a.*, *adv.*, *prep.*,
nīght, *n.*, darkness after
sunset [tertainment
nīght'clŭb, *n.*, place of en-
nīght'fǎll, *n.*, close of day,
dusk [gown
nīght'gōwn, *n.*, sleeping
nīght'ĭn-gāle, *n.*, thrush
nīght'lȳ, *a.*, *adv.*, every
night
nīght'māre, *n.*, frightening
dream; **marish**

ni'hil-ism, n., denial of law, religion, etc.; **ist; istic**

nil, n., nothing

nim'ble, a., agile, quick; **bly; -ness** [cloud

nim'bŭs, n., saint's halo,

nin'ny̆, n., fool

ni-ō'bi-ŭm, n., metallic element

nip, n., v., pinch, bite; n., small drink of liquor

nip'ple, n., breast part giving milk, nipplelike thing

nip'py̆, a., cold; **piness**

nit, n., egg or larva of a louse

nit'pick-ing, a., petty

ni'trāte, n., salt of nitric acid; v., make into nitrate; **tion**

ni'trô-gĕn, n., gaseous element essential to life; **-ize; trify; trifier; trification; tric; -ous**

ni-trô-glyc'êr-in, n., explosive oil

nit'wit, n., stupid person

nō, n., denial; a., not any; adv., not at all

nō-bil'i-ty̆, n., titled class

nō'ble, n., a., (one) of high rank; a., famous, highly moral, splendid; **bly; -ness**

nō'bŏd-y̆, n., pro., no one

nŏck, n., nock in bow or arrow [-ly

nŏc-tûr'năl, a., of night;

nŏc'tûrne, n., dreamy night music [-ness

nŏc'ū-oŭs, a., harmful; -ly;

nŏd, v., tilt head forward; -der [nodal

nōde, n., knot, swelling;

nŏd'ūle, n., small lump; **lar** a.; **lose** a.; **lous**

nŏg'gin, n., (coll.) head

nŏise, n., loud unpleasant sound; **-less; noisy** a.

nō'măd, n., wanderer; **-ism; -ic; -ically**

nō'mĕn-clā-tûre, n., system of names

nŏm'i-năl, a., in name only, very small; **-ly**

nŏm'i-nāte, v., appoint, select as candidate; **tor;**

nee; tion; tive

nŏn-, prefix, not

nŏn'ăge, n., state of being legally under age

nŏn-ă-gĕ-nār'i-ăn, n., one ninety years old

nŏn-chă-lănt', a., cool, indifferent; **lance; -ly**

nŏn-dĕ-scrĭpt', a., hard to describe

none (nŭn), n., a., not any; adv., not at all; pro., no one [tant person

nŏn-ĕn'ti̇-ty̆, n., unimportant

none-thĕ-lĕss (nŭn), adv., in spite of that

nŏn-môr'ăl, a., not moral or immoral

nŏŏk, n., corner

nŏŏse, n., rope loop, trap

nôr, conj., not either

nôrm, n., standard, average; **-ative; -atively**

nôr'măl, a., usual, natural; **-cy; -ity; -ize; -ly**

nôrth, n., direction to right when facing sunset; a., adv., in or of the north; **-erly; -ward, -wardly** a., adv.; **-ern** a.

nôrth-ēast', n., direction between north and east; **-erly, -ward, -wardly** a., adv.; **-ern** a.

nôrth-wĕst', n., direction between north and west; **-erly, -ward, -wardly** a., adv.; **-ern** a.

nōse, n., facial feature with openings for breathing and smelling; v., find by smell, meddle

nōse'gāy, n., small bouquet

nŏs-tăl'gi̇ă, n., longing for something; **gic; gically**

nŏs'trĭl, n., nose opening

nŏs'trŭm, n., remedy

nōs'y̆, a., curious, prying; **nosily; nosiness**

nŏt, adv., in no way

nō'tả-ble, n., a., (one who is) famous; **bly; bility**

nō'tả-rīze, v., certify; **zation**

nō-tā'tion, n., system of signs, note; **-al**

nŏtch, *n.,* V-shaped cut

nōte, *n.,* importance, mark, short writing, musical tone; *v.,* observe, indicate   [**-ness**

nōt'ĕd, *a.,* famous; **-ly;**

nōte'wŏr-thȳ, *a.,* outstanding; **thily; thiness**

nŏth'ĭng, *n.,* not anything, zero; **-ness**

nō'tĭce, *n.,* announcement, attention, *v.,* observe; **-able; -ably**

nō'tĭ-fȳ, *v.,* inform; **fier; fication; fiable** ·

nō'tion, *n.,* idea, small useful article; **-al**

nō-tô'rĭ-oŭs, *a.,* widely but unfavorably known; **riety; -ly; -ness**

nŏt-wĭth-stănd'ĭng, *adv., prep., conj.,* in spite of

noŭ'gàt, *n.,* chewy candy with nuts

noŭn, *n.,* name of person, place or thing

noûr'ĭsh, *v.,* feed, develop; **-er; -ment; -ing; -ingly**

nŏv'ĕl, *n.,* long fictional story; **-ist; -ize; -ization**

nŏv'ĕl, *a.,* new, unusual; **-ty**   [ateur

nŏv'ĭce, *n.,* beginner, am-

nŏw, *adv.,* at present, then; *conj.,* since

now'à-dāys, *n., adv.,* these days, at present

nō'whĕre, *n., adv.,* not in any place   [**-ness**

nŏx'ioŭs, *a.,* harmful; **-ly;**

nŏz'zle, *n.,* hose spout

nū'ànce, *n.,* slight difference

nū'bĭle, *a.,* marriageable; **bility**

nū'clē-ŭs, *n.,* central part ex. cell; **clear** *a.*

nūde, *a.,* unclothed; **nudity; -ly; -ness**

nūdge, *v.,* push gently; **-r**

nū'gà-tô-rȳ, *a.,* worthless

nŭg'gĕt, *n.,* lump of gold ore   [inconvenience

nūi'sànce, *n.,* annoyance,

nŭll, *a.,* not valid; **-ity; -ify; -ifier; -ification**

nŭmb, *a.,* not able to feel; **-ly; -ness**

nŭm'bêr, *n.,* symbol or word for how many, total; *v.,* count, limit

nŭm'bêr-lĕss, *a.,* countless   [ble

nū'mêr-à-ble, *a.,* counta-

nū'mêr-àl, *n.,* symbol for a number

nū'mêr-à-tōr, *n.,* counter, top part of fraction

nū-mĕr'ĭ-càl, *a.,* of number; **-ly**   [**-ness**

nū'mêr-oŭs, *a.,* many; **-ly;**

nū-mĭs-măt'ĭcs, *n.,* study or collection of money; **tist; ic**   [son

nŭm'skŭll, *n.,* stupid per-

nŭn, *n.,* religious woman living in convent

nŭn'nêr-ȳ, *n.,* convent

nŭp'tiàl, *n., pl.,* wedding; *a.,* of marriage

nûrse, *n., v.,* (person trained to) care for sick or young

nûrs'êr-ȳ, *n.,* room for children, place to raise plants, trees, etc.

nûr'tûre, *v.,* feed, train, raise; **-r; tural**

nŭt, *n.,* hard-shelled fruit, metal block with threaded hole for bolt; *pl.,* (coll.) crazy; **-ty** *a.*

nŭt'hătch, *n.,* bird

nŭt'mĕg, *n.,* spice

nū'trĭ-ĕnt, *a.,* nourishing

nū'trĭ-mĕnt, *n.,* food; **-al**

nū-trĭ'tion, *n.,* assimilation of food, study of proper diet; **-ist; tious; -al; -ally**

nŭz'zle, *v.,* rub nose against, snuggle; **-r**

nȳ'lŏn, *n.,* synthetic material   [maiden

nȳmph, *n.,* goddess,

O

ōaf, *n.,* clumsy person

ōak, *n.,* tree; **-en** *a.*

ôar, *n.,* rowing implement

ō-ā'sĭs, *n.,* place with water in desert

ōat, *n.,* cereal grain; **-en**

NO

a. [tion, curse
ōath, *n.*, formal declara-
ŏb′dū-ràte, *a.*, inflexible,
stubborn; **racy; -ly**
ō-bei′sànce (bā), *n.*,
showing of respect; **sant**
ŏb′è-lĭsk, *n.*, tall four-sided
pillar with pointed top
ō-bēse′, *n.*, very fat; **sity**
ō-bey′ (bā), *v.*, follow or-
ders; **-er**
ŏb′fŭs-cāte, *v.*, confuse;
tion [tice
ō-bĭt′ū-ār-ÿ, *n.*, death no-
ŏb′jĕct, *n.*, tangible thing,
recipient of action or
feeling, purpose; **-ive**
ŏb-jĕct′, *v.*, oppose; **-ion;
-ionable**
ŏb-jĕc′tĭve, *n.*, goal; *a.*,
real, without bias, fair;
tivity; -ly; -ness
ŏb′jûr-gāte, *v.*, scold, berate; **tor; tion; tory**
ŏb′lĭ-gāte, *v.*, bind by legal
or moral tie; **tion; tional;
tory** [-r; bliging
ò-blĭge′, *v.*, do a favor for;
ŏb-lĭque′, *a.*, slanting, indirect; **uity; -ly; -ness**
ŏb-lĭt′êr-āte, *v.*, erase; **tor;
tion; tive**
ŏb-lĭv′ĭ-oŭs, *a.*, forgetful,
unmindful; **ion; -ly;
-ness** [broad
ŏb′lŏng, *a.*, longer than
ŏb′lò-quÿ, *n.*, disgrace
from public blame
ŏb-nŏx′ioŭs, *a.*, unpleasant, offensive; **-ly; -ness**
ō′bōe, *n.*, woodwind musical instrument
ŏb-scēne′, *a.*, immoral,
lewd; **scenity; -ly**
ŏb-scūre′, *a.*, dark, not
clear, hidden; **rity; -ly;
-ness** [-ly; -ness
ŏb-sē′quĭ-oŭs, *a.*, servile;
ŏb-sêrv′à-tô-rÿ, *n.*, building for scientific obser-
vation
ŏb-sêrve′, *v.*, celebrate,
adhere to law, duty, etc.;
**-r; servance; servant;
servantly**
ŏb-sĕss′, *v.*, dwell in mind
persistently; **-ion; -ive;**

-ional; -ively; -iveness
ŏb-sò-lĕs′cènt, *a.*, going
out of use; **cence; -ly**
ŏb-sò-lēte′, *a.*, out of date,
old; **-ly; -ness**
ŏb′stà-cle, *n.*, hindrance
ŏb-stĕt′rĭcs, *n.*, medicine
of childbirth; **ic; cian** *n.*
ŏb′stĭ-nàte, *a.*, stubborn;
nacy; -ly; -ness
ŏb-strĕp′êr-oŭs, *a.*, noisy,
unruly; **-ly; -ness**
ŏb-strŭct′, *v.*, block,
hinder; **-er; -or; -ion;
-ive; -ively; -iveness**
ŏb-tāin′, *v.*, get possession of; **-er; -ment; -able**
ŏb-trŭde′, *v.*, force oneself
upon; **-r; trusion; tru-
sive; trusively;
trusiveness** [-ness
ŏb-tūse′, *a.*, dull; **sity; -ly;**
ŏb′vĭ-āte, *v.*, make unnecessary; **tion**
ŏb′vĭ-oŭs, *a.*, easy to understand; **-ly; -ness**
ŏc-cās′sion, *n.*, happening, opportunity; *v.*,
cause
ŏc-clūde′, *v.*, stop up,
close; **clusion; clusive;
-nt**
ŏc-cŭlt′, *a.*, secret, mysti-
cal; **-ism; -ist; -ly; -ness**
ŏc-cū-pā′sion, *n.*, control
of area, one's work; **-al;
-ally**
ŏc′cū-pÿ, *v.*, possess, live
in, fill; **pier; pancy; pant**
n.
ŏc-cûr′, *v.*, come to mind;
happen; **-rence**
ō′cèan (shĕn), *n.*, great
body of salt water; **-ic;
-ology; -ologist** [cat
ō′cè-lŏt, *n.*, large spotted
ō′chêr (kêr), *n.*, clay with
iron ore, dark yellow
ŏc′tà-gŏn, *n.*, eight-sided
plane; **-al; -ally**
ŏc′tāne, *n.*, gasoline
measure [tones; **val**
ŏc′tàve, *n.*, eight musical
ŏc-tĕt′, *n.*, group of eight
ŏc′tò-pŭs, *n.*, eight-armed
sea animal
ŏc′ū-làr, *a.*, of the eye; **-ly**

ŏc′ū-lĭst, *n.,* eye doctor

ŏdd, *a.,* left over, not even, strange; **-ity; -ly; -ness**

ŏdds, *n.,* advantage, betting ratio

ōde, *n.,* poem of praise

ō′dĭ-oŭs, *a.,* disgusting; **-ly; -ness**

ō′dŏr, *n.,* smell; **-ous; -ously; -ousness; -less**

ôf′fàl, *n.,* garbage

ŏf-fĕnd′, *v.,* anger, displease, commit crime; **-er; fense; fensive; fensively; fensiveness**

ŏf′fêr, *n.,* something offered; *v.,* present, propose, bid; **-er; -ing** *n.*

ŏff′hănd′, *a., adv.,* without preparation

ŏf′fĭce, *n.,* position, place of business; **ciate; ciator; ciation**

ŏf′fĭ-cêr, *n.,* person of authority, policeman

ŏf-fĭ′cioŭs, *a.,* meddlesome, domineering; **-ly; -ness**

ôff′sĕt, *n.,* compensation, type of printing; *v.* **(ôff-sĕt′)** balance

ôff′sprĭng, *n.,* child

ō′gle, *n., v.,* stare; **-r**

ō′gre (gêr), *n.,* fictitious monster

ŏil, *n.,* greasy combustile liquid; *v.,* lubricate; **-y** *a.*

ŏint′mėnt, *n.,* oily cream to soothe

ō′krà, *n.,* vegetable of sticky green pods

ōld, *a.,* existed for a long time, former, shabby; **-ster; -ish** [shrub

ō′lē-ăn-dêr, *n.,* flowering

ō-lē-ō-mâr′gà-rĭne, *n.,* butter substitute

ŏl-făc′tŏ-rȳ, *a.,* of the sense of smell

ŏl′ĭ-gâr-chȳ, *n.,* rule of a few [fruit

ŏl′īve, *n.,* tree, oval green

ŏm′e-lėt, *n.,* egg dish

ō′mėn, *n.,* sign

ŏm′ĭ-noŭs, *a.,* threatening; **-ly; -ness**

ō-mĭt′, *v.,* leave out, neg-

lect; **-ter; mission; missive; missively; missible** [bus

ŏm′nĭ-bŭs, *n.,* collection,

ŏm-nĭp′ŏ-tėnt, *a.,* all-powerful; **tence; -ly**

ŏm-nĭs′ciėnt, *a.,* knowing all things; **cience; -ly**

ŏm-nĭv′ŏ-roŭs, *a.,* devouring everything; **-ly; -ness**

once (wŭns), *adv.,* one time, long ago

ŏn′êr-oŭs, *a.,* troublesome; **-ly; -ness**

ŏn′ion, *n.,* edible bulb with strong taste

ŏn′lōok-êr, *n.,* spectator

ōn′lȳ, *a.,* alone, best; *adv.,* just, merely; *con.,* but

ŏn′sĕt, *n.,* attack, start

ŏn′slàught, *n.,* violent attack

ō′nŭs, *n.,* blame, burden

ŏn′ȳx, *n.,* semiprecious stone

ōoze, *n.,* slime; *v.,* leak slowly; **oozy** *a.* [stone

ō′pàl, *n.,* semiprecious

ō-pāque′, *n.,* impermeable to light; **pacity; -ly; -ness**

ō′pėn, *v.,* unfasten, expose, begin, be or make liberal; *a.,* not shut, unrestricted, free, frank; **-er; -ly; -ness**

ō-pėn-hănd′ėd, *a.,* generous; **-ly; -ness**

ō-pėn-heârt′ėd, *a.,* frank, generous; **-ly; -ness**

ō-pėn-mīnd′ėd, *a.,* free from bias; **-ly; -ness**

ō′pėn-wŏrk, *n.,* ornamental designs with openings in it

ŏp′êr-à, *n.,* musical drama; **-tic; -tically**

ŏp′êr-āte, *v.,* function, manage, perform surgery; **tor; tion; tional; tive; tively; able; ability; ably**

ŏp-êr-ĕt′tà, *n.,* light opera

ŏph-thăl-mŏl′ŏ-gȳ, *n.,* medicine of the eyes; **gist; logical**

ō'pǐ-āte, *n.,* narcotic drug with opium

ŏ-pǐn'ǐon, *n.,* one's judgment, belief; **-ative; -atively; -ativeness**

ŏ-pǐn'ǐon-āt-ĕd, *a.,* holding opinion stubbornly; **-ly; -ness**

ō'pǐ-ŭm, *n.,* narcotic drug

ŏ-pŏs'sŭm, *n.,* nocturnal tree-dwelling animal

ŏp-pō'nĕnt, *n.,* one against

ŏp-pŏr-tū'nǐ-tў, *n.,* chance

ŏp-pōse', *v.,* be against; **-r; position**

ŏp'pŏ-sǐte, *a.,* radically different, facing; **-ly; -ness**

ŏp-prĕss', *v.,* worry, rule harshly; **-or; -ion; -ive; -ively; -iveness**

ŏpt, *v.,* choose; **-ion; -ional**

ŏp'tǐc, *a.,* of eye; **-al; -ally**

ŏp-tǐ'cǐan, *n.,* maker of eyeglasses

ŏp'tǐ-mǐsm, *n.,* cheerful view of life; **mist; mistic; mistically** ·

ŏp'tǐ-mŭm, *n.,* best possible result; **mize; mization; mal; mally**

ŏp-tŏm'ĕ-trў, *n.,* examination of eyes; **trist; rical** [**ency; -ly**

ŏp'ū-lĕnt, *a.,* rich; **ence;**

ō'pŭs, *n.,* work, composition

ôr'ȧ-cle, *n.,* prophet, prophesy; **racular** *a.;* **racularity; racularly**

ô'rȧl, *a.,* of mouth, spoken; **-ly**

ŏr'ȧnge, *n.,* edible citrus fruit, reddish yellow

ŏ-răng'ū-tăn, *n.,* ape

ŏ-rā'tion, *n.,* speech; **tor**

ôr'ȧ-tôr-ў, *n.,* skill in public speaking; **torical; torically**

ôrb, *n.,* sphere, eye

ôr'bǐt, *n.,* eye socket, path of a heavenly body; **-er; -al** [**trees**

ôr'chȧrd, *n.,* land with fruit

ôr'chĕs-trȧ (kĕs), *n.,* many

musicians playing together; **-l**

ôr'chĕs-trāte, *v.,* arrange music; **tor; tion**

ôr'chǐd (kǐd), *n.,* decorative flower, pale purple; **-ology**

ôr-dāin', *v.,* decree, admit to ministry; **-er; -ment; dination** [**perience**

ôr-dēal', *n.,* difficult ex-

ôr'dêr, *n.,* position, system proper state, request; *v.,* command, arrange

ôr'dêr-lў, *n.,* attendant; *a.,* proper, methodical

ôr'dǐ'nȧl, *n.,* number indicating order ex. third

ôr'dǐ-nȧnce, *n.,* law

ôr'dǐ-nār-ў, *a.,* usual, common; **narily; nariness**

ôrd'nȧnce, *n.,* weapons, military equipment

ôre, *n.,* natural substance of minerals and/or elements

ô-rĕg'ȧ-nō, *n.,* seasoning

ôr'gȧn, *n.,* large musical instrument, body part with special function

ôr'gȧn-dў, *n.,* sheer fabric

ôr-gǎn'ǐc, *a.,* of body organ, of life, inborn, systematic; **-ally**

ôr'gȧn-ǐsm, *n.,* living thing

ôr'gȧn-ize, *v.,* arrange systematically, unite; **-r; zation** [**max; -ic**

ôr'gǎsm, *n.,* sexual cli-

ôr'gў, *n.,* wild party

ôr'ǐ-ĕnt, *n.,* Asia; *v.,* adjust, adapt; **-ation**

ôr'ǐ-fǐce, *n.,* opening; **cial**

ô-rǐ-gȧ'mǐ, *n.,* art of folding paper

ôr'ǐ-gǐn, *n.,* beginning; **-ate; -ator; -ation**

ŏ-rǐg'ǐ-nȧl, *a.,* first, new, inventive; **-ity; -ly**

ôr'nȧ-mĕnt, *n.,* decoration; *v.,* adorn; **-er; -al; -ation** [**-ness**

ôr-nāte', *a.,* fancy; **-ly;**

ôr'nêr-ў, *n.,* obstinate

ôr-nǐ-thŏl'ŏ-gў, *n.,* science of birds; **gist; logical**

ôr'phản, *n.*, child without parents; **-hood; -age**

ôr-thô-dŏn'tĭcs, *n.*, corrective dentistry; **tist; tic**

ôr'thô-dŏx, *a.*, conforming to established practices; **-y**

ôr-thô-pē'dĭcs, *n.*, bone surgery; **dist; dic**

ô'rўx, *n.*, antelope

ŏs'cĭl-lāte, *v.*, swing, waver; **tor; tion; tory**

ŏs'cŭ-lāte, *v.*, kiss; **tion; tory**

ŏs-mō'sĭs, *n.*, passage of fluid through thin membrane

ŏs'sē-oŭs, *a.*, of bone

ŏs'sĭ-fý, *v.*, change to bone; **fication**

ŏs-tĕn'sĭ-ble, *a.*, apparent; **bly; sive; sively**

ŏs-tĕn-tā'tion, *n.*, showy display; **tious; tiously; tiousness**

ŏs-tē-ŏp'ȧ-thȳ, *n.*, medicine of treating disease by massage; **path** *n.*; **pathic; pathically**

ŏs'trȧ-cīze, *v.*, banish; **ism**

ŏs'trĭch, *n.*, large bird

ō-tŏl'ȯ-gȳ, *n.*, medicine of ear; **gist; logical**

ŏt'têr, *n.*, weasellike animal

ôught, *v.*, be required to

oŭst, *v.*, force out; **-er**

oŭt, *a.*, external, away from; *adv.*, away from, outdoors, fully

oŭt-bĭd', *v.*, offer more

oŭt'bôard, *a., adv.*, outside main body of ship

oŭt'brēak, *n.*, sudden occurrence

oŭt'bûrst, *n.*, sudden release of feeling, energy, etc. [rejected

oŭt'cǎst, *n., a.*, (person)

oŭt'cȯme, *n.*, result

oŭt'crȳ, *n.*, protest

oŭt'do (dŭ), *v.*, surpass

oŭt'dôor, *a.*, in the open

oŭt'dôors, *n., adv.*, (place) outside of building

oŭt'êr, *a.*, external

oŭt'fĭt, *n.*, equipment, en-

semble, unit of people; *v.*, furnish

oŭt-fŏŏt', *v.*, go faster than

oŭt'gō-ĭng, *a.*, leaving, sociable

oŭt'grŏwth, *n.*, result

oŭt'hoŭse, *n.*, outside toilet [cursion

oŭt'ĭng, *n.*, pleasant ex-

oŭt-lǎnd'ĭsh, *a.*, strange; **-ly; -ness**

oŭt'lǎw, *n.*, criminal; *v.*, declare illegal

oŭt'lāy, *n.*, money spent

oŭt'lĕt, *n.*, way out, market, place to plug in to electricity [mary

oŭt'līne, *n.*, sketch, sum-

oŭt'lŏŏk, *n.*, viewpoint, prospect

oŭt'lȳ-ĭng, *a.*, remote

oŭt-mōd'ĕd, *a.*, obsolete

oŭt'pōst, *n.*, remote post

oŭt'pŭt, *n.*, amount done

oŭt'rāge, *n.*, violent act, great insult or anger; *v.*, offend greatly; **-ous; -ously; -ousness**

oŭt'right, *a.*, straight forward; *adv.*, fully, openly

oŭt'sīde, *n.*, exterior; *a.*, outer, from another place, slight; **-er**

oŭt'skîrt, *n.*, remote part of city [by cleverness

oŭt-smȧrt', *n.*, overcome

oŭt'spō'kĕn, *a.*, frank; **-ly; -ness** [prominent; **-ly**

oŭt-stǎnd'ĭng, *a.*, unpaid,

oŭt'strĭp, *v.*, surpass

oŭt'wȧrd, *a.*, outer, visible; **-ly; -ness**

oŭt-weigh' (wā), *v.*, be more valuable

oŭt-wĭt', *v.*, outsmart

ō'vȧl, *a.*, egg-shaped; **-ly; -ness**

ō'vȧ-rȳ, *n.*, female reproductive gland; **varian** *a.*

ō-vā'tion, *n.*, great applause [baking

ŏv'ĕn, *n.*, compartment for

ō'vêr, *a.*, finished; *adv.*, above, in excess, on other side, again; *prep.*, above, upon, across

ō'vêr-ǎlls, *n., pl.*, work

N O

pants with bib

ō-vêr-beār'ĭng, *a.*, arrogant; **-ly; -ness**

ō'vêr-bôard, *adv.*, over ship's side, to extremes

ō'vêr-cåst, *a.*, cloudy, dark

ō-vêr-cóme', *v.*, master, conquer, defeat

ō'vêr-drăft, *n.*, withdrawal of money in excess of that in account

ō-vêr-dūe', *a.*, late

ō-vêr-flōw', *v.*, flood

ō-vêr-häul', *v.*, repair

ō-vêr-hēar', *v.*, hear without speaker knowing

ō'vêr-lănd, *n.*, on land

ō-vêr-lăp', *v.*, cover, extend over

ō'vêr-lȳ, *adv.*, too

ō'vêr-păss, *n.*, bridge over road; *v.*, outdo, overlook

ō-vêr-pow'êr, *v.*, subdue

ō-vêr-rīde', *v.*, nullify

ō-vêr-rūle', *v.*, reverse

ō-vêr-rŭn', *v.*, spread rapidly

ō-vêr-sēe', *v.*, watch over, manage; **-r**

ō'vêr-shoe (shū), *n.*, protective boot worn over shoe

ō-vêrt', *a.*, open, public; **-ly** [with

ō-vêr-tāke', *v.*, catch up

ō-vêr-thrōw', *v.*, defeat

ō'vêr-tōne, *n.*, musical tone heard with another, implication

ō'vêr-tûre, *n.*, musical introduction

ō-vêr-tûrn', *v.*, turn over

ō'vêr-view, *n.*, survey

ō-vêr-whēlm', *v.*, crush, overpower; **-ing; -ingly**

ō-vêr-wrôught', *a.*, emotionally distressed

ō'vū-lāte, *v.*, produce and discharge ovum; **tion**

ō'vŭm, *n.*, female reproductive cell

ōwe, *v.*, be obliged to pay

ōwl, *n.*, night bird of prey; **-like; -ish; -ishly; -ishness**

ōwn, *v.*, possess, admit;

-er; -ership; -erless

ŏx, *n.*, castrated bull

ŏx'fôrd, *n.*, shoe, cotton cloth

ŏx'īde, *n.*, compound of oxygen and an element

ŏx'ī-dīze, *v.*, unite with oxygen; **-r; dizable**

ŏx'ȳ-gĕn, *n.*, gaseous element; **-ate; -ic; -ous**

oys'têr (ŏĭs), *n.*, edible mollusk

ō'zōne, *n.*, form of oxygen

P

păb'ū-lŭm, *n.*, food

pä'cå, *n.*, rodent

pāce, *n.*, walking step, rate; *v.*, walk; **-r**

păch'ȳ-dêrm, *n.*, large thick-skinned animal; **-al; -ic; -atous; -atously**

păc'ī-fȳ, *v.*, make calm; **fier; fiable; fic**

păck, *n.*, bundle, group; *v.*, put together, fill; **-er; -ing**

păct, *n.*, agreement

păd, *n.*, cushion, stacked and attached paper sheets; *v.*, walk softly; **-ding** *n.*

păd'dle, *n.*, flat blade with handle for canoeing, stirring, etc.; *v.*, canoe, beat; **-r**

păd'dóck, *n.*, small enclosed field [lock

păd'lóck, *n.*, removable

paē'ăn, *n.*, song of joy

pā'găn, *n.*, heathen; **-ize**

pāge, *n.*, leaf of a book, boy attendant; *v.*, call name out [show; **-ry**

păg'ĕant, *n.*, elaborate

på-gō'dån, *n.*, oriental towerlike temple

pāil, *n.*, bucket; **-ful**

pāin, *n.*, hurt felt in body, (*pl.*) great care; **-ful; -fully; -fulness; -less; -lessly; -lessness**

pāint, *n.*, colored pigment; *v.*, cover or draw with paint; **-er; -ing** *n.*

på-jă'mås, *n.*, *pl.*, pants

and shirt for sleeping

pǎl'ǎce, *n.,* royal residence; **latial; latially**

pǎl'ǎt-ǎ-ble, *n.,* pleasant tasting; **bility; bly; -ness**

pǎl'ǎte, *n.,* roof of mouth

pǎ-lǎv' êr, *n., v.,* talk

pāle, *n.,* white, colorless

pā-lē-ò-lǐth'ǐc, *a.,* of Stone Age   [artist's paint

pǎl'étte, *n.,* thin board for

pǎl'lét, *n.,* straw bed

pǎl'lǐ-āte, *v.,* excuse, ease, lessen; **tor; tion; tive**

pǎl'lǐd, *a.,* pale; **-ly; -ness**

pǎl'lǒr, *n.,* lack of color

pálm, *n.,* tall tropical tree, inside surface of hand

pálm'ǐs-trÿ, *n.,* fortune telling from reading palm; **ist**   [ored horse

pǎl-ò-mǐ'nō, *n.,* light col-

pǎl'pà-ble, *a.,* that can be felt, obvious; **bility; bly**

pǎl'pǐ-tāte, *v.,* throb; **tion**

pǎl'sÿ, *n.,* paralysis

pǎm'pêr, *v.,* spoil, indulge

pǎm'phlét, *n.,* unbound booklet

pǎn, *n.,* broad container for cooking; *v.,* (coll.) criticize

pǎn-à-cē'à, *n.,* cure-all

pǎn'crē-às, *n.,* gland aiding digestion; **atic**

pǎn'dà, *n.,* bearlike mammal   [confusion

pǎn-dè-mō'nǐ-ǔm, *n.,* wild

pāne, *n.,* sheet of glass

pǎn-è-gÿr'ǐc, *n.,* speech of praise; **gyrist; gyrize; -al; -ally**

pǎn'el, *n.,* wall section, group that judges, discusses, etc.; **-ing** *n.*

pǎn'ǐc, *n.,* hysterical fear; **-ky** *a.,* **-ally**

pǎn-ò-rǎ'mà, *n.,* wide view, extended picture; **ramic; ramically**

pǎnt, *v.,* breathe rapidly

pǎn-tà-lōons', *n., pl.,* trousers

pǎn'tò-mǐme, *n.,* acting without talking; **mimist; mimic**

pǎn'trÿ, *n.,* storeroom or

closet for food

pǎ'pà-cÿ, *n.,* authority of Pope; **pal; pally**

pà-pà'yà, *n.,* tree with edible fruit

pā'pêr, *n.,* thin sheet for writing; **-y** *a.*   [ing

pǎp'rǐ-kà, *n.,* red season-

pà-pÿ'rǔs, *n.,* water plant, ancient paper

pâr, *n.,* value, average

pǎr'à-ble, *n.,* story with moral; **bolic; bolical; bolically**

pǎr'à-chūte, *n.,* umbrella-like device to descend through air; **chutist**

pà-rāde', *n., v.,* march in public   [place

pǎr'à-dīse, *n.,* heavenly

pǎr'à-dǒx, *n.,* contrary statement; **-ical; -ically; -icalness**

pǎr'àf-fǐn, *n.,* waxy substance   [cellence

pǎr'à-gǒn, *n.,* model of ex-

pǎr'à-grǎph, *n.,* related sentences placed together

pǎr'à-kēet, *n.,* small parrot

pǎr'ǎl-lěl, *a.,* in same direction and distance apart

pà-rǎl'ÿ-sǐs, *n.,* loss of power to move body; **lyze; lyzation**

pǎr'à-mǒunt, *a.,* supreme; **-cy** *n.;* **-ly**

pǎr'à-nǒid, *a.,* oversuspicious   [wall

pǎr'à-pět, *n.,* protective

pǎr-à-phêr-nā'li-à, *n.,* belongings, equipment

pǎr-à-plē'gǐ-à, *n.,* paralysis from waist down; **gic** *n., a.*

pǎr'à-sīte, *n.,* one that lives off another; **sitic; sitical; sitically**

pǎr'à-sǒl, *n.,* woman's decorative umbrella

pâr'cél, *n.,* wrapped bundle; *v.,* divide

pârch, *v.,* make dry and thirsty

pârch'měnt, *n.,* animal skin used to write on

pâr'dòn, v., absolve, forgive, release; **-able; -ably**

pāre, v., peel, lessen

pâr-faìt' (fā), n., ice cream dessert in tall glass

pär'ĭsh, n., church district; **-ioner**

pär'ĭ-tў, n., equality

pârk, n., land for recreation; v., leave (car) temporarily

pâr'kà, n., hooded jacket

pâr'lāy, v., bet winnings

pâr'lèy, n., discussion

pâr'lià-mènt, n., legislative body; **-ary**

pâr'lŏr, n., living room

pâr'loùs, a., dangerous, clever

pà-rō'chĭ-àl (kĭ), a., of parish, restricted; **-ly**

pär'ò-dў, n., funny imitation; **dist**

pà-rōle', n. release from jail ending full term

pär'rў, v., deflect, evade

pâr-sĭ-mō'nĭ-oùs, a., stingy; **mony; -ly; -ness**

pârs'lèy, n., leafy plant for garnishing food

pârs'nĭp, n., white vegetable root [**-age**

pär'sòn, n., clergyman;

pârt, n., portion, segment; v., divide; **-ing** n.; **-ible**

pâr-tāke', v., share, participate

pâr-tĭc'ĭ-pāte, v., take a part, do; **tor; tant** n.; **tion; pance; tive; tory**

pâr'tĭ-cĭ-ple, n., verbal adjective [piece

pâr'tĭ-cle, n., very small

pâr-tĭc'ū-làr, a., special, hard to please; **-ity; -ize; -ly**

pâr'tĭ-sàn, n., supporter of one side, guerrilla

pâr-tĭ'tion, n., separation, divider; **-er; -ed**

pârt'nêr, n., one who shares, teammate; **-ship**

pâr'trĭdge, n., game bird

pâr'tў, n., political group, social gathering, person

pàss, n., free ticket, mountain gap; v., go forward or by, occur, decide

pàs'sàge, n., movement, journey, part of reading matter, hallway

pàs'sèn-gêr, n., traveler

pàs'sion, n., strong emotion; **-àte** a.; **àtely; -less; -lessly**

pàs'sĭve, a., inactive, yielding; **sivity; -ly; -ness**

pàss'pôrt, n., document of citizenship for travel abroad [aroni, etc.

pàs'tà, n., spaghetti, mac-

pāste, n., sticky mixture of flour and water; **pasty** a.; **pastiness**

pàs-těl', n., a., (color that is) soft and pale

pàs'têur-īze, v., kill bacteria in liquid; **-r; zation**

pàs'tŏr, n., clergyman; **-al**

pàs'tŏ-ràl, a., rural, rustic; **-ly** [good

pās'trў, n., fancy baked

pàs'tûre, n., animal's grazing ground

pàt, n., gentle tap, small lump; v., tap; a., suitable; **-ter**

pàtch, n., material to mend hole, small land plot, v., mend

pāte, n., top of head

pàt'ènt, n., exclusive right to invention

pāt'ènt, a., open, obvious; **ency; -ly**

pàth, n., course followed, trail [pity; **-ally**

pà-thět'ĭc, a., arousing

pà-thŏl'ò-gў, n., medicine of the nature of disease; **gist; logical**

pā'thòs, n., quality of arousing pity

pā'tĭènt, n., one under doctor's care

pā'tĭènt, a., calm, enduring; **tience; -ly**

pā'tĭ-ō, n., paved area of house [of family

pā'trĭ-ârch, n., father, head

pà-trĭ'cĭàn, n., nobleman

pā'trĭ-òt, n., one loyal to

his country; **-ism**

pā'trŏn, *n.*, sponsor, regular customer; **-age; -ize**

păt'têrn, *n., v.*, model

păt'tў, *n.*, small fish or meat cake

păunch, *n.*, large belly; **-y** *a.;* **-iness**

pău'pêr, *n.*, poor person

păuse, *n.*, temporary stop; *v.*, hesitate

pȧ-vĭl'ĭŏn, *n.*, large tent, exhibition building

păwn, *n., v.*, pledge; *n.*, lowest chessman

păwn'brō-kêr, *n.*, one who loans money on thing left as security

pāy, *n.*, salary; *v.*, give what is due ex. money, make; **-er; -ee; -ment; -able**

pēach, *n.*, fruit, orangish yellow; **-y** *a.*

pēa'cŏck, *n.*, bird with large colorful tail

pēak, *n.*, highest point

pēak'ĕd, *a.*, sickly; **-ness**

pēal, *n.*, ringing sound

pēa'nŭt, *n.*, vine with edible seeds

pêarl, *n.*, smooth round gem found in oyster; **-y** *a.*

pēas'ȧnt, *n.*, small farmer, ignorant person; **-ry**

pēat, *n.*, decayed plant matter [**bly**

pĕb'ble, *n.*, small stone;

pė-căn', *n.* tree with edible nut [**mal**

pĕc'cȧ-rў, *n.*, piglike animal

pĕck, *n.*, dry measure of eight quarts; *v.*, strike with beak, kiss

pė-cūl'ĭȧr, *a.*, out of ordinary, odd; **-ity; -ly**

pĕc'ū-lāte, *v.*, embezzle; **tor; tion**

pė-cū'nĭ-ār-ў, *a.*, of money, financial; **arily**

pĕd'ȧ-gŏ-gў, *n.*, teaching profession; **gogics; gogic; gogical; gogically** [**by foot**

pĕd'ȧl, *n.*, lever operated

pĕd'ȧnt, *n.*, one who ov-

erstresses his learning; **-ry; -ic; -ically**

pĕd'ĕs-tȧl, *n.*, base, ex. column, statue

pė-dĕs'trĭ-ȧn, *n.*, walker; *a.*, on foot, ordinary

pė-dī-ăt'rĭcs, *n.*, medicine of children; **cian** *n.*; **ric**

pĕd'ĭ-cūre, *n.*, care of feet; **curist**

pĕd'ĭ-grēe, *n.*, ancestry

pēel, *n.*, rind; *v.*, cut or strip away

pēer, *n.*, an equal, nobleman; **-less; -lessly; -lessness**

pēer, *v.*, look closely

pēe'vĭsh, *a.*, fretful; **-ly; -ness**

peign-oir', *n.*, (pān-wâr) woman's short robe

pĕl'ĭ-cȧn, *n.*, water bird

pĕl'lĕt, *n.*, little ball

pĕlt, *n.*, animal fur; *v.*, throw things at; **-er**

pĕl'vĭs, *n.*, body cavity of hip bones and lower backbone; **vic**

pĕn, *n.*, small enclosure for animals, writing device

pē'nȧl, *a.*, of legal punishment; **-ty; -ize; -ization; -ly** [of sin

pĕn'ȧnce, *n.*, repentance

pĕn'chȧnt, *n.*, inclination, liking

pĕnd'ȧnt, *n.*, hanging ornament, ex. locket, charm

pĕnd'ĭng, *a.*, not decided; *prep.*, during, until

pĕn'dū-lŭm (jŭ), *n.*, body hung to swing freely; **lous; lously; lousness**

pĕn'ė-trāte, *v.*, enter, affect; **tion; tive; trant**

pĕn'guĭn, *n.*, flightless bird [drug

pĕn-ĭ-cĭl'lĭn, *n.*, antibiotic

pĕn-ĭn'sū-lȧ, *n.*, land projecting into water; **-r** *a.*

pē'nĭs, *n.*, male sex organ; **nile** *a.*

pĕn'ĭ-tĕnt, *a.*, sorry for doing wrong; **tence; -ly**

pĕn-ĭ-tĕn'tiȧ-rў, *n.*, prison

pĕn'nȧnt, *n.*, long narrow

flag [**-ness**
pĕn'nĭ-lĕss, *a.*, very poor;
pĕn'sion, *n.*, regular payment for past services;
-er; -ary *a.;* **-able**
pĕn'sĭve, *a.*, thinking deeply; **-ly; -ness**
pĕnt, *a.*, held in
pĕn'tȧ-gŏn, *n.*, five-sided figure; **-al; -ally**
pĕnt'hoŭse, *n.*, rooftop apartment
pė-nū'rĭ-oŭs, *a.*, stingy; **-ly; -ness**
pĕn'ū-rȳ, *n.*, poverty
pē'ŏn, *n.*, laborer; **-age**
pēo'ple, *n.*, human beings, group members
pĕp'pėr, *n.*, spicy seasoning, vegetable; **-y** *a.*
pĕp'sĭn, *n.*, digestive enzyme; **peptic**
pėr-ăm'bū-lāte, *v.*, walk; **tor; tion; tory**
pėr-cāle', *n.*, fine cotton cloth
pėr-cēive', *v.*, grasp through senses; **-r; ceivable; ceivably**
pėr-cĕnt', *a., adv.*, out of a hundred; **-age; -ile** *n.*
pėr-cĕp'tion, *n.*, perceiving; **-al; tible; tibility; tibly; tive; tively; tiveness; tual; tually**
pĕrch, *n.*, fish; *v.*, sit
pėr'cȯ-lāte, *v.*, brew coffee; **tor; tion**
pėr-dĭ'tion, *n.*, hell
pėr'ė-grĭ-nāte, *v.*, travel; **tor; tion**
pėr-ĕn'nĭ-ȧl, *a.*, lasting for a long time; **-ly**
pėr-fĕct', *v.*, make perfect; *a.*, (**pėr'fĕct**) complete, exact, excellent; **-er; -ion; -ness; -ible; -ibility, -ly**
pėr'fĭ-dȳ, *n.*, treachery; **fidious; fidiously**
pėr'fȯ-rāte, *v.*, make holes in; **tor; tion; tive; rable**
pėr-fôrm', *v.*, do, accomplish, act; **-er; -ance; -able** [ing liquid
pėr'fūme, *n.*, sweet smell-
pėr-fŭnc'tȯ-rȳ, *a.*, done in-

differently; **rily; riness**
pėr-fūse', *v.*, spread with liquid; **sion; sive**
pėr'il, *n.*, danger, **-oŭs; -ously; -ousness**
pė-rĭm'ė-têr, *n.*, measurement of a boundary of area
pē'rĭ-ŏd, *n.*, portion of time, punctuation mark (.)
pė-rĭph'êr-ȳ, *n.*, edge, perimeter; **eral**
pėr'ĭ-scōpe, *n.*, tube with mirrors to see above; **scopic**
pėr'ĭsh, *v.*, die, be ruined; **-able; -ability; -ableness**
pėr'jû-rȳ, *n.*, lying under oath; **jure** *v.;* **jurer; jurious**
pėr'mȧ-nėnt, *a.*, lasting, forever; **nence; nency; -ly**
pėr'mē-āte, *v.*, pass or spread through; **tion; tive; ance; ant; able; ability; ably**
pėr-mĭs'sion, *n.*, consent; **sive; sively; siveness**
pėr-nĭ'cious, *a.*, harmful, deadly; **-ly; -ness**
pêr-pėn-dĭc'ū-lȧr, *a.*, exactly upright; **-ity; -ly**
pėr'pė-trāte, *v.*, do evil thing; **tor; tion**
pėr-pĕt'ū-ȧl, *a.*, lasting forever; **-ity; ate; ator; ation; -ly**
pėr-plĕx', *v.*, puzzle, confuse; **-ity; -ing; -ingly**
pėr'sė-cūte, *v.*, harass, punish; **tor; tion; tive; tory**
pėr-sė-vēre', *v.*, continue despite difficulties; **-nce; -nt**
pėr'sĭst, *v.*, continue steadily; **-ence; -ent; -ently**
pėr'sȯn-ȧ-ble, *a.*, attractive; **bly; -ness**
pėr'sȯn-ȧl, *a.*, individual, private; **-ity; -ize; -ism; -ly**
pėr-sŏn'ĭ-fȳ, *v.*, represent as a person; typify; **fier;**

fication [ees
pêr-sòn-nĕl', *n.*, employ-
pêr-spĕc'tĭve, *n.*, appearance at a distance, pro-
portion; **-ly**
pêr-spĭc'ū-oŭs, *a.*, easily
understood; **-ly; -ness;
cuity**
pêr-spīre', *v.*, sweat; **ration; spiratory**
pêrt, *a.*, impudent; **-ly;
-ness** [to
pêr-tāin',*v.*, belong, relate
pêr-tĭ-nā'cioŭs, *a.*, stubborn; **nacity; -ly**
pêr'tĭ-nént, *a.*, relevant;
nence; nency; -ly
pêr-tûrb', *v.*, alarm, worry;
-er; -ation; -able; -edly
pė-rūse', *v.*, study, read;
-r; rusal
pêr-vāde', *v.*, spread
throughout; **vasion; va-
sive; vasively; vasive-
ness**
pêr-vêrse', *a.*, improper,
contrary; **sion; sity;
sive; -ly; -ness**
pêr'vêrt,*n.*, perverted person; *v.*, **(pêr-vêrt')** lead
astray, distort; **-ed;
-edly; -edness**
pêr'vĭ-oŭs, *a.*, open to influence; **-ness**
pĕs'sĭ-mìsm, *n.*, tendency
to expect the worst;
mist; mistic; mistically
pĕst,*n.*, annoyance; **-er** *v.*
pĕs'tĭ-lénce, *n.*, contagious disease; **lent;
lently**
pĕs'tle, *n.*, club-shaped
tool for grinding
pĕt, *n.*, tamed animal,
cherished person; *v.*, caress; *a.*, favorite; **-ter**
pė-tĭ'tion, *n.*, written request; *v.*, appeal; **-er;
-ary**
pĕt'rĭ-fȳ, *v.*, change into
stone, frighten; **fied**
pė-trō'lē-ŭm,*n.*, oily liquid
found in rock layers
pĕt'tĭ-cōat, *n.*, female undergarment
pĕt'tȳ, *a.*, trivial, minor
pĕt'ū-lánt, *a.*, impatient;

lance; lancy; -ly
pė-tū'nĭ-å, *n.*, flower
pēw, *n.*, church bench
pēw'têr, *n.*, alloy of tin
phăl'lŭs, *n.*, image of
penis; **lic**
phâr'mà-cȳ, *n.*, preparing
and dispensing medi-
cine, drugstore; **cist;
cology; cological; col-
ogically; ceutics; ceut-
ical; ceutically**
phăr'ȳnx, *n.*, tube joining
mouth and esophagus
phāse,*n.*, aspect, stage of
development; **sic**
phė-nŏm'ė-nòn, *n.*, unusual happening; **nal;
nally**
phĭ-lăn'dêr, *v.*, make love
insincerely; **-er**
phĭ-lăn'thrò-pȳ, *n.*, charity; generosity; **pist;
pize; thropic; thropi-
cally**
phĭ-lăt'ė-lȳ, *n.*, collecting
stamps; **list; lic;
telically** [music
phĭl-hâr-mŏn'ĭc, *a.*, loving
phĭ-lŏs'ò-phȳ, *n.*, study of
truths, system of princi-
ples; **pher; phize;
sophic; sophically**
phlĕgm, *n.*, secreted
mucus [cool; **-al; -ally**
phlĕg-măt'ĭc, *a.*, dull,
phō'bĭ-å, *n.*, excessive
fear; **bic**
phŏn'ĭcs, *n.*, science of
sound, method of teach-
ing reading
phō'nò-grăph, *n.*, record
player; **-ic; -ically**
phŏs'phāte, *n.*, chemical
fertilizer; **tize; phatic**
phŏs'phô-rŭs, *n.*, white
chemical element;
phoric; rous
phò-tŏg'rà-phȳ, *n.*, art of
taking pictures with
camera; **pher; graphic;
graphically**
phrė-nĕt'ĭc, *a.*, insane
phȳ'lŭm,*n.*, division of animal kingdom
phȳs'ĭc, *n.*, laxative
phȳs'ĭ-cál, *a.*, of matter,

P
R

bodily, material; **-ity; -ly**

phý-sĭ'ciản, n., doctor, one who practices medicine

phýs-ĭ-ŏl'ŏ-gў, n., science of function of organisms; **gist**

pĭ-ăn'ŏ, n., large keyboard instrument; **anist**

pi'cả, n., type size

pĭc'cŏ-lŏ, n., small flute

pĭck, n., pointed tool, choice; v., dig at, pluck, select; **-er**

pĭck'le, n., food prepared in spicy vinegar solution

pĭc'nĭc, n., meal eaten outdoors; **nicker**

pĭc'tûre, n., visual representation, likeness, description

pĭc-tûr-ĕsque', a., quaint, beautiful; **-ly; -ness**

pĭe, n., bake pastry with filling

piĕce, n., part, single thing; v., join

piĕd'mŏnt, a., at base of mountain   [dock

piĕr, n., bridge support,

piĕrce, v., make a hole in, sound sharply; **-r; -ingly**

pi'ĕ-tў, n., religious devotion, loyalty

pĭg'hĕad-ĕd, a., stubborn; **-ly; -ness**

pĭg'mĕnt, n., coloring matter; **-ation; -ize; -ary**

pĭg'tāil, n., braid of hair

pĭke, n., freshwater fish

pĭle, n., heap, rug's fluffiness, heavy beam; v., load accumulate

pĭl'fêr, v., steal; **-er; -age**

pĭl'grĭm, n., traveler to holy place; **-age**

pĭl'lảge, n., v., plunder; **-r**

pĭl'lảr, n., upright support

pi'lŏt, n., person licensed to steer ship or plane

pĭ-mĕn'tŏ, n., sweet red pepper   [swelling

pĭm'ple, n., small skin

pĭn'ả-fôre, n., sleeveless dress

pĭn'cêrs, n. pl., gripping tool, lobster or crab claw

pĭnch, n., distress; v.,

squeeze between finger and thumb, steal

pĭne, n., evergreen tree; **naceous; -y** a.

pĭne, v., long for

pĭne'ăp-ple, n., tropical fruit

pĭnk, n., a., pale or light red   [point

pĭn'nả-cle, n., highest

pĭ-nŏch'le, n., card game

pĭn'pŏint, v., locate exactly; a., exact

pĭn'tŏ, n., spotted horse

pĭn'ŭp, n., sexy picture of girl   [discoverer

pĭ-ŏ-nēer', n., early settler,

pi'oŭs, a., holy, religious; **osity; -ly; -ness**

pĭpe, n., tube through which things pass; **-ful**

pi'quảnt, a., pugent, stimulating; **quancy; -ness; -ly**

pĭque, n., resentment; v., provoke, offend

pĭ-que' (quā), n., cotton cloth

pĭs-tă'chĭ-ō, n., edible nut, tree

pĭs'tĭl, n., seed-bearing part of flower

pĭs'tŏn, n., movable disk in cylinder

pĭt, n., stone in fruit, hole in ground, small scar; v., mark with pits, compete

pĭtch, n., tar, throw; v., set up, toss, degree, slope

pĭtch'êr, n., one who pitches, container for pouring liquid

pĭth, n., inner plant tissue, main part; **-y** a.

pĭt'tảnce, n., small amount (of money)

pĭt'ў, n., sorrow felt for another; **pitiful; pitiless**

pĭv'ŏt, n., point on which thing turns; v., turn; **-al**

plăc'ảrd, n., notice, sign

plā'cāte, v., appease; **-r; tion; tive; tory; able; ability; ably**

plăc'ĭd, a., calm; **-ity; -ly; -ness**

plā'giả-rĭze, v., take another's ideas as own; **-r; rism**

plāgue, *n.,* fatal epidemic disease; *v.,* annoy

plāin'tĭff, *n.,* one who brings law suit

plāin'tĭve, *a.,* sad; **-ly; -ness**

plāit, *n.,* braid (of hair)

plăn, *n.,* detailed method, arrangement; *v.,* make a plan, intend; **-ner**

plăn-ė-tār'ĭ-ŭm, *n.,* building to project heavenly images

plănk, *n.,* long thick board

plănt, *n.,* living thing that is stationary ex. tree, herb, factory; *v.,* put in soil to grow, set firmly

plăn-tā'tion, *n.,* large tropical farm

plăs'mȧ, *n.,* fluid part of blood; **-tic**

plăs'têr, *n.,* pasty mixture that hardens; **-er; -y** *a.*

plăs'tĭc, *n., a.* (synthetically made compound that is) flexible; **-ity; -ize; -ally**

plāte, *n.,* shallow dish, metal sheet, denture; *v.,* coat with gold or silver

plă-teau' (tō), *n.,* high level land

plăt'fôrm, *n.,* flat, raised flooring, political policy

plăt'ĭ-nŭm, *n.,* grey metallic chemical; **nize; tinic**

plăt'ĭ-tūde, *n.,* trite remark; **dinize; dinous; dinously**

plăt'ȳ-pŭs, *n.,* mammal

plău'sĭ-ble, *a.,* seemingly true; **bility; bly; -ness**

plāy'fŭl, *a.,* full of fun; **-ly; -ness**

plāy'ground, *n.,* outdoor recreation area

plāy'wright, *n.,* one who writes plays

plȧ'zȧ, *n.,* public square

plēad, *v.,* argue a law case, beg

plēase, *v.,* be agreeable, be kind enough of

plĕas'ûre, *n.,* enjoyment,

wish; **-ful; urable; urability; urableness; urably**

plēat, *n.,* fold in cloth

plė-bī'ȧn, *n.,* common person; **-ism; -ly**

plĕdge, *n.,* security, oath; *v.,* promise; **-r**

plė'nȧ-rȳ, *a.,* full, attended by membership; **rily**

plĕn'tȳ, *n.,* ample amount; **tiful; tifulness; tifully**

plĕth'ȯ-rȧ, *n.,* excess

plĕx'ŭs, *n.,* network

plī'ȧ-ble, *a.,* easily bent or influenced; **bility; bly; -ness**

plī'êrs, *n. pl.,* small gripping tool [tion

plĭght, *n.,* danger, condi-

plŏd, *v.,* move heavily; **-der; -dingly**

plŏt, *n.,* small area of ground, evil scheme

plow, *n., v.* (farm implement to) cut and turn up soil; **-er; -able**

ploy (plŏi), *n.,* outwitting maneuver [out

plŭck, *n.,* courage; *v.,* pull

plŭck'ȳ, *a.,* brave

plŭg, *n.,* hole stopper device to make electrical contact; *v.,* stop up, advertise

plŭm, *n.,* tree, fruit

plŭmb, *n.,* device to find water depth; *a.,* vertical

plŭm'mėt, *v.,* fall, drop

plŭmp, *v.,* drop; *a.,* full and rounded; **-per**

plŭn'dêr, *n.,* robbery, loot; *v.,* take by force; **-er; -age; -ous**

plŭnge, *n., v.,* dive, rush

plŭ-răl'ĭ-tȳ, *n.,* greatest number, ex. of votes

plŭsh, *n.,* thick, velvety fabric; *a.,* luxurious; **-y** *a.*

plŭ-tŏc'rȧ-cȳ, *n.,* government by wealthy; **crat**

plŭ-tō'nĭ-ŭm, *n.,* metallic element

plŭ'vĭ-ȧl, *a.,* of rain

plȳ, *n.,* single thickness; *v.,* bend, do work, ask,

travel

pneu-măt'ĭc, *a.,* filled with air; **-s; -ally**

pneu-mō'nĭ-à, *n.,* lung disease

pōach, *v.,* boil in water, hunt or fish illegally; **-er**

pŏd, *n.,* shell holding seeds or beans

pō-dī'à-trȳ, *n.,* treatment of human foot; **trist; ric**

pō'dĭ-ŭm, *n.,* raised platform

pō'ĕm, *n.,* rhythmical composition; **etry; etic; etical; etically**

pō-grŏm', *n.,* organized massacre

pōĭgn'ànt, *a.,* sharp, painful; **ancy; -ly**

pōĭnt'êr, *n.,* indicator, hint, hunting dog

pōĭnt'lĕss, *a.,* without meaning; **-ly; -ness**

pōĭse, *n.,* balance, dignity of manner

pōĭ'sòn, *n.,* substance causing death or illness; **-er; -ous; -ously; -ousness** [-r

pōke, *n., v.,* jab, search;

pŏk'êr, *n.,* card game

pō-lăr'ĭ-tȳ, *n.,* magnetic attraction to pole; **ize; ization; izer**

pò-lĕm'ĭc, *a.,* controversial; **-ally**

pò-līce, *n.,* governmental law enforcement, its members; *v.,* control by police; **-man** *n.*

pŏl'ĭ-cȳ, *n.,* principle, insurance contract

pō-lĭ-ō-mȳ-è-lī'tĭs, *n.,* virus disease of spine

pŏl'ĭsh, *v.,* rub to make smooth and glossy, refine; **-er**

pò-līte', *n.,* showing good manners; **-ly; -ness**

pŏl-ĭ-tī'cian, *n.,* one active in government

pŏl'ĭ-tĭcs, *n.,* science of government; **cal; calize; cally**

pŏl'kà, *n.,* fast dance

pōll, *n.,* head, counting of

votes, survey; *v.,* count

pŏl'lĕn, *n.,* powdery male sex cells of flower

pòl-lūte', *v.,* make dirty; **-r; tion**

pŏl'ȳ-ĕs-têr, *n.,* synthetic fiber

pò-lȳg'à-mȳ, *n.,* marriage to two or more spouses at once; **mist; mous; mously**

pŏl-ȳ-tĕch'nĭc, *a.,* of instruction in technical areas

pŏmp, *n.,* splendor

pŏm'pà-dôur, *n.,* hair style

pŏn'chō, *n.,* blanketlike cloak

pŏnd, *n.,* small lake

pŏn'dêr, *v.,* think deeply; **-er; -able; -ability**

pŏn'dêr-oŭs, *a.,* heavy; **osity; -ly; -ness**

pŏn'tĭff, *n.,* Pope, bishop

pŏn-tōon', *n.,* flat bottomed boat or float

pōol, *n.,* small garden pond, billiards, common fund

pôor, *a.,* lacking material things, inferior; **-ly**

Pōpe, *n.,* head of Catholic Church; **popish**

pŏp'lĭn, *n.,* ribbed cotton cloth

pŏp'ū-làce, *n.,* people

pŏp'ū-làr, *a.,* of common people, prevalent, well liked; **-ity; -ize; -izer; -ization** [ants

pŏp-ū-lā'tion, *n.,* inhabit-

pôr'cè-laĭn, *n.,* hard white ceramic ware; **laneous**

pôrch, *n.,* covered entrance to building

pôr'cū-pīne, *n.,* animal covered with sharp spines

pôre, *n.,* tiny opening; *v.,* study carefully, think

pôrk, *n.,* meat of pig

pôr-nŏg'rà-phȳ, *n.,* lewd writings or pictures; **pher, graphic; graphically**

pôr'rĭdge, *n.,* hot cereal

pôrt, *n.,* harbor, red wine,

left side of ship, opening

pôrt′à-ble, *a.*, easily carried; **bility**

pôr-tĕnd′, *v.*, be an omen

pôr′tĕnt, *n.*, omen

pôr-tĕn′toŭs, *a.*, ominous, pompous; **-ly; -ness**

pôrt-fō′lĭ-ō, *n.*, small case for papers

pôr′tĭ-cō, *n.*, large porch with columns

pôrt′lȳ, *a.*, fat and stately; **liness**

pôr′traĭt, *n.*, representation of a person; **-ist; -ure**

pôr-trāy′, *v.*, make a picture, describe; **-al** *n.*; **-er; -able**

pōse, *n.*, assumed manner; *v.*, present, model, pretend

pŏ-sĭ′tion, *n.*, opinion, place, status, job

pŏs′ĭ-tĭve, *a.*, very sure, greater than zero; **-ly; -ness**

pŏs-sĕss′, *v.*, own, have, control; **-or; -ion; -ed; -ive; -ively; -iveness**

pōst, *n.*, upright piece of wood, position, military camp, mail; *v.*, put up, assign to a post, mail

pōst′àge, *n.*, fee for sending mail

pōs-tē′rĭ-ôr, *a.*, behind, later; **-ity; -ly**

pōst′hŭ-moŭs, *a.*, occurring after death; **-ly**

pōst′mârk, *n.*, mark that cancels postage stamp

pōst-môr′tĕm, *a.*, done after death

pōst-nā′tàl, *a.*, after birth

pōst-nŭp′tiàl, *a.*, after marriage; **-ly**

pōst-pōne′, *v.*, delay; **-r; -ment; ponable**

pōst′scrĭpt, *n.*, addition to letter

pŏs′tûre, *n.*, position of body, attitude

pō′tà-ble, *a.*, fit to drink; **bility; -ness**

pŏ-tăs′sĭ-ŭm, *n.*, soft metallic element [tuber

pŏ-tā′tŏ, *n.*, vegetable

pō′tĕnt, *a.*, powerful, effective; **tency; -ly**

pō′tĕn-tāte, *n.*, ruler

pŏ-tĕn′tiàl, *n.*, undeveloped ability; *a.*, possible, latent; **-ity; -ly**

pō′tion, *n.*, drink

pōt-pôur′rĭ, *n.*, mixture

pŏŭch, *n.*, small bag; **-y** *a.*

pōul′trȳ, *n.*, fowls raised for meat or eggs; **-man**

pŏŭnd, *n.*, weight of 16 ounces, place of confinement; *v.*, beat

pôur, *v.*, flow freely, rain heavily; **-er**

pŏv′êr-tȳ, *n.*, being poor, need, inadequacy

pŏw′dêr, *n.*, fine, dustlike particles; **-y** *a.*

pŏw′êr, *n.*, ability, strength, authority; **-ful; -fully; -fulness; -less; -lessly; -lessness**

pŏx, *n.*, disease with skin eruptions

prăc′tĭce, *n.*, custom, habit, work in a profession; *v.*, do repeatedly

prăg-măt′ĭc, *a.*, practical; **tist; tism; -ally**

praĭ′riĕ, *n.*, level grassland

prāise, *v.*, express approval; **-r**

prănce, *v.*, strut with spirit

prănk, *n.*, mischievous trick; **-ster; -ish; -ishly; -ishness**

prāte, *n.*, *v.*, chatter; **-r**

prāwn, *n.*, shrimplike animal [God

prāy, *v.*, implore, ask of

prēach, *v.*, give moral or religious advice; **-er; -y** *a.* [tion

prē′ăm-ble, *n.*, introduc-

prè-cār′ĭ-oŭs, *a.*, risky; **-ly; -ness**

prè-cēde′, *v.*, come before; **-nce; cession; cessional**

prē′cĕpt, *n.*, rule of conduct; **-ive; -ively**

prē′cĭnct, *n.*, city district

prē′cioŭs, *a.*, of great value; **-ly; -ness**

prė-cĭp'ĭ-tāte, v., bring on; a., (tāte) sudden; **tor; tive; -ly; -ness**

prė-cĭp-ĭ-tā'tion, n., rain, snow, etc.

prė-clūde', v., prevent; **clusion; clusive; clu- sively**

prė-cō'cious, a., devel- oped beyond one's years; **city; -ly; -ness**

prė-cûr'sör, n., forerunner

prėd'ȧ-tô-rȳ, a., exploiting others; **tor; rily; riness**

prė-dĭc'ȧ-mėnt, n., diffi- cult situation; **-al**

prėd'ĭ-cāte, v., declare, base; **tion; tive; tively**

prė-dĭct', v., tell in ad- vance; **-or; -ion; -ive; -ively; -able; -ability; -ably** [ence

prė-dĭ-lĕc'tion, n., prefer-

prė-dŏm'ĭ-nāte, v., be greater, rule; **tor; tion; nant; nance; nancy; nantly**

prė-ėm'ĭ-nėnt, a., excel- ling others; **nence; -ly**

prēen, v., clean feathers, primp; **-er**

prė-fêr', v., like better, choose; **-rer; -ence; -ential; -able; -ability; -ableness; -ably**

prėg'nȧnt, a., carrying fe- tus in womb, filled; **nancy; -ly**

prėj'ůdĭce, n., unfair opin- ion, intolerance; **cial; cially**

prėl'ȧte, n., clergyman

prėl'ūde, n., introduction

prė-miêr', n., prime min- ister of a nation; a., chief

prĕm'īse, n., basic as- sumption, (pl.) property

prė'mĭ-ŭm, n., reward, in- surance payment, high value

prė-pāre', v., get ready; **ration; paratory; para- torily; -dly; -dness**

prė-pŏn'dêr-āte, v., sur- pass; **tion; ant; ance; ancy; antly**

pre-pŏs'têr- oŭs, a., ab- surd; **-ly; -ness**

prė-rŏg'ȧ-tĭve, n., privi- lege

prĕs'ȧge, n., warning; v., (āge) foretell; **-r**

prė'sci-ence, n., foresight

prė-scrībe', v., order, give medical advice; **-r; scription; scriptive; scriptively**

prĕs'ėnce, n., attendance, appearance

prĕs'ėnt, n., something given; a., existing; v., (prės-ĕnt') introduce, give, show; **-er; -ation**

prė-sêrve', n., jam; v., save, maintain; **serva- ble**

prĕs'ĭ-dėnt, n., highest of- ficer; **dency; -ial; -ially**

prĕss, n., pressure, crush- ing machine, printing, journalists; v., squeeze, iron clothes, urge; **-er**

prĕs'sure (shûr), n., force, urgency, influence

prĕs-tīge', n., influence, earned fame; **gious**

prė-sūme', v., take for granted; **-r; sumption; sumptive**

prė-tĕnd', v., claim falsely, make believe; **-er; tense**

prē'tĕxt, n., excuse, cover-up

prĕt'tȳ, a., pleasing and dainty; adv., somewhat; **tify; tily**

prė-vằr'ĭ-cāte, v., lie, tell falsehood; **tor; tion**

prė-vĕnt', v., keep from doing; **-er; -ion; -ive; -ively; -able**

prey (prāy), n., something hunted; v., plunder, hunt, weigh heavily; **-er**

prīce, n., v., cost, value; **-less**

prĭck, n., tiny hole made from sharp point; v., pierce; **-er**

prīde, n., self-respect; **-ful; -fully; -fulness**

prīest, n., one who leads religious rites; **-hood; -ly**

prĭg, *n.,* smug person; **-gish; -gishly; -gishness**

prī'mă-rÿ, *n.,* first, political party election; *a.,* first, basic; **rily**

prī'māte, *n.,* highest order of mammals; **-ship; tial**

prīme, *n.,* best part; *v.,* prepare; *a.,* first chief, basic

prĭm'ĭ-tĭve, *a.,* ancient, uncivilized, basic; **-ly; -ness**

prĭmp, *v.,* dress up fussily

prĭm'rōse, *n.,* flowering plant

prĭnce, *n.,* king's son, ruler; **-ss** *n.;* **cipality; -ly** *a.*

prĭn'cĭ-pȧl, *n.,* school director; money owed; *a.,* chief, first; **-ship; -ly**

prĭn'cĭ-ple, *n.,* basic truth, integrity

prĭnt, *n.,* mark made on something by pressure, photograph, copy; *v.,* mark by pressing; **-er; -ing** *n.;* **-able; -ability**

prī-ôr'ĭ-tÿ, *n.,* preference

prĭsm, *n.,* solid figure with equal and parallel sides; **-atic; -atically**

prĭs'ŏn, *n.,* jail

prī'vȧte, *a.,* limited to particular persons, secret; **vacy; -ly**

prĭv'ĭ-lège, *n.,* special right or favor

prĭv'ÿ, *n.,* outside toilet; *a.,* secret

prīze, *n.,* something won, reward; *v.,* value

prō'bāte, *v.,* validate a document

prō-bā'tion, *n.,* suspension of prison sentence, testing

prōbe, *n., v.,* (device that can) explore, investigate; **-r**

prŏb'lĕm, *n.,* perplexing question; **-atic; -atically**

prō-bŏs'cĭs, *n.,* long flexible snout, ex. elephant's trunk   [*n.*

prŏ-cēed', *v.,* go on; **-ing**

prŏ-cēed'ĭngs, *n., pl.,* transaction, legal action

prŏc'ĕss, *n.,* continuing development, method

prŏ-cĕs'sion, *n.,* parade

prō-clĭv'ĭ-tÿ, *n.,* tendency

prō-crăs'tĭ-nāte, *v.,* put off doing; **tor; tion**

prō'crē-āte, *v.,* beget offspring; **tor; tion; tive**

prŏc'tŏr, *n.,* supervisor

prŏd, *v.,* poke with pointed stick; **-der**

prŏd'ĭ-gȧl, *a.,* wasteful; **-ity; -ly**

prŏ-dĭ'gioŭs, *a.,* amazing, huge; **-ly; -ness**

prŏd'ĭ-gÿ, *n.,* marvel

prō'dūce, *n.,* farm products; *v.,* **(prŏ-dūce')** bring forth, make, cause, grow; **-r; duction; ducible; ducibility**

prŏ-fāne', *a.,* irreligious, contempt for sacred things; **fanity; nation; fanatory; -ness; -ly**

prŏ-fĕs'sion, *n.,* belief, learned occupation; **-al; -ally**   [teacher

prŏ-fĕs'sŏr, *n.,* college

prŏf'fêr, *n., v.,* offer

prŏ-fĭ'cĭent, *a.,* skilled; **ciency; -ly**

prŏf'ĭt, *n., v.,* benefit; *n.,* business gain; **-able; -ability; -ableness; -ably; -less**

prŏ-fŏūnd', *a.,* deep in feelings or ideas; **fundity; -ly; -ness**

prŏ-fūse', *a.,* abundant; **fusion; -ly; -ness**

prŏg'ė-nÿ, *n.,* offspring

prŏg-nō'sĭs, *n.,* medical prediction

prō'grăm, *n., v.,* plan; *n.,* schedule of events; **-matic**

prŏg'rĕss, *n.,* moving forward; *v.,* **(prŏg-rĕss')** advance; **-ion**

prō-hĭb'ĭt, *v.,* forbid; **-er; -or; -ion; -ive**

prŏj'ĕct, *n.,* organized undertaking; *v.,* **(prŏj-ĕct')** propose, send forth, stick out; **-or; -ion**

prō-lĕ-tār′ĭăt, *n.*, working class; **an** *n., a.*

prō-līf′ĕr-āte, *v.*, produce; **tion**   [**-ally**

prō-līf′ĭc, *a.*, fruitful; **-acy;**

prō′lŏgue, *n.*, introduction

prō-lŏng′, *v.*, extend; **-er; -ation**   [surely walk

prŏm-ĕ-nāde′, *n.*, lei-

prŏm′ĭ-nĕnt, *a.*, noticeable, famous; **nence; -ly**

prō-mĭs′cū-oŭs, *a.*, lack of discrimination; **cuity; -ly; -nous**

prŏm′ĭse, *n.*, agreement, vow, cause for hope; *v.*, pledge

prō-mōte′, *v.*, advance in position; **-r; tion; tional**

prŏmpt, *v.*, inspire, urge; *a.*, quick; **-er; -ly; -ness**

prōne, *a.*, lying flat; **-ly; -ness**   [fork

prŏng, *n.*, pointed end of

prō-noŭnce′, *v.*, declare, utter sounds, words, etc.; **-r**

prō-noŭnce′mĕnt, *n.*, authoritative statement

prōōf, *n.*, test, conclusive evidence

prŏp-ȧ-găn′dȧ, *n.*, systematic promotion of ideas; **dism; dist; dize; distic; distically**

prŏp′ȧ-gāte, *v.*, produce offspring, spread; **tor; tion; tive**

prō-pĕl′, *v.*, drive forward

prō-pĕn′sĭ-tȳ, *n.*, tendency

prŏp′ĕr, *a.*, suitable, correct; **-ly**

prŏp′ĕr-tȳ, *n.*, things owned, quality

prŏph′ĕ-cȳ, *n.*, prediction

prŏph′ĕ-sȳ, *v.*, predict

prō′phȳ-lăc-tĭc, *a.*, protective against disease; **laxis** *n.*

prō-pĭn′quĭ-tȳ, *n.*, nearness, kinship

prō-pĭ′tĭ-āte, *v.*, gain favor of; **tor; tion; pitious; pitiously; pitiousness; able**

prō-pôr′tion, *n.*, part, com-

parative relation between things; *v.*, balance; **-al; -ally; -āte** *n.;* **-ately; -able**

prō-pōse′, *v.*, suggest for consideration, offer marriage; **-r; position; positional; posal** *n.*

prō-prī′ĕ-tŏr, *n.*, owner; **-y**

prō-prī′ĕ-tȳ, *n.*, conformity to proper standards

prō-sā′ĭc, *a.*, commonplace; **-ally; -ness**

prō-scribe′, *v.*, outlaw; **-r; scription; scriptive; scriptively**   [word

prōse, *n.*, spoken or written

prŏs′ĕ-cūte, *v.*, take legal action against; **tor; tion; cutable**

prŏs′ĕ-lȳte, *n.*, convert to another belief; **lytism; lytize**

prŏs′pĕct, *n.*, outlook, anticipation, likely customer

prō-spĕc′tŭs, *n.*, outline of proposed plan

prŏs′pĕr, *v.*, succeed; **-ity; -ous; -ously**

prŏs′thĕ-sĭs, *n.*, artificial substitute of body part; **thetic**

prŏs′tĭ-tūte, *n.*, woman paid for sexual intercourse; **tor; tion**

prŏs′trāte, *v.*, lay flat; *a.*, prone; **tion**

prō-tăg′ō-nĭst, *n.*, main character in fiction

prō′tĕ-ge (gā), *n.*, one helped by a patron in a career

prō′tēin, *n.*, nitrogenous substance in all living things

prō′tĕst, *n.*, objection; *v.*, (prō-test′) oppose, assert; **-er; -or; -ation**

prō′tŏn, *n.*, positive particle in atom's nucleus

prō′tō-plăsm, *n.*, essential matter of all living things; **-ic**

prō′tō-tȳpe, *n.*, original model; **typal; typic; typical**

prō-tò-zō'àn, *n.*, microscopic animal; **zoic**

prō-tract'tör, *n.*, device to draw or measure angles

prō-trūde', *v.*, jut out; **trusion; trusive; trusively; trusiveness**

prō-tü'bêr-ànt, *a.*, swelling; **ance; -ly**

proŭd, *a.*, feeling pride, stately; **-ly**

prove (prūv), *v.*, show to be true; **-r; provable; provability; provably**

prŏv'êrb, *n.*, wise saying; **-ial; -ially**

prò-vīde', *v.*, supply, prepare, require; **-r**

prŏv'ĭ-dènt, *a.*, looking into future, economical; **dence; -ly**

prŏv'ĭnce, *n.*, geographical area, sphere

prò-vī'sion, *n.*, supplying, arrangement, requirement

prò-vī'sō, *n.*, condition; **-ry; -rily**

prò-vōke', *v.*, arouse action of feeling; **-r; ocation; vocative; vocatively; vocativeness; voking; vokingly**

prōw'ĕss, *n.*, bravery

prōwl, *v.*, wander stealthily; **-er**

prŏx'ĭ-màte, *a.*, nearest; **imity; -ly** [to vote

prŏx'ÿ, *n.*, agent, authority

prūde, a., one overly modest; **prudish; prudishly; prudishness**

prū'dènt, *a.*, wisely careful; **dence; -ly; -ial; -ially**

prÿ, *n.*, lever; *v.*, force up, look closely [**-ist**

psälm, *n.*, sacred song;

pseū'dò-nÿm, *n.*, false name used by author; **-ous; -ously**

psò-rī'à-sĭs, *n.*, skin disease [mind

psÿ'chē (kē) *n.*, human

psÿ-chè-dĕl'ĭc (kè), *a.*, of bright, vivid colors, intensification of percep-

tion; **-ally**

psÿ-chī'à-trÿ (kī), *n.*, medical study of mental illness; **trist; tric; trical; trically**

psÿ-chō-à-nàl'ÿ-sĭs (kō), *n.*, examination of mental process; **lyst** *n.*; **lyze** *v.*; **lytic; lytical; lytically**

psÿ-chŏl'ò-gÿ (kol), *n.*, science of behavior; **gist; gize; logical; logically**

psÿ'chò-päth (kò), *n.*, one with mental disorder; **-y; -ic; -ology; -ologist; -ological**

psÿ-chō'sĭs (kō), *n.*, severe mental disorder; **chotic**

psÿ-chō-sò-mät'ic (kō), *a.*, having bodily symptoms from mental origin; **-ally**

ptò'māine (tō), *n.*, poisonous substance found in decaying food

pū'bêr-tÿ, *n.*, physical development when sexual maturity begins

pŭb'lĭc, *n.*, people; *a.*, of the people, known by all; **-ly**

pŭb-lĭc'ĭ-tÿ, *n.*, notice to the people; **cize**

pŭb'lĭsh, *v.*, make known publicly, issue written work; **-er; -able**

pŭck, *n.*, hard rubber disk for ice hockey

pŭd'dĭng, *n.*, soft cooked food

pū'êr-īle, *a.*, childish; **il-ism; ility; -ly**

pŭg-nā'cioŭs, *a.*, quarrelsome; **nacity; -ly; -ness**

pŭl'chrĭ-tūde (krĭ), *n.*, physical beauty; **dinous**

pŭl'lèt, *n.*, young hen

pŭl'mò-när-ÿ, *a.*, of lungs

pŭlp, *n.*, soft moist mass; **-y** *a.* [platform

pŭl'pĭt, *n.*, church's raised

pŭlse, *n.*, beat of blood flow through arteries

pŭl'vêr-īze, *v.*, crush into powder; **-r; zation**

P
R

pū'má, *n.*, cougar

pŭm'īce, *n.*, light porous rock; **-ous**

pŭmp, *n.*, machine that forces liquid or gas in or out, low cut shoe; **-er**

pŭmp'kĭn, *n.*, large orange gourdlike fruit   [**-ster**

pŭn, *n.*, play on words;

pŭnch, *n.*, piercing tool, fruit drink; *v.*, hit with fist; **-er**

pŭnc-tĭl'ĭ-oŭs, *a.*, very exact; **-ly**; **-ness** [**-ness**

pŭnc'tū-ál, *a.*, on time; **-ly**;

pŭnc'tûre, *n.*, hole made by sharp point; *v.*, pierce

pŭn'gént, *a.*, sharp or strong in taste or smell; **gency**; **-ly**

pŭn'ĭsh, *v.*, make suffer for wrongdoing; **-er**; **-ment**; **-able**; **-ability**

pŭnt, *n.*, football kick, flat-bottomed boat

pū'nÿ, *a.*, inferior, weak

pū'pá, *n.*, insect in stage before adulthood

pū'pĭl, *n.*, student, dark opening in center of eye

pŭp'pét, *n.*, animated doll; **-eer** *n.*; **-ry**

pū-ree' (rā), *n.*, mashed, strained food

pûr-gá-tô'rÿ, *n.*, state of temporary punishment

pûrge, *v.*, cleanse, get rid of, **-r**

pū'rĭ-fÿ, *v.*, make pure; **fier**; **fication**; **ficatory**

pū-rĭ-tăn'ĭ-cál, *a.*, very strict; **-ly**

pûr'pôrt, *n.*, meaning; *v.*, imply

pûr'póse, *n.*, aim, intension; **-ful**; **-fully**; **-fulness**; **-less**; **-lessly**; **-lessness**; **-ly**

pûr-sūe', *v.*, chase, strive for   [**-ance**

pûr-vey' (vā), *v.*, supply;

pŭs, *n.*, discharge of an infection; **-sy** *a.*

pŭsh'ō-vêr, *n.*, goal easy to accomplish

pŭs'tūle, *n.*, small pimple containing pus

pū'trĭd, *a.*, rotten, bad smelling; **trefy**; **trefier**; **trefaction**; **-ity**; **-ness**; **-ly**

pŭtt, *v.*, tap golf ball into hole; **-er**

pŭt'tÿ, *n.*, soft plastic mixture

pŭz'zle, *n.*, very difficult problem; *v.*, confuse; **-r**; **-ment**

pÿg'mÿ, *n.*, very undersized person; **-ism**

pÿ'lön, *n.*, tall tower

pÿ-ór-rhē'á, *n.*, gum disease; **-l**

pÿre, *n.*, wood pile for burning dead

pÿ-rŏ-mā'nĭ-à, *n.*, compulsion to start fires; **-c** *n.*, *a.*; **-cal**

pÿ'thŏn, *n.*, large snake

Q

quăck, *n.*, fraudulent medical practitioner; **-ery**; **-ish**; **-ishly**

quád'ránt, *n.*, quarter part of a circle; **-al**

quád'rū-pĕd, *n.*, animal with four feet; **-al**

quád-rū'plét, *n.*, any of four offspring born together

quáff, *v.*, drink deeply

quăg'mīre, *n.*, land yielding under foot

quāil, *n.*, small game bird; *v.*, draw back in fear

quăint, *a.*, pleasingly old-fashioned, odd; **-ly**; **-ness**

quál'ĭ-fÿ, *v.*, make fit, limit, characterize; **fier**; **fication**; **fied**; **fiedly**; **fiedness**; **fiable**; **-ingly**

quál'ĭ-tÿ, *n.*, feature, nature, excellence; **tative**; **tatively**

quálm, *n.*, uneasy feeling; **-ish**; **-ishly**; **-ishness**

quán'da-rÿ, *n.*, state of uncertainty

quán'tĭ-tÿ, *n.*, amount

quâr'án-tĭne, *n.*, isolation for contagious disease

quâr′rėl, *n., v.,* dispute verbally; **-er; -some** *a.*

quâr′rÿ, *n.,* prey, place where rock is excavated

quar′ter (quôr), *n.,* fourth, city district, (pl.) lodgings

quartz (quôrtz), *n.,* bright mineral; **iferous**

quásh, *v.,* suppress; **-er**

quā′sī, *a.,* seeming; *adv.,* in part

quā′vêr, *v.,* tremble; **-er; -y** *a.;* **-ingly**

quéa′sÿ, *a.,* causing nausea; **sily; siness**

quēer, *a.,* strange; **-ly; -ness**   [**-er**

quéll, *v.,* subdue, quiet;

quénch, *v.,* put out, satisfy; **-er; -able; -less**

quêr′ŭ-loŭs, *a.,* complaining; **-ly; -ness**

quē′rÿ, *n., v.,* question

quést, *n.,* search

qués′tion, *n.,* inquiry, doubt, problem; *v.,* ask, challenge; **-er; -less**

queūe, *n.,* line of waiting people, hair braid

quĭb′ble, *n.,* minor objection; *v.,* evade; **-r**

quĭche, *n.,* custard pie

quĭck′sănd, *n.,* wet, loose sand yielding to weight

quĭck-wĭt′tėd, *a.,* alert; **-ly; -ness**   [**cence ;-ly**

quī-ĕs′cėnt, *a.,* quiet;

quī′ėt, *v., a.,* (make) still, silent, calm; **-ude** *n.***; -ly; -ness**

quĭll, *n.,* large feather, porcupine's spine

quĭlt, *n.,* layered bedcover; **-ing** *n.*   [malaria

quī′nĭne, *n.,* medicine for

quĭn-tĕt′, *n.,* any of five offspring born together

quĭn-tŭ′ple, *v., a.,* make five times as much

quĭp, *n.,* witty remark; *v.,* joke; **-ster**

quîrk, *n.,* peculiarity; **-y** *a.*

quĭt, *v.,* stop, leave; **-ter**

quĭte, *adv.,* completely, really

quĭv′êr, *v.,* shake

quĭx-ŏt′ĭc, *a.,* idealistic, impractical; **-ally**

quĭz′zĭ-cál, *a.,* comical, perplexed; **-ity; -ly**

quô′rŭm, *n.,* minimum number of members to legally do business

quô′tá, *n.,* assigned share

quōte, *v.,* repeat words exactly, state price of; **-r; tation; quotable**

quô′tiėnt, *n.,* resulting number from division

R

răb′bī, *n.,* Jewish clergyman; **-nic; -nical; -nically**

răb′bĭt, *n.,* long-eared rodentlike mammal

răb′ble, *n., v.,* mob

răb′īd, *a.,* fanatical, of rabies; **-ity; -ly; -ness**

rā′bĭes, *n.,* disease gotten from animal bite

rāce, *n.,* speed competition; *v.,* be in race, move swiftly

rāce, *n.,* division of mankind; **cial; cially**

răc′ĭsm, *n.,* racial discrimination; **ist**

răck, *n.,* framework for holding things, torture instrument, torment

răck′ėt, *n.,* noise, dishonest scheme, stringed frame for tennis

răc-ŏn-teûr′, *n.,* story teller

rāc′ÿ, *a.,* pungent, spirited; **raciness; racily**

rā′dâr, *n.,* radio detecting and ranging device

rā′dĭ-ánt, *a.,* shining brightly; *n.,* source of light or heat; **ance; -ly**

rā′dĭ-āte, *v.,* give forth, shine, send from center; **tion**

rā′dĭ-ā-tör, *n.,* heating device for homes

răd′ĭ-cál, *a.,* politically extreme, basic; **-ism; -ize; -ization; -ness; -ly**

rā′dĭ-ō, *n.,* device to send

and receive sound by electric waves

rā-dǐ-ō-ăc'tǐve, a., giving off radiant energy; **tivity; -ly**

rā-dǐ-ŏl'ò-gy, n., medical science of X-rays; **gist; logical; logically**

rǎd'ǐsh, n., edible root

rā'dǐ-ǔm, n., radioactive metallic element

rā'dǐ-ǔs, n., line from center to edge of circle

rǎf'fle, n., lottery of buying chances for prize

rǎft, n., floating platform, large number

rǎft'ẽr, n., roof support

rǎg, n., worn piece of cloth, (pl.) old worn clothes; **-ged**

rāge, n., furious anger, fad; v., be uncontrolled; **ingly**

rāid, n., hostile attack; **-er**

rāil, n., bar across posts, track for train; v., reproach

rāi'mènt, n., clothing

rāin, n., water dropping to earth; **-y** a.

rāin'bōw, n., arc of colors formed from sun on rain

rāise, n., increase; v., lift, construct, increase, bring up

rāi'sǐn, n., dried grape

rāke, n., long-handled tool with teeth; v., gather, scrape

rǎl'lY, n., mass meeting; v., gather together, revive

rǎm, n., male sheep; v., drive into, force; **-mer**

rǎm'ble, v., roam about; **-r**

rǎm-bǔnc'tioǔs, a., wild, unruly; **-ly; -ness**

rǎmp, n., sloping surface

rǎm-pāge', n., violent action; v., rage

rǎmp'ànt, a., widespread, wild; **ancy; -ly**

rǎm'shǎck-le, a., rickety

rǎnch, n., large animal farm; **-er**

rǎn'cǐd, a., smelling rotten,

spoiled; **-ly; -ness**

rǎn'cõr, n., bitter hate; **-ous; -ously**

rǎn'dòm, a., haphazard; **-ly; -ness**

rānge, n., extent, distance, open land, group of mountains, stove; v., extend, roam

rǎnk, n., relative position; v., place in order; a., extreme, rancid

rǎn'sǎck, v., search, plunder; **-er**

rǎn'sòm, n., price demanded to free kidnapped person; **-er**

rǎnt, v., talk wildly; **-er**

rà-pā'cioǔs, a., greedy, plundering; **city; -ly; -ness**

rāpe, n., crime of sexual intercourse by force

rǎp'ǐd, n., swift current; a., fast; **-ity; -ly; -ness**

rā'pī-êr, n., sword

rǎp-port' (pôr), n., close relationship

rǎpt, a., engrossed

rǎp'ture, n., great pleasure

rāre, a., scarce, of great value, partly raw; **-ness**

rāre'lY, adv., seldom

rǎs'càl, n., mischievous person; **-ly** a., adv.

rǎsh, n., red spots on skin

rǎsh, a., hasty; **-ly; -ness**

rǎsp, v., grate, irritate; **-er; -y** a.; **-ingly** [son

rǎt, n., rodent, sneaky per-

rāte, n., relative amount, evaluate; ratable

rǎt'ǐ-fY, v., approve officially; **fier; fication**

rā'tiō, n., comparison, proportion

rā'tion, n., fixed portion

rǎ'tion-àl, a., able to reason; **-ity; -ize; -ization; -ly**

rǎ-tion-ǎle', n., reason for something [wicker

rǎt-tǎn', n., cane to make

rǎt'tle, n., v., (thing that can) make quick sharp sounds

rǎt'tle-snāke, n., snake

with rattle at its tail
rău′coŭs, *a.,* loud; **-ly;
-ness**
răv′àge, *n.,* violent destruction; *v.,* ruin; **-er**
rave, *v.,* talk wildly, praise
greatly; **-r**
răv′ėl, *v.,* untwist; **-er;
-ment** [black
rā′vėn, *n.,* large crow; *a.,*
răv′ė-noŭs, *a.,* very hungry; **-ly; -ness**
răv′ĭsh, *v.,* carry away, enrapture; **-er; -ment**
răw, *a.,* in natural state,
sore, bleak [hide
răw′hīde, *n.,* untanned
rāy, *n.,* thin line of light,
straight line, flat fish
rāy′òn, *n.,* synthetic fiber
rāze, *v.,* destroy
rā′zŏr, *n.,* sharp-edged
device for shaving
rēach, *v.,* extend hand,
achieve, influence; **-er**
rē-āct′, *v.,* act in return,
respond; **-ion; -ive; -iv-
ity; -ively; -ivensss**
rē-ăc′tion-ār-ȳ, *a.,* politically very conservative;
tionist
rē-ăc′tŏr, *n.,* device producing atomic energy
rēad, *v.,* understand or say
aloud printed words,
study; **-er; -ing** *n.;* **-able;
-ability; -ableness;
-ably**
rĕad′ȳ, *a.,* prepared, apt,
willing, prompt; **readily;
readiness** [-ly
rē-àl, *a.,* true, existing; **-ity**
rē′àl-ĭsm, *n.,* tendency to
face facts; **ist; istic; istically**
rĕalm, *n.,* kingdom, area
rē′àl-tȳ, *n.,* land and whatever is part of it; **tor**
rēam, *n.,* large amount; *v.,*
enlarge [tain; **-er**
rēap, *v.,* gather crop, ob-
rēar, *n.,* back part; *v.,*
raise, stand on hind legs
rēa′sòn, *n.,* explanation,
cause, ability to think; *v.,*
think logically; **-ing** *n.;*
-able

rē-bāte′, *n., v.,* return of
part payment
rĕb′ėl, *n.,* one who resists
authority; *v.,* **(rĕb-ĕl′)** revolt against; **-lion;
-lious; -liously; -lious-
ness**
rė-bŭff′, *n.,* refusal, snub
rė-būke′, *n., v.,* reprimand
rē′bŭs, *n.,* puzzle
rė-bŭt′tàl, *n.,* argument in
debate
rė-căl′cĭ-trāte, *v.,* rebel;
**tion; trant; trance;
trancy; trantly**
rė-căll′, *v.,* call back, remember, cancel; **-able**
rē-cà-pĭt′ū-lāte, *v.,* repeat,
summarize; **tion; tory**
rē-căp′tûre, *v.,* retake,
remember [diminish
rė-cēde′, *v.,* move back,
rė-cēipt′ (cēt), *n.,* written
proof of something re-
ceived
rė-cēive′, *v.,* get, accept,
be given; **-er; ceivable**
rē′cėnt, *a.,* of time just
past; **cency; -ness; -ly**
rė-cėp′tà-cle, *n.,* container
rė-cĕp′tion, *n.,* receiving,
greeting, response; **-ist**
rė-cĕp′tĭve, *a.,* able to receive; **tivity; -ness; -ly**
rē′cĕss, *n.,* hollow place,
time of rest
rė-cĕs′sion, *n.,* withdrawal, temporary drop
in business
rė-cĕs′sion-àl, *n.,* concluding music
rė-cĕs′sĭve, *a.,* of latent
hereditary factor; **-ly;
-ness**
rĕc′ĭ-pē, *n.,* directions for
preparing food
rė-cĭp′ĭ-ėnt, *n.,* one who
receives
rė-cĭp′rò-càl, *a.,* done in
return, mutual; **-ity;
cate; cation; cator; ca-
tive; -ly** [action
rĕc-ĭ-prŏc′ĭ-tȳ, *n.,* mutual
rė-cĭt′àl, *n.,* telling, musical program
rĕc-ĭ-tā′tion, *n.,* public

speech

rĕ-cīte′, v., speak formally from memory; **-r**

rĕck′lĕss, a., careless; **-ly; -ness**

rĕck′ŏn, v., count, consider, settle; **-er**

rĕ-clăim′, v., rescue, recover; **-er; clamation; -able** [**nation**

rĕ-clīne′, v., lie back; **-r;**

rĕc′lūse, n., one living a secluded life; **sion; sive**

rĕc′ŏg-nīze, v., identify, accept; **-r; nition; nitive; nitory; nizable; nizability; nizably**

rĕc-ŏm-mĕnd′, v., suggest, advise; **-er; -ation; -atory; -able**

rĕc′ŏm-pĕnse, v., pay for

rĕc′ŏn-cīle, v., make friendly again, settle; **ciliation; ciliatory; cilable; cilability; cilably**

rĕc′ŏn-dīte, a., obscure; **-ly; -ness**

rĕ-cŏn′nais-sánce (ná), n., exploration, survey

rĕc′ŏrd, n., account, evidence, disc of recorded sound; a., best; v., **(rĕ-côrd′)** put in writing, register, put on disc; **-er**

rĕ-coŭp′, v., regain; **-ment; -able**

rĕ-cŏv′ĕr, v., get back, regain health; **-y**

rĕc-rĕ-ā′tion, n., form of amusement or relaxation; **-al**

rĕ-crĭm′ĭ-nāte, v., accuse in return; **tion; tive; tory**

rĕ-crūit′, n., new member; v., enlist; **-er; -ment**

rĕc′tĭ-fŷ, v., correct, adjust; **fier; fication; fiable**

rĕc′tĭ-tūde, n., honesty

rĕc′tŏr, n., clergyman; **-y**

rĕc′tŭm, n., end part of large intestine; **tal**

rĕ-cŭm′bĕnt, a., lying down; **bency; -ly**

rĕ-cū′pĕr-āte, v., restore health; **tor; tion; tive; tory**

rĕ-cûr′, v., occur again; **-rence; -rent; -rently**

rĕd, n., a., color of blood, communist; **-den; -dish; -dishness**

rĕ-dăct′, v., edit; **-or; -ion**

rĕ-dēem′, v., get back by paying; **-er; demption; demptive; -able**

rĕd′hănd′ĕd, a., adv., in the act of a wrongdoing

rĕ-doŭbt′, n., fort

rĕ-drĕss′, v., make right; **-er; -able**

rĕ-dūce′, v., lessen, lower, change form; **-r; duction; ductive; ducability; ducible; ducibly**

rĕ-dŭn′dánt, a., wordy, excess; **dancy; -ly**

rēed, n., hollow grass stem; **-y** a.

rēef, n., ridge just under water; v., take in part of sail

rēek, n., stench; v., smell offensively

rēel, n., lively dance, spool for winding thread, film, etc.; v., stagger

rĕ-fêr′, v., mention, direct to; **-rer; -ral** n.; **-rable**

rĕf-ĕr-ēe′, n., judge

rĕf′ĕr-ĕnce, n., regard, mention, information

rĕf-ĕr-ĕn′dŭm, n., direct vote by people

rē′fĭll, n., new supply

rĕ-fīne′, v., make pure, make elegant; **-r; -ry; -ment**

rĕ-flĕct′, v., give back an image of, result in, think; **-or; -ion; -ive; -ivity; -iveness; -ively**

rē′flĕx, n., involuntary response; **-ly**

rĕ-flĕx′īve, a., of verb with same subject and object; **flexivity; -ly; -ness**

rĕ-fôrm′, v., correct, change improve; **-er; -ation; -able; -ative**

rĕ-fôrm′á-tô-rŷ, n., prison for juveniles

rĕ-frăct′, v., bend light rays; **-or; -ion; -ive; -ive-**

ness; -ively

rè-frāin', *n.*, repeated verse of song or poem; *v.*, keep from doing

rè-frĕsh', *v.*, make fresh, renew; -er

rè-frĕsh'mènt, *n.*, light meal, food

rè-frĭg'êr-āte, *v.*, make or keep cold; tor; tion; tive

rĕf'ūge, *n.*, shelter

rē'fŭnd, *n.*, repayment; *v.*, (rè-fŭnd') pay back

rè-fûr'bĭsh, *v.*, renovate; -ment

rĕf'ūse, *n.*, trash

rè-fūse', *v.*, decline, reject; -r; fusal *n.*

rè-fūte', *v.*, prove to be wrong; -r; tation; futable; futably

rē'gàl, *a.*, royal, stately; -ity; -ly

rè-gàrd', *n.*, concern, esteem; *v.*, look at, consider; -less

rè-gârd'ĭng, *prep.*, about

rè-gĕn'êr-āte, *v.*, form again; *a.*, (āte) reborn; tor; tion; acy; -ness; -ly

rē'gĕnt, *n.*, one ruling for a monarch; gency

rè-gĭme', *n.*, ruling system or period

rĕg'ĭ-mènt, *n.*, military unit; *v.*, discipline; -ation; -al; -ally

rē'gĭon, *n.*, particular area, district; -al; -alism; -alist; -alistic; -ally

rĕg'ĭs-têr, *n.*, list, counting device, air ventilator; *v.*, list, enroll, show; trar; trary; tration

rè-grĕss', *v.*, go backward; -or; -ion; -ive; -ively

rè-grĕt', *v.*, feel sorry about; -er; -ful; -fully; -fulness; -able; -ably

rĕg'ū-làr, *a.*, usual, consistent; -ity; -ize; -ization; -ly

rĕg'ū-lāte, *v.*, control, adjust; tor; tion; tory

rè-gûr'gĭ-tāte, *v.*, throw up food; tion

rē-hà-bĭl'ĭ-tāte, *v.*, restore; tion; tive

rē-hăsh', *v.*, go over again

rè-hêarse', *v.*, perform for practice; hearsal *n.*

reign (rān), *n.*, time of rule

rē-ĭm-bûrse', *v.*, pay back; -ment; bursable

rein (rān), *n.*, strap for guiding horse

rē-ĭn-câr-nā'tion, *n.*, rebirth [deer

rein'dēer (rān), *n.*, large

rē-ĭt'êr-āte, *v.*, repeat; tion; tive; tively

rè-jĕct', *v.*, throw out, deny; -er; -or; -ion; -ive

rè-joīce', *v.*, be happy; joicing *n.*; joicingly

rè-jōin'dêr, *n.*, answer

rè-lāte', *v.*, tell, associate; -r; tion; tionship; latable [ily

rè-lāt'èd, *a.*, of same family

rĕl'à-tĭve, *n.*, person in same family; *a.*, having connection; tivity; -ly; -ness

rè-lăx', *v.*, be at ease, lessen, -er; -ation

rē'lāy, *n.*, fresh supply, team race; *v.*, (rè-lāy') send on [public

rè-lēase', *v.*, let go, make

rĕl'è-gāte, *v.*, exile, assign refer; tion

rĕl'è-vànt, *a.*, related to; vance; vancy; -ly

rē-lī'à-ble, *a.*, trustworthy; ability; -ness; ably

rĕl'ĭc, *n.*, thing from past

rè-lief', *n.*, aid, thing that lessens

rè-liĕve', *v.*, ease, help; -r; lievable

rè-lī'gĭon, *n.*, system of belief and worship; gious; giously; giousness

rè-lĭn'quĭsh, *v.*, give up; -ment

rĕl'ĭsh, *n.*, pleasing task, appetizer; *v.*, enjoy

rè-lŭc'tànt, *a.*, unwilling; tance; tancy; -ly

rè-lȳ', *v.*, trust, depend; liance; liant; liantly

rè-māin', *v.*, stay, continue

P
R

to be; **-der**
rè-mârk', *n.*, *v.*, comment
rè-mârk'á-ble, *a.*, unusual; **bly; -ness**
rĕm'è-dў,*n.*, *v.*, cure; **dial; dially; diable; diableness; diably**
rè-mĕm'bêr, *v.*, think of again, keep in mind; **brance** [**-er; -ful**
rè-mīnd', *v.*, remember;
rĕm-ĭ-nĭsce', *v.*, recall the past; **-nce; -nt; -ntly**
rè-mĭss', *a.*, careless; **-ly; -ness**
rè-mĭt', *v.*, forgive, send money, decrease; **mission; missive**
rè-mĭt'táncе, *n.*, money sent
rĕm'nánt, *n.*, remainder
rè-mŏn'strāte, *v.*, object; **tor; tion; tive; tively**
rè-môrse', *n.*, deep guilt; **-ful; -fully; -fulness; -less; -lessly; -lessness**
rè-mōte', *a.*, far off; **-ly; -ness**
rè-move' (mūv), *v.*, take, get rid of; **-r; moval; movable; movability; movably**
rĕn'àis-sánce, *n.*, rebirth, revival
rĕnd, *v.*, rip apart
rĕn'dêr,*v.*, give; **-er; -able**
rĕn-dĭ'tion, *n.*, performance
rĕn'è-gāde, *n.*, traitor
rè-nège', *v.*, go back on a promise
rè-new', *v.*, make new again by replacement; **-er; -al** *n.*; **-able; -ability**
rè-noúnce', *v.*, give up officially; **-r; -ment**
rĕn'ò-vāte, *v.*, make fresh again; **tor; tion; tive**
rè-nown', *n.*, great fame
rè-nŭn-cĭ-ā'tion, *n.*, renouncing; **tive; tory**
rè-pâir', *v.*, fix, mend; **-er; -able**
rĕp-à-rā'tion, *n.*, making amends, compensation
rĕp-ár-tée', *n.*, witty reply

rè-pást', *n.*, meal
rè-pāy',*v.*, pay back, compensate; **-ment; -able**
rè-pēal', *v.*, abolish; **-er; -able**
rè-pēat', *v.*, say or do again; **-er; -ability; -able**
rè-pĕl', *v.*, force back, reject, disgust; **-ler; -lent; -lence; -lency; -lently**
rè-pĕnt', *v.*, be sorry for; **-er; -ance; -ant; -antly**
rē-pêr-cŭs'sion, *n.*, reaction; **sive**
rĕp'êr-toire (twâr), *n.*, works a performer is familiar with
rĕp-è-tī'tion, *n.*, thing repeated; **tious; tiously; tiousness; tive; tively**
rē-phrāse', *v.*, phrase differently
rè-plāce', *v.*, put back, take place of; **-r; -ment; -able**
rè-plĕn'īsh, *v.*, supply again; **-er; -ment**
rĕp'lĭ-cà, *n.*, copy
rè-plў',*n.*, *v.*, answer; **plier**
rè-pôrt', *n.*, account, factual statement, rumor;*v.*, tell, present oneself; **-er; -edly** [**-fully**
rè-pōse', *n.*, *v.*, rest; **-ful**
rĕp-rè-hĕnd',*v.*, find fault; **hension; hensive; hensively; hensible; hensibility; hensibly**
rĕp-rè-sĕnt', *v.*, portray, symbolize; **-ation; -ational; -ative; -atively; -ativeness**
rè-prĕss', *v.*, hold back, control too strictly; **-er; -or; -ion; -ive; -ively; -iveness; -ible**
rè-priēve', *n.*, *v.*, delay of punishment
rĕp'rĭ-mănd, *n.*, *v.*, rebuke
rè-prīs'ál, *n.*, injury done in return
rè-prōach', *n.*, shame; *v.*, accuse; **-er; -ful; -fully; -fulness; -able; -ingly**
rĕp'rò-bāte,*n.*, scoundrel; *v.*, condemn; *a.*, de-

praved; **tion; tive**

rĕ-prò-dūce′, v., do again, produce offspring and copies; **-r; tion; tive; tively; tiveness; duci-ble**

rè-prōof′, n., blame; **proval**

rè-prove′ (prūv), v., criticize; **-r; provingly**

rĕp′tile, n., scaly, crawling animal

rè-pŭb′līc, n., government by elected representatives; **-an** n., a.

rè-pŭg′nànt, a., distasteful; **nance; nancy; -ly**

rè-pŭlse′, v., repel, reject; **sion** [**-ly; -ness**

rè-pŭl′sĭve, a., disgusting;

rĕp′ū-tà-ble, a., respectable; **bility; bly**

rè-pūte′, v., think to be; **-d; -dly**

rĕp-ū-tā′tion, n., others′ opinion of a person, fame [politely ask

rè-quĕst′, n., asking; v.,

rè-quire′, v., demand, need; **-ment**

rĕq′uĭ-sĭte, n., a., (thing) necessary

rĕq-uĭ-sĭ′tion, n., formal order; v., demand

rè-scĭnd′, v., cancel; **-er; scission; -able**

rĕs′cūe, v., save, free; **-r; cuable**

rè-sêarch′, n., careful study; v., investigate; **-er; -able** [**blance**

rè-sĕm′ble, v., be similar;

rè-sĕnt′, v., be angry at, feel hurt; **-ment; -ful; -fully; -fulness**

rĕs-êr-vā′tion, n., reserving, land put aside

rè-serve′, n., reticence, something held for later use; v., set aside, keep

rĕs′êr-voir (vwâr), n., large supply, place for storing water

rè-sīde′, v., live, dwell

rĕs′ĭ-dĕnce, n., place where one lives; **dency; dent** n., a., **dential;**

dentially [**ual; ually**

rĕs′ī-dūe, n., remainder;

rè-sĭgn′, v., give up, accept passively; **-ation; -ed; -edly**

rè-sĭl′iènt, a., elastic; **ience; iency; -ly**

rĕs′īn, n., gummy substance from trees

rè-sĭst′, v., oppose, fight against; **-er; -ence; -ant** n., a.; **-ive; -ively; -ivity; -ible; -ibility; -less; -lessly; -lessness**

rĕs′ò-lūte, a., determined; **-ly**

rĕs-ò-lū′tion, n., decision, formal statement

rè-sŏlve′, v., decide; **-r; -nt** n., a.; **-d; -dly; solvable; solvability**

rĕs′ò-nànt, a., of returning sound; **nance; nate; nator; -ly**

rè-sôrt′, n., vacation place; v., turn to

rè-sôurce′fŭl, a., capable; **-ly; -ness**

rè-spĕct′, n., honor; v., regard, consider; **-ful; -fully; -fulness**

rè-spĕct′à-ble, a., proper, moderate; **bility; bly**

rè-spĕc′tĭve, a., several; **-ly**

rè-spire′, v., breathe air; **rator; ration; ratory; rational**

rĕs′pĭte, n., postponement

rè-splĕnd′ènt, a., splendid; **ence; ency; -ly**

rè-spŏnd′, v., answer; **-er; sponse** n.; **-ent** n., a.; **sponsive; sponsively; sponsiveness**

rè-spŏn′sĭ-ble, a., liable for, accountable, dependable; **bility; bly; -ness**

rĕst, n., inactivity, peace, relief, remainder; v., be at ease, lie, stop

rĕs′tàu-rànt, n., place to buy and eat a meal

rĕs-tĭ-tū′tion, n., making good for loss; **tive**

rè-stôre′, v., give or bring

back, renew; **-r; stora-
tion; storative; stora-
ble**

rĕ-strāin′, v., hold back,
limit; **-er; straint** n.;
-able

rĕ-strĭct′, v., limit; **-ion;
-ive; -ively; -iveness;
-ed; -edly**

rĕ-sŭlt′, n., outcome, consequence; v., happen;
-ant n., a.; **-antly**

rĕ-sūme′, v., start again;
sumption; sumable

rĕ′sū-me′ (mā), n., summary

rĕ-sûr′gĕnt, a., rising
again; **gence**

rĕs-ûr-rĕct′, v., bring back
to life; **-ion; -ional**

rĕ-sŭs′cĭ-tāte, v., revive;
tor; tion; tive

rē′tāil, n., sale of goods to
consumer; **-er**

rĕ-tāin′, v., keep, hire, remember; **-er; -ment;
-able**

rĕ-tăl′ĭ-āte, v., get even;
tion; tive; tory

rĕ-târd′, v., delay, slow
down; **-er; -ation; -ative**

rĕtch, v., strain to vomit

rĕten′tion, n., capacity to
retain; **tive; tivity;
tively; tiveness**

rĕt′ĭ-cĕnt, a., silent, withdrawn; **cence; cency;
-ly**

rĕt′i-nȧ, n., eye part

rĕ-tīre′, v., go away, withdraw, go to bed, leave
job because of age;
-ment [**-ly**

rĕ-tīr′ĭng, a., shy, modest;

rĕ-tôrt′, v., reply sharply

rĕ-trāce′, v., go back over;
-able

rĕ-trăct′, v., draw or take
back; **-or; -ion; -ive;
-ability; -able**

rĕ-trēat′, n., withdrawal,
seclusion; v., go back

rē-trĕnch′, v., curtail,
economize; **-ment**

rĕt-rĭ-bū′tion, n., deserved
punishment or reward;
tive; tory; tively

rĕ-triēve′, v., get back, recover; **-r; trieval** n.,
trievable

rĕt-rō-ăc′tĭve, a., effective
as of a past date **tivity;
-ly**

rĕ-tûrn′, n., recurrence,
profit; v., go or come
back, answer, restore;
-er; -ee; -able

rē-ūn′iȯn, n., coming together again

rĕ-vămp′, v., make over

rĕ-vēal′, v., make known
a secret, tell; **-er; -ment;
-able** [waken soldiers

rĕ′vĕil-lē, n., signal to

rĕv′ĕl, v., make merry, delight; **-er; -ry**

rĕv-ĕ-lā′tion, n., disclosure, revealing; **-ist; tory**

rĕ-vĕnge′, n., v., harm in
return; **-r; -ful; -fully;
-fulness; vengingly**

rĕv′ĕ-nūe, n., income from
taxes

rĕ-vêr′bêr-āte, v., return,
re-echo, reflect; **tor;
tion; tive; tively; tory;
berant**

rĕ-vēre′, v., respect
greatly; **-nce; -nt; -ntly**

rĕv′êr-iĕ, n., daydream

rĕ-vêrse′, v., n., (change
to the) opposite; a., contrary; **-r; versal;** a.; **sion;
sionary; sional; versi-
ble; versibility; versi-
bly** [**-ible**

rĕ-vêrt′, v., go back to;

rĕ-vīle′, v., insult; **-r; -ment**

rĕ-vīse′, v., change, correct; **-r; -visal** n.; **vision;
visionist; visionary; vi-
sional; visȯry**

rĕ-vīve′, v., bring back to
life or health; **-r; vival** n.;
vivable; vivability

rĕ-vōke′, v., cancel, abolish; **ocation; ocable;
ocability**

rĕ-vōlt′, n., rebellion; v.,
rebel, disgust; **-er**

rĕv-ȯ-lū′tion, n., cycle,
complete change, rebel-
lion; **-ist; -ize; -ary**

rė·vŏlve′, v., turn in a circle, ponder

rė·vŏlv′ėr, n., handgun

rė·vūe′, n., musical show

rė·vŭl′sion, n., disgust

rė·ward′ (wôrd), n., thing given for a deed; **-er; -able** [ing of

rē·wŏrd′, v., change word-

rhăp′sŏ·dÿ, n., ecstasy, musical composition; **dize; sodic; sodically**

rhē′à, n., large non-flying bird

rhē′sŭs, n., monkey

rhĕt′ŏ·rĭc, n., art of effective language, eloquence; **-al; -ally**

rheū′mà·tĭsm, n., painful conditions of joints; **matic; matically**

rhine′stóne, n., artificial gem [imal

rhĭ·nŏc′ėr·ós, n., huge an-

rhĭ′zōme, n., rootlike stem

rhō·dŏ·dĕn′drón, n., flowering shrub

rhū′bárb, n., edible plant, (coll.) argument

rhўme, n., same ending sound in words

rhŷthm, n., regular pattern of beat or flow; **-ic; -ical; -ically; -icity**

rĭb, n., curved chest bone, ridge in cloth; **-bing** n.

rĭb′bón, n., narrow strip of cloth [grass

rice, n., aquatic cereal

rĭch, a., worth much, well supplied; **-en; -ly; -ness**

rĭch′ės, n., pl., wealth

rĭck′ėts, n., bone disease

rĭck′ėt·ÿ, n., weak; **etiness**

rĭd, v., free, relieve; **-dance**

rĭd′dle, n., puzzling problem; v., make holes in

ride, v., be carried, move along, control; **-r; -able**

rĭdge, n., raised strip, crest

rĭd′ĭ·cūle, v., make fun of

rĭ·dĭc′ū·loùs, a., absurd; **-ly; -ness**

rife, a., widespread, abundant; **-ness** [people

rĭff′räff, n., insignificant

rĭ′fle, n., long shoulder

gun; **-r; -man** n.; **-ry**

rĭft, n., v., crack, split

rĭg, n., equipment; v., equip, arrange dishonestly; **-ger**

rĭght, n., what is right, privilege; v., make amends; a., correct, virtuous, normal, of side to east when facing north; adv., straight, properly; **-ful; -fully; -ly**

rĭght′eoŭs, a., morally just; **-ly; -ness**

rĭght′ĭst, n., politically conservative person

rĭg′ĭd, a., stiff, strict; **-ity; -ify; -ly; -ness**

rĭg′or, n., severity, exactness; **-ous; -ously; -ousness**

rile, v., (coll.) anger

rĭm, n., edge [skin

rĭnd, n., firm outer layer,

rĭng, n., anything circular, resonant sound; v., encircle, make sound like bell; **-er**

rĭng′lėt, n., little curl

rĭng′worm, n., skin disease

rĭnk, n., skating arena

rĭnse, v., wash lightly, flush

rĭ′ót, n., wild public disorder, (coll.) funny person; **-er**

rĭp, v., tear, cut apart; **-per**

ripe, a., ready to be harvested, fully grown; **-n; -ly; -ness** [ply a.

rĭp′ple, n., small waves;

rise, n., ascent, slope, increase; v., get up, go up, increase, begin, rebel

rĭsk, n., dangerous chance; v., take the chance; **-er** [mony

rite, n., formal act, cere-

rĭt′ū·ál, n., system of rites; a., of rite; **-ism; -ist; -istic; -istically; -ize; -ly**

rĭ′vál, n., competitor; **-ry**

rĭv′ėr, n., large stream of flowing water [tener

rĭv′ėt, n., metal bolt, fas-

rōad, n., way for travelling, path [-er

rōam, v., travel aimlessly;

rôar, v., loud, deep, rumbling sound; -er; -ing n.

rōast, n., cut of meat; v., cook in oven or over fire; -er

rŏb, v., steal, take illegally; -ber; -bery   [ment

rōbe, n., long flowing garrŏb'ĭn, n., red-breasted bird   [being

rō'bŏt, n., mechanical

rō-bŭst', a., vigorous, healthy; -ious; -iously; -iousness; -ly; -ness

rŏck, n., large stone; -y a.; -iness   [forth; -er

rŏck, v., move back and

rŏck'ĕt, n., projectile propelled by combustible substance, missile; -ry

rŏd, n., straight, narrow stick, linear measure of 16½ feet   [mal

rō'dĕnt, n., gnawing mamrō'dē-ō, n., competition of cowboys skills

rōe, n., fish eggs

rōgue, n., scoundrel, fun-loving person; -ry; guish; guishly; guishness

rŏil, v., make cloudy, stir up; -y a.   [function

rōle, n., actor's part in play,

rŏll, n., cylinder, list, small cake of bread, loud echoing sound; v., move by turning, sway, start, flatten with roller

rŏll'ĕr, n., rolling cylinder

rŏl'lĭck-ĭng, a., lively, gay

rō'lȳ-pō'lȳ, n., pudgy

rō-māine', n., kind of lettuce

rō-mănce', n., tale of love and adventure, love affair; mantic; manticism; manticist; manticize; manticization; mantically

rŏmp, v., play boisterously

rŏmp'ĕrs, n., pl., loose pantlike garment for baby   [ing; -er

rōof, n., top cover of buildrŏŏk, n., crow, chess

piece; v., cheat   [ner

rŏŏk'ĭĕ, n., (slang) beginrōŏm, n., enough space, place enclosed by walls; -y a.; -iness; -ily

rōŏst, n., v., perch

rōŏs'tĕr, n., male chicken

rōŏt, n., plant part below ground, source; v., dig, (coll.) cheer; -y a.; -less

rōpe, n., strong twisted cord; v., fasten with rope; -r

rō'sȧ-rȳ, n., holy beads

rōse, n., flower, reddish pink; rosy

rōse'mär-ȳ, n., herb

rō-sē-ō'lȧ, n., rash

rŏs'ĭn, n., pine resin

rŏs'tĕr, n., list

rŏs'trŭm, n., speaker's platform

rŏt, n., decay; v., decompose, become sickly; -ten a.; -tenly; -tenness

rō'tȧ-rȳ, a., rotating

rō'tāte, v., turn on center point; tor; tion; tional; tive; tively

rōte, n., fixed routine

rō-tŭnd', a., round, plump; -ly; -ness

rouge, n., reddish cosmetic for coloring cheeks

rough'ȧge (rŭf), n., coarse food   [game

rou-lĕtte', n., gambling

rŏund, n., one of series, (pl.) circuit; v., make round, turn; a., circular, complete; adv., in circle or cycle; prep., about, throughout; -ish; -ly; -ness

rŏuse, v., wake, excite; -r

rŏut, n., disorderly mob in defeat; v., conquer, dig up

route, n., course travelled

rou-tine', n., regular procedure; a., customary; tinize; tinization; -ly

rōve, v., wander; -r

rōw, n., things in a line; v., propel boat with oars; -er

rŏw, *n.,* dispute, brawl

rŏw′dў, *a.,* disorderly; -ism; -ish; **dily; diness**

roy′ăl (rōī), *a.,* of a monarch of kingdom; **-ism; -ist; -ty; -ly**

rŭb, *v.,* move back and forth with pressure; **-ber**

rŭb′bĕr, *n.,* elastic substance, (*pl.*) overshoes; -y *a.*   [sense; **-y** *a.*

rŭb′bĭsh, *n.,* trash, non-

rŭb′ble, *n.,* fragmented rock   [sles

rū-bĕl′lă, *n.,* German mea-

rū′bў, *n.,* red gem

rŭck′ŭs, *n.,* (coll.) uproar

rŭd′dĕr, *n.,* steering device

rŭd′dў, *a.,* rosy; **diness**

rūde, *a.,* rough, unmannerly; **-ly; -ness**

rū′dĭ-mĕnt, *n.,* first principle; **-ary; -al; -arily**

rūe, *v.,* regret; **-ful; -fully; -fulness**   [person

rŭf′fĭ-ăn, *n.,* brutal, lawless

rŭf′fle, *n.,* pleated cloth trimming; *v.,* wrinkle, disturb

rŭg, *n.,* floor covering

rŭg′gĕd, *a.,* rough, strong, harsh; **-ly; -ness**

rū′ĭn, *n.,* destruction, downfall; *v.,* destroy; **-ous; -ously; -ousness**

rūle, *n.,* set guide, law, habit; *v.,* govern, determine, mark lines; **-r**

rŭm, *n.,* alcoholic drink

rŭm′bă, *n.,* dance

rŭm′ble, *n.,* deep, rolling sound; **-r; blingly; bly**

rū′mĭ-nāte, *v.,* chew cud, ponder; **tor; tion; tive; tively**

rŭm′măge, *n.,* miscellaneous items; *v.,* search thoroughly; **-r**

rŭm′mў, *n.,* card game

rū′mŏr, *n.,* unconfirmed report

rŭmp, *n.,* hind part

rŭm′ple, *n., v.,* wrinkle; **ply**

rŭm′pŭs, *n.,* (coll.) uproar

rŭn, *n.,* trip, race, rapid movement, course; *v.,*

go or move rapidly, race, spread, continue, operate; **-ner**

rŭn′-down′, *a.,* not running, in poor state

rŭng, *n.,* crosspiece of ladder or chair

rŭn-nêr-ŭp′, *n.,* second one in race

rŭnt, *n.,* undersized animal or thing

rŭn′wāy, *n.,* landing strip

rŭp′tûre, *n.,* bursting; *v.,* break apart

rū′răl, *a.,* of country life; **-ism; -ist; -ize; -ly**

rūse, *n.,* trick

rŭsh, *n.,* marsh plant, hurry, swift sudden attack; *v.,* move recklessly or quickly

rŭst, *n.,* russet oxidation on metal; **-y** *a.*

rŭs′tĭc, *a.,* rural, simple; **-ity; -ally**

rŭs′tle, *v.,* make soft rubbing sound, steal cattle; **-r**

rŭt, *n.,* groove, dull routine

rū-tă-bā′gă, *n.,* yellow turnip   [**-ness**

rŭth′lĕss, *a.,* cruel; **-ly;**

rўe, *n.,* cereal grain, whiskey

S

Săb′băth, *n.,* day of rest and worship   [rest

săb-băt′ĭ-căl, *n.,* period of

sā′bêr, *n.,* soldier's sword

săb′ȯ-tăge, *n.,* intentional destruction; **teur** *n.*

săc′chă-rĭn (kȧ), *n.,* sugar substitute

să-chet′ (shā), *n.,* small perfumed bag

săck, *n.,* large bag; *v.,* dismiss from job, plunder

săc′rȧ-mĕnt, *n.,* Christian rite; **-al; -ally**

săc′rĕd, *a.,* holy, consecrated; **-ly; -ness**

săc′rĭ-fīce, *n.,* offering of something valuable, loss; **cial; cially**

săc′rĭ-lĕge, *n.,* destruction

or disrespect of something holy; **gious; giously; giousness**

săd, *a.*, unhappy, sorrowful; **-den; -ly; -ness**

săd'dle, *n.*, rider's seat on horse

săd'ĭsm, *n.*, pleasure from hurting another; **ĭst; dĭstic; dĭstically**

sȧ-fȧ'rĭ, *n.*, hunting expedition

sāfe, *n.*, locked box for valuables; *a.*, free from danger; **-ty; -ly**

sāfe-kēep'ĭng, *n.*, protection [oil in seeds

săf'flow-êr, *n.*, flower with

săf'frŏn, *n.*, flowering plant, dye, medicine

săg, *v.*, hang down, droop

sȧ'gȧ, *n.*, long heroic story

sȧ-gā'cioŭs, *a.*, wise; **cĭty; -ly; -ness** [soning

sāge, *n.*, wise man, sea-

sāge'brŭsh, *n.*, shrub

sāil, *n.*, cloth that catches wind to move ship; *v.*, travel on water; **-or; -ing** *n.*

sāint, *n.*, holy or kind person; **-hood; -ly** *a.*; **-liness**

sāke, *n.*, reason, benefit

sȧ-lā'cioŭs, *a.*, obscene; **cĭty; -ly; -ness**

săl'ȧd, *n.*, cold vegetable or fruit dish

săl'ȧ-măn-dêr, *n.*, lizard-like amphibian

sȧ-lā'mĭ, *n.*, spiced sausage [work

săl'ȧ-rў, *n.*, payment for

sāle, *n.*, exchange of goods for money; **-sman** *n.*; **-able; salability**

sā'liĕnt, *a.*, noticeable; **lience; liency; -ly**

sā'līne, *a.*, salty

sȧ-lī'vȧ, *n.*, watery fluid in mouth; **-tion; -te** *v.*; **-ry** *a.*

săl'lōw, *a.*, of sickly yellow complexion; **-ish; -ness**

săl'lў, *n.*, sudden rush forth, witticism, jaunt

sȧ-lŏn', *n.*, reception hall, parlor [room

sȧ-lōōn', *n.*, large public

sălt, *n.*, sodium chloride, seasoning; **-y** *a.*; **-iness**

sȧ-lūte', *n.*, gesture to honor; *v.*, greet; **-r; tation; tatory**

săl-vā'tion, *n.*, saving

salve (săv), *n.*, medicinal ointment

săm'bȧ, *n.*, dance

sāme, *a.*, alike, identical; *adv.*, in like manner; **-ness** [tern

săm'ple, *n.*, example, pat-

sănc'tĭ-mō-nў, *n.*, pretended holiness; **nious; niously; niousness**

sănc'tion, *n.*, approval; *v.*, authorize, allow; **-able**

sănc'tĭ-tў, *n.*, holiness

sănc'tū-ār-ў, *n.*, holy place, shelter

sănd, *n.*, loose grains of rock; **-y** *a.*; **-iness**

săn'dȧl, *n.*, open shoe with straps

sănd'pā-pêr, *n.*, paper with sand for smoothing

sănd'pĭ-pêr, *n.*, small shore bird

sănd'wĭch, *n.*, filling, of meat, cheese, etc. between bread slices

sāne, *a.*, mentally healthy; **-ly; -ness**

săn'guĭ-nār-ў, *a.*, of bloodshed, bloodthirsty; **narily; nariness**

săn'guĭne, *a.*, ruddy, cheerful; **-ly; -ness**

săn-ĭ-tār'ĭ-ŭm, *n.*, institution to regain health

săn'ĭ-tār-ў, *a.*, clean and healthy; **tation; tize; tarily; tariness**

săp, *n.*, juice of plant, vigor; *v.*, undermine, weaken; **-py** *a.* [-ly

sā'pĭ-ĕnt, *a.*, wise; **ence;**

săp'lĭng, *n.*, young tree

săp'phĭre, *n.*, blue gem

sâr'căsm, *n.*, cutting ironical remark; **castic; castically** [fish

sâr-dīne', *n.*, small ocean

sâr-dŏn'ĭc, *a.*, bitterly sarcastic; **-ally**

sar-sa-pá-rïl′lá (säs), *n.*, soft drink

säsh, *n.*, band for waist or shoulder, frame for glass window   [*a.*

säss, *n.*, impudent talk; **-y**

sä-tän′ïc, *a.*, devilish, evil; **-al; -ally**   [case

sätch′él, *n.*, small carrying

säte, *v.*, satisfy

sät′él-līte, *n.*, small body revolving around larger one   [**tion**

sä′tï-āte, *v.*, satisfy fully;

sät′ïn, *n.*, smooth shiny fabric; **-y** *a.*

sät′īre, *n.*, literary ridicule; **rist; rize; tirical; tirically**

sät′ïs-fÿ, *v.*, fulfill needs, please; **fier; faction; factory**

sät′ü-rāte, *v.*, soak thoroughly; **tor; tion**

sāuce, *n.*, liquid served with food

sāu′cÿ, *a.*, rude, impudent; **cily; ciness**   [heat

sāu′ná, *n.*, bath of hot, dry

sāun′têr, *v.*, walk idly

sāu′ságe, *n.*, chopped, spicy meat in casing

sāu-te′ (tā), *v.*, fry quickly

säv′áge, *a.*, primitive, wild; crude; **-ry; -ly; -ness**

sāve, *v.*, keep safe, rescue, preserve for future, avoid waste; **-r; -able**

säv′ïng, *n.*, reduction, (pl.) money saved   [saves

säv′ior (yŏr), *n.*, one who

sä′vŏr, *n.*, special quality of taste or smell; **-less; -ous; -y** *a.*; **-ily; -iness**

säv′vÿ, *n.*, shrewdness; *v.*, understand; *a.*, shrewd

sāw, *n.*, cutting tool with series of sharp teeth

säx′ò-phōne, *n.*, woodwind instrument; **phonist; phonic**

säy, *n.*, chance to speak, power; *v.*, express in words, state; **-er**

säy′ïng, *n.*, expression of

wisdom   [sore; **-by** *a.*

scăb, *n.*, crust formed over

scăb′bárd, *n.*, sword holder   [**-ness**

scăb′roŭs, *a.*, rough; **-ly;**

scăf′fóld, *n.*, temporary framework for workers

scăld, *v.*, burn with hot liquid or steam

scāle, *n.*, weighing instrument, ratio of size, graduated series; fish's hard covering; *v.*, go up, weigh, remove scales

scăl′lïón, *n.*, onion

scăl′lóp, *n.*, shellfish, curved fancy edge

scăl′pèl, *n.*, surgical knife

scămp, *n.*, rascal; **-ish**

scăm′pêr, *v.*, run hurriedly

scăn, *v.*, glance at quickly, examine; **-ner**

scăn′dál, *n.*, disgrace, slanderous talk; **-ize; -izer; -ization; -ous; -ously; -ousness**

scănt, *a.*, meager, not enough; **-y** *a.*; **-ily; -iness**

scāpe′gōat, *n.*, one blamed for others' mistakes

scăr′áb, *n.*, beetle, its image cut on stone

scārce, *a.*, rare; **city; -ly; -ness**   [**scary** *a.*

scāre, *n.*, fear; *v.*, frighten;

scârf, *n.*, cloth worn about neck, head or shoulders

scâr′lèt, *n.*, *a.*, bright red

scăth′ïng, *a.*, harsh; **-ly**

scăt′têr, *v.*, throw about loosely

scăv′ĕng-êr, *n.*, collector of disgarded things

scè-nār′ï-ō, *n.*, outline of play, script of movie

scēne, *n.*, place setting, view, part of play, emotional display; **scenic**

scē′nêr-ÿ, *n.*, painted surroundings for play, view outdoors

scĕnt, *n.*, *v.*, smell

scēp′têr, *n.*, ruler's rod of authority

schĕd′üle (skĕd), *n.*, list,

S
T

scheme 146 **scurrilous**

timed plan; v., place in schedule, plan

schēme (skēm), n., plan, secret project; v., plot; **matize; matic; matically**

schĭsm (skĭsm), n., split; **matic; matical; matically**

schĭz-ȯ-phrē'nĭ-á (skĭz), n., mental disorder; **ic** n., a.

schŏl'år (skŏl), n., learned person, pupil; **-ship; -ly** a.

schȯ-lăs'tĭc (skȯ), a., of school, academic; **-ally**

schōol (skul), n., place for learning, group, group of fish; v., instruct

sci'ĕnce, n., systematized knowledge, group of facts; **entist; entific; entifically**

scĭn'tĭl-lāte, v., sparkle, be clever; **tor; tion**

sci'ȯn, n., bud, offspring

scĭs'sȯrs, n., cutting tool with opposing blades

scŏff, n., v., jeer, ridicule; **-er; -ingly** [**-er**

scŏld, v., find fault angrily;

scō-lĭ-ō'sĭs, n., curvature of spine; **otic**

scŏnce, n., candleholder on wall

scōne, n., tea cake

scōop, n., small shovel; v., take up and carry, dig; **-er**

scōot'êr, n., child's two-wheeled vehicle, small motorcycle

scōpe, n., extent, range of understanding

scŏrch, v., burn lightly

scōre, n., mark, notch, debt, points made in game, rating, twenty; v., mark, tally, make point(s); **-r**

scŏrn, n., contempt; v., reject; **-er; -ful; -fully; -fulness** [bing; **-er**

scōŭr, v., clean by rubbing

scoûrge, n., whip, punishment [spy, search

scout, n., v., (one sent to)

scrăg'glȳ, a., ragged; **gliness**

scrăm, v., get out

scrăm'ble, v., climb hurriedly, struggle, mix; **-r**

scrăp, n., bit, discarded piece, fight; v., junk

scrătch, n., skin wound; v., cut surface, rub, write hurriedly; **-er; -y** a.; **-ily; -iness**

scrăwl, v., write carelessly; **-er; -y** a.

scrăw'nȳ, a., skinny; **niness**

scrēam, n., loud, high piercing sound; **-er**

scrēen, n., partition, coarse mesh of wire, surface to show movies on; v., separate, protect, sift; **-er; -able; -less**

scrēw, n., grooved naillike fastener; v., twist, fasten

scrībe, n., writer

scrĭm'måge, n., confused struggle

scrĭmp, v., be frugal; **-er; -y** a.; **-ily; -iness**

scrĭpt, n., handwriting, copy of play

scrĭp'tûre, n., Bible

scrŏll, n., roll of paper with writing

scrō'tŭm, n., testicles' pouch; **tal** [pilfer; **-r**

scrōŭnge, v., (coll.) beg,

scrŭb, n., stunted tree; a., undersized; **-by** a.; **-bily; -biness** [clean; **-ber**

scrŭb, v., rub hard to

scrŭff, n., nape of neck

scrŭmp'tioŭs, a. (coll.) delicious; **-ly; -ness**

scrŭ'tĭ-nȳ, n., close examination; **nize; nizer**

scū'bà, n., underwater breathing apparatus

scŭd, v., move swiftly

scŭf'fle, n., v., fight

scŭlp'tûre, n., art of carving, modeling and welding; **tor; tural; turally**

scŭm, n., filth, impurities; **-my** a. [**-ness**

scûr'rĭl-oŭs, a., vulgar; **-ly;**

scûr'rÿ, v., run hastily

scûr'vÿ, n., disease; a., vile; **vily; viness**

scŭt'tle, v., move quickly

scÿthe, n., tool with long blade for cutting

sēa, n., body of salt water

sēa'fār-êr, n., sailor

sēal, n., sea mammal with flippers, official mark; v., close securely, certify

sēam, n., line made by joining two pieces; v., join

sēam'strėss, n., woman who sews for money

se'ȧnce (sā), n., meeting of spiritualists

sēar, v., burn the surface

sēarch, n., inquiry; v., examine; **-er; -able; -ing; -ingly**

sēa'sĭck, a., of nausea from travelling on sea; **-ness**

sēa'sȯn, n., time of year, spring, summer, autumn or winter; v., add spices, herbs to food, mature; **-er** [for food

sēa'sȯn-ĭng, n., flavoring

sēat, n., place to sit, part one sits on; v., put on seat; **-ing** n.

sēa'wȯr-thy, a., fit to travel on sea

sė-cēde', v., withdraw from; **-r; cession; cessional**

sė-clūde', v., isolate; **clusion; clusive; clusively; clusiness**

sĕc'ȯnd-hănd', a., used previously

sĕc'rėt, n., a., (something) hidden from others, mysterious; **recy; -ive; -ively; -iveness; -ly**

sĕc'rė-tār-ÿ, n., corresponding or recording officer, cabinet minister; **tariat** n.

sė-crēte', v., hide, discharge body substance; **tion; tory**

sĕct, n., group with same beliefs; **-arian** a.

sĕc'tion, n., part; v., cut into divisions; **-al**

sė-cūre', v., protect, make firm, get; a., safe, stable; **-r; rity; curance; curable; -ness; -ly**

sė-dȧn', n., enclosed automobile

sė-dāte', v., reduce excitement; a., serious, calm; **tion**

sĕd'ėn-tār-ÿ, a., sitting

sĕd'ĭ-mėnt, n., matter settling to bottom of liquid; **-ation; -al; -ary**

sė-dūce', v., lead astray; **-r; duction; -ment; ductive; ductively; ductiveness; ducible**

sĕd'ū-loŭs, a., working hard; **lity; -ly; -ness**

sēe, n., bishop's official seat; v., look at, understand, make sure, meet

sēed, n., plant part from which new one grows, source; v., plant or remove seeds; **-er; -less**

sēed'ÿ, a., shabby; **seedily; seediness**

sēem'lÿ, a., handsome; **liness** [**-age; -y** a.

sēep, v., leak out, ooze;

sēer'sŭck-êr, n., light fabric

sēe'sȧw, n., plank for riding up and down

sēethe, v., boil, be very angry

sĕg'mėnt, n., part, division; **-ation; -ary; -al; -ally**

sĕg'rė-gāte, v., set apart from group; **tion; tionist; tive** [ing net

seine (sān), n., large fishseis'mĭc, a., of earthquake; **-ity; mism, mology; mologist; -ally**

sēize, v., take forcibly; **-r; seizable**

sĕl'dȯm, adv., rarely; **-ness**

sė-lĕct', v., choose; a., chosen; **-or; -ion; -ness; -ive; -ivity; -ively; -iveness**

sĕlf, *n.*, one's own person

sĕlf'ĭsh, *a.*, too interested in oneself; **-ly; -ness**

sĕlf'lĕss, *a.*, interested in others; **-ly; -ness**

sĕlf-rīght'eoŭs, *a.*, feeling morally superior; **-ly; -ness**   [**-ness**

sĕlf'sāme, *a.*, identical;

sĕlf-wĭll', *n.*, stubbornness

sĕll, *v.*, trade for money, deal in, betray; **-er**

sĕ-măn'tĭcs, *n.*, study of words and meanings; **ti-cist; tic**   [ance

sĕm'blănce, *n.*, appear-

sē'mĕn, *n.*, male reproductive fluid

sĕ-mĕs'tĕr, *n.*, half year, college term

sĕm'ĭ-nâr, *n.*, course for research or advanced study

sĕm'ĭ-nâr-ȳ, *n.*, school for clergymen; **narian** *n.*

sĕn'ăte, *n.*, lawmaking assembly; **tor; torial**

sĕnd, *v.*, cause to go or be carried; **-er**

sē'nĭle, *a.*, of old age, mentally feeble; **nility; -ly**   [rank; **-ity**

sēn'iŏr, *a.*, older, of higher

sĕnse, *n.*, ability to feel, hear, see, smell and taste, feeling, sound judgment, meaning; *v.*, perceive, understand; **sory** *a.*

sĕnse'lĕss, *a.*, foolish, meaningless; **-ly; -ness**

sĕn'sĭ-ble, *a.*, wise, aware; **bility; bly**

sĕn'su-ăl, *a.*, of bodily pleasure; **-ism; -ist; -ity; -ize; -istic; -ly**

sĕn'tĕnce, *n.*, group of words stating a thought, judge's decision

sĕn'tĭ-mĕnt, *n.*, feeling opinion

sĕn-tĭ-mĕn'tăl, *a.*, emotionally nostalgic; **-ity; -ism; -ist; -ize; -ization; -ly**

sĕn'tĭ-nĕl, *n., v.*, guard

sĕn'trȳ, *n.*, guard

sĕp'ȧ-rāte, *v.*, divide, keep apart; *a.*, **(rāte)** distinct; **tor; tion; tive; -ly; -ness**

sĕp'ŭl-chêr, *n.*, tomb; **chral**

sē'quĕl, *n.*, result

sē'quĕnce, *n.*, succession, order, series; **quent; quential; quentially**   [seize

sĕ-quĕs'tĕr, *v.*, seclude,

sē'quĭn, *n.*, small shiny ornament

sĕr-ĕ-nāde', *n.*, outdoor lover's music; **-r**

sĕr-ĕn-dĭp'ĭ-tȳ, *n.*, good luck

sĕ-rēne', *a.*, calm; **renity; -ly; -ness**

sĕrf, *n.*, person bound to master's land; **-dom**

sêrge, *n.*, twilled fabric

sē'rĭ-ăl, *n.*, separately published episodes

sē'rĭĕs, *n., pl.*, number of related things coming in order; **riate; ration; rial; rially**

serĭ-grăph, *n.*, original print by silkscreen

sē'rĭ-oŭs, *a.*, thinking deeply, important, dangerous; **-ly; -ness**

sêr'mon, *n.*, serious speech, religious lecture; **-ize; -ic**

sĕr'rāte, *v.*, make toothlike notches on edge; **tion**

sē'rŭm, *n.*, watery animal fluid, liquid antitoxin; **rous; rology; rologist**

sêr'vănt, *n.*, one hired to perform services for another; **-less**

sêrve, *v.*, assist, spend time, supply, offer food; **-r**

sêr'vĭce, *n.*, job, ceremony, assistance; *v.*, repair, supply; **-able; -ability; -ableness; -ably**

sêr'vĭ-tūde, *n.*, slavery

sĕs'ȧ-mē, *n.*, edible seed

sĕs'sion, *n.*, meeting of a group, period of time

sĕt, *n.*, stage scenery, group of like things or people, firmness; *v.*, put, arrange, become hard or firm, establish start; *a.*, established, rigid, ready

sē'tå, *n.*, bristle

sĕt-tēe', *n.*, sofa

sĕt'tle, *v.*, arrange, go to live, calm, sink, decide, pay; **-r; -ment**

sĕv'êr, *v.*, cut, separate; **-ance; -able; -ability**

sé-vēre', *a.*, harsh, strict, serious; **verity- -ly; -ness**

sew (sō), *v.*, fasten with needle and thread; **-er**

sēw'êr, *n.*, underground pipes to carry water and waste; **sewage**

sex, *n.*, one of two divisions of living things: male or female, living reproduction; **-ual; -uality; -less; -lessly; -lessness; -ly**

sĕx'tȯn, *n.*, church official

sĕx'ÿ, *a.*, sexually exciting; **sexily; sexiness**

shăb'bÿ, *a.*, worn out, disgraceful; **bily; biness**

shăck, *n.*, small crude cabin

shăck'le, *n.*, wrist or ankle restraint, fastener; *v.*, hamper

shāde, *n.*, part darkness caused by blocking light, color gradation, small degree; *v.*, screen from light; **-r; -less; shady** *a.*; **shadily; shadiness**

shăd'ōw, *n.*, dark image cast by body in light, small amount; *v.*, follow; **-er; -less; -y** *a.*

shăft, *n.*, long, slender part, arrow, vertical tunnel

shăg, *n.*, long, rough nap, disorderly mass; **-gy** *a.*; **-gily; -giness**

shāke, *n.*, tremor; *v.*, move with abrupt, brisk motions, tremble, upset; **-r;**

-able; shaky *a.*

shāle, *n.*, rock of clay

shȧl-lȯt', *n.*, small onion

shȧl'lōw, *a.*, not deep; **-ly; -ness**

shăm, *v.*, pretend; *a.*, false

shăm'bles, *n., pl.*, disorderly scene

shāme, *n.*, feeling of having lost respect, dishonor; *v.*, disgrace; **-ful; -fully; -fulness; -less; -lessly; -lessness**

shăm-pōō', *n., v.*, (soap to) wash hair

shăn'tÿ, *n.*, small, run-down dwelling

shāpe, *n.*, physical form, *v.*, form, mold; **-less; -lessly; -lessness; -ly; -liness**

shāre, *n.*, one's portion; *v.*, divide, participate in together

shârk, *n.*, large fish

shāve, *v.*, cut off, scrape into thin slices, graze; **-r; -n** *a.*

shãwl, *n.*, large cloth worn on head and shoulders

shēaf, *n.*, bundle

shēath, *n.*, close fitting case

shĕd, *n.*, small building; *v.*, flow, radiate, lose

shēen, *n.*, brightness

shēep'ĩsh, *a.*, shy; **-ly; -ness**

shēer, *n., v.*, swerve; *a.*, transparent, pure; **-ly; -ness**

shēet, *n.*, large thin piece of cloth, paper, etc.

shĕll, *n.*, hard outer covering, framework; *v.*, remove shell

shĕl-lăc', *n., v.*, varnish

shĕl'têr, *n.*, covered protection; *v.*, protect; **-er; -less**

shĕlve, *v.*, put on shelf

shĕp'hêrd, *n.*, one who tends sheep

shêr'bĕt, *n.*, frozen dessert

shêr'rÿ, *n.*, wine

shiēld, *n.*, thing that protects, protective armor;

S
T

v., defend, screen; **-er**

shift, *n.*, change, work period; *v.*, move from one to another; **-er; -able**

shift'less, *a.*, lazy; **-ly; -ness**

shim'mer, *v.*, shine; *a.*, wavering light

shine, *n.*, brightness, polish; *v.*, emit light, glow; **-r; shiny** *a.*

shin'gle, *n.*, thin piece of wood to cover roof, woman's short haircut

ship, *n.*, large water vessel; *v.*, transport; **-per; -ment; -ping** *n.;* **-pable**

ship'wright, *n.*, one who makes and repairs ships

shirk, *v.*, neglect work; **-er**

shiv'er, *n.*, splinter; *v.*, shake, shatter; **-y** *a.*

shoal, *n.*, school of fish, shallow place in water; **-y** *a.*

shoat, *n.*, young hog

shock, *n.*, sudden impact, great surprize, extreme nerve stimulation; *v.*, startle; **-er**

shod'dy, *a.*, cheap, inferior; **dily; diness**

shoot, *n.*, new growth; *v.*, move quickly, send forth, discharge a gun, photograph; **-er**

shop, *n.*, place to sell goods or do work; *v.*, buy; **-per** [store; **-er**

shop'lift, *v.*, steal from

shore, *n.*, edge of land bordering water; *v.*, prop, make stable

short, *a.*, low in height, brief, lacking; *adv.*, abruptly; **-en; -ly**

short-change', *v.*, cheat by not returning change due; **-r**

short'com-ing, *n.*, defect

short'en-ing, *n.*, making short, edible fat for cooking [ing

short'hand, *n.*, speed writ-

short'wave', *n.*, radio band for broadcasting

shoul'der, *n.*, joint connecting arm to body; *v.*, push or hold with shoulder [**-er**

shout, *n.*, loud call or cry;

shove, *n., v.*, push; **-r**

show, *n.*, display, trace, pretense entertainment; *v.*, bring into view, complete exhibit, point out; **-er**

show'er, *n.*, rain, party for an occasion, bath with spraying of water; *v.*, pour forth

shred, *n.*, torn strip, fragment; *v.*, tear

shrew, *n.*, nagging woman; **-ish; -ishly; -ishness**

shrewd, *a.*, clever, astute; **-ly; -ness**

shrill, *a.*, piercing in tone; **-y** *adv.;* **-ness**

shrimp, *n.*, small edible shellfish

shrine, *n.*, sacred place

shrink, *v.*, become smaller, contract, avoid; **-age; -able**

shriv'el, *v.*, shrink and become wrinkled

shroud, *n.*, burial cloth

shrub, *n.*, bush; **-bery; -by** *a.;* **-biness**

shuck, *v.*, remove pod, husk or shell [ror

shud'der, *v.*, shake in horror

shuf'fle, *v.*, drag feet as walking, mix; **-r**

shun, *v.*, keep away from

shush, *int.*, be quiet

shut, *v.*, close, lock up, stop [opening

shut'ter, *n.*, cover for an

shut'tle, *n., v.*, (thing on which to) go back and forth

shy, *a.*, shrinking from notice, bashful; **-ly; -ness**

sib'ling, *n.*, child born of same parents as another child

sick, *a.*, in bad health, disgusted, upset; **-ness; -en; -ening; -ish; -ly; -liness** [tool

sick'le, *n.*, curved cutting

sīde, *n.,* right or left half, bounding line, position, surface; *a.,* of side, secondary

sīde'bûrns, *n.,* hair growing in front of ears

sīde'lông, *a.,* sloping, indirect; *adv.,* on side

sī-dè'rē-ȧl, *a.,* of stars; **-ly**

sīde'splīt-tĭng, *a.,* causing laughter

sīd'ĭng, *n.,* covering for outside wall

sī'dle, *v.,* move sideways

sīege, *n.,* persistent attack, blockade [range

sī-ĕr'rȧ, *n.,* mountain

sī-ĕs'tȧ, *n.,* afternoon nap

sĭft, *v.,* pass through a sieve, distinguish; **-er**

sīght, *n.,* seeing, view, aiming device; *v.,* see

sīght'lĕss, *a.,* blind; **-ly; -ness**

sīgn, *n.,* something to convey meaning, symbol, display board; *v.,* write one's name, signal

sĭg'nȧl, *n.,* notice to impel action; *v.,* communicate; **-er; -ize; -ly**

sĭg'nȧ-tûre, *n.,* one's name written by oneself; **tory** *a.*

sĭg'nĕt, *n.,* official seal

sī'lĕnt, *a.,* not speaking, quiet; **lence; lencer; -ly**

sĭl-hŏu-ĕtte', *n.,* black outline of thing

sĭl'ĭ-cȯn, *n.,* nonmetallic chemical element

sĭlk, *n.,* fine soft fiber from silkworm; **-en; -y** *a.*

sĭll, *n.,* bottom of door or window frame

sĭl'lў, *a.,* ridiculous, of little sense, foolish; **lily; liness** [fodder

sī'lō, *n.,* tower for storing

sĭlt, *n.,* fine-grained sediment

sĭl'vêr-wāre, *n.,* household articles made of silver

sĭm'ĭ-lȧr, *a.,* nearly the same; **-ity; -ly**

sĭm'mêr, *v.,* boil gently

sĭm'ple, *a.,* easy, not complex, plain, natural, common; **plicity; plify; plifier; plification; -ness**

sĭm'ū-lāte, *v.,* pretend; **tor; tion; tive**

sī-mŭl-tā'nē-oŭs, *a.,* done at same time; **neity; -ly; -ness**

sĭn, *n.,* breaking moral law; *v.,* do wrong; **-ful; -fully; -fulness**

sĭn-cēre', *a.,* truthful, honest, genuine; **cerity; -ly; -ness**

sĭn'ew̄, *n.,* tendon; **-y** *a.*

sĭng, *v.,* produce music with voice; **-er; -able**

sĭnge, *v.,* burn slightly

sĭn'gle, *a.,* one only, alone, unmarried; **gly**

sĭng'sŏng, *n.,* monotonous rhythm [ous

sĭn'īs-têr, *a.,* evil, dangerous

sĭnk, *v.,* go under water, descend, lower; **-er; -age; -able**

sĭn'ū-oŭs, *a.,* crooked; **-ly**

sī'nŭs, *n.,* air cavity in skull

sī'phȯn, *n., v.,* (tube to) drain liquid from one container to another

sī'rèn, *n.,* warning signal with wailing sound

sīte, *n.,* piece of land, location

sĭt-ū-ā'tion, *n.,* position, state; **-al; -ally**

sīz'ȧ-ble, *a.,* quite large; **bly; -ness**

sīze, *n.,* amount of space occupied, graded measures

sĭz'zle, *v.,* hiss when hot

skĕl'ė-tȯn, *n.,* animal's bony framework, outline; **tal** [-ally

skĕp'tĭc, *n.,* doubter; **-al;**

skĕtch, *n.,* rough drawing, outline; **-er; -y** *a.*

skī, *n.,* shoe runner for gliding on snow or water; **-er**

skĭll, *n.,* expertness, art, craft; **-ful; -fully; -fulness**

skĭl'lĕt, *n.,* frying pan

S
T

skĭm, v., remove floating matter from liquid, glance over; **-mer**

skĭmp, v., be stingy; **-y** a., **-ily**; **-iness**

skĭn, n., outer covering; v., remove skin from; **-less**

skĭp, v., jump from leg to leg, omit

skĭr'mĭsh, n., brief fight

skĭrt, n., woman's garment from waist down; v., go along edge

skĭt, n., short play

skĭt'tĭsh, a., lively, nervous; **-ness**; **-ly**

skŭlk, v., lurk stealthily

skŭnk, n., mammal emitting foul odor, (coll.) offensive person

skȳ, n., air above, heavens

skȳ'līght, n., window in ceiling

slăb, n., flat, broad piece

slăck, a., loose, slow, lax; **-er**; **-ness**; **-en**; **-ly**

slăm, n., noisy impact; v., shut, throw or hit forcibly

slăn'dêr, n., false statement said about another; **-er**; **-ous** [guage

slăng, n., informal language

slănt, n., slope, attitude, bias; v., incline, distort

slăp, n., v., hit with palm of hand; adv., straight; **-per** [rough play

slăp'stĭck, n., comedy with

slăsh, v., cut or whip viciously, reduce; **-er**

slăt, n., thin strip

slăugh'têr, n., brutal killing; **-ous**; **-ously**

slāve, n., person totally owned by another; **-ry**

slāy, v., kill; **-er**

slēa'zȳ, a., flimsy; **ziness**; **zily**

slĕdge'hăm-mêr, n., long, heavy hammer

slēek, a., glossy, stylish; **-ness**; **-en**; **-ly**

slēet, n., partially frozen rain

slĕn'dêr, a., small in width, thin; **-ness**; **-ize**; **-ly**

sleŭth, n., detective

slīce, n., thin, cut piece, part; v., cut into slices; **-r**

slĭck, n., oily film on water; v., a., (make) glossy; a., clever; **-ness**; **-ly**

slīde, n., sliding, surface on which to slide, photographic transparency; v., move smoothy on surface, slip; **-r**

slīght, v., neglect; a., thin; **-ness**; **-ly**

slīme, n., wet slippery matter; **slimy**

slīng, n., v., (looped or hanging band used to) support, carry, throw

slĭnk, v., sneak, lurk; **-y** a.; **-ingly**

slĭp, n., woman's undergarment, error, small piece of paper; v., go quietly or quickly, slide accidently, err

slĭt, n., narrow opening; v., cut open; **-ter** [a.

slĭth'êr, v., slide, glide; **-y**

slĭv'êr, n., splinter

slŏb'bêr, v., drip saliva from mouth, drool; **-er**; **-y** a. [phrase

slō'găn, n., motto, catch

slōop, n., sailing vessel

slŏp, n., unappetizing food mixture; v., splash; **-py**; **-piness**; **-pily**

slōpe, n., raising or falling plane; v., go up or down at an angle

slŏt, n., narrow opening, position

slŏth, n., tree-dwelling mammal, laziness; **-ful**; **-fulness**; **-fully**

slōugh, n., swamp

slough (slŭf), v., shed, discard

slŏv'ĕn-lȳ, a., careless in appearance; **liness**

slōw, a., taking a long time, dull; v., make slow; **-ness**; **-ly**

slŭg, n., small land mollusk, false coin; v., hit hard

slŭm, n., poor, over-

crowded neighborhood
slŭm'bêr, n., v., sleep; **-er; -ous**
slŭmp, n.,v., fall, decline
slûr, n., insult; v., say indistinctly, slander
slûrp, v., drink or eat noisily   [snow
slŭsh, n., partly melted
slŭt, n., slovenly woman
slў, a., skillful at deceit; **-ness; -ly**
smăck, n., sharp noise, loud kiss, slap, trace; v., make a smack; **-er**
smăll, a., little, limited in size, trivial; **-ness; -ish**
smăll'pŏx, n., contagious disease
smârt, v., cause pain; a., sharp, intelligent, stylish; **-ness; -en; -ly**
smăsh, v., break violently, hit; **-er**   [amount
smăt'têr-ĭng, n., small
smêar, n., smudge mark; v., rub, spread dirt, slander; **-y** a.
smĕll, n., quality perceived through nose, odor; v., detect a smell, sniff; **-er**
smĕlt, n., small silvery fish; v., melt ore or metal; **-er**
smīle, n., grin; v., curve mouth upward to show pleasure; **-r; smilingly**
smīte, v., strike, distress; **-r**
smĭth, n., one who makes or repairs metal things
smŏck, n., protective outer garment
smŏg, n., fog and smoke
smōke, n., vapor arising from fire; v., give off smoke, use cigarettes, etc.; **-r; -able; -less; smoky** a.
smōl'dêr, v., burn without flame, be supressed
smôr'gàs-bôrd, n., many foods served buffet style
smŏth'êr, v., keep from getting air, suffocate, stifle; **-er; -y** a.

smŭdge, n., dirty spot; v., soil; **smudgy**
smŭg, a., annoyingly self-satisfied; **-ness; -ly**
smŭg'gle, v., import or export illegally; **-r**
smŭt, n., dirty matter, pornography; **-ty** a.
snăg, n., rough, sharp part, hidden difficulty; v., tear on snag; **-gy** a.
snāil, n., mollusk with spiral shell   [reptile
snāke, n., long limbless
snăp'shŏt, n., photograph
snāre, n., trap
snârl, n., v., growl, tangle; **-y** a.
snătch, n., v., grab; n., brief period, bit; **-er**
snēak, v., move or act underhandedly; **-y** a., **-iness; -ily**
snēer, v., smile scornfully; **-er; -ingly**
snēeze, v., exhale breath from mouth and nose in explosive action; **-r**
snĭck'êr, v., laugh slyly; **-ingly**   [**-ness; -ly**
snīde, a., malicious;
snĭff, v., breathe in through nose forcibly; **-er**
snĭp, v., cut quickly with scissors; **-per**
snīpe, v., shoot from a hidden place; **-r**
snŏb, n., one who acts superior; **-bery; -bish; -bishness; -bishly**
snōoze, n., v., (coll.) nap; **-r**   [while asleep; **-r**
snōre, v., breathe loudly
snôrt, v., breath making harsh sound; **-er; -ingly**
snōw, n., flakes of frozen water vapor from sky; **-y** a.   [**-ber; -by** a.
snŭb, v., show contempt;
snŭff, n., smokeless tobacco; v., inhale through nose, put out candle
snŭg, a., warm and cozy, tight in fit; **-gery; -ness; -ly**
sōak, v., make very wet, take in; **-age**

S
T

sōap, *n.,* washing substance; **-y** *a.;* **-iness; -ily**

sōap'bŏx, *n.,* improvised platform

sôar, *v.,* fly high in air; **-er**

sŏb, *v.,* cry aloud; **-ingly**

sŏc'cêr, *n.,* team ball game

sō'cĭál, *a.,* of people, of society; **-ity; -ize; -izer; -ization; -ly**

sō'cĭál-ĭsm, *n.,* public ownership of industry; **ist; istic; istically**

sò-cĭ'ė-tȳ, *n.,* community of people, all people, wealthy class; **tal**

sō-cĭ-ŏl'ò-gȳ, *n.,* study of society and human relations; **gist; logical**

sŏck, *n.,* short stocking; *v.,* hit hard

sŏck'ĕt, *n.,* hollow part into which a thing fits

sŏd'dĕn, *a.,* soaked, soggy; **-ness; -ly**

sō'dĭ-ŭm, *n.,* soft metallic element

sŏd'òm-ȳ, *n.,* abnormal sexual behavior

sôft, *a.,* pleasing to senses, yielding easily to touch, smooth, mild, easy; **-ness; -en; -ener; -ly** [ball

sôft'bǎll, *n.,* kind of base-

sôft'ȳ, *n.,* sentimental person [giness; gily

sŏg'gȳ, *a.,* wet and heavy;

sŏil, *n.,* top layer of earth, ground, stain; *v.,* make dirty

sō'joŭrn, *n., v.,* visit; **-er**

sŏl'áce, *n., v.,* comfort; **-r**

sō-lǎr'ĭ-ŭm, *n.,* glassed-in room exposed to sun

sŏl'dier (jêr), *n.,* member of army; **-y; -ly** *a.;* **-liness**

sōle, *n.,* bottom of foot; fish

sōle, *a.,* single, alone; **-ly**

sŏl'ĕmn, *a.,* sacred, formal, serious, awesome; **-ity; -ify; -ize; -ness; -ly**

sò-lĭc'ĭt, *v.,* seek, ask for **-ation; -ant** *n., a.*

sò-lĭc'ĭ-tŏr, *n.,* lawyer

sŏl-ĭ-dǎr'ĭ-tȳ, *n.,* complete unity

sò-lĭl'ò-quȳ, *n.,* talking aloud to oneself; **quize**

sŏl'ĭ-tār-ȳ, *a.,* alone, single; **tariness; tarily**

sò-lū'tion, *n.,* answer, being dissolved

sŏl'vĕnt, *n.,* solution; *a.,* able to pay debts, dissolving; **vency**

sō-mǎt'ĭc, *a.,* of the body; **-ally** [-ness; -ly

sŏm'bêr, *a.,* gloomy, sad;

sòme'bŏd-ȳ, *pro.,* a person [time

sòme'dāy, *adv.,* at a future

sòme'how, *adv.,* in an unknown way [body

sòme'òne, *pro.,* some-

sòm'êr-säult, *n.,* turning the body head over heels

sòme'times, *adv.,* occasionally

sòme'whĕre, *adv.,* at an unknown place

sō'nànt, *a.,* of sound; **nance**

sò-nä'tá, *n.,* musical piece

sòng, *n.,* music to be sung; **-ster**

sŏn'ĭc, *a.,* of sound

sŏn'nĕt, *n.,* poem with fourteen lines

sò-nô'roŭs, *a.,* rich in sound; **nority; -ness; -ly**

soot, *n.,* black particles of smoke; **-y** *a.*

soothe, *v.,* calm, pacify; **-r; soothingly**

sooth'sāy, *v.,* predict; **-er**

sŏph'ĭsm, *n.,* false reasoning

sò-phĭs'tĭ-cāt-ĕd, *a.,* knowledgeable, complex; **tion**

sò-prä'nō, *n.,* highest singing voice

sôr'cĕr-ȳ, *n.,* witchcraft; **cerer; cerous; cerously**

sôr'dĭd, *a.,* dirty, mean; **-ness; -ly**

sôre, *n.,* infected spot on body; *a.,* painful, distressing; **-ness; -ly**

sò-rôr'ĭ-tȳ, *n.,* woman's club

sŏr'rĕl, *n., a.,* (horse of) reddish-brown

sŏr'rŏw, *n.,* mental pain, sadness, distress; *v.,* grieve; **-er; -ful; -fulness; -fully**

sor'rȳ (săr), *a.,* feeling regret, grieved, poor; **riness; rily**

sôrt, *n.,* type; *v.,* arrange, classify; **-er; -able**

souf-fle' (flā), *n.,* light, puffy baked dish

sōul, *n.,* spiritual part of person, vital part; **-ful; -fulness; -fully; -less**

sŏūnd, *n.,* inlet of sea

sŏūnd, *a.,* in good condition, valid, deep; **-ness; -ly**

sŏūr, *a.,* tasting unplesant and sharp, fermented; **-ness; -ly**

sôurce, *n.,* starting point

sŏūth, *n.,* direction to left when facing sunset; *a., adv.,* in or of south; **-erly** *a., adv.;* **-ern** *a.;* **-ward, -wardly** *a., adv.*

soū-vĕ-nĭr', *n.,* thing kept as a reminder

sŏv'er-eĭgn, *n., a.,* (person) supreme in power; **-ty**

sŏw, *n.,* adult female pig

sōw, *v.,* plant seed, scatter; **-er**

soy'bēan (sŏī), *n.,* plant of legume family, seed

spå, *n.,* mineral spring, health resort

spāce, *n.,* unlimited expanse, area, room; **-less**

spā'cioŭs, *a.,* vast, large; **-ness; -ly**

spāde, *n.,* digging tool, black card suit

spå-ghĕt'tĭ, *n.,* long thin noodles

spăn, *n.,* measurement, extent, period of time; *v.,* reach across; **-ner**

spăn'gle, *n.,* small decorative metal piece; **gly** *a.*

spănk, *v.,* hit on buttocks as punishment; **-ing** *n.*

spâr, *n.,* long thick pole; *v.,* box with fists, dispute

spāre, *n.,* extra part; *v.,* save, give up; *a.,* extra; **-r; -ness; -ly**

spårk, *n.,* particle of fire or electricity, trace; *v.,* stir up; **-er**

spâr'kle, *n., v.,* glitter

spârse, *a.,* meager; **-ness; -ly**

spăsm, *n.,* sudden muscle contraction; **-odic; -odical; -odically**

spăt, *n., v.,* quarrel

spā'tiăl, *a.,* of space; **-ity; -ly** [drops

spăt'têr, *v.,* splash in

spăt'ŭ-lå, *n.,* utensil with flexible blade

spāwn, *n.,* mass of eggs, or young; *v.,* produce young

spēar, *n.,* long pointed weapon

spēar'mĭnt, *n.,* fragrant plant for flavoring

spē'ciăl, *a.,* distinctive, extraordinary; **-ty; -ize; -ization; -ly**

spē'ciĕs, *n., pl.,* distinct kind, biological classification

spė-cĭf'ĭc, *a.,* definite, explicit; **-ity; -ally**

spĕc'ĭ-mĕn, *n.,* sample

spĕck, *n.,* particle

spĕc'tå-cle, *n.,* unusual display, (pl.) pair of eyeglasses; **cular** *a.;* **cularly**

spĕc'tå-tŏr, *n.,* onlooker

spĕc'têr, *n.,* ghost; **tral** *a.;* **trality; tralness; trally**

spĕc'trŭm, *n.,* band of colors formed by diffusing light

spĕc'ū-lāte, *v.,* ponder, take business risk; **tor; tion; tive; tively**

spēech, *n.,* talk, address given to audience; **-less; -lessness; -lessly**

spēēd, *n.,* quick motion; *v.,* move rapidly, aid; **-er; -y** *a.*

S
T

spéed-ŏm′ė-têr, *n.,* device showing rate of speed

spĕll, *n.,* charm, period of time

spĕll, *v.,* give letters in word in order, signify; **-er; -ing** *n.*

spĕnd, *v.,* use up, pay out money; **-er** [derer

spĕnd′thrĭft, *n.,* squan-

spêr-măt-ȯ-zō′ŏn, *n.,* male reproductive cell; **zoal; zoan** *a.;* **zoic**

spĕw, *v.,* vomit, gush forth; **-er**

sphēre, *n.,* round body, ball; **spheric; spherical; spherically**

sphĭnx, *n.,* statue with human head and lion's body

spī′dêr, *n.,* eight-legged animal that spins web; **-y** *a.*

spīke, *n.,* large nail, sharp-pointed projection; *v.,* fasten [**-age**

spĭll, *v.,* drop, overflow;

spĭn, *n.,* ride; *v.,* twist fibers into thread, make a web, rotate; **-ner; -ning** *n.* [vegetable

spĭn′ảch, *n.,* green leafy

spĭn′dle, *n.,* rod used in spinning thread

spīne, *n.,* backbone, quill, thorn; **nal; nous; spiny** *a.* [**-ness; -ly**

spīne′lĕss, *a.,* cowardly;

spĭn′ét, *n.,* upright piano

spĭn′stêr, *n.,* older unmarried woman

spī′rảl, *n.,* coil, helix; *a.,* circling around a center; **-ly** [a point

spīre, *n.,* thing tapering to

spĭr′ĭt, *n.,* soul, ghost, courage, meaning, (pl.) frame of mind; **-less; -lessness; -lessly**

spĭr′ĭt-ū-ảl, *n.,* Negro folk song; *a.,* of spirit, religious; **-ity; -ize; -ization**

spĭt, *n.,* rod to roast meat over fire, saliva; *v.,* eject from mouth; **-ter**

spīte, *n.,* malice; *v.,* hurt; **-ful; -fulness; -fully**

splăsh, *v.,* scatter liquid; **-er; -y** *a.*

splēen, *n.,* abdominal organ

splĕn′dĭd, *a.,* brilliant, grand, glorious; **dor** *n.;* **dorous; drous; -ness; -ly**

splīce, *v.,* join together; **-r**

splĭnt, *n.,* device to hold broken bone together

splĭn′têr, *n.,* sliver; *v.,* break into small parts; **-y** *a.*

splĭt, *n.,* break; *v.,* separate, break, divide; **-ter**

splûrge, *n.,* (coll.) showy display; *v.,* be extravagant; **-r**

spŏil, *n.,* conquered property; *v.,* damage, ruin, overindulge; **-er; -age**

spōke, *n.,* wheel brace, ladder rung

spōkes′mản, *n.,* one who speaks for another

spŏnge, *n.,* porous plant-like animal of sea, absorbent material; *v.,* absorb, wipe clean; **-r; gy** *a.;* **giness**

spŏn-tā′nė-oŭs, *a.,* occurring naturally; **neity; -ness; -ly**

spook, *n.,* ghost; *v.,* haunt, frighten; **-y** *a.*

spool, *n.,* cylinder for thread, wire, etc.

spô-răd′ĭc, *a.,* happening from time to time; **-ally**

spôre, *n.,* reproductive cell

spôrt, *n.,* athletic game, fun; *v.,* play; *a.,* informal; **-er; -ive; -iveness; -ively; -ful; -fully; -y** *a.;* **-ness; -ily**

spŏt, *n.,* small area different from the rest, *v.,* stain, locate; **-ter; -less; -lessness; -lessly; -ty** *a.;* **-tiness; -tily**

spoŭse, *n.,* partner in marriage; **spousal**

spoŭt, *n.,* lip or tube for

pouring liquid; *v.*, shoot out; **-er; -less**

sprāin, *v.*, twist a muscle

sprāwl, *v.*, spread limbs to relax; **-er; -y** *a.*

sprāy, *n.*, mist of fine liquid drops; *v.*, apply a spray; **-er**

sprĕad, *n.*, extent, cover; *v.*, stretch out, scatter, cover; **-er**

sprēe, *n.*, lively time

sprĭng, *n.*, leap, resilient coil, source of water, season for beginning plant growth; *v.*, bounce, rise, come from

sprĭn'kle, *v.*, scatter in drops or particles

sprĭnt, *n., v.*, race fast

sprŏut, *n.*, new growth; *v.*, begin growing

sprȳ, *a.*, active, agile; **-ness; -ly**

spŭnk, *n.*, (coll.) courage; **-y** *a.;* **-ness; -ily**

spŭr, *n., v.*, (pointed attachment to horseman's heel to) urge to action

spū'rĭ-oŭs, *a.*, artificial; **-ness; -ly**   [**-er**

spŭrn, *v.*, reject scornfully;

spŭrt, *n.*, sudden burst of energy; *v.*, gush

spŭt'nĭk, *n.*, manmade satellite

spȳ, *n.*, one who spies; *v.*, watch closely and secretly

squăb, *n.*, young pigeon

squăb'ble, *n., v.*, quarrel

squăd, *n.*, small group

squăll, *n.*, violent storm; shrill cry; *v.*, scream harshly   [**fully**

squăn'dêr, *v.*, use waste-

squāre, *n.*, figure with four equal sides, city block; *v.*, adjust; multiply by itself; *a.*, squarelike, straight, even, fair; **-ness; -ly**

squăsh, *n.*, fleshy vegetable, tennislike game; *v.*, crush, suppress; **-y** *a.*

squăt, *v.*, crouch, settle public land; *a.*, short and

thick; **-ter; -ty** *a.*

squăw, *n.*, Indian woman

squēal, *n.*, shrill cry or sound; *v.*, (coll.) informer; **-er**

squēam'ĭsh, *a.*, easily nauseated or shocked; **-ness; -ly**   [**hug**

squēeze, *v.*, press closely,

squĕlch, *v.*, suppress

squĭd, *n.*, ten-armed sea mollusk

squĭg'gle, *n.*, short curved line; **gly** *a.*

squire, *n.*, country gentleman [**body**; **-y** *a.*

squîrm, *v.,* twist and turn

squîr'rĕl, *n.*, tree-dwelling rodent   [**jet; -er**

squîrt, *v.*, shoot liquid in

stăb, *n.*, wound; *v.*, pierce with something sharp; **-ber**

stā'ble, *n.*, building for horses and cattle

stā'ble, *a.*, firm, enduring; **bility; bilize; bilizer; bilization; bly**

stăff, *n.*, rod or stick, group of workers

stăg, *n.*, male deer, party for only men

stăge, *n.*, platform, theater, growth period; *v.*, present

stăg'gêr, *v.*, move unsteadily; **-er**   [**ing; -ly**

stăg'gêr-ĭng, *a.*, astonish-

stăg'nănt, *a.*, not moving, foul; **nancy; nate; nation; -ly**

stāid, *a.*, settled, steady; **-ness; -ly**

stāin, *n., v.*, spot, dishonor, color; **-er; -able; -less; -lessly**

stāke, *n.*, pointed stick, wager, prize; *v.*, mark off, hitch

stă-lăc'tīte, *n.*, lime deposit hanging from cave; **titic**

stă-lăg'mīte, *n.*, lime deposit sticking up from cave floor; **mitic**

stāle'māte, *n.*, deadlock

stălk, *n.*, plant stem; *v.*,

walk or spread grimly;
-er

ställ, *n.,* animal compartment in stable, booth; *v.,* delay

stăl'liŏn, *n.,* male horse

stăl'wȧrt, *a.,* strong, sturdy; **-ness; -ly**

stăm'ĭ-nȧ, *n.,* endurance

stăm'mêr, *v.,* talk with involuntary pauses, stutter; **-er; -ingly**

stămp, *n.,* gummed paper for postage, mark from die, sign; *v.,* put foot down forcibly, imprint mark; **-er**   [rush

stăm-pēde', *n.,* headlong

stănce, *n.,* standing posture [support beam

stăn'chiŏn, *n.,* upright

stănd, *n.,* position, halt, platform, booth; *v.,* be or set upright, tolerate, remain, rank; **-er**

stănd'ȧrd, *n.,* established rule or model, basis of measurement; *a.,* typical; **-ize; -izer; -ization**

stănd'ĭn, *n.,* substitute

stănd'pŏint, *n.,* point of view

stănd'stĭll, *n.,* halt

stăn'zȧ, *n.,* division of poem; **-ic**

stā'ple, *n.,* main commodity; *a.,* principal

stā'ple, *n.,* U-shaped wire fastener; *v.,* fasten with staple; **-r**

stȧr, *n.,* heavenly body, flat figure with five or six points, celebrated person; *a.,* outstanding

stȧr'bŏȧrd, *n.,* ship's right side when facing bow

stȧrch, *n.,* carbohydrate food substance, clothes stiffener; **-y** *a.;* **-iness; -ily**

stāre, *v.,* look intently; **-r**

stȧrk, *a.,* prominent, bare, rigid, utter; **-ness; -ly**

stȧrt, *n.,* beginning, shock; *v.,* set into motion, move suddenly; **-er**

stȧrve, *v.,* suffer from hunger; **vation**

stāte, *n.,* condition, political unit; *v.,* declare; *a.,* formal

stāte'mĕnt, *n.,* declaration, financial account, bill

stăt'ĭc, *n.,* electrical interference; *a.,* motionless; **-ally**

stā'tion, *n.,* assigned place, stopping place, position

stā'tion-ār-ȳ, *a.,* fixed, unchanging

stā'tion-ĕr-ȳ, *n.,* writing supplies

stȧ-tĭs'tĭcs, *n.,* science of numerical data; **cian** *n.;* **cal; cally**

stăt'ūe, *n.,* carved or modeled figure; **uary**

stăt'ûre, *n.,* height, level of attainment

stăt'ŭs, *n.,* position

stăt'ūte, *n.,* law; **tory** *a.*

stäunch, *v.,* stop flow; *a.,* firm, loyal; **-ness; -ly**

stāve, *n.,* barrel slat

stāy, *n., v.,* support, stop, delay, continuing; *v.,* remain

stĕad, *n.,* position for a replacement

stĕad'ȳ, *a.,* fixed, regular; **steadiness; steadily**

stĕal, *v.,* take without permission; **-er**

stĕalth, *n.,* secret behavior; **-y** *a.;* **-iness; -ily**

stēam, *n.,* water vapor; **-y** *a.;* **-iness; -ily**

stēel, *n.,* tough metal of iron and carbon; **-y** *a;* **-iness**

stēep, *v.,* soak in liquid

stēep, *a.,* having sharp slope, extreme; **-ness; -en; -ly**

stēe'ple, *n.,* high tower on building   [**-able**

stēer, *v.,* guide, direct; **-er;**

stēer'ȧge, *n.,* poorest accommodations aboard ship

stein, *n.,* beer mug

stĕl'lȧr, *a.,* of star, important

stĕm, *n.*, main upward axis of plant, stemlike thing; *v.*, derive, stop; **-less**

stĕnch, *n.*, offensive odor

stĕn'cĭl, *n.*, cut-out pattern; *v.*, make or mark with stencil; **-er**

stĕ-nŏg'rȧ-phў, *n.*, shorthand writing; **pher; graphic; graphical; graphically**

stĕp'lăd-dêr, *n.*, ladder with flat rungs and wide base

stĕr-ē-ȯ-phŏn'ĭc, *a.*, of sounds from two or more directions; **ny; -ally**

stĕr'ē-ȯ-tȳpe, *n.*, fixed pattern

stĕr'ĭle, *a.*, unable to reproduce, not stimulating, free of germs; **rility; lize; lizer; lization**

stĕr'lĭng, *n.*, real silver; *a.*, excellent

stêr'nŭm, *n.*, breastbone

stĕth'ȯ-scōpe, *n.*, device to hear chest sounds; **py; scopic; scopical; scopically**

stē'vȧ-dôre, *n.*, one who loads and unloads ships

stēw, *n.*, mixture of meat and vegetables; *v.*, boil slowly

stēw'ȧrd, *n.*, one in charge; **-ess** *n.*; **-ship**

stĭck'lêr, *n.*, uncompromising person

stĭck'ў, *a.*, adhesive, humid; **stickiness; stickily**

stĭff, *a.*, hard to bend, firm, rigid; **-ness; -en; -ish; -ly**

stĭ'fle, *v.*, smother, suppress; **-r; fling; flingly**

stĭg'mȧ, *n.*, mark of disgrace, plant part; **-tize; -tization; -tic; -tical; -tically**

stĭll, *n.*, device for distilling liquids

stĭll, *a.*, quiet, inactive; *adv.*, continuously, yet; **-ness; -y** *a.*, *adv.*

stĭll'bôrn, *n.*, dead at birth

stĭlt, *n.*, supporting pole

stĭlt'ĕd, *a.*, raised, pompous; **-ness; -ly**

stĭm'ū-lāte, *v.*, excite; **-r; tor; lant,** *n.*, *a.*; **lus** *n.*; tion; tive

stĭn'gў, *a.*, miserly; **giness; gily**

stĭnt, *n.*, limit, task; *v.*, restrict; **-er**

stĭ'pĕnd, *n.*, fixed payment; **-iary** *a.*

stĭp'ple, *v.*, mark with dots

stĭp'ū-lāte, *v.*, specify, require; **tor; tion; tory**

stĭr'rŭp, *n.*, footrest on saddle

stĭtch, *n.*, single loop in sewing; *v.*, sew; **-er; -ery**

stŏck, *n.*, lineage, supporting part, livestock, goods in store, share in a business; *v.*, supply; *a.*, common

stŏck-āde', *n.*, enclosure, jail

stŏck'brō-kêr, *n.*, agent for stocks and bonds; **-age**

stŏck'ĭng, *n.*, closefitting cover for leg and foot

stŏck'pīle, *n.*, supply in reserve; **-r**

stŏck'ў, *a.*, short and heavy; **stockiness**

stō'ĭc, *n.*, *a.* (one who is) indifferent; **-al; -ally**

stōke, *v.*, feed full, fill; **-r**

stōle, *n.*, large shoulder scarf   **[-ness; -ly**

stŏl'ĭd, *a.*, unexcitable;

stōne, *n.*, hard nonmetallic mineral matter, rock

stōol, *n.*, backless seat, feces

stōop, *n.*, small porch; *v.*, bend body forward, lower oneself

stŏp'găp, *n.*, temporary substitute

stôr'ȧge, *n.*, place for keeping goods

stôre, *n.*, supply, place to sell goods; *v.*, put aside for future

stôrk, *n.*, large wading bird

stôrm, *n.*, atmospheric disturbance wind, rain,

S
T

snow, etc.; v., attack; **-y**
a.

stô'rӯ, n., series of connected events, tale, one level of building

stŏŭt, a., fat, brave; **-ness; -ish; -ly**

stōve, n., device for heating or cooking

stŏw, v., pack away; **-age**

străd'dle, v., put leg on either side; **-r**

străfe, v., attack with gunfire; **-r**

straight (strāt), a., not crooked, even, sincere; v., directly; **-en**

straight-fôr'wård (strāt), a., direct, honest; **-ness; -ly**

strāin, n., effort, breed; v., stretch or exert to utmost, filter, strive hard; **-er**

strāit, n., narrow waterway, emergency

strănd, n., shore, thread; v., be helpless; **-er**

strănge, a. unfamiliar, foreign, odd; **-r; -ness; -ly**

străn'gle, v., choke; **-r**

străp, n., leather strip; **-less**

străt'à-gėm, n., trick

străt'ė-gӯ, n., plan, maneuver; **gist; gic; gical; gically**

străt'ō-sphēre, n., upper atmosphere

strā'tŭm, a., layer

străw, n., hollow grain stalk, tube used for sucking; **-y** a. [fruit

străw'bĕr-rӯ, n., small red

strāy, v., roam; a., lost, incidental; **-er**

strēam, n., small river; n., v., flow [banner

strēam'ẽr, n., ribbonlike

strēam'līne, v., design for efficiency; **-d**

strēet'câr, n., passenger car on rails

strĕngth, n., strong quality, durability, force; **-en; -ener**

strĕn'ū-oŭs, a., showing great effort; **-ness; -ly**

strĕss, n., strain, emphasis, tension; **-ful; -fully**

strĕtch, v., reach out, extend; **-ability; -able; -y** a.

strī'āte, v., make with lines; **tion**

strĭck'ĕn, a., afflicted

strĭct, a., exact, closely enforced; **-ness; -ly**

strĭc'tûre, n., sharp criticism

strīde, n., long step

strī'dĕnt, a., shrill; **dence; dency; -ly**

strīfe, n., struggle, discord

strīke, v., hit, sound by hitting, ignite, find, stop work for new demands; **-r** [-ly

strĭk'ĭng, a., outstanding;

strĭn'gĕnt, a., strict; **gency; -ness; -ly**

strĭp, n., narrow piece, runway; v., remove covering, deprive

strīpe, n., long narrow mark

strĭp'lĭng, n., grown boy

strīve, v., try hard, fight; **-r**

strōke, n., sudden action, single effort, sound from striking; v., caress

strōll, v., walk leisurely; **-er**

strŏng'-ârm, a., physical force [place

strŏng'hōld, n., fortified

strŏn'tĭ-ŭm, n., chemical element

strŭc'tûre, n., building, organization; v., organize; **tural; turally**

strŭg'gle, n., great effort; n., v., conflict; **-r**

strŭm, v., stroke strings of instrument

strŭt, v., walk arrogantly

strӯch'nīne, n., poisonous substance

stŭb, n., short remaining piece; v., hit against

stŭb'bôrn, n., unyielding, resistant; **-ness; -ly**

stŭc'cō, n., coarse plaster

stŭd, n., ornamental nailhead, wall support, male breeder [room

stū′dī-ō, *n.,* artist's work-

stŭd′y,*n., v.,* act to acquire knowledge, examine carefully; *n.,* place to study; **dious; dious-ness; diously**

stŭff, *n.,* substance, objects; *v.,* fill, pack; **-er**

stŭl′tĭfy, *v.,* make absurd; **fier; fication**

stŭm′ble,*n.,* error; *v.,* miss one's step, happen; **-r; blingly**

stŭmp, *n.,* remaining part; *v.,* speak on tour; **-y** *a.*

stŭn, *v.,* shock, make unconscious; **-ner**

stŭnt, *n.,* daring trick; *v.,* hinder growth

stū′pĕ-fy, *v.,* shock, amaze; **fier; faction; facient**

stū-pĕn′doŭs, *a.,* astonishing; **-ly**

stū′pŏr,*n.,* loss of senses, lethargy; **-ous**

stŭr′dy, *a.,* physically strong, firm; **diness; dily**

stŭr′geón, *n.,* large fish

stŭt′tĕr, *v.,* talk with involuntary repeat of sounds; **-er** [eyelid

sty,*n.,* pigpen, swelling of

style, *n.,* manner, artistic expression, fashion; **stylist; stylize**

sty′lŭs, *n.,* marking tool

sty′miĕ, *v.,* obstruct

suáve, *a.,* smoothly gracious; **suavily; -ness; -ly** [rank

sŭb-äl′têrn, *a.,* of lower

sŭb-cŏn′scioŭs, *a.,* happening without awareness; **-ness; -ly**

sŭb′cŭl-tûre, *n.,* culture within larger society; **tural**

sŭb-dī-vīde′, *v.,* divide land into smaller areas

sŭb-dūe′, *v.,* conquer, lessen; **duct; dual; duable**

sŭb′jĕct, *n.,* one controlled, theme, course of

study, word discussed

sŭb-jĕct′, *v.,* control, undergo; **-ion**

sŭb-jĕc′tĭve, *a.,* of one's own feelings; **tivity; -ness; -ly**

sŭb′jŭ-gāte, *v.,* control, conquer; **tor; tion**

sŭb′lĭ-māte, *v.,* express impulses in acceptable forms; **tion**

sŭb-līme′, *a.,* exalted, splendid; **limity**

sŭb-mêrge′, *v.,* put under water; **gence; gible**

sŭb-mĭt′, *v.,* yield, surrender; **-ter; mission; missive; missiveness; missively; -table**

sŭb-poĕ′na, *n.,* written order to appear in court

sŭb-scrībe′, *v.,* agree to pay, support; **-r; scription**

sŭb-sīde′, *v.,* sink lower, abate; **-nce** [illiary

sŭb-sĭd′ĭ-är-y, *n., a.,* aux-

sŭb′sĭ-dy, *n.,* grant of money; **dize; dizer; dization**

sŭb-sĭst′, *v.,* exist, remain alive; **-ence; -ent**

sŭb′stánce, *n.,* essence, matter, character

sŭb-stăn′tĭ-āte, *v.,* prove; **tor; tion; tive**

sŭb′stĭ-tūte, *n.,* one in place for another; *v.,* replace; **tion; tive; tional; tionally; tionary; tutable** [action

sŭb′têr-fūge, *n.,* evasive

sub-tle (sŭt′l), *a.,* delicate, clever, keen; **-ty; -ness; -ly**

sŭb-trăct′, *v.,* take away from; **-er; -ion; -ive**

sŭb′ûrb, *n.,* residential district near city; **-anize; -anization; -an** *a.*

sŭb-vêrt′, *v.,* destroy, undermine; **-er; version; versive; versiveness; versively**

sŭc-cēed′, *v.,* follow, achieve goal; **-er**

sŭc-cĕss,*n.,* favorable re-

S
T

sult, gaining wealth; **-ful;
-fulness; -fully**
sŭc-cĕs'sĭon,n., following
in order, series; **sor;
sive; siveness; sively;
-al; -ally**
sŭc-cīnct', a., briefly and
clearly stated; **-ness; -ly**
sŭc'cŏr, n., v., help
sŭc'cū-lĕnt, a., juicy;
lence; lency; -ly
sŭc-cŭmb', v., yield, die
sŭck, v., draw into or up,
dissolve in mouth; **-er**
sŭck'le, v., suck at breast;
-r
sū'crōse, n., pure sugar
sŭd'dĕn, a., unexpected,
abrupt; **-ness; -ly**
sŭds,n., pl., foam of soapy
water; **-y** a.
sūe, v., take legal action
against, plead; **-r**
sū'ĕt, n., hard animal fat
sŭf'fĕr,v., experience pain
or grief, endure; **-er;
-ance; -ing** n.; **-able**
sŭf-fī'ciĕnt,a., as much as
is needed; **ciency; -ly**
sŭf'fŏ-cāte, v., deprive of
air; **tion; tive; catingly**
sŭf'frăge, n., right to vote
sŭf-fūse', v., overspread;
sion; sive
sŭg'år, n., sweet crystalline carbohydrate; **-like;
-less; -y** a.
sŭg-gĕst', v., bring to
mind, propose; **-er; -ion;
-ive; -iveness; -ively;
-ibility; -ible**
sū'ĭ-cīde, n., killing oneself; **dal; dally**
sŭit, n., set of clothes or
playing cards, legal ac-
tion; v., be right for,
please; **-ability; -able;
-ableness; -ably**
suite (swēt), n., set of
rooms of furniture
sŭit'ŏr, n., man wooing
woman
sŭl'fŭr, n., chemical element; **-ic; -ous**
sŭlk, v., be aloof and
ill-humored; **-y** a.;
-iness; -ily

sŭl'lĕn, a., silently resentful; **-ness; -ly**
sŭl'lў, v., soil, stain
sŭl'trў, a., hot and humid;
triness; trily
sŭm, n., whole amount,
amount of money; v., to-
tal; **-mation; -mational**
sŭm'mĭt, n., highest point
sŭm'mŏn, v., order to
come; **-er**
sŭmp'tū-oŭs, a., costly,
lavish; **-ness; -ly**
sŭn'bŭrn, n., skin inflammation for exposure to
sun
sŭn'daē, n., ice cream
topped with syrup
sŭn'dĕr, v., break apart;
-ance; -able
sŭn'drў, a., various
sŭn'glăss-ĕs, n., pl.,
tinted eyeglasses for
protection from sun
sŭnk'ĕn, a., submerged,
depressed
sŭn'nў,a., bright like sun-
shine; **niness; nily**
sŭn'tăn, n., skin's dark-
ened condition from ex-
posure to sun
sū'pêr, a., outstanding,
large
sū-pêrb', a., splendid;
-ness; -ly
sū'pêr-chärge, v., in-
crease power; **-r**
sū-pêr-fī'ciăl, a., on the
surface, obvious; **-ity;
-ness; -ly**
sū-pêr'flū-oŭs, a., excessive; **-ness; -ly**
sū-pêr-ĭm-pōse',v., put on
top of; **position**
sū-pêr-ĭn-tĕnd'ĕnt, n.,
one in charge
sū-pē'rĭ-ŏr,a., higher, better, greater; **-ity; -ly**
sū-pêr'lå-tĭve, n., highest
degree; a., exceeding
all; **-ness; -ly**
sū-pêr-sēde', v., replace;
-r; dure; -nce
sū-pêr-sŏn'ĭc, a., faster
than speed of sound, be-
yond human hearing; **-s**
sū-pêr-stĭ'tĭon, n., belief

in magic or charm;
tious; tiousness; tiously

su'per-vīse, v., oversee, direct; **sor; sion; sory**

sŭp'per, n., evening meal

sŭp-plănt', v., replace; **-er; -ation**

sŭp'ple, a., flexible; **-ness; -ly**

sŭp'ple-mėnt, n., added part; **-ation; -al, -ary**

sŭp'plĭ-cāte, v., ask humbly; **tion; pliance; pliant** n., a.; **tory**

sŭp'plў, n., available amount; v., meet needs of, furnish; **plier**

sŭp-pôrt', n., aid; n., v. (that which can) hold up, help, be in favor of, maintain; **-er; -ive; -able; -ably**

sŭp-pŏs'ĭ-tô-rў, n., medicine put into a body passage

sŭp-prĕss', v., put down by force, stop; **-or; -ion; -ive; -ively; -ible**

sŭ-prēme', a., highest, utmost; **premacy; -ness; -ly** [charge, overload

sûr'chârge, n., v., over-**sure (sŏr),** a., without doubt, certain; **-ty; -ly**

sûrf, n., sea waves at shore

sûr'fāce, n., exterior; v., rise to top; a., superficial

sûr'feĭt, n., excess

sûrge, n., sudden rush, wave; v., increase suddenly

sûr'gėr-ў, n., medical treatment by operations; **geon** n.; **gical; gically**

sûr'lў, a., bad-tempered; **liness**

sûr-mīse', n., v., guess

sûr-mŏūnt', v., overcome, rise above; **-able**

sûr'nāme, n., family name

sûr-prīse', n., unexpected event; v., come upon unexpectedly; **prising; prisingly**

sûr-rē'ăl-īsm, n., modern art movement; **ist; istic; istically**

sûr-rĕn'dêr, n., yielding; v., give up

sûr-rĕp-tĭ'tioŭs, a., secret; **-ness; -ly**

sûr'rēy, n., horse-drawn carriage with top

sûr'rȯ-gāte, n., v., substitute

sûr-rŏūnd', v., enclose

sûr-vey' (vā), n., detailed inspection, view; v., examine, determine land boundaries; **-or; -ing** n.

sûr-vīve', v., continue to live; **vor; vorship; vival; vivability; vivable**

sŭs-cĕp'tĭ-ble, a., easily affected; **bility; -ness; bly** [mise

sŭs-pĕct', v., distrust, sur-**sŭs-pĕnd',** v., stop temporarily, exclude, hang; **pension; pensive**

sŭs-pĕnd'êrs, n., shoulder straps to hold up pants

sŭs-pĕnse', n., anxious uncertainty; **-ful**

sŭs-pĭ'ciȯn, n., suspecting, trace; **cious; ciousness; ciously**

sŭs-tāin', v., support, endure; **-er; -ment; -able**

sŭs'tė-nánce, n., nourishment

su'tŭre, n., join by sewing

swăb, n., (thing used to) clean or medicate

swăd'dle, v., bind in cloth

swăg'gêr, n., v., strut

swămp, n., wet, spongy land; v., flood, overwhelm; **-ish; -y** a.; **-iness**

swănk, a., ostentatiously stylish; **-y** a.; **-iness; -ily**

swarm (swôrm), n., v., (colony of bees that) fly together

swarth'ў (swôrth), a., darkish; **swarthiness; swarthily**

swäsh'bŭck-lêr, n., swaggering fighting man; **ling** n. [-ter

swät, n., quick sharp hit;

swätch, n., sample of cloth

swāthe, v., wrap a bandage around; **-r**

swāy, n., power; v., move back and forth, lean, influence; **-er**

sweār, v., vow, curse; **-er**

swĕat, n., salty liquid given off from skin; v., give forth sweat; **-y** a.; **-iness; -ily**

swēep, n., flowing movement, extent; v., clean with broom, win; **-er**

swēep'stākes, n., lottery

swēet, n., candy; a., tasting like sugar, pleasant; **-en; -ener; -ening** n.

swēet'heàrt, n., lover

swĕll, n., bulge, increase; v., become larger, expand; **-ing** n.

swĕl'tèr, v., feel intense heat

swêrve, v., turn aside; **-r**

swĭll, n., garbage; v., drink greedily

swĭm, v., move through water, be dizzy; **-mer; -ming** n.

swĭn'dle, n., v., cheat, fraud; **-r**

swĭne, n., pig

swĭng, n., swinging motion; v., sway when hanging; **-er**

swîrl, v., twist; **-y** a.

swĭsh, n., sharp, hissing sound; **-y** a.

swĭtch, n., stick for whipping, control device; n., v., lash, shift, change

swĭtch'bôard, n., control panel for electrical circuits

swĭv'èl, v., rotate

swōl'lèn, a., swelling

swōōn, n., v., faint; **-er**

sword (sôrd), n., weapon with sharp blade

sỳc'ò-phànt, n., one seeking favors by flattery; **phancy; -ish; -ishly; -ic; -ically**

sỳl'là-bŭs, n., summary of course of study

sỳl'lò-gĭsm, n., form of reasoning; **gize; gistic; gistical; gistically**

sýlph, n., thin graceful woman [est

sỳl'vàn, a., wooded, of forest

symbol, n., representation, sign; **-ize; -izer; -ization; -ism; -ist; -istic; -istically; -ic; -ical; -ically**

sým'mė-trỹ, n., balance of opposite parts; **trize; trization; trical; trically**

sým'pà-thỹ, n., sharing another's feeling, agreement; **thize; thizer; thizingly; thetic; thetically**

sým'phò-nỹ, n., harmony, musical composition for orchestra; **phonic; phonically**

sỳm-pō'sī-ŭm, n., meeting with intellectual discussion

sỳmp'tòm, n., outward sign, indication; **-atic; -atically**

sỳn'à-gŏgue, n., Jewish place of worship

sỳn'chrò-nīze, v., regulate together; **-r; zation; nous; nousness; nously**

sỳn'drōme, n., set of symptoms in a disease; **dromic**

sỳn'òd, n., council of churches; **-al; -ical; -ically**

sỳn'ò-nỹm, n., word with same meaning as another; **-ic; -ical; -ous; -ously**

sỳn-ŏp'sĭs, n., summary; size; **optic; optical; optically**

sỳn'tăx, n., word arrangement in sentence; **tactic; tactical; tactically**

sỳn'thė-sĭs, n., uniting parts into whole; **size; sizer**

sỳ-rĭnge', n., ball with tube for drawing in or ejecting liquid [uid; **-y** a.

sỳr'ŭp, n., sweet thick liq-

sỳs'tĕm, n., plan, method, orderly arrangement; **-atize; -atizer; -atiza-**

tab 165 tarnish

tion; -atic; -atical; -atically

T

tăb, *n.,* small flat, (coll.) bill for expenses

tăb'ér-năc-le, *n.,* place of worship; **nacular**

tā'ble, *n.,* furniture of flat surface and legs, systematic list; *v.,* postpone

tăb'lĕt, *n.,* flat inscribed stone slab, writing pad, compressed piece of medicine

tă-boo', *n.,* sacred or social prohibition; *a.,* forbidden

tăc'ĭt, *a.,* silent, implied; **-ness; -ly**

tăck, *n.,* short nail, course of action, ship's course; *v.,* fasten with tack, change course

tăck'le, *n.,* equipment; *v.,* undertake, bring down football carrier

tăct, *n.,* diplomatic skill; **-ful; -fulness; -fully; -less; -lessness; -lessly**

tăc'tĭcs, *n., pl.,* skillful method; **tic; tical; tically**

tăc'tĭle, *a.,* of touch; **tility**

tăf'fy, *n.,* chewy candy

tăg, *n.,* label, chase game; *v.,* fasten tag, touch; **-ger**

tāil, *n.,* rear part, appendage to body's hind part; *v.,* (coll.) follow; **-less**

tāint, *v.,* spoil; **-less**

tāke, *n.,* amount taken; *v.,* get hold of, seize, obtain, use, receive, lead, carry; **-r; -able**

tāke'ôff, *n.,* leaving the ground   [control

tāke'ō-vêr, *n.,* assuming

tăl'cŭm, *n.,* body powder

tāle, *n.,* story, be

tăl'ĕnt, *n.,* natural ability; **-ed**   [-ical

tăl'ĭs-mán, *n.,* charm; **-ic;**

tălk, *n.,* speech, discussion, rumor; *v.,* say words, gossip; **-er;**

-ative

tăll, *a.,* high; **-ness**

tăl'lōw, *n.,* animal fat; **-y** *a.*

tăl'lÿ, *n., v.,* record, score; *v.,* agree

tăl'ón, *n.,* claw

tăm, *n.,* flat, round cap

tăm-bóu-rĭne', *n.,* hand drum with jingling metal discs

tāme, *v., a.,* (make) domestic, gentle, obedient; **-r; -ness; -less; -able; -ly**

tămp, *v.,* pack down; **-er**

tăm'pêr, *v.,* interfere; **-er**

tăn, *n., a.,* yellowish brown; *v.,* make hide into leather, become sunburned, heat

tăn'à-gêr, *n.,* songbird

tăn'dĕm, *n.,* horse team, bicycle for two; *adv.,* one behind another

tăng, *n.,* strong taste or odor; **-y** *a.* **; -iness**

tăn'gĕnt, *a.,* touching at a point; **gency; -ial**

tăn'gĭ-ble, *a.,* real; **bility; -ness; bly**

tăn'gō, *n.,* dance

tănk, *n.,* large container, large armored vehicle

tănk'êr, *n.,* vehicle carrying liquids

tăn'tà-līze, *v.,* tease; **-r; zation; lizingly**

tăn'tà-moùnt, *a.,* equal

tăn'trŭm, *n.,* fit of temper

tāpe, *n.,* strong narrow strip   [*v.,* lessen

tā'pêr, *n.,* slender candle;

tăp'ĕs-trÿ, *n.,* cloth with woven designs

tāpe'wŏrm, *n.,* worm living in intestines

tăp-ĭ-ō'cà, *n.,* starchy food

tā'pĭr, *n.,* hoglike mammal

tăp'rŏot, *n.,* main root

tär, *n.,* thick dark liquid made from coal

tär'dÿ, *a.,* late, slow; **tardiness; tardily**

tär'gĕt, *n.,* thing aimed at

tăr'ĭff, *n.,* tax

tär'nĭsh, *n.,* dullness, stain; *v.,* discolor; **-able**

S T

târ-päu'lĭn, *n.,* water-proofed canvas

tăr'rў, *v.,* linger, stay

târt, *n.,* pastry

târt, *a.,* sour; **-ness; -ly**

târ'tăr, *n.,* deposit on teeth

tăsk, *n.,* assigned work; *v.,* labor

tăs'sĕl, *n.,* ornamental tuft of threads

tāste, *n.,* sense, flavor, sample, liking; *v.,* detect flavor in mouth, experi-ence; **-r; -less; -lessness; -lessly**

tăt'tĕr, *n.,* rag, shred

tăt'tle, *v.,* tell tales; **-r**

tăt-tōo', *v.,* mark skin with permanent design

täunt, *n.,* scornful remark; *v.,* ridicule; **-er; -ingly**

taupe (tōp), *n., a.,* brown-ish gray   [**-ly**

täut, *a.,* tight, tense; **-ness;**

tăv'ĕrn, *n.,* place for sell-ing liquor   [yellow

täw'nў, *n., a.,* brownish

tăx, *n.,* payment required by government, burden; *v.,* levy, strain; **-er; -ation; -ability; -able**

tăx'ĭ-căb, *n.,* automobile for hire

tēa, *n.,* beverage made from leaves, afternoon meal

tēach, *v.,* impart knowl-edge, instruct; **-er; -ing** *n.*; **-ability; -able; -ableness**

tēak, *n.,* yellowish brown wood   [grayish blue

tēal, *n.,* wild duck, dark

tēam, *n.,* group working together

tēam'stêr, *n.,* truck driver

tēar, *n.,* liquid drop from eye; **-y** *a.*; **-iness; -ily; -ful; -fulness; -fully; -less; -lessness; -lessly**   [dash; **-er**

teār, *v.,* force apart, rip,

tēase, *v.,* comb out, annoy, poke fun; **-r; teasingly**

tēat, *n.,* nipple

tĕch'nĭ-căl, *a.,* of mechan-ical arts, skilled; **-ly**

tĕch-nĭ-căl'ĭ-tў, *n.,* detail

tĕch-nïque', *n.,* method

tē'dĭ-oŭs, *a.,* boring, tire-some; **dium** *n.*; **-ness; -ly**   [or football

tēe, *n.,* holder for golf ball

tēem, *v.,* pour, swarm

tēens, *n., pl.,* years from thirteen through nine-teen

tēethe, *v.,* grow teeth

tĕl'ė-căst, *n., v.,* broadcast of television; **-er**

tĕl'ė-grăph, *n., v.,* (device to) send message elec-trically by wire; **-er; -y; -ic; -ically**

tė-lĕp'ȧ-thў, *n.,* thought transference; **thist; pathic; pathically**

tĕl'ė-phōne, *n.,* electrical device to convey speech; **-r; phonic; phonically**

tĕl'ė-scōpe, *n.,* instrument that makes objects seem nearer; **scopic; scopi-cally**

tĕl'ė-vĭ-sión, *n.,* transmis-sion of scenes by radio waves; **vise; -al; -ally**

tĕl'ĕx, *n.,* teletypewriter with a dial

tĕll, *v.,* say, relate, recog-nize, order; **-er; -able**

tĕll'êr, *n.,* counter, bank cashier

tĕll'tāle, *a.,* revealing

tĕl-lū'rĭ-ŭm, *n.,* chemical element

tė-mĕr'ĭ-tў, *n.,* rash bold-ness; **erarious**

tĕm'pêr, *n.,* state of mind, mood, rage; *v.,* reduce intensity; **-er; -ability; -able**   [paint

tĕm'pêr-ȧ, *n.,* water-base

tĕm'pêr-a-mėnt, *n.,* frame of mind

tĕm'pêr-ȧtė, *a.,* moderate; **ance; -ness; -ly**

tĕm'pêr-a-tûre, *n.,* degree of hot and cold, fever

tĕm'pĕst, *n.,* violent storm; **-uous; -uousness; -uously**

tĕm'ple, *n.,* place for wor-

ship, area on head be-
tween eye and ear

tĕm′pō, *n*., rate of speed

tĕm′pō-rār-ў, *a*., of limited
time; **rariness; rarily**

tĕm′pō-rīze, *v*., delay,
evade; **-r; zation**

tĕmpt, *v*., lure, attract; **-er;
-ation; -ing; -able**

tĕ-nā′cioŭs, *a*., holding
fast, retentive; **nacity;
-ness; -ly**

tĕn′ȧnt, *n*., one renting living space; **ency; -able;
-less**   [inclined

tĕnd, *v*., take care of, be

tĕn′dẽr, *n*., *v*., offer; **-er**

tĕn′dẽr, *a*., delicate, soft,
gentle; **-ness; -ly**

tĕn′dẽr-fŏŏt, *n*., beginner

tĕn′dẽr-lŏin, *n*., choice cut
of meat

tĕn′dȯn, *n*., fibrous cord
connecting muscle to
bone; **dinous**

tĕn′ė-mėnt, *n*., slum apartment house

tĕn′nĭs, *n*., sport played
with racket and ball

tĕn′ōr, *n*., high male voice,
general meaning

tĕnse, *n*., verb form of time

tĕnse, *a*., showing strain,
anxious; **sion; sity;
sive; sile** *a*.

tĕn′tȧ-cle, *n*., long flexible
growth on head; **tacular**

tĕn′tȧ-tĭve, *a*., temporary;
-ness; -ly

tĕn′ū-oŭs, *a*., thin, flimsy;
nuity; -ness; -ly

tĕn′ûre, *n*., right or time
holding a position

tĕp′ĭd, *a*., lukewarm; **-ity;
tepefy; -ness; -ly**

tẽr′bĭ-ŭm, *n*., metallic element

tẽrm, *n*., set period of time,
contractual condition,
word

tẽr′mĭ-nāte, *v*., end; **tor;
tion; tive**

tẽr-mĭ-nŏl′ō-gў, *n*., system
of terms; **gist; logical;
logically**

tẽr′mīte, *n*., insect of colony eating wood

tẽrn, *n*., sea bird

tẽr′rȧce, *n*., reused flat
land, paved garden area

tẽr̆rȧ-cŏt′tȧ, *n*., unglazed
earthenware

tẽr′rāin, *n*., land features

tẽr-rār′ĭ-ŭm, *n*., container
for small garden   [**-ly**

tẽr-rĕs′trĭ-ȧl, *a*., earthly;

tẽr′rĭ-ble, *a*., frightful, extreme, very bad; **bly**

tẽr-rĭf′ĭc, *a*., dreadful,
(coll.) great; **-ally**

tẽr′rĭ-fў, *v*., frighten; **-ingly**

tẽr′rĭ-tō-rў, *n*., land region,
area as part of country;
**rial; riality; rialism; rial-
ize; rialization; rially**

tẽr′rōr, *n*., intense fear

tẽr′rōr-ĭsm, *n*., intimidation by force and threats;
ist; ize; ization   [**-ly**

tẽrse, *a*., concise; **-ness;**

tĕst, *n*., examination, trial;
v., try, take test; **-er;
-able**

tĕs′tȧ-mėnt, *n*., Bible part,
legal will; **-al**

tĕs′tĭ-cle, *n*., male sex
gland; **ticular**

tĕs′tĭ-fў, *v*., give evidence;
fier; fication

tĕs′tĭ-mō-nў, *n*., proof

tĕs′tў, *a*., irritable; **tiness;
tily**   [disease

tĕt′a-nŭs, *n*., infectious

tĕth′ẽr, *n*., *v*., rope to confine animal

tĕxt, *n*., wording, main part
of book, subject; **-ual**

tĕx′tĭle, *n*., *a*., (fabric) that
has been woven

tĕx′tûre, *n*., appearance or
feel of surface; **tural;
turally**

thănk, *v*., express gratitude; **-ful; -fulness;
-fully; -less; -lessness;
-lessly**

thătch, *n*., roof of straw,
etc.

thăw, *v*., melt

thē′ȧ-tẽr, *n*., place for
viewing plays, etc.,
drama; **atrics; atrical;
atric; atrically**

thĕft, *n*., stealing

thē′ĭsm, *n.,* belief in God; **ist; istic; istically**

thēme, *n.,* topic, short essay, main tune; **matic**

thĕn, *adv.,* at that time, next, therefore, besides

thē-ŏl′ō-gў, *n.,* study of God and religions; **gist; logical; logically**

thē′ō-rĕm, *n.,* statement that can be proved; **-atic**

thē′ō-rў, *n.,* unproven idea, guess; **rize; rizer; rization; retical; retically**

thĕr-à-peū′tĭc, *a.,* serving to cure; **-s; -al; -ally**

thĕr′à-pў, *n.,* treatment of disease; **pist**

thēre′à-bouts, *adv.,* near that place [that

thĕre-ăf′tĕr, *adv.,* after

thĕre′fôre, *adv., conj.,* as a result of this

thĕre-tȯ-fôre′, *adv.,* up to then

thĕre-ŭp-ŏn′, *adv.,* at once

thêr′măl, *a.,* of heat; **-ly**

thêr-mō-dў-năm′ĭcs, *n.,* relationship of heat and mechanical power; **ic**

thêr-mŏm′é-têr, *n.,* device to measure temperature; **try; metric; metrically**

thêr′mȯ-stăt, *n.,* device to regulate temperature

thē-sau′rŭs (sô), *n.,* book of words

thē′sĭs, *n.,* unproved premise, lengthy research paper

thī′à-mīne, *n.,* vitamin B₁

thĭck, *a.,* of great depth, not thin, dense; **-ness; -en; -ener; -ening** *n.;* **-ish; -ly** [of plants

thĭck′ĕt, *n.,* dense growth

thiĕf, *n.,* one who steals

thiĕve, *v.,* steal; **-ry; thievish**

thĭm′ble, *n.,* protective cap for finger when sewing

thĭn, *a.,* of little depth, slender, sparce, sheer; **-ness; -ly**

thĭnk, *v.,* use mind, consider, reason, recall; **-er;**

-ing *n., a.;* **-able**

thîrst, *n.,* need for water; **-y** *a.;* **-iness; -ily**

thĭs′tle, *n.,* prickly plant

thông, *n.,* leather strap

thô′răx, *n.,* body between neck and abdomen

thô′rĭ-ŭm, *n.,* chemical element

thôrn, *n.,* sharp point on plant; **-y** *a.;* **-iness**

thŏr′ough, *a.,* complete, very exact; **-ness; -ly**

thŏr′ough-brĕd, *n., a.,* (animal) of pure breed

thou, *pro.,* you

thōugh, *adv., conj.,* nevertheless

thôught, *n.,* act or result of thinking, idea; consideration; **-ful; -fulness; -fully; -less; -lessness; -lessly**

thrăsh′ĕr, *n.,* songbird

thrĕad, *n.,* fine, spun cord, groove on screw; **-er; -like** *a.* [shabby

thrĕad′bāre, *a.,* worn,

thrĕat, *n.,* sign of danger, intention to hurt; **-en; -ener; -eningly**

thrĕsh, *v.,* beat grain out of husk; **-er**

thrĕsh′ōld, *n.,* doorway, entrance

thrĭft, *n.,* careful money management; **-y** *a.;* **-iness; -ily; -less; -lessness; -lessly**

thrĭll, *n.,* excitement; *v.,* excite; shiver; **-er**

thrive, *v.,* prosper, succeed

thrŏb, *v.,* vibrate strongly; **-ber; -bingly**

thrōe, *n.,* struggle

thrŏm-bō′sĭs, *n.,* blood clot; **botic** [chair

thrōne, *n.,* king's official

thrông, *n., v.,* crowd

thrŏt′tle, *n.,* valve controlling power flow

thrōugh, *a.,* open, finished; *adv.,* in and out, to the end; *prep.* from end to end, by way of

thrōw, *v.,* send through air

from hand, hurl, direct; **-er**

thrŭsh, *n.,* songbird, infant disease in mouth

thrŭst, *n.,* shove, sudden attack; *v.,* push with force

thŭg, *n.,* hoodlum; **-gery; -gish** [nearest wrist

thŭmb, *n.,* thick finger

thŭmp, *n.,* heavy blow, its sound; **-er**

thŭn'dêr, *n.,* loud sound after lightning; **-ous; -ously**

thwart (thwôrt), *v.,* frustrate, hinder; **-er**

thȳme, *n.,* herb

thȳ'rŏid, *n.,* gland in neck that regulates growth

ti-ār'à, *n.,* woman's crown-like headdress

tĭck, *n.,* light tapping sound, insect, mattress covering

tĭck'ĕt, *n.,* paper giving one a right, label, list of candidates

tĭde, *n.,* regular rise and fall of ocean

tĭ'dȳ, *a.,* neat, orderly; **di-ness; dily**

tĭe, *n.,* neckwear, link railroad beam; *v.,* connect as with string, etc., make knot, equal a score

tĭêr, *n.,* row of seats

tĭff, *n.,* argument

tĭght, *a.,* close fitting, compact, taut, constricting; **-ness; -en; -ly**

tĭle, *n.,* piece of glazed clay for covering floor or roof

tĭll, *n.,* cash drawer; *prep; conj.,* until [**-age**

tĭll, *v.,* cultivate land; **-er;**

tĭlt, *n., v.,* slope, slant

tĭm'bêr, *n.,* wood for building, trees

tĭme, *n.,* duration, period, measured interval, tempo, occasion

tĭme'lĕss, *a.,* eternal; **-ness; -ly**

tĭme'lȳ, *a.,* done at suitable time; **liness**

tĭm'ĭd, *a.,* shy, afraid; **-ity; -ness; -ly**

tĭm'pà-ni, *n.,* set of kettle drums

tĭn, *n.,* soft metallic element; **-ny; -niness; -nily**

tĭn'dêr, *n.,* dry easily flammable material

tĭne, *n.,* prong

tĭnge, *n.,* tint, slight trace; *v.,* color, give a trace

tĭn'gle, *n., v.,* sting, prickle; **-r; gly** *a.;* **glingly**

tĭn'kêr, *v.,* mend, fuss aimlessly; **-er**

tĭn'sĕl, *n.,* decorative stripes of foil; *a.,* gaudy; **-ly** *a.*

tĭnt, *n.,* shading of color; **-er**

tĭp, *n.,* pointed end, light blow, warning, secret information; *v.,* give money for service, tilt, overturn

tĭp'sȳ, *a.,* shaky, somewhat drunk; **siness; sily**

tĭ'rāde, *n.,* long, angry speech

tĭre, *n.,* rubber wheel for vehicle; *v.,* become weary, lose strength

tĭred, *a.,* fatigued, stale; **-ness; -ly**

tĭs'sūe, *n.,* body substance, thin paper or cloth

tĭthe, *n.,* tenth part of income paid to church; **-r; tithable**

tĭt'ĭl-lāte, *v.,* excite; **-r; tion; tive**

tĭ'tle, *n.,* name, word showing rank, legal right; **titular** *a.;* **titularly**

tĭt'mouse, *n.,* small bird

tĭz'zȳ, *n.,* state of excitement

to (tōo), *adv.,* forward; *prep.,* toward, as far as, on, until, for, as compared with [imal

tōad, *n.,* froglike land an-

tōad'stōol, *n.,* poisonous mushroom

tōad'ȳ, *n.,* sycophant; *v.,* flatter; **-ism**

tȯ-băc′cō, *n.,* plant, its leaves used to smoke

tȯ-bŏg′gȧn, *n.,* flat sled without runners

tȯ-gĕth′êr, *adv.,* in one group, at same time, in agreement

tȯil, *n.,* hard work; *v.,* labor; **-er; -ful; -some** *a.;* **-someness; -somely**

tȯi′lĕt, *n.,* fixture receiving body waste, grooming; **-ry**

tō′kĕn, *n.,* sign, keepsake, metal piece for fare

tŏl′êr-ȧnce, *n.,* enduring another's way; **ant; antly**

tōll, *n.,* tax, charge, number lost; *v.,* ring bell; **-er**

tŏm, *n.,* male of some animals

tŏm′ȧ-hȧwk, *n.,* light ax

tȯ-mā′tō, *n.,* red fruit, eaten as vegetable

tomb (tōōmb), *n.,* chamber for dead; **-like**

tōme, *n.,* large scholarly book [drum

tŏm′-tŏm, *n.,* primitive

tŏn, *n.,* two thousand pounds; **-nage**

tōne, *n.,* musical sound, attitude, style, shade; **tonal; tonality; tonally**

tŏngs, *n., pl.,* hinged device for seizing and lifting

tȯngue, *n.,* movable structure in mouth; **-less**

tŏn′ĭc, *n.,* substance that invigorates; **-ally**

tŏn′sĭl, *n.,* tissue at back of mouth; **-lar**

tōō, *adv.,* in addition, very

tōōl, *n.,* work instrument

tōōth, *n.,* bony structure set in jaw, toothlike part; **-like** [**-ness; -ly**

tōōth′sȯme, *a.,* tasty;

tŏp, *n.,* highest part or rank, spinning toy; *v.,* be better

tō′păz, *n.,* gem

tŏp′ĭc, *n.,* subject for discussing or writing; **-al; -ality; -ly**

tŏp-nŏtch′, *a.,* first-rate

tȯ-pŏg′rȧ-phȳ, *n.,* science of geographic features and maps; **pher; graphic; graphical; graphically**

tŏp′ple, *v.,* fall over

tŏp′sȳ-tûr′vȳ, *a., adv.,* upside down, in disorder; **viness; vily**

tôr′mĕnt, *n.,* suffering; *v.,* **(tôr-mĕnt′)** cause agony; **-or; -ingly**

tôr-nā′dō, *n.,* violently whirling funnellike cloud

tôr-pē′dō, *n.,* explosive missile or its case

tôr′rĕnt, *n.,* violent flow; **-ial; -ially**

tôr′rĭd, *a.,* very hot; **-ity; -ness; -ly** [**-ally**

tôr′sion, *n.,* twisting; **-al;**

tôr′sō, *n.,* trunk of body

tôrte, *n.,* rich cake

tôr′toȋse, *n.,* land turtle

tôr′tûre, *n.,* inflicting great pain, agony; *v.,* torment; **-r; turous; turously**

tŏss, *n.,* pitch; *v.,* throw about, fling; **-er**

tō′tȧl, *n.,* whole amount; *v.,* add; *a.,* complete; **-ity; -ize; -izer; -ly**

tō-tăl-ĭ-tār′ĭ-ȧn, *a.,* of dictatorship; **-ism**

tōte, *v.,* carry

tŏt′têr, *v.,* be unsteady; **-y** *a.;* **-ing; -ingly**

toǔ′căn, *n.,* tropical bird

toǔch, *n.,* tap, sense of feeling, small amount, contact; *v.,* feel; come into contact with, mention; **-er; -able; -ability**

toǔ-che′ (shā), *int.* expression to acknowledge a point

tough (tŭf), *a.,* hard to chew, cut, break, etc., strong, difficult; **-ness; -en; -ly** [wig

toǔ-pee′ (pā), *n.,* man's

toǔr, *n.,* trip, circuit; **-ist**

toǔr′nȧ-mĕnt, *n.,* contest

toǔr′nĭ-quĕt, *n.,* device to stop bleeding

tou′sle, *v.,* dishevel

tŏw, *v.,* pull, drag; **-er;**

-age

to͞w'el, *n.*, cloth or paper for drying

to͞w'êr, *n.*, high narrow structure; *v.*, rise high; **-ing**

to͞wn, *n.*, small city, business district

tŏx'ĭn, *n.*, poison; **ic; icant** *a.*

trāce, *n.*, sign, small amount; *v.*, follow the trail, copy; **-r; -able; -ability; -ableness; -ably**

trā'chē-à, *n.*, windpipe; **-l**

trà-chō'mà, *n.*, eye infection; **-tous**

trăck, *n.*, mark left as evidence, path, parallel rails for train, running sports; *v.*, follow the track, leave footprints; **-less**

trăct, *n.*, area, booklet

trăc'tà-ble, *a.*, manageable; **bility; -ness; bly**

trăc'tion, *n.*, pulling, adhesive friction

trāde, *n.*, skilled work, buying and selling; *v.*, swap, buy and sell; **-r**

trāde'mârk, *n.*, manufacturer's distinguishing mark

trà-dūce', *v.*, slander, betray; **-r; -ment**

trăf'fĭc, *n.*, business, vehicles or people on street; *v.*, trade; **-ker**

trăg'ê-dy̆, *n.*, serious drama ending unhappily

trāil, *n.*, path; *v.*, track, follow behind

trāin, *n.*, thing that drags, procession, series, connected railroad cars; *v.*, guide, instruct; **-er; -ee; -ing** *n.*

trāit, *n.*, characteristic

trāi'tör, *n.*, unfaithful person; **-ous; -ousness; -ously**

trămp, *n.*, vagrant; *v.*, walk heavily, hike; **-er**

trăm'ple, *v.*, step on, crush; **-r**

trănce, *n.*, altered consciousness, daze

trăn'quĭl, *a.*, calm; **-ity; -ize; -izer; -ization; -ness; -ly**

trăns-ăct', *v.*, do, complete; **-or; -ion; -ional**

trăn-scĕnd', *v.*, excel; **-ent; -ence; -ency; -ently**

trăn-scrībe', *v.*, write out; **-r; script; scription; scriptional**

trăns'fêr, *n.*, *v.*, move or change to another; **-rer; -ence; -al** *n.*; **-ential; -able**

trăns-fôrm'êr, *n.*, device that changes voltage

trăns-fū'sion, *n.*, transfer of blood to another

trăns-grĕss', *v.*, sin, break law; **-or; -ion; -ive**

trăn'sĭent, *a.*, temporary; **science; sciency; -ly**

trăn-sĭs'tör, *n.*, small electronic device; **-ize**

trăn-sĭ'tion, *n.*, change, passing stage; **-ary; -al; -ally**

trăns-lāte', *v.*, put into different language; **tor; tion; tional; latable**

trăns-lĭt'êr-āte, *v.*, express in alphabet of another language; **tion**

trăns-mĭs'sion, *n.*, transmitting, auto part sending power to wheels; **-al**

trăns-mūte', *v.*, transform; **tation; tational; tative; mutable; mutably**

trăn'sŏm, *n.*, small window over doorway

trăns-pār'ént, *a.*, easily seen through, clear; **ency; -ness; -ly**

trăn-spīre', *v.*, happen

trăns-plănt', *v.*, move from one to another; **-er; -ation; -able**

trăns-pōse', *v.*, interchange; **-r; sition; posable**

trăns-vêrse', *a.*, across, crosswise; **sal** *n.*; **-ly**

trăns-vĕs'tīte, *n.*, one

dressing in clothes of opposite sex

trăp, n., device for catching animals; v., catch; **-per**

tră-pēze', n., high swing

trăp'pĭngs, n., adornments

tráu'má, n., shock; **-tize; -tic; -tically**

trăv'ăil, n., hard work, agony; v., work

trăv'ĕl, n., trip; v., go from place to place; **-er; -ler**

tră-vêrse', v., move across

trăv'ĕs-tÿ, n., farcical imitation

trăwl, n., fishing net

trāy, n., flat carrying board

trēach'êr-oŭs, a., disloyal, unsafe; **ery; -ness; -ly**

trĕad, v., walk, trample

trĕad'mĭll, n., monotonous routine

trēa'sŏn, n., betrayal of one's country; **-ous; -able; -ably**

trĕas'ûre, n., stored wealth; v., value greatly

trĕat, n., delight, something paid by another; v., deal with, pay another's expense, give medical care; **-ment**

trēa'tĭse, n., formal composition

trēa'tÿ, n., agreement between nations

trĕ'ble, n., highest musical part, v., a., triple

trēe, n., large woody plant

trĕk, n., slow journey; v., travel slowly; **-ker**

trĕl'lĭs, n., lattice for plants

trĕm'ble, v., shake, quiver; **-r; bly** a.; **blingly**

trè-mĕn'doŭs, a., great; **-ness; -ly**

trĕnch, n., long ditch

trĕnd, n., general direction, current style

trĕp-ĭ-dā'tĭon, n., fear

trĕs'păss, v., sin, intrude another's land or privileges; **-er**

trĕss, n., lock of hair

trĕs'tle, n., framework for

support [**-ic**

trī'ăd, n., group of three;

trī'ăl, n., test, formal court hearing, effort

trĭbe, n., primitive communal group; **tribal; tribally**

trĭb-ū-lā'tĭon, n., affliction

trī-bū'năl, n., court of law

trĭb'ū-tār-ÿ, n., river flowing into larger one

trĭb'ūte, n., forced payment, praise

trĭck, n., clever act; n., v., (thing done to) deceive or outwit; **-er; -ery; -ish; -ishness; -y** a.; **-iness; -ily**

trĭed, a., proven

trī'fle, n., thing of little value, dessert; v., deal lightly; **-r**

trĭg'gêr, n., gun lever

trĭg-ò-nŏm'è-trÿ, n., mathematics of angles and lines; **ric; rical; rically**

trĭll, n., vibrating sound

trĭl'lĭon, n., number followed by twelve zeros; **-th** a.

trĭl'ō-gÿ, n., set of three plays or books

trĭm, n., good condition, decoration; v., make neat, clip, decorate; a., neat; **-mer; -ness; -ly**

trĭn'kĕt, n., trifle, small ornament

trĭp, n., short course of travel; v., stumble, skip, err

trī'plĕt, n., group of three, three of same birth

trī'pŏd, n., three-legged stand, stool, etc.

trīte, a., worn-out, stale; **-ness; -ly**

trī'ŭmph, n., victory, success; **-al; -ant** a.; **-antly**

trĭv'ĕt, n., small stand for hot dishes [**matters**

trĭv'ī-à, n., pl., unimportant

trōll, v., fish with moving line; **-er** [**car**

trōl'lēy, n., electric street-

trŏl'lŏp, n., prostitute

trŏm-bōne', n., brass horn

with sliding tube; **bonist**

troōp, *n.*, military unit, group of people; *v.*, go in group

trō′phў, *n.*, prize or memento for victory

trŏp′ĭc, *n.*, one of two latitudes on either side of equator; (pl.) hot region between these latitudes; **-al; -ally**

troŭ′ble, *n.*, distress, difficulty, bother; *v.*, disturb; **-r; -some** *a.*; **-someness; -somely**

trough (trôf), *n.*, long, narrow container for animal's food and water

troŭpe, *n.*, company of actors; **-r**

troŭs′seau (sō), *n.*, bride's clothing, linens, etc.

trōw′ĕl, *n.*, hand tool for smoothing, scooping, etc.

trū′ȧnt, *n.*, *a.*, (one) absent without permission; **ancy**

trūce, *n.*, halt in fighting

trŭc′ū-lĕnt, *a.*, fierce, harsh; **lency; lently**

trūe, *a.*, loyal, factual, real; **-ness; truly**

trŭf′fle, *n.*, edible fungus

trū′ĭsm, *n.*, statement of truth; **istic**

trŭmp, *n.*, playing card of highest suit

trŭm′pĕt, *n.*, brass horn; **-er** [**tion**

trŭn′cāte, *v.*, cut off a part;

trŭn′chĕon, *n.*, club, authority [*v.*, roll; **-r**

trŭn′dle, *n.*, small wheel;

trŭss, *n.*, framework for support, bundle; *v.*, fasten; **-er; -ing** *n.*

trŭst, *n.*, faith, custody, business monopoly, care of another's property; *v.*, believe in, rely on; **-er; -ee; -eeship; -ful; -fulness; -fully; -less**

trŭth, *n.*, being true, real fact; **-ful; -fulness; -fully**

trў, *n.*, *v.*, attempt; *v.*, test,

determine judicially

trўst, *n.*, appointment to meet

tŭb, *n.*, large open container, especially for washing

tŭ′bȧ, *n.*, large brass horn

tū′bêr, *n.*, fleshy part of underground stem

tŭ-bêr-cū-lō′sĭs, *n.*, infectious disease of lungs; **lar; lous**

tŭck, *n.*, sewed fold; *v.*, gather into folds, wrap snuggly, cram; **-er**

tŭf′fĕt, *n.*, low stool

tŭft, *n.*, cluster of hairs or feathers; **-er; -y** *a.*

tŭg′bȯat, *n.*, small boats for pulling ships

tŭ-ĭ′tion, *n.*, charge for instruction; **-al**

tŭm′ble, *n.*, fall, confusion; *v.*, do acrobatics, fall suddenly [**glass**

tŭm′blêr, *n.*, acrobat,

tū′mĭd, *a.*, swollen; **-ity; -ness; -ly**

tū′mŏr, *n.*, abnormal body growth or swelling; **-ous**

tū′mŭlt, *n.*, uproar, confusion; **-uous; -uousness; -uously**

tŭn′drȧ, *n.*, nearly treeless plains of arctic area

tūne, *n.*, musical pitch, melody, agreement; *v.*, put in tune; **-r; -ful; -fulness; -less; -lessness; -lessly**

tŭng′stĕn, *n.*, heavy metallic element

tū′nĭc, *n.*, loose, belted garment

tûr′bȧn, *n.*, cloth wrapped around head

tûr′bĭd, *a.*, muddy, not clear; **-ity; -ness; -ly**

tûr′bĭne, *n.*, engine powered by air, steam or water

tûr′bȯt, *n.*, edible fish

tŭ-rēen′, *n.*, large deep dish with lid

tûrf, *n.*, grass-covered layer of earth

tûr′gĭd, *a.*, swollen, pomp-

S T

ous; **-ity; -ness; -ly**

tûr′mŏĭl, *n.,* confusion, up-roar

tûrn′cōat, *n.,* traitor

tûr′nĭp, *n.,* plant with edible leaves and root

tûrn′pīke, *n.,* highway with toll   [platform

tûrn′tā-ble, *n.,* rotating

tûr′pĭ-tūde, *n.,* vileness

tûr′quŏise, *n., a.,* (gem of) greenish-blue

tûr′rĕt, *n.,* small tower on building   [in shell

tûr′tle, *n.,* reptile encased

tŭsk, *n.,* long projecting animal tooth

tŭs′sle, *n., v.,* struggle

tū′tŏr, *n.,* private teacher, guardian; *v.,* teach; **-age; -ship; telage; -ial**

tŭx-ē′dō, *n.,* man's semi-formal jacket

twēak, *n.,* twisting pinch

twēed, *n.,* rough wool fabric; **-y** *a.;* **-iness**

twēez′êrs, *n., pl.,* small pincers

twĭd′dle, *v.,* toy with, twirl; **-r; dly** *a.*

twĭg, *n.,* small tree branch

twī′līght, *n.,* subdued light after sunset

twĭll, *n.,* rubbed cloth

twĭn, *n.,* one of a pair that are alike; *a.,* paired

twine, *n.,* strong cord

twĭnge, *n.,* sudden pain

twĭn′kle, *n., v.,* sparkle; **-r; kling** *n.*

twĭst, *n.,* thing twisted; *v.,* wind together, put out of shape, turn; **-er**

twĭtch, *n.,* quick slight jerk

twĭt′ter, *v.,* chirp, chatter, flutter; **-er; -y** *a.*

two′fold (tōo), *a.,* double; *adv.,* twice

tȳ-cōon′, *n.,* industrialist

tȳpe, *n.,* group having common characteristics, metal pieces for printing; *v.,* classify, use typewriter; **-able**

tȳ′phoid, *n.,* infectious disease; **-al**   [phonic

tȳ-phōon′, *n.,* hurricane;

tȳ′phŭs, *n.,* infectious disease; **phous**

tȳ′rånt, *n.,* cruel, absolute ruler; **anny; annize; annizer; rannical; rannically; annous; annously**

tȳ′rō, *n.,* beginner

tzâr, *n.,* czar

U

ū-bĭq′uĭ-toŭs, *a.,* being everywhere; **uity; -ness; -ly**

ŭd′dêr, *n.,* mammary   [gland

ŭg′lȳ, *a.,* unpleasant to see, bad; **liness; lify; lily**

ū′kāse, *n.,* official order

ū-kŭ-le′lē (lā), *n.,* small guitarlike instrument

ŭl′cêr, *n.,* open sore; **-ous; -ously**

ŭl-tē′rĭ-ŏr, *a.,* beyond what is said; **-ly**

ŭl′tĭ-måte, *a.,* farthest, final, utmost; **macy; -ness; -ly**   [mand

ŭl-tĭ-mā′tŭm, *n.,* final de-

ŭl′trå, *a.,* extreme

ŭl-trå-sŏn′ĭc, *a.,* beyond human hearing; **-s; -ally**

ŭl′ū-lāte, *v.,* wail; **tion; lant**

ŭm-bĭl′ĭ-cŭs, *n.,* navel; **cal**

ŭm-brĕl′là, *n.,* cloth covered frame as rain protector   [judge

ŭm′pīre, *n.,* game or sports

ū-năn′ĭ-moŭs, *a.,* agreeing completely; **nimity; -ly**

ŭn-, *prefix* not, reverse of,

ŭn-åp-prōach′å-ble, *a.,* aloof, unmatched; **bility; -ness; bly**

ŭn-åp-prō′prĭ-āt-ĕd, *a.,* not granted for use

ŭn-ârmed′, *a.,* defenseless

ŭn-åsked′, *a.,* not invited

ŭn-ås-sŭm′ĭng, *a.,* modest

ŭn-åt-tăched′, *a.,* not connected, unmarried

ŭn-åt-tĕnd′ĕd, *a.,* neglected

ŭn-băl′ánced, *a.,* not equal, mentally ill

ŭn-bear′à-ble, *a.,* not tolerated; **-ness; bly**

ŭn-bĕ-cŏm′īng, *a.,* unattractive; **-ness; -ly**

ŭn-bĕ-liēv′à-ble, *a.,* incredible; **bly**

ŭn-bĕnd′, *v.,* relax, straighten

ŭn-bŏs′ŏm, *v.,* reveal

ŭn-bûr′dĕn, *v.,* reveal, disclose

ŭn-căn′nў, *a.,* eerie; **niness; nily**

ŭn-cĕr-ĕ-mō′nĭ-oŭs, *a.,* informal; **-ness; -ly**

ŭn-cŏn-cĕrn′, *n.,* apathy; **-ed; -edness; -edly**

ŭn-cŏn-dĭ′tion-ál, *a.,* absolute, **-ly**

ŭn-cŏn′scion-à-ble, *a.,* unreasonable; **bly**

ŭn-coŭ′ple, *v.,* unfasten

ŭn-coŭth′, *a.,* crude; **-ness; -ly**

ŭnc′tion, *n.,* annointment with oil; **tuous; tuousness; tuously**

ŭn′dĕr-, *prefix,* beneath, below normal, too little

ŭn′dĕr, *a.,* lower; *adv.,* beneath; *prep.,* lower than, covered, controlled by

ŭn′dĕr-brŭsh, *n.,* shrubs below large trees

ŭn-dĕr-clăss′màn, *n.,* student below senior

ŭn-dĕr-cŏv′êr, *a.,* secret

ŭn′dĕr-dŏg, *n.,* one expected to lose

ŭn-dĕr-gō′, *v.,* experience

ŭn-dĕr-grăd′ŭ-àte, *n.,* college student not ready to receive degree

ŭn′dĕr-ground′, *a., adv.,* below ground, secret

ŭn-dĕr-hănd′ĕd, *a.,* secret, sly; **-ness; -ly**

ŭn′dĕr-līng, *n.,* subordinate

ŭn-dĕr-mīne′, *v.,* dig beneath, weaken

ŭn-dĕr-nēath′, *a.,* lower; *adv., prep.,* below

ŭn-dĕr-pĭn′, *n.,* support from below; **-ning** *n.*

ŭn-dêr-prĭv′ĭ-lĕged, *a.,* poor

ŭn-dêr-sĭgn′, *v.,* sign name at end

ŭn-dêr-stănd′, *v.,* know meaning of, infer, take as fact, learn

ŭn-dêr-stănd′īng, *n.,* knowledge, intelligence, agreement

ŭn-dêr-stāte′, *v.,* say too weakly [tute actor

ŭn′dêr-stŭd-ў, *n.,* substi-

ŭn-dêr-tāke′, *v.,* agree to do, promise; **taking** *n.*

ŭn-dêr-tāk′êr, *n.,* funeral director

ŭn′dêr-wear, *n.,* clothes worn under outer clothes

ŭn′dêr-wörld, *n.,* hell, organized crime

ŭn′dêr-wrīte′, *v.,* agree to buy or pay

ŭn-do′(doo), *v.,* open, destroy; **-ing** *n.*

ŭn-drĕss′, *v.,* remove clothing

ŭn-dūe′, *a.,* excessive, improper; **duly**

ŭn′dū-lāte, *v.,* move in waves; **tion; tory; lant**

ŭn-êarth′, *v.,* dip up, learn

ŭn-êarth′lў, *adv.,* weird

ŭn-ēas′ў, *a.,* uncomfortable, perturbed; **easiness; easily**

ŭn-ĕ-quĭv′ŏ-cál, *a.,* clear; **-ly** [tant; **-ly**

ŭn-ĕ-vĕnt′fŭl, *a.,* unimpor-

ŭn-fāil′īng, *a.,* certain; **-ly**

ŭn-fōld′, *v.,* open, reveal

ŭn-fôr-gĕt′à-ble, *a.,* never to be forgotten; **bly**

ŭn-fôrmed′, *a.,* shapeless

ŭn-fôr′tu-nàte (chu), *a.,* unlucky; **-ly**

ŭn-foŭnd′ĕd, *a.,* not based on truth

ŭn-fûrl′, *v.,* unfold

ŭn-gāin′lў, *a.,* clumsy; **liness** [ness

ŭn-gŏd′lў, *a.,* wicked; **li-**

ŭn′guĕnt, *n.,* ointment

ŭn-hăp′pў, *a.,* unlucky, sad; **piness; pily**

ŭn-hĕalth′ў, *a.,* sickly, harmful; **healthiness**

ū-nĭ-căm′êr-ȧl, *a.,* of single legislature

ū′nĭ-côrn, *n.,* mythical one-horned horse

ū′nĭ-fôrm, *n.,* official clothes of group; *a.,* all alike, unchanging; **-ity; -ly**

ū′nĭ-fŷ, *v.,* combine into one; **fier; fication; fiable**

ū-nĭ-lăt′êr-ȧl, *a.,* of one side; **-ism; -ly**

ūn′ĭȯn, *n.,* joining, united group; **-ize**

ū-nïque′, *a.,* one and only, unusual; **-ness; -ly**

ū′nĭ-sȯn, *n.,* harmony, agreement

ū′nĭt, *n.,* one, single part, fixed amount; **-ary**

ū-nīte′, *v.,* join into whole

ū′nĭ-tŷ, *n.,* oneness, agreement

ū-nĭ-vêr′sȧl, *a.,* of all, present everywhere; **-ity; -ize; -ly**

ū′nĭ-vêrse, *n.,* world

ū-nĭ-vêr′sĭ-tŷ, *n.,* school of higher learning

ŭn-kĕmpt′, *a.,* not neat; **-ness** [**-ness; -ly**

ŭn-lăw′fŭl, *a.,* illegal;

ŭn-lĕad′ĕd, *a.,* not containing lead

ŭn-lêarn′, *v.,* forget

ŭn-lĕss′, *conj., prep.,* except [not like

ŭn-līke′, *a.,* not alike; *prep.*

ŭn-māke′, *v.,* revert to original, ruin

ŭn-măn′nêr-lŷ, *a.,* rude; **liness**

ŭn-mêr′cĭ-fŭl, *a.,* cruel; **-ly**

ŭn-nêrve′, *v.,* upset

ŭn-ŏc′cū-pied, *a.,* empty, idle [qualed

ŭn-păr′ȧl-lĕled, *a.,* une-

ŭn-prĕc′ė-dĕnt-ĕd, *a.,* unique

ŭn-quĕs′tion-à-ble, *a.,* certain; **bly**

ŭn-răv′ĕl, *v.,* undo threads, make clear; **-ment** [ble

ŭn-rė-lĕnt′ĭng, *a.,* inflexi-

ŭn-rĕst′, *n.,* angry discon-tent

ŭn-rūl′ŷ, *a.,* hard to restrain; disorderly; **ruliness**

ŭn-sā′vȯr-ŷ, *a.,* disgusting; **voriness; vorily**

ŭn-scāthed′, *a.,* unharmed

ŭn-sĕt′tle, *v.,* disturb; **-d**

ŭn-sīght′lŷ, *a.,* ugly; **liness**

ŭn-soŭnd′, *a.,* defective, not safe; **-ness; -ly**

ŭn-spēak′à-ble, *a.,* wicked; **bly**

ŭn-strŭc′tūred, *a.,* loose

ŭn-sŭng′, *a.,* not honored

ŭn-tĕn′à-ble, *a.,* not defensible; **bility**

ŭn-tĭl′, *prep.,* up to the time of, before; *conj.,* to the point, before

ŭn-toŭch′à-ble, *n., a.,* (one that) should not be touched; **bility**

ŭn-trŭth′fŭl, *a.,* dishonest; **-ness; -ly**

ŭn-veil′ (vāl), *v.,* reveal; **-ing** *n.*

ŭn-wȯnt′ĕd, *a.,* rare

ŭp, *a., adv., prep.,* to a higher place or condition

ŭp-brāid′, *v.,* scold

ŭp′brĭng-ĭng, *n.,* child's training

ŭp′grāde, *n.,* upward slope; *v.,* raise upward

ŭp-hēav′ȧl, *n.,* violent change

ŭp-hōld′, *v.,* support; **-er**

ŭp′kēep, *n.,* maintenance

ŭp-ŏn′, *adv., prep.,* on

ŭp′pêr, *a.,* higher than

ŭp-pêr-clăss′mȧn, *n.,* junior or senior student

ŭp′pêr-mōst, *a.,* highest

ŭp′rīght, *a.,* straight up, honest, just; **-ness; -ly**

ŭp′rīs-ĭng, *n.,* revolt

ŭp′rôar, *n.,* loud commotion; **-ious; -iousness; -iously**

ŭp-rōot′, *v.,* pull up by roots, remove

ŭp′sĕt, *n.,* disorder, unexpected defeat; *v.,* **(ŭp-sĕt′)** overturn, defeat, disturb; **-ter**

ŭp′shŏt, *n.*, outcome

ŭp′stāirs′, *a.*, *adv.*, on upper level

ŭp-stănd′ĭng, *a.*, erect, honorable

ŭp′stârt, *n.*, *a.*, (one) newly rich or powerful

ŭp′tĭght′, *a.*, very tense

ŭp′-tȯ-dāte′, *a.*, most recent

ŭp′wȧrd, *a.*, *adv.*, toward higher place

ū-rā′nĭ-ŭm, *n.*, radioactive metallic element

ûr′bȧn, *a.*, of city; **-ism; -ize; -ization**

ûr-bāne′, *a.*, refined, suave; **banity**

ûr′chĭn, *n.*, mischievous child

ûrge, *n.*, impulse; *v.*, persuade, provoke; **-r**

ûr′gĕnt, *a.*, needing immediate action; **gency; -ly**

ū′rĭne, *n.*, liquid body waste; **nate; nation; nary**

ûrn, *n.*, footed vase

ū-rŏl′ȯ-gȳ, *n.*, medicine of urinary system; **gist; logic; logical; logically**

ŭs, *pro.*, objective case of **we**

ŭs′ȧ-ble, *a.*, fit for use; **bility; -ness; bly**

ŭs′ȧge, *n.*, treatment, habit

ūse, *n.*, **(ūs)** worth, function; *v.*, **(ūz)** put into action, treat, consume; **-er; -less; -lessness; -lessly**   [**-ly**

ūse′fŭl, *a.*, helpful; **-ness;**

ŭsh′êr, *n.*, *v.*, (one who can) show the way

ū′sū-ȧl, *a.*, common, expected; **-ness; -ly**

ū′sū-rȳ, *n.*, lending money at high interest rate; **rer; rious; riousness; riously**

ū-sûrp′, *v.*, take without right; **-er; -ation; -ingly**

ū-tĕn′sĭl, *n.*, tool, implement   [*a.*

ū′têr-ŭs, *n.*, womb; **terine**

ū-tĭl′ĭ-tȳ, *n.*, usefulness, public service giving power; **lize; lizer; lization; tarian**

ŭt′mōst, *n.*, *a.*, greatest, farthest

ū-tō′pĭ-ȧ, *n.*, ideal society of perfection; **-n** *a.*

ŭt′têr, *v.*, express with voice; **-er; -ance; -able**

ŭt′têr, *a.*, complete; **-ness; -ly**

ŭx-ô′rĭ-oŭs, *a.*, submissive to one's wife; **-ly**

V

vā′cȧnt, *a.*, empty; **cancy; -ness; cate; -ly**

vȧc-cīne′, *n.*, preparation to cause immunity to a disease

vȧc′ĭl-lāte, *v.*, waver, show indecision; **tor; tion; tory; lant; lating; latingly**

vȧc′ū-ŭm, *n.*, completely empty space

vȧ-gār′ȳ, *n.*, odd action or idea; **garious**

vā′grȧnt, *n.*, idle wanderer; **grancy; -ly**

vāgue, *a.*, not clear, undefinite; **-ness; -ly**

vȧl-ė-dĭc′tȯ-rȳ, *n.*, school farewell speech; **rian** *n.*

vȧl′ĭȧnt, *n.*, brave; **iance; iancy; -ly**

vȧl′ĭd, *a.*, being legal, sound; **-ity; -ness; -ate; -ly**

vȧl′lĕy, *n.*, area between hills

vȧl′ūe, *n.*, worth in money, importance; *v.*, place value on, regard highly; **-r; uation; uate; uator**

vȧlve, *n.*, device that controls flow of liquid; **vular**

vȧn′dȧl, *n.*, one who purposely destroys property; **-ism; -ize**

vāne, *n.*, swinging device that shows wind direction   [front

vȧn′guȧrd, *n.*, group in

văn'ĭ-tў, *n.,* false pride

văn'quĭsh, *v.,* conquer, defeat; **-er**

vā'pör, *n.,* mist, gas; **-ize; -izer; -like; -ish; -ous**

vār'ĭ-cōse, *a.,* swollen; **cosity**

vār'nĭsh, *n.,* liquid to make surface glassy; **-er**

vār'ў, *v.,* change, differ

văs'cū-lår, *a.,* of body or plant vessels; **-ity**

văs-ĕc'tȯ-mў, *n.,* male operation for sterility

văs'sȧl, *n.,* feudal tenant, underling; **-age** [**-ly**

văst, *a.,* very great; **-ness;**

vaude'vĭlle, *n.,* stage show of many acts

vȧunt, *n., v.,* boast; **-er; -ed; -y** *a.*

vēer, *v.,* deviate, shift; **-ingly**

vĕg-ė-tār'ĭȧn, *n.,* one eating no meat; **-ism**

vē'hė-mėnt, *a.,* showing strong feeling; **mence; mency; -ly**

vein (vān) *n.,* blood vessel to heart, mineral deposit, leaf tube, quality; **-y** *a.*

vė-lŏc'ĭ-tў, *n.,* speed

vĕnd, *v.,* sell; **-or; -ee; -ition; -ible**

vĕn'êr-āte, *v.,* respect deeply; **tor; tion; able; ability; ableness; ably**

vė-nė'rē-ȧl, *a.,* of sexual intercourse

vē'nĭ-ȧl, *a.,* pardonable; **-ity; -ly**

vĕn'ȯm, *n.,* animal poison; **-ous; -ousness; -ously**

vĕnt, *n.,* outlet, escape; *v.,* let out, relieve feelings

vĕn'trĭ-cle, *n., a.,* lower chamber of heart

vĕn'ūe, *n.,* locality of trial

vė-răn'dȧ, *n.,* porch

vêr-bā'tĭm, *n.,* word for word

vêr'dĭct, *n.,* legal decision

vêr'ĭ-fў, *v.,* prove to be true; confirm; **fier; fica-tion; fiable**

vêr'mĭn, *n.,* troublesome

animal or insect; **-ous**

vêr-năc'ū-lȧr, *a.,* of commonly spoken language; **-ly**

vêr'sȧ-tĭle, *a.,* skilled in many areas; **tility; -ly**

vêr'sion, *n.,* translation, report; **-al**

vêr'tė-brȧte, *n.,* animal with segmented spine

vêr'tĕx, *n.,* top, corner point

vêr'tĭ-gō, *n.,* dizziness

vĕs'tĭge, *n.,* trace; **tigial; tigially**

vĕt-êr-ĭ-nār-ў, *n.,* medicine of animals; **narian**

vētō, *n.,* power to reject; *v.,* prevent from becoming law; **-er**

vī'ȧ-ble, *a.,* workable; **bil-ity; bly**

vī'brāte, *v.,* quiver, swing; **tor; tion; tory**

vī-cār'ĭoŭs, *a.,* experienced by imaginary participation; **-ness; -ly**

vĭ-cĭn'ĭ-tў, *n.,* nearness, neighborhood; **nal**

vĭ-cĭs'sĭ-tūde, *n.,* constant change, shifting circumstances; **dinary; dinous**

vĭc'tȯ-rў, *n.,* winning, success; **tor; rious; riously**

vīe, *v.,* compete; **-r**

view, *n.,* seeing, sight, scene, opinion; *v.,* look at, consider; **-er; -less; -lessly**

vĭg'ĭl, *n.,* night watch

vĭg'ör, *n.,* strength, energy; **-ous; -ousness; -ously**

vīle, *a.,* disgusting, very bad; **-ness; -ly**

vĭm, *n.,* energy

vĭn'dĭ-cāte, *v.,* clear name, absolve; **tor; tion; tive; tory**

vĭn'ė-gȧr, *n.,* sour liquid from fermenting liquor; **-y** *a.*

vī'ȯ-lāte, *v.,* break law, desecrate, rape; **tor; tion; tive**

vī'pêr, *n.,* venomous snake, spiteful one; **-ous; -ouslу**

vĭr'ĭle, *a.,* manly; **rility**

vĭr'tūe, *n.,* moral goodness, value; **tuous;
tuousness; tuously**

vī'rŭs, *n.,* microscopic
agent causing disease

vī'sion, *n.,* seeing, mental
image, foresight; **-al**

vĭs'ĭt, *v.,* go or come to
see, stay as a guest; **-or;
-ation; -ational; -able**

vī'tå-mĭn, *n.,* organic food
substance for good
health; **-ic**

vī'tĭ-āte, *v.,* spoil; **tor; tion;
able**

vĭv'ĭd, *a.,* lively, bright, active; **ify; ifier; ification;
-ness; -ly**

vō-cā'tion, *n.,* career,
trade; **-al**

vŏĭce, *n.,* sound made by
mouth, opinion; *v.,* utter;
**-less; -lessness;
-lessly**

vŏl'å-tĭle, *a.,* changeable,
explosive; **tility; -ness**

vŏl'lēy, *n.,* discharge of
firearms, burst of words;
-er

vŏl'ume (yŭm), *n.,* book,
space occupied, bulk;
**minous; minosity; min-
ousity**

vŏ-lŭp'tū-oŭs, *a.,* sensual;
-ness; -ly

vŏ-rā'cioŭs, *a.,* greedy,
hungry; **racity; -ness;
-ly**

vŏte, *n.,* formal choice, decision reached; *v.,* cast
a vote; **-r** [antee

vŏŭch, *v.,* uphold, guar-

vŏw, *n.,* holy or solemn
pledge; *v.,* promise; **-er**

vŭl'cån-ize, *v.,* treat crude
rubber; **zation**

vŭl'nêr-å-ble, *a.,* easily
hurt; **bility; bly**

W

wåd, *n.,* small soft mass;
v., crumple, roll up; **-der**

wāde, *v.,* walk in shallow
substance, do with ef-
fort; **-r**

wā'fêr, *n.,* thin flat cracker

wåf'fle, *n.,* batter cake with
gridlike surface

wåft, *v.,* float; **-er**

wåg, *v.,* move back and
forth; **-ger** [gage in

wāge, *n.,* salary; *v.,* en-

wā'gêr, *n.,* *v.,* bet; **-er**

wāif, *n.,* homeless person

wāil, *n.,* pitiful cry; *v.,* cry
with grief; **-er; -ful; -fully**

wāin'scòt, *n.,* paneling on
lower part of wall

wāist, *n.,* body between
ribs and hips

wāit, *v.,* remain in readiness, serve food; **-er;
-ress** [-r

wāive, *v.,* give up rights;

wāke, *v.,* come out of
sleep, become alert; **-n;
-ner; -ful; -fulness;
-fully**

wāke, *n.,* track gone before

wålk, *n.,* walking, path; *v.,*
go along on foot; **-er**

wåll, *n.,* upright structure,
building side

wål'lå-bÿ, *n.,* small kan-
garoolike animal

wål'lèt, *n.,* pocket case for
money

wål'lòp, *n.,* hardblow; *v.,*
strike; **-er**

wål'lōw, *v.,* roll in mud,
indulge oneself; **-er**

wål'nŭt, *n.,* tree, nut, wood

wål'rŭs, *n.,* large sea
mammal

wåltz, *n.,* ballroom dance
with three-fourth time;
-er [-ness; -ly

wån, *a.,* pale, sickly;

wånd, *n.,* thin rod

wån'der, *v.,* go aimlessly,
stray; **-er**

wāne, *v.,* fade, decline; **-y**
a. [need

wånt, *n.,* *v.,* lack, desire,

wăn'tòn, *a.,* immoral,
senseless; **-ness; -ly**

wåp'ĭ-tĭ, *n.,* large deer

war (wôr), *n.,* armed conflict, hostility; *v.,* fight;
-like [bird; -r

war'ble (wôr), *v.,* sing like

ward (wôrd), *n.,* one under

guardian's care, division of hospital, jail or city; *v.*, turn aside

war'dèn (wôr), *n.,* head of prison

ward'rōbe (wôrd), *n.,* movable closet, clothes supply   [pottery

wāre, *n.,* kind of goods,

wāre'hoŭse, *n.,* storage building   [conflict

war'fāre (wôr), *n.,* armed

warm (wôrm), *v., a.,* (make or be) of moderate heat, friendly, lively, angry; **-th** *n.;* **-ness; -ly**

warn (wôrn), *v.,* tell of danger, inform; **-ing** *n.*

warp (wôrp), *n.,* distortion, lengthwise thread; *v.,* distort, pervert; **-er**

war'rànt (wôr), *n.,* legal sanction, *n., v.,* guarantee; **-or; -ee**

war'ràn-tÿ (wôr), *n.,* guarantee

wart (wôrt), *n.,* small tumorous growth on skin

wäsh, *n.,* clothes to be washed; *v.,* clean with water, purity; **-er; -ing** *n.;* **-able**   [sect

wàsp, *n.,* large stinging in-

wāste, *n.,* empty land refuse, neglect, excrement; *v.,* use up, make weak, consume; **-r; -ful; -fulness; -fully**

wàtch, *n.,* guarding, small timepiece; *v.,* guard, be alert, observe; **-er; -ful; -fulness; -fully**

wä'têr, *n.,* colorless liquid of rivers, etc., rain, body fluid; *v.,* supply water; **-y** *a.;* **-iness; -less; -lessness**

wä'têr-crĕss, *n.,* plant, its leaves used in salad

wä'têr-frònt, *n.,* land at edge of river, etc.

wä'têr-lĭl-ÿ, *n.,* aquatic flowering plant

wä'têr-lŏgged, *a.,* soaked

wä'têr-mĕl-òn, *n.,* large melon with juicy red pulp

wä'têr-shĕd, *n.,* area drained by river

wä'têr-wörks, *n.,* system of public water supply

wätt, *n.,* unit of electrical power; **-age**

wāve, *n.,* curving swell in water, curls, hand signal rise; *v.,* move to and fro; **wavy** *a.;* **-less; -like**

wăx, *n.,* plastic substance made by bees, similar substance; *v.,* polish, with wax, become larger; **-en** *a.*

wāy, *n.,* route, course, method, manner, wish

wāy'fār-êr, *n.,* traveler

wāy-lāy', *v.,* ambush; **-er**

wāy'wàrd, *a.,* disobedient, erratic; **-ness; -ly**

wēak, *a.,* lacking strength, or power, deficient; **-en; -ener**

wēak'nĕss, *n.,* fault, fondness

wēalth, *n.,* riches, large amount; **-y** *a.,* **-iness; -ily**

wēan, *v.,* stop suckling, withdraw in degrees from habit

wēap'òn, *n.,* device used for fighting; **-ry**

wear, *n.,* fashion, damage; *v.,* have on body, impair by use, tire, last; **-able; -ability**

wēa'rÿ, *a.,* tired; **riness; risome** *a.,;* **riless; rily**

wēas'êl, *n.,* small slender mammal

wĕath'êr, *n.,* condition of atmosphere; *v.,* survive

wēave, *v.,* interlace threads to make fabric; **-r**

wĕb, *n.,* woven network animal membrane connecting digits

wĕd'dĭng, *n.,* marriage ceremony

wĕdge, *n.,* wood or metal piece tapered to point; *v.,* jam in

wēe, *a.,* very small

wēed, *n.,* undesired plant; *v.,* remove; **-er; -less;**

-y *a.*

wēep, *v.*, shed tears, mourn; **-er; -y** *a.*

wēe'vĭl, *n.*, beetle

weight (wāt), *n.*, heaviness, importance; **-less; -lessness; -y** *a.;* **-iness**

wēird, *a.*, very strange, mysterious; **-ness; -ly**

wĕld, *v.*, unite by fusing; **-er; -ability; -able**

wĕl'fâre, *n.*, prosperity, public agencies giving aid to needy

wĕll, *n.*, shaft to tap underground water, source; *v.*, pour forth; *a.*, in good health; *adv.*, satisfactorily, prosperously

wĕll-brĕd', *a.*, courteous

wĕll-măn'nêred, *a.*, courteous [intentions

wĕll-mēan'ĭng, *a.*, of good

wĕll-ôff', *a.*, prosperous

wĕlt, *n.*, raised ridge on skin, shoe leather piece

wĕlt'êr, *n.*, confusion; *v.*, wallow

wĕnch, *n.*, young woman

wĕnd, *v.*, go on

wĕst, *n.*, direction left of one facing north; *a.*, *adv.*, in, of or to west; **-ern** *a.;* **-erly; -ward** *a.*, *adv.*, **-wardly**

wĕt, *v.*, *a.*, (become) soaked with liquid, rainy; **-ter; -ness; -tability; -table; -tish**

whāle, *n.*, large fishlike mammal

wharf (wôrf), *n.*, platform to dock ships

whăt, *pro.*, which thing, event, etc.?, that which; *a.*, which kind of, as much as; *adv.*, how, in part; *int.*, exclamation of surprize

whăt'nŏt, *n.*, nondescript thing or person

whēat, *n.*, cereal grass, its grain; **-en** *a.*

whēe'dle, *v.*, coax

whēel, *n.*, disk turning on axis; *v.*, roll, turn; **-er**

whēel'chāir, *n.*, mobile chair for one unable to walk

whēeze, *v.*, breathe with difficulty; **-r; wheezy** *a.;* **wheezingly**

whĕlp, *n.*, puppy

whĕn, *adv.*, at what time or point?; *conj.*, if, at that time

whêre, *adv.*, in or at what place?; *conj.*, at that place

whêre'wĭth-äl, *n.*, necessary means, ex. money

whĕt, *v.*, sharpen, stimulate; **-ter**

whĕth'êr, *conj.*, in either case that

whĕt'stōne, *n.*, abrasive stone for sharpening tools

whĭch, *a.*, *pro.*, what one or ones, that

whĭff, *n.*, light puff or smell

whīle, *n.*, time period; *v.*, spend time; *conj.*, during the time that

whĭm, *n.*, passing notion; **-sical; -sicality; -sically**

whĭm'pêr, *n.*, *v.*, cry in broken sounds; **-ingly**

whĭp, *n.*, rod with strap; *v.*, beat, move suddenly; **-per; -ping**

whĭp'lăsh, *n.*, sudden jolt of neck

whĭp'pĕt, *n.*, small greyhoundlike dog

whîr, *v.*, move with buzzing sound

whîrl'pōol, *n.*, water in whirling motion

whĭsk, *n.*, *v.*, (utensil or small broom to) brush quickly

whĭsk'êrs, *n.*, *pl.*, hair growing on face

whĭs'tle, *n.*, clear, shrill sound; *n.*, *v.*, (device to) make whistling sound; **-r; ling** *n.*

whĭt, *n.*, least bit

white, *n.*, color of white; *a.*, of color of snow, pale, pure, of light skin; **-n; -ner; -ness; -ly**

white-cŏl'lâr, *a.*, of cleri-

U
Z

cal and professional workers

whĭth'êr, a., where

whĭt'tle, v., cut wood shavings, reduce gradually; **-r**

who (hū), pro., what or which person, that

whōle (hōl), a., entire, unity; **-ness**

whole'sāle (hōl), n., selling large amounts to retailer; a., extensive; **-r**

whole'sóme (hōl), a., healthy, morally good; **-ness; -ly**

whoop (hūp), n., loud shrill shout

whŏp'pêr, n., something very large, lie

whore (hōr), n., prostitute

whose (hūz), pro., of who or which

whȳ, adv., for what reason?; conj., because of which

wĭck, n., cord in candle

wĭck'ĕd, a., morally bad; **-ness; -ly**   [twig

wĭck'êr, n., thin flexible

wĭde, a., of great extent, ample; adv., to full extent; **-ness; -n; -ner; -ly**

wiĕld, v., handle with skill, use; **-er; -y** a.

wiē'nêr, n., smoked sausage

wĭg, n., false covering of hair   [gler; gly a.

wĭg'gle, v., twist and turn;

wĭg'wäm, n., Indian tent

wĭld, a., in its natural state, uncivilized, unruly, imprudent; **-ness; -ly**

wĭl'dêr-nêss, n., uninhabited, wild area

wĭle, n., sly trick

wĭll, n., choice, determination, wish, legal paper disposing of property after death; v., choice, bequeath

wĭll'ĭng, a., consenting, done readily; **-ness; -ly**

wĭl'lōw, n., tree

wĭlt, v., become limp, droop

wī'lȳ, a., sly

wĭn, v., gain victory, achieve, get; **-ner**

wĭnce, v., draw back; **-r**

wĭnd, n., moving air; **-less; -lessness; -lessly; -y** a.; **-iness; -ily**

wĭnd, v., twist around, tighten spring, ex. clock; **-er; -ing** n.

wĭnd'bǎg, n., great talker who says little

wĭnd'fäll, n., stroke of luck

wĭn'dōw, n., glass opening in building; **-less**

wĭnd'pīpe, n., trachea

wĭnd'shiēld, n., glass screen in car's front

wine, n., liquor fermented from grapes; **-ry**

wĭng, n., feathered limb of bird, winglike part; **-less**

wĭnk, n., instant; v., close and open eyelid quickly; **-er**   [**-ness; -ly**

wĭn'sóme, a., charming;

wĭn'têr, n., coldest season of year; **try** a.; **triness; trily**   [**-r**

wipe, v., rub clean or dry;

wire'tǎp, n., v., (device to) secretly intercept information; **-per**

wise, a., having good judgment, learned; **-ly**

wise'crǎck, n., flippant remark

wĭsh, n., v., want, desire, request; **-er; -ful; -fulness; -fully**

wĭst'fŭl, a., yearning; **-ness; -ly**

wĭt, n., good sense, cleverness; **-less; -lessness; -lessly**

wĭtch, n., woman supposedly having magical power

wĭth, prep., in company of, concerning, of same opinion as, because of, using

wĭth-dräw', v., remove from, go away; **-er; -al** n.

wĭth'êr, v., dry up, wilt

wĭth-hōld', v., keep back,

refuse; **-er**
wǐth-stǎnd′, v., endure
wǐt′nėss, n., testimony, firsthand observer of occurrence; v., testify
wǐt′tỹ, a., cleverly amusing; **tiness; tily**
wǐz′ȧrd, n., magician; **-ry**
wǐz′ėned, a., withered
wōe, n., sorrow, trouble; **-ful; -fulness; -fully**
wǒk, n., metal cooking pan
wǒlf, n., flesh-eating doglike mammal; **-ish**
wȯl-vêr-īne′, n., large weasellike animal
wȯm′ȧn, n., adult female; **-hood; -ish; -ishness; -ishly; -ly**
womb (wūmb), n., uterus
wǒm′bȧt, n., burrowing marsupial
wȯn′dêr, n., astonishment, miracle; v., marvel, be curious; **-ment**
wōnt, n., habit; a., accustomed; **-ed; -edness**
wōō, v., court, coax
wōōd, n., hard material under tree's bark, lumber; **-en; -enness; -y** a.; **-iness**
wōōd′cǒck, n., game bird
wōōd′pěck-êr, n., bird that pecks holes in wood
wōōd′wȯrk, n., wooden doors, frames, etc.
wōōl, n., hair of sheep, yarn or cloth from wool; **-en** a.; **-ly** a.; **-liness**
wȯrd, n., unit of language, sound or sounds having meaning, promise; v., phrase; **-age; -less**
wȯrk, n., effort put forth, result, job; v., exert oneself, operate; **-er; -able; -ability; -ableness**
wȯrk′mȧn-shǐp, n., skill of workman [ercise
wȯrk′ōut, n., strenuous ex-
wȯrld, n., plant earth, universe, sphere
wȯrm, n., long slender creeping animal; **-like; -y** a.; **-iness**
wȯr′rỹ, n., troubled state;

v., feel uneasy; **rier; riment; risome**
wȯrse, a., less good, more ill; **-n**
wȯr′shǐp, n., religious service, extreme devotion; v., pray, adore; **-er**
wȯrst, a., least good, lowest
wor′stėd (wōōs), n., smooth wool fabric
wȯrth, n., material value, importance; a., deserving equal in value; **-y** a.; **-iness; -ily; -less; -lessness; -lessly**
wound, n., injury; v., hurt
wrǎn′gle, n., v., quarrel; **-r**
wrǎp, n., outer covering; v., enclose in covering, envelop
wrǎth, n., anger; **-ful; -fulness; -fully; -y** a.
wrēak, v., inflict, give vent to; **-er**
wrēath, n., ring of leaves
wrēathe, v., make wreath, encircle
wrěck, n., destruction, ill person; v., damage, ruin; **-er; -age**
wrěn, n., songbird
wrěnch, n., v., twist; n., tool to turn nuts
wrěst, v., take by force; **-er**
wrěs′tle, v., struggle, force opponent to ground; **-r; tling** n. [son
wrětch, n., miserable per-
wrětch′ėd, a., miserable, poor; **-ness; -ly**
wrǐg′gle, v., twist and turn; **-r; gly**
wrǐn′kle, n., tiny ridge; v., crease; **kly**
wrǐst, n., joint between hand and forearm
wrǐt, n., formal legal order
write, v., form visible letters or words, be author of; **-r; writing** n. [-r
writhe, v., squirm in pain;
wrông, n., violation; v., treat badly; a., unlawful, improper, false; adv., incorrectly; **-er; -ness; -ful; -fulness; -fully; -ly**

wrôught, *a.,* formed, shaped by hammering

wrÿ, *v.,* twist; *a.,* distorted; **-ness; -ly**

X

xē'bĕc (zē), *n.,* small ship

xē'nŏn (zē), *n.,* colorless gaseous chemical element

xĕn-ò-phō'bĭ-á (zĕn), *n.,* fear of strangers; **phobe** *n.;* **bic**

xè-rŏg'rà-phÿ (zè), *n.,* process of copying written material; **phic**

X-rāy, *n., v.,* (radiation used to) photograph or treat body tissues

xÿ'lò-phōne (zī), *n.,* musical percussion instrument

Y

yăcht, *n.,* small pleasure ship; **-sman** *n.;* **-ing** *n.*

yăk, *n.,* large ox

yăm, *n.,* edible root

yănk, *n., v.,* pull, jerk

yârd, *n.,* length measure of three feet, land around building; **-age**

yârn, *n.,* spun strand of fiber, (coll.) tale

yāwl, *n.,* small sailboat

yāwn, *v.,* open mouth wide when sleepy or bored; **-er**

yēar, *n.,* period of 365 days; **-ly** *a., adv.*

yēar'lĭng, *n.,* one year old animal [*n.*

yêarn, *v.,* desire; **-er; -ing**

yēast, *n.,* frothy substance used as fermenting or leavening agent; **-y** *a.*

yĕll, *n., v.,* shout, scream; **-er**

yĕl'lōw, *n.,* color; *a.,* of ripe lemon color; **-ness**

yĕn, *n.,* strong desire

yeō'mán, *n.,* naval clerk

yĕs, *n.,* affirmative reply; *adv.,* it is so

yĕt, *adv.,* now, still; *conj.,* however

yiēld, *n.,* product; *v.,* produce, surrender, grant; **-er**

yō'dèl, *v.,* sing with abrupt alternating sounds; **-er**

yō'gà, *n.,* body exercising system

yōke, *n.,* wooden neck harness for oxen, slavery, thing that binds, garment pair at shoulders; *v.,* harness, join together

yōlk, *n.,* yellow of egg

yŏn'dêr, *a., adv.,* farther

yôre, *n., adv.,* (time) long ago

youñg, *a.,* being in early period of life, fresh; **-ster; -ling** *n.;* **-ish**

yôur-sĕlf', *pro.,* reflexive or intensive form of you

youth, *n.,* state of being young, young people; **-ful; -fulness; -fully**

yŭc'cà, *n.,* shrub

yūle, *n.,* Christmas

yŭm'mÿ, *a.,* (coll.) delicious

Z

za'ny, *n.,* clown; comical foolish; **niness; nily**

zarf, *n.,* an ornamental holder for a hot coffee cup, used in the Levant

zax, *n.,* a tool for trimming slates

zeal, *n.,* enthusiasm, passion; **-ous; -ousness; -ously**

zeal-ous, *adj.,* eager in the pursuit of an object, enthusiastic

ze'bra, *n.,* striped horse like mammal

ze-bec, *n.,* a small three-masted ship, sometimes seen in the Mediterranean

ze'-bu, *n.,* the Indian ox or cow, with long ears and a large hump on the shoulders

Zech-a-ri-ah, *n.*, a book of the Old Testament containing the message of the Hebrew prophet Zechariah

zed, *n.*, the English name for the last letter of the alphabet

ze'nith, *n.*, highest point; -al

zeph'yr, *n.*, soft gentle breeze

ze-ta, *n.*, in the Greek alphabet, the sixth letter

Zep'-pe-lin, *n.*, a cigar-shaped dirigible balloon, named after its inventor, Count von Zeppelin of Germany , and able to fly long distances and to carry a large weight: used by Germany in bombing raids over England and France during the World War

ze-ro, *n.*, a cipher, nothing; neutral point (°) on a scale, of temperature, etc., from which reckoning begins: zero hour, the hour fixed for beginning a military engagement, as an advance or attack

zest, *n.*, flavor, enthusiasm; **-ful; -fullness; -fully; -y** *a.*

zig-zag, *n.*, a course or line the direction of which changes in sharp turns or angles alternately to left and right

zilch, *n.*, nothing

zinc, *n.*, bluish-white metallic element

zip, *n.*, energy; *v.*, fasten zipper; **-py** *a.*

zir'con, *n.*, mineral

zith'er, *n.*, stringed instrument

zo'-di-ac, *n.*, imaginary belt near sun's path divided into twelve signs; **-al**

zo-ic, *adj.*, pertaining to, or connected with, animal life; containing fossils or preserved animals or plants: said of rocks

zone, *n.*, distinct area; *v.*, divide into districts; **zonal**

zoo, *n.*, a park or other large enclosure in which live animals are kept for public exhibition; a zoological garden

zo'-ol'o-gy(zu), *n.*, science of animals and animal life; gist; logical; logically

zoom, *v.*, make a loud buzzing sound, rise rapidly

zo-ot-omy, *n.*, the dissection of animals, especially of animals other than man

zounds, *interj.*, an exclamation expressing anger or wonder;

Zu-lu, *n.*, one of a warlike native tribe of Natal, South Africa

zwie-back, *n.*, a kind of biscuit or roll first baked in a loaf and then cut and toasted

zy'gote, *n.*, fertilized egg

zy-mol-o-gy, *n.*, the science or study of the principles of fermentation.

U
Z

Directory of Computer Terms and Meanings

The computer has become commonplace in most homes and businesses. The following section of computer terms will help in your understanding of this important area of interest.

Adapter: A circuit as an interface board that serves between the system unit, typically a motherboard and the devices that attach to it.

Address: A location where a piece of information is stored within the computer.

Alphanumeric: An association of characters whose group is comprised of both Alphabetic (A-Z) and Numeric (0-9) symbols.

ANSI: American National Standards Institute. An organization that develops standards and guidelines for both the computer and electronics industries.

ASCII: American Standard Code for Information Interchange. A code used by computers to represent characters such as letters, numbers punctuation marks and other symbols.

Asynchronous: A term used typically to describe a method of data transfer. The timing of which is not directly tied to an external clock. but instead dictated by either of the computers involved in the communication.

Backup: A process of copying data from one type of media to another, for the purpose of preventing data loss in the event the original may become unusable.

Baud: A term used to describe the rate at which data is transferred between two computers. As originally used it was equivalent to the number of bits transmitted per second.

Binary: The Base 2 numbering system used by computers comprised of 1's and 0's.

BIOS: Basic Input/Output System. The part of a computer operating system that is responsible for communications with the machines peripheral components such as the monitor, printer, and keyboard.

Bit: The smallest unit of measure used by computers. The electronic equivalent to a switch which can be either on; high or 1 or off; low or 0. Eight associated bits comprise one byte.

Boot: A term to turning on of a computer and the subsequent describe the loading of its operating system.

Buffer: A section allocated to of memory temporarily store data during transfer.

Bug: A glitch or error in the expected operation of a program.

Byte: The equivalent of one character, typically eight bits.

Clock: A time regulated electronic signal used by the computer to coordinate its operation.

Cluster: The allocation for disk files. Clusters are smallest unit of comprised of one or more sectors.

CPU: Central Processing Unit. The main computer chip used within a computer where the bulk of the processing of data is done. Can also refer to the chassis or box in which this chip is located.

Cursor: The small flashing mark usually a line or box that appears on your computer screen signifying the location of where typed key will be located.

Directory: A location on a disk where the names, locations and other information related to files located on that disk are kept.

DMA: Direct Memory Access. An electronic path within a computer for high-speed data transfer. The computers CPU is not utilized in this operation that neither the transfer or system is impacted.

Disk: A magnetic storage device used to store computer information.

Encryption: A method of securing data by changing the codes to unrelated characters which can later be deciphered by use of a key, usually algorithm.

File: A collection of related information or instructions that is usually stored on a disk.

Fixed Disk: A non removable magnetic storage device which retains its memory after power to the computer is turned off. Also referred to as a hard disk.

Format: Preparing a magnetic disk or tape so that data may be stored. This process typically deletes any prior information stored while also checking for any defects or flaws in the surface being prepared.

Gigabyte: A quantity of storage approximately equivalent to one billion bytes. Exactly 1,073,741,824 bytes.

Head: The electromagnetic component responsible for reading and writing information on magnetic media.

I/O: Input/Output. A term used to relate to the flow of information to or from a source.

Interface: To attach through a common point of access two disparate systems.

Interrupt: Abbr. IRQ. An electrical signal with a computer used to temporarily suspend a task in process so that another task may be performed.

Kilobyte: Abbr. Kbyte. or KB. A quantity of storage approximately equivalent to one thousand bytes. Exactly 1024 bytes.

Logical Drive: A function of creating through the operating system the appearance of a specific physical device, but instead may represent another disk drive or directory.

Megabyte: Abbr. Mbyte. or MB. A quantity of storage approximately equivalent to one million bytes. Exactly 1,048, 576 bytes.

Memory: The electronic components within a computer used to temporarily hold information as its being processed. Also referred to as RAM.

Modem: Modulator/Demodulator. A device used to interface computers to telephone lines to link them together. A modem must be in use at each computer to translate the digital signals to its telephone line in compatible analog form.

Network: The linking of several computers together so that physical and data resources may be shared.

Output: Data that is sent to a device such as a monitor, printer, speaker or another physical device.

Parallel: The process of transferring data where the electrical signals are sent over multiple wires simultaneously.

Parity: A method of

insuring data integrity by adding an extra bit to each byte in a process similar to check summing.

Partition: A section of a hard disk that has been set aside for use by an operating system.

Peripheral: A piece of equipment connected to the computer. Some typical examples are modems, monitors, printers and disk drives.

Port: The connector that allows for the attaching of external peripherals.

Program: A series of instructions which allow a computer to perform a specific task.

Random-Access Memory: Abbr. RAM. The memory accessed by the computer to run a program or temporarily store data. This memory is cleared and the data lost when the computer is turned off.

Read-Only Memory: Abbr. ROM. This type of memory has the information permanently placed into it which cannot be altered. The information contained in ROM is not lost when power is turned off.

Sector: A sub section of a track of a disk. The size of a sector may vary depending on the drive and operating system in use.

Serial: The process of transferring data or executing tasks one after the other in succession.

Terminal: A separate piece of equipment that is used to input and process information to prepare it for its end use. A complete computer processing station.

Terminate and Stay Resident: Abbr. TSR. A program that remains in memory after it has been loaded and exited.

Track: On a disk it represents one of the concentric circles in which data stored. On a tape the concept is similar but data is stored in parallel lines extending the entire tape length.

Virus: A program designed to attach itself to other programs for the purpose of being unknowingly propagated from computer to computer. The affects of a virus may range from a simple annoyance to the loss of data.

METRIC CONVERSION CHART
APPROXIMATIONS

When You Know	Multiply by	To Find
Length		
millimeters	0.04	inches
centimeters	0.04	inches
meters	3.3	feet
meters	1.1	yards
kilometers	0.6	miles
Area		
square centimeters	0.16	square inches
square meters	1.2	square yards
square kilometers	0.4	square miles
hectares 10,000m^2	2.5	acres
Mass and Weight		
grams	0.035	ounce
kilograms	2.2	pounds
tons (1000kg)	1.1	short tons
Volume		
millimeters	0.03	fluid ounces
liters	2.1	pints
liters	1.06	quarts
liters	0.26	gallons
cubic meters	35	cubic feet
cubic meters	1.3	cubic yards
Temperature (exact)		
Celsius temperature	9/5, + 32	Fahrenheit temp.
Fahrenheit temperature	-32, 5/9 x remainder	Celsius temp.
Length		
inches	2.5	centimeters
feet	30	centimeters
yards	0.9	meters
miles	1.6	kilometers
Area		
square inches	6.5	square centimeters
square feet	0.09	square meters
square yards	0.8	square meters
square miles	2.6	square kilometers
acres	0.4	hectares
Mass and Weight		
ounces	28	grams
pounds	0.45	kilograms
short tons (2000 lb)	0.9	tons
Volume		
fluid ounces	30	milliliters
pints	0.47	liters
quarts	0.95	liters

WEIGHTS AND MEASURES

U.S. Customary Unit	U.S. Equivalents	Metric Equivalents
Length		
inch	0.083 foot	2.54 centimeters
foot	1/3 yard. 12 inches	0.3048 meter
yard	3 feet. 36 inches	0.9144 meter
rod	51/2 yards. 161/2 feet	5.0292 meters
mile (statute, land)	1,760 yards. 5,280 feet	1.609 Kilometers
mile (nautical international)	1.151 statute miles	1.852 kilometers
Area		
square inch	0.007 square foot	6.4516 square centimeters
square foot	144 Square inches	929.030 square centimeters
square yard	1,296 square inches. 9 square feet	0.836 square meter
acre	43,560 square feet. 4,840 square yards	4,047 square meters
square mile	640 acres	2,590 square kilometers
Volume or Capacity		
cubic inch	0.00058 cubic foot	16,387 cubic centimeters
cubic foot	1,728 cubic inches	0.028 cubic meter
cubic yard	27 cubic feet	0.765 cubic meter

U.S. Customary Liquid Measure	U.S. Equivalents	Metric Equivalents
fluid ounce	8 fluid drams 1.804 cubic inches	29,573 milititers
pint	16 fluid ounces 28,875 cubic inches	0.473 liter
quart	2 pints. 57.75 cubic inches	0.946 liter
gallon	4 quarts. 231 cubic inches	3l.785 liters
barrel	varies from 31 to 42 gallons, established by law or usage	

U.S. Customary Dry Measure	U.S. Equivalents	Metric Equivalents
pint	1/2 quart. 33.6 cubic inches	0.551 liter
quart	2 pints. 67.2 cubic inches	1.101 liters
peck	8 quarts. 537.605 cubic inches	8.810 liters
bushel	4 pecks. 2,150.42 cubic inces	35.238 liters

UNITED STATES STATISTICS

State	Capital	Admitted to the Union	Population
Alabama	Montgomery	1819	3,444,165
Alaska	Juneau	1959	302,173
Arizona	Phoenix	1912	1,772,482
Arkansas	Little Rock	1836	1,923,295
California	Sacramento	1850	19,953,134
Colorado	Denver	1876	2,207,259
Connecticut*	Hartford	1788	3,032,217
Delaware*	Dover	1787	548,104
Florida	Tallahassee	1845	6,789,443
Georgia*	Atlanta	1788	4,589,575
Hawaii	Honolulu	1959	769,913
Idaho	Boise	1890	713,008
Illinois	Springfield	1818	11,172,000
Indiana	Indianapolis	1816	5,172,000
Iowa	Des Moines	1846	2,825,041
Kansas	Topeka	1861	2,249,071
Kentucky	Frankfort	1792	3,219,311
Louisiana	Baton Rouge	1812	3,643,180
Maine	Augusta	1820	999,663
Maryland*	Annapolis	1788	3,922,399
Massachusetts*	Boston	1788	5,689,170
Michigan	Lansing	1837	8,875,083
Minnesota	St. Paul	1858	3,805,069
Mississippi	Jackson	1817	2,216,9123
Missouri	Jefferson City	1821	4,677,395
Montana	Helena	1889	694,405
Nebraska	Lincoln	1867	1,483,791
Nevada	Carson City	1864	488,738
New Hampshire*	Concord	1788	737,681
New Jersey*	Trenton	1787	7,168,164
New Mexico	Santa Fe	1912	1,016,000
New York*	Albany	1788	18,241,266
North Carolina*	Raleigh	1789	5,082,059
North Dakota	Bismarck	1889	617,761
Ohio	Columbus	1803	10,652,012
Oklahoma	Oklahoma City	1907	2,559,253
Oregon	Salem	1859	2,091,385
Pennsylvania*	Harrisburg	1787	11,793,909
Rhode Island*	Providence	1790	946,723
South Carolina*	Columbia	1788	2,590,516
South Dakota	Pierre	1889	666,257
Tennessee	Nashville	1796	3,924,164
Texas	Austin	1845	11,196,730
Utah	Salt Lake City	1896	1,059,273
Vermont	Montpelier	1791	444,732
Virginia*	Richmond	1788	4,648,494
Washington	Olympia	1889	3,409,165
West Virginia	Charleston	1863	1,744,237
Wisconsin	Madison	1848	4,417,933
Wyoming	Cheyenne	1890	332,416

*One of the thirteen original states

GIFT GIVING

WEDDING
ANNIVERSARY SYMBOLS

	Traditional	Modern
1st	paper	clocks
2nd	cotton	china
3rd	leather	crystal, glass
4th	books	electrical appliances
5th	wood	silverware
6th	sugar, candy	wood
7th	wood copper	desk sets
8th	bronze, pottery	linens, laces
9th	pottery, willow	leather
10th	tin, aluminum	diamond jewelry
11th	steel	fashion jewelry
12th	silk, linen	pearls, colored gems
13th	lace	textiles, furs
14th	ivory	gold jewelry
15th	crystal	watches
20th	china	platinum
25th	silver	silver
30th	pearl	diamond
35th	coral	jade
40th	ruby	ruby
45th	sapphire	sapphire
50th	gold	gold
55th	emerald	emerald
60th	diamond	diamond
75th	diamond	diamond

BIRTHSTONES

January	Garnet
February	Amethyst
March	Bloodstone or Aquamarine
April	Diamond
May	Emerald
June	Pearl or Alexandrite
July	Ruby
August	Sardonyx or Peridot
September	Sapphire
October	Opal or Tourmaline
November	Topaz
December	Turquoise or Zircon

ROGETS THESAURUS

A DICTIONARY OF

SYNONYMS & ANTONYMS

1994 EDITION

Published by PSI & Associates, Inc.
13322 SW 128th Street, Miami, FL 33186
(305) 255-7959

CONTENTS

SYNONYMS...

Are those words which appear
under the alphabetical listing.
All have the same meaning.

ANTONYMS...

Are those words which appear
under the alphabetical listing in
parentheses. All have the
opposite or different meanings.

PARTS OF SPEECH...

Abbreviations:

n- noun
v- verb
adv- adverb
adj- adjective

Insert compiled by Jane Solmson.

A
B

A

abandon—*v.* abdicate, leave, jilt, desert, vacate, cease, resign, drop, waive, discontinue, yield, surrender, forsake, retire, quit, relinquish, let go, repudiate, part with. *(cherish, keep, retain, adopt, pursue, uphold, occupy, support, favor, depend, maintain, vindicate, assert, advocate, claim, seek, embrace.)*

abase—*v.* disgrace, debase, mock, scorn, belittle, mortify, reduce, degrade, dishonour, despise, shame, lower, expose, humble, confuse, humiliate. *(elevate, uplift, exalt, honour, cherish, respect, praise, dignify, glorify, lift, laud, extol.)*

abate—*v.* alleviate, terminate, wane, reduce, diminish, ebb, decrease, restrain, lessen, allay, lower, decline, subside, slacken, slow down, ease. *(increase, prolong, extend, intensify, enlarge, magnify, amplify, enhance, aggravate, grow, accelerate, speed.)*

abbreviate—*v.* curtail, shorten, clip, reduce, lessen, condense, prune, abridge, cut short, cut down, trim, diminish, compress. *(lengthen, increase, expand, distend, dilate, prolong, swell, amplify, enlarge, augment, add to, supplement.)*

abdicate—*v.* cede, renounce, yield, resign, abandon, give up, relinquish, quit, forego, surrender, waive. *(claim, retain, hold, assume, maintain, challenge, defy, seize, possess.)*

abet—*v.* help, encourage, assist, aid, condone, uphold, stimulate, sustain, support, promote, incite, subsidize, sanction. *(hinder, impede, thwart, obstruct, discourage, frustrate, deter, oppose, resist, counteract, dampen, baffle.)*

abeyance—*n.* inactivity, recess, suspension, expectation, rest, reservation, pause, adjournment, latency. *(continuation, operation, exercise, enjoyment, force, possession, revival, enforcement, renewal, action.)*

abhor—*v.* loathe, detest, avoid, abominate, shun, scorn, distain, hate, dislike, recoil from. *(cherish, adore, prize, love, desire, enjoy, treasure, admire, value, approve, covet.)*

abide—*v.* stay, dwell, sojourn, rest, remain, lodge, anchor, exist, live, settle, tarry, confront, sit, bide, endure, await. *(move, proceed, go, leave, migrate, despise, journey, avoid, deport, mistake.)*

ability—*n.* aptitude, capability, power, energy, skill, talent, knack, cleverness, strength, qualification, flair, know-how, vigor. *(inabili-*

ty, weakness, helplessness, incompetence, ineffectiveness, unreadiness, inadequacy.)

abject—*adj.* base, mean, degrade, low, vile, worthless, contemptible, dishonourable, sordid, miserable, hangdog, outcast, hopeless, wretched, fawning, servile. (*noble, haughty, proud, dignified, honorable, magnificent, lofty, bold, arrogant, worthy, aristocratic, vain, respected, exalted, hopeful, staunch, manly.*)

able—*adj.* skillful, adroit, competent, strong, accomplished, gifted, clever, capable, expert, proficient, adept, powerful, apt, talented, highly qualified. (*incapable, weak, incompetent, inept, unqualified, inefficient, mediocre, indifferent, useless, stupid, delicate, fair.*)

ablution—*n.* purification, bathing, cleansing, washing, lavation, ceremonial washing. (*soil, soiling, tainting, pollution, contaminating, taint, defiling.*)

abnormal—*adj.* eccentric, weird, exceptional, irregular, unnatural, peculiar, atypical, bizarre, strange, devious, monstrous, queer, odd, unconventional. (*natural, customary, common, routine, normal, ordinary, familiar, usual, conventional, typical.*)

abode—*n.* residence, home, nest, pad, lodgings, berth, habitat, domicile, house, address, quarters. (*halt, tent, pilgrimage, ramble, perch, bivouac, peregrenation.*)

abolish—*v.* eliminate, efface, annihilate, destroy, cancel, repeal, annul, erase, revoke, repudiate, nullify, end, suppress, obliterate, quash, extinguish, overturn. (*introduce, enforce, restore, support, sustain, establish, continue, create, renew, enact, repair, promote, reinstate, legalize.*)

abominable—*adj.* vile, detestable, despicable, contemptible, hateful, horrid, revolting, repugnant, wretched, offensive, nauseous, infamous, foul, atrocious. (*choice, select, delightful, attractive, pure, charming, typical, routine, conventional, admirable, familiar, enjoyable.*)

aboriginal—*adj.* original, native, earliest, indigenous, ancient, primary, first, prime, primitive. (*foreign, immigrant, alien, late, imported, exotic, recent, modern.*)

abortion—*n.* disaster, failure, miscarriage, unsuccessful attempt, fiasco, blunder, termination, ending, mishap, misproduction. (*achievement, delivery, success, childbirth, perfection, development, realization, feat, parturition, completion.*)

abound—*v.* swarm, increase, flow, multiply, teem, overflow, be numerous, swell, luxuriate, flourish, be rich in, revel, be well supplied, stream, superabound. (*lack, have too few, fall, want, waste, decay, be scant, dry, die, lessen, vanish, wane, fail, need, be destitute of.*)

about—*adj.* around, nearly, regarding, relative to, concerning, approximately, connected with, over, surrounding, generally, almost, round, touching, respecting. *(unlike, afar, precisely, exactly, remote, distant, separated.)*

above—*adv.* over, aloft, overhead, beyond, higher, on top of, exceeding. *(within, beneath, below, under.)*

abridge—*v.* condense, compress, curtail, abbreviate, lessen, reduce, diminish, digest, epitomize, recap, summarize, telescope, shorten. *(amplify, expand, exténd, spread out, enlarge, lengthen, detail.)*

abrupt—*adj.* rude, curt, harsh, sudden, craggy, zigzag, jagged, sharp, brusque, uneven, violent, broken, blunt. *(civil, easy, blending, gliding, gracious, polite, polished, smooth.)*

absent—*adj.* missing, listless, gone away, truant, pre-occupied, oblivious, inattentive, elsewhere, dreamy, out, heedless. *(present, aware.)*

absolute—*adj.* unrestricted, pure, perfect, dogmatic, full, supreme, irrespective, complete, unqualified, despotic, certain, arbitrary, unconditional, entire. *(mild, conditional, gentle, dubious, meek, relative, imperfect, incomplete, dependent, accountable, docile, qualified.)*

absolve—*v.* pardon, acquit, clear, excuse, exonerate, forgive, release, deliver, condone, liberate. *(accuse, bind,* blame, censure, condemn, hold to, convict, compel.)

absorb—*v.* sponge up, suck up, swallow, devour, monopolize, drink in, drown, engulf, consume, engross, exhaust, merge. *(impart, cast off, emit, belch, dissipate, distil, eject, disperse, distract, disgorge, eliminate, weary.)*

abstain—*v.* avoid, eschew, withhold, forgo, scruple, decline, forbear, refrain, discontinue, refuse, desist, avoid, demur. *(yield to, wanton, overdue, reveal, indulge, exceed.)*

abstract—*v.* discriminate, subtle, abridge, purloin, outline, separate, appropriate, detach, take away, eliminate, steal, withdraw. *(mend, add, unite, concrete, return, specific, restore, impose, conjoin, adduce, surrender.)*

absurd—*adj.* ludicrous, silly, stupid, comical, ridiculous, funny, unreasonable, asinine, monstrous, senseless, foolish, listless. *(smart, judicious, wise, sensical, prudent, sensible, reflective, sound, rational, consistent, logical, sagacious, reasonable.)*

abundant—*adj.* enough, copious, replete, overflowing, profuse, large, liberal, lavish, rich, plentiful, teeming, luxuriant. *(meager, poor, scant, skimpy, uncommon, rare, drained, deficient, scarce, short, sparing, dry, exhausted.)*

abuse—*v.* harm, hurt, injure, misuse, desecrate, disparage, damage, ill-use, revile, malign, pervert, maltreat, upbraid, prostitute, defame, asperse, vilify. *(eulogize, shield, care for, extol, laud, cherish, flatter, tend, regard, consider, respect, protect, sustain.)*

abuse—*n.* unfair use, ill treatment, imposition, invective, improper use, ribaldry, reproach, insolence, ill usage, disgrace, blame, censure. *(praise, laudation, commendation, approval, sanction, deference, respect, kindness, good treatment.)*

academic—*adj.* learned, lettered, classical, bookish, scholarly, collegiate, pedantic. *(non-scholarly, untaught, unschooled, illiterate, ordinary, plain.)*

accelerate—*v.* quicken, rush, spur, urge, hasten, further, speed, hurry, promote, expedite, forward, precipitate. *(slow, hinder, resist, embarrass, impede, clog, delay, retard, obstruct, drag.)*

accent—*n.* stress, force, cadence, modulation, beat, pulsation, emphasis, rhythm. *(flow, smoothness, babble, monotony, inaccentuation, equableness.)*

accept—*v.* receive, concur, hail, allow, recognize, take, avow, admit, accede to, believe, agree. *(yield, spurn, disown, disacknowledge, deny, decline, refuse, ignore.)*

acceptable—*adj.* fitting, suitable, worthy, good, gratifying, agreeable, grateful, welcome, pleasant. *(repugnant, unfitting, annoying, poor, below par, disagreeable, unpleasant, unsuitable, ungrateful.)*

accessory—*n.* retainer, associate, colleague, complement, aide, additional, assistant, crutch, auxiliary, accomplice, henchman, helper. *(opponent, spy, adversary, rival, enemy, foe, antagonist, irrelevant, immanent, superfluous, cumbersome.)*

accident—*n.* hazard, collision, chance, wreck, fortuity, crash, calamity, misadventure, incident, mishap, adventure, misfortune. *(intent, design, purpose, plan, decree, appointment, law, ordainment, provision.)*

accommodate—*v.* oblige, provide, aid, suit, help, supply, fit, adapt, serve, harmonize, reconcile, lodge. *(disturb, impede, deprive, censure, aggravate, inconvenience, hinder, hissing, block.)*

accommodating—*adj.* courteous, gracious, neighborly, polite, kind, yielding, obliging, unselfish, considerate. *(churlish, exacting, rude, disobliging, selfish, imperious, dictatorial, hostile.)*

accomplice—*n.* cohort, coworker, assistant, aide, supporter, ally, colleague, henchman, partner, accessory, associate, helper. *(objector, rival, foe, denouncer, opponent, betrayer, enemy, antagonist.)*

accomplish—*v.* conclude, do, discharge, effect, perform, carryout, fulfil, perfect, realize, attain, execute, achieve, associate, manage, finish. *(give up, leave undone,* *fall short, defeat, baffle, fail, destroy, spoil.)*

accord—*v.* give, admit, cede, allow, tally, render, agree, answer, consist, consent, grant, bequeath. *(deny, disagree, clash, collide, differ, refuse, misfit, withhold, discord.)*

accordingly—*adv.* whence, whereupon, thence, suitably, conformably, hence, agreeably, conversely.

accost—*v.* solicit, confront, stop, waylay, greet, salute. *(avoid, shun, overlook, slight.)*

account—*n.* narrative, reckoning, value, charge, bill, recital, motive, description. *(riddle, silence, puzzle, unknown quantity, mystery, project.)*

account—*v.* think, judge, view as, rate, calculate, estimate, deem, value, hold, explain, reckon. *(leave unexplained, leave unsolved, mystify, perplex.)*

accountable—*adj.* answerable, censurable, responsible, beholden, liable, delegated, guilty, subordinate, blameworthy. *(innocent, despotic, autocratic, guiltless, absolute, supreme, unreliable.)*

accredit—*v.* delegate, commission, license, entrust, authorize, endorse, believe, sanction. *(distrust, discard, recall, supersede, disbelieve, suspect, dismiss.)*

accumulate—*v.* gather, pile up, amass, hoard, collect, add to, garner, augment, assemble, accrue. *(waste, scatter, disperse, distribute,*

dissipate, get rid of, throw out.)

accumulation—*n.* store, amassing, agglomeration, gathering, heap, hoard, pile, mass, bulk, lot. *(division, separation, scattering, unit, individual, segregation, dispersal.)*

accurate—*adj.* minute, careful, nice, unerring, true, scrupulous, just, correct, close, strict, exact, faithful, truthful. *(false, wrong, deceptive, careless, faulty, loose, inexact, defective, sloppy.)*

accuse—*v.* indict, summon, impeach, against, incriminate, tax, blame, censure, taunt. *(plea, pardon, blame, vindicate, acquit, condone, exonerate, deny, rebut.)*

accustom—*v.* form, ingrain, train, discipline, harden, incure, reconcile, familiarize. *(disaccustom, estrange, alienate, dishabituate, wean.)*

achieve—*v.* accomplish, dispatch, attain, fulfill, realize, win, procure, finish. *(be deprived of, lose, fail, miss.)*

achievement—*n.* realization, fulfillment, exploit, performance, accomplishment. *(frustration, defeat, failure, loss, waste.)*

acknowledge—*v.* recognize, admit, confess, accept, profess, concede, yield, own, grant. *(disclaim, slight, reject, repudiate, ignore, deny, abandon.)*

acme—*n.* height, peak, apex, summit, zenith, pinnacle, crown. *(bottom, depth,* base, nadir, low point, foundation.)

acquaint—v. familiarize, inform, reveal, advertise, enlighten, divulage, notify, tell, apprise. (hide, misinform, withhold, reserve, deceive, conceal, delude.)

acquaintance—n. relationship, experience, dealings, association, knowledge, intimacy. (stranger, ignore, inexperience, ignorance.)

acquiesce—v. allow, yield, concur, assent, comply, submit, bow to, grant. (contest, demur, protest, veto, resist.)

acquire—v. get, obtain, attain, gain, secure, achieve. (lose, relinquish, give up, forgo, be deprived of.)

acquit—v. clear, excuse, release, discharge, exonerate, vindicate, deliver, pardon. (convict, declare, charge, constrain, compel, bind, condemn, damn, indict, accuse.)

acquittance—n. discharge, voucher, release, receipt. (obligation, bond, charge, claim.)

across—prep. & adv. against, transversely, athwart, crosswise, thwart. (lengthwise, parallel, along, concurrently.)

act—n. statute, movement, play, degree, bill, performance, operation, measure, pose, deed, (inactivity, quiet, repose, inertia, rest, stop, procrastinate, suspension, immobility, sluggishness.)

activate—v. turn on, drive, stimulate, impel, energize, nudge. (stop, halt, paralyze, weaken, turn off, check.)

active—adj. energetic, vigorous, brisk, supple, nimble, busy, vibrant, agile, prompt, dexterous, ambitious, forceful, bubbling. (quiet, dormant, sluggish, heavy, inactive, inert.)

actual—adj. concrete, positive, authentic, tangible, sure, certain, unquestionable, prevailing. (fictional, hypothetical, probable, possible, potential, fabulous, unreal, made-up.)

acumen—n. insight, keenness, sharpness, cleverness, wisdom, intelligence. (dullness, ignorance, apathy, slowness, stupor, bad judgment.)

acute—adj. clever, ingenious, severe, sharp, shrewd, violent, astute, sagacious, smart, fierce. (stupid, obtuse, dense, mild, dull, stolid, blunt, heavy.)

adamant—adj. determined, unbending, stubborn, firm, set, insistent, immovable. (lax, yielding, flexible, indifferent, easy-going, undemanding.)

adapt—v. adjust, temper, qualify, fit, attune, harmonize, comply, assimilate. (confuse, jumble, misapply, misfit, disturb, displace.)

add—v. enlarge, extend, increase, affix, append, adduce, sum up, count up, amplify. (deduct, subtract, remove, withdraw, reduce, exclude.)

addicted—adj. attached, prone, devoted, given, accustomed, disposed, dedicated. (unaddicted, averse, free, contrary, opposed, indisposed, reluctant.)

addition—*n.* totaling, appendage, enlargement, increase, adjunct, summation, enumeration, extension. *(subtraction, loss, deterioration, deduction, decrease, shrinkage.)*

address—*n.* speech, discourse, tact, oration, ability. *(awkwardness, rudeness, folly, stupidity.)*

address—*v.* approach, implore, solicit, greet, salute, appeal, invoke, hail, memorialize. *(pass, shun, elude, avoid, ignore.)*

adept—*n.* soothsayer, wizard, expert, master, peer, artist, performer, magician. *(faker, blunderer, novice, hypocrite, pretender, awkward, clumsy.)*

adequate—*adj.* suitable, fit, equal, capable, ample, able, enough, satisfactory, competent. *(unsuited, imperfect, inadequate, incompetent, unfit, inferior, worthless.)*

adherence—*n.* loyalty, attachment, endearment, fidelity, allegiance, devotion, constancy, adhesion. *(slickness, disunion, infidelity, unfaithfulness, desertion, disloyalty, breaking.)*

adherent—*n.* accessory, ally, follower, devotee, fan, disciple, backer, pupil, admirer. *(detractor, betrayer, opponent, renegade, opposer, adversary.)*

adhesive—*adj.* glutinous, gummy, waxy, sticky, adherent. *(attachment, free, apart, unattachable, oily, open, loose.)*

adieu—*n.* farewell, departure, parting, leave, good-bye, leave-taking, setting out. *(salutation, greeting, recognition, welcome.)*

adipose—*adj.* fat, greasy, obese, oily, corpulent, sebaceous, oleoginous. *(thin, bony, leathery, mummified.)*

adjacent—*adj.* next to, beside, neighboring, close, bordering, attached, adjoining, near. *(beyond, afar, remote, distant, detached, apart.)*

adjoin—*v.* border upon, near to, annex, adjacent to, connect, unite, add, touch, affix, join on, approximate, abut. *(dismember, part, remote, disunite, detach, disconnect, removed, distant, recede.)*

adjourn—*v.* suspend, recess, close, postpone, defer, delay, procrastinate, put off, dismiss. *(convene, stimulate, conclude, hasten, gather, convoke, expedite, consummate, protract, impel.)*

adjunct—*n.* accessory, auxiliary, addition, complement, attachment, aid, acquisition, dependency. *(lessening, removal, hindrance, essence, clog, separation, impediment, drawback, detriment.)*

adjust—*v.* arrange, regulate, harmonize, localize, organize, acclimate, callocate, set in order, compose, classify, prepare. *(scatter, disorder, dislocate, jumble, dismember, derange, disturb, involve, confuse.)*

ad-lib—*n.* wisecrack, extemporaneous, improvisation, speak off the cuff, speak impromptu. *(follow the script, speak from notes.)*

administer—*v.* supply, direct, accord, dole, furnish, govern, award, discharge, afford, execute, superintend, distribute, dispense. *(foil, resign, withhold, frustrate, refuse, resume, deny, nullify, betray, forego.)*

admirable—*adj.* worthy, excellent, captivating, pleasing, praiseworthy, astonishing, enticing, good. *(repelling, ridiculous, displeasing, unworthy, hateful, mediocre, repulsive.)*

admissible—*adj.* worthy, permissible, probable, proper, fair, just, likely, reasonable, qualified. *(intolerable, wrong, irrelevant, absurd, preposterous, unfair, excluded, inadmissible.)*

admit—*v.* invest, pass, accept, own, avow, welcome, acknowledge, receive, grant, tell. *(deny, shut, debar, repel, reject, dismiss, eject, repudiate, disavow, confute.)*

admonish—*v.* counsel, advise, rebuke, remind, censure, scold, criticize, forewarn, reprove, warn. *(laud, urge, extol, instigate, applaud, chide, abet, praise.)*

adolescent—*n.* teenager, lad, lass, youth, schoolboy, schoolgirl, young man or woman. *(adult, grown-up, child, mature.)*

adopt—*v.* acknowledge, select, affiliate, elect, endorse, espouse, avow, choose, accept, conform to, assume. *(annul, reject, discard, disinherit, repudiate,*

abrogate, decline, disclaim, disown.)*

adoration—*n.* worship, exaltation, glorification, veneration, honor, magnification, devotion. *(denunciation, blasphemy, reviling, execration, belittling.)*

adore—*v.* exalt, revere, praise, admire, idolize, glorify, hallow, reverence. *(loathe, dislike, revile, exercrate, abhor, blaspheme, abominate.)*

adorn—*v.* beautify, gild, garnish, embellish, bejewel, illustrate, ornament. *(mock, despise, curse, condemn, strip, bare, simplify, mar, spoil.)*

adulation—*n.* compliment, praise, fawning, flattering, courtship, cringing, fulsome, incense. *(loathing, dislike, hatred, defamation, obloquy, satire, sarcasm, detraction, abuse, censure.)*

advance—*v.* prosper, rise, go, proceed, promote, elevate, lend, increase, exalt, allege. *(stop, withhold, depress, hesitate, halt, withdraw, degrade, retreat, oppose, yield.)*

advantage—*n.* boon, success, interest, blessing, comfort, gain, help, superiority, utility, profit, victory, avail. *(hindrance, curse, loss, frustration, obstacle, disadvantage, dilemma, disservice, burden, barrier.)*

adventurous—*adj.* challenging, brave, risky, gallant, bold, fearless, rash, audacious, valiant. *(cautious, nervous, hesitant, dull, routine,* boring, hesitating, cowardly, unenterprising.)

adversary—n. opponent, rival, enemy, competitor, foe, antagonist. (colleague, aider, friend, teammate, accessory, ally, accomplice, help, cooperation.)

adverse—adj. contrary, negative, hostile, harmful, antagonistic, unfriendly, detremental, injurious. (favorable, helpful, supporting, agreeable, auspicious, beneficial.)

adversity—n. trial, calamity, woe, misfortune, misery, disaster, bad luck, affliction, ruin, unsuccess. (blessings, prosperity, help, aid, happiness, approval.)

advertise—v. call attention to, publicize, show, circulate, inform, advise, notify, proclaim, tout, display. (hide, warn, deliberate, conceal, ignore, proclaim, hush, misinform, hoodwink.)

advise—v. counsel, direct, acquaint, warn, deliberate, prompt, inform, admonish, show, apprise. (fool, deter, curb, mislead, dissuade, inhibit, remonstrate, delude, misinform.)

advocate—n. counsellor, propagator, champion, defender. (opponent, impugner, accuser, enemy, antagonist.)

affable—adj. kindly, genial, courteous, condescending, polite, easy, civil, pleasant, mild, gracious. (haughty, exclusive, sour, arrogant, surly, distant, unapproachable, contemptuous.)

affect—v. soften, favor, assume, thrill, agitate, influence, like, overcome, interest, subdue, modify. (repudiate, dislike, scorn, repel, shed, shun, feign.)

affectation—n. airs, artifice, mannerism, pretext, frills, simulation, hypocrisy, pretense, sham. (sincerity, naturalness, simplicity, artlessness, genuineness, unaffectedness.)

affection—n. friendship, state love, desire, fondness, solicitude, mood, warmth, attachment, tenderness. (hate, repugnance, indifference, insensibility, antipathy, loathing, coldness.)

affinity—n. relation, harmony, attraction, alliance, connection, sympathy, compatibility, likeness, homology, interdependence. (aversion, antipathy, disconnection, repugnance, repulsion, discordance, dissimilarity.)

affirm—v. swear, tell, ratify, validate, declare, endorse, warrant, approve, state, aver, maintain. (refute, deny, rescind, dispute, demur, impugn, oppose, veto, nullify, disallow.)

affix—v. attach, fasten, fix, add on, set to, seal, glue, paste, stick. (detach, unfasten, take off, unglue.)

affliction—n. calamity, distress, trial, pain, curse, misery, woe, torment, misfortune. (relief, blessing, pleasure, joy, solace, comfort, consolation, boon.)

affluent—adj. rich, wealthy, prosperous, moneyed, well-off, well-fixed. (poor, indigent, *impoverished, impecunious, destitute.)*

afford—*v.* supply, offer, produce, yield, furnish, impart, grant, give, extend, bestow. *(grudge, retain, stint, withhold, deny, withdraw.)*

affront—*v.* insult, outrage, wrong, vex, provoke, abuse, annoy, displease, shame. *(compliment, placate, soothe, mollify, please.)*

afloat—*adj.* loose, distracted, dazed, adrift, wrong. *(snug, tight, close, fast, collected, ashore, concentrated.)*

afoot—*adj.* instituted, started, established, afloat, launched, working, agoing. *(contemplated, designed, projected, incomplete, uncommenced, proposed.)*

afraid—*adj.* panicky, alarmed, terrified, faint-hearted, apprehensive, uneasy, aghast, cautious, fearful. *(unafraid, bold, hopeful, fearless, inapprehensive, unsolicitous, secure, reckless, eager, audacious, confident.)*

afresh—*adv.* over again, anew, repeatedly, again, intermittently, frequently. *(unintermittently, connectedly, uniformly, continuously, uninterruptedly.)*

after—*prep.* afterwards, following, latter, behind, subsequent. *(introducing, preceeding, afore, before.)*

again—*adv.* another, frequently, over, afresh, once more, anew. *(uninterruptedly, uniformly, continuously, once, unintermittently.)*

against—*prep.* abreast of, close to, over, despite, counter, opposing, fronting, resisting. *(aiding, promoting, with, accompanying, suiting, for.)*

age—*n.* generation, date, forever, millennium, era, century, senility, duration, period, epoch. *(infancy, moment, instant, childhood, adolescence, second.)*

agent—*n.* executor, performer, force, mechanic, deputy, doer, operator, cause, envoy, delegate. *(opponent, neutralizer, counteragent, counteraction, counteractor.)*

aggravate—*v.* annoy, provoke, vex, intensify, nettle, affront, irritate, exasperate, enhance, embitter, inflame, worsen. *(soften, soothe, mitigate, diminish, assuage, neutralize, lessen, alleviate.)*

agile—*adj.* limber, active, brisk, quick, dexterous, lithe, fleet, nimble, supple, swift, rapid, lively, graceful. *(sluggish, inert, awkward, bulky, clumsy, lethargic, ponderous, slow.)*

agitate—*v.* trouble, ruffle, shake, excite, oscillate, fluster, convulse. *(soothe, compose, quiet, pacify, smooth, still.)*

agog—*adj.* thrilled, astir, awestruck, enthralled, excited. *(bored, uninterested, indifferent.)*

agony—*n.* torture, distress, affliction, anxiety, pain, anguish, torment, woe, suffering. *(pleasure, enjoyment, ease, consolation, ecstacy, comfort, joy, relief, gratification.)*

agree—*v.* match, tally, harmonize, concur, chime, suit, consent, consort, coincide, dovetail, square. *(dispute, oppose, protest, demur, refute, contradict, revolt, disagree.)*

agreeable—*adj.* concurring, pleasant, enticing, suitable, acceptable, amenable, ready, willing, accommodating, loving. *(unfitting, harsh, unpleasant, ungrateful, offensive, unacceptable, disobliging, repugnant, revolting, odious.)*

agreement—*n.* compact, unison, mutuality, welcome, harmony, contract, bond, undertaking, concord, bargain, compliance. *(disagreement, difference, discrepancy, discord.)*

aid—*v.* assist, support, minister to, favor, help, sustain, serve, protect, encourage, befriend, foster, promote, instigate, encourage. *(harm, oppose, resist, hurt, obstruct, thwart, discourage, baffle, deter, impede, hinder.)*

ailment—*n.* malady, sickness, disease, infection; complaint, affliction, weakness. *(health, fitness, sanity, robustness, vigor, convalescence.)*

aim—*n.* goal, design, aspiration, purpose, endeavor, wish, tendency, scope. *(oversight, neglect, carelessness.)*

airy—*adj.* light, sprightly, frolicsome, jaunty, animated, joyous, fairylike. *(heavy, gloomy, dark, doleful, stony, ponderous, cheerless.)*

akin—*adj.* homogeneous, allied, related, analogous, similar, sympathetic, agnate, cognate. *(unrelated, dissimilar, unconnected, alien, unsympathetic, hostile, antagonistic.)*

alacrity—*n.* agility, briskness, animation, compliance, speed, promptitude, eagerness, zeal, alertness. *(repugnance, apathy, dislike, slowness, lethargy, dullness, laziness.)*

alarm—*n.* terror, fright, distress, fear, misgiving, dread, panic, apprehension, agitation. *(quiet, security, calmness, coolness, tranquillity, peace, repose.)*

alarming—*adj.* imminent, formidable, perilous, terrible, frightful, ominous, fearful. *(assuring, hopeful, attractive, soothing, inviting, alluring.)*

alert—*adj.* diligent, brisk, lively, vigilant, watchful, sprightly, hustling, prompt, nimble, wary. *(lazy, oblivious, heavy, stupid, lethargic, languid, dilatory, slow, absent, lackadaisical.)*

alien—*adj.* foreign, strange, remote, undomesicated, hostile, estranged, irrelevant. *(germane, akin, alike, congenial, pertinent, proper, naturalized, native.)*

alike—*adj.* identical, uniform, similar, equal, same, kindred, parallel, homogeneous, resembling. *(apart, unlike, distinct, different, heterogeneous.)*

alive—*adj.* together, animate, breathing, equal, vivacious, alert, brisk, agile, resembling, safe. *(departed, lifeless, inanimate, cold, dull,* dead, apathetic, morose, drowsy.)

allay—v. ease, soften, soothe, pacify, diminish, appease, quiet, calm, tranquilize. (agitate, aggravate, provoke, stimulate, stir, arouse, intensify, magnify.)

allege—v. profess, affirm, assert, contend, accuse, cite, plead, maintain, state, aver. (neutralize, repel, retract, deny, refute, disclaim, contradict, quash.)

allegiance—n. homage, devotion, loyalty, fealty, faithfulness, deference, fidelity, duty. (treason, rebellion, treachery, sedition, alienation, deceit, ressistance, disloyalty.)

alleviate—v. soften, lessen, mitigate, diminish, subdue, mollify, remove. (enhance, embitter, intensify, increase, multiply, augment.)

alliance—n. treaty, union, junction, coalition, partnership, friendship, confederation, association, syndicate. (secession, enmity, discord, disunion, rebellion, separation, divorce, revolution.)

allot—v. destine, award, tabulate, grant, mete out, catalogue, classify, distribute, parcel, yield. (resume, repudiate, grasp, resist, withstand, guard, shuffle, refuse, protest, retain.)

allow—v. acknowledge, confess, apportion, recognize, authorize, warrant, approve, avow, grant, tolerate, concede, admit. (withdraw, forbid, prohibit, withstand, reject, deny, resume, protest, disallow.)

alloy—n. deterioration, lower impairment, debasement, adulteration, admixture, abatement, degradation. (enhancement, integrity, purity, genuineness.)

allude—v. mention, glance, hint, point, refer, insinuate, cite, quote, imply, remark. (keep secret, state, declare, be closemouthed about, specify.)

ally—n. supporter, helper, confederate, league, affiliate, accomplice, colleague. (rival, competitor, foe, opponent, antagonist, adversary, enemy.)

aloft—adv. overhead, heavenward, high up, in the clouds, above. (down, below, beneath, lower, earthward, low.)

aloud—adv. plainly, clearly, audibly, sonorously, clamorously, loudly. (silently, suppressedly, softly, inaudibly.)

alter—v. transform, substitute, vary, convert, modify, diversify, recast, regulate, twist. (keep, retain, stay, arrest, refrain, continue, stereotype, solidify, preserve.)

altercation—n. disagreement, controversy, wrangle, spat, fracas, dissension, dispute. (union, accord, agreement, unity, peace, harmony, consonance.)

alternative—n. option, choice, preference, pick, election. (necessity, fix, quandry, urgency, obligation, coercion.)

altogether—adv. thoroughly, collectively, totally, quite, fully, perfectly, completely, on the whole. *(incompletely, partially, separately, partly, somewhat, individually.)*

altruistic—*adj.* humane, kind, charitable, philanthropic, generous. *(selfish, self-centered, malevolent, mean.)*

amass—*v.* assemble, heap, aggregate, muster, pile up, gather, collect, hoard. *(squander, dispense, scatter, portion, divide, waste, parcel, distribute.)*

amazement—*n.* admiration, wonder, awe, shock, astonishment, confusion, perplexity, surprise. *(indifference, coolness, calmness, anticipation, preparation, composure, steadiness.)*

ambiguous—*adj.* indefinite, puzzling, vague, equivocal, uncertain, perplexing, dubious, doubtful, misleading, cryptic. *(explicit, clear, obvious, necessary, frank, uncertain, perplexing, plain, lucid, unequivocal.)*

ambition—*n.* goal, aim, hope, longing, intent, yearning, dream, desire, enterprise. *(indolence, sloth, indifference, laziness, modesty, simplicity.)*

ameliorate—*v.* correct, raise, amend, reform, rectify, elevate, advance, promote. *(impair, injure, depress, debase, vitiate, mar, spoil.)*

amend—*v.* better, rectify, mend, repair, meliorate, promote, cleanse, mitigate, correct. *(harm, corrupt, spoil, vitiate, blemish, tarnish, mar, impair, hurt.)*

amiable—*adj.* gentle, engaging, benevolent, cordial, pleasing, gracious, lovable, fascinating, charming, polite, genial. *(hostile, hateful, churlish, sullen, surly, offensive, abminable, repellent.)*

amiss—*adj.* untrue, bad, faulty, mistaken, defective, wrong, incorrect, false, inappropriate, erroneous. *(good, proper, suitable, right, complete, successful, opportune, expedient.)*

amnesty—*n.* absolution, pardon, truce, reprieve, condonation, dispensation, remission. *(penalty, retribution, requital, trial, retaliation, account, punishment.)*

ample—*adj.* abundant, liberal, copious, generous, enough, bountiful, adequate. *(sparse, narrow, scant, mean, insufficient, meager, scrimpy, bare, stint.)*

amplify—*v.* increase, augment, widen, dilate, expand, stretch, magnify, develop, swell, unfold, deepen. *(gather, epitomize, curtail, reduce, amputate, condense, collect, lessen, compress, abbreviate, shorten.)*

amuse—*v.* divert, occupy, charm, cheer, entertain, please, engross. *(bore, sadden, tire, weary, annoy, vex.)*

analogy—*n.* resemblance, metaphor, relation, affinity, parallelism, simile, comparison, likeness. *(difference, dissimilarity, incongruity, inaffinity, heterogeneousness, disharmony.)*

A
B

analysis—*n*. judgement, separation, partition, reduction, segregation, investigation, inquiry. *(synthesis, combination, union, aggregation, coalition, uniting.)*

anarchy—*n*. chaos, tumult, riot, misrule, rebellion, insubordination, disorder. *(control, law, order, organization, government, subjection.)*

anatomy—*n*. structure, framework, dissection, segregation, resolution, division. *(structure, union, organization, synthesis, body, form, collocation.)*

ancestry—*n*. family, parentage, genealogy, progenitors, pedigree, line, stock. *(posterity, descendants, issue, progeny.)*

ancient—*adj*. aged, old-time, antiquated, obsolete, archaic, primeval, olden, remote. *(modern, new, recent, fresh, young, newfangled, modish, juvenile.)*

anger—*n*. outrage, vexation, gall, bile, exasperation, petulance, fury, irritation, grudge, hostility, hatred, ire, choler. *(patience, peace, contentment, mildness, goodwill, peacefulness, gratitude.)*

anger—*v*. ruffle, vex, fret, provoke, embitter, annoy, irritate, wound. *(compose, calm, please, delight, soothe, conciliate, heal, gratify.)*

animosity—*n*. rancor, anger, hatred, feud, acrimony, enmity, malice, resentment, bitterness, virulence, strife, dislike. *(love, friendship, harmony, sympathy, congeniality, companionship, alliance, kindliness.)*

annex—*v*. attach, incorporate, acquire, subjoin, unite, add, expropriate, seize, appendage. *(detachment, detach, disconnect, remove, separate, disengage.)*

annihilate—*v*. nullify, destory, exterminate, eradicate, abolish, extirpate, liquidate, demolish, efface, erase, uproot, end. *(create, keep, cherish, build, make, develop, augment, cultivate, construct, foster, perpetuate, let live.)*

announce—*v*. speak, enunciate, circulate, herald, trumpet, broadcast, declare, publish, report, divulge, reveal. *(refrain, hush, suppress, withhold, silence, hide, stifle, smother, reserve, bury.)*

annoy—*v*. bore, badger, irritate, tease, plague, nag, exasperate, provoke, pester, incommode, harass, chafe, inconvenience, molest. *(appease, calm, foster, mollify, console, conciliate, cherish, solace, calm, please.)*

anomaly—*n*. rarity, abnormality, eccentricity, exception, aberration, oddity, peculiarity. *(the norm, the rule, conformity, specimen, illustration, regularity, exemplification.)*

anonymous—*adj*. nameless, unsigned, unacknowledged, unattested, authorless, unauthenticated, unnamed. *(acknowledged, signed, identified, known, attested, verified, named, authorized.)*

answer—*n*. plea, reply, defense, solution, vindication, apology, retort, counterpart, acknowledgment, confutation, response. *(question, inquiry, call, summons, interrogation, challenge, ask.)*

antecedent—*adj.* anterior, earlier, prior, previous, preliminary, former. *(later, posterior, consequent, succeeding, following.)*

anticipate—*v.* await, expect, prevent, count upon, hope for, prepare, forecast, forsee, apprehend, forestall. *(despair of, fear, remember, cure, doubt, dread, misapprehend, remedy, recollect.)*

anticipation—*n.* prospect, awaiting, foresight, prevention, preclusion, preconception, prelibation, provision, antepast. *(non-expectation, realization, unprepardness, surprise, consummation, enjoyment.)*

antipathy—*n.* dislike, hatred, aversion, enmity, rancor, bitterness, repugnance, ill-will, digust, abhorrence. *(affinity, respect, regard, sympathy, love, approval, esteem, reverence, affection.)*

antique—*adj.* ancient, quaint, relic, curio, objet d'art. trinket, antiquated, pristene, immemorial. *(new, modern, recent, modish, fashionable, current, up-to-date, stylish.)*

anxiety—*n.* unease, worry, trouble, solicitude, misgiving, anguish, concern, apprehension, fear. *(contentment, relief, apathy, ease, aplomb, nonchalance, tranquility, composure.)*

anxious—*adj.* uneasy, keen, watchful, solicitous, ardent, concerned, careful, intent, restless. *(careless, cool,* inert, certain, confident, ease, unruffled, nonchalent.)*

apathy—*n.* insensibility, unconcern, passiveness, indifference, coolness, lack of interest. *(concern, interest, care, sensibility, eagerness, fervor, zeal, irritability.)*

ape—*v.* simulate, copy, mimic, echo, mock, follow, imitate, emulate. *(vary, change, modify, not to imitate, originate.)*

apiece—*adv.* analytically, each, respectively, severally, individually. *(together, en masse, synthetically, collectively, overall, as a group.)*

apology—*n.* explanation, plea, defense, confession, pretext, evasion, vindication, excuse, acknowledgment of error. *(wrong, censure, offense, impeachment, insult, charge, complaint, accusation, injury.)*

appal—*v.* daunt, dismay, shock, alarm, horrify, revolt, discourage, abash, sicken, frighten, cow, nauseate. *(rally, calm, reassure, please, attract, console, comfort, encourage.)*

apparel—*n.* garments, robes, attire, vesture, habit, togs, costume, dress, clothing, gear. *(rags, nudity, divestiture, dishabille, tatters.)*

apparent—*adj.* understandable, evident, obvious, visible, likely, overt, presumable, ostensible, conspicious, certain, distinct, open. *(hidden, real, veiled, disguised, obscure, uncertain, improbable, inapparent, dubious.)*

appeal—v. invoke, beseech, urge, request, apply, plea, petition, solicit, address, invite, apostrophize. (deny, disclaim, recall, refuse, repudiate, protest, reject, disavow.)

appearance—n. advent, arrival, appearing, aspect, manner, look, pretense, manifestation, emergence, coming. (vanishing, passing, concealment, departure, unlikelihood, presumption.)

append—v. add, attach, join, supplement, fasten, affix, hang. (remove, omit, separate, disconnect, subtract, detach, take away.)

appetite—n. passion, yearning, craving, tendency, gusto, thirst, proclivity, zest, impulse, want, propension. (apathy, dislike, surfeit, loathing, repugnance, aversion, fill, revulsion, hatred.)

applause—n. plaudits, eulogy, cheers, acclamation, ovation, fanfare, praise, commendation, homage, compliments, encoring, approval. (disapproval, blame, condemnation, criticism, contempt, ridicule, hissing, obloquy, vituperation.)

applicable—adj. germane, useful, apropos, pertinent, appropriate, apt, suitable. (unfit, wrong, irrelevant, inconducive, useless, unsuitable.)

appoint—v. establish, arrange, allot, apportion, nominate, select, employ, choose, fix, prescribe, elect, invest, institute, ordain. (fire, cancel, dismiss, discharge, reverse, withdraw, suspend,

disappoint, strip, dismantle, divest, recall.)

apportion—v. allocate, ration, distribute, administer, dole out, dispense, share, deal, consign, prorate, adjust. (resume, reappoint, collect, give all, divert, assemble, retain, receive, reserve, withhold, gather.)

appreciate—v. cherish, recognize, regard, value, relish, admire, savor, acknowledge, respect, treasure. (disparage, depreciate, misconceive, ignore, misjudge, deflate, underrate, belittle.)

apprehend—v. seize, detect, arrest, dread, comprehend, fear, discern, anticipate, catch, capture, understand, perceive. (lose, liberate, ignore, misconjecture, misapprehend, release, free, discharge, let go.)

apprentice—n. pupil, novice, neophyte, beginner, student, indentured assistant. (master, expert, professional.)

approach—v. advance, gain upon, near. (leave, retreat, diverge, exist, retire.)

appropriate—v. take, confiscate, expropriate, allocate, allot, set apart, assign, earmark. (donate, relinquish, cede.)

approve—v. praise, sanction, respect, authorize, second, prize, cherish, value. (repudiate, censure, dislike, criticize, reject, refute, disown.)

approximate—adj. resemble, near, border, nearly equal, abut, closely resemble, suggest, verge on. *(precise, vary, exact, accurate, correct, recede, deviate, differ.)*

apt—*adj.* clever, suitable, proper, liable, relevant, pertinent, ready, seemly, apropos, **appropriate.** *(awkward, averse, slow, inapt, illtimed, dull, improper.)*

arbitrary—*adj.* despotic, harsh, willful, capricious, fanciful, tyrannical, selfish, irresponsible, domineering, whimsical. *(lenient, impersonal, modest, objective, limited, constitutional, lawful.)*

arbitrate—*v.* adjust, compose, mediate, adjudicate, settle, umpire, judge, referee, decide. *(claim, negotiate, dispute, litigate, misjudge, appeal.)*

ardent—*adj.* fervent, eager, warm, passionate, vehement, fierce, emotional, lusty, keen, feverish, zealous, burning, earnest. *(cold, nonchalant, apathetic, unloving, frigid, phlegmatic, passionless, detached, indifferent.)*

argue—*v.* dispute, battle, wrangle, reason, question, imply, demonstrate, bicker, quibble, denote. *(propound, agree, concur, assert, doubt, conceal, command, assent.)*

argument—*n.* controversy, quarrel, dispute, reasoning, debate, embroilment, altercation, clash. *(assumption, agreement, harmony, assertion, rebuttal, response, accord.)*

arid—*adj.* barren, sterile, dry, unproductive, lifeless, dreary, dull. *(damp, fertile,* lush, pithy, luxuriant, moist, productive, lively, verdant.)

aromatic—*adj.* sweet smelling, scented, fragrant, spicy, pungent, odoriferous. *(unscented, rank, putrid, acrid, bad smelling, malodorous.)*

arouse—*v.* stimulate, animate, spur, kindle, stir, incite, provoke, foster, quicken, whet, goad, excite. *(mollify, pacify, still, alleviate, calm, quell, allay, mitigate, dampen.)*

arraign—*v.* impute, cite, accuse, indict, impeach, denounce, prosecute. *(condone, pardon, discharge, acquit, vindicate, absolve, exonerate.)*

arrange—*v.* array, classify, marshall, rank, adjust, pose, systematize, sort, harmonize, prepare, order, parcel. *(scatter, disarray, strip, jumble, confuse, disperse, derange, divest, disturb.)*

array—*v.* deploy, don, garnish, place, dispose, arrange, attire, decorate. *(confuse, jumble, strip, mess up, disarray, denude.)*

arrest—*v.* capture, hold, halt, retain, apprehend, catch, detain, hinder, obstruct, suspend, incarcerate. *(free, release, let go, discharge, liberate, dismiss.)*

arrive—*v.* approach, near, enter, attain, land, come, reach, succeed, make good. *(start, leave, depart, retire, embark, withdraw.)*

arrogance—*n.* contemptuousness, hauteur, assurance, loftiness, vanity, conceit, egoism, self-importance, discourtesy, swagger, contempt. *(shyness, modesty, meekness, bashfulness, humility, simplicity, deference, courtesy, politeness, self-effacement.)*

artful—*adj.* maneuvering, subtle, shrewd, diplomatic, scheming, contriving, deceitful, underhand. *(innocent, open, natural, candid, unsophisticated, frank, naive, simple.)*

artificial—*adj.* false, invented, manmade, imitation, fake, simulated, concocted, unnatural, phony, synthetic. *(genuine, real, natural, spontaneous, artless, unaffected, sincere, candid, actual, frank.)*

ascertain—*v.* establish, verify, confirm, prove, learn, detect, settle, ferret out. *(surmise, suppose, conjecture, presume, guess.)*

ascribe—*v.* credit, refer, render, trace to, charge, arrogate, impute, assign. *(discount, refuse, dissociate, deny, disconnect.)*

askew—*adv., adj.* crooked, awry, lopsided, aslant, crookedly. *(line, aligned, plumb, straight as an arrow.)*

aspiration—*n.* ambition, hope, yearning, endeavor, daydream, purpose, desire, effort, craving. *(dullness, inertia, aversion, aimlessness, callousness, repudiation.)*

assembly—*n.* throng, council, conclave, meeting, conference, collection, pack, gathering, body, flock, congregation. *(disunion, dismissal, disruption, dissipation.)*

assent—*v.* accede, acquiesce, agree, approve, allow, comply, concur, yield, permit, acknowledge. *(differ, dissent, deny, repudiate, disclaim, reject, negate, refuse, veto.)*

assign—*v.* name, apportion, refer, allot to, convey, specify, stipulate, determine, prescribe. *(retain, disconnect, withhold, discharge, keep, open, divest, hold in abeyance.)*

assist—*v.* collaborate, reinforce, succor, support, cooperate, aid, boost, help, second, uphold, abet, serve. *(hamper, impede, obstruct, antagonize, clog, counteract, oppose.)*

assistant—*n.* aider, attendant, ally, partner, adjutant, aide, auxiliary, colleague, accomplice, helper. *(rival, foe, opposer, hinderer, antagonist.)*

association—*n.* companionship, alliance, membership, society, fellowship, partnership, corporation, league, intimacy, friendship, community. *(solitude, avoidance, severance, disunion, disconnection, separation, alienation, independence.)*

assortment—*n.* quantity, stock, collection, variety, miscellany, lot, motley, store, conglomeration, diversity, array. *(misplacement, sameness, monotony, mixing, heaping together, displacement.)*

assume—*v.* arrogate, postulate, uphold, certify, wear, fancy, infer, presume, judge, surmise, gather. *(allow, render, concede, know, prove, leave, relinquish, put aside.)*

assure—*v.* promise, rally, encourage, aid, uphold, guarantee, clinch, secure, confirm, ensure, advise, certify. *(deter, warn, age, unsettle, intimidate, deny, refute, lie, disavow, fib, doubt.)*

astonish—*v.* amaze, surprise, startle, stun, shock, alarm, stupefy, daze, stagger, dumb, perplex, confuse, bewilder. *(rally, embolden, encourage, assure, anticipate, foresee, bore, count upon.)*

astray—*adj., adv.* loose, missing, erring, wrong, amiss, afield, off, into error. *(close, safe, at home, right, on course.)*

athletic—*adj.* muscular, powerful, brawny, burly, strong, strapping, manly, vigorous, herculean, sinewy, hardy. *(puny, feeble, effeminate, fragile, weak, frail, strengthless.)*

atrocious—*adj.* diabolical, wicked, shameful, infamous, ruthless, savage, monstrous, cruel, flagrant, nefarious, brutal. *(humane, kind, admirable, benevolent, gentle, chivalrous, merciful, noble.)*

attach—*v.* conciliate, tie, adhere, couple, add, secure, bind, unite, fasten, append, annex, join. *(loosen, detach, estrange, untie, release, disconnect, alienate.)*

attack—*v.* censure, invade, besiege, storm, threaten, assault, aggress, criticize. *(vindicate, retreat, defend, support, sustain, excuse, uphold, resist, befriend, cover.)*

attack—*n.* assault, onset, pelt, invasion, stone, aggres-sion, onslaught, trespass. *(protection, aid, withdrawal, support, flight, defense, resistance.)*

attain—*v.* grasp, acquire, procure, win, master, fulfill, execute, reach, accomplish, reap, score. *(forfeit, lose, miss, let go, fail at, abandon, fall short of.)*

attempt—*v.* strive, venture, force, experiment, undertake, effort, violate, aim, hazard. *(abandon, dismiss, neglect, shun, disregard, drop, pretermit.)*

attend—*v.* observe, escort, oversee, listen, mark, watch, superintend, mind, notice, guard, serve, note. *(disregard, forsake, miss, leave, skip, ignore, desert, disassociate, abandon, wander.)*

attention—*n.* alertness, care, consideration, study, respect, civility, concentration, thought, note, observation, concern. *(remission, carelessness, absence, neglect, rudeness, abstraction, negligence, unconcern.)*

attest—*v.* certify, corroborate, display, support, vouch, aver, show evidence, seal, testify, prove, authenticate, imply, ratify, warrant, demonstrate, suggest. *(contradict, exclude, refute, deny, belie, disprove, negate, falsify, exclude.)*

attire—*v.* garb, costume, dress, outfit. *(strip, bare, undress, disrobe, unclothe.)*

attract—*v.* dispose, allure, pull, fascinate, enchant, evoke, influence, captivate, invite, precipitate. *(estrange,* repel, alienate, disgust, offend, deter.)

attractive—adj. magnetic, winning, alluring, enticing, handsome, fetching, chic, elegant, tasteful, charming, lovely, fair, captivating. (repugnant, deformed, loathsome, ugly, repulsive, repellent, unattractive, unpleasant, deterrent.)

attribute—v. assign, arrogate, refer, connect, credit, blame, associate. (disconnect, divorce, dissever, dissociate.)

attribute—n. characteristic, sign, indication, reduction, erosion, weakening, quality. (essence, substance, its correlative, viz, etc. misnomer, mask, semblance.)

attrition—n. repentance, erosion, remorse, friction, sorrow, self-reproach, grinding. (cállousness, buildup, relentlessness, strengthening, impenitence.)

audacious—adj. adventurous, reckless, rash, hardy, brave, valiant, impudent, insolent, fearless, dauntless. (cautious, timid, unenterprising, shy, humble, polite, cowardly, unventuresome.)

audacity—n. temerity, boldness, daring, recklessness, spunk, nerve, effrontery, arrogance. (self-preservation, prudence, forethought, calculation, caution, timidity, meekness, gentility.)

augment—v. enlarge, swell, inflate, increase, add, acquire, supply, deepen, amplify, widen, magnify. (withdrawal, lose, reduce, diminish, subside, curtail, detract, waste,

abridge, narrow, shrink, lessen.)

augury—n. omen, prediction, conjecture, forerunner, indication, herald, forecasting. (science, experience, observation.)

auspicious—adj. lucky, successful, hopeful, timely, felicitous, right, golden, fortunate, opportune, encouraging. (unfavorable, abortive, hopeless, ill-fated, unpromising, doomed, pathetic, unlucky.)

austere—adj. rigid, strict, spartan, grave, severe, stiff, rigorous, harsh, chaste, stark. (affable, tender, cheerful, sunny, mild, lavish, indulgent, relaxed.)

authentic—adj. real, true, accurate, genuine, actual, bona fide, legitimate, reliable, dependable, factual, accredited, trustworthy. (false, fake, disputed, unauthorized, sham, unreliable, deceptive, corrupt, fraudulent, counterfeit, fictitious, untrue, phony.)

authoritative—adj. conclusive, sure, potent, imperious, sanctioned, ruling, lordly, dogmatic, firm, arrogant, autocratic, tyrannical, commanding, peremptory. (vague, vacillating, deceptive, weak, inconclusive, servile, meek, bland, indefinite, conciliatory, affable, frivolous, invalid.)

authority—n. authenticity, control, weight, supremacy, jurisdiction, sufferance, prestige, rule, esteem, force, command, direction, respect, administration, influence. (indecision, weakness, groundlessness, servility, wrong, inconclusiveness, servitude, incompetency, inoperativeness.)

autocratic—adj. arbitrary, absolute, tyrannical, depotic, czaristic, dictatorial, irresponsible. (subordinate, limited, democratic, lenient, indulgent, constitutional, responsible.)

auxilliary—adj. abetting, conducive, helping, secondary, backup, ancillary. (superfluous, cumbersome, chief, primary, irrelevant, unassisting.)

avail—v. hold, endure, service, aid, utilize, profit, answer, suffice, benefit, use. (fall, betray, harm, ignore, hinder, disappoint.)

available—adj. convertible, handy, on tap, obtainable, accessible, applicable, helpful, suitable. (inappropriate, inoperative, inconducive, unobtainable, unserviceable.)

avarice—n. cupidity, stinginess, griping, venality, greed, covetousness, penury, miserliness, greediness, rapacity. (bountifulness, extravagance, waste, generosity, liberality, munificence.)

aver—v. oblige, protest, affirm, insist, profess, avow, maintain. (contradict, repudiate, disclaim, doubt, dispute, deny, be uncertain.)

avidity—n. eagerness, longing, varacity, hankering, greed, ravenousness, desire. (apathy, nausea, repugnance, loathing, coldness, unwillingness, disdain, aversion.)

avoid—v. abandon, forsake, eschew, shun, fly, elude, escape, dodge, shirk, evade. (approach, address, court, invite, pursue, find, solicit, accost.)

award—v. attribute, accord, divide, give, confer on, assign, decree, grant, determine. (withdraw, retain, withhold, refuse, deny, misappropriate.)

aware—adj. sensible, certified, knowledgeable, mindful, conversant, cognizant, informed, known. (insensible, unaware, ignorant, unmindful, oblivious, unconscious.)

awful—adj. appalling, ugly, dreadful, solemn, horrendous, deplorable, ghastly, hideous, portentous. (unalarming, alluring, terrific, pretty, unnoticeable, likeable, delightful, unimposing.)

awkward—adj. clownish, unhandy, unskillful, uncouth, boorish, stiff, gauche, ungainly. (agile, neat, dexterous, deft, adroit, supple, nimble.)

axiom—n. Truth, aphorism, postulate, maxim, principle, self-evidence. (absurdness, paradox, absurdity, nonsense, contradiction.)

B

babble—n. dribble, gabble, jabbering, twaddle, cackle, chatter, prattle, chitchat.

(sense, wisdom, learning, knowledge, understanding, erudition.)

babel—*n.* clamor, din, clang, turmoil, confusion, bedlam, hubbub, discord, jargon. *(articulation, calm, intonation, monotony, elocution, enunciation, tranquility, distinctness, consecutiveness.)*

backing—*n.* help, assistance, sanction, endorsement, succor, aid, championing, cooperation. *(opposition, hindrance, resistance, subversion, repudiation.)*

bad—*adj.* defective, useless, imperfect, faulty, unfit, awful, inferior, below par, inadequate. *(excellent, fine, first rate, superior, exemplary, healthful, agreeable, pleasant.)*

baffle—*v.* disconcert, defeat, mystify, frustrate, elude, neutralize, amaze, counteract, perplex, dodge, foil, mar, restrain, balk, estop, counterfoil, upset, mock. *(aid, promote, transmit, point, assist, allow, encourage, advance, abet, enforce.)*

bait—*n.* decoy, allurement, hound, snare, inducement, badger, morsel, tease. *(intimidation, calm, deterrent, soothing, warning, prohibition, lull, dissuasion.)*

balance—*v.* estimate, weigh, pit, equalize, counteract, adjust, set, redress. *(tilt, subvert, overbalance, upset, cant, mispoise.)*

balk—*v.* thwart, nullify, defeat, impede, baffle, circumvent, hinder, prevent, bar, foil, estop, frustrate, stop, counteract. *(promote, aid, cooperate, encourage, in-stigate, progress, advance, abet.)*

balm—*n.* solve, emollient, sedative, narcotic, panacea, comfort, tranquilizer. *(stimulant, abrasive, irritant, nuisance.)*

balmy—*adj.* mild, pleasant, temperate, soft, gentle, refreshing, soothing. *(inclement, stormy, unpleasant, irritating, chafing, sensible, sound, normal.)*

banish—*v.* abandon, extrude, relegate, exile, repudiate, eject, eliminate, expel, expatriate, disclaim, eradicate. *(admit, cherish, protect, accept, foster, encourage, entertain, harbor, domiciliate, locate, retain.)*

banquet—*n.* festivity, carouse, dine, feast, treat, entertainment, cheer, repast. *(starvation, fast, snack, abstinence.)*

banter—*n.* mockery, irony, chaff, joshing, jesting, ridicule, badinage, ragging. *(discourse, kid, needle, argument, discussion, jolly, ride.)*

bar—*v.* obstruct, hinder, impede, thwart, restrain, exclude, forbid. *(allow, permit, let, accept, admit, welcome, receive, invite.)*

bargain—*n.* business, gain, agreement, speculation, pact, profit, treaty, transaction, hawking, haggling. *(misprofit, extravagance, swindle, loss.)*

barren—*adj.* depleted, useless, futile, ineffectual, dull, unfruitful, prosaic, uninformative, unrewarding, stale. *(productive, fertile, prolific, lush, rich, luxuriant, fruitful, interesting, instructive.)*

base—*adj.* vile, sordid, mean, pedestal, infamous, ignoble, source, cheap, corrupt, worthless, shameful, vulgar, dishonorable. *(exalted, noble, esteemed, correct, pure, precious, virtuous, shrill, honored, lofty, refined, valued.)*

bashful—*adj.* diffident, shy, timorous, modest, sheepish, retiring, reserved. *(impudent, forward, brazen, bold, impudent, arrogant, pert, unreserved, conceited.)*

basic—*adj.* fundamental, vital, essential, cardinal, key, necessary, care, prime, prerequisite. *(supporting, secondary, frill, trivial, accessory, superfluous, extra.)*

battle—*n.* skirmish, contest, engagement, fight, massacre, action, encounter, conflict, combat. *(harmony, truce, council, peace, reconcile, arbitrament, mediation.)*

bawl—*v.* roar, bellow, yell, clamor, vociferate, shout. *(babble, whisper, whimper, mumble, weep, wail.)*

beach—*n.* coast, seaboard, shore, seashore, rim, sands, water edge. *(deep, main, ocean, sea.)*

beaming—*adj.* radiant, bright, transparent, happy, gleaming, glowing, beautiful, translucid. *(opague, wan, gloomy, dingy, matt, sullen, morose.)*

bear—*v.* transport, maintain, brace, tolerate, sustain, lift, undergo, buttress, carry, admit, suffer, support, harbor, enact, endure, generate, produce. *(protest, eject, stroke, surrender, shed, resent, defend, relinquish, drop, reject, repel, decline.)*

beat—*v.* whack, conquer, pound, pommel, strike, batter, overcome, truncheon, surpass, vanquish, thrash, belabor. *(stroke, shield, defend, submit, relinquish, fall, surrender, protect, caress.)*

beauty—*n.* grace, exquisiteness, embellishment, radiance, picturesqueness, adornment, attractiveness, bloom, comeliness. *(ugliness, bareness, repulsiveness, foulness, hideousness, homeliness, unattractiveness.)*

because—*conj.* consequently, accordingly, owing, on account of. *(independently, inconsequently, unconnectedly, irrespectively.)*

becoming—*adj.* neat, proper, seemly, enhancing, comely, graceful, befitting, pleasing, decorous, improving, beseeming, fit. *(unseemly, indecent, unattractive, uncomely, unbecoming, ungraceful, unsuitable, incongruous, derogatory.)*

befitting—*adj.* becoming, expedient, proper, relevant, desirable, appropriate, consistent, seemly, fitting, decent. *(unsuitable, improper, obligatory, unseemly, improper, inexpedient, compulsory, meaningless, incomptible, unbecoming.)*

before—*adv.* anteriorly, prior to, foremost, precedently, first. *(subsequently, later, afterwards, following, behind, after.)*

beg—*v.* request, supplicate, implore, plead, ask, petition, pray, crave, solicit.

(exact, require, demand, insist, give, bestow.)

begin—*v.* prepare, originate, inaugurate, initiate, start, arise, create, commence. *(complete, conclude, stop, finish, achieve, consummate, terminate, expire.)*

beginning—*n.* start, rise, outbreak, opening, source, foundation, precedent, prelude, inception, commencement, preface, threshold, outset, initiation, preparation. *(finale, close, conclusion, completion, end, termination, consummation.)*

behavior—*n.* comportment, manner, deportment, actions, conduct, demeanor, proceeding, attitude. *(misbehavior, misconduct, misdemeanor.)*

belief—*n.* credence, faith, opinion, acceptance, trust, confidence, creed, persuasion, admission, concession, avowal, reliance, permission. *(distrust, misgiving, skepticism, unbelief, denial, incredulity, disavowal, rejection.)*

belligerent—*adj.* hostile, pugnacious, quarrelsome, combative, defiant, argumentative, warlike, embattled, cantankerous. *(easygoing, cool, compromising, pacific, conciliatory, amicable.)*

belonging—*adj.* connected, obligatory, congenial, cognate, accompanying, related. *(alien, uninvolved, independant, optional, unrelated, discretional, irrelevant, unconnected, impertinent, unimplied, uncongenial.)*

bend—*v.* incline, swerve, curve, bias, buckle, mold, influence, accompany, twist, deviate, lean. *(extend, advance, straighten, proceed, stiffen, crush, resist, continue.)*

benediction—*n.* commendation, blessing, thanksgiving, gratitude, boon, dedication, prayer. *(censure, curse, calumniation, obloquy, execration, malediction, disapproval.)*

benefactor—*n.* contributor, upholder, welldoer, backer, subscriber, friend, donor, subsidizer, well-wisher. *(antagonist, foe, rival, backfriend, oppressor, disfavor, opponent.)*

beneficial—*adj.* salutory, wholesome, valuable, profitable, healthful, advantageous, good. *(noxious, detrimental, prejudicial, destructive, unprofitable, hurtful, baneful.)*

benefit—*n.* service, utility, good, profit, asset, advantage, blessing, reward, favor, avail, use. *(damage, injury, privation, detriment, handicap, calamity, bereavement, hinder.)*

benign—*adj.* kindly, warm, generous, amiable, benevolent, altruistic, affable. *(cold, hostile, violent, malign, nasty, mean, inclement.)*

bequeath—*v.* grant, devise, bestow, endow, give, impart, demise, leave, render, *(alienate, withhold.)*

bereavement—*n.* affliction, loss, destitution, adversity, tragedy, deprivation. *(donation, restoration, gift, substitution, consolation, blessing.)*

bestial—*adj.* animalistic, barbaric, wild, brutish, inhuman, disgusting. *(human, benevolent, compassionate, gentle, humane.)*

betray—*v.* delude, circumvent, abandon, deceive, dupe, defect, reveal, manifest, dishonor, ensnare. *(foster, dare, overlook, be faithful, support, protect, guard, cherish, adhere, preserve, cover.)*

better—*adj.* superior, finer, preferable, choicer, worthier. *(poorer, worse, inferior, lesser, second-rate.)*

beware—*v.* refrain, heed, take warning, care, fear, mind, consider, avoid. *(overlook, neglect, brave, dare, incur, ignore.)*

bewilder—*v.* confound, puzzle, muddle, astonish, nonplus, disconcert, daze, perplex, fluster, mystify, mislead. *(inform, instruct, advise, guide, edify, lead, educate.)*

bewitch—*v.* fascinate, charm, entrance, beguile, enchant, enrapture, captivate. *(disgust, disillusionize, exorcise, disenchant, repulse.)*

bias—*n.* prejudice, bent, proclivity, feeling, idea, preconception, inclination, bigotry. *(fairness, impartiality, objectivity, tolerance, dispassionateness.)*

bid—*v.* request, direct, tell, charge, offer, summon, command, propose, enjoin, greet. *(deter, restrain, forbid, prohibit, ban, dissallow.)*

bide—*v.* remain, stay, await, continue, tolerate, tarry, anticipate, suffer, stand, expect, abide. *(depart, move, resent, abominate, quit, move, repel, go, migrate, rebel, resist.)*

big—*adj.* wide, proud, fat, arrogant, mammoth, huge, pompous, enormous, massive, large, bulky. *(narrow, slight, easy, microscopic, lean, affable, petite, small, minute, little.)*

binding—*adj.* restraining, costive, mandatory, obligatory, styptic, compelling, astringent, restrictive. *(enlarging, flexible, loosening, elastic, opening, distending.)*

birth—*n.* nativity, origin, parentage, lineage, inception, source, race, nobility, beginning, rise, family, extraction. *(plebeianism, death, miscarriage, extinction, end.)*

bitter—*adj.* sharp, tart, severe, caustic, acrimonious, intense, afflictive, astringent, harsh, sarcastic, sad, stinging, pungent, cutting, acrid. *(pleasant, trivial, light, kindly, bland, mellow, genial, insipid, affable, mitigated, sweet.)*

blacken—*v.* befowl, defame, calumniate, asperse, discredit, malign, bespatter, slander, vilify, smear, dishonor, decry. *(eulogize, praise, vindicate, clear, exalt.)*

blame—*v.* chide, reproach, dispraise, reprove, condemn, accuse, reprobate, reprehend, rebuke, censure, vituperate, disapprove, burden. *(exonerate, praise, approve, excuse, acquit, encourage, vindicate, exculpate.)*

bland—*adj.* gentle, courteous, gracious, monotonous, soft, complaisant, mild, tender, benign, prosaic, affable. *(abrupt, exciting, harsh, severe, rough.)*

blank—*adj.* vacant, clean, dull, empty, hollow, plain, futile, void. *(full, marked, busy, alert, sharp, valuable, significant, consequential.)*

blast—*v.* wither, shrivel, destroy, blight, ruin, wreck. *(swell, restore, expand, enlarge.)*

blast—*n.* explosion, burst, destruction, gale, tempest, tornado, squall, breeze, afflation, flurry, squall, frustration. *(neutralization, zephyr, gentle breeze, puff.)*

blatant—*adj.* gross, cheap, unpolished, harsh, noisy, crude, uncouth, tawdry, vulgar, tasteless. *(subtle, delicate, cultured, agreeable, unobtusive, acquiescent, genteel.)*

bleak—*adj.* bare, exposed, stormy, grim, open, dreary, nipping, blank, cold. *(verdant, halcyonic, balmy, warm, sheltered, lush, luxuriant, zephyrous, flourishing.)*

blemish—*n.* blot, speck, stain, obvious, blur, spot, tarnish, dishonor, gross, taint, disfigurement, disgrace, defect, daub, flow, discoloration. *(honor, purity, perfection, intactness, refinement, unsulliedness.)*

blend—*v.* harmonize, combine, merge, fuse, mingle, coalesce, amalgamate, unite, complement, assimilate. *(divide, separate, split, run, dissociate, confound, divide.)*

bless—*v.* gladden, endow, thank, consecrate, enrich, cheer, sanctify, felicitate, rejoice. *(ignore, sadden, condemn, deprive, curse, impoverish, harm, anathematize.)*

blind—*eyeless, ignorant, visionless, unseeing, unaware, depraved, prejudiced, unperceptive, unconscious, undiscerning, irrational. (penetrating, keen, clearsighted, aware, concerned, conscious, rational, farsighted, sensitive, discriminating.)*

blink—*v.* connive, ignore, wink, squint, overlook, peer. *(note, mark, visit, notice, be aware of.)*

bliss—*n.* joy, rapture, luxury, ectasy, blessedness, paradise. *(woe, suffering, agony, condemnation, misery, accursedness, grief, gloom.)*

blockhead—*n.* dunce, dullard, booby, numskull, clod, dolt, ignoramus, ninny, chump, simpleton, dunderhead, loggerhead. *(luminary, adept, sage, savant, scholar, philosopher, schoolman.)*

bloom—*v.* blossom, height, perfection, prime, flourish, prosper, succeed, blush, florescence. *(decay, dwindle, wane, languish, waste away.)*

blooming—*adj.* flowering, young, flourishing, vigorous, beautiful, fair, blossoming, exuberant. *(blighted, old, fading, unsightly, withering, waning, paralysed, deformed, declining, blasted.)*

blot—*v.* tarnish, sully, discolor, obliterate, blur, blotch, smear, stain, erase, daub, obscure, pollute, smutch, spoil, stigma. *(clear, perpetuate, cleanse, honor, elucidate, conserve, credit.)*

blow—*n.* breath, knock, bang, puff, stroke, crack, shock, wound, calamity, disappointment, blast, affliction, misfortune, tragedy. *(consolation, comfort, sparing, calm, assuagement, relief, caress.)*

bluff—*adj.* bold, frank, rude, swaggering, blunt, gruff, surly, open, brusk, discourteous, rough, bullying, hectoring, coarse, blustering. *(courteous, polite, inclined, undulating, suave, inabrupt, reserved, polished.)*

blunder—*n.* mistake, fault, inaccuracy, indescretion, slip, oversight, delusion, fumble, error, omission. *(exactness, prevention, correction, success, foresight, accuracy, achievement, truthfulness, faultlessness, atonement, hit.)*

blush—*n.* flush, carnation, confusion, bloom, glow, color, shame, self-reproach, guiltiness, aspect, complexion. *(unconsciousness, purity, effrontery, paleness, innocence, ashen, boldness, quiltlessness.)*

boast—*v.* brag, swell, bluster, flaunt, truimph, vapor, glory, exhibit. *(be ashamed, disclaimer, cover up, deprecate, disavow.)*

body—*n.* mass, collection, organization, assemblage, association, whole, matter, substantiality, corporation, substance, denseness. *(soul, individual, intellect, spirit, mind.)*

boggle—*v.* blunder, halt, demur, blotch, spoil, vacillate, botch, hesitate, falter, dubitate. *(advance, face, beautify, clear, perfect, refine, encounter, advance, complete.)*

boisterous—*adj.* tumultuous, rowdy, obstreperous, shrill, clamorous, rambunctious, unruly, wild, loud. *(well-behaved, orderly, quiet, restrained, calm, tranquil, sedate, serene, disciplined.)*

bold—*adj.* fearless, brave, forward, dauntless, audacious, courageous, stout, daring, intrepid, brazen, lionhearted, adventurous. *(bashful, fearful, meek, timid, shy, weak, retiring.)*

bombast—*n.* braggadocio, bluster, pomposity, fustian, extravagance, tumidity, rhodomontade, gasconade, bravado. *(humility, truthfulness, refrain, modesty, veracity, reserve, shyness.)*

bond—*n.* association, compact, obligation, cement, link, tie, chain, security, fastening, manacle. *(honor, option, freedom, discretion, detachment.)*

bondsman—*n.* serf, captive, vassal, toiler, prisoner, slave. *(freeman, yeoman, master, lord, gentleman, aristocrat.)*

boost—*v.* lift, hoist, raise, elevate, pitch, shove, press, push, promote. *(reduce, decline, diminish, lessen, curtail, ease, deduct, belittle.)*

border—*n.* brink, rim, edge, circumference, limit, boundry, perimeter, hem, confine, enclosure, brim, band. *(tract,* space, middle, center, land, inside, interior.)

border on—v. be adjacent to, adjoin, be conterminous with, approach, come near. (be remote from, be away from.)

botch—v. jumble, mar, blunder, fumble, patch, disconcert, muff, cabble, spoil, mess, fail. (trim, mend, perform, embroider, master, harmonize, beautify, handle, manipulate, perfect.)

bother—n. worry, fuss, excitement, confusion, flurry, trouble. (orderliness, quiet, comfort, calm, composure, peace, solace.)

boundless—adj. infinite, illimitable, immense; unlimited, endless, unbounded, immeasurable. (limited, circumscribed, restricted, small, confined, narrow, bounded.)

bounty—n. benevolence, donation, charity, assistance, munificence, gratuity, liberality, gift, generosity, aid. (closeness, stinginess, niggardliness, avarice, hardness, churlishness, greed.)

brag—v. swagger, extol, bully, boast, crow, vaunt. (whimper, deprecate, cringe, whine.)

branch—n. bough, member, limb, channel, shoot, twig, ramification, relative, tributary, scion, bifurcation, offspring. (house, trunk, stock, race, family, mass, stem, conglomerate.)

brave—adj. courageous, valiant, heroic, dauntless, unafraid, plucky, fearless, stalwart. (cowardly, fearful,

craven, timid, timorous, frightened, faint hearted.)

break—v. rupture, shatter, destroy, fragment, demolish, fracture, tame, burst, mangle, infringe, violate, subdue, smash, shiver, sever, split, tear. (conjoin, observe, obey, repair, heal, conserve, rally, service, protect, piece.)

breath—n. inspiration, respiration, exhalation, aspiration, expiration, inhalation. (passing, death, perishing, cessation, departure, dying.)

breeding—n. education, training, nurture, manners, air, decorum, discipline, gentility, culture. (ill-training, ill-manners, ill-breeding, ignorance, ill-behavior.)

brevity—n. compendiousness, abbreviation, terseness, curtness, shortness, conciseness, closeness, briefness, pointedness. (diffuseness, tediousness, verbosity, length, elongation, prolixity, extension, garrulity.)

bright—adj. luminous, happy, joyous, glowing, shining, cheerful, brilliant, intense, burnished, lucid, witty, radiant, sparkling, vivid. (dull, joyless, imbecile, pallid, opaque, dead, sullen, cheerless, morose, muddy, slow, stupid.)

brilliant—adj. shining, beaming, glorious, gleaming, flashing, radiant, luminous, resplendent, sparkling, lustrous. (opaque, dull, tarnished, lusterless, lifeless.)

bring—v. convey, bear, import, transport, fetch, carry, induce, produce, initiate, procure, cause. (debar, prevent, subtract, quash, remove, exclude, dispel, abstract, export.)

brisk—*adj.* vivacious, alert, quick, animated, vigorous, lively, active, prompt, spry, spirited, nimble, sprightly. *(dull, indolent, lethargic, slow, stagnant, heavy, lazy, inactive, unenergetic.)*

broad—*adj.* expansive, liberal, indelicate, voluminous, wide, coarse, extensive, spacious, generic, unreserved, ample. *(confined, prejudiced, narrow-minded, slender, restricted, pointed, delicate, veiled, shaded, precise, specific, enigmatical, illiberal, reserved, bigoted.)*

brotherhood—*n.* association, fellowship, society, affiliation, sodality, comradeship. *(no antonyms).*

brutal—*adj.* inhuman, violent, intemperate, fierce, savage, rude, bloodthirsty, stolid, cruel, primitive, unfeeling, vindictive, dense, ignorant, barbarous, brutish, sensual. *(civilized, self- controlled, sympathetic, generous, chivalrous, polished, intelligent, conscientious, merciful.)*

bubble—*n.* fancy, trash, effervescence, conceit, froth, percolate, trifle, toy, bead. *(treasure, good, advantage, be flat, reality, verity, acquisition, substance, prize, jewel.)*

budge—*v.* change, influence, persuade, sway, convince, shift. *(remain, stay, stick, halt, pause.)*

building—*n.* architecture, fabric, structure, house, erection, frame, construction, domicile. *(dismantlement, delapidation, demolition, ruin, destruction.)*

bulk—*n.* entirety, mass, body, bigness, weight, dimension, largeness, bigness, enormity, whole, integrity, volume, magnitude, majority, size, greatness. *(diminution, atom, disintegration, tenuity, lesser part, smallest part, minority, portion, section.)*

bungler—*n.* fumbler, novice, clown, blunderer, botcher, muffer, lubber. *(artist, professor, expert, master, proficient, adept, workman, adroit.)*

buoyant—*adj.* vivacious, light, spirited, floating, elated, sprightly, energetic, lively, joyous, elastic, hopeful. *(moody, heavy, cheerless, sullen, joyless, depressed, doleful, dejected, desponding.)*

burden—*n.* incubus, load, grief, stress, weight, affliction, hamper, difficulty, obstruction, oppression. *(expedition, lightness, ease, abjugation, free, facility, consolation, mitigation, airiness, alleviation, lighten, facility, disburdenment, assuagement, light-heartedness.)*

burn—*v.* brand, cauterize, flash, scorch, ignite, consume, cremate, glow, singe, kindle, rage, incinerate, smoulder, blaze. *(cool, wane, pale, chill, lower, extinguish, soothe, glimmer, stifle.)*

bury—*v.* conceal, suppress, cancel, compose, screen, hush, entomb, inter, obliterate, repress, veil. *(resus-*

citate, bruit, expose, reveal, exhume, aggravate, excavate, air.)

business—*n.* profession, affair, office, concern, career, trade, duty, interest, occupation, calling, activity, vocation, employment, matter. (inactivity, hobby, leisure, stagnation, avocation.)

bustle—*n.* stir, commotion, excitement, scramble, business, flurry, haste, energy, dash, eagerness, hurry. (indifference, calm, stagnation,

procrastinate, idleness, inactivity, indolence, quiet, loaf, desertion, vacation, coolness.)

busy—*adj.* diligent, engaged, industrious, laboring, occupied, toiling, assiduous. (indolent, slothful, relaxed, idle, unoccupied, lazy.)

but—*conj.* except, yet, moreover, save, beside, excluding, notwithstanding, still, though, barring. (nevertheless, not withstanding, inclusive, with, including, however.)

C

cage—*n.* coop, pen, receptacle, cell, enclosure, box. (free, liberate, let out.)

calamity—*n.* misfortune, trouble, mishap, fatality, disaster, catastrophe, affliction, tragedy, reverse. (blessing, luck, boon, God-send.)

calculate—*v.* weigh, reckon, apportion, consider, compute, estimate, investigate, count, rate, gauge, proportion. (chance, stake, guess, hit, risk, speculate, conjecture, miscalculate.)

calculation—*n.* consideration, regard, care, judgement, estimation, balance, caution, apportionment, vigilance, investigation, watchfulness, anticipation, reckoning, computation, forethought, thought. (exception, inconsideration, carelessness, incaution, omission, exclusion, inconsiderateness, indiscretion, miscalculation,

misconception, supposition, mistake.)

calibre—*n.* diameter, capacity, force, endowment, character, strength, quality, power, scope.

called—*v.* denominated, termed, named, designated. (misnamed, unnamed, misdesignated, undesignated.)

calm—*v.* compose, still, appease, sedate, smooth, tranquilize, assuage, quiet, soothe, allay, relax. (agitate, lash, stir, disconcert, tense, ruffle, heat, discompose, excite.)

calumny—*n.* libel, opprobrium, slander, aspersion, defamation, back-biting, traducement, detraction, scandal. (eulogy, panegyric, vindication, testimonial, clearance.)

cancel—*v.* annul, obliterate, erase, delete, efface, nullify, discharge, abolish, repeal, blot out, expunge, countervail, quash, rescind, abrogate, revoke. *(ratify, contract, enforce, confirm, perpetuate, re-enact, enact.)*

candid—*adj.* frank, aboveboard, plain, ingenious, blunt, open, fair, unreserved, impartial, transparent, honest, artless, just. *(biased, jesuitical, unfair, mysterious, shuffling, reserved, disingenuous, close, insincere.)*

candidate—*n.* claimant, aspirant, petitioner, solicitor, canvasser, applicant, nominee, contender. *(abjurer, decliner, waiver, abandoner, resigner, noncompetitor.)*

cantankerous—*adj.* crotchety, cranky, irritable, cross, contrary, bad-tempered, quarrelsome, perverse. *(serene, affable, pleasant, equable, debonair, good-humored.)*

canvass—*v.* examine, request, question, challenge, discuss, sift, test, analyze, ventilate, investigate, contemplate, solicit. *(admit, pretermit, pass, allow, disregard, misexamine, ignore, misinvestigate.)*

capacity—*n.* volume, space, scope, calibre, talents, comprehensiveness, magnitude, accommodation, range, parts, competency, cleverness, tonnage, aptitude, size, ability, faculty. *(restriction, coarctation, contractedness, narrowness, incapacity.)*

capital—*n.* important, high, wealth, chief, cleverness, wherewithal, cardinal, principal. *(minor, defective, inferior, poor, unimportant, subordinate, awful.)*

capricious—*adj.* humorsome, uncertain, erratic, wayward, crotchety, whimsical, fanciful, fitful, inconstant, changeful, fickle, giddy. *(unchanging, constant, steadfast, firm, inflexible, unswerving, decided.)*

captivated—*adj.* smitten, enslaved, taken, enthralled, enchanted, captured, charmed. *(free, unscathed, insensitive, uninfluenced, unaffected, insensible, unfeeling.)*

capability—*n.* capacity, skill, competence, power, talent, flair, knack, qualification, attainment. *(inadequacy, impotency, inability, ineptitude, incompetence.)*

care—*n.* prudence, attention, thrift, consideration, pains, economy, heed, wariness, anxiety, foresight, effort, caution, preservation, custody, regard, solicitude, circumspection, prevention, trouble, concern. *(unguardedness, neglect, incaution, recklessness, inattention, improvidence, disregard, remissness, indifference, temerity, carelessness, abandon.)*

career—*n.* walk, progress, way of life, employment, course, race, history, passage, activity. *(unsuccess, miscarriage, avocation, misproceeding, misdeportment.)*

caress—*n.* stroking, embrace, endearment, wheedling, blandishment, fondling. *(annoyance, persecution, melancholy, vexation, provocation, irritation, teasing.)*

careless—*adj.* negligent, rash, thoughtless, heedless,

slack, unthinking, inconsiderate, slipshod. *(cautious, alert, careful, wary, mindful, diligent, concerned, neat, orderly.)*

caricature—*n.* parody, farce, mimicry, travesty, satire, extravagance, burlesque, exaggeration, hyperbole, monstrosity. *(justice, representation, portraiture, resemblance, truthfulness, fidility, likeness.)*

carnival—*n.* festivity, revel, masquerade, rout, celebration. *(mortification, retirement, fast, lent.)*

carpet—*n.* consideration, table, consultation, board, mat. *(disposal, rejection, oblivion, shelf, discharge.)*

carriage—*n.* bearing, vehicle, gait, transportation, coach, conveyance, deportment, bearing, behavior, walk, mien, conduct, manner, stance. *(misconduct, misconveyance, miscarriage, misconsignment.)*

case—*n.* contingency, plight, episode, condition, fact, instance, predicament, occurrence, circumstance, event, incident. *(supposition, hypothesis, presumption, theory, fancy, conjecture.)*

cast—*v.* throw, fling, frame, construct, pattern, mold, hurl, impel, project, pitch, send down. *(dissipate, approve, retain, ignore, dismember, misprovide, erect, raise, dislocate, break, recover, elevate, accept, carry, miscalculate.)*

cast--*n.* plight, fact, event, condition, subject, instance, occurrence, predicament,

contingency, catapult. *(supposition, theory, hypothesis, fancy, conjecture, speculation.)*

caste—*n.* rank, blood, order, station, class, lineage, race, respect, dignity. *(taboo, reproach, degradation, disrepute, abasement, depravation.)*

casual—*adj.* occasional, contingent, fortuitous, accidental, chance, incidental, unforeseen. *(ordinary, fixed, systematic, calculated, regular, certain, periodic.)*

catastrophe—*n.* disaster, blow, misadventure, visitation, calamity, devastation, revolution, reverse, misfortune, tragedy. *(triumph, success, benefit, blessing, godsend, felicitation, ovation, achievement, victory.)*

catch—*v.* capture, corner, snag, grab, seize, arrest, apprehend, snare, trap. *(free, liberate, let go, fumble, lose, release, give up, drop.)*

cause—*n.* agent, inducement, suit, reason, action, source, motive, producer, stimulus, object, origin, creator, account, purpose, principle, motivation. *(result, end, production, issue, preventive, effect, accomplishment, conclusion.)*

cease—*v.* desist, pause, quit, stop, leave off, adjourn, intermit, abstain, refrain, end, discontinue. *(commence, persist.)*

celebrated—*adj.* notable, renowned, distinguished, exalted, popular, famed, eminent, noted, famous, glorious. *(disgraced, obscure, mean, in-*

significant, unrenowned, unknown, nondescript.)

celebrity—*n.* eminence, honor, renown, fame, notoriety, personality, notability, distinction, star, glory. *(cipher, obscurity, ingloriousness, indolence, meaness, ignominy, disgrace, nobody, contempt.)*

celestial—*adj.* ethereal, elysian, heavenly, atmospheric, blissful, godlike, supernatural, radiant, angelic, immortal, divine. *(hellish, earthly, mundane, infernal, mortal, terrene, sublunary, human, wordly.)*

censure—*n.* reprimand, blame, dispraise, stricture, rebuke, reproach, criticism, disapproval, admonition. *(eulogy, encouragement, praise, approbation, support, commendation.)*

ceremonial—*adj.* functional, imposing, scenic, ritualistic, pompous, sumptuous, official, ministerial. *(unostentatious, private, casual, undramatic, unimposing, ordinary.)*

certain—*adj.* regular, infallible, sure, actual, convinced, real, confident, unfailing, unmistakable, indubitable, incontrovertible, undoubtful, true, fixed, established, secure, reliable. *(undecided, casual, dubious, irregular, unsettled, uncertain, occasional, doubtful, exceptional, vacillating, unsure, fallible.)*

certify—*v.* prove, aver, vouch, demonstrate, protest, assure, inform, ratify, evidence, testify, acknowl-

edge, avow, declare, avouch, underwrite. *(misinform, repudiate, disprove, misadvise, disavow.)*

challenge—*v.* dare, question, brave, demand, defy, investigate, canvass, summon. *(allow, believe, pass, grant, acquiesce, concede, yield.)*

chance—*n.* hazard, luck, fate, fortuity, befallment, accident, haphazard, casualty, destiny, fortune. *(design, consequence, rule, intent, certainty, law, causation, sequence, purpose, premeditation, casualty.)*

changeless—*adj.* settled, firm, consistent, constant, immovable, reliable, regular, uniform, immutable, steady, stationary, undeviating, resolute, fixed, abiding. *(mutable, irregular, plastic, unsettled, wavering, fluctuating, vacillating, capricious, unsteady, irresolute, variable.)*

character—*n.* mark, symbol, sign, record, letter, figure, nature, type, genius, class, quality, tone, part, disposition, temperament, repute, cast, kind, order, individuality, species, stamp, makeup. *(vagueness, non-description, dishonesty, anonymousness, disrepute, dishonor.)*

characteristic—*n.* singularity, distinction, specialty, peculiarity, idiosyncrasy, individuality, personality. *(miscellany, nondescription, mannerism, generality, abstractedness.)*

charge—*v.* command, instruct, bid, direct, call, order, accuse, incriminate, assign, indict, blame. *(vindicate, par-*

C
D

don, withdraw, retreat, imply, absolve, exonerate, acquit.)

charitable—*adj.* benevolent, kind, inextreme, forgiving, liberal, compassionate, generous, placable, philanthropic, considerate, inexacting, benign. *(extreme, harsh, revengeful, exacting, stingy, retaliative, uncharitable, selfish, censorious, uncompassionate, unforgiving, illiberal, unkind, parsimonious.)*

charm—*v.* enchant, subdue, transport, delight, captivate, attract, entrance, bewitch, fascinate, soothe, entice, lay, mesmerize, gratify. *(irritate, rouse, annoy, disgust, terrify, excite, offend, disenchant, disturb, disillusionize, repel, alarm.)*

charm—*n.* attraction, incantation, allurement, spell, magnetism, spell, enchantment. *(repulsion, disgust, fear, disenchantment, displeasure.)*

chaste—*adj.* uncontaminated, nice, pure, virtuous, modest, celibate, incorrupt, unaffected, undefiled, simple, spotless, wholesome. *(meretricious, flashy, impure, lewd, corrupt, gaudy, overdecorated.)*

cheap—*adj.* low-priced, mean, inexpensive, vile, economical, common, uncostly, worthless. *(worthy, honorable, valuable, high, costly, expensive, rare, noble.)*

cheat—*v.* fleece, inveigle, gull, silence, beguile, hoodwink, dissemble, deceive, overreach, victimize, prevar-icate, trick, cozen, defraud, juggle, dupe, deprive, shuffle, swindle.

cheat—*n.* charlatan, fraud, trick, imposter, artifice, fake.

check—*v.* halt, constrain, brake, curb, harness, arrest, prevent, stay, restrain, suppress, retard, impede, thwart. *(initiate, unleash, encourage, aid, support, begin, accelerate, spur, foster, help, abet.)*

cheer—*n.* conviviality, hope, comfort, hospitality, plenty, happiness, optimism. *(unsociableness, dejection, gloom, niggardliness, pessimism, sullenness, churlishness, dearth, inhospitableness, starvation.)*

cheerful—*adj.* joyous, lively, happy, sprightly, joyful, merry, jovial, gay, buoyant, blithe, in good spirits, bonny, glad, enlivening, pleasant, bright. *(despiriting, lifeless, unhappy, depressing, dull, dejected, melancholy, gloomy, morose, sullen, joyless, depressed.)*

chief—*n.* boss, administrator, supervisor, master, chairman, overseer, chieftain, overlord, monarch, potentate, director. *(underling, subject, subordinate, secondary, subsidiary, follower.)*

childish—*adj.* silly, paltry, foolish, infantine, adolescent, weak, trivial, trifling, imbecile, puerile. *(chivalrous, judicious, strong, polite, mature, resolute, wise, manly, sagacious, profound.)*

chivalrous—*adj.* generous, heroic, gallant, valiant, courtly, high-minded, spirited, handsome, courageous, adventurous, knightly, polite. *(dirty, ungenerous, unhandsome, sneaking, ungentlemanly, recreant, scrubby, dastardly, pettifogging, borish, cruel.)*

choice—*n.* preference, selection, option, election, discretion, alternative, adoption. *(indifference, refusal, compulsion, rejection, refuse, coercion, necessity, unimportance.)*

chuckle—*v.* cackle, laugh, grin, crow, chortle. *(grumble, wail, whine, cry, whimper, moan.)*

churlish—*adj.* brusque, crusty, petulant, irritable, bilious, sour, rude, grouchy, sullen. *(amiable, kind, pleasant, gallant, noble, cultivated, humble, polite.)*

cipher—*n.* dot, button (fig.), rush, straw, nonentity, naught, pin, nothing, trifle, mole-hill, nil. *(colossus, notability, triton, star, somebody, infinity, something, bigwig, celebrity.)*

circumstance—*n.* feature, point, event, incident, position, topic, episode, detail, specialty, condition, particular, occurrence, situation, fact. *(case, deed, transaction, performance.)*

civil—*adj.* political, polite, respectful, well-mannered, civilized, affable, obliging, accommodating, courteous, well-bred, complaisant, cordial. *(unaccommodating, boorish, churlish, impolite, uncivil, clownish, disrespectful, disobliging.)*

claim—*v.* ask, insist, privilege, maintain, profess, demand, require, title, right, pretense, request, avow. *(abandon, surrender, waive, deny, abjure, disavow, concede, repudiate, disclaim, forego.)*

claim—*n.* vindication, demand, right, assertion, pretension, title, arrogation, request, privilege. *(surrender, abjuration, waiving, disclaimer, denial.)*

claimant—*n.* appellant, assertor, vindicator, petitioner, litigrant. *(conceder, abjurer, relinquisher, quiter, resigner, waiver, renouncer.)*

classification—*n.* nature, sect, designation, genus, order, section, division, species, character, description, assortment, category, kind, group, cast, stamp. *(isolation, division, hetergeneity, specialty, individuality, compartment, exclusion, alienation, singularity, distinction.)*

clause—*n.* paragraph, article, section, chapter, passage, portion, term, stipulation, proviso, condition, provision. *(instrument, document, muniment, charter.)*

clear—*v.* exonerate, disentangle, clarify, emancipate, extricate, whitewash, disencumber, set free, disembarrass, liberate, absolve, retrieve, acquit, justify, exculpate, eliminate, release, rid. *(pollute, embarrass, clog, implicate, contaminate, condemn, encumber, involve, befowl.)*

clear—*adj.* intelligible, pure, lucid, transparent, obvious, open, plain, free, unobstructed, patent, unequivocal, conspicuous, manifest, apparent, evident, unclowded, serene, acquitted, absolved, disentangled, disengaged, disencumbered. *(condemned, dubious, muddy, thick, opaque, fowl, entangled, convicted, encumbered, blurred, indistinct, turbid, unintelligible, limpid.)*

clemency—*n.* mercy, compassion, leniency, forbearance, tolerance, charity, understanding, sympathy, benevolence. *(vindictiveness, cruelty, illwill, vengefulness, intolerance, brutality.)*

clever—*adj.* talented, gifted, expert, well-contrived, adroit, nimble, able, skillful, ingenious, quick-witted, dexterous, quick, ready. *(botched, weak, clumsy, dull, slow, awkward, incompetent, bungling, stupid, ill-contrived, uninventive, doltish, inept.)*

cling—*v.* adhere, hug, hang, fasten, embrace, linger, hold, twine, cleave, stick. *(surrender, drop, relax, swerve, abandon, forsake, apostatize, forego, secede, recede.)*

cloak—*v.* extenuate, conceal, screen, mask, disguise, cover, mitigate, camouflage, veil, palliate, hide. *(propound, exhibit, promulge, expose, reveal, protray, unmask, aggravate, demonstrate.)*

close—*adj.* condensed, compressed, dense, niggardly, secret, narrow, fast, limited, adjacent, restricted, shut, reserved, firm, compact, packed, solid. *(liberal, ample, frank, wide, spacious, rarefied, vaporous, public, roomy, open, advertised, open-handed, patent, airy, subtle, dispersed, unconfined.)*

cloudy—*adj.* misty, smoky, gray, overcast, hazy, vaporous, soupy, dreary, gloomy. *(clear, fair, bright, sunny, cloudless, azure, transparent.)*

clownish—*adj.* foolish, cloddish, bucolic, clumsy, comical, rude, rustic, untutored, boorish, awkward. *(intelligent, civil, polite, educated, urbane, high-bred, sedate, courtly, affable, graceful, polished, refined.)*

clumsy—*adj.* uncouth, bungling, unhandy, botching, ill-shaped, awkward, inept, unwieldy, inexpert, maladroit, unskillful. *(dexterous, artistic, adroit, neat, expert, workmanlike, handy, nimble, skillful.)*

coarse—*adj.* indelicate, rough, immodest, unrefined, crude, vulgar, common, unpolished, ordinary, gross, rude. *(choice, refined, elegant, delicate, gentle, fine, polished.)*

cognizance—*n.* recognition, notice, observation, knowledge, perception, experience. *(oversight, neglect, connivance, inadventure, ignorance, unawareness, inexperience.)*

coherent—*adj.* complete, compact, consecutive, united, close, sensible, logical, consistent, adhering. *(illogical, loose, inconsecutive, discursive, rambling, confused, aberrant, disunited, silly, inconsistent.)*

coincide—*v.* square, tally, agree, accord, harmonize, dovetail, correspond, equal, meet. *(diverge, conflict, differ, disagree, clash.)*

coincidence—*n.* consent, casualty, contemporaneousness, chance, agreement, fortuity, simultaneous, concurrence, harmony, correspondence, commensurateness. *(purpose, difference, incommensurateness, design, variation, premeditation, adaption, discordance, disharmony, asynchronism, anachronism.)*

colleague—*n.* adjutant, partner, helper, associate, assessor, companion, ally, collaborator, confederate, coadjutor, assistant. *(competitor, co-rival, counteragent, adversary, co-opponent, co-antagonist.)*

collect—*v.* gather, sum, muster, accumulate, collate, marshal, garner, convoke, glean, convene, amass, congregate, infer, learn, assemble. *(arrange, sort, dispose, classify, deal, scatter, dispense, distribute, divide.)*

collection—*n.* store, assemblage, collation, gathering, compilation, assembly. *(disposal, division, classification, arrangement, distribution, assortment, dispersion, dispensation.)*

color—*n.* complexion, speciousness, falsification, perversion, hue, pretense, pigment, varnish, tint, distortion, garbling, tinge. *(transparency, achromatism, pallor, nakedness, paleness, openness, truthfulness, genuineness.)*

combination—*n.* association, coalition, co-operation, cabal, blending, union, synthesis, alliance, league, confederacy, concert, consortment. *(analysis, resistance, inter-repellence, separation, division, opposition, disunion, disruption, dispersion, dissolution.)*

comely—*adj.* becoming, tasteful, proper, pleasant, charming, appealing, unaffected, decorous, nice, simple. *(homely, unsightly, ugly, faded, unattractive, improper, repulsive, affected, plain, unbecoming.)*

comfortable—*adj.* convenient, snug, consoled, satisfied, agreeable, congenial, commodious, cozy, pleasant. *(disagreeable, uncomfortable, forlorn, unhappy, dissatisfied, unsuitable, cheerless, wretched, troubled, miserable.)*

command—*v.* govern, conduct, guide, supervise, administer, rule, boss, direct, superintend. *(supplicate, follow, plead, beg, deter, discourage, repel, obey.)*

commerce—*n.* merchandize, barter, dealing, trade, intercourse, communication, exchange, business, industry, traffic. *(interdict, stagnation, dullness, inactivity, embargo, standstill, exclusion.)*

common—*adj.* everyday, universal, ordinary, mean, habitual, low, prevalent, familiar, coarse, frequent, vulgar. *(exceptional, rare, egregious, unusual, excellent, peculiar, scarce, uncommon, partial, refined, sporadic, infrequent.)*

community—*n.* association, unity, aggregation, homogeneity, polity, society, brotherhood, co-ordination, fellowship, similarity, nationality, commonwealth, fraternity, class, order, sympathy. *(contrariance, segregation, heterogeneity, hostility, estrangement, secession, polarity, animosity, independence, disconnection, dissociation, dissimilarity, rivalry.)*

company—*n.* union, aggregation, firm, sodality, concourse, assembly, order, congregation, association, audience, society, fraternity, corporation, guild, assemblage, community, gang, troop, posse, crew, establishment. *(antagonism, competition, counter-association, rivalry, isolation, opposition, counter-agency, disqualification.)*

compass—*v.* complete, circumvent, encompass, effectuate, embrace, consummate, surround, enclose, achieve, circumscribe. *(misconceive, liberate, expand, miscontrive, mismanage, despond, discard, fail, exclude, amplify, display, dismiss, bungle, unfold.)*

compatible—*adj.* consentaneous, consonant, consistent, congenial, harmonious, sympathetic, co-existent, agreeable, accordant, congruous. *(inter-repugnant, impossible, contradictory, divergent, incompatible, destructive, hostile, insupposable, adverse, in-*

congruous, antagonistic, discordant, inconsistent.)

compel—*v.* coerce, force, blind, make, oblige, constrain, domineer, drive, necessitate. *(cozen, persuade, liberate, induce, thwart, release, convince, egg, tempt, coax, seduce, acquit, allure.)*

compensation—*n.* restoration, pay, damages, remuneration, restitution, indemnification, amercement, equivalent, settlement, wages, allowance, satisfaction, atonement, expiation. *(fraudulence, deprivation, damage, loss, injury, donation, non-payment, gratuity.)*

competition—*n.* emulation, race, rivalry, contention, two of a trade, conflict. *(colleagueship, confederation, association, copartnership, collaboration, alliance, teamwork.)*

complacement—*adj.* kind, mannerly, pleased, amiable, acquiescent, affable, easygoing, satisfied, content, pleasant. *(morose, austere, grudging, dissatisfied, sullen, irritated, unmannerly, churlish.)*

complaint—*n.* repining, disease, murmur, lamentation, criticism, discontent, expostulation, sickness, annoyance, grievance. *(boon, sanity, benefit, congratulation, complacency, rejoicing, approbation, salve, applause, jubilee, health.)*

complement—*n.* totality, counterpart, completion, supply, fulfilment, correlative, supplement. *(defalcation, abatement, insufficiency, drawback, lessening, defi-*

C
D

ciency, diminution, deficit, detraction.)

complete—*adj.* perfect, thorough, accomplished, full, exhaustive, intact, finished, total, consummate, adequate, entire. *(partial, imperfect, incomplete, inadequate, deficient, unfinished.)*

complexion—*n.* feature, indication, face, interpretation, makeup, aspect, hue, color, look, appearance, character. *(reticence, heart, unindicativeness, inexpression, core, concealment, reserve.)*

complicated—*adj.* involved, entangled, confused, perplexed, intricate, complex. *(simple, lucid, uninvolved, obvious, clear, unraveled.)*

compliment—*n.* courtesy, praise, homage, flattery, tribute. *(discourtesy, contempt, insolence, insult.)*

complimentary—*adj.* ecomiastic, lavish of praise, flattering, commendatory, laudatory, panegyrical, eulogistic. *(vituperative, condemnatory, disparaging, abusive, insulting, objurgatory, damnatory, reproachful, defamatory, denunciatory.)*

composition—*n.* combination, adjustment, commutation, mixture, settlement, compound, creation, conformation, compromise, structure. *(perpetuation, analysis, aggravation, criticism, segregation, discussion, examination, disturbance.)*

comprehend—*v.* embody, understand, apprehend, include, perceive, embrace, grasp, involve, enclose, comprise, conceive. *(misunder-*

stand, reject, except, exclude.)

comprehensive—*adj.* general, large, capacious, pregnant, embracing, inclusive, wide, extensive, all, universal, compendious, ample, significant, generic, brood. *(shallow, narrow, exceptive, exclusive, limited, restricted, adversative.)*

compromise—*v.* adjust, settle, implicate, involve, arbitrate, reconcile, compose, endanger. *(disengage exempt, exonerate, enfranchise, aggravate, extricate, excite, foster, perpetuate, arbitrate.)*

conceal—*v.* keep secret, screen, hide, disguise, suppress, shield, dissemble, secrete, camouflage. *(divulge, manifest, publish, reveal, promulgate, disclose, expose, exhibit, avow, confess.)*

concentrate—*v.* muster, convene, centralize, conglomerate, assemble, converge, cluster, localize, condense, draw, congregate. *(dismiss, disperse, scatter, decentralize, dissipate.)*

concerning—*prep.* relating, about, touching, with respect to, relative to, of, with regard to, apropos of, with reference to, respecting, in relation to, regarding. *(disregarding, omitting, neglecting.)*

concert—*n.* combination, union, co-operation, concord, agreement, collaboration, association, harmony. *(counteraction, dissociation, disconnection, opposition.)*

conciliate—*v.* appease, disarm, placate, mollify, soothe, pacify, arbitrate.

(arouse, stir up, antagonize, alienate.)

concrete—*adj.* explicit, precise, specific, actual, tangible, definite, material. *(general, vague, abstract, intangible, immaterial.)*

condescension—*n.* graciousness, stooping, affability, favor, humility. *(pride, haughtiness, superciliousness, scorn, arrogance, superiority, disdain.)*

condition—*n.* mood, qualification, situation, plight, requisite, state, circumstances, proviso, case, mode, stipulation, predicament, term, shape. *(fulfilment, relation, circumstances, adaptation, dependence, connection, situation, concession.)*

conducive—*adj.* promotive, effective, contributive, caustive, calculated, subsidiary, productive. *(contrariant, destructive, counteractive, repugnant, hindering, preventive.)*

conduct—*v.* transfer, manage, guide, administer, lead, control, bring, behavior, carry, direct. *(misconduct, mislead, follow, miscarry, misadminister, mismanage.)*

confer—*v.* deliberate, present, compare, give, palaver, collate, discuss, consult, converse. *(contrast, withhold, hazard, withdraw, dissociate, deny, conjecture.)*

confession—*n.* catechism, tenets, subscription, creed, articles, doctrine, declaration, revelation, profession. *(renunciation, refutation, heresy, protest, concealment, apos-*

tasy, index, abjuration, condemnation.)

confidant—*n.* advisor, confederate, confessor, trusty companion. *(betrayer, rival, traitor, turncoat.)*

confident—*adj.* assured, bold, certain, impudent, sure, positive, undaunted, sanguine. *(diffident, apprehensive, despondent, dubious, uncertain.)*

confidential—*adj.* trustworthy, private, intimate, secret, honorable. *(open, official, treacherous, insidious, disloyal, public, patent.)*

confirm—*v.* stabilitate, settle, substantiate, perpetuate, verify, strengthen, sanction, ratify, establish, corroborate, prove, fix. *(annul, refute, upset, weaken, abrogate, confute, nullify, shake, cancel, repeal.)*

conform—*v.* fit, harmonize, reconcile, correspond, adapt, comply, agree, acquiesce, submit. *(diverge, deviate, disagree, oppose, differ.)*

confront—*v.* face, resist, encounter, menace, challenge, intimidate, oppose. *(encourage, abet, evade, countenance, rally.)*

confused—*adj.* perplexed, dazed, disordered, promiscuous, abashed, chaotic, disarranged, embarrassed, involved, disconcerted, complex, disorganized. *(unembarrassed, unconfused, unabashed, systematic, arranged, organized.)*

congregate—*v.* get together, flock, assemble, collect, convene, rally, meet, throng. *(scatter, part,* *disperse, separate, spread out.)*

congress—*n.* parliament, convention, synod, conclave, assembly, conference, council, legislature. *(conclave, cabal, mob, session.)*

conjecture—*v.* divination, guess, supposition, notion, estimate, hypothesis, surmise, theory. *(calculation, proof, computation, certainty, inference, deduction, reckoning.)*

connection—*n.* relation, kindred, union, junction, relationship, conjunction, kinsman, association, coherence, communication, concatenation, affinity, relevance, intercourse. *(irrelevance, disunion, disconnection, separation, disjunction, independence, dissociation.)*

conquer—*v.* vanquish, master, prevail over, subdue, surmount, subjugate, quell, crush, defeat, overthrow, overcome, overpower. *(forfeit, fail, cede, fall, resign, retreat, sacrifice, succumb, lose, capitulate, fly, submit, surrender.)*

conscious—*adj.* cognizant, alert, aware, sensible. *(unconscious, insensible, asleep, unaware.)*

consecutive—*adj.* coherent, continuous, orderly, subsequent, arranged. *(undigested, discursive, rambling, disordered, simultaneous, inconsecutive, inconsequent, incoherent.)*

consent—*v.* agree, concur, acquiesce, submit. *(disagree, refuse, dissent, disapprove, resist, decline.)*

consequence—*n.* dignity, effect, moment, issue, note, result, importance, inference, sequel, coherence, outcome, deduction, conclusion. *(paltriness, cause, meanness, antecedence, causation, irrelevance, inconsecutiveness, premise, inconsequence, precursor, origin, insignificance, unimportance, axiom, postulate, datum.)*

consider—*v.* revolve, think, deem, weigh, attend, ponder, judge, deliberate, mediate, cogitate, deduce, infer, investigate, reflect, opine, observe, regard, contemplate. *(hazard, disregard, conjecture, ignore, guess, pretermit, despise, omit.)*

considerate—*adj.* cautious, patient, thoughtful, careful, attentive, reflective, forbearing, circumspect, prudent, unselfish, judicious, serious. *(careless, rash, thoughtless, inconsiderate, injudicious, inattentive, rude, overbearing, heedless, selfish.)*

consistency—*n.* proportion, mass, consistence, analogy, congruity, harmony, composition, uniformity, substance, coherence, material, compactness, amalgamation, compound, density, closeness, compatibility, solidity. *(contrariety, volatility, subtility, contradiction, vaporousness, disproportion, incongruity, tenuity, variance, sublimation, incoherence, inconsistency.)*

consistent—*adj.* harmonious, congruous, compatible, accordant, agreeing, consonant, congenial. *(not agreeing with, incongruous, inharmonious, at variance with, incompatible, illogical.)

conspicuous—*adj.* magnified, uniform, noticeable, visible, seen, observable, easily, prominent, salient, noted, eminent, famous, manifest, distinguished, evident. *(microscopic, invisible, unobservable, inconspicuous, noticeable, shrouded.)*

constant—*adj.* regular, trustworthy, true, uniform, faithful, perpetual, immutable, firm, continuous, stalwart, fixed, steady, invariable. *(exceptional, false, irregular, treacherous, variable, untrustworthy, faithless, fickle, vacillating, casual, incidental, accidental, broke, interrupted, inconsistent.)*

constitution—*n.* frame, regulation, temperament, law, structure, habit, temper, organization, texture, character, substance, nature, government, composition, state, consistence, policy. *(destruction, accident, demolition, habituation, disorganization, modification, dissipation, interference, change, revolution, anarchy, depotism, rebellion, tyranny.)*

construction—*n.* view, composition, interpretation, fabrication, fabric, creation, explanation, reading, rendering, understanding, erection, edifice. *(misconception, dislocation, misinterpretation, dismemberment, razing, demolition, misunderstanding, displacement, misconstruction, misplacement.)*

consult—*v.* ask advice of, confer, promote, interrogate, care for, canvass, consider, question, advise, deliberate, regard, counsel. *(contravene, resolve, counteract, explain, dictate, expound, instruct, direct, bypass.)*

consumption—*n.* lessening, decay, decrease, decline, waste, decrement, expenditure, depletion. *(development, growth, augmentation, conservation, enlargement.)*

contact—*n.* continuity, adjunction, touch, contiguity, collision, apposition. *(adjacence, non-contact, proximity, isolation, distance, interruption, separation, disconnection.)*

contagious—*adj.* infectious, catching, epidemic, transmitted, pestilential, communicated, transferred, spreading. *(preventive, sporadic, antipathetic, endemic, noninfectious.)*

contaminate—*v.* taint, corrupt, soil, pollute, defile, sully, befoul. *(chasten, purify, sanctify, cleanse, clarify, lave, ameliorate.)*

contemplate—*v.* project, mediate, intend, behold, design, survey, observe, purpose, study, ponder. *(waive, overlook, ignore, disregard, abandon.)*

contemptible—*adj.* trivial, mean, despicable, vile, paltry, pitiful, disreputable, trifling, detestable. *(venerable, grave, important, weighty, respectable, honorable, laudable.)*

content—*adj.* satisfied, gratified, resigned, full, willing, pleased, contented, happy. *(reluctant, unwilling, unsatisfied, discontented, dissatisfied, restless.)*

contentious—*adj.* perverse, exceptious, litigious, wayward, quarrelsome, splenetic, cantankerous. *(obliging, easy, pacific, obsequious, considerate, accommodating, harmonious.)*

contingent—*adj.* incidental, conditional, dependent, uncertain, provisional, co- efficient, hypothetical. *(irrespective, positive, uncontrolled, absolute, unaffected, unmodified, independent, contrived.)*

continually—*adv.* persistently, ever, repeatedly, continuously, frequently, constantly, always, perpetually, incessantly, unceasingly. *(intermittently, casually, fitfully, occasionally, rarely, spasmodically, sometimes, contingently.)*

contract—*v.* lessen, curtail, form, retrench, abridge, compress, diminish, abbreviate, agree, decrease, reduce, narrow. *(dilate, elongate, cancel, abandon, magnify, expand, amplify, reverse.)*

contract—*n.* agreement, compact, bargain, pact, covenant, treaty, bond, stipulation. *(assurance, promise, parole, discourse.)*

contradict—*v.* negate, refute, contravene, oppose, controvert, impugn, dissent, deny, confute, disprove. *(propound, argue, affirm, state, maintain, endorse, corroborate, confirm.)*

contrary—*adj.* incompatible, opposed, inconsistent,

repugnant, opposite, adverse, antagonistic, negative. *(coincident, agreeing, kindred, consentaneous, consistent, obstinate, compatible.)*

contribute—*v.* supply, add, give, assist, cooperate, tend, conduce, bestow, subscribe. *(misapply, refuse, contravene, withhold, deny, misconduce.)*

contrive—*v.* arrange, plan, adjust, scheme, design, intrigue, fabricate, concert, devise, manage, adapt. *(overdo, hazard, chance, over-vault, demolish, bungle, hit, venture, run.)*

control—*v.* administer, curb, coerce, govern, manipulate, check, manage, restrain, regulate, guide, moderate, repress. *(liberate, abandon, misconduct, neglect, mismanage, license, release.)*

convenient—*adj.* seasonable, apt, opportune, handy, timely, fitted, adapted, useful, helpful, commodious, suitable, beneficial. *(untimely, awkward, inopportune, inconvenient, useless, unseasonable, obstructive, superfluous, unsuitable.)*

conventional—*adj.* usual, prevalent, customary, social, ordinary, traditional, stipulated. *(unsocial, natural, invariable, unusual, innovative, legal, immutable, statutable, compulsory.)*

conversant—*adj.* proficient, learned, familiar, versed, experienced, acquainted. *(strange, unfamiliar, inconversant, unacquainted, unversed, ignorant, unlearned.)*

C
D

convertible—*adj.* identical, equivalent, commensurate, equipollent, conterminous, transformable. *(contradictory, variant, contrariant, incommensurate, contrary, unequivalent, converse.)*

conviction—*n.* persuasion, faith, assurance, belief. *(misgiving, doubt, skepticism, disbelief.)*

co-operate—*v.* abet, concur, work together, conspire, assist, collaborate, help, contribute. *(oppose, rival, thwart, nullify, counteract.)*

copy—*n.* portraiture, transcript, image, imitation, likeness, reproduction, duplicate, counterfeit, facsimile. *(example, original, prototype, pattern, model, creation.)*

cordial—*adj.* earnest, hearty, invigorating, warm, sincere, affectionate, reviving, genial. *(formal, cold, hostile, distant, ceremonious.)*

corner—*n.* hole, recess, retreat, nook, cavity, confound. *(protection, coin, convexity, abutment, prominence, angle, elbow, protrusion, salience.)*

corpulent—*adj.* lusty, stout, fat, gross, fleshy, obese, plethoric, portly, burly. *(attenuated, emaciated, lean, slight, thin, gaunt.)*

correct—*adj.* exact, accurate, decorous, true, right, faultess, proper, strict. *(untrue, wrong, falsify, imprecise, false, incorrect.)*

correct—*v.* rectify, amend, set right, chasten, remedy, punish, improve, redress, emend, reform. *(ruin, falsify, corrupt, spare.)*

correction—*n.* discipline, chastisement, amendment, punishment, emendation, reparation. *(retrogradation, deterioration, recompense, debasement, reward, compensation.)*

correspond—*v.* fit, harmonize, agree, match, answer, correlate, suit, tally. *(disagree, vary, clash, jar, differ, deviate.)*

correspondence—*n.* adaptation, match, fitness, answerableness, letter, correlation, depatches, agreement, congruity, congeniality, writing, communication. *(colloquy, reservation, difference, withholding, conversation, repugnance, withdrawal, confabulation, dissimilarity, non-intercourse.)*

corrupt—*adj.* polluted, depraved, tainted, contaminated, defiled, vitiated, wicked, decayed, putrid, profligate, infected, rotten. *(undefiled, pure, moral, uncorrupt.)*

corruption—*n.* putrescence, taint, putrefaction, decomposition, evil, contamination, decay, debasement, adulteration, deterioration, depravity, rottenness, perversion, defilement. *(purification, vitality, amelioration, morality, organization, purity.)*

cost—*n.* outlay, expense, payment, expenditure, worth, outgoings, precious, charge, price, compensation, disbursement, *(emolument, profit, revenue, return, income,* *resources, perquisite, receipt.)*

costly—*adj.* expensive, precious, high-priced, exorbitant, valuable, rich, sumptuous. *(cheap, beggarly, mean, valueless, paltry, worthless, reasonable, low-priced.)*

council—*n.* consultation, parliament, synod, convocation, cabinet, convention, bureau, company, conference, chamber, conclave, meeting, congress, assembly, legislature. *(conspiracy, mob, crowd, league, cabal, intrigue, multitude, alliance.)*

counsel—*n.* instruction, monition, warning, recommendation, advice, admonition, consultation. *(misinstruction, betrayal, subversion, misguidance.)*

count—*v.* enumerate, reckon, compute, calculate, estimate, sum, total, number. *(conjecture, confound, guess, exclude, hazard, lump.)*

countenance—*v.* favor, support, help, encourage, patronize, abet, sanction, tolerate, aid. *(discourage, confront, discountenance, oppose, browbeat, condemn.)*

counteract—*v.* counterfoil, baffle, thwart, hinder, neutralize, counterinfluence, foil, negate, rival, oppose. *(conserve, promote, co-operate, aid, subserve, help, encourage, abet.)*

counterpart—*n.* fellow, brother, correlative, supplement, match, parallel, tally, complement, twin, copy. *(reverse, opposite, contradiction, counter-agent, contrary,*

opponent, observe, antithesis, contrast.)

countryman—*n.* husbandman, clown, compatriot, yeoman, native, inhabitant, swain, rustic, citizen, boor, subject, fellow-citizen, provincial, fellow-subject, peasant, fellow-countryman, laborer, agriculturist. *(townsman, alien, cockney, oppidan, foreigner, stranger, emigrant.)*

couple—*v.* conjoin, bracket, unite, button, brace, yoke, link, connect, tie, buckle, splice, clasp, amalgamate, pair. *(part, separate, untie, loosen, detach, divorce, sever, uncouple, unclasp, isolate.)*

courage—*n.* fortitude, gallantry, intrepidity, boldness, pluck, heroism, bravery, fearlessness, resolution, valor. *(poltroonery, timidity, pusillanimity, cowardice, faintheartedness, dastardliness.)*

course—*n.* sequence, direction, race, order, method, continuity, conduct, plain, trail, manner, line, progress, succession, series, passage, route, mode, career, way, round, road. *(solution, disorder, conjecture, caprice, deviation, interruption, speculation, error, discursion, hazard, hindrance, cogitation.)*

courtly—*adj.* polished, aristocratic, mannerly, dignified, refined, high-bred, elegant. *(rough, awkward, unrefined, rustic, unmannerly, vulgar, undignified, coarse, unpolished, plebeian, boorish.)*

covetous—*adj.* avaricious, greedy, rapacious, acquisitive, lustful, grasping. *(bountiful, unselfish, profuse, generous, liberal, charitable, self-sacrificing.)*

coward—*n.* dastard, poltroon, renegade, craven, recreant, milquetoast. *(daredevil, champion, desperado, hero, lion.)*

coy—*adj.* shrinking, modest, shy, bashful, sheepish, reserved, retreating. *(rompish, bold, hoydenish, saucy, forward.)*

craft—*n.* underhandedness, art, dodge, artifice, chicanery, guile, intrigue, ingenuity, cunning, stratagem, wiliness, maneuver, duplicity, trickery. *(ingenuousness, candor, openness, straightforwardness, fairness, reliability, honesty, frankness, sincerity, artlessness.)*

cram—*v.* squeeze, gorge, ram, compress, stuff, choke, pack. *(vent, empty, unload, eliminate, deplete, disgorge, eviscerate, discharge, unpack.)*

crash—*n.* clang, resonance, clash. *(babble, din, murmur, silence, reverberation, whisper, rumbling.)*

crave—*v.* pine for, desire, want, covet, require, need, yearn for, wish for. *(repudiate, spurn, detest, abominate, despise, scorn, abhor.)*

cream—*n.* pith, acme, gist, marrow. *(offal, dross, garbage, refuse, dregs.)*

credential or credentials—*n.* seal, diploma, vouchers, missive, recommenda-

tion, title, letter, testament, warrant, certificates, testimonials. *(self-appointment, self license, autocracy, self constitution, self-derived power.)*

credit—*n.* trustworthiness, faith, honor, relief, reputation, merit, reliance, confidence, praise, security. *(insecurity, disbelief, untrustworthiness, disgrace, skepticism, distrust, shame, censure.)*

creed—*n.* articles, subscription, catechism, belief, doctrine, confession. *(abjuration, disbelief, protest, recantation, non-subscription, retractation, rejection.)*

criminal—*adj.* felonious, wrong, sinful, nefarious, indictable, flagitious, guilty, illegal, vicious, iniquitous, immoral, culpable. *(virtuous, laudable, right, lawful, honorable, just, blameless, praise-worthy, innocent, meritorious, moral, creditable.)*

critical—*adj.* exact, censorious, momentous, precarious, severe, nice, hazardous, important, delicate, crucial, fastidious, accurate, discriminating, dubious, ticklish. *(settled, popular, redressed, inexact, retrieved, supportive, loose, easy, determined, undiscriminating, safe, decided.)*

criticism—*n.* censure, evaluation, animadversion, stricture. *(praise, approval, acclaim, rave.)*

crude—*adj.* undigested, unrefined, raw, half-studied, unchastened, unfinished, unconsidered, harsh, ill-prepared, unshaped, churlish. *(well-digested, artistic, well-prepared, highly-wrought, ripe, classical, well-considered, elaborate, well-adapted, refined, finished, classical, well-expressed, elegant.)*

cruel—*adj.* barbarous, truculent, malignant, inhuman, maleficent, sanguinary, savage, brutal, unmerciful, pitiless, ruthless, unrelenting, inexorable, hardhearted, harsh. *(forbearing, beneficent, humane, generous, forgiving, benevolent, beneficial, merciful.)*

crush—*v.* pound, crumble, pulverize, demolish, granulate, triturate, bray, overpower. *(compact, aggrandize, consolidate, solidify, liberate, stabilitate, compress, upraise, amalgamate, cake.)*

cuff—*v.* box, punch, buffet, slap, smack, pummel, hustle, smite. *(flagellate, cane, lash, whip, cudgel, thrash, strap, maul.)*

cultivate—*v.* foster, improve, till, improve, nourish, advance, cherish, promote, study, nurture, civilize, refine, fertilize. *(desert, uproot, neglect, extirpate, abandon, prevent, paralyze, stifle, abolish, discourage, impair, blight, blast, eradicate.)*

cupidity—*n.* acquisitiviness, stinginess, avarice, repacity, covetousness. *(extravagance, prodigality, generosity, liberality.)*

cure—*n.* restorative, renovation, convalescence, medication, remedy, heal-all, alleviation, restoration, amelioration, reinstatement. *(confirmation, disease, inoculation, corruption, aggravation, inflamation, complaint, ailment, contagion.)*

curiosity—*n.* interest, marvel, lion, celebrity, prying, wonder, inquisitiveness, interrogativeness, phenomenon, oddity, rarity. *(heedlessness, drug, song, abstraction, disregard, dirt, apathy, bagatelle, indifference, cipher, absence, weed.)*

curious—*adj.* inquisitive, odd, inquiring, recondite, meddling, unique, questioning, scrutinizing, rare, prying, peering, searching, peeping, singular. *(uninquiring, trite, superficial, blasè, indifferent, incurious, common, uninterested.)*

current—*adj.* prevalent, exoteric, general, running, vulgar, floating, widespread, ordinary, popular, present. *(private, secret, confined, obsolete, rejected, previous, esoteric, exploded.)*

custody—*n.* guardianship, care, conservation, protection, keeping. *(betrayal, jeopardy, abandonment, liberation, release, neglect, discharge, desertion, exposure.)*

cynical—*adj.* snarling, sneering, currish, cross-grained, sarcastic, contemptuous, snappish, carping. *(complaisant, lenient, sanguine, urbane, genial.)*

D

daft—*adj.* innocent, silly, light-headed, lunatic, foolish, idiotic, cracked. *(sensible, sane, practical, shrewd, palpable, deft, sound.)*

dainty—*adj.* rare, tasty, epicurean, choice, refined, delicate, luxurious, exquisite. *(unrelishing, dirty, gluttonous, nasty, greedy, gross, common, omnivorous, coarse.)*

damage—*n.* harm, impairment, injury, defacement, mutilation, loss, ruin, destruction. *(reparation, mend, improvement, betterment, repair.)*

damp—*adj.* moist, drizzly, humid, dewy, wet, vaporous.

dapper—*adj.* neat, smart, dashing, spruce, natty. *(unwieldy, untidy, slovenly, sloppy, awkward.)*

daring—*adj.* fearless, valorous, adventurous, intrepid, dashing, brave, bold, imprudent, courageous, foolhardy, venturesome, dauntless. *(timid, prudent, cautious, inadventurous.)*

dark—*adj.* sable, obscure, recondite, blind, benighted, inexplicable, dismal, sombre, sorrowful, opaque, black, swarthy, abstruse, ignorant, dim, secret, nebulous, joyless, dingy, dusky, enigmatical, besotted, unintelligible, shadowy, mysterious, hidden, murky, cheerless, gloomy, mournful. *(fair, luminous, white, radiant, festive, illumined, light, dazzling, radiant, glaring, brilliant, enlightened, bright, intelligible, lucid, transparent, crystalline.)*

dash—*v.* throw, scatter, hurl, course, fly, cast, shatter, subvert, drive, send, strike, dart, speed, rush, detrude. *(erect, lag, raise, support, reinstate, creep, hobble, crawl.)*

daunt—*v.* scare, intimidate, terrify, confront, frighten, appall, alarm, dishearten, cow. *(encourage, inspirit, countenance, fortify, rally.)*

dawdle—*v.* dally, lag, loiter, idle, loaf. *(speed, rush, fag, hustle, work, haste, dash.)*

dead—*adj.* departed, inanimate, still, deserted, spiritless, heavy, defunct, inert, torpid, deceased, cheerless, dull, unconscious, insensible, gone, lifeless. *(thronged, living, susceptible, joyous, bustling, stirring, responsive, vivacious, vital, animate, alive.)*

deadly—*adj.* venomous, fatal, pernicious, destructive, murderous, mortal, implacable, malignant, destructive, noxious, baneful. *(healthful, vital, wholesome, nutritious, innocuous, life-giving.)*

deaf—*adj.* disinclined, averse, dead, inaudible, surd, heedless, hard of hearing, inexorable, rumbling, insensible, inattentive. *(interested, acute, disposed, susceptible, alive, listening, sensible, willing, attentive, penetrating.)*

dear—*adj.* costly, beloved, loved, precious, priceless, expensive, high-priced. *(inex-*

pensive, vile, nominal, cheap, misliked.)

death—*n.* decease, exit, fall, expiration, departure, release, demise, cessation, dissolution, mortality, failure, eradication, termination. *(life, auspices, rise, inauguration, commencement, vigor, birth, existence, spirit, operation, animation, activity, vitality, action, growth.)*

debatable—*adj.* problematical, unsettled, doubtful, disputable, undecided, dubious, floating, uncertain, inestimable. *(sure, incontestible, certain, unquestionable, self-evident, settled, indisputable.)*

debauchery—*n.* revelry, orgies, gluttony, riot, excess. *(frugality, maceration, moderation, abstinence, asceticism, refraining.)*

debase—*v.* disgrace, corrupt, adulterate, desecrate, lower, degrade, defile, befowl, corrupt, deteriorate. *(elevate, heighten, enhance, improve, uplift.)*

debt—*n.* liability, obligation, something due, debit, score, default, claim, bill. *(assets, gift, grace, accommodation, gratuity, credit, liquidation, trust, favor, obligation, grant.)*

decay—*v.* sink, wither, decrease, perish, decline, waste, wane, dwindle, ebb, rot, shrivel. *(grow, enlarge, rise, expand, flourish, increase, luxuriate, vegetate.)*

decay—*n.* waning, decadence, wasting, declension, dry rot, decline, sinking,

corruption, putrefaction, consumption, rottenness, decrease, collapse. *(growth, increase, exuberance, prosperity, rise, birth, fertility, luxuriance, vigor.)*

deceit—*n.* imposition, fraud, artifice, hypocrisy, cunning, cheat, sham, trick, duplicity, deception, guile, indirection, double-dealing, circumvention, insidiousness, treachery, beguilement, delusion. *(honesty, verity, reality, openness, instruction, guidance, fair dealing, enlightenment, candor.)*

deceitful—*adj.* delusive, fallacious, deceptive, dishonest, fraudulent. *(fair, veracious, open, honest, truthful, delude.)*

deceive—*v.* beguile, gull, entrap, take in, trick, circumvent, ensnare, overreach, mislead, betray, cheat, dupe, delude. *(advise, deliver, illumine, be honest to, enlighten, guide, undeceive, disabuse.)*

decide—*v.* settle, terminate, resolve, determine, fix, adjudicate, arbitrate. *(drop, misdetermine, waive, raise, misjudge, suspend, waver, vacillate, moot, doubt.)*

decipher—*v.* spell, solve, unravel, unfold, read, explain, interpret, translate. *(symbolize, mystify, enigmatize, cipher, impuzzle, illustrate.)*

decision—*n.* resolve, conviction, determination, firmness, will, strength, perseverance, certainty, decisiveness. *(vagueness, weakness, vacillation, uncertainty, evasion, indecisiveness.)*

C
D

declaration—*n.* exhibition, avowal, manifestation, ordinance, affirmation, profession, assertion, statement, testimony. *(concealment, denial, retraction, suppression.)*

decompose—*v.* individualize, dissolve, analyse, segregate, spoil, resolve. *(mix, organize, compound, concoct, compose, brew.)*

decorum—*n.* propriety, order, good manners, modesty, seemliness, respectability, dignity, good behavior. *(impropriety, disorder, rudeness, unseemliness, disturbance.)*

decrease—*v.* lessen, abate, decline, curtail, wane, diminish, abbreviate, subside, lower, retrench, reduce. *(grow, expand, extend, enlarge, increase, escalate, amplify, augment.)*

decrepit—*adj.* weak, enfeebled, aged, infirm, superannuated, broken down, dilapidated, effete, tottering, crippled. *(robust, agile, youthful, strong, active, in good shape.)*

dedicate—*v.* consecrate, assign, set, devote, set apart, separate, hallow, apportion, offer, apply. *(misconvert, alienate, misapply, misuse, devolve, misappropriate, desecrate.)*

deed—*n.* commission, instrument, muniment, act, feat, action, accomplishment, achievement, document, perpetration, exploit. *(failure, recall, undoing, omission, reversion, abortion, non-performance, false-witness, innocent, disproof, cancelling, invalida-*

tion, retraction, impossiblity, collapse.)

deep—*adj.* subterranean, thick, heartfelt, occult, obscure, penetrating, profound, abstruse, submerged, learned, designing, recondite, sagacious, mysterious, intense, subtle. *(superficial, familiar, commonplace, undesigning, shallow, artless, obvious.)*

deface—*v.* spoil, disfigure, mar, destroy, damage, injure, mutilate, deform, bruise. *(adorn, embellish, beautify, decorate.)*

defame—*v.* libel, disparage, vilify, insult, slander, discredit, malign, stigmatize, belittle. *(flatter, laud, applaud, extol, compliment, boost, praise.)*

default—*n.* forfeit, delinquency, want, lapse, failure, defect, absence, omission. *(appearance, supply, maintenance, presence, compliance, plea, forthcoming, satisfaction.)*

defeat—*n.* discomfiture, frustration, disaster, overthrow. *(triumph, success, killing, victory.)*

defeat—*v.* worst, foil, baffle, conquer, frustrate, rout, overcome, vanquish, overthrow, overpower. *(establish, promote, advance, secure, aid, speed, insure, strenghten.)*

defect—*n.* blemish, shortcoming, want, fault, flaw, omission, deficiency, imperfection. *(sufficiency, virtue, emendation, complement, supply, ornament, strength, compensation.)*

defective—*adj.* insufficient, short, faulty, wanting, inadequate, imperfect, deficient. *(complete, ample, perfect, satisfactory, correct, sufficient, abundant, full.)*

defense—*n.* protection, excuse, apology, resistance, rampart, preservation, vindication, plea, justification, shelter, bulwark. *(surrender, exposure, prosecution, abandonment, betrayal.)*

defer—*v.* postpone, adjourn, put off, prolong, delay, retard, waive, procrastinate, shelve, prorogue, hinder, protract. *(hasten, press, hurry, expedite, dispatch, urge, quicken, overdrive, facilitate.)*

deference—*n.* consideration, honor, allegiance, respect, condescension, homage, contention, obedience, esteem, regard, reverence, submission, veneration. *(contumacy, defiance, attention, disrespect, contumely, disregard, impudence, rudeness, non-allegiance, slight, disobedience.)*

defiant—*adj.* mutinous, fractious, rebellious, ungovernable, lawless, willful, audacious, bold, stubborn. *(obedient, dutiful, meek, submissive, timid, docile.)*

definite—*adj.* specified, certain, clear, positive, limited, exact, determined, precise, bounded, definitive, specific, fixed, concrete, ascertained, restricted. *(confused, vague, obscure, unspecified, ambiguous, undetermined, intermingled, indefinite.)*

definition—*n.* specification, determination, restriction, clarification, limitation. *(vagueness, misconception, confusion, misstatement, ambiguity, acceptation, explanation, description.)*

defray—*v.* liquidate, bear, quit, discharge, meet, settle, pay, dispose of. *(misappropriate, repudiate, embezzle, dishonor, dissatisfy, swindle.)*

defy—*v.* challenge, despite, brave, scorn, provoke, spurn. *(agree, comply, obey, cooperate, submit, yield.)*

degree—*n.* stage, amount, grade, quantity, rank, station, step, order, class, limit, extent, mark, position, quality, level, rate, measure, range. *(magnitude, numbers, space, size, mass, volume.)*

deliberate—*v.* meditate, perpend, ponder, consider, reflect, debate, consult, weigh, contemplate. *(discard, risk, shelve, hazard, burke, haphazard, chance.)*

deliberate—*adj.* intentional, resolute, unbiased, determined, grave, unprejudiced, thoughtful, earnest, designed, purposed. *(playful, biased, jocose, prejudiced, facetious, instigated, irresolute, dictated, spontaneous, suggested, dubious, unresolved, compulsory, undetermined.)*

delicious—*adj.* luxurious, choice, exquisite, dainty, savory, delightful. *(common, nauseous, loathsome, unpalatable, coarse, unsavory, inedible.)*

delight—*n.* pleasure, happiness, esctasy, bliss, gratification, enjoyment, rapture, joy, transport, gladness, felicity. *(suffering, trouble, discontent, dissatisfaction, pain, sorrow, melancholy, misery, distress, displeasure, depression, discomfort, disappointment, dejection, disgust.)*

delinquent—*n.* culprit, criminal, violator, offender. *(paragon, worthy, pattern, model.)*

deliver—*v.* free, utter, consign, liberate, entrust, save, give up, set free, hand, surrender, give, yield, pronounce, rescue, transmit, concede, distribute. *(misdeliver, confine, suppress, appropriate, retain, assume, betray, withdraw, conserve.)*

deluxe—*adj.* choice, prime, posh, grand, luxurious, select, costly, sumptuous, elegant, splendid. *(ordinary, everyday, common, run of the mill, mediocre, cheap.)*

democratic—*adj.* autonomous, popular, republican, leveling, destructive, radical, unlicensed, subversive, anarchical. *(despotic, regal, autocratic, imperial, tyrannical, conservative, oligarchical, dictatorial, constitutional, aristocratic.)*

demonstrate—*v.* show, manifest, illustrate, describe, prove, exhibit, evince. *(conceal, obscure, misexemplify, disprove, misdemonstrate.)*

demure—*adj.* grave, discreet, sedate, prudish, staid, dispassionate, modest, sober, downcast, retiring. *(vivacious, indiscreet, boisterous, lively, hoydenish, facetious,* wanton, noisy, rompish, wild, aggressive.)

denial—*n.* rejection, declination, negation, refusal, veto, repulsion, prohibition, rebuff. *(acceptance, approval, permission, allowance, yes, affirmation.)*

denomination—*n.* designation, appellation, class, name, order, description, category, kind. *(misnomer, pseudonym, non-description.)*

dense—*adj.* thick, solid, stout, consolidated, thick-set, slow, stupid, dull, compact, close, condensed, stolid. *(uncompacted, quick, sparse, intelligent, clever, rare, meager, rarefied.)*

deny—*v.* withhold, oppose, refuse, disclaim, disown, reject, disavow, contradict, nullify, gainsay, negative. *(accept, indulge, afford, yield, grant, concede, affirm, acquiesce, confirm, admit.)*

department—*n.* division, portion, line, section, province, dominion, branch, function, office. *(establishment, body, society, institution, community, art, organization, whole, service, science, state, literature, conformity.)*

dependent—*adj.* contingent, resting, relative, hanging, relying, trusting, subject, subordinate. *(irrelative, free, independent, absolute, autonomous, irrespective.)*

deplorable—*adj.* lamentable, sorry, calamitous, regrettable, distressing, unfortunate, grievous, ill-fated, miserable. *(happy, felicitious,* cheering, fortunate, gratifying, pleasant, agreeable.)

depression—n. degradation, valley, dip, discouragement, hollow, dejection, despondency. (prominence, raising, mound, elevation, eminence, exaltation, rising, promotion, encouragement, amelioration, preferment, rallying, optimism.)

deprive—v. bereave, rob, hinder, despoil, dispossess, prevent, depose, strip, divest, abridge, confiscate. (indemnify, invest, present, compensate, reinstate, endow, supply, enrich, furnish.)

derision—n. contempt, irony, disrespect, scorn, contumely, sarcasm, mockery, isdain. (admiration, respect, reverence, regard, esteem.)

descendant—n. progeny, lineage, branch, offspring, family, stock, house, scion, posterity, issue, seed. (source, progenitor, parent, author, origin, root, founder, ancestor, stock, forebear.)

describe—v. explain, draw, depict, delineate, recount, picture, narrate, illustrate, define, relate, portray, represent, chronicle. (confuse, distort, confound, caricature, mystify, misrepresent, contort.)

desert—n. wilderness, void, wild, waste, solitude. (field, pasture, oasis, civilization, enclosure, garden.)

design—v. purpose, plan, project, contemplate, intend, prepare, fashion. (conjecture, miscontrive, risk, hit, fluke guess, misconceive, chance, peril.)

design—n. intention, sketch, plan, artifice, scheme, contemplation, pattern, project, purpose, intent, preparation, contrivance, draft, delineation, guile, drawing, artfulness, cunning. (performance, accident, execution, change, result, simplicity, sincerity, issue, artlessness, construction, openness, candor, structure, fairness, frankness.)

desirable—adj. advisable, beneficial, valuable, expedient, judicious, profitable, acceptable, delightful, good, proper, enviable, worthwhile. (unadvisable, evil, improper, undesirable, deplorable, injudicious, inexpedient, objectionable, unprofitable.)

desire—n. affection, craving; appetency, yearning, concupiscence, longing, propension. (abomination, loathing, reject, hate, repugnance, aversion, disgust, horror.)

despair—n. despondency, alienation, desperation, hopelessness. (expectation, hilarity, hopefulness, anticipation, elation, optimism, confidence, sanguineness.)

desperate—adj. inextricable, audacious, frantic, irremediable, daring, hopeless, determined, mad, desponding, reckless, regardless, abandoned, furious, rash, despairing, heedless. (propitious, cool, promising, calm, hopeful, shy, remediable, prudent, irresolute, timid, cautious.)

despotic—adj. arbitrary, cruel, tyrannical, autocratic, self-willed, absolute, irresponsible, domineering, arrogant, dictatorial, imperious.

C
D

(constitutional, merciful, limited, yielding, humane.)

destination—*n.* design, aim, end, purpose, goal, intention, location, design, point, consignment, scope, appointment, object, use, application, fate, doom, aspiration. *(effort, operation, project, tendency, initiation, exercise, design, action, movement, activity.)*

destiny—*n.* doom, fate, end, decree, necessity, fortune, lot, predestination, providence. *(volition, freedom, free will, choice, will, deliberation, selection.)*

destroy—*v.* annihilate, ruin, consume, demolish, waste, overthrow, subvert, undo, extinguish. *(construct, restore, repair, create, fabricate, make, reinstate, erect.)*

destructive—*adj.* hurtful, baleful, damaging, detrimental, subversive, deleterious, ruinous, injurious, baneful, noxious. *(conservative, restorative, constructive, wholesome, preservative, beneficial, subsidiary, reparatory.)*

determination—*n.* settlement, verdict, decision, arbitration, judgement, verification, corroboration, confirmation, resolution, authentication. *(uncertainty, vacillation, indecision, irresolution, hesitation, spinelessness.)*

detraction—*n.* backbiting, slander, diminution, depreciation, derogation, aspersion, deterioration. *(compliment, eulogy, augmentation, flattery, respect, improvement, enhancement.)*

detriment—*n.* prejudice, harm, inconvenience, loss, damage, hurt, disadvantage, deterioration, impairment, injury, disservice. *(improvement, remedy, augmentation, repair, benefit, reinstatement, enhancement.)*

detrimental—*adj.* hurtful, pernicious, prejudicial, injurious. *(profitable, augmentative, beneficial, advantageous.)*

develop—*v.* eliminate, expand, educe, enlarge, enucleate, amplify, lay open, enunciate, disclose, clear, unravel, unfold, mature. *(wrap, involve, narrow, er.velop, conceal, obscure, compress, mystify, contract, restrict, condense, recede.)*

device—*n.* expedient, emblem, show, cognizance, invention, artifice, contrivance, design, implement, symbol, stratagem, project, plan. *(hazard, incognito, fairdealing, abortion, openness, fortune, miscontrivance, hit, luck, camouflage.)*

devil—*n.* lucifer, arch-fiend, demon, satan, foul fiend, fiend, villain. *(angel, cherub, saint, archangel, seraph.)*

devise—*v.* plan, concert, manage, contrive, maneuver, create. *(mismanage, disorder, miscontrive.)*

devoid—*adj.* destitute, unprovided, void, unendowed, wanting, depleted. *(supplied, gifted, provided, furnished, replete, laden.)*

devotion—*n.* love, attachment, piety, self-sacrifice, devoutness, dedication, religiousness, loyalty, self-aban-

C
D

donment, ardor, consecration, self-surrender. *(apathy, impiety, indifference, profanity, alienation, selfishness, antipathy, coolness.)*

devour—*v.* consume, gorge, absorb, eat, bolt, swallow, gulp. *(vomit, regurgitate, disgorge.)*

dictate—*v.* suggest, order, decree, command, prompt, enjoin, rule, prescribe, instruct, direct, propose. *(obey, follow, answer, submit to, repeat, echo.)*

dictatorial—*adj.* domineering, autocratic, despotic, bossy. *(democratic, liberal, reasonable, tolerant, flexible, open-minded.)*

die—*v.* decay, cease, expire, perish, decrease, languish, sink, decline, disappear, wane, fade, wither, succumb. *(originate, regetate, begin, rise, luxuriate, live, strenghten, grow, blossom, flourish, develop.)*

difference—*n.* dissimilarity, dissent, variety, dissimilitude, separation, destruction, dissonance, estrangement, distinction, contrariety, unlikeness, discord, disagreement, individuality. *(consociation, identity, community, uniformity, condonation, reconciliation, similarity, harmony, consentaneousness, consonance, sympathy, likeness, agreement, resemblance.)*

difficult—*adj.* intricate, opposed, perplexing, reserved, hard, obscure, unamenable, complicated, involved, uphill, unmanageable, troublesome, enigmatical, arduous, trying. *(unreserved, plain, favorable,* easy, amenable, lucid, tractable, categorical, straight, simple, complaisant.)*

digest—*v.* arrange, tabulate, sort, methodize, dispose, convert, order, incorporate, classify, ponder, prepare, assimilate, consider, study, recapitulate. *(disturb, discompose, displace, complicate, reject, eject, confound, derange, refuse, disorder, dislocate.)*

dignity—*n.* honor, loftiness, worth, stateliness, worthiness, grandeur, excellence, solemnity, behavior, decorum. *(disrepute, ignobility, shame, guilt, humility, lowness, unimportance.)*

dilemma—*n.* quandry, doubt, scrape, fix, difficulty, hobble, plight. *(rebutment, retort, superiority, solution, extrication, freedom, escape, solvent.)*

diligence—*n.* attention, industry, care, heed, assiduity, application, meticulousness. *(desultoriness, indifference, idleness, neglect, carelessness, inattention, inertness, heedlessness, lethargy.)*

dingy—*adj.* rusty, sombre, bright, dull, bedimmed, soiled, dusky, obscure, tarnished, colorless, dead, dirty, shabby. *(gleaming, burnished, lustrous, bright, luminous, high-colored, glossy, radiant, sparkling.)*

diplomacy—*n.* circumvention, tact, ministry, contrivance, negotiation, out- witting, ambassadorship, management, discretion, savoir-faire. *(recall, miscontrivance, self-defeat, mismanagement,* cancel, ineptness, crassness, self-entanglement, mal-administration, over vaulting.)

diplomatic—*adj.* sagacious, wise, well-managed, judicious, prudent, politic, astute, clever, well-contrived, discreet, delicate, knowing, well-planned. *(bungling, rude, ill-managed, injudicious, stultifying, undiplomatic, tactless.)*

direction—*n.* tendency, order, course, superscription, address, command, control, inclination, bearing, charge, trend. *(miscontrol, deviation, misinstruction, aberration, departure, alteration.)*

directly—*adv.* immediately, at once, quickly, straightaway, soon, promptly, instantly, speedily, precisely. *(by-and-by, indirectly, eventually, there-after, later.)*

dirty—*adj.* soiled, stained, foul, contaminated, polluted, unclean, filthy, grimy, tarnished, messy. *(spotless, clean, immaculate, pure, decent, respectable, washed.)*

disability—*n.* impotency, forfeiture, incompetency, infirmity, defect, incapacity, disqualification. *(fitness, merit, qualification, recommendation, capacity, deserving, strength.)*

disappoint—*v.* defeat, frustrate, foil, deluxe, betray, delude, baffle, mortify, vex, deceive, thwart. *(justify, fulfil, gratify, encourage, realize, satisfy, please, delight, verify.)*

discern—*v.* understand, discover, notice, behold, as-certain, note, recognize, apprehend, observe, perceive, distinguish. *(disregard, slight, neglect, overlook, pass by, fail to see.)*

discharge—*v.* remove, unburden, debark, unload, activate, explode, detonate, launch, propel, project. *(detain, keep, hire, load, maintain, fill, stow, burden.)*

discipline—*n.* strictness, drilling, coercion, organization, order, government, chastisement, rule, training, punishment, control. *(confusion, reward, disorganization, mutiny, disorder, chaos, turbulence, encouragement, rebellion.)*

discomfort—*n.* vexation, trouble, disagreeableness, disquiet, ache, annoyance, anguish, unpleasantness. *(ease, pleasure, agreeableness, comfort, pleasantness.)*

disconcert—*v.* confuse, derange, thwart, defeat, interrupt, ruffle, embarrass, frustrate, disorder, vex, abash, confound, upset, perplex, disturb, fret, unsettle, baffle, discompose. *(scheme, design, rally, encourage, prepare, order, hatch, reassure, countenance, pacify, aid, arrange, contrive, concoct.)*

discourtesy—*n.* incivility, rudeness, impoliteness, brusqueness, insolence, surliness, impudence, boorishness. *(civility, refinement, politeness, graciousness.)*

discreet—*adj.* wise, circumspect, wary, sensible, discerning, prudent, judicious, regulative, cautious, tactful, guarded. *(injudicious, blind,* silly, foolish, indiscreet, reckless, undiscerning, insensitive, imprudent, unrestrained.)

discrimination—n. discernment, sagacity, distinction, penetration, judgement, insight, acuteness, shrewdness, perception, acumen. (hebetude, dullness, shortsightedness, carelessness, fairness, insensitivity, indescernment, confusedness.)

disease—n. malady, complaint, sickness, affliction, disorder, ailment, illness, distemper, indisposition. (sanity, health, vitality, convalescence, salubrity, strength.)

disgrace—n. discredit, dishonor, disfavor, reproach, debase, infamy, degradation, tarnish, embarrassment, blemish. (credit, glory, pride, reverence, honor, distinguish.)

disgust—n. loathing, abhorrence, repugnance, nausea, dislike, irritate, abomination, aversion, distaste, revolt. (liking, relish, fondness, avidity, desire, partiality, delight, longing, please, affection.)

dismal—adj. tragic, dreary, sad, lonesome, melancholy, blank, funereal, somber, gloomy, depressed, foreboding, cheerless, doleful, pessimistic, sorrowful. (ridiculous, gay, lively, promising, comic, elated, propitious, cheerful, exhilarating, joyous, pleasing.)

dispatch—v. send, execute, conclude, hasten, expedite, accelerate, settle, push. (obstruct, retard, stall, impede, detain, delay.)

dispel—v. scatter, dissipate, dismiss, disperse, banish, drive away, disseminate, rout. (mass, summon, congregate, recall, convene, assemble, collect, accumulate, conglomerate.)

disperse—v. separate, dispel, distribute, dealout, disseminate, dissipate, scatter, dissolve, break up, spread abroad. (summon, gather, meet, collect, concentrate, recall, congregate.)

dispute—v. question, contest, quarrel, difference, argue, canvass, debate, altercation, controvert, challenge, squabble, contend, controversy, gainsay, impugn. (forego, waive, allow, acquiesce, concede, agree.)

dissemble—v. feign, repress, cloak, smother, disguise, restrain, conceal, pretend. (manifest, feign, proclaim, pretend, exhibit, protrude, expose, evidence, vaunt, simulate, assume, profess, show.)

dissiminate—v. propagate, claim, circulate, spread, promulgate, distribute, scatter, preach. (suppress, extirpate, repress, eradicate, discountenance, stifle, quell, annihilate.)

dissolute—adj. profligate, wanton, abandoned, loose, vicious, libertine, licentious, rakish. (self-controlled, upright, correct, virtuous, strict, conscientious.)

distance—n. absence, removal, remoteness, length, interspace, interval, aloofness, separation, space, gap. (neighborhood, contact, prox-

C
D

imity, adjacency, presence, nearness, propinquity, closeness, warmth, contiguity.)

distinct—*adj.* independent, unlike, conspicuous, perspicuous, plain, separate, unconnected, disjoined, clear, obvious, dissimilar, detached, definite, different, transparent. *(confused, united, conjoined, indistinct, dim, one, consolidated, obscure, blurred, indefinite.)*

distinction—*n.* separation, dignity, eminence, characteristic, mark, difference. *(debasement, unity, insignificance, identity, degradation, anonymity.)*

distinguish—*v.* perceive, know, separate, discern, discriminate, divide, make famous, differentiate, descry, dissimilate, see, discover, characterize, isolate. *(confound, miss, overlook, confuse, oversee.)*

distinguished—*adj.* noted, famous, illustrious, celebrated, eminent, conspicuous, marked, dignified. *(inconspicuous, hidden, obscure, not famous, mediocre.)*

distress—*v.* embarrass, worry, disturb, afflict, harass, trouble, pain, vex, annoy, mortify, grieve, perturb, sadden. *(gratify, console, comfort, soothe, please, gladden, elate, compose, solace, sustain.)*

disturb—*v.* discompose, disquiet, derange, molest, disorder, vex, discommode, worry, plague, confuse, interrupt, rouse, trouble, agitate, annoy, upset, distract. *(collocate, soothe, leave, order,* pacify, compose, arrange, quiet, organize.)

diversion—*n.* divergence, detour, enjoyment, pastime, sport, deviation, recreation, amusement, entertainment. *(procedure, task, avocation, study, continuity, directness, labor, work, business, drudgery.)*

divide—*v.* dissect, portion, part, segregate, sunder, disunite, allot, keep apart, distribute, part among, multiply, separate, bisect, divorce, sever, deal out, partition. *(consociate, unite, join, collocate, convene, conglomerate, classify, congregate, conglutinate, co-ordinate, commingle, cement, splice.)*

divorce—*n.* divert, separate, alienate, dissever, disconnect, dissolution. *(unite, apply, reunite, conjoin, connect, reconcile, fusion.)*

do—*v.* accomplish, work, achieve, complete, finish, act, execute, perform, transact, enact, produce. *(mar, omit, neglect, undo, fail.)*

docile—*adj.* amenable, managed, yielding, quiet, tractable, tame, teachable, pliant, gentle, easily, compliant, submissive. *(obstinate, intractable, self-willed, dogged, stubborn, defiant.)*

dogmatic—*adj.* theological, arrogant, positive, magisterial, doctrinal, imperious, dictatorial, settled, authoritative, self-opinionated. *(active, diffident, vacillating, modest, practical, moderate, uncertain.)*

doleful—*adj.* rueful, piteous, somber, sorrowful,

dismal, dolorous, melancholy, woebegone, mournful. *(joyful, blithe, gay, merry, beaming, cheerful.)*

dominion—*n.* tyranny, power, rule, government, empire, realm, jurisdiction, supremacy, territory, sway, control, despotism, authority. *(inferiority, weakness, servitude, subjugation, submission, docility.)*

dormant—*adj.* slumbering, quiescent, sleeping, latent, inert, oblivious, undeveloped. *(wakeful, energetic, vigilant, active, developed, operative, functioning.)*

doubt—*n.* scruple, suspense, distrust, indecision, dubiousness, hesitation, suspicion, difficulty, uncertainty, ambiguity, perplexity, challenge, demur. *(clearness, determination, satisfaction, certainty, precision, conviction, decision, belief, trust.)*

dowdy—*adj.* shabby, slovenly, unfashionable, seedy, frumpy, unfashionable, sloppy, drab, bedraggled, unattractive. *(smart, stylish, chic, elegant, fashionable, modish, tidy, trim.)*

drain—*v.* percolate, exhaust, dry, draw, drip, strain, drop, empty, withdraw, discharge. *(supply, moisten, fill, inundate, swill, replenish, pour, energize, drown, drench, stimulate.)*

dramatize—*v.* intensify, highlight, punctuate, exaggerate, rant, embroider, spout, embellish, emote, color, interpret. *(play down, minimize, understate.)*

draw—*v.* pull, induce, sketch, entice, describe, delineate, rouse, inhale, drag, haul, attract, solicit. *(propel, drive, thrust, push, throw, carry, compel, repel, impel, shove, disperse.)*

dreadful—*adj.* monstrous, terrible, awful, horrible, fearful, dire, shocking, alarming, frightful, terrific, distressing, tragic. *(assuring, hopeful, promising, encouraging, suitable, inspiriting, cheerful.)*

dreamy—*adj.* visionary, absent, fanciful, speculative, foggy, abstracted, fabulous, rapt. *(earnest, practical, collected, attentive, awake, energetic, active, vigilant, aware.)*

dress—*n.* preparation, accoutrements, garniture, vestments, clothing, don, lively, habiliments, uniform, apparel, raiment, investiture, garb, costume, array, arrangement, garments, drape, ornament. *(disorder, undress, nudity, disarrangement, deshabille, disrobe, divest.)*

drift—*n.* direction, tenor, scope, issue, conclusion, course, aim, tendency, motion, meaning, design, purport, intention, object, purpose, result, end, inference, vein. *(vagueness, indefiniteness, pointlessness, aberrancy, unmeaningness, confusedness, aimlessness, motionlessness, inertia.)*

drink—*v.* quaff, absorb, draught, imbibe, drain, guzzle, swallow, gulp. *(replenish, exude, water, disgorge, moisten, pour, dampen.)*

drivel—*n.* nonsense, snivel, fatuity, trifling, babble, rambling. *(coherence, solidity, soundness, substance, essence.)*

droll—*adj.* queer, funny, comic, farcical, whimsical, odd, quaint, fantastic, amusing, comical, laughable. *(lugubrious, sad, funereal, lamentable, ordinary, tragic.)*

drop—*v.* emanate, percolate, fall, faint, decline, descend, ooze, droop, trickle, distil. *(rise, recover, soar, rally, evaporate, climb, ascend.)*

drown—*v.* overwhelm, submerge, deluge, sink, swamp, engulf, perish, inundate, immerse, overflow. *(drain, ventilate, dry, expose, air, rescue, perserve.)*

dry—*adj.* parched, monotonous, dull, arid, juiceless, sarcastic, tame, moistureless, uninteresting, vapid, evaporated, barren, lifeless, tedious, withered. *(fresh, lively, damp, entertaining, juicy, soaked, moist.)*

due—*adj.* unpaid, payable, mature, accrued, owed, owing, outstanding, in arrears, demandable. *(unsuitable, inapt, wrong, undeserved, inappropriate.)*

dull—*adj.* stolid, insensible, heavy, dismal, turbid, dowdy, sad, commonplace, stupid, dead, doltish, callous, gloomy, clowdy, opaque, sluggish, tiresome, faded, muted. *(clever, animated, bright, burnished, exhilarating, sharp, lively, sensible, transparent, brilliant, cheerful, keen, intense.)*

durable—*adj.* permanent, firm, abiding, continuing, lasting, stable, sturdy, persistent, constant. *(transient, unstable, impermanent, perishable, evanescent.)*

duty—*n.* part, responsiblity, function, province, trust, service, liability, obligation, business, allegiance, office, calling, commission, task. *(exemption, license, desertion, freedom, direliction, dispensation, immunity, liberation.)*

dwindle—*v.* diminish, fall off, melt, pine, decline, waste, decrease, lessen, degenerate. *(enlarge, grow, flourish, expand, develop, augment, strenghten, increase, multiply.)*

dynamic—*adj.* vigorous, energetic, vital, forceful, active, oscillating, impelling, powerful. *(fixed, still, inert, stable, dead, passive, weak, enverated.)*

E

early—*adj.* forward, quickly, anon, beforehand, soon, first, betimes, matutinal, shortly, premature. *(backward, belated, late, vespertinal, tardily, retarded.)*

earn—*v. acquire, obtain, gain, realize, merit, achieve, win, deserve, collect. (forego, lose, squander, forfeit, waste, spend, exhaust, dissipate.)*

earnest—*adj.* serious, determined, solemn, warm, ardent, eager, fervent, intent, strenuous, grave, intense, devoted. *(playful, unearnest, jesting, indifferent, flippant, idle, desultory, irresolute, sportive, superficial.)*

easy—*adj.* comfortable, indulgent, lenient, gentle, self-possessed, not difficult, unconcerned, quiet, manageable, facile, unpretentious. *(disturbed, difficult, hard, embarrassed, uneasy, exacting, anxious, painful, unmanageable, awkward, uncomfortable.)*

ebb—*v.* recede, fall, decline, wane, lessen, shrink, dwindle, sink, diminish, weaken, decrease. *(grow, wax, enlarge, increase, swell, prosper, flowish, build.)*

economical—*adj.* thrifty, spare, frugal, saving, prudent, chary, careful, parsimonious, cheap, scrimping. *(prodigal, lavish, improvident, spendthrift, elaborate, ample, generous, liberal.)*

economy—*n.* dispensation, rule, administration, management, distribution, arrangement, frugality, thrift. *(waste, mismanagement, prodigality, misrule, disorder, maladministration, imprudence, extravagance.)*

ecstasy—*n.* inspiration, frenzy, emotion, delight, happiness, rapture, fervor, enthusiasm, joy, transport, exhilaration. *(coolness, weariness, tedium, fidget, misery, bore, dullness, indifference, sorrow.)*

edifice—*n.* building, tene-ment, structure, house, fabric, institute. *(heap, dismantlement, ruin, demolition, devastation.)*

educate—*v.* nurture, train, develop, school, initiate, teach, instruct, discipline, ground, enlighten, cultivate. *(misinstruct, misnurture, miseducate, mistrain.)*

effective—*adj.* conducive, cogent, able, powerful, telling, talented, efficient, effectual, serviceable, operative, patent, efficacious, competent. *(futile, nugatory, ineffective, inoperative, weak, inconducive, inadequate, useless.)*

effete—*adj.* barren, sterile, exhausted, worn-out, sere, unproductive, decadent, morally, decayed, spent, deteriorated. *(fruitful, inventive, prolific, creative, teeming, vital, vigorous, youthful.)*

effort—*n.* attempt, exertion, trial, endeavor, struggle, stress. *(misadventure, facility, spontaneity, ease, failure, unsuccess, futility, inactivity, frustration, collapse.)*

egotism—*n.* vanity, self-assertion, conceit, self-exaltation, pride, self-praise, narcissism, arrogance. *(deference, modesty, self-abnegation, considerateness.)*

ejaculation—*n.* utterance, cry, exclamation, vaciferation. *(silence, speech, dumbfoundedness, obmutescence, speechlessness, drawl, oration, address.)*

elastic—*adj.* extensile, resilient, flexible, springy, modifiable, buoyant, ductile, alterable, supple. *(unchangeable, inert, tough, brittle,*

E
F

rigid, inflexible, obstinate, dull, crystallized.)

elated—*adj.* inspirited, proud, cheered, inflated, joyed, gleeful, jubilant. *(dispirited, dejected, disappointed, depressed, sad, humiliated, gloomy, abashed, confounded.)*

elegance—*n.* refinement, taste, grandeur, beauty, symmetry, gracefulness, luxuriousness. *(awkwardness, rudeness, ungracefulness, plainness, deformity, coarseness, crudeness, disproportion.)*

elegant—*adj.* lovely, well made, accomplished, refined, graceful, handsome, symetrical, polished, luxurious, well formed, graud. *(deformed, coarse, rude, unsymmetrical, plain, ungraceful, inelegant, crude.)*

elementary—*adj.* material, simple, ultimate, physical, constituent, primary, physical, basic, natural, component, inchoate, fundamental. *(incorporeal, compound, aggregate, organized, complicated, immaterial, collective, impalpable, developed, complex.)*

elevate—*v.* basic, fundamental, elemental, rudimentary, primary, original, initial, simple, primitive. *(debase, belittle, degrade, reduce, weaken, impair, depreciate.)*

eligible—*adj.* suitable, desirable, choice, preferable, capable, prime, worthy, chosen, proper. *(worthless, ordinary, indifferent, unprofitable, undesirable, unacceptable, ineligible, unsuitable.)*

eloquent—*adj.* forceful, fluent, articulate, inspired, passionate, persuasive, cogent, inspired, vivid, emphatic. *(inarticulate, dull, hesitant, clumsy, routine, commonplace, prosaic, weak.)*

elude—*v.* avoid, baffle, parry, frustrate, wade, eschew, shun, escape, fence, dodge, mock, flee. *(court, defy, encounter, confront, dare, meet, challenge.)*

emaciated—*adj.* wasted, thin, scrawny, famished, gaunt, haggard, frail, atrophied, wizened, skeletal. *(well-fed, fat, corpulent, plump, obese, hardy, robust.)*

embarrass—*v.* desconcert, confuse, clog, entangle, puzzle, encumber, distress, trouble, hamper, perplex, mortify. *(expedite, assist, extricate, disencumber, liberate, facilitate, accelerate, put at ease.)*

embezzle—*v.* confuse, piculate, appropriate, falsify, misappropriate, pilfer, steal. *(balance, square, recompense, clear, remunerate.)*

embody—*v.* methodize, codify, aggregate, compact, enlist, express, systematize, incorporate, integrate, introduce, combine, consolidate. *(segregate, dissipate, dismember, disband, eliminate, analyse, disintegrate, colliquate, disembody, divide, disunite.)*

embrace—*v.* comprehend, hug, contain, incorporate, clasp, close, encompass, include, comprise, embody. *(reject, except, repudiate, ex-*

clude, decline.)

emergency—*n.* conjuncture, strait, exigency, difficulty, crisis, casualty, pitch, necessity, embarrassment, tension. *(solution, provision, arrangement, rescue, anticipation, subsidence, deliverance, stability.)*

eminent—*adj.* excellent, foremost, outstanding, esteemed, celebrated, noted, renowned, distinguished, honored, famous, laureate, paramount. *(obscure, humble, mediocre, undistinguished, unknown, modest, unpretentious, petty.)*

emotion—*n.* feeling, agitation, trepidation, passion, excitement, tremor, perturbation, worry, turmoil. *(impassiveness, peace, stoicism, indifference, harmony, insensibility, imperturbability.)*

emphatic—*adj.* forceable, energetic, positive, special, consummate, earnest, strong, impressive, important, egregious, decisive. *(cool, ordinary, commonplace, mild, unnoticeable, unimpassoned, unimportant, hesitant.)*

employ—*v.* apply, occupy, engross, use, economize, engage, hire, enlist. *(dismiss, misemploy, discard, misuse, discharge, fire.)*

empower—*v.* commission, qualify, warrant, direct, enable, encourage, delegate, sanction, authorize, permit. *(prevent, disable, disqualify, hinder, discourage, forbid, disbar.)*

empty—*adj.* void, unobstructed, waste, unfre-

quented, vacuous, unfilled, untenanted, deficient, silly, senseless, vacant, idle, unencumbered, unoccupied, devoid, uninhabited, destitute, unfurnished, evacuated, weak, frivolous. *(occupied, obstructed, substantial, colonized, informed, experienced, significant, important, full, encumbered, abundant, sensible, cultivated, inhabited, well-instructed, forcible.)*

enamor—*v.* fascinate, charm, bewitch, captivate, enchain, enslave, endear, infatuate. *(disgust, disenchant, repel, horrify, estrange, revolt.)*

enclose—*v.* encircle, afforest, include, envelop, shut, circumscribe, wrap, surround. *(disclose, bare, develop, open, exclude, expose, disencircle, boycott, disenclose.)*

encourage—*v.* rally, abet, inspirit, embolden, enhearten, incite, urge, foster, promote, advance, impel, forward, animate, prompt, reassure, countenance, cherish, stimulate, cheer, advocate. *(discourage, dispirit, deter, dissuade, dishearten, daunt.)*

end—*n.* stop, terminus, limit, tip, boundary, point, finish, close, conclusion, finale, cessation, point, expiration, aftermath. *(origin, beginning, source, start, commencement, infancy, inception, outset.)*

endanger—*v.* risk, imperil, jeopardize, peril, commit, expose, hazard, compromise. *(defend, screen, cover, protect, safeguard, shield.)*

E
F

endear—v. gain, attach, make dear, conciliate, idolize, treasure. (alienate, embitter, estrange, provoke.)

endless—adj. illimitable, eternal, uncensing, deathless, infinite, everlasting, interminable, unending, perpetual, boundless, imperishable, immortal. (temporary, transient, ephemeral, finite, terminable, limited, brief, periodic, fugitive, measured.)

endowment—n. provision, capacity, qualification, gift, benefaction, donation, benefit, attainment, grant. (incapacity, impoverishment, lack, loss, poverty, detriment, drawback, harm.)

enforce—v. compel, exact, strain, urge, require, exert, administer, impose. (forego, abandon, relax, disregard, waive, remit, default.)

engage—v. vouch, promise, buy, involve, undertake, employ, occupy, attract, adopt, agree, hire, gain, stipulate, commit, pledge, enlist. (refuse, dismiss, extricate, disengage, decline, withdraw, discard, fire, cancel.)

enhance—v. magnify, intensify, heighten, elevate, lift, boast, embellish, augment, fortify, escalate. (diminish, detract, undermine, reduce, lessen, depreciate, minimize, weaken.)

enigmatical—adj. perplexing, elusive, mystic, puzzling, obscure, cryptic. (explanatory, self-evident, lucid, plain, candid, frank.)

enlarge—v. expand, broaden, stretch out, dilate, augment, swell, increase, extend, amplify, magnify, widen. (lessen, restrict, curtail, narrow, reduce, contract, diminish, dwindle, condense.)

enlighten—v. edify, illuminate, teach, illumine, instruct, inform, educate, apprise. (darken, obscure, perplex, mislead, mystify, confound, delude, deceive.)

enlist—v. register, embody, enroll, enter, incorporate, recruit, obtain. (erase, dismiss, retire, disembody, withdraw, expunge, disband, resign.)

enmity—n. asperity, bitterness, animosity, malignity, maliciousness, hostility, discord, hate, malevolence, aversion, ill-feeling, opposition, acrimony, malice, antipathy. (love, esteem, cordiality, friendship, affection, friendliness, harmony, amicability.)

enormous—adj. immense, gross, colossal, vast, monstrous, huge, prodigious, elephantine, gigantic, astronomic. (insignificant, venial, ordinary, trivial, diminutive, regular, average, puny, undersized.)

enough—adj. ample, abundance, plenty, sufficient, adequate. (scant, inadequate, short, bare, insufficient, deficient.)

ensue—v. accrue, befall, follow, supervene, result. (threaten, forewarn, precede, herald, premonish.)

ensure—v. determine, seal, secure, fix, guarantee. (hazard, forfeit, imperil, jeopardize, endanger.)

enterprising—adj. bold,

dashing, active, adventurous, forceful, speculative, venturesome, daring. *(inadventurous, inactive, cautious, timid, apathetic.)*

entertain—*v.* maintain, foster, recreate, harbor, amuse, receive, conceive, engross. *(exclude, debar, tire, weary, eject, deny, bore, annoy, ignore.)*

enthusiasm—*n.* frenzy, passion, fervor, devotion, excitement, sensation, transport, warmth, vehemence, ardor, inspiration, zeal, rapture, fervency, ebullience. *(callousness, disaffection, alienation, coldness, contempt, repugnance, indifference, apathy.)*

entire—*adj.* complete, total, all, undiminished, solid, whole, integral, unimpaired, full, perfect, intact. *(impaired, partial, broken, incomplete, fragmentary.)*

entitle—*v.* empower, characterize, denominate, qualify, fit, name, designate, style, enable, permit. *(disable, disqualify, not characterize, desentitle, not designate, unfit.)*

entreat—*v.* obsecrate, beseech, crave, supplicate, ask, petition, implore, beg, importune, solicit, pray, urge, plead with. *(insist, enjoin, bid, command, demand.)*

enumerate—*v.* name, recount, reckon, calculate, over, specify, number, detail, compute, call, list. *(miscount, miscalculate, misreckon, confound.)*

ephemeral—*adj.* evanescent, fugacious, momentary, transient, fleeting, fugitive, temporary. *(persistent, perpetual, perennial, abiding, immortal, external, permanent, lasting.)*

equable—*adj.* regular, even, easy, smooth, uniform, tranquil, proportionate. *(uneasy, desultory, fitful, irregular, agitated, variable, disjointed.)*

equal—*adj.* commensurate, alike, even, sufficient, co-extensive, uniform, smooth, impartial, co-ordinate, identical, adequate, equivalent, equable. *(incommensurate, inadequate, unequal, partial, incoordinate, variable, disparate.)*

equitable—*adj.* proportionate, fair, honest, reasonable, just, proper, even-handed, impartial, upright honorable. *(disproportionate, unfair, partial, biased, unjust.)*

erase—*v.* efface, blot, eradicate, cancel, expunge, obliterate. *(write, stamp, delineate, mark.)*

erect—*v.* institute, establish, set up, elevate, manufacture, raise, build plant, found, construct, uplift. *(supplant, remove, demolish, raze, subvert, destroy, depress, lower.)*

erratic—*adj.* aberrant, capricious, desultory, abnormal, changeful, unpredictable, flighty. *(normal, calculable, undeviating, regular, predictable, methodical, steady, unalterable.)*

error—*n.* mistake, deception, untruth, fault, hallucination, blunder, misunderstanding, falsity, fallacy. *(correctness, soundness, truth, rec-*

E F

tification, correction, flaw-
lessness, accuracy.)

escape—v. decamp, avoid,
fly, elude, evade, shun, flee,
abscond. (meet, confront, suffer, trap, incur, encounter.)

esoteric—adj. cryptic,
obscure, arcane, abstruese,
inscrutable, mysterious, private, veiled, occult, hidden.
(clear, simple, open, exoteric,
obvious, plain.)

essential—adj. inherent,
leading, immanent, innate,
requisite, crucial, necessary,
indispensable, vital, key,
main. (qualitative, option, promotive, induced, ascititious,
superfluous, adventitious,
minimal, accidental, quantita-
tive, regulative, imported,
redundant.)

establish—v. settle,
substantiate, plant, found,
prove, organize, inaugurate,
confirm, fix, demonstrate, institute. (presume, surmise,
guess, supplant, break-up,
misstate, refute, subvert, conjecture, suppose, unsettle,
disestablish, upset, confute,
invalidate.)

esteem—n. value, deem,
believe, think, affect, revere,
respect, venerate, love, price,
consider, admiration, like, admire, honor, appreciate, regard, judge, estimate, prize,
treasure. (disconsider, dislike, underrate, deprecate,
disregard, disaffect, undervalue, decry, contempt.)

eternal—adj. endless,
deathless, never-dying, ever-
living, undying, infinite, unceasing, immortal, perpetual,
ceaseless, everlasting, imperishable, constant. (temporal,

fleeting, ephemeral, evanescent, mortal, transient, perishable.)

etiquette—n. fashion, manners, conventionality, proto-
cal, breeding, decorum. (rudeness, singularity, nonconfor-
mance, boorishness, vulgarity, misobservance.)

evaporate—v. exhale, colliquate, distil, melt, liquefy,
dissolve, vaporize, dehydrate,
disappear. (crystallize, solidify, consolidate, indurate,
condense, compact.)

even—adj. level, smooth,
flush, regular, straight, flat,
uniform, tranquil, serene,
calm. (jagged, askew, unfair,
uneven, rough, lumpy, jumpy,
unstable, biased.)

event—n. circumstance,
adventure, accident, fact, occurence, incident, happening,
issue, episode, result. (predisposition, cause, tendency,
antecedent, union, conver-
gence, contribution, operation, inducement.)

eventful—adj. memorable,
marked, critical, notable, remarkable, signal, active, stirring, noted, important. (un-
marked, trivial, ordinary, unimportant, empty, characterless, uninteresting, event-
less.)

evidence—n. attraction,
testimony, declaration, sign,
proof, exemplification, token,
illustration, manifestation,
averment, disposition, appearance, corroboration, indication. (conjecture, fallacy,
surmise, counter-evidence,
refutation, suppression, disproof, concealment, misindication, disguising.)

evident—*adj.* visible, manifest, obvious, palpable, plain, clear, incontrovertible, indisputable, conspicuous, apparent. *(questionable, doubtful, dubious, obscure, uncertain, unsure.)*

evil—*adj.* deleterious, bad, hurtful, unhappy, unpropitious, corrupt, unfair, miserable, ill, sorrowful, noxious, wrong, mischievous, sinful, adverse, wicked, harmful, notorious, immoral. *(beneficial, virtuous, pure, fortunate, joyous, grateful, welcome, good, wholesome, right, holy, happy, felicitous, noble.)*

exactly—*adv.* correspondently, truly, precisely, accurately, literally. *(inadequately, loosely, otherwise, approximately, differently, incorrectly.)*

exaggerate—*v.* enlarge, magnify, overdraw, over-paint, strain, overestimate, embellishment, amplify, heighten, overstate, inflate. *(attenuate, lenify, soften, modify, disparage, palliate, mitigate, qualify, understate, minimize, underestimate.)*

examine—*v.* ponder, perpend, scrutinize, prove, discuss, search, explore, weigh, inspect, overhaul, inquire, study, test, criticize, investigate, survey. *(conjecture, slur, guess, discard, misinvestigate, misconsider, ignore.)*

example—*n.* specimen, model, copy, illustration, issue, development, sample, pattern, instance, standard. *(material, law, stock, character, substance, rule, case,* principle, quality, system, anomaly.)

excellent—*adj.* superior, great, fine, splendid, exceptional, superb, remarkable, outstanding, magnificent, choice. *(average, inadequate, mediocre, deficient, rotten, worthless, so-so, inferior.)*

except—*v.* save, segregate, exclude, bar, negate, omit, ignore. *(include, state, propound, admit, count, reckon, classify, affirm, attest.)*

exceptional—*adj.* peculiar, unusual, rare, uncommon, irregular, abnormal, outstanding. *(regular, ordinary, common, normal, usual, typical.)*

excessive—*adj.* undue, overmuch, extravagant, immoderate, enormous, inordinate, exorbitant, unreasonable, superfluous, superabundant, extreme. *(scant, inadequate, insufficient, want, shortage.)*

excuse—*v.* pardon, exculpate, condone, exonerate, release, absolve, extenuate, defend, forgive, vindicate, overlook, remit, mitigate, indulge, free, justify, acquit, exempt, alibi. *(inculpate, sentence, strain, charge, condemn, exact, accuse, blame, criticize.)*

exemplary—*adj.* praiseworthy, honorable, meritorious, excellent, laudable, conspicuous, wary, worthy, commendable. *(objectionable, regrettable, exceptionable, detestable, worthless.)*

exempt—*adj.* irresponsible, free, clear, privileged, unamenable, absolved, liberated, special, responsible, liable, amenable, subject, accountable.

exercise—*n*. use, application, drill, employment, exertion, training, practice, discipline, preparation. *(idleness, ease, recreation, relaxation, inactivity, rest.)*

exhaust—*v*. spend, weaken, void, drain, debilitate, deplete, weary, waste, empty, consume. *(replenish, refresh, obtain, fill, invigorate, augment.)*

existence—*n*. entity, creature, being, subsistence, life. *(non-existence, chimera, nothingness, nonenity.)*

expand—*v*. dilate, open, spread, amplify, unfold, distend, swell, enlarge, diffuse, extend, develop. *(curtail, restrict, contract, diminish, condense, attenuate, deflate.)*

expect—*v*. await, forebode, anticipate, wait for, foresee, forecast, contemplate, hope, rely on, predict. *(recognize, realize, welcome, fear, greet, hail, dread.)*

expediency—*n*. advantage, aptness, utility, interest, usefulness. *(disadvantage, inutility, idealism, detriment, inexpediency.)*

expend—*v*. disburse, waste, use, exhaust, spend, lay out, consume, dissipate. *(economize, preserve, husband, save, hoard.)*

expense—*n*. cost, payment, outlay, price, amount, charge, expenditure. *(receipt, income, proceeds, profit, gain.)*

experience—*v*. feel, encounter, suffer, try, undergo, endure, perceive. *(miss, e-vade, foil, escape, lose, baffle.)*

experience—*n*. test, proof, habit, knowledge, experiment, trial, observation. *(theory, surmise, inexperience.)*

explain—*v*. teach, decipher, interpret, expound, elucidate, illustrate, demonstrate, clear up, describe. *(obscure, bewilder, mystify, confuse, misinterpret, darken.)*

explanation—*n*. interpretation, description, explication, sense, exposition, reason, analysis. *(obscuration, misinterpretation, mystification, confusion, complication.)*

explicit—*adj*. detailed, declaratory, stated, determinate, express, plain, precise, inobscure, categorical, distinctly, definite. *(implied, vague, obscure, implicit, hinted, suggestive.)*

expression—*n*. indication, term, lineament, phrase, delivery, countenance, feature, look, face. *(enigma, suppression, falsification, solecism, restraint, misstatement.)*

exquisite—*adj*. refined, perfect, intense, delicious, choice, elegant, rare, consummate, matchless, delicate. *(coarse, ordinary, gross, common, uncouth.)*

extend—*v*. expand, increase, reach, apply, spread, avail, prolong, augment, unfurl, stretch, amplify, enlarge. *(contract, narrow, fail, return, curtail, constrict, miss, restrict, limit, recur, shorten.)*

extinguish—*v*. quench, put out, abolish, extirpate, annihilate, destroy, eradicate, kill, douse, smother. *(replen-*

ish, promote, propagate, confirm, implant, secure, establish, ignite, cherish, invigorate, light

extraneous—adj. irrelevant, extra, immaterial, incidental, external, accidental, superfluous, nonessential, peripheral. (apropos, apt, inherent, germane, pertinent, relevant, essential.)

extraordinary—adj. uncommon, preposterous, unwonted, wonderful, strange, monstrous, unprecedented, peculiar, marvelous, prodigious, amazing, unusual, remarkable. (unimportant, frequent,

wonted, usual customary, common, ordinary, unremarkable, expected.)

extravagant—adj. abnormal, wild, profuse, monstrous, lavish, wasteful, profligate, reckless, prodigal, absurd, preposterous, excessive. (usual, frugal, sound, consistent, fair, sober careful, thrifty, economical, regular, rational.)

extreme—adj. ultimate, final, distant, immoderate, severe, terminal, remote, extravagant, last, utmost, farthest, most violent. (moderate, judicious, initial, primal, average, mild.)

F

fable—n. fiction, falsehood, romance, fabrication, romance, parable, apologue, fantasy, allegory, untruth, novel, invention. (narrative, truth, history, fact, authenticity.)

fabrication—n. deceit, fiction, forgery, lie, deception, fib, untruth, prevarication, creation. (fact, verity, destruction, truth, reality, actuality.)

facetious—adj. jocular, droll, pungent, comical, jesting, humorous, clever, flippant, witty, funny. (matter-of-fact, saturnine, lugubrious, grave, heavy, sombre, dull, serious, sedate, sad.)

facile—adj. tractable, indulgent, irrisolute, affable, pliable, docile, characterless, easy, weak, flexible, manageable, dexterous. (obstinate, crusty, self-willed, self-

reliant, sturdy, determined, inflexible, resolue, independent, pig-headed, arduous.)

facility—n. address, quickness, dexterity, adroitness, proficiency, ease, readiness, pliancy, skill. (awkwardness, labor, ineptness, difficulty, exertion.)

fact—n. deed, certainty, event, truth, reality, incident, occurence, circumstance. (supposition, unreality, delusion, romance, fiction, opinion, falsehood, invention, lie, chimera.)

fade—v. decline, etiolate, pale, vanish, fall, droop, dissolve, set, fail, bleach, dwindle, change, blur, taper. (increase, endure, bloom, stand, rise, brighten, grown, flourish, last, abide.)

failure—n. lapse, miscarriage, decline, disappointment, collapse, ruin, insolvency, defeat, bankruptcy. *(victory, conquest, prosperity, luck, success, hit, fortune.)*

faint—*adj.* languid, inconspicious, weak, fatigued, irresolute, exhausted, obscure, faded, collapse, unenergetic, feeble, timid, pale, half-hearted, dim. *(glaring, strong, fresh, vigorous, conspicuous, energetic, marked, resolute, daring, courageous, prominent.)*

fair—*adj.* clear, unspotted, reasonable, serene, just, equitable, open, impartial, attractive, spotless, untarnished, unblemished, beautiful, honorable. *(fraudulent, dull, disfigured, lowering, fowl, inclement, unfair, ugly, dishonorable.)*

faithful—*adj.* firm, loyal, close, correspondent, equivalent, incorruptible, true, staunch, attached, accurate, consistent, exact, trustworthy. *(fickle, inexact, false, capricious, faithless, treacherous, untrue, wavering, inaccurate.)*

fallacy—*n.* error, misconception, chimera, fiction, saphistry, blunder, delusion, bugbear, deception. *(verity, logic, proof, axiom, truth, certainty, fact, argument, postulate, soundness.)*

false—*adj.* faithless, untrue, fiction, fallacious, spurious, fabrication, mendacious, mock, unfaithful, falsity, dishonorable, fib, bagus, sham, counterfeit, deceptive, sophistical, hypocritical, erroneous. *(correct, faithful, true, sound, authentic, genuine, real, honorable, candid, conclusive, staunch.)*

falsify—*v.* misinterpret, cook, mistake, garble, misrepresent, betray, distort, belie. *(correct, declare, verify, expose, rectify, publicate, confirm, exhibit, check, justify, certify.)*

falter—*v.* hesitate, slip, flinch, halt, vacillate, fluctuate, hobble, dubitate, demur, stammer, waver. *(career, proceed, resolve, run, persevere, speed, persist, flow, determine, discourse.)*

fame—*n.* renown, eminence, repute, notice, reputation, prominence, notability, esteem, notoriety. *(anonymity, seclusion, retirement, oblivion, dishonor, infamy.)*

familiar—*adj.* common, intimate, household, conversant, free, apprised, accustomed, frank, well-acquainted, affable, every-day. *(rare, unfamiliar, new, unaccustomed, uncommon, extraordinary, strange, ignorant, unacquainted, inconversant.)*

famous—*adj.* glorious, eminent, celebrated, prominent, illustrious. *(obscure, unknown, unsung, inglorious, humble.)*

fanciful—*adj.* chimerical, fitful, grotesque, unreal, quaint, absurd, whimsical, erroneous, imaginary, eccentric, humorous, freakish, capricious, erratic, fantastic. *(literal, calculable, natural, regular, sober, real, truthful, correct, ordinary, accurate, orderly, prosaic.)*

fancy—*n.* belief, supposition, idea, caprice, conceit, inclination, humor, desire, thought, illusion, imagination, notion, vagary, whim, predilection. *(horror, object, fact, aversion, subject, verity, reality, unadorned, system, order, law, truth.)*

far—*adj.* remote, removed, long-distant, estranged, alienated, faraway, separated, yonder. *(close, adjacent, near, familiar, neighboring, contiguous, handy, convenient.)*

fashion—*n.* mold, shape, ceremony, form, vague, way, guise, manner, style, usage, appearance, figure, practice, character, custom, mode. *(strangeness, work, outlandishness, person, speech, eccentricity, dress, derangement, shapelessness, formlessness.)*

fast—*adj.* gay, firm, dissipated, secure, reckless, fixed, wild, constant, accelerated, steadfast, rapid, stable, unswerving, unyielding, immovable. *(virtuous, loose, slow, sober, insecure, tardy, steady, tenuous, wavering.)*

fastidious—*adj.* dainty, critical, squeamish, over-nice, particular, censorious, punctilious, over-refined, meticulous. *(omnivorous, easy, uncritical, neglectful, coarse, indulgent.)*

fat—*adj.* oleaginous, corpulent, obese, fleshy, unctuous, brawny, pursy, fertile, rich, stout, luxuriant, portly, rotund. *(anatomical, lean, exsanguineous, slender, scant, attenuated, poor, emacinated, barren, marrowless, gaunt, cadaverous.)*

fatal—*adj.* lethal, calamitous, mortal, deadly, destructive, terminal, pernicious. *(harmful, beneficial, superficial, wholesome, slight, nutritious, restorative, salubrious, vitalizing, nonlethal.)*

fate—*n.* doom, necessity, fortune, lot, destiny, end, providence. *(independence, choice, freedom, will, chance, decision.)*

fault—*n.* error, drawback, flow, defect, want, imperfection, misdeed, omission, failure. *(perfection, sufficiency, goodness, completeness, correctness.)*

favor—*n.* patronage, permission, countenance, grace, boon, gift, concession, preference, civility, accomodation, condescension, goodwill, regard, predilection, benefit, kindness. *(discountenance, refusal, withholding, injury, denial, frown, prohibition, disfavor, withdrawal, malice, disapproval.)*

favorable—*adj.* friendly, fond, permissive, auspicious, partial, indulgent, liberal, propitious, concessive, advantageous, beneficial. *(unpropitious, impartial, contrary, unsatisfactory, reluctant, unfavorable.)*

fear—*n.* solicitude, awe, fright, apprehension, timidity, alarm, dread, trepidation, horror, dismay, panic, terror, consternation, misgiving. *(boldness, fearlessness, assurance, bravery, confidence, trust, courage.)*

feasible—*adj.* practicable, attainable, possible, suitable, practical, operable, reasonable, expedient, desirable. *(impractical, unworkable, unsuitable, impossible, unfeasible.)*

feeble—*adj.* scanty, weak, vain, pitiable, wretched, fruitless, poor, frail, incomplete, infirm, debilitated, dull, invalid, forceless, faint, puny, enervated, enfeebled, nerveless. *(robust, effective, abundant, vigorous, strong, active, successful.)*

feeling—*n.* sensation, passion, touch, sensitiveness, pathos, sentiment, contact, emotion, tenderness, impression, sensibility, awareness, consiousness. *(insensateness, callousness, coldness, apathy, insensibility, inexcitability, imperturbability, numbness.)*

felicitous—*adj.* timely, opportune, happy, successful, joyous, appropriate, apropos. *(unhappy, sad, unsuccessful, unfortunate, inopportune, irrelevant, disastrous, untimely.)*

feminine—*adj.* womanly, modest, delicate, soft,tender, gentle, ladylike. *(manly, rude, unfeminine, robust, indelicate, rough, masculine.)*

ferment—*v.* stir up, incite, agitate, trouble, disturb, rouse, shake, seethe, fester, perturb, provoke, effervesce, foam. *(soothe, relax, calm, compose, allay, still, quiet.)*

fertile—*adj.* inventive, rich, copious, ingenious, luxuriant, fruitful, teeming, fecund, productive, prolific, exuberant, causative, pregnant, fraught, conducive. *(unimaginative, poor, uninventive, sterile, in-operative, barren, fruitless, inconducive, ineffective, unproductive, unyielding.)*

fickle—*adj.* unstable, fanciful, inconstant, fitful, restless, capricious, variable, irresolute, shifting, unpredicitable, changeable, veering, unrealiable, vacillating, mutable. *(uniform, sober, steady, orderly, trustworthy, reliable, calculable, well-regulated, faithful.)*

fiction—*n.* myth, invention, romance, fabrication, falsehood, creation, fable, fantasy, figment. *(truth, reality, accuracy, fact, verity.)*

fidelity—*n.* attachment, loyalty, truthfulness, integrity, fealty, honesty, allegiance, faithfulness, devotion, accuracy, exactness, closeness. *(disloyalty, infidelity, treachery, inexactness, disaffection, inaccuracy, untruthfulness, unrealiability.)*

fierce—*adj.* furious, cruel, enraged, violent, ravenous, extreme, savage, ferocious, brutal. *(gentle, docile, mild, harmless, moderate, meek, calm, submissive, placid, domesticated.)*

fiery—*adj.* hot-brained, vehement, irritable, hot, impassioned, ardent, fervid, fervent, glowing, fierce, smoldering, enkindled, passionate, excited, irascible, choleric. *(tame, cold, quenched, icy, extinguished, indifferent, mild, apathetic, unimpassioned, passionless, phlegmatic.)*

fight—*n.* engagement, battle, action, struggle, encounter, contention, skirmish, conflict, combat, contest.

(reconciliation, compromise, pacification, appeasement.)

figure—*n.* illustration, aspect, delineation, shape, likeness, emblem, metaphor, type, symbol, imagine, form, appearance, condition, silhouette. *(deformity, defigurement, malformation, misrepresentation.)*

fill—*v.* content, expand, replenish, increase, glow, supply, swell, satisfy, rise, gorge, store, glut, appoint, occupy, stuff, saturate. *(diminish, exhaust, evaporate, deprive, ebb, drain, shrink, dissatisfy, subside, stint, misappoint, vacate, empty.)*

filthy—*adj.* polluted, foul, dirty, putrid, sordid, stained, unclean, unwashed, slimy, piggish, squalid. *(washed, hygienic, cleansed, purified, sanitary, decent, virtuous, pure.)*

final—*adj.* terminal, last, decisive, ultimate, latest, irrevocable, definite, conclusive, extreme, developed. *(rudimental, open, nascent, initiative, inchoate, unconcluded, inaugural, dynamic, incipient, current, continuous, progressive.)*

find—*v.* confront, furnish, meet, invent, ascertain, discover, experience, observe, perceive. *(elude, miscontrive, overlook, miss, withdraw, lose, withhold, misplace.)*

fine—*adj.* minute, casuistical, thin, subtle, slender, nice, delicate, high, presumptuous, pure, ostentatious, grand, elegant, noble, showy, pretty, sensitive, beautiful, refined, generous, handsome,

honorable, dull, exemplary, pretentious, excellent, superior, finished, smooth, choice, filmy, artistic, gauzy, keen, pulverized. *(indissective, coarse, unreflective, large, unanalytical, rough, plainspoken, blunt, rude, categorical, unfinished, affable, mean, unaffected, petty, modest, illiberal, unimposing, paltry, mediocre.)*

finesse—*n.* tact, savior faire, discretion, skill, polish, artfulness, cleverness, diplomacy, adroitness, delicacy. *(clumsiness, stupidy, ineptitude, crudeness, tactlessness, maladroitness.)*

finish—*v.* terminate, complete, shape, perfect, end, accomplish, achieve, conclude, cease, desist. *(commence, botch, miscontrive, begin, mar, start, mismanage, undertake, fail, launch.)*

first—*adj.* onmost, leading, chief, primary, highest, pristine, primeval, original, principal, foremost, primitive, earliest. *(secondary, hindmost, subsequent, last, subordinate, unimportant, subservient, lowest, terminating, concluding.)*

fit—*adj.* befitting, proper, decent, ripe, expedient, meet, contrived, apt, calculated, fitting, adequate, adapted, prepared, seemly, suitable, appropriate, particular, becoming, peculiar, decorous, congruous, qualified, germane. *(improper, awkward, unfit, ungainly, inexpedient, misfitting, miscontrived, ill-suited, miscalculated, unseemly, inadequate, inap-*

propriate, unprepared, amiss, unsuitable, out of place.)

fix—*v.* fasten, secure, attach, plant, decide, place, determine, settle, position, link, root, locate, establish, tie, immobilize. *(unsettle, change, shake, remove, transfer, disestablish, unfix, displace, uproot, disconnect, reverse, disarrange, transplant, weaken, disturb.)*

flagrant—*adj.* brazen, scandalous, outrageous, glaring, indecent, blatant, disgraceful, shocking, shameless, notorious, infamous, audacious. *(clandestine, sneaky, concealed, hidden, surreptitious, undercover.)*

flat—*adj.* insipid, mawkish, dull, level, lifeless, tame, vapid, tasteless, downright, horizontal, even, spiritless, absolute, uniform. *(rugged, interesting, sensational, exciting, thrilling, animated.)*

flexible—*adj.* lithe, yielding, elastic, ductile, pliable, easy, pliant, indulgent, rubbery, supple. *(hard, inelastic, inexorable, rigid, tough, inflexible, brittle.)*

flimsy—*adj.* thin, superficial, gauzy, shallow, poor, weak, fragile, transparent, trifling, puerile, trivial, inane, slight. *(substantial, sound, irrefragable, cogent, durable, solid.)*

flippant—*adj.* forward, malapert, thoughtless, pert, saucy, brazen, superficial. *(deferential, servile, accurate, complimentary, flattering, respectful, polite, obsequious, considerate.)*

flood—*n.* abundance, drench, inundation, deluge, shower. *(ebb, subsidence, drought, scarcity, drain, shortage.)*

florid—*adj.* sanguine, overwrought, rubicund, meretricious, flowery, embellished, ornate. *(exsanguineous, unadorned, sober, pallid, nude, understated, chaste, bare.)*

flounder—*v.* blunder, wallow, roll, bungle, tumble, struggle, boggle. *(career, rise, emerge, skim, course, flow, emanate, speed, flourish.)*

flourish—*v.* thrive, triumph, wave, flower, prosper, speed, brandish. *(decline, ground, arrest, fail, miscarry, sheathe, wither, fade, founder.)*

flow—*v.* issue, course, run, surge, stream, career, glide, progress. *(stick, hesitate, halt, recoil, abate, regurgitate, stint, ebb, stickle, stop, fail, beat.)*

fluent—*adj.* facile, flowing, glib, graceful, articulate, smooth, ready, effusive, uninterrupted, expert, constrained. *(halting, hesitant, limping, constrained, stammering, uneven.)*

flurry—*v.* ruffle, excite, fluster, agitate, disturbance, worry. *(compose, calm, soothe, tranquilize, mesmerize, quiet.)*

foible—*n.* failing, weakness, peccadillo, infirmity, defect, fault. *(atrocity, sin, crime, strength, enormity.)*

follow—*v.* accompany, succeed, attend, copy, pursue, observe, chase, shadow, ensue, supplant, obey, imitate, result. *(elude, abandon, quit, produce, forerun, shun, cause avoid, disobey, precede.)*

folly—*n.* nonsense, imbecility, absurdity, madness, silliness, misconduct, weakness, irrationality, foolishness, imprudence. *(wisdom, judgment, sobriety, sense prudence, allay, rationality.)*

foment—*v.* cherish, propagate, fan, agitate, encourage, excite. *(extinguish, extirpate, allay, quench, discourage, hinder.)*

fond—*adj.* attached, foolish, weak, empty, devoted, silly, loving, doting, enamored, affectionate, friendly. *(sensible, unloving, undemonstrative, averse, hostile, well-groomed, unaffectionate, rational, strong-minded, austere.)*

foolish—*adj.* idiotic, shallow, simple, ridiculous, senseless, crazed, weak, asinine, nonsensical, injudicious, contemptible, absurd, brainless, witless, preposterous, silly, imbecile, objectionable, irrational. *(sane, advisable, deep, sensible, eligible, clearsighted, wise, calculating, sagacious, intelligent, strongminded, judicious, prudent, sound.)*

forbearance—*n.* restraint, sympathy, meekness, mildness, temperance, gentleness, mercy, clemency, patience, tolerance, self-control. *(vindictiveness, rancor, ruthlessness, impatience, intolerance, vengefulness.)*

forbidding—*adj.* deterrent, offensive, repulsive, prohibitory, menacing. *(encouraging,*

permissive, attractive, cordial, alluring, seductive.)*

force—*n.* strength, instrumentality, cogency, violent, coercion, power, agency, validity, compulsion, army duress, host, vehemence, pressure, dint, might, vigor. *(counteraction, inefficiency, pointlessness, inconclusiveness, weakness, debility, feebleness, impotence, neutralization.)*

foreign—*adj.* outlandish, strange, extraneous, exotic, alien, imported, irrelevant. *(native, pertinent, domestic, germane, indigenous, congenial.)*

forfeit—*n.* mulct, loss, penalty, damages, transgress, amercement, fine. *(reward, douceur, compensation, gratuity, entice, premium, remuneration, bribe.)*

forget—*v.* unlearn, overlook, lose, oblivate, pretermit, unintentionally. *(learn, recollect, mind, treasure, reminisce, retain, acquire, remember.)*

form—*v.* mould, constitue, frame, devise, produce, create, shape, fashion, contrive, make, scheme, arrange, construct. *(analyze, deform, distort, disorganize, disintegrate, dislocate, dissipate, derange, dismember, subvert.)*

formal—*adj.* complete, sufficient, stately, ceremonious, stiff, explicit, affected, systematic, methodical, exact, regular, shapely, precise, pompous, dignified, correct. *(incomplete, easy, unceremonious, irregular, informal,* *nonconformist, inadequate, unassuming, incorrect.)*

formality—*n.* parade, stateliness, ritualism, punctiliousness, ceremony, etiquette, affectation. *(casualness, ease, nonconformism, eccentricity, informality.)*

former—*adj.* antecedent, ancient, anterior, foregoing, preceding, previous, preliminary, bygone, first- mentioned, prior, earlier. *(subsequent, latter, succeeding, future, modern, ensuing, posterior, coming.)*

fortunate—*adj.* propitious, happy, felicitous, auspicious, successful, blessed, lucky, prosperous, providential. *(unhappy, disastrous, unlucky, infelicitous, unfortunate.)*

forthright—*adj.* direct, candid, blunt, honest, frank, sincere, explicit, plain, straightforward, truthful. *(guarded, equivocal, misleading, devious, indirect, circuitous.)*

forward—*adj.* ready, anxious, bold, self-assertive, presumptuous, advanced, eager, brash, obtrusive, impertinent, confident, progressive, onward. *(reluctant, slow, modest, timid, backward, tardy, retiring, indifferent.)*

found—*v.* institute, fix, root, ground, establish, set, endow, plant, originate, build, base, setup, rest. *(supplant, uproot, disestablish, annihilate, subvert.)*

foundation—*n.* establishment, basis, ground, rudiments, underlying, institution, footing, skeleton, base, origin, groundwork, principle,

substratum. *(superstructure, pinnacle, disestablishment, summit.)*

fragrant—*adj.* scented, balmy, aromatic, odoriferous, redolent, odorous, perfumed, sweet-smelling, sweet-scented, spicy. *(scentless, fetid, malodorous, inodorous, mephitic.)*

frail—*adj.* erring, delicate, mutable, irresolute, wispy. *(virtuous, robust, lasting, resolute, vigorous.)*

frank—*adj.* candid, unreserved, free, honest, sincere, plain, evident, ingenious, open, artless, familiar, easy, outspoken. *(close, guarded, disingenious, reserved, devious.)*

freakish—*adj.* whimsical, erratic, sportful, capricious, grotesque, frisky, fanciful, strange. *(sober, unwhimsical, reliable, uniform, temperate, equable, demure, consistent, unfanciful, steady.)*

free—*adj.* playing, open, unoccupied, unimpeded, unhindered, gratuitous, at liberty, liberal, unconfined, loose, munificent, frank, gratis, generous, detached, operating, unobstructed, permitted, exempt, unconditional, bounteous, clear, untrammelled, careless, easy, unreserved, bountiful. *(stingy, qualified, intern, amenable, unlawful, impeded, occupied, restricted, bound, biased, enslaved, subservient, shocked, clogged, obstructed, compulsory, liable, conditional, niggardly.)*

frequent—*adj.* repeated, recurrent, continual, common, many, numerous, usual, habitual, general. *(solitary, scanty, few, sporadic, casual, rare.)*

fresh—*adj.* young, cool, renewed, untarnished, blooming, novel, modern, flourishing, unskilled, untried, ruddy, unfaded, new, unimpaired, recent, vigorous. *(stale, weary, stagnant, original, tarnished, decayed, sickly, mouldy, fusty, polluted, musty, putrid, pallid, faded, impaired, ordinary, former, old, jaded.)*

fretful—*adj.* fractious, impatient, waspish, cranky, petulant, peevish, irritable. *(forbearing, meek, unmurmuring, agreeable, patient, contented, resigned.)*

friction—*n.* grating, abrasion, rubbing, attrition, contact, grinding. *(detachment, harmony, lubrication, isolation, compatibility.)*

friend—*n.* companion, familiar, chum, coadjutor, adherent, ally, intimate, confidant, messmate, acquaintance, associate. *(foe, antagonist, rival, opponent, adversary, enemy, competitor.)*

friendly—*adj.* well-disposed, kindly, neighborly, affectionate, cordial, comradely, well-inclined, amicable, social, sociable, favorable. *(ill-disposed, inimical, distant, antagonistic, averse, hostile, aloof, ill-inclined.)*

frightful—*adj.* horrible, ugly, monstrous, direful, shockful, terrific, horrendous, horrid, awful, dreadful, hideous, grim, alarming, terrible. *(at-tractive, fair, lovely, charming, encouraging, beautiful, pleasing.)*

frivolous—*adj.* silly, petty, worthless, flighty, trifling, trivial, giddy. *(earnest, grave, significant, important, serious.)*

frolic—*n.* game, festivity, gambol, lark, merry-making, play, sport, entertainment, gayety, spree, prank, outing. *(undertaking, engagement, obligation, study, occupation, purpose.)*

frugal—*adj.* economical, abstinent, temperate, thrifty, sparing, provident, parsimonious, abstemious, saving, cautious. *(luxurious, prodigal, intemperate, generous, self-indulgent, extravagant, profuse.)*

fruitful—*adj.* prolific, fraught, effectual, successful, abundant, fecund, productive, pregnant, causative, useful, fertile, plenteous, plentiful, valuable. *(sterile, fruitless, useless, futile, abortive, ineffectual, barren, unproductive.)*

fulfill—*v.* complete, verify, achieve, effect, consummate, execute, fill, accomplish, discharge. *(sober, delicate, nice, chaste, abandon.)*

function—*n.* part, capacity, duty, administration, operation, power, office, character, business, role, discharge, exercise, employment, pursuit. *(maladministration, misdemeanor, misconduct, misdeed.)*

fundamental—*adj.* important, essential, primary, foremost, indispensable. *(unimportant, ascititious,*

E
F

secondary, superficial, non-essential, adventitious.)

funny—*adj.* droll, laughable, jocose, ludicrous, ridiculous, amusing, diverting, humorous, comical, sportive. *(tedious, lugubrious, grave, sad, sober, lamentable, serious, dismal, mournful, dull.)*

furnish—*v.* provide, afford, bestow, give, provide, purvey, yield, equip, supply. *(with-*

draw, demolish, dismantle, withhold.)

fuss—*n.* excitement, worry, ado, bustle, fidget, flurry, tumult, stir, agitation. *(peace, tranquility, silence, calm, quiet, composure, sedateness.)*

future—*n.* coming, destiny, advenient, forthcoming, forecast. *(bygone, previous, past, gone, prior.)*

G

gabby—*adj.* loquacious, wordy, chatty, talkative, garrulous, windy, talky, glib, talkative, voluble. *(terse, quiet, taciturn, reticent, laconic, reserved.)*

gain—*v.* get, procure, reach, profit, earn, realize, reap, acquire, win, accomplish, obtain, benefit, attain, achieve. *(suffer, deplete, forfeit, lose, squander.)*

gallant—*adj.* chivalrous, courteous, fearless, valiant, splendid, gay, undaunted, showy, bold, courageous, heroic, intrepid, brave. *(discourteous, timid, churlish, cowardly, fearful.)*

game—*n.* recreation, amusement, diversion, contest, play, frolic, pastime, sport. *(labor, duty, flagging, weariness, study, trust, toil, business, occupation.)*

garble—*v.* misquote, cook, color, pervert, misstate, distort, falsify, dress, misrepresent, mutilate. *(recite, quote, cite, clarify, extract.)*

gather—*v.* assemble, mass, store, accumulate, muster,

collect, marshal, congregate, group, deduce, pile. *(disperse, scatter, separate, distribute, spread, dissipate, allot.)*

gaudy—*adj.* fine, bespangled, gay, showy, garish, ostentatious, showy, tawdry, meretricious. *(simple, chaste, fine, subtle, rich, handsome.)*

gauge—*v.* fathom, probe, assess, measure, evaluate, appraise, calculate. *(conjecture, scan, observe, survey, view, guess, mismeasure, analyze.)*

gawky—*adj.* ungainly, clumsy, awkward, foolish, uncouth, clownish. *(handy, handsome, polished, neat, graceful.)*

gay—*adj.* merry, lively, sportive, smart, gladsome, cheerful, blithe, joyous, jolly, sprightly, festive, pleasuresome. *(melancholy, sad, sombre, dowdy, miserable, heavy, grave, dull.)*

general—*adj.* universal, comprehensive, broad, prevalent, common, impartial, collective, generic, panoramic, vague, categorical. *(ex-*

clusive, limited, individual, local, specific, precise, explicit.)

generous—*adj.* chivalrous, honorable, disinterested, magnanimous, munificent, noble, benevolent, liberal, bountiful, open-hearted. *(ignoble, selfish, mean, illiberal, churlish, stingy, petty.)*

genial—*adj.* cordial, cheering, festive, hearty, restorative, warm, balmy, merry, joyous, revivifying, affable. *(cutting, deleterious, deadly, destructive, lethal, cold, surly, harsh, noxious, blighting, uncongenial.)*

genteel—*adj.* well-bred, courteous, elegant, polished, cultured, polite, refined, aristocratic, graceful, fashionable. *(boorish, clownish, unpolished, plebeian, rude, ill-bred, churlish, unfashionable, inelegant.)*

gentle—*adj.* polite, mild, tame, amiable, soft, tender, serene, placid, meek, docile, bland, high-bred, courteous. *(rude, fierce, heartless, savage, coarse, rough.)*

genuine—*adj.* true, pure, natural, sincere, veritable, proven, real, authentic, unalloyed, unaffected, sound, unadulterated. *(apocryphal, fictitious, counterfeit, spurious, adulterated, fake.)*

get—*v.* procure, earn, attain, achieve, acquire, secure, obtain, gain, receive. *(forfeit, forego, lose, avoid, surrender.)*

ghastly—*adj.* wan, cadaverous, pallid, shocking, hideous, spectral, grim, deathlike, appalling. *(bloom-*

ing, buxom, ruddy, seemly, fresh, comely, beautiful.)

giddy—*adj.* vertiginous, inconstant, lofty, dizzy, flighty, whirling, thoughtless, unsteady, faint, beetling, harebrained. *(slow, thoughtful, steady, unelevated, circumspect, serious, wary, low, earnest, ponderous, stationary.)*

gift—*n.* present, boon, benefaction, talent, alms, donation, douceur, faculty, endowment, gratuity, grant, contribution. *(refusal, purchase, compensation, inanity, forfeit, fine, penalty, reservation, wages, earnings, remuneration, stupidy, surrender, confiscation.)*

gigantic—*adj.* huge, enormous, mammoth, colossal, tremendous, immense, gargantuan, vast, stupendous, prodigious. *(miniature, tiny, dwarfish, small, microscopic, infinitesimal.)*

gist—*n.* pith, substance, force, essence, main point, marrow, kernel, core, meaning. *(redundancy, environment, garb, surplusage, additament, accessories, clothing, excess.)*

give—*v.* grant, impart, produce, concede, afford, furnish, donate, bestow, confer, yield, surrender, present, communicate. *(withdraw, retain, fail, deny, accept, withhold, refuse, grasp, restrain.)*

glad—*adj.* joyous, gratified, gleeful, delighted, elated, happy, merry, joyful, cheerful, gladsome, blithesome, pleased. *(sorrowful, disap-*

G
H

pointed, tearful, dismal, sorry, unhappy, disastrous.)

glare—v. shine, ray, glow, stare, dazzle, beam, gleam, radiate. (scintillate, smoulder, glisten, sparkle, flicker, glance, shimmer, glitter, glimmer, glister, flash.)

glassy—adj. smooth, glacial, brittle, crystalline, limpid, silken, expressionless, glossy, pellucid, transparent, glabrous, polished, vitreous. (scabrous, muddy, opaque, pliant, uneven, bright, rough, rugged, tough, luteous, turbid.)

gloom—n. depression, despair, woe, melancholy, despondency, sorrow, pessimism, misery, sadness, dejection. (glee, happiness, joy, delight, mirth, frivolity, cheerfulness.)

glory—n. radiance, honor, fame, pomp, magnificence, renown, prestige, splendor, luster, celebrity, brightness, effulgence. (igonominy, dishonor, obscurity, cloud, degradation, infamy.)

glut—v. fill, cram, cloy, gorge, satiate, surfeit, stuff, devour. (empty, disgorge, vacant, void.)

go—v. depart, travel, reach, evaporate, move, budge, pass, vanish, extend, stir, set out. (stay, remain, abide, endure, fail, approach, lack, stand, come, persist, rest.)

good—adj. complete, sound, pious, propitious, suitable, sufficient, valid, actual, honorable, righteous, true, just, efficient, excellent, right, virtuous, benevolent, serviceable, admirable, competent, real, considerable, reputable, proper, upright. (imperfect, vicious, evil, niggardly, unserviceable, inefficient, incompetent, fictitious, inconsiderable, disgraceful, bad, mediocre, disreputable, mean, supposititious, invalid, inadequate, unsuitable, unpropitious, profane, unsound, wrong.)

good—n. benefit, gain, mercy, prosperity, profit, welfare, enjoyment, interest, boon, weal, advantage, blessing, virtue. (loss, disadvantage, calamity, hurt, catastrophe, curse, ill, injury, infliction, evil, detriment.)

goodly—adj. desirable, fair, fine, personable, pleasant, excellent, comely, graceful, considerable. (uncomely, unpleasant, inconsiderable, disagreeable, undesirable.)

goodness—n. honesty, integrity, morality, virtue, righteousness, merit, innocence, benevolence, worth, quality. (dishonesty, vice, evil, wickedness, corruption, malice, imperfection, cruelty, spite.)

gorgeous—adj. splendid, rich, grand, magnificent, glorious, costly, superb, strong, beautiful. (naked, bare, dingy, poor, homely, threadbare, cheap.)

govern—v. direct, moderate, conduct, manage, rule, influence, control, guide, sway, command, supervise. (misdirect, misrule, submit, comply, miscontrol, follow.)

grace—n. beauty, kindness, charm, pardon, favor, refinement, condescension, elegance, mercy, excellence. *(deformity, pride, awkwardness, ugliness, gawkiness, inelegance, unkindness, disfavor.)*

gracious—*adj.* courteous, kind, condescending, friendly, gentle, affable, beneficent, compassionate, benignant, civil, merciful, tender. *(discourteous, churlish, uncivil, haughty, illdisposed, ungracious, austere.)*

gradual—*adj.*step by step, slow, progressive, continuous, steady, gradational, unintermittent, successive. *(instantaneous, recurrent, disconnected, abrupt, sudden, broken, intermittent, momentary, periodic, hasty, discontinuous.)* .

grand—*adj.* dignified, important, magnificent, majestic, exalted, impressive, splendid, elevated, gorgeous, superb, large, imposing, eventful, grandly, august, stately, lofty, pompous, sublime. *(undignified, secondary, unimportant, little, ignoble, insignificant, mean, paltry, unimposing, inferior, petty, beggarly, common.)*

grant—*v.* award, accord, bestow, donate, impart, confer, allow, give. yield, concede, apportion, allocate. *(refuse, deny, reject, renounce, forbid, despite, repel, withdraw, disclaim, withhold.)*

graphic—*adj.* illustrative, pictorial, vivid, described, striking, forcible, picturesque, descriptive, emphatic, comprehensible. *(unrealistic, dull, undescriptive, unpictur-*

esque, hazy, unillustrative, dubious.)

grateful—*adj.* acceptable, thankful, welcome, pleasant, appreciative, agreeable, obliged. *(disagreeable, rude, disobliged, unpleasant, careless, ungrateful.)*

gratify—*v.* satisfy, humor, charm, please, delight, indulge, regale, exhilarate. *(dissatisfy, stint, curb, inure, deprive, displease, deny, disappoint, discipline, harden, frustrate.)*

gratitude—*n.* gratefulness, obligation, thankfulness, acknowledgment, thanks, recognition. *(resentment, ingratitude, indignation, unthankfulness, beholdenness, thanklessness.)*

grave—*adj.* serious, weighty, sedate, thoughtful, sombre, important, heavy, sad, cogent, subdued, momentous, pressing, demure, sober, solemn, aggravated. *(merry, unimportant, trivial, frivolous, joyous, inconsequential, futile, light, ridiculous, facetious.)*

great—*adj.* huge, protracted, large, bulky, gigantic, grand, august, magnanimous, powerful, noticeable, stupendous, big, numerous, wide, excellent, immense, majestic, vast, sublime, eminent, noble, exalted. *(narrow, scanty, short, ignoble, unimportant, little, few, diminutive, puny, mean, weak.)*

greedy—*adj.* voracious, desirous, gluttonous, mercenary, avaricious, hungry. *(abstinent, contented, philan-*

G
H

thropic, abstemious, indifferent.)

grief—*n.* tribulation, mourning, affliction, sadness, heartbreak, trouble, woe, regret, sorrow. *(exultation, elation, bliss, joy, hilarity, solace, delight.)*

grieve—*v.* burden, distress, wound, sorrow, affict, lament, deplore, weep, trouble, annoy, bewail, pain, hurt, mourn, complain. *(console, please, exult, alleviate, gladden, ease, soothe, rejoice, gratify.)*

grim—*adj.* ferocious, hideous, ghastly, stern, fierce, terrible, savage, ugly, sullen. *(docile, placid, mild., amiable, benign, attractive.)*

groan—*v.* whine, grumble, moan, lament, growl, complain. *(cackle, titter, chuckle, laugh, giggle, snicker.)*

gross—*adj.* flagrant, deplorable, grievous, shocking, glaring, dreadful, outrageous, obvious, unmitigated. *(minor, trivial, small, graceful, elegant, refined, cultivated, inoffensive.)*

groundless—*adj.* suppositious, baseless, gratuitous, false, unwarranted, vain, unfounded, fanciful, chimerical. *(substantial, actual, authentic, well-founded, logical, authoritative, justified.)*

group—*n.* bunch, assemblage, class, clump, assembly, order, cluster, knot, collection, congregation, collocation. *(individual, confu-sion, isolation, crowd, medley, disperse.)*

grudge—*v.* retain, envy, spare, resent, covet, withhold, stint. *(welcome, spend, impart, gratify, please, satisfy.)*

grudge—*n.* grievance, rancor, pique, discontent, spite, aversion, resentment, refusal, dissatisfaction, hatred. *(satisfaction, bestowal, approval, benefaction, liberality, complacency, welcome, contentment.)*

gruff—*adj.* surly, harsh, blunt, impolite, rough, bearish, rude. *(mild, courteous, genial, affable, smooth.)*

guess—*v.* surmise, suppose, fancy, estimate, imagine, suspect, conjecture, divine. *(prove, establish, deduce, elaborate, examine, certainty, investigate, demonstrate.)*

guide—*v.* direct, pilot, superintend, train, lead, manage, shield, conduct, regulate, influence. *(misconduct, mismanage, misguide, betray, mislead, dupe, deceive, miseducate, misregulate, misdirect, ensore.)*

gush—*v.* stream, gush, rush, flow-out, burst, eject, flow, pour out, spout. *(drop, trickle, drain, filter, drip, dribble, ooze, percolate, strain, discharge.)*

guttural—*adj.* harsh, gruff, deep, hoarse, rasping, cracked, rough, gargling, throaty, inarticulate. *(high, ringing, musical, clear, pleasant, dulcet, nasal, squeaky.)*

H

habit—*n.* custom, association, usage, way, routine, manner, practice, inurement, familiarity, habituation. *(inexperience, desuetude, irregularity, dishabituation, inconversance.)*

habitual—*adj.* ordinary, customary, familiar, wonted, chronic, regular, perpetual, usual, accustomed. *(extraordinary, unusual, rare, sporadic, irregular, occasional, exceptional.)*

hail—*v.* salute, applaud, greet, acclaim, cheer, call, honor, signal, summon, accost, welcome. *(ignore, avoid, shun, neglect, pass over, disregard, rebuff, insult.)*

half—*n.* bisection, partial, dimidiation, moiety, divided. *(entirety, whole, total, integrity, totality, aggregate.)*

halt—*v.* rest, falter, stammer, dubitate, hold, still, restrain, stop, limp, hammer, demur, pause, stand still. *(decide, speed, career, continue, advance, determine, flow.)*

handsome—*adj.* good-looking, liberal, ample, graceful, elegant, stately, comely, generous, beautiful, pretty, lovely. *(ill-looking, illiberal, uncomely, unhandsome, repulsive, ungenerous.)*

handy—*adj.* convenient, helpful, dexterous, expert, accessible, near, useful, manageable, ready. *(inconvenient, useless, unwieldy, worthless, remote, awkward, cumbrous, unhandy.)*

haphazard—*adj.* aimless, random, accidental, purposeless, casual, fortuitous, incidental, arbitrary, unmethodical, unsystematic. *(controlled, planned, deliberate, intentional, designed, organized, thoughtful, premeditated, systematic.)*

happy—*adj.* fortunate, successful, joyous, blithesome, glad, ecstatic, lucky, felicitous, delighted, merry, prosperous, blissful. *(unfortunate, sorry, unsuccessful, unlucky, unhappy, lugubrious, ecstatic, infelicitous, sorrowful, disappointed, dull, desponding.)*

hard—*adj.* dense, compact, impenetrable, difficult, distressing, oppressive, unfeeling, born, forced, inexplicable, severe, obdurate, callous, hardened, cruel, flinty, constrained, harsh, stubborn, exacting, rigorous, firm, grievous, arduous, unyielding, solid, formidable. *(fluid, elastic, penetrable, mild, tender, uninvolved, intelligible, soft, liquid, brittle, easy, pliable, lenient, ductile, simple, perspicuous, resilient.)*

hardship—*n.* burden, grievance, infliction, affliction, ordeal, endurance, calamity, annoyance, trouble. *(amusement, recreation, relief, facilitation, treat, pleasure, happiness, alleviation, boon, gratification, assuagement.)*

hardy—*adj.* robust, resolute, stout-hearted, intrepid, manly, sturdy, valiant, brave, vigorous, inured, strong. *(un-*

G
H

inured, irresolute, debilitated, fragile, weak, delicate, enervated, tender, dainty.)

harm—n. mischief, detriment, evil, misfortune, mishap, injury, hurt, trauma, damage, wrong, ill. *(boon, improvement, compensation, remedy, benefit, amelioration, reparation, healing, welfare, cure.)*

harmonious—adj. accordant, uniform, musical, tuneful, peaceful, amicable, concordant, compatible, congruous, proportioned, melodious, dulcet, consistent, agreeable, friendly. *(discordant, unshapely, unmelodious, grating, riotous, quarrelsome, conflicting, incongruous, disproportioned, harsh, sharp, unfriendly, unpeaceful.)*

hasty—adj. rapid, hurried, impetuous, head-long, incomplete, immature, precipitate, passionate, quick, rash, prompt, speedy, superficial, irascible, reckless, crude, undeveloped, swift, fiery, slight, excitable, cursory. *(leisurely, close, developed, complete, thoughtful, meticulous, slow, careful, reflective, matured, deliberate, elaborate.)*

hateful—adj. detestable, odious, execrable, repulsive, offensive, abominable, vile, heinous, loathsome. *(lovely, delightful, enticing, tempting, agreeable, pleasant, lovable, desirable, attractive, enjoyable.)*

have—v. possess, entertain, bear, keep, acquire, own, feel, accept, enjoy. *(need,*

forego, reject, desiderate, desire, crave, want, lose, discard, miss, covet.)

hazard—n. risk, danger, imperil, venture, dare, peril, jeopardy, chance. *(security, warrant, calculation, safety, assurance, protection, certainty, law.)*

hazy—adj. nebulous, filmy, cloudy, caliginous, smoky, murky, gauzy, misty, foggy. *(clear, transparent, distinct, crystalline, diaphanous.)*

head—n. crown, leader, mind, section, topic, culmination, leadership, commander, summit, superior, top, chief, ruler, source, division, gathering, crisis, guide, acme. *(bottom, servant, tail, subordinate, inferiority, bulk, continuation, worker, follower, retainer, subordination, body, subject.)*

healthy—adj. hale, sound, hearty, vigorous, in the pink, robust, virile, strong, hygienic, healing, lusty. *(sickly, ill, weak, delicate, feeble, emaciated, ailing, infirm, debilitated, unsound.)*

hearty—adj. robust, sound, honest, genuine, sincere, hale, generous, healthy, cordial, warm, earnest, well, heart felt. *(delicate, cold, frail, insincere, infirm, unhealthy.)*

heat—n. ardor, excitement, ebullition, temperature, intensity, fever, passion, warmth. *(indifference, calmness, reflection, tranquillity, composure, subsidence, coolness.)*

heavy—adj. ponderous, slow, inert, stupid, impenetrable, cumbrous, afflictive, burdensome, laborious, weighty, dull, stolid, grievous, oppressive, sluggish, depressed, substantial. *(trifling, agile, light, quick, alleviative, skimpy, buoyant, weightless, trivial, active, joyous, consolatory, animating.)*

heighten—*v.* increase, intensify, vivify, raise, lift up, strengthen, amplify, exalt, enhance, color, aggravate, exaggerate. *(depress, deteriorate, temper, extenuate, qualify, abate, lower, diminish, abase, tone, modify.)*

heinous—*adj.* hateful, detestable, atrocious, abominable, enormous, repugnant, flagrant, flagitious, odious, execrable. *(laudable, praiseworthy, justifiable, palliable, creditable, excellent, meritorious, distinguished, excusable.)*

help—*v.* succor, prevent, assist, co-operate, second, befriend, aid, remedy, avoid, promote, relieve. *(obstruct, incur, hinder, aggravate, oppose.)*

herculean—*adj.* formidable, mighty, prodigious, heroic, titanic, exhausting, difficult, arduous, overwhelming, stupendous. *(feeble, delicate, weak, restful, effortless, frail, easy.)*

hereditary—*adj.* ancestral, inbred, lineal, inherited, congenital. *(won, conferred, acquired, earned.)*

heroism—*n.* bravery, valor, courage, daring, gallantry, prowess, boldness, chivalry. *(cowardice, timidity, meanness, weakness, baseness, cravenness.)*

hesitate—*v.* waver, scruple, stammer, doubt, tentative, dubitate, demur, falter, pause. *(determine, flow, positive, career, run, decide.)*

hide—*v.* secrete, dissemble, protect, ensconce, cover, camouflage, burrow, screen, disguise, store, mask, conceal. *(discover, manifest, strip, reveal, expose, exhibit, betray.)*

hideous—*adj.* unshapely, horrid, ugly, grim, repulsive, ghastly, grisly, horrible, monstrous, frightful. *(beautiful, charming, attractive, graceful, captivating.)*

high—*adj.* lofty, eminent, noble, violent, exalted, prominent, elevated, tall, excellent, haughty, proud. *(low, ignoble, mean, affable, insignificant, depressed, stunted, base.)*

hilarious—*adj.* laughable, comical, uproarious, riotous, gleeful, mirthful, boisterous, funny. *(serious, depressed, miserable, melancholy, sad, woebegone.)*

hinder—*v.* interrupt, retard, embarrass, thwart, stop, delay, block, impede, debar, obstruct, prevent. *(expedite, promote, accelerate, enable, support, facilitate, encourage.)*

hoarse—*adj.* grating, raucous, gruff, guttural, rough, harsh, husky. *(mellow, sweet, full, mellifluous, rich, melodious.)*

hold—*v.* grasp, support, defend, occupy, sustain, consider, have, continue, occupy, keep, retain, restrain, maintain, possess, regard, cohere. *(abandon, fail, desert, vacate,*

G
H

break, relinquish, cease, drop, surrender, release, forego, concede.)

hollow—*adj.* concave, weak, insincere, unsubstantial, flimsy, senseless, unsound, empty, foolish, faithless, artificial, void, transparent, vacant, false, sunken. *(solid, strong, sincere, genuine, sound, cogent, full, wellstored, firm, true, substantial.)*

homely—*adj.* coarse, modest, uncomely, plain. *(beautiful, courtly, ostentatious, handsome, refined.)*

honest—*adj.* upright, proper, sincere, reliable, conscientious, honorable, virtuous, right. *(dishonorable, improper, wrong, deceitful, dishonest, vicious, insincere.)*

honor—*n.* reverence, dignity, reputation, high-mindedness, self-respect, grandeur, glory, esteem, respect, nobility, eminence, fame, spirit, renown. *(contempt, slight, degradation, abasement, cowardice, infamy, humiliation, disrespect, irreverence, obscurity, disgrace, demoralization, dishonor.)*

honorary—*adj.* unofficial, nominal, titular, complimentary, gratuitous, unremuneration. *(remuneration, jurisdictional, official, professional, skilled.)*

hope—*n.* prospect, longing, desire, trust, contemplation, anticipation, vision, confidence, expectation. *(despondency, disbelief, abjuration, doubt, abandonment, distrust, despair.)*

horrible—*adj.* destestable, fearful, ghastly, hateful, horrid, frightful, shocking, abominable, dreadful, hideous, terrific, direful, awful. *(desirable, attractive, fair, amiable, lovely, enjoyable, beautiful, pleasant, delightful.)*

hostility—*n.* enmity, will, dislike, animosity, defiance, spite, hatred, contempt, abhorrence, antagonism. *(goodwill, warmth, benevolence, cordiality, friendliness, affability.)*

huge—*adj.* monstrous, vast, large, prodigious, stupendous, mammoth, gigantic, immense, enormous, colossal, bulky, great. *(undersized, puny, petty, pigny, microscopic.)*

humane—*adj.* kind, merciful, compassionate, charitable, benign, tender, benevolent. *(cruel, inhuman, unkind, brutal, unmerciful.)*

humble—*adj.* lowly, meek, low, unassuming, submissive, obscure, modest, unpretending, insignificant. *(lofty, proud, high, arrogant, pretentious, eminent, boastful, assuming, haughty.)*

humor—*n.* temper, caprice, pleasantry, drollery, disposition, nonsense, fun, frame, jocoseness, mood. *(personality, will, purpose, nature, mind, seriousness, sadness.)*

hurt—*v.* bruise, injure, pain, ache, grieve, damage, wound, harm. *(soothe, repair, reinstate, benefit, alleviate, compensate, heal, console.)*

hurt—*n.* injury, wound, detriment, harm, laceration, mischief, damage. *(pleasure, benefit, content, comfort.)*

hurtful—*adj.* injurious, baleful, baneful, detrimental, harmful, mischievous, pernicious, deleterious, noxious, moleficent. *(remedial, good, advantageous, helpful.)*

hypocritical—*adj.* sanctimonious, smooth, unctuous, pharisaical, faultfinding, mincing, mealy, smug. *(candid, sincere, transparent, plain-spoken, lenient, genuine, truthful.)*

hysterical—*adj.* distraught, crazed, frenzied, overwrought, distracted, ludicrous, droll. *(composed, poised, grave, sad, calm, somber, serious.)*

I

idea—*n.* notion, belief, supposition, fiction, thought, fantasy, image, sentiment, opinion, fancy, doctrine, understanding, conception, impression. *(form, thing, fact, reality, subject, object, weight.)*

ideal—*adj.* notional, intellectual, spiritual, supposititious, unreal, chimerical, imaginative, visionary, mental, creative, poetical, fictitious, fanciful, imaginary. *(visible, tangible, real, palpable, factual, substantial, physical, material, historical, actual.)*

identical—*adj.* same, uniform, twin, equal, duplicate, alike, one, synonymous, equivalent, substitute, indistinguishable. *(separate, diverse, contrary, different, divergent, opposite, unlike, distinct.)*

idle—*adj.* unoccupied, vain, empty, useless, lazy, jobless, indolent, void, waste, unemployed, inactive. *(occupied, filled, helpful, assiduous, industrious, tilled, populated, employed.)*

ignoble—*adj.* base, humble, lowly, unworthy, mean, dishonorable, plebeian, inferior. *(noble, exalted, grand, illustrious, admirable, honorable, eminent, lordly, notable.)*

ignominious—*adj.* scandalous, infamous, humiliating, shameful, dishonorable. *(reputable, honorable, worthy, creditable, estimable.)*

ignorant—*adj.* uneducated, stupid, unlearned, unlettered, untaught, uninformed, illiterate. *(learned, cultivated, intelligent, well-informed, wise, cultured.)*

illegal—*adj.* illicit, banned, wrong, unlawful, prohibited, criminal, felonious, unconstitutional, illegitimate. *(lawful, sanctioned, permitted, legal, authorized, permissible, licit.)*

illegible—*adj.* cramped, obscure, scribbled, unreadable, indecipherable, unintelligible. *(clear, plain, legible, readable, intelligible.)*

illusion—*n.* mockery, delusion, phantasm, myth, show, fallacy, mirage, dream, deception, error, hallucination, vision, false. *(reality, substance, actuality, form, body, truth.)*

illustrious—*adj.* glorious,

exalted, eminent, celebrated, noble, famous, remarkable, renowned, brillant, conspicuous, splendid. *(disgraceful, inglorious, obscure, ignominious, infamous, notorious, disreputable.)*

ill-will—*n.* hatred, dislike, spite, antipathy, malevolence, malice, aversion. *(beneficence, favor, congeniality, good-will.)*

imagine—*v.* suppose, understand, fabricate, presume, apprehend, think, create, conceive, deem, surmise, fancy, envision. *(exhibit, prove, verify, validate, depict, represent, demonstrate, substantiate.)*

imitate—*v.* copy, follow, depict, pattern, mock, counterfeit, duplicate after, mimic, represent, ape, resemble, portray, repeat, echo. *(caricature, vary, differentiate, remodel, change, distort, misrepresent, alter, dissimilate, modify.)*

immaculate—*adj.* spotless, clean, unsoiled, untarnished, stainless, untainted, spic-and-span. *(unclean, soiled, tarnished, dirty, spotted, stained.)*

immediate—*adj.* contigious, direct, next, closest, proximate, present, instant. *(remote, mediate, indirect, distant, future.)*

immoral—*adj.* bad, wicked, unprincipled, corrupt, evil, heinous, obscene, indecent, unethical. *(good, ethical, honest, moral, decent, noble, virtuous, honorable, chaste.)*

impair—*v.* injure, damage, vitiate, lessen, obstruct, deteriorate, reduce, enfeeble, diminish. *(improve, repair, amend, enhance, augment, facilitate.)*

impassive—*adj.* phlegmatic, calm, insensible, reserved, unmoved, unemotional, aloof, sedate, apathetic, indifferent. *(theatrical, expressive, demonstrative, responsive, dramatic, emotional, perturbed.)*

impediment—*n.* obstacle, barrier, stumbling block, hinderance, obstruction, delay. *(help, succor, furthermore, relief, furtherance, support, assistance, aid, encouragement.)*

imperative—*adj.* irresistable, inexorable, compulsory, mandatory, obligatory, urgent, dictatorial, peremptorily. *(lenient, entreative, optional, voluntary, indulgent, mild, supplicatory, discretional.)*

implement—*n.* utensil, appliance, instrument, tool, apparatus. *(work, art, labor, agriculture, manufacture, science.)*

implicate—*v.* associate, criminate, entangle, compromise, embroil, connect, charge, involve, infold. *(dissociate, extricate, exclude, acquit, disconnect.)*

imply—*v.* mean, suggest, denote, import, include, connote, hint, involve, indicate. *(pronounce, declare, express, describe, state.)*

important—*adj.* expressive, main, considerable, dignified, weighty, material, essential, serious, significant, relevant, leading, great, influential, momentous, grave. *(trivial, irrelevant, petty, uninfluential, negligible, unimportant, insignificant, minor, inexpressive, inconsiderable, mean, secondary.)*

impotent—*adj.* powerless, feeble, nerveless, incapacitated, enfeebled, weak, useless, helpless. *(vigorous, virile, forceful, strong, powerful.)*

impractical—*adj.* unfeasible, inoperable, unrealistic, ideal, unintelligent, careless, speculative, quixotic, romantic. *(practical, viable, prosaic, pragmatic, realistic, sensible, systematic.)*

impressive—*adj.* solemn, grand, imposing, magnificent, important, forcible, affecting, effective. *(unimpressive, tame, dry, unimportant, ordinary, insignificant, weak, feeble, jejune, vapid.)*

improvement—*n.* amendment, increase, proficiency, enrichment, advancement, progress, correction, beneficial. *(degeneration, debasement, retrogression, ruination, degeneracy, deterioration, retrogradation.)*

impudent—*adj.* insolent, shameless, rude, immodest, presumptuous, impertinent, saucy, brazen, bold. *(obsequious, bashful, diffident, modest, timid, servile, sycophantic, retiring, deferential.)*

impulse—*n.* push, force, instigation, motive, stimulus, incentive, incitement, thought, feeling. *(repulse, denial, deliberation, premeditation, rebuff, rejection.)*

inactive—*adj.* inert, stationary, inoperative, dormant, dilatory, idle, languid, indolent, dull, sedentary. *(operative, active, functional, dynamic, vigorous, energetic, busy, industrious.)*

inadequate—*adj.* deficient, lacking, unequal, unqualified, unfit, imperfect, meager, scant, slight, incapable, inept. *(adequate, fit, abundant, enough, sufficient, competent, capable, ample, equal.)*

inadvertent—*adj.* accidental, fortuitous, chance, thoughtless, unobservant, inconsiderate, careless, involuntary, unpremeditated. *(deliberate, careful, intentional, aware, premeditated, calculated, planned, studied.)*

inaudible—*adj.* inarticulate, muttering, stifled, silent, low, muffled, suppressed, mumbling. *(outspoken, loud, articulate, ringing, clear, audible, sonorous, candid.)*

incapable—*adj.* unable, weak, feeble, insufficient, inadequate, unqualified, unfitted, disqualified, incompetent. *(able, clever, fitted, qualified, skilled, strong.)*

incidental—*adj.* occasional, concomitant, accidental, casual, subordinate, appertinent, concurrent, fortuitous. *(regular, disconnected, essential, inherent, invariable, fundamental, systematic, independent, irrelative, imminent, uniform.)*

incivility—*n.* ill-breeding, uncourteousness, ill-manners, discourtesy, rudeness, impudence. *(urbanity, polite-*

I
K

ness, good-manners, civility, respect.)

inclement—*adj.* tyrannical, raw, unmerciful, stormy, rigorous, tempestuous, harsh, cruel, severe, rough. *(benign, genial, pleasant, merciful, clement, mild.)*

inclination—*n.* slope, disposition, aptness, bias, attachment, liking, leaning, tendency, wish, proneness, predelection, bent, affection, desire. *(inaptness, disinclination, dislike, distate, inaptitude, repulsion.)*

incoherent—*adj.* incongruous, loose, illogical, unconnected, inconsequential. *(connected, plain, coherent, articulate, clear.)*

incomparable—*adj.* unique, transcendent, matchless, superlative, consummate. *(ordinary, mediocre, average, common.)*

inconsistent—*adj.* incompatible, incoherent, contrary, opposed, careless, remiss, thoughtless, vacillating, volatile, changing. *(coherent, uniform, steady, reliable, homogeneous, orderly, suitable, constant.)*

inconsolable—*adj.* joyless, melancholy, disconsolate, forlorn, heartbroken, cheerless, spiritless, gloomy, comfortless, heartsick. *(hopeful, consolable, enthusiastic, cheerful.)*

inconstant—*adj.* mutable, fitful, unsteadfast, erractic, fickle, changeable, variable, unstable. *(reliable, steady, constant, steadfast, loyal.)*

incontestable—*adj.* impregnable, indisputable, unassailable, undeniable, unquestionable, irrefutable. *(questionable, supposititious, dubious, problematical, hypothetical, arbitrary, assumptive, unctuous.)*

inconvenient—*adj.* annoying, awkward, cumbersome, bothersome, troublesome, tiresome, inopportune, untimely, unwieldy. *(opportune, helpful, convenient, handy, advantageous, timely.)*

increase—*n.* advance, development, augmentation, extension, addition, expansion, grouth, enlargement, spread, benefit. *(diminution, loss, decrease, reduction, drop, contraction.)*

incredible—*adj.* unbelievable, marvelous, remarkable, surpassing, fabulous, preposterous. *(believable, usual, ordinary, credible, common, unremarkable.)*

inculcate—*v.* urge, infuse, instill, implant, teach, impart, press, impress, enforce. *(suggest, disavow, denounce, intimate, insinuate, abjure.)*

incumbent—*adj.* binding, urgent, indispensable, devolvent, imperative, pressing, coercive, obligatory, persistent. *(discretional, exempt, optional, privileged.)*

incurable—*adj.* irredeemable, terminal, cureless, irremediable, hopeless. *(remediable, tractable, curable, removable, correctable.)*

indecent—*adj.* immodest, improper, distasteful, indelicate, lewd. *(proper, delicate, modest, virtuous, ethical.)*

indelible—*adj.* indefeasible, persistent, permanent, irreversible, indestructible, ineffaceable. *(evanescent, effaceable, temporary, mutable, transient.)*

indescribable—*adj.* inexpressible, unutterable, overwhelming, unaccountable, ineffable. *(ordinary, familiar, commonplace, predictable.)*

indestructible—*adj.* indiscerptible, everlasting, imperishable, unbreakable. *(dissoluble, perishable, fragile, destructible.)*

indicate—*v.* evidence, evince, declare, denote, betaken, mark, suggest, show, betray, manifest, specify, point out, designate. *(contradict, misindicate, falsify, disguise, conceal, negative, misdirect.)*

indifference—*n.* unimportant, coolness, apathy, composure, nonchalance, triviality, insignificance, carelessness, insensibility. *(significance, gravity, interest, ardor, affection, importance, weight, eagerness, affection.)*

i n d i g e n o u s—*a d j.* aboriginal, natural, native, endemic, innate, autochthonous, domestic, inherent, homegrown. *(introduced, exotic, naturalized, foreign, alien, imparted.)*

indescriminate—*adj.* confused, promiscuous, undiscerning, undiscriminating, casual, mixed, medley, illassorted, undistinguishing. *(sorted, discerning, exclusive, careful, select.)*

indispensable—*adj.* essential, needful, critical, necessary, requisite, expedient, vital. *(unessential, dispensable, superfluous, unnecessary, inexpedient, expendable.)*

individual—*adj.* specific, indivisible, singular, personal, special, separate, solitary, particular, peculiar, identical, indiosyncratic, single. *(common, plural, ordinary, general collective, typical.)*

indorse—*v.* approve, accept, ratify, scantion, subscribe, comment. *(repudiate, abjure, renounce, condemn, protest, cancel.)*

induce—*v.* cause, prompt, actuate, instigage, influence, prevail on, encourage, produce, persuade, impel, urge, move. *(prevent, disincline, hinder, dissuade, slave, deter.)*

indulge—*v.* pamper, gratify, bask, gravel, favor, placate, allow, spoil, humor, cherish, revel, foster. *(contradict, discard, counteract, nortify, frustrate, thwart, deny, disappoint, abjure, renounce, discipline.)*

i n d u s t r i o u s—*a d j.* laborious, assiduous, hardworking, busy, energetic, diligent, active. *(idle, inactive, slothful, sluggish, indolent, inert, lazy, unoccupied, listless.)*

ineffable— *adj.* inconceivable, indeclarable, exquisite, perfect, unutterable, inexpressible, insurpassable, indescribable. *(trivial, vulgar, colloquial, commonplace, frivolous, common, superficial, conversational, obvious.)*

ineffectual—*adj.* useless, idle, abortive, ineffective, unsuccessful, fruitless, vain, unavailing, inoperative. *(successful, effective, profitable, effectual, useful.)*

inexcusable—*adj.* unpardonable, unjustifiable, outrageous, unmitigated, indefensible, unforgiving. *(pliable, vindicable, pardonable, forgivable, mitigable, justifiable, defensible.)*

inexhaustible—*adj.* unwearied, perennial, unlimited, illimitable, incessant, indefatigable. *(poor, measured, limited, scant, wearied.)*

inexpedient—*adj.* inadvisable, imprudent, disadvantagious, undesirable, indiscreet. *(expedient, advisable, judicious, profitable.)*

infallible—*adj.* perfect, sure, reliable, foolproof, dependable, all-wise, incontestable, tested, unimpeachable, certain. *(errant, dubious, refutable, uncertain, doubtful, unsure, contestable, unreliable.)*

infamy—*n.* degradation, ignominy, extreme, dishonor, corruption, despair, disgrace, obloquy, vileness. *(reputation, glory, integrity, renown, honor, celebrity.)*

inference—*n.* corollary, deduction, consequence, assumption, conclusion. *(enunciation, anticipation, proposition, statement.)*

inferiority—*n.* minority, mediocrity, servitude, insignificance, poverty, subordination, subjection, depression, inadequacy. *(majority, edge, eminence, mastery, ele-vation, advantage, superiority, excellence, independence, exaltation.)*

infidel—*n.* unbeliever, heretic, freethinker, pagan, skeptic. *(pietist, Christian, religionist, believer, devotee.)*

infinitesimal—*adj.* tiny, wee, microscopic, diminutive, insignificant, imperceptible, minute. *(vast, colossal, huge, enormous, tremendous, gargantuan, great.)*

inflame—*v.* kindle, rouse, fire, incense, infuriate, irritate, fan, anger, ignite, enrage, excite, madden, exasperate, imbitter. *(extinguish, cool, quiet, soothe, quench, allay, pacify.)*

inflexible—*adj.* firm, steadfast, determined, rigid, mulish, resolute, adamant, stubborn, obstinate, stringent. *(elastic, resilient, pliable, supple, flexible, springy, malleable, fluid.)*

influence—*n.* control, affection, power, character, weight, prestige, supremacy, authority, effect, causation, impulse, credit, sway, ascendancy. *(ineffectiveness, nullity, inefficacy, aloofness, inefficiency, inoperativeness, neutrality.)*

information—*n.* advice, notice, knowledge, evidence, counsel, instruction, notification. *(occulatation, ignorance, unawareness, concealment, mystification, hiding.)*

infringe—*v.* violate, contravene, intrude, break, transgress. *(conserve, satisfy, keep within bounds, observe, preserve.)*

ingenious—*adj.* adept, inventive, frank, creative, skillful, clever, ready, sincere, imaginative. *(slow, unready, unskillful, clumsy, inept, uninventive.)*

ingenuous—*adj.* candid, frank, straightforward, open, honest, unsophisticated, noble, generous, sincere, honorable, artless. *(reserved, subtle, disingenuous, insincere, sly, mean.)*

ingrained—*adj.* innate, inborn, inherent, intrinsic, rooted, organic, inbred, implanted. *(surface, alien, external, superficial, learned, superimposed, acquired.)*

ingredient—*n.* component, factor, constituent, element, module, section. *(refuse, counter-agent, non-ingredient, incongruity, residuum.)*

inherent—*adj.* congenial, ingrained, intrinsic, inbred, essential, innate, immanent, inborn, natural. *(ascititious, separable, foreign, extraneous, superficial, temporary.)*

initiative—*n.* leadership, start, example, independence, commencement, enterprise. *(termination, wake, prosecution, rear.)*

injunction—*n.* order, exhortation, requirement, mandate, precept, command. (insubordination, infraction, non-observance, non-compliance, disobedience.)

injurious—*adj.* deleterious, noxious, baleful, wrongful, damaging, abusive, baneful, hurtful, prejudicial, detrimental, pernicious, mischievous. *(advantageous, helpful, con-*

structive, healing, beneficial.)

innocence—*n.* inoffensiveness, guiltlessness, purity, sinlessness, innocuousness, guilelessness, simplicity, harmlessness. *(offensiveness, guilt, corruption, sinfulness, reprehensibility, hurtfullness, guile, contamination, impurity.)*

innocent—*adj.* blameless, pure, spotless, harmless, sinless, guiltless, naive, unsophisticated, unwordly, ingenuous, honest, chaste, virginal. *(sinful, guilty, corrupt, impure, wily, evil, culpable, immoral, nefarious, tainted, dishonest.)*

innocuous—*adj.* harmless, moderate, wholesome, bland, inoffensive. *(deleterious, obnoxious, insidious, hurtful, pernicious.)*

inquiry—*n.* question, investigation, examination, scrutiny, probe, exploration, interrogation, asking, search, research, analysis. *(supposition, hypothesis, guess, theory, conjecture, intuition, assumption.)*

insatiable—*adj.* unappeasable, ravenous, greedy, unlimited, voracious, omnivorous, rapacious. *(delicate, dainty, appeasable, moderate, fastidious, squeamish, limited.)*

insidious—*adj.* treacherous, dangerous, sly, artful, wily, underhanded, designing, deceitful, crafty. *(undesigning, straightforward, innocuous, overt, sincere, frank.)*

insincere—*adj.* false, deceitful, fraudulent, hollow,

perfidious, hypocritical, dishonest, guileful, double-dealing, devious. *(earnest, honest, sincere, direct, truthful, genuine, candid, straightforward.)*

insinuate—*v.* insert, ingratiate, suggest, hint, convey, introduce, worm, intimate, infuse. *(retract, extract, withdraw, remove, alienate.)*

insipid—*adj.* vapid, uninteresting, flavorless, pointless, prosy, monotonous, stupid, tasteless, characterless, flat, lifeless, dull. *(savory, tasty, flavorful, delicious, pungent, stimulating, piquant, lively, provocative, spirited.)*

insist—*v.* demand, contend, persist, urge, vouch, stand, maintain, persevere, assert. *(waive, yield, plead, abandon, forego, concede, surrender.)*

insolent—*adj.* overbearing, abusive, impertinent, offensive, surly, outrageous, rude, insulting, haughty, contemptuous, saucy, opprobrious, pert, scurrilous. *(courteous, civil, polite, obedient, deferential, respectful.)*

insolvent—*adj.* ruined, penniless, overextended, beggared, bankrupt. *(flourishing, solid, thriving, flush, monied, sound.)*

inspire—*v.* inspirit, imbue, encourage, enliven, breathe in, exhilarate, influence, animate, inflame, impel, inhale, cheer, infuse. *(dispirit, deter, discourage, stifle, depress, squelch.)*

instance—*n.* request, persuasion, solicitation, illustration, entreaty, occurrence, precedence, specimen, prompting, example, case, exemplification, point. *(warning, statement, misexemplification, breach, dissuassion, rule, depreciation, principle.)*

instill—*v.* infuse, import, insinuate, indoctrinate, pour, inculcate, introduce, implant. *(strain, eradicate, remove, discard, drain, extract, extirpation, eliminate.)*

instinctive—*adj.* voluntary, intuitive, innate, impulsive, natural, spontaneous. *(forced, willed, rationalistic, premeditated, cultivated, reasoning.)*

instruction—*n.* education, counsel, direction, command, guidance, teaching, information, advice, order. *(misinformation, misdirection, obedience, pupilage, misteaching, misguidance, misinstruction.)*

insufferable—*adj.* unpermissible, unendurable, outrageous, unbearable, unallowable, intolerable. *(allowable, supportable, bearable, tolerable, endurable.)*

insupportable—*adj.* intolerable, unendurable, obnoxious, unbearable, insufferable. *(comfortable, to be borne, tolerable, endurable.)*

integrity—*n.* honor, probity, candor, conscientiousness, rectitude, parity, virtue, uprightness, honesty, truthfulness, single-mindedness, entireness, completeness. *(sleight, meanness, duplicity, roguery, immorality, rascality,*

unfairness, underhanded-
ness, chicanery, fraud.)

intellectual—*adj.* metaphysical, inventive, cultured,
mental, psychological, learned, knowledgeable. (*unlearned, unintellectual, illiterate,
unmetaphysical.*)

intelligence—*n.* ap-
prenhension, conception,
report, tidings, information,
rumor, intellectual, capacity,
knowledge, news, notice, intellect, perception, publication, understanding, com-
prehension, mind, announcement, advice, instruction.
(*misinformation, stupidy, suppression, darkness, silence,
misguidance, misrepart, dullness, ineptitude, misap-
prehension, misunderstan-
ding, misconception, ig-
norance, concealment, non-
publication, misintelligence.*)

intensity—*n.* force, strain,
energy, eagerness, strength,
tension, concentration, attention, ardor. (*debility, languor,
coolness, diminution, de-
crease, laxity, relaxative, indifference, coolness, hebetude.*)

Intentional—*adj.* designed,
intended, contemplated,
studied, planned, purposed,
deliberate, done on purpose,
premeditated. (*casual, accidental, haphazard, undersigned, unintentional, fortuitous.*)

intercourse—*n.* dealing, intimacy, commerce, conversation, connection, corres-
pondence, intercommunica-
tion. (*suspension, disconnection, interpellation, restraint,*

reticence, cessation, in-
terception.)

interest—*n.* business, profit, share, curiosity, cause,
consequence, concern, ad-
vantage, attention, behalf.
(*disconnection, disadvantage,
inattention, loss, indif-
ference, boredom, unconcern,
repudiation, incuriosity.*)

interior—*adj.* inside, inner,
proximal, enclosed, internal,
encapsulated, remote, inland.
(*exterior, outer, external, outside,exposed, distal, surface.*)

intermediate—*adj.* includ-
ed, comprised, moderate,
transitional, interjacent, in-
tervening, interposed, middle.
(*surrounding, embracing, extreme, exclusive, advanced,
circumjacent, enclosing, outside, excluded.*)

interpret—*v.* render, explain, expone, declare, elucidate, solve, unravel, translate,
construe, expound, represent,
understand, decipher. (*misunderstand, misconceive,
distort, misrepresent, confuse, misinterpret, mistake,
falsify, misdeclare.*)

interrupt—*v.* disconnect,
obstruct, intersect, stop,
hinder, break, discontinue,
distrub. (*prosecute, resume,
expedite, continue.*)

interval—*n.* meantime, gap,
interspace, space between,
pause, season, interim,
period, intermission, cessation. (*perpetuity, uninter-
ruptedness, continuity, simul-
taneousness.*)

intimate—*v.* communicate,
declare, suggest, insinuate,
allude, mention briefly, impart, announce, tell, hint.

(repress, withhold, proclaim, reserve, conceal.)

intoxication—*n.* poison, bewilderment, hallucination, ecstasy, alcoholism, drunkenness, venom, obfuscation, delirium, ravishment, inebriation, inebriety. *(clarification, sanity, melancholy, antidote, temperance, depression, sobriety, ebriety.)*

intricate—*adj.* involved, labyrenthine, tortuous, perplexing, complicated, mazy, entangled. *(uninvolved, direct, plain, unadorned, obvious, simple.)*

introduction—*n.* importation, taking, insertion, preliminary, initiative, vestibule, gate, prelude, conducting, induction, leading, presentation, commencement, preface, portico, entrance, preamble. *(extraction, elimination, estrangement, completion, egress, withdrawal, education, exportation, ejection, conclusion, end.)*

intuition—*n.* apprehension, insight, clairvoyance, instinct, recognition. *(learning, elaboration, induction, reasoning, information, instruction, acquirement, experience.)*

invalid—*adj.* sick, frail, incapacitated, infirm, wealthy, feeble. *(healthy, strong, hearty, well, vigorous.)*

invent—*v.* contrive, imagine, conceive, devise, originate, frame, feign, create, discover, concoct, elaborate, design, fabricate, find out, forge. *(copy, reproduce, simulate, imitate, execute.)*

invincible—*adj.* immovable, unsubduable, indomitable, insupirable, impregnable, unyielding, inexpugnable, irresistible, unconquerable, insurmountable. *(spiritless, weak, puny, vulnerable, effortless, powerless.)*

invisible—*adj.* ultimate, minute, concealed, atomic, mysterious. *(separable, obvious, divisible, discerptible, visible.)*

involve—*v.* confound, envelop, include, entangle, contain, implicate, mingle, compromise, complicate. *(extricate, liberate, disconnect, separate.)*

irreligious—*adj.* ungodly, profane, blasphemous, impious, godless, undevout. *(godly, reverential, devout, worshipful, religious, reverent, pious.)*

irrepressible—*adj.* ungovernable, insuppressible, unconfined, vibrant, excitable, unrepressible, uncontrollable, free. *(governable, calm, depressed, bound down, repressible, controllable.)*

irresponsible—*adj.* unencumbered, not answerable, lawless, despotic, unreliable. *(obligatory, imperative, under obligation, legal, trustworthy, legitimate, responsible, binding, chargeable on, lawful.)*

irritate—*v.* annoy, exasperate, anger, provoke, agitate, irk, trouble, pester, offend. *(calm, soothe, appease, please, placate, pacify, comfort.)*

isolate—*v.* segregate, insulate, quarantine, sequester, detach, separate, exile, set apart. *(unite, mix, join, combine, blend, merge, coordinate.)*

J

jealous—*adj.* self-anxious, invidious, resentful, suspicious, envious, covetous. (*liberal, self-denying, unjealous, tolerant, unenvious, genial, indifferent.*)

jejune—*adj.* deficient, inadequate, lacking, wanting, inane, dull, insubstantial, insipid, prosaic. (*invigorating, vital, nourishing, solubrious, exciting, mature, inspired.*)

jeopardy—*n.* danger, exposure, risk, hazard, peril, insecurity, precariousness, liability. (*safety, security, certainty.*)

jingle—*n.* tinkle, jangle, ring, clink, rattle. (*harmony, melody, euphony, consonance, chord.*)

jocular—*adj.* humorous, witty, funny, whimsical, droll, jovial, frolicsome, amusing, jolly, comical. (*solemn, earnest, grave, sober, serious, sedate, humorless.*)

join—*v.* adhere, add, connect, annex, combine, accompany, splice, confederate, unite, link, adjoin, couple, associate, append. (*disjoin, disconnect, sever, separate, subtract, deviate, quit, disassociate.*)

jolly—*adj.* joyful, mirthful, jovial, robust, plump, gay, cheerful, merry, gladsome, genial, jubilant, lively. (*mournful, cheerless, lugubrious, gloomy, saturnine, lean, sad, joyless, unmirthful, morose.*)

jostle—*n.* push, jog, hustle, thrust, shake, tremor, jolt, collison. (*lead, guidance, convoy, escort, squire, pilot.*)

jovial—*adj.* gay, gleeful, blithe, cheerful, jocular, delightful, humorous, merry, animated, buoyant. (*dour, gloomy, melancholy, saturnine, somber, pensive, sober, cheerless, morose.*)

joy—*n.* pleasure, happiness, transport, ecstasy, bliss, mirth, festivity, charm, delight, blessedness, gladness, elation, exultation, felicity, rapture, gaiety, merriment, hilarity. (*pain, misery, grief, tears, despondency, distress, despair, sorrow, trouble, melancholy, affliction, depression.*)

jubilant—*adj.* triumphant, glad, congratulatory, joyous, exultant, elated, festive, ecstatic, radiant. (*mournful, wailing, penitential, remorseful, dejected, doleful, sorrowful, penitent, lugubrious, forlorn.*)

judgment—*n.* determination, sagacity, judiciousness, intellect, estimation, verdict, discernment, intelligence, award, arbitration, condemnation, decision, adjudication, penetration, sense, belief, opinion, sentence, discrimination, prudence. (*consideration, inquiry, speculation, investigation, insagacity, evidence, obtuseness, pronunciation, argument, proposition, pleading, injudiciousness.*)

judicious—*adj.* sagacious, wise, sensible, discreet, well-advised, discerning, cautious, thoughtful, expedient, prudent, well-judged, polite. (unwise, foolish, imprudent, ill-judged, silly, impolitic, rash, injurious, unreasonable, indiscreet, ill-advised, inexpedient, blind.)

juggle—v. cheat, shuffle, beguile, swindle, mystify, manipulate, mislead, conjure, bamboozle, trick, circumvent, overreach. (correct, guide, undeceive, detect, direct, expose, enlighten, lead, disillusionize.)

junior—adj. secondary, younger, subordinate, minor, inferior, youthful, immature, juvenile, adolescent. (superior, older, advanced, elder, senior, primary, mature, adult.)

just—adj. fitting, fair, harmonious, reasonable, honorable, impartial, upright, orderly, right, proper, decent, exact, true, proportioned, honest, sound, normal, equitable, regular, lawful, righteous. (misfitted, ill- pro-

portioned, inharmonious, unreasonable, biased, dishonorable, unequitable, irregular, disorderly, inexact, disproportioned, untrue, unfair, unsound, partial, unjust, abnormal.)

justice—n. impartiality, right, propriety, desert, virtue, integrity, equity, fairness, reasonableness, uprightness. (wrong, unfairness, unlawfulness, dishonor, inadequateness, injustice, partiality, unreasonableness.)

justify—v. defend, vindicate, excuse, exonerate, acquit, warrant, advocate, plead for, varnish, clear. (incriminate, tax, accuse, blame, censure, denounce, indict, implicate, condemn.)

juvenile—adj. young, boyish, early, adolescent, childish, unsophisticated, puerile, youthful, infantine, girlish, immature, pubescent. (later, womanly, aged, anile, adult, developed, superannuated, mature, manly, elderly, senile.)

K

keen—adj. vehement, piercing, acute, biting, sarcastic, ardent, shrewd, knife-like, eager, sharp, penetrating, cutting, severe, satirical, prompt. (languid, dull, flat, obtuse, blind, indifferent.)

keep—v. restrain, detain, guard, suppress, conceal, support, tend, conduct, obey, observe, celebrate, adhere to, hinder, possess, hold, retain, preserve, repress, maintain,

continue, haunt, frequent, sustain, protect, practice. (acquit, send, betray, divulge, abandon, disobey, transgress, desert, ignore, release, liberate, dismiss, neglect, discard, intermit, disregard, obviate, forsake.)

key—adj. crucial, salient, decisive, vital, essential, basic, chief, fundamental, indispensable, material. (immaterial, secondary, insignifi-

cant, minor, peripheral.)

kind—*n.* character, designation, genus, sort, nature, breed, progeny, style, description, denomination, species, class, set. *(dissimilarity, unlikeness, variety.)*

kind—*adj.* benign, indulgent, clement, compassionate, good, forbearing, charitable, benevolent, tender, humane, lenient, gentle, gracious, kind-hearted. *(harsh, cruel, illiberal, bitter, unkind, severe, hard, ruthless.)*

kindle—*v.* light, ignite, provoke, inflame, arouse, excite, stir, enkindle, awaken, set fire to. *(douse, smother, quench, stifle, extinguish.)*

kindred—*adj.* akin, fraternal, familial, allied, harmonious, congenial, related, united, germane. *(uncongenial, dissimilar, different, unlike, alien, unrelated.)*

king—*n.* sovereign, lord, czar, tycoon, master, potentate, leader, monarch, chief. *(subject, slave, serf, follower, dependent, vassal, servant.)*

knack—*n.* skill, ability, gift, genius, aptitude, facility, flair, dexterity, cleverness. *(ineptitude, gaucherie, clumsiness, awkwardness, disability.)*

knit—*v.* join, fasten, affix, link, attach, connect, unite, secure, weave, bind. *(part, divide, separate, split.)*

knot—*n.* bond, difficulty, twist, cluster, band, protuberance, joint, tie, intricacy, perplexity, collection, group. *(unfastening, solution, unraveling, multitude, untie, indentation, smoothness, cavity, loosening, dissolution, crowd, explication, dispersion, evenness.)*

knotty—*adj.* gnarled, bumpy, knotted, rough, lumpy, uneven, nodular, coarse, rugged. *(flat, level, smooth, plane, obvious, clear.)*

knowing—*adj.* astute, sharp, sagacious, proficient, acute, intelligent, well-informed, perceptive, accomplished, shrewd, discerning, penetrating, skillful, experienced. *(dull, gullible, stolid, unwise, silly, simple, innocent, undiscerning.)*

knowledge—*n.* comprehension, understanding, experience, familiarity, notice, instruction, enlightenment, attainments, erudition, apprehension, recognition, conversance, acquaintance, cognizance, information, learning, scholarship, ability, wisdom. *(inobservance, deception, misunderstanding, inconversance, ignorance, incognizance, rudeness, uneducatedness, illiterateness, incapacity, misapprehension, incomprehension, misconception, inexperience, unfamiliarity, misinformation, misinstruction, untutoredness.)*

L

M

L

laborious—*adj.* diligent, indefatigable, burdensome, wearisome, hard-working, difficult, tedious, strenuous, assiduous, painstaking, arduous, toilsome, industrious, active. *(indiligent, easy, indolent, facile, simple, idle, dainty, lazy, light, feasible.)*

lack—*n.* deficiency, absence, shortcoming, want, gap, failure, insufficiency, dearth,omission. *(surplus, extra, excess, sufficiency, plethora, adequacy, amplitude.)*

laconic—*adj.* curt, epigrammatic, concise, terse, concentrated, summary. *(wordy, prosy, circumlocutory, prolix, tedious, talkative, garrulous, loquacious.)*

laggardly—*adv.* tardily, slowly, belatedly, dilatorily, hesitantly, languidly, sluggishly, slackly, backwardly. *(quickly, speedily, willingly, smartly, readily, briskly.)*

lame—*adj.* faltering, hesitating, impotent, imperfect, crippled, weak, hobbling, ineffective, deformed, defective. *(agile, efficient, cogent, telling, nimble, robust, potent, satisfactory, convincing, effective.)*

language—*n.* talk, dialect, tongue, phraseology, accents, expression, verbalization, speech, conversation, discourse, diction, articulation, vernacular. *(jabber, babel, cry, bark, roar, dumbness, jargon, inarticulateness, chatter, gabble, speechlessness, gibberish, whine, howl, obmutescence, muteness.)*

languid—*adj.* weary, unnerved, pining, enervated, flagging, apathetic, spiritless, faint, feeble, unbraced, drooping, exhausted. *(healthy, strong, vigorous, braced, fatigued, robust, active.)*

large—*adj.* bulky, abundant, ample, comprehensive, catholic, vast, substantial, wide, big, extensive, capacious, liberal, enlightened, great. *(mean, circumscribed, scanty, niggardly, petty, minute, sordid,small, narrow, contracted, illiberal, bigoted.)*

last—*v.* remain, endure, live, persevere, continue,hold, abide. *(fail, fly, depart, terminate, expire, cease, fade, wane, disappear.)*

last—*adj.* ending, concluding, past, lowest, ultimate, terminal, latest, final, hindmost, extreme, remotest. *(introductory, opening, ensuing, minor, nearest, temporary, first, initiatory, foremost, highest, next.)*

latent—*adj.* hidden, potential, dormant, quiescent, suspended, inactive, smoldering, passive, concealed, covert. *(evident, active, apparent, manifest, kinetic, patent, activated, developed.)*

laud—*v.* extol, glorify, honor, applaud, esteem, compliment, approve, acclaim, praise. *(denigrate, belittle, decry, censure, disparage, minimize.)*

laughter—*n.* glee, ridicule, contempt, mocking, merriment, derision, cachinnation. *(tears, sorrow, veneration, whimper, wailing, weeping, mourning, admiration, respect, whine.)*

law—*n.* edict, decree, order, enactment, method, principle, legislation, jurisdic-

tion, ordinance, jurisprudence, rule, regulation, command, statute, mode, sequence, code, adjudication. *(disorder, rebellion, hazard, irregularity, casualty, chaos, accident, misrule, anarchy, insubordination, chance, caprice.)*

lawful—*adj.* permissible, right, fair, rightful, permitted, legitimate, legal, orderly, allowable, constitutional. *(impermissible, wrong, unfair, prohibited, illegal, unlawful, lawless.)*

lay—*v.* establish, allay, arrange, put, set down, repose, place, deposit, prostrate, dispose, spread. *(raise, excite, disorder, abrade, elevate, erect, lift, disarrange, scrape.)*

lead—*v.* guide, induce, pass, inaugurate, persuade, conduct, influence, accompany, precede, spend, commence, convoy, direct. *(mislead, dissuade, leave, depart, misguide, misconduct, follow, abandon.)*

lead—*n.* prominence, guidance, direction, control, priority. *(inferiority, followership, submission, subordination.)*

lean—*v.* rest, tend, depend, repose, slope, slant, incline, support, bend, hang, confide. *(re-erect, rise, reject, straighten, stabilitate, erect, raise.)*

lean—*adj.* lank, emaciated, bony, scraggy, slender, skeletal, scanty, meagre, tabid, shrivelled, thin, skinny. *(brawny, fleshy, well-conditioned, fat, plump.)*

learning—*n.* erudition, lore, acquirements, scholarship, tuition, wisdom, knowledge, literature, letters, attainments, education, culture, skill. *(boorishness, emptiness, intuition, inspiration, nescience, ignorance, sciolism, illiterateness, revelation.)*

leave—*n.* permission, concession, sanction, liberty, license. *(prohibition, veto, inhibition, refusal, restriction, prevention.)*

leery—*adj.* wary, suspicious, cautious, dubious, skeptical, unsure, uncertain, shy, distrustful. *(credulous, gullible, confident, trustful, secure, assured.)*

legal—*adj.* legitimate, lawful, licit, rightful, legalistic, judiciary, statutory, juristic, permissible, legislative. *(illegal, unlawful, illicit, extrajudicial, invalid, illegitimate.)*

legend—*n.* fable, story, saga, myth, marvelous, fiction. *(fact, occurrence, event, history, actual.)*

lengthy—*adj.* prolix, longdrawn, diffuse, verbase, interminable, tedious, elongated. *(compendious, short, laconic, condensed, fleeting, succinct, concise, curt, brief, compact.)*

leniency—*n.* indulgence, patience, mercifulness, softness, pity, charity, benevolence, compassion, mildness, mercy, gentleness. *(roughness, severity, sternness, harshness, mercilessness, implacability.)*

lesson—*n.* warning, lecture, information, exercise, precept, instruction, homily. *(misguidance, misinstruction, deception, misinformation.)*

lethargic—*adj.* apathetic, lazy, sluggish, drowsy, languid, dull, comatose, slow, sleepy, slothful, indolent, idle. *(vigorous, vital, energetic, alert, animated, lively, strenuous, spirited.)*

level—*n.* surface, equality, plane, platform, coordinateness, floor, position, horizontalness, aim, ground. *(acclivity, inequality, verticality, elevation, declivity, unevenness, uncoordinateness.)*

level—*v.* smooth, flatten, raze, align, plane, roll, equalize. *(furrow, graduate, engrave, roughen, disequalize.)*

libel—*n.* detraction, calumny, defamatory, lampoon, innuendo, defamation, traducement, slander, publication. *(vindication, eulogy, puff, encomium, retraction, cancellation, apology, panegyric, advocacy.)*

liberal—*adj.* gentle, polished, free, bountiful, enlarged, ample, large, munificent, noble-minded, tolerant, lavish, plentiful, refined, generous, catholic, capious, profuse, handsome, abundant, bounteous. *(low, boorish, illiberal, niggardly, greedy, narrow-minded, prejudiced, scanty, bigoted, mean, inadequate, churlish, ungenerous, grasping, avaricious, gainful, conservative, contracted.)*

liberty—*n.* leave, permission, license, immunity, impropriety, voluntariness, audacity, exemption, freedom, independence, privilege, franchise, insult, volition. *(servitude, constraint, dependence, compulsion, respect, necessity, predestination, bondage, slavery, restraint, submission, obligation, deference, considerateness, fatality.)*

licentious—*adj.* dissolute, lax, debauched, loose, libertine, unbridled, voluptuous, rakish, self-indulgent, profligate. *(strict, self-controlled, self-denying, rigid, puritanical, temperate, sober, ascetic.)*

lie—*n.* untruth, subterfuge, fib, falsity, deception, falsehood, fabrication, evasion, fiction. *(veracity, truth, reality, fact.)*

lie—*v.* repose, remain, lounge, be, rest. *(stir, change, rise, move.)*

life—*n.* duration, condition, spirit, animation, personality, society, history, vitality, career, existence, vigor, state, morals, activity, conduct, vivacity. *(decease, non-existence, torpor, lethargy, extinction, lifelessness, mortality, death, dullness, portraiture.)*

lift—*v.* elevate, upheave, hoist, erect, heighten, raise, upraise, exalt, elate. *(sink, crush, overwhelm, plunge, lower, depress, hurl, degrade, cast, dash.)*

light—*n.* radiance, gleam, scintillation, flash, brilliancy, splendor, candle, lantern, instruction, understanding, day, luster, life, luminosity, beam, phosphorescence, coruscation, brightness, effulgence, blaze, lamp, explanation, illumination, interpretation. *(dimness, shade, night, gloom, misinterpretation, dusk, misunderstanding, death, tenebrosity, mystification, extinguish, darkness, obscurity, duskiness, extinction, ignorance, confusion.)*

light—*adj.* portable, buoyant, easy, scanty, unencumbered, slight, unsteady, vain, characterless, unthoughtful, inadequate, unsubstantial, not difficult, bright, trifling, sparse, imponderous, unweighty, volatile, digestible, active, empty, gentle, capricious, frivolous, thoughtless, unconsidered, incompact, inconsiderable, whitish. *(dark-colored, heavy, weighty, leaden, hard, full, encumbered, oppressed, loaded, ballasted, serious, violent, firm, cautious, reliable, sensible, thoughtful, adequate, compact, ponderous, immovable, solid, indigestible, lazy, burdened, weighed, laden, grave, important, steady, principled, reflective, liable, earnest, well-considered, stiff, dark, substantial.)*

likeness—*n.* resemblance, similitude, copy, portrait, image, carte de visite, appearance, picture, similarity, correspondence, parity, imitation, representation, effigy. *(dissimilitude, inequality, original, difference, dissimilarity, disparity, unlikeness.)*

line—*n.* thread, outline, direction, course, succession, continuity, filament,

cord, length, row, verse, method, sequence. *(contents, divergency, fluctuation, interruption, discontinuance, constancy, breath, space, deviation, variation, solution.)*

link—*v.* couple, combine, merge, attack, join, consolidate, fuse, fasten, splice, connect. *(untie, sever, divide, disconnect, part, detach, divorce, disengage, uncouple.)*

liquid—*adj.* liquescent, running, fluent, mellifluous, flowing, smooth, moist, fluid, melting, watery, soft, limpid, clear. *(solidified, congealed, dry, insoluble, discordant, hard, cohesive, solid, concrete, harsh, indissolvable.)*

listen—*v.* attend, incline, heed, eavesdrop, hear, hearken, give ear, overhear. *(ignore, repudiate, neglect, disregard, refuse.)*

literal—*adj.* grammatical, close, positive, plain, precise, exact, verbal, real, actual. *(substantial, free, allegorical, spiritual, general, metaphorical.)*

literature—*n.* erudition, study, attainment, literary works, writings, lore, reading, learning, scholarship. *(genius, inspiration, creation, intuition.)*

little—*adj.* tiny, diminutive, brief, unimportant, slight, inconsiderable, illiberal, petty, dirty, dwarf, miniature, small, pigmy, short, scanty, insignificant, weak, trivial, mean, paltry, shabby. *(bulky, enormous, long, monstrous, big, developed, large, important, serious, liberal, huge, noble, handsome, magnanimous,* full, full-sized, much, grave, momentous, generous, high-minded.)

live—v. grow, continue, dwell, act, subsist, exist, prevail, vegetate, survive, abide, last, behave, breathe. (perish, demise, vanish, fail, depart, decrease, expire, die, wither, migrate, fade, languish, drop.)

live—adj. vital, animate, energetic. (defunct, inert, inanimate.)

load—n. lading, oppression, drag, encumbrance, burden, weight, cargo, incubus. (support, alleviation, lightness, consolation, solace, refreshment, emptiness.)

load—v. charge, cargo, oppress, weight, burden, lade, cumber. (unload, lighten, believe, liberate, disburden, disencumber, alleviate.)

loan—n. mortgage, hypothecation, accommodation, advance, credit. (foreclosure, recall, return, resumption.)

loathsome—adj. detestable, evil, repulsive, abominable, obnoxious, disgusting, horrible, revolting, contemptible, nasty. (delightful, sweet, beautiful, lovely, charming, engaging, alluring, attractive.)

locate—v. establish, fix, lodge, detect, place, settle, dispose, discover, pinpoint. (disestablish, remove, leave, displace, dislodge, conceal.)

lofty—adj. towering, dignified, stately, majestic, tall, sublime, elevated, high, eminent, haughty, airy. (low, undignified, unstately, unimposing, affable, dwarfed,

depressed, stunted, ordinary, mean, unassuming.)

logical—adj. argumentative, close, rational, sound, cogent. (fallacious, inconclusive, confused, illogical.)

lonesome—adj. dreary, wild, desolate, isolate, lonely, forlorn, forsaken, solitary. (befriended, frequented, gay, bustling, cheerful, happy, festive, populous, animated.)

long—adj. produced, lengthy, prolix, diffuse, interminable, protracted, dilatory, tedious, extensive, far-reaching. (curt, brief, quick, condensed, small, short, curtailed, speedy, concise.)

loose—v. unfasten, let go, free, untie. (fasten, retain, hold, secure, tie.)

loose—adj. detached, scattered, incompact, inexact, dissoluted, released, licentious, unbound, flowing, sparse, vague, rambling. (tied, tight, lashed, thick, dense, pointed, exact, strict, conscientious, precise, bound, fastened, moored, close, secured, compact, accurate, consecutive, logical, scientific.)

loquacious—adj. chatty, wordy, talkative, garrulous, verbose, vociferous, voluble, gushy, profuse. (reticent, silent, reserved, taciturn, terse, quiet.)

lose—v. drop, forfeit, vanish, miss, mislay, misplace, waste, flounder, fail. (retain, recover, earn, treasure, utilize, abandon, reject, vanquish, keep, find, locate, guard, economize, preserve, discard.)

loss—*n.* dropping, missing, waste, damage, depletion, mislaying, forfeiture, privation, detriment. *(recovery, satisfaction, economy, advantage, preservation, gain, profit, earning, restoration, augmentation.)*

lot—*n.* fortune, hazard, doom, destiny, chance, fate, ballot, heritage. *(provision, disposal, purpose, portion, grant, law, allotment, arrangement, design, plan.)*

loud—*adj.* sonorous, noisy, vociferous, obstreperous, tumultuous, sounding, resonant, audible, clamorous. *(gentle, whispering, murmuring, pattering, dulcet, quiet, peaceful, soft, subdued, rustling, babbling, tinkling, inaudible.)*

love—*n.* attachment, devotion, charity, fondness, kindness, affection, passion, benevolence. *(dislike, alienation, bitterness, indifference, infidelity, unkindness, uncharitableness, loathing, hatred, disaffection, estrangement, coldness, repugnance, desertion, malice.)*

lovely—*adj.* lovable, beautiful, delightful, gracious, charming, amiable, enchanting, pleasing. *(unamiable, hateful, plain, unattractive, distasteful, unlovely, unlovable, hideous, homely.)*

lover—*n.* wooer, swain, fiance, beau, suitor, sweetheart. *(wife, spouse, mate, husband.)*

low—*adj.* sunk, stunted, deep, inaudible, gentle, degraded, poor, abject, unworthy, feeble, frugal, subdued, insignificant, humble, abated, depressed, declining, cheap, subsided, dejected, mean, base, lowly, moderate, repressed, reduced. *(lofty, ascending, high, violent, excited, eminent, strong, influential, honorable, intensified, wealthy, ample, rich, elevated, tall, rising, exorbitant, loud, elated, considerable, high-minded, proud, aggravated, raised.)*

lower—*v.* decrease, bate, drop, sink, humble, submerge, diminish, depress, reduce, abate, humiliate, debase. *(raise, exalt, superior, aggrandize, elevate, hoist, heighten, increase.)*

lower—*adj.* secondary, inferior, subordinate. *(superior, elevate, higher.)*

loyal—*adj.* obedient, allegiant, true, constant, staunch, submissive, faithful. *(insurgent, rebellious, unfaithful, untrue, disaffected, treacherous, insubmissive, malcontent, disobedient, unallegiant, inconstant.)*

lucid—*adj.* understandable, plain, transparent, pellucid, distinct, evident, comprehensible, clear, bright. *(dark, fuzzy, vague, confusing, unintelligible, gloomy, opaque, turgid.)*

lucky—*adj.* auspicious, successful, blessed, favorable, fortunate, prosperous. *(unfortunate, unprosperous, ill-fated, luckless, unpromising, unlucky, inauspicious, adverse, disastrous.)*

ludicrous—*adj.* farcical, comic, funny, preposterous, comical, ridiculous, laugh-

L
M

able, droll. (*momentous, sad, mournful, lugubrious, sombre, solemn, doleful, serious, grave, sorrowful, tragic, melancholy.*)

lugubrious—*adj.* mournful, dismal, sad, doleful, melancholy, gloomy, woeful, depressed, downcast, sorrowful. (*happy, content, joyous, cheerful.*)

lunatic—*n.* maniac, psychopath, madman, schizophrenic. (*philosopher, genius, solon, luminary, rational.*)

lurid—*adj.* lowering, dismal, sensational, gloomy, murky, wan. (*luminous, bright, sunny.*)

luscious—*adj.* delicious, honied, toothsome, delectable, sweet, sugary, delightful, savory. (*sharp, bitter, unpalatable, sour, tart.*)

luxury—*n.* epicurism, wantonness, softness, delicacy, profuseness, wealth, effeminacy, voluptuousness, self-indulgence, animalism, dainty. (*asceticism, self-denial, penury, hardness, stoicism, hardship, need.*)

lying—*adj.* false, untruthful, deceit, mendacious, untrue. (*veracious, honesty, true.*)

M

macabre—*adj.* ghastly, gruesome, horrible, weird, grim, eerie, dreadful, deathly, horrid. (*lovely, delightful, appealing, pleasant, beautiful, inviting.*)

mad—*adj.* demented, lunatic, crazy, frantic, wild, unbalanced, distracted, insane, furious, infuriated, maniacal, rabid. (*sound, quiet, lucid, unexcited, sane, sober, sensible, composed.*)

madden—*v.* enrage, inflame, provoke, infuriate, exasperate. (*pacify, mesmerize, soothe, lay, calm, assuage.*)

magnanimous—*adj.* highminded, high-souled, lofty, chivalrous, honorable, noble, exalted, liberal. (*petty, mean, selfish, vindictive.*)

magnetic—*adj.* captivating, alluring, tantalizing, entrancing, hypnotic, enthralling, fascinating, intriguing, dynamic. (*repulsive, offensive, repellent, forbidding, antimagnetic.*)

magnificent—*adj.* magnanimous, splendid, august, gorgeous, grand, majestic, sublime, exalted, noble, pompous, superb, imposing, stately, dignified. (*mean, paltry, beggarly, ordinary, unimposing, unpretentious, petty, little, flat, humble, tawdry, tame.*)

maid—*n.* girl, lass, virgin, maiden, damsel, miss. (*married woman, matron, dowager, matriarch.*)

maintain—*v.* carry on, protract, preserve, perpetuate, continue, extend, overhaul, fix, mend, secure. (*discontinue, refrain, cease, ruin, demolish, quit, wreck.*)

majority—*n*. predominance, priority, preponderance, bulk, minority, superiority, seniority, lion's share. *(juniority, childhood, minority, inferiority, little.)*

make—*v*. produce, frame, create, construct, do, execute, gain, find, establish, reach, shape, bring about, fashion, fabricate, effect, perform, compel, constitute, mould, form. *(unmake, dismember, destroy, miss, mar, dismantle, disestablish, annihilate, undo, disintegrate, defeat, lose.)*

malaise—*n*. disquiet, alienation, uneasiness, anxiety, apprehension, nervousness, discontent, qualm, exhaustion, fatigue. *(serenity, well-being, vim, contentment, restfulness, vigor, hardiness.)*

malevolent—*adj*. vicious, spiteful, hostile, pernicious, malign, mean, malignant, evil, hateful, antagonistic. *(kind, friendly, amicable, benevolent, cordial, compassionate.)*

manage—*v*. manipulate, conduct, mould, contrive, husband, wield, operate, handle, control, administer, regulate, train, direct. *(impracticable, unmanageable, refractory, spoil, follow, difficult, impossible, intractable.)*

management—*n*. conduct, government, skill, skillful treatment, operation, treatment, administration, address, superintendence. *(misconduct, misgovernment, maladroitness, maltreatment, maladministration, mismanage.)*

manifest—*adj*. obvious, conspicuous, clear, plain, apparent, evident, open, candid, visible, distinct, indubitable, patent. *(dubious, indistinct, vague, invisible, inconspicuous.)*

manly—*adj*. courageous, open, frank, noble, fine, masculine, fearless, vigorous, manful, virile, dignified, bold, generous, chivalrous, firm, stately, mature, brave, hardy, manlike. *(childish, unmanly, weak, ungrown, cowardly, womanish, timid, dastardly, puny, boyish.)*

manner—*n*. method, form, kind, carriage, deportment, sort, practice, mode, style, fashion, behavior, habit. *(project, performance, action, appearance, creation, being, work, design, life, proceeding.)*

manners—*n*. behavior, courtesy, intercourse, refinement, demeanor, deportment, carriage, politeness. *(misbehavior, coarseness, unmannerliness, misdemeanor.)*

manufacture—*v*. production, make, composition, manipulation, devise, molding, fabrication, construction. *(employment, wear, destroy, use, consumption.)*

many—*adj*. abundant, manifold, sundry, myriad, multifarious, numerous, frequent, divers. *(scarce, infrequent, several, few, rare.)*

marginal—*adj*. insignificant, minor, unimportant, slight, trivial, expendable, borderline, indifferent replaceable. *(principal, capital,*

L
M

sovereign, crucial, primary, compelling.)

mark—n. token, symptom, vestige, note, score, trace, sign, impression, indication. (obliteration, plainness, erasure, deletion, effacement, unindicativeness.)

mark—v. label, indicate, brand, signalize, observe, heed, specialize, identify, stamp, sign, decorate, stigmatize, note, regard, specify. (overlook, mislabel, misindicate, misspecify, omit, obliterate, ignore, mismark, misobserve.)

martial—adj. brave, warlike, belligerent, military. (unmilitary, peaceful, conciliatory, unmartial.)

marvel—n. prodigy, portent, wonder, astonishment, phenomenon, miracle, spectacle, admiration, amazement. (unconcern, trifle, bagatelle, cipher, imposture, incuriosity, joke, farce, moonshine, drug.)

masculine—adj. manly, hardy, virile, sturdy, male, manful, courageous. (feminine, weak, womanly, effeminate, female, womanish.)

mask—n. screen, ruse, hypocrisy, camouflage, pretext, pretense, cover. (nakedness, exposure, verity, candor, unfolding, truth, detection, unmasking, openness.)

mask—v. screen, cloak, shroud, disguise, hide, blink. (unmask, divulge, detect, expose.)

master—n. ruler, owner, proprietor, professor, chief, controller, adept, lord, governor, possessor, teacher.

(slave, property, tyro, pupil, subordinate, learner, servant, subject.)

master—v. overcome, overpower, dominate, conquer, subdue. (fail, succumb, capitulate to, yield, surrender.)

masterful—adj. skillful, virtuoso, sharp, accomplished, commanding, able, authoritative, canny, wise, superb, deft. (amateurish, inept, unable, incompetent, clumsy, unskillful, meek, spineless.)

match—n. mate, contest, tally, pair, duplicate, equal, companion, competition, equality. (inferior, oddity, inequality, unequal, superior, mismatched, disparity.)

match—v. compare, pit, sort, mate, unite, equal, oppose, adapt, suit. (exceed, surpass, dissociate, misfit, missort, divide, fail, predominate, mismatch, separate, misadapt.)

matchless—adj. incomparable, surpassing, unrivaled, peerless, inimitable, consummate. (ordinary, commonplace, undistinguished, common, every-day.)

matter—n. stuff, body, material, substance, object, essence, gist, theme, content, sense. (mind, intellect, moral, soul, ego, vision, thought, spirit.)

mature—adj. grown, mellow, developed, fullgrown, ripe, enriched, capable, complex, detailed, practiced. (unripe, unfledged, raw, immature, tender, green, embryonic, young.)

meagre—*adj.* lean, scanty, dry, paltry, thin, lank, barren, tame, sparse. *(fat, abundant, copious, generous, stout, brawny, fertile.)*

mean—*adj.* low, spiritless, contemptible, beggarly, vulgar, vile, intermediate, miserable, average, common, base, dishonorable, despicable, sordid, niggardly, middle. *(exalted, spirited, lordly, munificent, generous, excessive, superior, high, eminent, honorable, princely, liberal, extreme, exorbitant, deluxe.)*

mean—*n.* moderation, average, balance, medium, compromise, norm, rule. *(excess, disproportion, shortcoming, ultimate, inadequacy, extreme, preponderance, deficiency.)*

mean—*v.* purpose, signify, indicate, suggest, aim, intend, design, denote, hint. *(state, execute, declare, perform, say, enunciate, do.)*

means—*n.* instrument, media, resources, funds. *(object, end, purpose, point.)*

mechanical—*adj.* automatic, spontaneous, unimpassioned, routine, habitual, unreflective, effortless. *(self-conscious, forced, appreciative, lively, impassioned, manual, labored, feeling, spirited, lifelike, animated.)*

meddlesome—*adj.* obtrusive, officious, interfering, impertinent, intrusive. *(reserved, inobtrusive, unofficious, aloof.)*

mediocrity—*n.* commonplace, average, inferiority, sufficiency, mean, medium. *(superiority, rarity, distinc-*

tion, brilliance, uniqueness, excellence.)

meek—*adj.* gentle, modest, docile, unassuming, mild, submissive, yielding. *(arrogant, irritable, high-spirited, domineering, bold, self-asserting, proud.)*

melancholy—*adj.* sad, disconsolate, moody, cast down, unhappy, gloomy, dejected, dismal, hypochondriac. *(sprightly, merry, gleesome, happy, gamesome, vivacious, lively, gladsome, blithesome, cheerful, mirthful.)*

mellow—*adj.* rich, jovial, soft, velvety, ripe, full-flavored, mature. *(harsh, acid, crabbed, dry, gruff, unripe, sour, acrid, sober.)*

memorable—*adj.* striking, conspicuous, noticeable, extraordinary, eminent, distinguished, great, remarkable, prominent, illustrious, famous. *(trifling, trivial, insignificant, slight, ordinary, petty, prosaic, unnoticeable, mediocre.)*

memory—*n.* reminiscence, tribute, recollection, retrospect, fame, remembrance, perpetuation, retention. *(oblivion, amnesia, forgetfulness, blank.)*

mend—*v.* restore, promote, rectify, amend, better, recondition, repair, correct, improve, reform, ameliorate. *(impair, retard, falsify, corrupt, injure, damage, pervert, deteriorate, spoil.)*

mendacious—*adj.* dishonest, false, guileful, deceitful, untruthful, fraudulent, deceptive, double-dealing, lying, tricky. *(honest, true,* *creditable, sincere, veracious, truthful.)*

menial—*adj.* attendant, servile, lackey, drudge, domestic, dependent. *(sovereign, lordly, uncontrolled, dignified, autocratic, paramount, supreme, independent.)*

mental—*adj.* subjective, psychical, conscious, intellectual, psychological, metaphysical. *(objective, bodily, unconscious, corporal, physical.)*

mention—*n.* notice, observation, hint, indication, communication, declaration, announcement, remark. *(suppression, omission, disregard, silence, forgetfulness.)*

mercantile—*adj.* interchangeable, retail, business, marketable, commercial, wholesale. *(unmercantile, unmarketable, stagnant, inactive.)*

merchant—*n.* dealer, tradesman, trader, importer, shopkeeper, vendor. *(salesman, huckster, chandler, costermonger, shopman, hawker, peddler.)*

merciful—*adj.* kindhearted, gracious, humane, kind, compassionate, clement. *(unrelenting, inexorable, callous, pitiless, remorseless.)*

mercurial—*adj.* flighty, volatile, capricious, fickle, unstable, changeable, erratic, impulsive, fluctuating, impetuous. *(steadfast, stable, predictable, constant, fixed, phlegmatic, callous.)*

mere—*adj.* unmixed, uninfluenced, unaffected, mundane, simple, pure, absolute,

unadulterated. *(compound, biased, mixed, blended, impure.)*

merit—*n.* worth, desert, integrity, excellence, goodness, worthiness, virtue, ability. *(demerit, worthlessness, imperfection, defect, failing, dishonor, badness, unworthiness, weakness, error, fault.)*

meteoric—*adj.* phosphorescent, flashing, coruscant, brilliant, volcanic, momentary, displosive, pyrotechnic. *(beaming, steady, enduring, inconspicuous, permanent, burning, persistent.)*

method—*n.* system, way, mode, process, arrangement, technique, order, rule, manner, course, regularity, procedure. *(conjecture, empiricism, assumption, chaos, guess-work, disorder, quackery, experimentation.)*

meticulous—*adj.* scrupulous, fastidious, finicky, careful, perfectionistic, exacting, nice, punctilious. *(careless, inexact, negligent, slovenly, perfunctory, sloppy.)*

middling—*adj.* average, well enough, mediocre, not bad, ordinary, moderate. *(firstrate, fine, good, glowing, splendid, excellent.)*

midst—*n.* center, throng, core, heart, middle, thick, nucleus, interior. *(confine, limit, purlieu, periphery, outskirt, edge, margin, extreme.)*

might—*n.* force, ability, potency, strength, power. *(infirmity, frailty, feebleness, weakness.)*

migrate—*v.* journey, emigrate, relocate, move, travel,

resettle. *(bide, alight, settle, sojourn, remain, alight.)*

mild—*adj.* lenient, gentle, calm, tempered, meek, placid, genial, amiable, moderate, soft, tender. *(wild, savage, severe, harsh, balmy, bitter, violent, fierce, strong, merciless.)*

mind—*n.* spirit, memory, understanding, will, sentiment, belief, inclination, purpose, impetus, conception, remembrance, recollection, soul, liking, opinion, judgement, choice, desire, intellect. *(organization, proceeding, object, coolness, forgetfulness, body, action, conduct, resist, obviousness, indifference, aversion, ignore.)*

mindful—*adj.* attentive, careful, cautious, recollective, regardful, thoughtful. *(inattentive, oblivious, thoughtless, regardless, mindless.)*

mingle—*v.* compound, confound, intermingle, amalgamate, coalesce, mix, blend, confuse, associate. *(segregate, sort, discompound, classify, avoid, divide, separate, sift, analyze, eliminate, unravel.)*

minimize—*v.* little, diminutive, small, dwarf, microscopic, petite, tiny, minute, mini, wee. *(enlarge, expand, exaggerate, increase, maximize, stress, emphasize, magnify.)*

minister—*n.* officer, official, subordinate, clergyman, parson, preacher, shepherd, curate, religious, vicar, servant, delegate, ambassador, ecclesiastic, priest, divine, pastor, reverend. *(government, superior, head, fold, congregation, secular, monarch, master, principal, layman, flock.)*

minute—*adj.* microscopic, miniature, exact, specific, diminutive, tiny, searching, detailed, petite. *(enormous, tremendous, general, comprehensive, huge, monstrous, superficial, broad, momentous.)*

mischief—*n.* hurt, disservice, injury, damage, devilment, harm, damage, detriment, annoyance, ill-turn. *(good-turn, favor, advantage, gratification, benefit, compensation.)*

mischievous—*adj.* injurious, wanton, annoying, detrimental, spiteful. *(advantageous, conservative, protective, orderly, beneficial, reparatory, careful.)*

miser—*n.* churl, curmudgeon, scrimp, cheapskate, hoarder, niggard, skinflint, screw. *(spendthrift, wastrel, rake, prodigal.)*

miserable—*adj.* forlorn, wretched, despicable, pathetic, disconsolate, abject, pitiable, worthless. *(happy, worthy, comfortable, joyous, respectable, contented.)*

misery—*n.* heartache, unhappiness, anguish, wretchedness, woe. *(glee, cheerfulness, joy, happiness.)*

misguided—*adj.* ill-advised, misled, mistaken, unwarranted, foolish, indiscreet, misdirected, unwise, erroneous. *(wise, sound, judicious, sagacious, prudent.)*

L M

mitigate—*v.* alleviate, extenuate, relieve, temper, soothe, placate, mollify, allay, moderate, ameliorate. *(aggravate, intensify, increase, harden, magnify, augment, enhance.)*

mock—*v.* ridicule, mimic, ape, deceive, taunt, imitate, jeer, flout, insult, deride. *(welcome, admire, esteem, salute, respect, compliment, praise.)*

model—*n.* pattern, type, design, facsimile, standard, kind, example, mold. *(copy, execution, work, imitation, deformity, distortion.)*

moderate—*v.* soften, regulate, govern, abate, temper, control, allay, repress. *(disorganize, misconduct, aggravate, disturb, excite.)*

moderate—*adj.* temperate, sober, dispassionate, abstinent, steady, typical, ordinary, limited, calm, sparing. *(intemperate, excessive, extraordinary, drastic, extravagant, rigorous, violent.)*

modern—*adj.* existent, new-fangled, recent, novel, contemporary, later, present, new, new-fashioned, late. *(bygone, olden, old-fashioned, obsolete, archaic, past, former, ancient, antiquated.)*

modesty—*n.* diffidence, humility, simplicity, puremindedness, sobriety, bashfulness, reserve, shyness. *(conceit, self-admiration, coxcombry, shamelessness, pride, effrontery, vanity, self-sufficiency, foppery, wantonness.)*

moisture—*n.* dampness, wet, damp, humidity, dew, evaporation, vapor, mist, drizzle, perspiration. *(aridity, dryness, dehumidification, drought, barrenness, dehydration.)*

moment—*n.* second, twinkling, weight, gravity, avail, jiffy, instant, importance, trice, force, consequence. *(period, generation, insignificance, unimportance, unconcern, inefficacy, age, century, triviality, worthlessness.)*

monopoly—*n.* engrossment, trust, exclusiveness, impropriation, privilege, appropriation, cartel, preoccupancy. *(partnership, competition, accessory, free-trade, participation, community.)*

monotonous—*adj.* unvaried, humdrum, tedious, repetitious, uniform, dull, undiversified. *(changing, diversified, varying.)*

monstrous—*adj.* portentous, deformed, hideous, intolerable, grotesque, prodigious, marvelous, abnormal, preposterous. *(familiar, fair, shapely, natural, just, typical, ordinary, unnoticeable, comely, regular, reasonable.)*

moody—*adj.* sullen, temperamental, unstable, melancholy, erratic, morose, petulant, dismal, pessimistic, lugubrious, unhappy. *(cheerful, amiable, happy, stable, phlegmatic, stoic, calm, compatible.)*

moral—*adj.* ideal, spiritual, probable, presumptive, virtuous, scrupulous, mental, intellectual, ethical, inferential, analogous, well-conducted, honest. *(material, demonstrative, immoral, unethical, vicious, physical, practical, mathematical, unprincipled.)*

mortal—*adj.* ephemeral, short-lived, fatal, destructive, corporeal, human, sublunary, deadly, perishable. *(immortal, life-giving, eternal, divine, celestial, venial, imperishable.)*

m o t i v e—*n.* p u r p o s e, prompting, reason, incitement, motivation, inducement, design, stimulus, impulse. *(action, deed, project, deterent, maneuver, execution, dissuasive, effort, attempt, preventive.)*

move—*v.* go, stir, agitate, impel, advance, instigate, migrate, provoke, change, progress, affect, actuate, propose, propel. *(stop, rest, allay, prevent, withdraw, remain, stand, lie, stay, deter, arrest.)*

much—*adj.* plenteous, abundantly, considerable, ample, abundant, greatly, far, substantial. *(scant, shortly, near, sparse, little, slightly, short.)*

muddle—*v.* waste, confuse, misarrange, entangle, fail, fritter away, derange. *(manage, classify, organize, clarify, economize, arrange, simplify.)*

muggy—*adj.* misty, damp, dim, cloudy, humid, foggy, dank, murky, vaporous. *(bright, vaporless, airy, pleasant, clear.)*

multitude—*n.* swarm, throng, number, mob, horde, rabble, crowd, accumulation, assemblage, host. *(scantiness, paucity, sprinkling, minority, nothing.)*

munificent—*adj.* princely, generous, lavish, liberal, bounteous, philanthropic. *(beggarly, stingy, niggardly, penurious.)*

murmur—*v.* whisper, grumble, mutter, complain, drone, repine, purr. *(vociferate, clamor, bawl.)*

muscular—*adj.* brawny, sinewy, stalwart, lusty, husky, sturdy, powerful, robust, strong, athletic. *(flabby, lanky, frail, debile, feeble, soft.)*

musical—*adj.* harmonious, concordant, tuneful, euphonious, mellifluous, melodious, dulcet, rythmical. *(inharmonious, discordant, unmelodious, harsh, dissonant.)*

musty—*adj.* rank, frowzy, sour, mildewed, decaying, fusty, moldy, stale, fetid. *(fresh, aromatic, refreshing, odorous, fragrant, balmy.)*

mutter—*v.* mumble, sputter, murmur, grunt, grumble. *(exclaim, vociferate, enunciate, pronounce, articulate.)*

mysterious—*adj.* obscure, unexplained, reserved, hidden, incomprehensible, inexplicable, cryptic, dim, veiled, unrevealed, unaccountable, secret, mystic. *(plain, explained, easy, simple, communicative, apparent, clear, obvious, understood, explainable, frank.)*

mystery—*n.* puzzle, secrecy, shrowd, quandry, arcanum, enigma, obscurity, veil. *(solution, truism, answer, publication, matter-of-fact, commonplace.)*

mystify—*v.* bamboozle, puzzle, mislead, perplex, confuse, hoodwink, confound,

L
M

obfuscate, elude. *(enlighten, guide, interpret, illumine, inform, disclose.)*

mythical—*adj.* fictitious, unreal, fantastic, imaginary, legendary, fabricated, invented, fanciful, nonexistent. *(actual, true, factual, palpable, real.)*

N

nadir—*n.* foundation, floor, zero, base, root, rock bottom, nothing, minimum, bedrock. *(acme, summit, apex, zenith, peak, pinnacle.)*

naked—*adj.* bare, denuded, defenseless, unqualified, nude, unvarnished, simple, stripped, unclothed, undraped, destitute, uncolored, mere. *(robed, muffled, qualified, shrouded, varnished, embellished, dressed, draped, protected, veiled, colored.)*

name—*n.* cognomenation, title, reputation, appointment, fame, representation, nomenclature, designation, appelation, stead, authority. *(anonymousness, alias, pseudonym, ingloriousness, individuality, namelessness, misnomer, obscurity, disrepute, person.)*

name—*v.* designate, indicate, label, specify, call, nominate, title. *(miscall, misindicate, suggest, adumbrate, mention, misname, misdesignate, hint, shadow.)*

narrate—*v.* recite, tell, rehearse, describe, portray, relate, reveal, recapitulate, enumerate, paint. *(cover, withhold, veil, screen, smother, hide, conceal, shade.)*

narrow—*adj.* straightened, thin, contracted, cramped, scant, slender, scrutinizing, bigoted, tight, straight, confined, spare, near, limited, pinched, close, niggardly. *(broad, thick, easy, spacious, liberal, wide, ample, expanded.)*

nasty—*adj.* offensive, disagreeable, impure, unclean, loathsome, obscene, fowl, odious, indelicate, gross. *(pleasant, savory, agreeable, kind, pure, nice, sweet, admirable.)*

natural—*adj.* essential, normal, true, consistent, artless, inherent, original, intrinsic, regular, cosmical, probable, spontaneous. *(adventitious, monstrous, fictitious, affected, unsupposable, artful, ascetitious, incidental, abnormal, unnatural, improbable, forced.)*

nature—*n.* creation, structure, truth, kind, character, affection, attributes, naturalness, essence, constitution, disposition, sort, regularity, species. *(object, man, creature, unnaturalness, fiction, thing, invention, subject, being, art, monstrosity, romance, soul.)*

near—*adj.* close, neighboring, adjoining, nigh, adjacent. *(distant, remote, past, far.)*

neat—*adj.* immaculate, tidy, orderly, methodical, clean, shipshape, uncluttered, trim. *(disorderly,* slovenly, unkempt, messy, disorganized.)

necessary—adj. inevitable, certain, requisite, compulsory, expedient, unavoidable, indispensable, essential, needful. (casual, free, discretional, unessential, optional, contingent, unnecessary, unrequired.)

nefarious—adj. atrocious, evil, despicable, odious, foul, vile, heinous, wicked, detestable, horrendous. (honest, virtuous, noble, exalted, just, laudable, praiseworthy.)

neglect—v. overlook disregard, despise, omit, fail, slight, abandon, forget. (respect, observe, esteem, attend, study, care for, consider, notice, regard, tend faster.)

neglect—n. disregard, failure, slight, remissness, oversight, negligence, omission, default, carelessness. (consideration, notice, esteem, care, attention, respect, regard.)

nerve—n. firmness, boldness, resolution, endurance, strength. (forceless, weak, impotent, cowardice, nerveless, feeble, enfeebled, palsied, bashfulness.)

neutral—adj. impartial, remote, uninvolved, unbiased, indifferent, withdrawn, aloof, peaceful, pacifist. (partisan, prejudiced, committed, biased, definite, active, belligerent.)

new—adj. recent, modern, unused, current, novel, fresh, original. (ancient, antiquated, passe, used, obsolete, old, antique.)

nice—adj. scrupulous, neat, dainty, agreeable, fine, exact, particular, delightful, fastidious, accurate, discerning, pleasant, finished. (unscrupulous, rude, undiscriminating, nauseous, miserable, coarse, disagreeable, inaccurate, rough, nasty.)

niggardly—adj. penurious, miserly, cheap, parsimonious, small, mercenary, frugal, stingy, thrifty, avaricious. (liberal, generous, munificent, lavish, charitable, bountiful, profuse, ample.)

nobility—n. dignity, peerage, loftiness, rank, grandeur, aristocracy, distinction, lordship, generosity. (meanness, serfdom, contemptibleness, simplicity, plebeianism, obscurity, commonalty, paltriness.)

noble—adj. aristocratic, illustrious, worthy, dignified, lofty-minded, fine, patrician, grand, generous, exalted, excellent, magnanimous, honorable. (plebeian, paltry, humble, mean, ignoble, despicable.)

noisome—adj. harmful, odorous, pestilential, hurtful, nocuous. (salutary, beneficial, curative, wholesome, salubrious.)

noisy—adj. clamorous, loud, stunning, riotous, uproarious, hectic, deafening. (soft, whispering, musical, harmonious, subdued, noiseless, peaceful, still, inaudible, soothing, melodious, tuneful, gentle.)

nominal—adj. suppositious, professed, formal, trivial, trifling, ostensible,

NO

pretended. *(deep, important, substantial, intrinsic, essential, genuine, real, serious, grave, actual, veritable.)*

nondescript—*adj.* indefinite, colorless, commonplace, vague, unclassifiable, indistinct, characterless, stereotyped. *(unusual, distinctive, definite, vivid, unique, extraordinary.)*

nonsense—*n.* trash, pretense, balderdash, foolishness, absurdity, folly, jest. *(wisdom, fact, philosophy, reason, reality, sense, truth, gravity, science.)*

notice—*n.* cognizance, advice, consideration, mark, attention, note, observation, heed, news, visitation. *(disregard, mistidings, slight, ignorance, heedlessness, omission, misjudge, oversight, misinformation, neglect, amnesty, connivance, incognizance.)*

notion—*n.* idea, judgment, belief, sentiment, thought, apprehension, conception, opinion, expectation. *(falsification, misjudgment, misconception, misunderstanding, misapprenhension, misbelief, frustration.)*

notorious—*adj.* undisputed, allowed, scandalous, known, recognized. *(reputed, suspected, decent, reported.)*

nude—*adj.* bare, naked, stark, undressed, denuded, disrobed, unadorned, exposed. *(covered, clad, dressed, robed, appareled, clothed.)*

nuisance—*n.* annoyance, pest, vexation, trouble, offense, plague. *(delight, gratification, pleasure, benefit, blessing, joy.)*

nullify—*v.* veto, cancel, repeal, abolish, revoke, rescind, annul, invalidate, obliterate, abrogate. *(decree, ratify, establish, power, existence, viability.)*

O

oasis—*n.* retreat, shelter, haven, sanctum, refuge, sanctuary, asylum, island. *(desert, jungle, crossroads, thick, mainstream.)*

obedience—*n.* compliance, meekness, subservience, submission. *(rebellion, obstinate, transgression, disobedience, resistance, violation, antagonism.)*

obese—*adj.* corpulent, fleshy, fat, stout, heavy, rotund, portly, plump, gross, overweight. *(thin, emaciated, gaunt, lean, slender, angular, lanky, skinny.)*

obey—*v.* comply, concur, yield, submit. *(disobey, refuse, transgress, resist.)*

object—*n.* sight, end, motive, view, goal, target, appearance, design, aim, intent. *(notion, fancy, idea, proposal, effect, illusion, conception, subject, purpose.)*

object—*v.* contravene, demur to, gainsay, protest, oppose, obstruct, disapprove, complain. *(approve of, applaud, agree, justify.)*

oblige—*v.* coerce, force, favor, gratify, constrain, please, compel, necessitate, benefit, accommodate, bind. *(acquit, persuade, disoblige, inconvience, release, induce, annoy.)*

obliterate—*v.* eradicate, raze, destroy, ruin, pulverize, crush, extinguish, annihilate, level, abolish. *(create, reconstruct, rehabilitate, restore, preserve, build.)*

oblivious—*adj.* distracted, heedless, unconscious, careless, forgetful, unaware, inattentive, disregardful. *(aware, alert, careful, watchful, mindful, cognizant, concerned, worried.)*

obscene—*adj.* immodest, lewd, indelicate, disgusting, vulgar, foul-mouthed, impure, foul, indecent, filthy. *(modest, pure, decent, innocent, respectable.)*

obscure—*adj.* dim, indistinct, uncertain, unascertained, unintelligible, cloudy, dark, mean, lowering, enigmatical, doubtful, humble. *(luminous, lucid, plain spoken, unambiguous, eminent, resplendent, prominent, bright, distinct, plain, intelligible, ascertained.)*

observance—*n.* fulfilment, rule, celebration, ceremony, form, practice, adherence, attention, respect, performance, custom. *(inattention, disuse, disrespect, desuetude, omission, non-performance, unceremoniousness, evasion, inobservance,* breach, disregard, informality.)*

observation—*n.* study, attention, comment, watching, contemplation, remark, notice. *(oversight, inattention, ignorance, apathy, disregard, inadvertence, silence.)*

obsolete—*adj.* archaic, outmoded, old-fashioned, passé, ancient, antiquated, out-of-date, old, extinct. *(up-to-date, modern, current, prevalent, new, present-day.)*

obstacle—*n.* obstructive, objection, difficulty, hurdle, check, bar, impediment, hindrance. *(proceeding, course, advancement, support, career.)*

obstinate—*adj.* stubborn, self-willed, obdurate, intractable, determined, headstrong, refractory, pertinacious, perverse. *(complaisant, docile, characterless, wavering, flexible, amenable, yielding, ductile, irresolute.)*

obvious—*adj.* self-evident, explicit, open, perceptible, patent, plain, manifest, apparent. *(obscure, involved, vague, latent, remote, far-fetched.)*

occasion—*n.* opportunity, cause, event, necessity, ground, happening, conjucture, occurrence, need, reason, opening. *(unseasonableness, frustration, untimeliness.)*

occult—*adj.* hidden, mysterious, dark, mystic, unknown, latent, unrevealed, secret, supernatural. *(plain, clear, exposed, aware, open, developed, patent, familiar.)*

NO

occupation—*n.* vocation, usurpation, tenure, pursuit, business, career, holding, employment, possession, encroachment, calling, trade. *(vacancy, abandonment, resignation, loafing, idleness, leisure, vacation.)*

odd—*adj.* sole, remaining, alone, fragmentary, singular, queer, fantastical, nondescript, unique, unmatched, over, uneven, peculiar, quaint, uncommon. *(consociate, balanced, integrant, common, regular, systematic, normal, aggregate, matched, squared, even, usual.)*

odious—*adj.* offensive, abominable, repugnant, hated, hateful, detestable. *(grateful, acceptable, agreeable, delectable, pleasant, delightful.)*

odorous—*adj.* redolent, scented, fragrant, odoriferous, aromatic, heady, perfumed, spicy, ambrosial. *(smelly, rancid, noxious, malodorous, fetid.)*

offense—*n.* sin, umbrage, misdeed, wrong, outrage, trespass, vice, misdemeanor, attack, crime, transgression, injury, affront, insult, indignity. *(innocence, virtue, guiltlessness, defense, honor.)*

offensive—*adj.* obnoxious, displeasing, fetid, repugnant, unsavory, aggressive, distasteful, foul. *(grateful, pleasant, amiable, savory, defensive.)*

offer—*v.* exhibit, present, extend, volunteer, donate, propose, proffer, tender, adduce. *(withdraw, retain, divert,*

deny, withhold, retract, alienate.)

office—*n.* duty, function, station, post, incumbency, service, appointment, employment, business. *(vacancy, sinecure, loafing, resignation, leisure.)*

officious—*adj.* interfering, forward, intermeddling, snooping, meddling, pushing, intrusive. *(negligent, unofficious, modest, reticent, backward, remiss, retiring.)*

often—*adv.* repeatedly, habitually, frequently. *(seldom, infrequently, scarcely.)*

old—*adj.* pristine, ancient, antiquated, senile, sedate, antique, aged, long-standing, preceding, obsolete. *(young, fresh, immature, subsequent, current, youthful, recent, modern, new-fashioned.)*

ominous—*adj.* suggestive, foreboding, unpropitious, sinister, portentous, threatening, premonitory. *(propitious, encouraging, promising, auspicious.)*

oncoming—*adj.* impending, imminent, approaching, looming, immediate, arriving, growing, successive, developing. *(retiring, distant, subsiding, retreating, receding, remote.)*

ongoing—*adj.* progressing, growing, continuing, advancing, prosperous, successful, viable, evolving, proceeding, unfolding. *(declining, flagging, terminating, abortive, concluding, regressive, deteriorating.)*

onslaught—*n.* assult, foray, raid, invasion, charge, offense, encounter, coup, aggression. *(retreat, stampede, recession, flight, counterattack, defense.)*

opaque—*adj.* murky, dense, clouded, obscure, impervious, hazy, muddy, nontranslucent. *(transparent, shiny, clear, lucid, limpid, translucent, pellucid.)*

open—*v.* lay-open, expose, disclose, begin, unfasten, commence, unclose, lay bare, explain, initiate. *(shut up, inclose, misinterpret, cover, seal, close, conceal, mystify, conclude.)*

open—*adj.* free, unshut, public, unrestricted, unaffected, accessible, barefaced, above-board, available, unclosed, frank, unsettled, unbarred, undetermined, genuine, liberal, candid, ingenuous, unfolded, unreserved, undisguised. *(closed, unavailable, close, reserved, determined, blocked, inaccessible, barred, shut, secretive, settled.)*

opening—*n.* gap, space, chasm, initiation, inauguration, start, fissure, beginning, aperture, hole, opportunity, commencement, chink. *(obstruction, end, unreasonableness, inopportuneness, termination, conclusion, close, blockage, occlusion, stopgap, contretemps, enclosure.)*

operation—*n.* action, production, performance, manipulation, agency, exercise, influence, functioning *(inaction, cessation, inoperativeness, inefficiency, powerlessness, rest, inefficacy, misoperation, repose.)*

opinion—*n.* view, notion, idea, impression, theory, sentiment, conviction, judgment, estimation. *(actuality, fact, act, certainty, reality, happening, deed.)*

opportune—*adj.* auspicious, apt, favorable, timely, seasonable, convenient, fortunate, appropriate, suitable, proper. *(untimely, unfortunate, inopportune, unseasonable, inconvenient, unsuitable.)*

opposition—*n.* hostility, obstruction, antagonism, resistance, obstacle, rejection, aversion. *(cooperation, attraction, collaboration, combination, synergism, approval.)*

opposite—*adj.* adverse, opposed, inconsistent, contrary, counter, facing, repugnant, irreconcilable, antagonistic, contradictory. *(coincident, similar, identical, consentaneous, agreeing.)*

oppressive—*adj.* overpowering, galling, grinding, tyrannical, heavy, unjust, extortionate. *(just, lenient, compassionate, light.)*

oratorical—*adj.* eloquent, rhetorical, sermonizing, declamatory, orotund, elecutionary, bombastic. *(intimate, chatty, conversational, informal.)*

order—*n.* condition, direction, grade, decree, series, injunction, command, system, arrangement, sequence, rank, class, method, succession, precept. *(mess, jumble, chaos, disorder, anarchy.)*

order—*v.* dispose, adjust, command, ordain, appoint,

N O

mandate, manage, arrange, regulate, direct, classify, enjoin, prescribe. *(confusion, inversion, disorder, scramble, disarrangement, unsettlement, execution.)*

ordinary—*adj.* wonted, plain, commonplace, matter of fact, habitual, settled, conventional, inferior, humdrum. *(unusual, rare, superior, extraordinary, uncommon.)*

organization—*n.* form, method, construction, structure. *(disorder, disorganization, confusion.)*

origin—*n.* commencement, cause, rise, inception, beginning, source, spring, derivation. *(conclusion, extinction, finish, termination.)*

original—*adj.* initiatory, peculiar, ancient, first, fundamental, primary, primordial, pristine, former. *(terminal, later, ultimate, derivative, subsequent, modern.)*

ostentatious—*adj.* showy, flashy, pretentious, flamboyant, immodest, garish, grandiose, overdone, gaudy. *(modest, plain, inconspicuous, reserved, somber, sedate, unpretentious.)*

ostracize—*v.* avoid, banish, expel, isolate, boycott, blackball, reject, shun, exclude, blacklist. *(accept, invite, include, welcome, embrace, acknowledge.)*

oust—*v.* dispossess, evict, dislodge, banish, remove, eject, deprive. *(reinstate, restore, induct, install, readmit.)*

outbreak—*n.* epidemic, invasion, eruption, outburst, explosion, display, demonstra-

tion. *(recession, decline, waning, decrease, subsidence, tranquillity, quiet.)*

outcast—*n.* reprobate, vagabond, fugitive, exile, castaway, vagrant. *(hero, saint, leader, philanthropist, gentleman, queen, angel.)*

outlandish—*adj.* queer, foreign, barbarous, bizarre, rude, strange, grotesque, rustic. *(modish, ordinary, native, fashionable, commonplace.)*

outline—*n.* sketch, draft, plan, diagram, delineation, contour. *(substance, object, field, bulk, core, space, form, figure, subject, ground.)*

outrage—*n.* offense, mischief, ebullition, indignity, insult, cruelty, outbreak, wantonness, abuse, violence, affront. *(self-control, soothe, subsidence, calmness, moderation, self-restraint, coolness.)*

outrageous—*adj.* unwarrantable, wanton, nefarious, violent, diabolical, excessive, flagrant, unjustifiable, atrocious. *(reasonable, equitable, moderate, justifiable.)*

outset—*n.* start, exordium, opening, inauguration, inception, preface, commencement, beginning. *(termination, peroration, finale, close, conclusion.)*

outward—*adj.* apparent, sensible, ostensible, extrinsic, perceptible, extraneous, external, visible, superficial, forthcoming. *(intrinsic, inner, inapparent, interior, inward, internal, withdrawn.)*

overcome—*v.* conquer, exhaust, overwhelm, vanquish,

defeat, surmount. *(capitulate to, give up, admit defeat, surrender to, give in to.)*

overflow—*v.* exuberance, deluge, surge, inundation, redundancy, superabundance. *(subsidence, dearth, deficiency, exhaustion.)*

overlook—*v.* connive, oversee, inspect, review, pardon, neglect, slight, condone, disregard, supervise, survey, excuse, forgive. *(scrutinize, mark, remember, visit, investigate.)*

oversight—*n.* omission, neglect, inadvertence, superintendence, heedless, error, mistake, slip, inspection. *(correction, attention, notice, diligence, scruting, emendation, mark.)*

overthrow—*v.* subvert, overturn, demolish, rout, discomfit, overset, capsize, reverse, destroy, upset, ruin, defeat, overcome, invert. *(reinstate, regenerate, revive, conserve, re-edify, restore, construct, reintegrate.)*

overwhelm—*v.* quell, drawn, swamp, inundate, crush, extinguish, subdue. *(reinvigorate, reestablish, extricate, capitulate, raise, reinstate, rescue.)*

owing—*adj.* imputable, overdue, attributable, due, ascribable. *(perchance, by accident, settled, casually, by chance, paid.)*

own—*v.* hold, acknowledge, admit, maintain, confess, possess, have, avow. *(forfeit, disclaim, disinherit, abjure, deprive, alienate, lose, disavow, abandon, disown.)*

P

pacify—*v.* conciliate, still, quiet, placate, tranquilize, appease, calm, soothe. *(agitate, irritate, provoke, aggravate, exasperate, excite, rouse.)*

pack—*v.* compact, cook, cram, stow, compress. *(unsettle, displace, dissipate, unload, neutralize, unpack, jumble, misarrange.)*

pack—*n.* bundle, lot, load, weight, burden, package, parcel.

pain—*n.* suffering, uneasiness, labor, anguish, agony, torment, penalty, distress, grief, effort, torture. *(remuneration, delight, gratification, pleasure, relief, enjoyment, gladness, reward,* ease, joy, felicity, alleviation.)*

pain—*v.* grieve, torment, hurt, agonize, torture, annoy, harass, distress, afflict, rack, trouble, aggrieve. *(please, rejoice, relieve, refresh, comfort, gratify, delight, charm, ease.)*

painstaking—*adj.* attentive, laborious, meticulous, careful, diligent. *(negligent, careless, sloppy, haphazard.)*

palatable—*adj.* savory, delicious, delectable, toothsome, tasteful, appetizing. *(unsavory, bitter, nauseating, distasteful, repugnant.)*

palatial—*adj.* splendid, glorious, superb, grand, im-

P
R

posing, luxurious, majestic, stately, grandiose. *(humble, mean, unpretentious, ramshackle.)*

pale—*adj.* wan, dim, etiolated, cadaverous, ashen, pallid, faint, undefined, sallow. *(high-colored, deep, florid, ruddy, conspicuous.)*

palliate—*v.* extenuate, minimize, excuse, soften, apologize for, mitigate, varnish, alleviate. *(inflame, intensify, magnify, exaggerate, aggravate.)*

palmy—*adj.* glorious, victorious, enjoyable, flourishing, prosperous, distinguished. *(inglorious, gloomy, unflourishing, depressed, undistinguished.)*

paltry—*adj.* shabby, trifling, shifty, pitiable, worthless, trashy, niggardly, mean, vile, shuffling, prevaricating, contemptible, beggarly. *(honorable, conscientious, straightforward, admirable, magnificent, weighty, noble, candid, determined, estimable, worthy.)*

pamper—*v.* indulge, cater to, cosset, spoil, cherish, please, satisfy, flatter, fondle, humor. *(mistreat, domineer, oppress, abuse, maltreat, bully, intimidate, chastise.)*

pang—*n.* throe, convulsion, anguish, twinge, discomfort, paroxysm, agony, smart, pain. *(enjoyment, delight, fascination, solace, refreshment, pleasure, gratification, delectation.)*

panicky—*adj.* alarmed, shocked, panic-stricken, stunned, fearful, stupefied, aghast, immobilized, speechless. *(imperturbable, cool, unruffled, steady, composed.)*

paradox—*n.* enigma, absurdity, dilemma, ambiguity, contradiction, mystery. *(proposition, truism, proverb, postulate, precept, axiom.)*

parallel—*adj.* congruous, abreast, analogous, equidistant, correspondent, correlative, concurrent. *(opposed, irrelative, divergent, distinct, different, contrariant, incongruous, unanalogous.)*

paralyze—*v.* benumb, enervate, enfeeble, stupefy, deaden, prostrate, debilitate. *(strengthen, lift up, sustain, restore, give life, nerve.)*

paramount—*adj.* principal, main, leading, dominant, superior, greatest, supreme, cardinal, primary, utmost, essential. *(minimum, immaterial, least, minor, slightest, secondary, subordinate, inconsequential.)*

pardon—*v.* condone, acquit, excuse, discharge, overlook, forgive, absolve, remit. *(visit, accuse, condemn, punish, incriminate.)*

part—*n.* piece, fraction, member, element, share, concern, lot, participation, party, faction, duty, ingredient, portion, side, fragment, division, constituent, ingredient, interest, behalf, item. *(completeness, integrity, mass, body, transaction, unite, affair, whole, entirety, totality, bulk, compound.)*

partake—*v.* participate, derive, share, accept, sample, enjoy. *(relinquish, cede, afford, abstain, forfeit, forego, yield.)*

partial—*adj.* local, specific, inequitable, biased, peculiar, fragmentary, restricted, favoring, unfair, particular. *(total, general, equitable, fair, thorough, unbiased, unrestricted, universal, impartial, just.)*

particular—*adj.* specific, detail, special, minute, careful, exact, precise, nice, unique, local, subordinate, partial, fastidious, scrupulous, accurate, delicate, circumstantial. *(general, uncareful, comprehensive, inexact, coarse, undiscriminating, abundant, universal, unspecial, inaccurate, unscrupulous, rough, indiscriminate.)*

partisan—*n.* follower, henchman, supporter, promoter, disciple, adherent, party man, clansman. *(renegade, apostate, maverick, independent.)*

partition—*n.* division, compartment, separation, allotment, severance, screen, barrier, enclosure, demarcation, distribution. *(non-distinction, inclusion, combination, juncture, union, incorporation, generalization, collection, non-partition, non-separation, comprehension, coalition, amalgamation, concatenation.)*

partner—*n.* sharer, colleague, confederate, partaker, spouse, collaborator, associate, coadjutor, participator, accomplice, companion. *(opponent, alien, counter-agent, rival, enemy, competitor.)*

passable—*adj.* navigable, admissible, ordinary, mediocre, traversable, tolerable, penetrable. *(impervious, inadmissible, superior, excellent, impassable, impenetrable).*

passage—*n.* thoroughfare, course, route, clause, sentence, corridor, paragraph, journey, road, avenue, channel, phrase. *(book, chapter, part, clause.)*

passionate—*adj.* fiery, emotional, excitable, avid, impassioned, eager, enthusiastic, zestful, ardent. *(apathetic, unresponsive, phlegmatic, unconcerned, serene, placid.)*

passive—*adj.* inert, unresisting, negative, patient, apathetic, inactive, quiescent, unquestioning, enduring. *(alert, positive, malcontent, impatient, aggressive, active, resistant, insubmissive, vehement.)*

pastime—*n.* entertainment, diversion, sport, relaxation, recreation, amusement, play. *(study, task, work, profession, business, labor, occupation.)*

patent—*adj.* evident, plain, apparent, obvious, indisputable. *(questionable, cryptic, ambiguous, dubious.)*

pathetic—*adj.* moving, tender, poignant, meeting, affecting, emotional. *(unimpassioned, unaffecting, humorous, ludicrous, farcical.)*

patience—*n.* resignation, perseverance, sufferance, endurance, submission. *(insubmissiveness, rebellion, impatience, resistance, exasperation, repining, inconsistency.)*

pattern—*n.* sample, exemplar, shape, mold, prototype, model, archetype, specimen, precedent, design. *(cari-*

**P
R**

cature, mockery, misrepresentation, perversion, monstrosity.)

pause—*n.* cessation, halt, rest, interlude, stop, suspension, intermission. (advancement, perseverance, continuance, furtherance.)

pause—*v.* suspend, forbear, wait, demur, desist, cease, delay, intermit, stay, hesitate, stop. (proceed, persist, maintain, perserve, advance, continue.)

peace—*n.* tranquility, repose, order, reconciliation, concord, amity, quiet, calm, pacification, calmness, harmony. (disturbance, agitation, disorder, war, variance, conflict, strife, noise, tumult, hostility, embroilment, discord.)

peaceable—*adj.* inoffensive, peaceful, mild, serene, orderly, placid, unwarlike, quiet, innocuous, unquarrelsome. (warlike, fierce, quarrelsome, violent, restless, chaotic, pugnacious, litigious, savage, hostile, bellicose.)

peculiar—*adj.* personal, special, exceptional, particular, singular, strange, odd, eccentric, private, characteristic, exclusive, specific, unusual, uncommon, rare. (common, universal, ordinary, conventional, public, general, unspecial.)

peevish—*adj.* testy, crabby, irritable, grouchy, touchy, petulant, querulous, sullen. (amiable, genial, complaisant, jovial, good-natured, affable.)

penetrating—*adj.* piercing, acid, sharp, severe, pungent,

caustic, biting, shrill, harsh, deafening. (dull, muted, bland, blunt, soft, mild, shallow, apathetic, dense.)

pensive—*adj.* dreaming, sad, wistful, melancholy, somber, serious, solemn, thoughtful, reflective. (happy, gay, jovial, carefree, frivolous, joyous, cheerful.)

people—*n.* community, mob, herd, vulgar, mass, inhabitants, fellow-creatures, race, society, group, nation, populace, crowd, persons, commonalty, tribe. (nobility, ruler, gentry, oligarchy, aristocracy, government, blue bloods.)

perceive—*v.* distinguish, observe, touch, recognize, know, detect, discern, descry, feel, see, understand. (misobserve, misunderstand, misperceive, miss, ignore, overlook, misconceive.)

perception—*n.* apprehension, sight, understanding, vision, discernment, cognizance. (ignorance, misapprehension, unawareness, incognizance, misunderstanding, imperception.)

peremptory—*adj.* express, absolute, dictatorial, imperious, positive, categorical, decisive, authoritative, dogmatic, despotic. (entreative, mild, postulatory, untenable, docile, flexible, suggestive.)

perfect—*adj.* complete, indeficient, absolute, impeccable, unblemished, unexceptionable, ripe, flawless, pure, consummate, full, mature, immaculate, faultless, infallible, blameless. (meagre, scant, deficient, imperfect, fallible, marred, defective, spoilt, incomplete, faulty, short, defective, blemished, inept.)

perform—v. do, transact, enact, execute, fulfil, complete, perpetrate, accomplish, act, achieve, discharge, effect, consumate. (mar, misexecute, misenact, spoil, neglect, miss, misperform, botch, misconduct.)

perhaps—adv. peradventure, maybe, probably, possibly, perchance. (inevitably, certainly, positively.)

perilous—adj. dangerous, risky, insecure, hazardous, tricky. (secure, certain, guarded, safe.)

period—n. date, era, duration, limit, end, determination, interval, time, epoch, age, continuance, bound, conclusion. (datelessness, infinity, illimitability, indefiniteness, beginning, indeterminateness, eternity, immemoriality, perpetuity, endlessness.)

periodic—adj. recurrent, stated, systematic, alternate, calculable, regular. (eccentric, incalculable, fitful, incessant, indeterminate, irregular, spasmodic.)

peripheral—adj. borderline, marginal, surrounding, outlying, tangential, incidental, exterior, outer, surface. (primary, basic, intrinsic, proximal, central, inner, essential.)

permanence—n. endurance, stability, survival, permanency, continuance, duration, perpetuity. (mortality, brevity, transience, evanescence.)

perpetual—adj. unceasing, eternal, unfailing, continual, incessant, infinite, constant, uninterrupted, endless, everlasting, perennial, enduring. (periodic, temporary, falling, occasional, casual, unstable, inconstant, recurrent, transient, exhaustible, momentary.)

perplex—v. puzzle, involve, complicate, bewilder, harass, nonplus, entangle, embarrass, entangle, encumber, confuse, mystify. (enlighten, disentangle, elucidate, explain, disencumber, clear, explicate, simplify.)

perseverance—n. steadfastness, indefatigability, tenacity, endurance, persistence, constancy, resolution, stamina. (unsteadfastness, caprice, vacillation, indecision, levity, hesitation, volatility, inconstancy, fitfulness, irresoluteness, wavering, variableness.)

persuade—v. influence, convince, urge, incite, cajole, induce, incline, dispose, allure. (disincline, compel, mispersuade, coerce, discourage, deter, indispose, misinduce.)

pertinent—adj. applicable, material, apropos, suited, relevant, apt, germane, significant, fitting, appropriate. (foreign, irrelevant, unrelated, alien, unsuitable, extraneous, impertinent.)

perverse—adj. untoward, fractious, unmanageable, crochety, forward, eccentric, stubborn, wayward, intractable. (ductile, governable, accommodating, obliging, normal, docile, amenable, complacent, pleasant.)

pet—*adj.* favorite, darling, dear, cherished, precious, beloved, dearest. *(despised, unloved, detested, scorned, disliked.)*

petite—*adj.* dainty, little, diminutive, small, wee, undersized, slight. *(large, big, gross, ample.)*

petition—*n.* entreaty, application, salutation, request, invocation, instance, supplication, craving, appeal, prayer. *(expostulation, command, claim, requirement, dictation, censure, deprecation, protest, injunction, demand, exaction.)*

petty—*adj.* mean, ignoble, narrow, contemptible, insignificant, small, paltry, trifling, trivial. *(large, chivalrous, broad, magnificent, great, magnanimous, liberal, noble, generous.)*

philanthropy—*n.* generosity, charity, munificence, benevolence, humanity, charitableness, beneficence. *(stinginess, cynicism, misanthropy, ill will, selfishness, hostility.)*

philosopher—*n.* savant, master, thinker, schoolman, doctor, teacher. *(sciolist, tyro, foal, dunce, simpleton, ignoramus, freshman, greenhorn, apprentice.)*

philosophical—*adj.* sound, calm, scientific, enlightened, tranquil, unprejudiced, wise, conclusive, rational, accurate. *(crude, loose, popular, sciolistic, emotional, unphilosophical, unsound,*

vague, inaccurate, unscientific.)

physical—*adj.* material, tangible, corporeal, concrete, natural, visible, substantial, objective, real. *(moral, immaterial, intangible, supernatural, psychic, mental, intellectual, hyperphysical, invisible, unsubstantial, spiritual.)*

picture—*n.* resemblance, painting, image, photograph, engraving, likeness, drawing, representation. *(mirror, original, pattern.)*

picturesque—*adj.* seemly, scenic, pictorial, photogenic, graphic, comely, graceful, artistic. *(uncouth, dead, unpicturesque, flat, monotonous, unseemly, banal, rude, ugly, tame.)*

piece—*n.* element, fragment, portion, section, share, unit, swatch, quantity, amount, bit, division. *(whole, sum, entirety, assemblage, set, total, zero, none.)*

piquant—*adj.* sharp, racy, biting, smart, keen, tart, savory, pungent, lively, severe, cutting, stimulating, stinging. *(dull, characterless, bland, insipid, tame, flat.)*

pithy—*adj.* forceful, expressive, spongy, succinct, terse, laconic, concise. *(characterless, weak, pointless, vapid, redundant, diluted, flat.)*

pity—*n.* compassion, commiseration, sympathy, empathy, condolence, mercy, tenderness, ruth. *(hardheartedness, scorn, pitilessness, apathy, rancor, ruthless-*

ness, cruelty, rage, relentlessness.)

place—*v.* assign, establish, attribute, put, situate, set, locate, fix, settle, deposit. *(remove, unsettle, disestablish, misattribute, uproot, extirpate, transport, detach, disturb, disarrange, misplace, misassign, transplant, eradicate.)*

plain—*adj.* even, smooth, clear, unobstructed, manifest, obvious, simple, natural, homely, open, unembellished, artless, lucid, level, feat, unencumbered, uninterrupted, evident, unmistakable, easy, unaffected, unvarnished, unsophisticated, unreserved. *(undulating, rough, abrupt, confused, obstructed, questionable, dubious, enigmatical, obtruse, fair, sophisticated, varnished, complicated, embellished, uneven, rugged, broken, encumbered, uncertain, interrupted, ambiguous, hard, affected, beautiful, artful.)*

plan—*n.* drawing, sketch, scheme, project, stratagem, system, design, draft, contrivance, device.

plan—*v.* devise, design, picture, contrive, sketch out, hatch, illustrate. *(confuse, twist, distort, falsify, obscure, perplex.)*

platonic—*adj.* intellectual, cold, mental, ecstatic, philosophical, unsensual. *(animal, sexual, passionate, intense, ardent, sensual.)*

plausible—*adj.* superficial, unctuous, pretentious, right, colorable, probable, credible, specious, passable, fairspoken, ostensible, apparent, feasible. *(sterling, absurd, unlikely, profound, genuine, unmistakable.)*

playful—*adj.* sportive, frolicsome, vivacious, frisky, sprightly, lively, jocund, gay. *(dull, somber, sedate, earnest, grave.)*

plea—*n.* vindication, ground, apology, request, appeal, excuse, justification, defense, entreaty. *(accusation, action, charge, impeachment, indictment.)*

pleasure—*n.* gratification, choice, self-indulgence, will, purpose, favor, indulgence, entertainment, enjoyment, sensuality, voluptuousness, preference, inclination, determination, satisfaction. *(suffering, trouble, self-denial, disinclination, indisposition, refusal, elation, pain, affliction, asceticism, abstinence, aversion, denial.)*

plebian—*adj.* vulgar, lowbred, ignoble, crude, low, lowborn, coarse. *(noble, refined, high-bred, elite, patrician, aristocratic, high-born.)*

pliable—*adj.* limber, plastic, supple, lithe, docile, flexible, pliant. *(stiff, firm, rigid, hard, stubborn.)*

plot—*n.* plan, combination, machination, scheme, intrigue, stratagem, conspiracy.

plot—*v.* concoct, contrive, hatch, scheme, devise, conspire, frame, plan.

plump—*adj.* bloated, distended, fat, chubby, massive, swollen, portly, rotund, corpulent. *(lean, emaciated,*

P R

angular, slender, skinny, thin, bony, lank, weazen.)

plunge—v. dive, duck, sink, immerse, thrust under, spurt, pitch headlong, dip, douse, submerge, precipitate, overwhelm. (issue, raise, rescue, rise, emerge, soar, extricate.)

plural—adj. many, manifold, multiple, several, numerous, multiplex. (singular, unique, solitary, lone, single, sole.)

poetic—adj. lyric, creative, imaginative, inspired, metrical, dreaming, rhythmic, lilting. (prosaic, literal, stolid, unimaginative, routine, matter-of-fact.)

poisonous—adj. infectant, toxic, corruptive, noxious, malignant, peccant, pestiferous, deleterious, venomous, vicious, vitiative, baneful, morbific, virulent, mephitic. (genial, sanative, healthful, restorative, hygeian, salubrious, wholesome, beneficial, invigorative, innoxious, remedial.)

polite—adj. refined, courteous, complaisant, courtly, genteel, gracious, accomplished, elegant, well-bred, obliging, civil, polished. (rude, ill-bred, boorish, disobliging, insolent, awkward, uncouth, discourteous, clownish.)

politic—adj. wise, provident, judicious, wary, discreet, tactful, prudent, sagacious, diplomatic, cunning, well, devised. (unwise, undiplomatic, blundering, impolitic, imprudent, improvident.)

pompous—adj. gorgeous, showy, ostentatious, lofty, bombastic, stiff, pretentious, assuming, arrogant, magnificent, splendid, sumptuous, stately, grand, turgid, inflated, coxcombical. (unobtrusive, unassuming, humbleminded, retiring, unpretending, modest, plain-mannered.)

ponderous—adj. bulky, heavy, massive, cumbersome, hefty, big, weighty, enormous, awkward. (flimsy, airy, fragile, delicate, light, small, dainty.)

poor—adj. moneyless, penniless, meager, deficient, unsatisfactory, thin, bold, destitute, indigent, impecunious, weak, insufficient, faulty, inconsiderable, scanty. (wealthy, affluent, liberal, ample, sufficient, considerable, prosperous, rich, copious, abundant, large, moneyed, satisfactory.)

popular—adj. current, public, received, beloved, approved, liked, prevalent, common, vulgar, general, favorite, prevailing, wide-spread. (restricted, detested, esoteric, odious, disliked, exclusive, scientific, unpopular.)

positive—adj. actual, absolute, real, unconditional, explicit, settled, indisputable, express, assured, direct, overbearing, decisive, dogmatical, substantial, fixed, independent, unequivocal, definitive, conclusive, enacted, confident, dogmatic. (insubstantial, fictitious, relative, dependent, implied, questionable, uncertain, indirect, suspicious, doubtful, negative, unreal, imaginary, contingent, conditional, dubious, moral, fallacious, occasional.)

possess—*v.* enjoy, hold, own, inherit, occupy, have, entertain. *(renounce, resign, surrender, forfeit, abandon, abjure, lose, submit.)*

possible—*adj.* feasible, potential, conceivable, practicable, likely. *(impossible, impracticable, absurd, unfeasible.)*

postpone—*v.* delay, procrastinate, suspend, defer, prorogue. *(accelerate, sustain, dispatch, expedite.)*

posterity—*n.* progeny, children, issue, heirs, descendents, offspring, scions. *(forbears, ancestors, progenitors, forefathers.)*

potent—*adj.* effective, stiff, strong, powerful, compelling, powerful, impressive, serious, cogent, vigorous, solid. *(feeble, weak, mild, impotent, ineffectual, dubious, frail, inefficient.)*

poverty—*n.* need, destitution, penury, want, indigence. *(wealth, affluence, prosperity.)*

power—*n.* capacity, potentiality, strength, might, susceptibility, dominion, command, agency, rule, effectiveness, strength, faculty, capability, ability, force, energy, influence, sway, government, authority, jurisdiction. *(incapability, inability, imbecility, insusceptibility, powerlessness, subservience, feebleness, incapacity, impotence, weakness, inertness, subjection, obedience, ineffectiveness.)*

practice—*n.* habit, experience, action, manner, routine, performance, usage, exercise, exercitation, custom. *(dishabituation, theory, nonperformance, disuse, inexperience, speculation, abolition.)*

practice—*v.* exercise, carry on, perform, deal in.

praise—*v.* laud, honor, puff, compliment, applaud, flatter, panegyrize, eulogize, commend, glorify, celebrate, extol. *(censure, reprove, disparage, blame, discommend.)*

prayer—*n.* supplication, orison, suit, worship, request, petition, entreaty, benediction. *(expostulation, restriction, disrespect, irreverence, mockery.)*

precaution—*n.* provision, anticipation, care, prudence, providence, forethought, premonition, pre-arrangement. *(improvidence, thoughtlessness, carelessness, negligence.)*

precede—*v.* forego, lead, preface, introduce, herald, usher, anticipate, head, pave the way, forerun. *(follow, result, ensue, succeed, postdate.)*

precious—*adj.* valuable, cherished, beloved, of great value, dear, priceless, costly, treasured, estimable. *(valueless, unvalued, unappreciated, useless, vile, cheap, worthless, disesteemed.)*

precise—*adj.* exact, pointed, correct, formal, scrupulous, punctilious, formal, explicit, definite, nice, accurate, particular, specific, terse, ceremonious. *(vague, rough, loose, ambiguous, informal, casual, unceremonious, indefinite, inexact, inac-*

P R

curate, circumlocutory, tortuous.)

predict—v. foretell, prognosticate, foreshadow, anticipate, prophesy, forecast, forebode.)

preface—n. proem, prologue, premiss, preliminary, introduction, prelude, preamble. (sequel, epilogue, supplement, postscript, peroration, appendix.)

prefer—v. elect, fancy, advance, favor, further, choose, select, promote. (postpone, withhold, depress, exclude, reject, defer, degrade.)

prejudice—n. prejudgment, bias, injury, impairment, partiality, damage, preconception, prepossession, predisposition, unfairness, harm, detriment, disadvantage. (fairness, judgment, advantage, detachment, impartiality.)

premature—adj. crude, untimely, precipitate, rash, inopportune, unseasonable, hasty, precocious, unauthenticated, too early. (timely, opportune, mature, ripe, seasonable.)

premium—n. guerdon, douceur, bribe, bonus, bounty, reward, remuneration, encouragement, enhancement, recompense, prize. (fine, mulct, penalty, amercement, forfeit.)

preparation—n. readiness, provision, development, apprenticeship. (without, provision, unpreparedness, unawareness.)

prepare—v. adapt, adjust, fit, arrange, lay, equip, ready, qualify, groom, provide, order, plan, furnish. (misadapt, derange, demolish, discon-

cert, confuse, misfit, misprovide, disarrange, subvert.)

prepossessing—adj. alluring, winning, engaging, personable, attractive, charming, taking. (sinister, repulsive, unpleasant, unattractive.)

preposterous—adj. exorbitant, absurd, foolish, fantastic, ridiculous, monstrous, unreasonable, irrational. (due, sound, reasonable, right, orderly, sensible, just, fair, moderate, judicious.)

presence—n. influence, closeness, attendance, nearness, intercourse. (absence, distance, remoteness, separation, distraction.)

preserve—v. guard, keep safe, protect, rescue, shield, spare, defend, save, uphold, maintain. (destroy, damage, ruin, dilapidate.)

president—n. moderator, chairman, superintendent, commander-in-chief, principal. (subordinate, corporation, ward, component, institution, member, constituent, society.)

press—v. crowd, force, squeeze, compress, constrain, instigate, impress, encroach, harass, palpate, urge, compel, crush, express, hurry, inculcate, throng. (inhibit, entice, solicit, skim, free, ease, relieve, touch, relax, persuade, allure, graze, liberate, avoid, manipulate.)

presume—v. anticipate, venture, conjecture, deem, surmise, assume, suppose, apprehend, take for granted, believe. (deduce, argue, withdraw, distrust, conclude, infer, prove, retire, hesitate.)

pretend—*v.* simulate, allege, propound, profess, imitate, feign, offer, exhibit, affect. *(unmask, test, refute, verify, detect, substantiate, corroborate.)*

pretense—*n.* pretext, simulation, mask, show, plea, make believe, pretension, mimicry, excuse, fabrication, cloak, color, garb, assumption, hoax. *(reality, simplicity, guilelessness, veritableness, fact, frankness, verity, truth, candor, openness, actuality.)*

pretty—*adj.* attractive, trim, pleasing, fine, delicate, comely, handsome, neat, tasteful, beautiful. *(grotesque, homely, ugly, ungainly, plain.)*

prevailing—*adj.* ruling, operative, prevalent, ascendant, most, common, current, controlling, influential, predominant, rife, most general. *(diminishing, powerless, uneffectual, mitigated, subordinate.)*

prevent—*v.* obstruct, neutralize, thwart, anticipate, frustrate, checkmate, preclude, hinder, bar, nullify, intercept, forefend, obviate. *(aid, expedite, instigate, advance, induce, produce, promote, facilitate, encourage, accelerate, cause.)*

price—*n.* figure, compensation, appraisement, expenditure, worth, cost, charge, expense, value. *(discount, remittance, reduction, abatement, donation, allowance.)*

pride—*n.* haughtiness, self-exaltation, conceit, vanity, loftiness, lordliness, arrogance, gratification. *(meekness, self-distrust, humility, lowliness, modesty.)*

prim—*adj.* precise, starched, self-conscious, priggish, puritanical, formal, demure, stiff, unbending. *(easy, unaffected, free, libertine, naive, unformal, genial, natural.)*

primary—*adj.* original, elementary, chief, important, primitive, first, embryonic, pristine, earliest, main, principal, leading. *(subordinate, unimportant, subsequent, later, following, secondary, posterior, inferior.)*

primitive—*adj.* primeval, pristine, simple, archaic, aboriginal, old-fashioned, quaint, unsophisticated. *(new-fangled, modish, civilized, modern, sophisticated.)*

princely—*adj.* munificent, superb, regal, supreme, distinguished, imperial, august, magnificent, royal. *(mean, ignoble, beggarly,' niggardly, vulgar.)*

principal—*adj.* first, leading, primary, pre-eminent, main, paramount, prominent, highest, chief, foremost. *(subordinate, minor, supplemental, auxiliary, peripheral, inferior, secondary subject.)*

principle—*n.* origin, cause, substance, power, truth, law, axiom, rule, postulate, ethics, source, motive, energy, element, faculty, tenet, doctrine, maxim. *(manifestation, action, development, exercise, formation, dishonesty, exhibition, application, issue, operation.)*

private—*adj.* peculiar, secret, retired, secluded,

P R

privy, special, individual, not public. *(public, unconcealed, general, open, available.)*

privilege—*n.* immunity, right, advantage, exemption, priority, prerogative, franchise, liberty, claim. *(disqualification, prohibition, subordination, inhibition, disfranchisement, exclusion.)*

prize—*n.* spoil, prey, trophy, guerdon, honors, palm, award, booty, plunder, forage, laurels, premium, ovation. *(forfeiture, penalty, sacrifice, failure, stigma, mulct, taint, loss, fine, amercement, disappointment, brand, infamy.)*

probability—*n.* presumption, chance, expectation, verisimilitude, appearance, likelihood. *(improbability, inconceivableness, unlikelihood, impossibility, doubtfulness.)*

probable—*adj.* presumable, reasonable, anticipated, likely, credible. *(incredible, unlikely, unreasonable, implausible.)*

problem—*n.* question, dilemma, puzzle, conundrum, query, riddle, difficulty, predicament, paradox, mystery. *(answer, solution, response, discovery, finding out, deciphering.)*

proceed—*v.* pass, progress, issue, flow, initiate, arise, move, advance, continue, emanate. *(deviate, stand, stop, stay, discontinue, retire, ebb, regress, recede, retreat, desist.)*

procession—*n.* march, file, train, cavalcade, parade, retinue, caravan, cortege. *(herd, rush, mob, rout, rabble, disorder, confusion, disarray.)*

prodigal—*adj.* profuse, reckless, squandering, profligate, improvident, lavish, extravagant, wasteful. *(saving, economical, miserly, closefisted, cautious, frugal, hoarding, niggardly, close.)*

prodigious—*adj.* portentous, vast, astounding, monstrous, huge, surprising, extraordinary, marvelous, wonderful, gigantic, enormous, amazing, remarkable. *(common-place, usual, moderate, picayune, ordinary, every-day, familiar.)*

produce—*n.* yield, profit, effect, consequence, amount, product, agricultural products, fruit, result.

produce—*v.* bear, afford, create, yield, prolong, render, cause, furbish, lengthen, exhibit, originate, extend. *(retain, withhold, destroy, curtail, contract, stifle, withdraw, neutralize, annihilate, shorten, reduce, subvert.)*

product—*n.* result, consequence, emanation, generate, work, fruit, issue, effect. *(principle, motive, operation, tendency, cause, law, power, energy, action, force.)*

production—*n.* evolution, genesis, manufacture, creation, growth, origination, formation, product. *(consumption, use.)*

profane—*v.* secular, unsanctified, irreligious, ungodly, godless, blasphemous, pervert, temporal, unconsecrated, unholy, irreverent, wicked, impious. *(consecrated, spiritual, reverent,* *godly, devout, glorify, holy, sacred, sanctified, religious, pious.)*

profess—*v.* avow, own, pretend, lay claim to, certify, declare, acknowledge, confess, proclaim. *(suppress, disavow, renounce, rebuff, abjure, conceal, disown, repudiate.)*

profit—*n.* emolument, avail, benefit, use, value, gain, advantage, acquisition, service, improvement. *(detriment, disadvantage, harm, waste, loss, damage.)*

program—*n.* notice, catalogue, performance, calendar, plan, advertisement, schedule. *(rehearsal, resume, précis, recital, review, analysis, repetition.)*

progress—*n.* advance, proceeding, journey, speed, progression, growth, advancement, movement, way, proficiency. *(stoppage, stay, delay, failure, relapse, retardation, retreat, retrogression.)*

project—*n.* purpose, scheme, device, undertaking, venture, plan, design, contrivance. *(chance, hazard, peril.)*

prominent—*adj.* protuberant, embossed, manifest, eminent, main, leading, distinctive, jutting, protrusive, relieved, extended, conspicuous, distinguished, important, characteristic. *(concave, indented, engraved, withdrawn, minor, unimportant, undistinguishable, secondary, subordinate, receding, rebated, hallowed, entailed, average, inconspicuous, indistinctive.)*

promiscuous—*adj.* confused, unselected, undistributed, common, casual, unordered, heterogeneous, mingled, undistinguished, unarranged, unassorted, unreserved, disorderly. *(select, arranged, reserved, exclusive, homogeneous, nice, sorted, orderly, distributed, assorted.)*

promise—*v.* engage, covenant, stipulate, guarantee, pledge, assure, warrant.

promise—*n.* assurance, pledge, covenant, stipulation, engagement, word, oath.

promote—*v.* further, excite, raise, prefer, encourage, aid, advance, exalt, elevate. *(repress, check, depress, dishonor, disable, discourage, hinder, allay, degrade.)*

prompt—*v.* alert, active, brisk, unhesitating, incite, ready, responsive, quick, apt. *(sluggish, inactive, deter, unready, irresponsive.)*

pronounce—*v.* utter, propound, express, assert, enunciate, proclaim, articulate, declare, affirm, deliver. *(mispropound, suppress, silence, swallow, mumble, subdue, mispronounce, misaffirm, stifle, choke, gabble.)*

proof—*n.* trial, criterion, test, establishment, demonstration, testimony, verification, essay, examination, comprobation, evidence, scrutiny, authentication. *(failure, short-coming, undemonstrativeness, error, reprobation, disproof, invalidity, fallacy.)*

proper—*adj.* appertinent, own, special, adapted, suit-

P
R

able, just, equitable, decent, fit, applicable, peculiar, personal, constitutional, befitting, suited, appropriate, fair, right, becoming. (*inappertinent, universal, unbefitting, unsuited, indecent, inappropriate, improper, common, incongruous, alien, nonspecial, unadopted, unsuitable, wrong, unbecoming, unorthodox.*)

property—*n.* attribute, nature, possessions, wealth, gear, ownership, acquisitions, quality, peculiarity, characteristic, goods, estate, resources.

proportion—*n.* relation, distribution, symmetry, uniformity, harmony, correlation, adaptation, rate, adjustment, interrelationship. (*misadjustment, disparity, disorder, disproportion, irregularity, misproportion, incongruity, disharmony, irrelation.*)

propose—*v.* tender, bring forward, intend, propound, design, move, suggest, offer, proffer, purpose, mean. (*denounce, deprecate, dispute, discount, deny, protest, contradict.*)

prosaic—*adj.* matter-of-fact, prolix, unimaginative, dull, tedious. (*animated, lively, eloquent, provocative, graphic, poetic, interesting, fervid.*)

prospect—*n.* vision, landscape, anticipation, assurance, view, field, hope, probability, promise. (*dimness, darkness, veiling, hopelessness, shadow, improbability, viewlessness, obscurity, cloud, occultation.*)

prospectus—*n.* plan, announcement, scheme, brochure, synopsis, program, catalogue, bill, compendium. (*proceeding, subject, transaction, enactment.*)

prosperity—*n.* weal, good fortune, good luck, affluence, success, welfare, well-being. (*woe, failure, depression, reverse, unsuccess, adversity.*)

protect—*v.* fortify, shield, cover, save, screen, vindicate, defend, guard, preserve, secure. (*endanger, abandon, forsake, expose, betray, imperil.*)

prototype—*n.* original, first, norm, example, precedent, sample, absolute, pattern, model. (*imitation, rerun, facsimile, reproduction, copy.*)

protracted—*adj.* prolonged, lengthy, extensive, extended, diffuse, rambling, interminable. (*short, concise, brief, abbreviated, limited.*)

proud—*adj.* haughty, supercilious, boastful, vain, elated, lofty, magnificent, appreciative, self-conscious, arrogant, imperious, presumptuous, prideful, imposing, ostentatious, self-satisfied. (*humble, unpresuming, lowly, unimposing, humiliated, deferential, affable, meek, mean, ashamed.*)

prove—*v.* assay, establish, ascertain, show, examine, validate, attest to, verify, try, test, demonstrate, argue, confirm, substantiate. (*pretermit, misindicate, disprove, disestablish, invalidate, pass, misdemonstrate, refute, contradict, neutralize.*)

proverbial—*adj.* current, customary, unquestioned, notorious, acknowledged. *(unfounded, suspected, unfamiliar, dubious, questionable, suspicious.)*

provide—*v.* arrange, afford, cater, contribute, get, produce, stipulate, donate, prepare, procure, supply, yield, furnish, agree, collect. *(neglect, withhold, appropriate, deny, divert, retain, mismanage, disallow, overlook, misprovide, refuse, alienate, misemploy.)*

province—*n.* region, section, domain, precinct, territory, tract, department, sphere. *(capital, metropolis, center, center of government.)*

provision, provisions—*n.* arrangement, supply, food, victuals, eatables, rations, preparations, produce, anticipation, supplies, edibles. *(pittance, misprovision, thoughtlessness, destitution, dearth, dole, neglect, scantiness, forgetfulness, want, oversight, starvation.)*

provoke—*v.* summon, irritate, challenge, impel, exasperate, tantalize, infuriate, educe, rouse, excite, vex, offend, anger. *(relegate, soothe, propitiate, conciliate, allay, pacify.)*

proxy—*n.* substitution, agent, representative, commissioner, delegate, deputy, agency, representation, substitute, surrogate, lieutenant. *(personality, person, deputer, principalship, principal, authority, superior.)*

prudent—*adj.* wary, circumspect, careful, vigilant, judicious, wise, cautious, discreet. *(unwary, indiscreet, uncircumspect, imprudent, reckless, foolish, incautious, rash, audacious, silly, liberal.)*

prudish—*adj.* over-modest, squeamish, demure, puritanical, coy, over-nice, reserved. *(promiscuous, free, uninhibited.)*

public—*adj.* notorious, social, open, exoteric, generally known, universal, common, national, general. *(secret, domestic, close, solitary, individual, parochial, private, secluded, personal.)*

pull—*v.* drag, extract, haul, tug, magnetize, pluck, draw, adduce. *(eject, propel, thrust, push, extrude.)*

punch—*v.* pierce, pommel, bore, strike, perforate, poke, puncture. *(plug, bung, stop, seal, snap.)*

punish—*v.* castigate, correct, discipline, scourge, penalize, chastise, chasten, whip. *(recompense, indemnify, exonerate, reward, remunerate.)*

pupil—*n.* learner, tyro, ward, disciple, scholar, student, novice. *(master, adept, tutor, guardian, teacher, proficient.)*

pure—*adj.* unmixed, genuine, mere, quietless, unadulterated, unsullied, chaste, clean, immaculate, unspotted, sheer, innocent, unpolluted, clear, simple, absolute, uncorrupted, unblemished, real, spotless, undefiled, guileless. *(turbid, adulterated, corrupt, stained, defiled, guilty, faulty, foul, impure, mixed.)*

purpose—*n.* design, meaning, object, end, point, objective, resolve, intention, mind, view, aim, scope. *(fortune, accident, lot, lottery, incident, hit, chance, fate, hazard, casualty.)*

purpose—*v.* determine, resolve, propose, persist, intend, design, mean. *(risk, revoke, venture, jeopardize, stake, chance, hazard, miscalculate.)*

push—*v.* drive, shove, press against, butt, urge, accelerate, jostle, reduce, press, impel, propel, thrust, expedite. *(draw, adduce, pull, drag, haul.)*

put—*v.* lay, propose, situate, place, set. *(raise, transfer, dislodge, withdraw, remove, displace.)*

putrid—*adj.* rancid, decaying, spoiled, moldering, moldy, rotten, contaminated, decomposed, bad. *(pure, fresh, wholesome, healthy, untainted.)*

puzzle—*n.* bewilderment, confusion, intricacy, enigma, embarrassment, doubt, conundrum, labyrinth, quandary. *(solution, extrication, lucidity, clue, disentanglement, explanation.)*

puzzle—*v.* perplex, bewilder, mystify, complicate, confuse, pose, embarrass, confound. *(instruct, clarify, illumine, enlighten.)*

Q

quack—*n.* mountebank, impostor, humbug, fraud, empiric, charlatan, pretender. *(gull, victim, dupe, prey.)*

quaint—*adj.* recondite, elegant, odd, affected, archaic, singular, charming, old-fashioned, curious, abstruse, nice, whimsical, antique, fanciful. *(ordinary, coarse, modern, fashionable, current, dowdy, commonplace, usual, common, modish.)*

qualified—*adj.* adapted, suitable, eligible, fitted, competent. *(unable, deficient, impotent, inept.)*

quality—*n.* character, attribute, disposition, sort, description, power, nature, stature, tendency, condition, property, peculiarity, temper, kind, capacity, virtue. *(heterogeneousness, incapacity, indistinctiveness, disqualification, disability, mediocrity, anomalousness, nondescript, weakness, triviality, ineffectiveness, negation.)*

qualm—*n.* scruple, uneasiness, regret, pang, twinge, fear, compunction, apprehension, uncertainty. *(security, comfort, firmness, confidence, invulnerability, easiness.)*

quandry—*n.* dilemma, perplexity, entanglement, impasse, crisis, plight, predicament, fix, doubt. *(relief, assurance, ease, certainty, plain sailing.)*

quantity—*n.* amount, size, measure, portion, magnitude, share, volume, division, bulk, sum, aggregate, part. *(defi-*

ciency, want, scantiness, loss, diminution, wear, dearth, margin, waste, deduction, inadequacy, leakage, insufficiency, deterioration.)

quarrel—*n.* altercation, squabble, tumult, wrangle, disagreement, hostility, embroilment, broil, controversy, brawl, affray, feud, dispute, variance, misunderstanding, quarreling, bickering. *(conversation, pleasantry, friendliness, amity, agreement, goodwill, confabulation, chat, conciliation, peace.)*

quarrelsome—*adj.* irascible, litigious, brawling, hot-tempered, choleric, irritable, argumentative, petulant, pugnacious, fiery, contentious. *(amenable, mild, unquarrelsome, conciliatory, bland, meek, suave, accommodating, peaceable, genial, inoffensive.)*

quarter—*n.* district, territory, forbearance, source, pity, region, locality, mercy. *(mercilessness, cruelty, pitilessness, extermination, ruthlessness, unsparingness.)*

queasy—*adj.* sick, nauseated, edgy, squeamish, restless, upset, giddy. *(relaxed, content, comfortable, easy, untroubled.)*

queer—*adj.* whimsical, cross, crochety, eccentric, weird, odd, quaint, strange, singular. *(common, familiar, orthodox, customary, ordinary, usual.)*

quell—*v.* quiet, subdue, reduce, disperse, scatter, vanquish, pacify, tranquillize, curb. *(excite, stimulate, kin-*

dle, incite, spur, irritate, enrage.)

question—*v.* inquire, doubt, ask, dubitate, dispute, catechize, interrogate, investigate, controvert. *(state, pronounce, concede, affirm, allow, answer, dictate, assert, enunciate, grant, endorse.)*

question—*n.* interrogation, inquiry, scrutiny, topic, investigation, doubt, debate. *(response, answer, admission, retort, concession, reply, solution, explanation.)*

questionable—*adj.* dubious, suspicious, disputable, uncertain, hypothetical, doubtful, problematical, debatable. *(evident, obvious, unequivocal, indisputable, certain, self-evident.)*

quick—*adj.* rapid, expeditious, hasty, ready, sharp, adroit, keen, active, nimble, agile, sprightly, fast, intelligent, precipitous, irasible, speedy, swift, prompt, clever, shrewd, fleet, brisk, lively, alert, transient. *(tardy, inert, dull, gradual, insensitive, slow, sluggish, inactive.)*

quiet—*n.* repose, calm, rest, pacification, peace, stillness, tranquillity, appeasement, silence. *(motion, agitation, disturbance, tumult, uproar, unrest, noise, excitement, turmoil.)*

quiet—*v.* appease, pacify, lull, soothe, silence, calm, allay, still, hush, tranquilize. *(excite, agitate, urge, blare, goad, rouse, disturb, stir.)*

quit—*v.* resign, relinquish, cease, release, give up, forsake, leave, abandon, discharge, surrender, depart

P
R

from. *(occupy, bind, haunt, continue, enter, seek, invade, enforce.)*

quite—*adv.* entirely, wholly, altogether, fully, totally, perfectly, completely, truly. *(imperfectly, scarcely, insufficiently, partially, hardly, barely.)*

quixotic—*adj.* impractical, idealistic, romantic, lofty, fantastic, chivalrous, visionary. *(practical, prosaic, pragmatic, realistic, hardheaded.)*

quote—*v.* name, plead, note, cite, repeat, paraphrase, adduce, allege. *(refute, oppose, traverse, misadduce, deny, rebut, disprove, retort, contradict, misquote.)*

R

rabid—*adj.* zealous, dedicated, fanatical, bigoted, unreasonable, deranged, frantic, maniacal, frenzied. *(reasonable, normal, moderate, sound, sober, lucid, rational, sane, steady.)*

racy—*adj.* fresh, piquant, spicy, smart, vivacious, animated, rich, fine-flavored, pungent, spirited, lively. *(stupid, flavorless, languid, dull, morose.)*

radiant—*adj.* luminous, bright, lustrous, sparkling, shining, brilliant, ecstatic, beaming, elated, merry. *(dull, murky, dim, gloomy, downcast, somber, sad, blurred.)*

radical—*adj.* fundamental, natural, unsparing, entire, immanent, underived, profound, deep-seated, original, thorough-going, extreme, innate, essential, ingrained. *(ascititious, partial, superficial, conservative, derived, traditional, acquired, adventitious, extraneous, moderate.)*

rage—*n.* rabidity, indignation, fury, anger, dudgeon, passion, ferocity, wrath, choler, frenzy, ire, mania, madness. *(moderation, temperateness, quiescence, assuagement, mildness, serenity, softness, reason, gentleness, calmness, mitigation.)*

rage—*v.* storm, be furious, rave, seethe, be violent, fume. *(be peaceful, be calm, mollify, be composed, lull.)*

raise—*v.* heave, exalt, promote, lift, enhance, rouse, call forth, rear, collect, erect, propagate, intensify, elevate, advance, heighten, awaken, excite, cultivate, produce, summon, originate. *(cast, degrade, dishonor, depreciate, compose, calm, destroy, disband, hush, neutralize, curtail, confute, lay, depress, retard, lull, lower, quiet, blight, disperse, stifle, silence.)*

rampant—*adj.* wild, flagrant, excessive, unrestrained, prevalent, menacing, boisterous, ungovernable, comprehensive, universal. *(bland, mild, calm, decorous, local, moderate, contained, dispassionate.)*

range—*n.* dispose, place,

collocate, concatenate, stroll, scope, rove, rank, class, order, file, ramble. *(disconnection, derangement, disturbance.)*

rank—*n.* line, order, grade, series, dignity, row, tier, degree. *(disorder, incontinuity, intermission, plebianism, commonalty, breach, hiatus, disconnection, solution, meanness.)*

rank—*adj.* exuberant, excessive, proliferating, luxuriant, rampant, extreme. *(sparse, fragrant, scanty, pure, wholesome.)*

rankle—*v.* smoulder, irritate, disquiet, embitter, fester, burn, gall. *(cool, calm, compose, improve, heal, close, quiet.)*

rapid—*adj.* swift, accelerated, instantaneous, flying, quick, speedy. *(tardy, cumbrous, deliberate, slow, lazy, retarded.)*

rapture—*n.* delight, exultation, joy, ecstasy, felicity, bliss, passion, rejoicing, transport. *(misery, revulsion, disgust, distress, discontent, affliction.)*

rare—*adj.* choice, excellent, volatile, exceptional, unusual, uncommon, extraordinary, dispersed, precious, sporadic, scarce, infrequent, few, sparse, singular, incomparable, unique, valuable, thin. *(frequent, numerous, ordinary, regular, dense, common, worthless, valueless, mediocre, abundant, mean, usual, crowded, vulgar, cheap.)*

rash—*adj.* audacious, precipitate, foolhardy, adventurous, indiscreet, overventuresome, unwary, impulsive, headstrong, hasty, reckless, careless, thoughtless, venturesome, heedless, incautious. *(cautious, discreet, dubitating, reluctant, prudent, timid, wary, calculating, unventuresome, hesitating.)*

rate—*n.* impost, duty, allowance, quota, price, status, tax, assessment, standard, ratio, worth, value. *(rebate, discount, allowance, percentage.)*

rate—*v.* calculate, value, abuse, evaluate, appraise, compute, estimate, scold. *(repose, be quiescent, loaf.)*

rational—*adj.* sound, reasoning, judicious, sensible, equitable, fair, logical, sane, intelligent, reasonable, sober, probable, moderate. *(unsound, silly, absurd, fanciful, preposterous, unreasonable, exorbitant, emotional, insane, weak, unintelligent, injudicious, extravagant, unreasoning, irrational.)*

ravel—*v.* undo, unwind, fray, disentangle, separate, untwist. *(complicate, confuse, mend, entangle, conglomerate.)*

ravish—*v.* transport, enrapture, violate, debauch, captivate, entrance, enchant, charm, outrage. *(disgust, pique, rile, displease, provoke, harass.)*

raw—*adj.* unprepared, unripe, unseasoned, fresh, unpracticed, bare, exposed, chill, piercing, crude, uncooked, unfinished, bleak, inexperienced, green, untried, bald, galled, unrefined.

(dressed, finished, cooked, mature, seasoned, expert, healed, habituated, practiced, tried, genial, processed, prepared, ripe, mellow, experienced, adept, familiar, trained, covered, balmy.)

reach—v. thrust, obtain, attain, grasp, strain, lengthen, aim, extend, stretch, arrive at, gain, penetrate. (stop, revert, miss, drop, recoil, fail, cease, rebate.)

read—v. interpret, unravel, recognize, comprehend, learn, persue, decipher, discover. (misinterpret, misobserve, misunderstand, overlook.)

ready—adj. responsive, alert, speedy, dexterous, skillful, expert, easy, fitted, disposed, free, compliant, quick, accessible, prompt, expeditious, unhesitating, apt, handy, facile, opportune, prepared, willing, cheerful. (tardy, hesitating, dubitating, unhandy, remote, unavailable, unsuited, unwilling, unprepared, grudging, incompliant, difficult, unready, slow, reluctant, awkward, clumsy, inaccessible, inopportune, unfitted, indisposed, constrained, unaccommodating, irresponsive, doubtful.)

real—adj. veritable, authentic, true, developed, tangible, actual, existent, legitimate, genuine. (imaginary, non-existent, false, adulterated, pretended, possible, counterfeit, fictitious, unreal, untrue, artificial, assumed, potential.)

really—adv. truly, unquestionably, indubitably, veritably, indeed. (possibly, falsely, fictitiously, doubtfully, questionably, perhaps, untruly.)

reason—n. account, explanation, proof, understanding, rationality, propriety, order, sake, target, purpose, ground, cause, motive, apology, reasoning, right, justice, object. (pretense, falsification, disproof, absurdity, irrationality, unreason, unfairness, aimlessness, nonsense, unaccountableness, pretext, misinterpretation, misconception, unreasonableness, fallacy, wrong, impropriety, folly.)

reason—v. discuss, infer, deduce, conclude, cogitate, debate, argue. (back up, comply, abet, encourage, agree.)

reassure—v. restore, inspirit, countenance, bolster, rally, encourage, animate. (cow, intimidate, unnerve, discountenance, discourage, brow-beat.)

rebuff—v. repel, check, oppose, reject, rebuke, repulse, snub. (encourage, welcome, abet, accept, support.)

rebuff—n. discouragement, check, refusal, rebuke, repulsion. (encouragement, spur, acceptance, welcome.)

rebuke—v. chide, reprimand, berate, censure, reprove, rebuff. (encourage, applaud, extol, incite, approve, eulogize.)

receipt—n. reception, acknowledgement, acquisition, voucher, custody. (rejection, exclusion, emission, expulsion.)

receive—v. accept, hold,

assent to, acquire, take, admit, entertain. *(impart, reject, emit, expend, give, afford, discharge.)*

reception—*n.* admittance, acceptation, salutation, entertainment, admission, acceptance. *(protest, rejection, dismissal, renunciation, abjuration, denial, repudiation, non-acceptance, discardment, adjournment.)*

recess—*n.* nook, retirement, seclusion, vacation, depression, holiday, cavity, withdrawal, retreat, privacy. *(protrusion, publicity, promontory, work time, projection, discharge.)*

reckless—*adj.* heedless, foolhardy, rash, regardless, improvident, venturesome, careless, incautious, thoughtless, precipitate, inconsiderate. *(heedful, timid, thoughtful, provident, wary, prudent, circumspect, careful, cautious, chary, calculating, considerate.)*

reckon—*v.* calculate, regard, value, consider, infer, enumerate, judge, compute, count, estimate, account, argue. *(miscalculate, misreckon, miscompute, misestimate, miscount.)*

reclusive—*adj.* solitary, recluse, secluded, isolated, cloistered, ascetic, withdrawn, eremitic. *(sociable, gregarious, convivial, companionable, wordly, accessible.)*

recognize—*v.* acknowledge, know, avow, allow, discern, identify, concede, own, recollect. *(overlook, repudiate, disown, scrutinize, disallow, ignore, misobserve, disavow.)*

recollect—*v.* recall, bethink, reminisce, think of, recreate, recover, remember, bring to mind. *(lose, forget, obliterate, overlook.)*

recommend—*v.* confide, applaud, advise, sanction, commend, praise, approve. *(disapprove, warn, dissuade, disparage, condemn, deter.)*

recompense—*v.* remunerate, indemnify, repay, compensate, repair, requite, reward, satisfy, reimburse. *(injure, spoil, dissatisfy, damnify, mar, misrequite.)*

recompense—*n.* indemnification, remuneration, requital, reward, amends, satisfaction.

reconcile—*v.* conciliate, pacify, adjust, suit, appease, reunite, unite, propitiate, harmonize, adapt. *(sever, estrange, derange, antagonize, separate, incite, disharmonize, alienate, conflict.)*

record—*n.* entry, list, inventory, catalogue, schedule, scroll, roll, instrument, remembrance, memorandum, chronicle, register, enrollment, index, registry, archive, enumerative, memento. *(oblivion, desuetude, immemorality, amnesty, disremembrance, obliteration, nonregistration, obsolescence.)*

recover—*v.* repossess, retrieve, save, heal, revive, reanimate, recapture, regain, resume, recruit, cure, restore. *(forfeit, sacrifice, impair, decline, succumb, relapse, lose, miss, deteriorate, decay.)*

P R

recovery—*n.* regaining, vindication, restitution, retrieval, replacement, revival, improvement, redemption, repossession, reinstatement, renovation, re-establishment, rectification, reanimation. *(forfeiture, deprival, loss, abandonment, retrogression, ruin, dec'ension, defection, privation, sacrific?, relapse, decay, incurableness.)*

recreation—*n.* cheer, amusement, revival, sport, relaxation, regeneration, refreshment, holiday, reanimation, diversion, pastime. *(toil, labor, work, employment, drudgery, weariness, lassitude, fatigue, assiduity.)*

redeem—*v.* regain, make amends for, ransom, rescue, satisfy, liberate, discharge, reconvert, repurchase, retrieve, recompense, recover, fulfill. *(lose, abandon, surrender, rescind, sacrifice, pledge, forfeit, betray.)*

reduce—*v.* diminish, attenuate, narrow, weaken, subdue, bring, subject, curtail, convert, lessen, abridge, impoverish, contract, impair, subjugate, refer, classify. *(magnify, augment, exalt, extend, broaden, renovate, expand, restore, liberate, except, transform, enlarge, increase, produce, amplify, invigorate, repair, free, dissociate.)*

redundant—*adj.* expendable, extra, superfluous, marginal, wasteful, additional, dispensable, repetitious, unnecessary. *(essen-*

tial, central, necessary, concise, brief, indispensable.)

refer—*v.* associate, advert, relate, belong, apply, relegate, attribute, assign, connect, point, allude, appeal. *(dissociate, misappertain, misbeseem, disunite, disresemble, disconnect, misapply, alienate.)*

refinement—*n.* purification, sublimation, elegance, civilization, finesse, polish, clarification, filtration, delicacy, cultivation, subtility, sophistry, discernment. *(grossness, turbidity, coarseness, unrefinement, foulness, inelegance, broadness, vulgarity, bluntness, impurity, rudeness, boorishness, unsophisticatedness.)*

reflect—*v.* image, mirror, consider, cogitate, contemplate, muse, heed, animadvert, reverberate, return, exhibit, think, meditate, ponder, ruminate, advert. *(dissipate, dream, rove, wool-gather, disregard, absorb, overlook, divert, idle, wander, star-gaze, connive.)*

reform—*v.* ameliorate, rectify, reclaim, remodel, reorganize, regenerate, improve, amend, correct, better, rehabilitate, reconstitute. *(vitate, deteriorate, stabilitate, impair, stereotype, degenerate, corrupt, worsen, perpetuate, confirm, deform.)*

refresh—*v.* refrigerate, revive, renovate, renew, cheer, brace, revitalize, cool, invigorate, reanimate, recreate, restore, freshen. *(oppose, burden, annoy, fatigue, debilitate, relax, depress,* heat, weary, afflict, tire, exhaust, enervate.)

refuse—*v.* withhold, decline, veto, repudiate, deny, reject. *(afford, concede, permit, acquiesce, grant, yield.)*

refuse—*n.* scum, sediment, sweepings, offscourings, remains, waste, dross, offal, dregs, recrement, trash, debris. *(pickings, flower, prime, merchandise, cream, firstfruits, chattels.)*

regard—*v.* view, esteem, deem, respect, revere, conceive, notice, behold, mind, contemplate, consider, affect, reverence, value, heed, scrutinize. *(overlook, despise, miss, contemn, loathe, misconceive, misjudge, reject, disregard, dislike, hate, misconsider, misestimate.)*

regenerate—*v.* rehabilitate, improve, remedy, edify, reform, uplift, redeem, rejuvenate, reanimate, redo, recreate, convert, better, civilize. *(debase, lower, corrupt, degenerate, defile, demolish, crush, deprove.)*

regret—*v.* lament, miss, deplore, brood, grieve, repent, desiderate. *(hail, abandon, forget, overlook, disregard, welcome, approve, abjure.)*

regret—*n.* grief, remorse, concern, repentance, sorrow, lamentation, anguish. *(contentment, tranquillity, peace of mind, comfort, solace.)*

regular—*adj.* normal, orderly, stable, recurrent, systematic, established, formal, certain, customary, ordinary, stated, periodical, methodic, recognized, symmetrical. *(exceptional, capricious, irreg-*

ular, fitful, variable, erratic, abnormal, uncertain, unusual, habitual, rare, disordered, unsymmetrical, eccentric.)*

regulation—*n.* law, disposal, rule, government, control, organization, arrangement, adjustment, method, order, statute. *(disorder, misgovernment, disarrangement, caprice, insubjection, license, uncontrol, misrule, anarchy, maladministration, nonregulation, chaos.)*

reject—*v.* renounce, cast away, repel, decline, refuse, ignore, exclude, throw out, repudiate, discard. *(welcome, appropriate, hail, select, endorse, admit, accept, choose.)*

rejoice—*v.* glory, joy, gladden, revel, cheer, enliven, jubilate, gratify, delight, exult, triumph, be glad, please. *(grieve, weep, repent, afflict, weary, disappoint, darken, pain, vex, mope, annoy, mourn, lament, sorrow, trouble, oppress, depress, burden, distress, sadden.)*

relation—*v.* aspect, narration, fitness, bearing, homogeneity, relevancy, ratio, agreement, kindred, reference, correlation, appurtenancy, connection, proportion, affinity, association, pertinency, harmony, relative, kinsman. *(disconnection, irrelevancy, disproportion, unfitness, heterogeneity, disagreement, isolation, alien, irrelation, dissociation, disharmony, impertinency, misproportion, independence, unsuitableness.)*

release—*v.* loose, discharge, acquit, extricate,

indemnify, exempt, free, liberate, quit, parole, disengage. *(constrain, shackle, fetter, enslave, yoke, bind, confine.)*

relevant—*adj.* apt, contingent, pertinent, apropos, related, germane, suitable, appropriate, connected, applicable, on target. *(inappropriate, alien, unrelated, irrelevant, foreign, immaterial.)*

relief—*n.* support, extrication, respite, mitigation, help, remedy, exemption, refreshment, succor, comfort, release, alleviation, aid, assistance, redress, deliverance. *(aggravation, burdensomeness, exhaustion, discomfort, hamper, oppression, intensification, trouble, weariness.)*

religion—*n.* creed, belief, piety, godliness, denomination, holiness, faith, theology, profession, sanctity. *(irreligion, atheism, unbelief, sacrilege, blasphemy, profanity, sanctimoniousness, formalism, irreverence, reprobation, scoffing, skepticism, hypocrisy, pharisaism, godlessness, impiety.)*

religious—*adj.* godly, devotional, holy, reverent, sacred, pious, devout, divine. *(ungodly, sacrilegious, skeptical, agnostic, impious, profane, undevout, blasphemous.)*

relish—*n.* recommendation, flavor, gusto, appetite, sapidity, allure, zest, enhancement, savor, taste, piquancy. *(disflavor, nauseousness, insipidity, antipathy, unsavoriness, drawback, disrecommendation, disrelish.)*

remain—*v.* continue, stop, halt, rest, abide, endure, loi-ter, accrue, stay, wait, tarry, sojourn, dwell, last. *(vanish, depart, hasten, flit, pass, transfer, fly, remove, speed, press, disappear.)*

remarkable—*adj.* noticeable, unusual, striking, notable, famous, rare, prominent, eminent, singular, observable, extraordinary, noteworthy, distinguished, peculiar. *(unnoticeable, mean, every-day, inconspicuous, undistinguished, unremarkable, ordinary, commonplace.)*

remedy—*v.* restorative, reparation, relief, specific, rectify, cure, counteraction, redress, help. *(disease, infection, ill, deterioration, provocation, undermine, evil, hurt, plague, impairment, aggravation.)*

remember—*v.* recall, bear in mind, review, mind, recollect, retain. *(obliviate, overlook, forget, disregard, ignore.)*

remembrance—*n.* memory, token, memento, nostalgia, reminiscence, recollection, memorial, souvenir. *(oblivion, forgetfulness, obscurity.)*

remiss—*adj.* careless, inattentive, slow, idle, dilatory, remissful, delinquent, slack, negligent, wanting, slothful, lax, tardy. *(careful, active, alert, diligent, meticulous, strict, energetic, attentive, assiduous, painstaking.)*

remit—*v.* pardon, forego, surrender, resign, condone, relax, absolve, discontinue, forgive. *(intensity, exact, deteriorate, increase, enforce.)*

remorse—*n.* anguish,

penitence, qualm, contrition, compunction, self-condemnation, regret. *(self-approval, pride, self-congratulation, complacency, satisfaction.)*

remote—*adj.* indirect, unrelated, alien, separate, inaccessible, contingent, distant, unconnected, foreign, heterogeneous. *(close, connected, actual, homogeneous, proximate, present, urgent, current, near, direct, related, immediate, essential, pressing.)*

remove—*v.* separate, transport, transfer, oust, suppress, depart, uproot, displace, abstract, carry, eject, dislodge, migrate, obliterate. *(conserve, perpetuate, reinstate, install, fasten, fix, stand, remain, abide, sustain, restore, stabilitate, establish, reinstall, dwell, stay.)*

render—*v.* present, restore, give, apportion, surrender, requite, submit, deliver, return, give up, assign, pay. *(retain, appropriate, misapportion, misrequite, refuse, keep, withhold, alienate, misappropriate.)*

renegade—*adj.* heretical, insurgent, rebellious, traitorous, dissident, mutinous, maverick, apostate, disloyal. *(faithful, obedient, loyal, steadfast, unswerving.)*

renew—*v.* restore, renovate, furbish, repeat, reissue, reform, modernize, transform, recreate, refresh, rejuvenate, recommence, reiterate, regenerate. *(wear, vitiate, discontinue, weaken, deprove, cancel, impair, deteri-*

orate, exhaust, corrupt, defile.)

renounce—*v.* abjure, disown, disavow, quit, abandon, resign, relinquish, reject, repudiate, disclaim, forego, deny, resign, recant. *(recognize, maintain, propound, vindicate, profess, retain, accept, defend, acknowledge, claim, assert, own, avow, hold.)*

renowned—*adj.* celebrated, famous, illustrious, prominent, wonderful. *(obscure, unknown, anonymous, unrecognized.)*

repay—*v.* reimburse, reward, requite, indemnify, refund, remunerate, recompense, retaliate. *(misappropriate, waste, extort, exact, circumvent, defraud, embezzle, alienate, confiscate.)*

repeal—*n.* rescission, annulment, termination, abrogation, recall, revocation. *(establishment, perpetuation, endurance, continuance.)*

repeal—*v.* revoke, cancel, recall, reverse, invalidate, abolish, rescind, annul, abrogate, discontinue, delete. *(establish, institute, enact, confirm, secure, continue, pass, sanction, perpetuate.)*

repeat—*v.* iterate, cite, relate, quote, recapitulate, reaffirm, reproduce, reiterate, renew, rehearse. *(drop, abandon, suppress, misquote, misrepresent, misconvey, discontinue, discard, ignore, misrepeat, misrecite, neglect, misinterpret.)*

repentance—*n.* contrition, regret, sorrow, self-condemnation, remorse, contrition,

P
R

penitence, compunction, self-reproach. *(obduracy, hardness, self-approval, smugness, impenitence, recusancy, reprobation.)*

repetition—*n.* reiteration, iteration, diffuseness, relation, verbosity, recapitulation, dwelling upon. *(precedence, newness, freshness, singularity, uniqueness.)*

replace—*v.* supply, reinstate, re-establish, supersede, restore, substitute, rearrange. *(abstract, remove, move, deprive, deviate, withdraw, damage.)*

reply—*v.* answer, rejoin, rebut, replicate, respond. *(drop, pass, question, disregard, ignore, pretermit.)*

reply—*n.* rejoinder, replication, retaliation, answer, response. *(ignoring, pass by, stimulus.)*

report—*v.* relate, circulate, narrate, describe, communicate, divulge, declare, announce, tell, notify, recite, detail. *(hush, misreport, misrelate, expunge, falsify, silence, suppress, misrepresent.)*

report—*n.* announcement, narration, description, declaration, rumor, repute, reverberation, disclosure, tidings, relation, recital, news, communication, fame, noise. *(suppression, silence, fabrication, reticence, noiselessness, misannouncement.)*

represent—*v.* delineate, exhibit, state, indicate, enact, denote, dramatize, symbolize, resemble, portray, play, reproduce, personate, describe, embody, illustrate. *(mis-delineate, falsify, misrepresent, misportray, distort, caricature, minimize.)*

representative—*n.* commissioner, agent, deputy, embodiment, delegate, proxy, vicigerent, soverign, emissary, constituency, substitute, personation, vicar, principal. *(dictator, autocrat, despot.)*

repress—*v.* control, inhibit, block, restrain, hinder, stifle, squelch, swallow, curb, quell, subdue. *(liberate, encourage, allow, permit, free, sanction, authorize.)*

reproach—*n.* censure, rebuke, blame, reprobate, lecture, taunt, reprove, upbraid. *(praise, approval, laud, glory, esteem.)*

reprobate—*n.* villain, miscreant, scalawag, degenerate, castaway, ruffian, rascal. *(pattern, model, paragon, example, mirror, saint.)*

repudiate—*v.* disown, abjure, disclaim, revoke, disavow, discard, divorce, renounce, contradict. *(own, assert, vaunt, profess, acknowledge, concede, accept, avow, vindicate, retain, claim, recognize.)*

repulsive—*adj.* deterrent, odious, unattractive, revolting, repugnant, forbidding, ungenial, ugly, disagreeable. *(agreeable, winning, fascinating, seductive, enchanting, pleasant, charming, attractive, captivating, alluring.)*

reputable—*adj.* creditable, reliable, estimable, dependable, honorable, respectable. *(discreditable, disgraceful, unrespectable, dis-*

honorable, disreputable, notorious.)

rescue—*v.* recover, liberate, save, preserve, salvage, retake, recapture, extricate, deliver. *(imperil, surrender, expose, endanger, betray, abandon, impede.)*

resemblance—*n.* similarity, affinity, semblance, portrait, likeness, reflection, image, similitude, representation. *(dissimilarity, difference, contrast, contrariety, unlikeness, disresemblance.)*

resent—*v.* resist, recalcitrate, be indignant at, repel, rebel, take exception to. *(submit, pardon, approve, overlook, acquiesce, condone.)*

reserve—*n.* retention, accumulation, shyness, modesty, reservation, limitation, coldness, coyness, evasiveness. *(rashness, immodesty, spontaneity, boldness, recklessness.)*

residence—*n.* stay, home, domicile, dwelling, mansion, sojourn, abode, habitation.

resist—*v.* oppose, check, baffle, disappoint, frustrate, withstand, hinder, thwart. *(yield, surrender, comply, weaken, capitulate.)*

resolute—*adj.* decided, constant, steadfast, bold, unshaken, decisive, determined, fixed, steady, persevering, firm. *(infirm, cowardly, faltering, inconstant, weak, shy.)*

resource—*n.* means, expedients, riches, assets, material, supplies, wealth. *(exhaustion, drain, poverty, want, destitution, lack, nonplus.)*

respect—*v.* esteem, revere, appreciate, regard, honor, venerate. *(disrespect, deride, dishonor, scorn.)*

respond—*v.* rejoin, answer, reply, acknowledge, notice. *(disregard, neglect, ignore, overlook.)*

rest—*n.* relaxation, indolence, lassitude, idleness, leisure, retirement, siesta, repose, tranquillity, calm. *(work, activity, exertion, sweat, toil, turmoil, agitation.)*

restless—*adj.* uneasy, disquieted, agitated, unsettled, wandering, turbulent, unquiet, disturbed, sleepless, anxious, roving. *(settled, steady, calm, quiet, peaceful.)*

restrain—*v.* hinder, withhold, curb, coerce, abridge, confine, tether, check, stop, repress, suppress, restrict, limit. *(let go, free, liberty, give full rein to, release, flow.)*

result—*n.* consequence, inference, event, effect, conclusion, issue, aftermath. *(origin, beginning, cause, seed.)*

retain—*v.* restrain, keep, hold, withhold. *(give up, yield, abandon.)*

retire—*v.* leave, secede, abdicate, withdraw, deport, recede. *(continue, advance, proceed.)*

retort—*v.* answer, repartee, retaliate.

retreat—*n.* departure, seclusion, privacy, shelter, evacuation, refuge, retirement, withdrawment, solitude, asylum. *(forward march, progress, advance.)*

return—*v.* requite,

recompense, remit, restore, repay, render, report, remember. *(question, assert, claim, displace, remove.)*

reveal—*v.* disclose, unveil, open, impart, announce, show, communicate, divulge, uncover, discover. *(withhold, conceal, disguise, hide, keep secret, cover.)*

revengeful—*adj.* resentful, spiteful, malicious, vindictive, merciless. *(ingenuous, hearty, kind, charitable, cordial, open, frank, generous.)*

revenue—*n.* returns, proceeds, result, wealth, dividends, receipts, income. *(outgo, expense, disbursements.)*

reverence—*n.* honor, adoration, esteem, veneration, awe. *(disdain, contempt, scorn, arrogance.)*

review—*n.* resurvey, survey, revise, revision, evaluation, re-examination, retrospect, reconsideration.

reward—*n.* compensation, pay, retribution, accolade, recompense, remuneration, requital. *(fine, punishment, penalty, damages.)*

rhetorical—*adj.* eloquent, articulate, fluent, pompous, expressive, pretentious. *(inarticulate, ill-spoken, tongue-tied, fumbling.)*

rich—*adj.* affluent, ample, abundant, costly, precious, luscious, lavish, wealthy, opulent, copious, fruitful, sumptuous, generous. *(weak, cheap, sordid, destitute, poor, straitened, scanty.)*

ridicule—*n.* wit, raillery, irony, mockery, satire, gibe, sneer, sarcasm, derision, ban-

ter, burlesque, travesty, jeer. *(praise, respect, honor, homage, deference.)*

ripe—*adj.* mellow, finished, developed, mature, complete. *(young, unfinished, tender, green, incomplete.)*

rise—*v.* ascend, mount, climb, arise, scale, emanate. *(sink, decline, fall, slump.)*

risk—*n.* hazard, jeopardy, peril, vulnerability, exposure, danger. *(security, safeness, safety, protection.)*

rival—*n.* emulator, competitor, antagonist, opponent. *(colleague, associate, collaborator, ally, partner.)*

road—*n.* highway, lane, route, course, way, street, pathway, passage, thoroughfare.

robbery—*n.* depredation, despoliation, pillage, piracy, theft, steal, plunder, caper, looting.

romance—*n.* novel, tale, mystery, fable, fiction.

romantic—*adj.* fanciful, glamorous, extravagant, chimerical, wild, sentimental, fictitious. *(familiar, timorous, aloof, unromantic, frigid, cold.)*

room—*n.* compass, latitude, space, apartment, scope, chamber.

rotund—*adj.* rounded, spherical, circular, globular, plump, fat, corpulent, chubby, stout. *(slim, lean, trim, svelte, thin, slender.)*

round—*adj.* spherical, globose, orbed, full, rotund, curved, circular, globular, orbicular, cylindrical, plump.

(oblong, lean, slender, thin, square, angular.)

rout—*v.* smite, conquer, defeat, vanquish. *(recede, retire, withdraw.)*

route—*n.* path, track, roadway, passage. *(drift, digression, twist, meander.)*

royal—*adj.* regal, imperial, noble, princely, majestic, splendid, magnanimous, aristocratic, kingly, monarchical, kinglike, august, superb, illustrious. *(low, humble, plebian, coarse, vulgar, tawdry, common.)*

ruin—*n.* downfall, fall, defeat, subversion, bane, mischief, destruction, perdition, overthrow, pest, collapse. *(construction, creation, improve, enhance, build.)*

rule—*n.* law, maxim, canon, method, control, sway, authority, empire, regulation, precept, guide, order, direction, government. *(misrule, violence, revolt, misgovernment, confusion, riot, rebellion, conflict.)*

rustic—*adj.* rude, inelegant, honest, awkward, coarse, unadorned, artless, uncouth, rural, plain, unpolished, untaught, rough, simple. *(stylish, elegant, sophisticated, blasé, chic.)*

ruthless—*adj.* pitiless, heartless, unfeeling, hardened, cold, cruel, brutal, relentless, merciless. *(tenderhearted, gentle, indulgent, compassionate, sympathetic.)*

S

sabotage—*v.* disable, sap, wreck, subvert, vandalize, hamper, damage, obstruct, incapacitate. *(enhance, strengthen, abet, assist, cooperate, reinforce.)*

sacred—*adj.* divine, consecrated, devoted, venerable, blessed, holy, hallowed, dedicated, religious, reverend, sanctified. *(secular, sinful, profane, violable, impious, temporal, unconsecrated.)*

sacrifice—*n.* slaughter, offering victim, martyr, scapegoat, oblation, homage, holocaust, corban, hecatomb. *(gain, seizure, usurpation, confiscation, appropriation, profit.)*

sad—*adj.* mournful, dejec-

ted, cheerless, sedate, grave, afflictive, sorrowful, despondent, calamitous, gloomy, depressed, downcast, serious, grievous. *(lively, spirited, jolly, seductive, cheerful, gay, happy, sprightly, fortunate.)*

safe—*adj.* unendangered, sure, protected, secure, unscathed. *(hazardous, dangerous, risky, exposed, in danger.)*

sagacious—*adj.* acute, keen, judicious, intelligent, shrewd, cunning, wise, rational, prudent, sensible, tactful. *(irrational, stupid, foolish, obtuse, silly, ignorance, fatuous.)*

salient—*adj.* outstanding, noticeable, striking, signal,

S T

conspicuous, prominent, obvious, palpable, manifest. *(depressed, minor, trifling, insignificant, trivial, unimportant.)*

sample—*n.* illustration, specimen, instance, example.

sanction—*v.* endorse, support, approve, ratify. *(disapprove, forbid, hinder, censure.)*

sarcasm—*n.* irony, ridicule, sneering, scorn, contempt, jeer, taunting, vitrial, bitterness. *(compliment, praise, flattery, admiration, eulogy, commendation, enthusiasm.)*

satire—*n.* sarcasm, ridicule, burlesque, humor, pasquinade, lampoon, irony, mockery, wit.

satisfaction—*n.* content, pleasure, compensation, remuneration, atonement, felicity, contentment, gratification, recompense, amends, indemnification, *(discomfort, want, displeasure, discontent, resentment, shame, unhappiness.)*

satisfy—*v.* content, gratify, fulfill, compensate, indemnify, satiate, please, recompense, remunerate. *(renege, fail, trouble, sadden, deplete, drain, vex.)*

saucy—*adj.* insolent, impudent, disrespectful, impertinent, rude. *(well-bred, demure, respectful, mannerly, amiable.)*

savage—*adj.* wild, untaught, feral, unpolished, brutish, heathenish, cruel, fierce, merciless, murderous, ferocious, uncultivated, rude, uncivilized, brutal, barbarous, inhuman, pitiless, unmerciful.

(refined, gentle, humane, domesticated, tame, cultured, kind, merciful, human.)

save—*v.* rescue, protect, reserve, redeem, prevent, preserve, deliver, spare. *(expose, throw away, sacrifice, abandon, give up.)*

saying—*n.* speech, maxim, by-word, apothegm, proverb, utterance, declaration, adage, aphorism, saw.

scandal—*n.* detraction, calumny, reproach, disgrace, outrage, defamation, slander, opprobrium, shame. *(glory, respect, honor, esteem, praise.)*

scanty—*adj.* gaunt, scarce, deficient, meager, inadequate. *(plenty, full, ample, copious.)*

scarce—*adj.* infrequent, uncommon, rare, unique, deficient. *(general, frequent, common, usual, abundant.)*

scatter—*v.* dissipate, strew, diffuse, sprinkle, disperse, spread. *(keep together, preserve, assemble, gather, collect, unite.)*

scheme—*n.* project, contrivance, device, strategy, plot, plan, design, purpose.

scholar—*n.* intellectual, sage, pupil, disciple, professor, academician. *(ignoramus, illiterate, simpleton, dunce, dolt.)*

science—*n.* art, knowledge, literature, expertness, skill. *(illiteracy, ignorance, sciolism.)*

scoff—*v.* mock, jeer, ridicule, belittle, sneer, deride, taunt, revile. *(exalt, extol, value, praise, appreciate.)*

scorn—*n.* disdain, contumely, slight, contempt, disregard, derision, despite, dishonor. (respect, admiration, approval, flattery, love, honor.)

scrimp—v. save, stint, economize, hoard, grudge, scrape, withhold, be parsimonious. (spend, pour, lavish, squander, waste.)

scrupulous—adj. careful, hesitating, meticulous, cautious, ethical, conscientious. (careless, daring, reckless, dishonest, negligent, unscrupulous, scatterbrained.)

scurrilous—adj. abusive, low, insulting, offensive, vile, mean, foul-mouthed, scurrile, obscene, opprobrious, reproachful, insolent, gross, vulgar, foul, indecent. (proper, delicate, polite, decent, refined, well-bred.)

seasoned—adj. mature, knowing, ripe, weathered, experienced, veteran, practiced, hardened. (immature, green, innocent, starry-eyed, untried.)

secret—adj. concealed, unseen, private, recondite, covert, privy, confidential, hidden, secluded, unknown, obscure, latent, clandestine. (free, public, revealed, known, open.)

sectarian—adj. partisan, heretic, schismatic, fanatic, clannish. (nonpartisan, broadminded, nonsectarian.)

section—n. division, portion, segment, part, component. (entirety, all, whole, totality.)

security—n. defense, shelter, certainty, assurance, confidence, pledge, invulnerability, protection, guard, safety, ease, carelessness, surety. (exposure, uncertainty, hazard, danger, doubt.)

sedate—adj. demure, calm, quiet, settled, passive, unruffled, sober, serious, grave, serene. (frolicsome, ruffled, disturbed, excitable, flighty, indiscreet, agitated.)

seem—v. look, appear, manifest.

seemly—adj. fit, proper, congruous, decent, conventional, becomingly, suitable, appropriate, meet, decorous, polite. (immodest, gross, outrageous, rude, improper, unconventional.)

segregate—v. disconnect, seclude, isolate, sequester, exclude, quarantine, ghettoize, divorce, disunite. (blend, integrate, unify, desegregate, mix.)

seize—v. grasp, snatch, arrest, capture, embrace, catch, clutch, append, take. (relinquish, liberate, free, let go, loose, let pass.)

selective—adj. choosy, critical, discriminating, finicky, fastidious, percipient, exacting, cautious, careful. (random, inclusive, promiscuous, careless, unselective, undemanding.)

self-control—n. self-discipline, independence, self-restraint, equilibrium, stability, balance, fortitude, willpower. (instability, weakness, hotheadedness, excitability.)

selfish—adj. egotistic, self-centered, greedy, mean, tight, egotistical, self-interested, mercenary, rapacious, stingy. (selfless, generous, altruistic, giving, magnanimous, charitable.)

sense—*n.* reason, sensation, meaning, signification, opinion, reaction, judgment, understanding, perception, feeling, import, notion. *(anesthesia, atrophy, paralysis, numbness.)*

sensible—*adj.* wise, satisfied, astute, persuaded, intelligent, cognizant, logical. *(foolish, dense, obtuse, scatterbrained, impractical.)*

sentiment—*n.* opinion, sensibility, emotion, feeling, thought, notion.

sepulchral—*adj.* funereal, dismal, somber, dreary, morbid, ghastly, melancholy, cheerless, lugubrious. *(bright, vivacious, lively, inviting, cheerful.)*

serene—*adj.* fair, balmy, cool, peaceful, tranquil, placid, relaxed, dignified, nonchalant. *(agitated, anxious, excitable, stormy, turbulent, hectic.)*

serious—*adj.* solemn, weighty, pensive, grave, important, thoughtful. *(lively, light, happy, frivolous, gay, unimportant.)*

serve—*v.* minister to, promote, obey, help, benefit, officiate, succor, subserve, aid, assist, support. *(obstruct, dissatisfy, thwart, hinder, betray, deceive.)*

set—*v.* settle, decline, consolidate, establish, harden, sink, subside, compose. *(ascend, mount, agitate, run, melt, fuse, dislodge, flow, rise, soar, stir, loosen, soften, mollify.)*

set—*adj.* established, determined, formal, conventional, fixed, firm, regular. *(unorthodox, eccentric, unusual, unconventional.)*

settle—*v.* establish, arrange, adjust, decide, quiet, still, fall, lower, acquiesce, agree, stabilize, fix, regulate, compose, determine, allay, adjudicate, sink, subside, calm, abate. *(disestablish, derrange, aggravate, disturb, misdetermine, misplace, rise, move, increase, scramble, remove, misregulate, discompose, disorder, confuse, heighten, misarrange, unsettle, ascend, disagree.)*

settlement—*n.* dregs, precipitation, location, stabilization, colony, subsidence, residuum, colonization, arrangement. *(perturbation, fluctuation, disorder, turbidity, excitement.)*

several—*adj.* distinct, sundry, various, numerous, different, separate, diverse, divers. *(same, indistinguishable, united, integral, communal, one, identical, inseparable, total.)*

severe—*adj.* austere, grave, harsh, rigorous, afflictive, violent, exact, censorious, sarcastic, keen, cruel, serious, stern, strict, rigid, sharp, distressing, extreme, critical, caustic, cutting, better, demanding. *(smiling, relaxed, mild, jocund, indulgent, trivial, loose, inconsiderable, lenient, moderate, considerate, tender, compassionate, gentle, gay, genial, cheerful, jocose, joyous, light, trifling, inexact, uncritical, inextreme, kind, feeling.)*

shabby—*adj.* threadbare, beggarly, impoverished, ragged, contemptible, paltry, mangy. *(dapper, debonair, admirable, new, spendthrift.)*

shadowy—*adj.* cloudy, dark, gloomy, somber, mysterious, dim, obscure, murky. *(brilliant, sunny, bright, clear, sharp, dazzling.)*

shallow—*adj.* slight, trifling, superficial, trivial, unprofound, shoal, flimsy, simple. *(profound, deep, serious, meaningful.)*

sham—*n.* ghost, illusion, delusion, shadow, counterfeit, deception, phantom, mockery, pretense, unreality, affectation. *(reality, substantiality, authenticity, sincerity, verity, truth, substance.)*

shame—*n.* humiliation, decorum, shamefacedness, dishonor, contempt, discredit, remorse, dispraise, abashment, modesty, decency, reproach, ignominy, degradation. *(barefacedness, impudence, indecorum, honor, exaltation, credit, shamelessness, glory, immodesty, indecency, impropriety, renown, pride.)*

shameful—*adj.* degrading, outrageous, indecent, despicable, unbecoming, disgraceful, scandalous, dishonorable. *(respectable, estimable, honorable, reputable.)*

shape—*v.* mould, adapt, adjust, create, make, fashion, form, figure, delineate, contrive, execute. *(distort, misdelineate, discompose, misproduce, destroy, pervert, misadapt, derange, miscontrive, caricature, ruin.)*

shape—*n.* form, mould, pattern, model, silhouette, figure, outline, fashion, cost. *(disorder, disarray, confusion.)*

share—*n.* apportionment, division, allowance, contingent, segment, portion, lot, participation, quota, allotment, dividend. *(mass, entirety, aggregate, whole, total.)*

sharp—*adj.* fine, shrewd, clever, acute, aculeated, pungent, shrill, afflictive, harsh, cutting, active, sore, animated, perceptive, spirited, thin, keen, discerning, sarcastic, pointed, penetrating, acid, piercing, distressing, severe, eager, ardent, hard. *(indifferent, blunt, obtuse, light, rounded, mellow, hollow, trivial, gentle, tender, sluggish, indifferent, spiritless, ambiguous, tame, thick, dull, knobbed, bluff, bass, deep, trifling, mild, soft, lenient, inactive.)*

shatter—*v.* dissipate, derange, rend, shiver, disintegrate, burst, split, disrupt, break in pieces, demolish, dismember. *(organize, fabricate, rear, strengthen, constitute, construct, collocate, compose.)*

sheer—*adj.* mere, unqualified, absolute, unadulterated, gauzy, pure, unmixed, unmitigated, simple. *(qualified, modified, partial, limited, adulterated.)*

shelve—*v.* discard, stifle, postpone, dismiss, swamp, shift. *(prosecute, revive, expedite, agitate, start, pursue.)*

S
T

shift—*v.* alter, shelve, remove, rearrange, change, transfer, displace. *(fasten, insert, plant, restrain, place, fix, locate, pitch.)*

shift—*n.* expedient, pretext, change, device, resource, deviation, transference, contrivance, artifice, substitute, motive, evasion. *(fixity, retention, gripe, permanence, miscontrivance, steadiness, location.)*

shocking—*adj.* horrible, hateful, abominable, foul, astounding, sad, disgraceful, revolting, loathsome. *(honorable, delightful, edifying, attractive, enticing, comforting, pleasing, charming, creditable, exemplary, alluring.)*

short—*adj.* limited, inadequate, near, condensed, lacking, defective, weak, incomplete, inextensive, abrupt, brief, concise, abridged, scanty, insufficient, less, deficient, imperfect, soon, narrow, incomprehensive, blunt. *(protracted, unlimited, ample, adequate, exuberant, long, large, complete, deferred, strong, extensive, bland, inabrupt, diffuse, elongated, extended, plentiful, abundant, sufficient, liberal, copious, distant, wide, comprehensive, exceeding, courteous, expanded.)*

shortsighted—*adj.* imprudent, myopic, unthinking, unwise, reckless, impulsive, indiscreet, thoughtless, foolish. *(prudent, circumspect, cautious, thoughtful, sagacious.)*

show—*v.* present, unfold, teach, conduct, evince, prove, verify, explain, exhibit, demonstrate, reveal, inform, manifest. *(suppress, withhold, mystify, misdemonstrate, contradict, deny, misinterpret, misexplain, screen, conceal, hide, obscure, wrap, misdeclare, refute, disprove, falsify.)*

show—*n.* exhibition, parade, illusion, semblance, pretext, pretense, pageantry, appearance, pomp, demonstration, likeness, profession. *(disappearance, suppression, disguise, unlikeness, reality, substance, deception, nonappearance, concealment, secrecy, sincerity, dissimilarity, ungenuineness.)*

showy—*adj.* gaudy, gorgeous, tinsel, garish, gay, high-colored, flashy. *(unnoticeable, quiet, subdued, dingy, inconspicuous.)*

shrewd—*adj.* penetrating, discriminating, discerning, perceptive, sagacious, astute, intelligent, acute, keen. *(undiscerning, dull, stupid, ignorant, stolid, unsagacious.)*

shrink—*v.* shrivel, retire, revolt, deflate, contract, withdraw, recoil. *(expand, venture, dare, dilate, amplify, stretch.)*

shrivel—*v.* dry up, wrinkle, decrease, degenerate, contract, wither, corrugate. *(flatten, unfold, dilate, rejuvenate, expand, develop, spread.)*

shuffle—*v.* interchange, intershift, derange, wade, equivocate, cavil, mystify, dissemble, jumble, confuse, shift, intermix, agitate, prevaricate, quibble, sophisticate, palter. *(distribute, arrange, reveal, confuse, declare, elucidate, deal, apportion, order, com-*

pose, propound, explain.)

shy—*adj.* reserved, bashful, chary, shrinking, sheepish, timid, modest, suspicious. *(brazen-faced, audacious, aggressive, reckless, bold, impudent.)*

sick—*adj.* ill, distempered, weak, disgusted, feeble, nauseated, corrupt, valetudinarian, queasy, disordered, indisposed, ailing, morbid, impaired, diseased. *(well, sound, strong, salubrious, vigorous, whole, healthy, robust, well-conditioned.)*

side—*n.* edge, border, face, plane, interest, policy, boundary, behalf, margin, verge, laterality, aspect, party, cause. *(body, interior, neutrality, severance, opposition, detachment, center, core, essence, disconnection, secession.)*

sight—*n.* perception, vision, spectacle, inspection, representation, image, appearance, seeing, view, visibility, show, examination. *(invisibility, obscuration, oversight, undiscernment, blunder, non-perception, blindness, disappearance, non-appearance.)*

sign—*n.* indication, memorial, symbol, prefiguration, type, symptom, mark, presage, gesture, token, proof, expression, emblem, badge, premonition, prognostic, signal, wonder. *(misrepresentation, misleader, misindication, falsification.)*

signal—*adj.* conspicuous, extraordinary, memorable, important, distinguished, prominent, eminent, remarkable, notable, illustrious, salient. *(common, mediocre, unimportant, obscure, ordinary, unnoticeable, unmemorable.)*

signify—*v.* purport, mean, indicate, denote, declare, forebode, imply, presage, portend, prognosticate, represent, communicate, betaken, utter. *(suppress, misdenote, refute, preclude, obviate, conceal, misindicate, nullify, neutralize.)*

silence—*n.* stillness, peace, quiet, muteness, oblivion, taciturnity, calm, hush, secrecy, lull. *(loquacity, chatter, brawl, clatter, babel, agitation, storm, roar, reverberation, fame, commotion, proclamation, celebrity, remembrance, effusiveness, garrulity, talkativeness, noise, clamor, din, tumult, restlessness, unrest, bruit, resonance, cackling, publicity, rumor, repute.)*

silly—*adj.* foolish, shallow, weak, unwise, imprudent, fatuous, absurd, simple, witless, indiscreet. *(intelligent, wise, discreet, sound, mature, rational, deep, sagacious, astute, prudent.)*

similar—*adj.* resembling, common, concordant, congruous, kindred, correspondent, alike, homogeneous, harmonious. *(unlike, alien, discordant, contrary, incongruous, different, dissimilar, heterogeneous.)*

simple—*adj.* incomplex, unblended, pure, mere, plain, unartificial, sincere, single-minded, silly, homely, unsophisticated, elementary, primal, transparent, rudimen-

S
T

tary, single, uncompounded, isolated, unmixed, absolute, unadorned, artless, undesigning, unaffected, weak, humble, lowly, ultimate. *(complex, blended, fused, multigenerous, compound, eminent, subdivided, connected, complicated, artificial, designing, double-minded, self-conscious, sophisticated, complete, perfect, embellished, double, compounded, mixed, multi-form, various, articulated, organized, modified, elaborate, artful, insincere, affected, sagacious, great, illustrous, developed.)*

simultaneous—*adj.* concomitant, synchronous, contemporary, con-current, synchronic. *(separate, intermittent, diachronic, periodic, inconcurrent, apart.)*

sin—*n.* iniquity, ungodliness, evil, crime, immorality, wrongdoing, transgression, unrighteousness, wickedness, impurity. *(obedience, righteousness, godliness, virtue, goodness, sinlessness, holiness, purity.)*

sincere—*adj.* unmixed, unadulterated, honest, unvarnished, cordial, unfeigned, genuine, true, pure, heartfelt, hearty, unaffected, candid, frank. *(adulterated, insincere, feigned, false, duplicity, impure, dishonest, hypocritical, pretended.)*

single—*adj.* one, alone, individual, solitary, sole, uncombined, separate, unmarried, private, isolated, unaccompanied. *(many, united, frequent, conglomerate, plural, collective, numerous, married, blended.)*

singular—*adj.* individual, eminent, conspicuous, unusual, odd, quaint, unexampled, solitary, eccentric, exceptional, remarkable, queer, unparalleled, single, unique, extraordinary, consummate, uncommon, peculiar, whimsical, unprecedented, sole, fantastic, particular, curious. *(frequent, ordinary, unnoticeable, customary, regular, nondescript, common, numerous, usual, every-day, general.)*

sinister—*adj.* evil, pernicious, malevolent, noxious, ominous, corrupt, malign, disastrous, menacing. *(good, auspicious, benign, fortunate, promising.)*

situation—*n.* position, state, post, condition, aspect, office, plight, standing, dilemma, locality, birth, topography, seat, place, residence, footing, predicament. *(non-location, non-assignment, displacement, non-appearance, dislodgement, non-situation, absence, unfixedness.)*

skeptical—*adj.* suspicious, cynical, doubtful, agnostic, dubious, questioning, quizzical, incredulous, unbelieving, unconvinced. *(credulous, certain, gullible, confident, believing, sure.)*

skillful—*adj.* skilled, polished, expert, proficient, adroit, deft, capable, clever, competent, versed. *(clumsy, awkward, inept, unskilled, bungling, unqualified.)*

slander—*v.* injure, malign, discredit, asperse, smear, defame, libel, vilify, denigrate. *(commend, defend, praise, eulogize, laud, extol.)*

slender—*adj.* narrow, slim, trivial, inadequate, feeble, meagre, superficial, spindly, thin, slight, small, spare, fragile, flimsy, inconsiderable. *(thick, robust, considerable, deep, pudgy, stout, broad, massive, ample.)*

sloppy—*adj.* messy, dirty, careless, tacky, slovenly, untidy, slipshod, substandard, frowzy. *(careful, trim, clear, immaculate, meticulous, tidy.)*

slow—*adj.* inactive, lazy, tardy, gradual, dull, lingering, inert, deliberate, sluggish, unready, slack, late, tedious, dilatory. *(quick, rapid, ready, early, immediate, punctual, active, fast, alert, prompt, sudden.)*

slur—*n.* smear, affront, insult, innuendo, detraction, disparagement, insinuation, reproach. *(commendation, honor, eulogy, compliment, praise, homage.)*

sly—*adj.* subtle, artful, underhanded, stealthy, covert, cunning, crafty, wily, astute. *(frank, undesigning, candid, open, artless.)*

small—*adj.* diminutive, minute, trivial, paltry, mean, slender, inferior, modest, little, slight, feeble, insignificant, narrow, weak, fine. *(large, considerable, extensive, spacious, strong, liberal, broad, weighty, great, big, bulky, ample, stout, important.)*

smart—*adj.* pungent, quick, sharp, active, brilliant, witty, spruce, fresh, showy, intelligent, keen, piercing, vigorous, severe, clever, vivacious,

ready, brisk, dressy. *(heavy, slow, stupid, unready, unwitty, shabby, bland, clownish, dull, aching, inactive, sluggish, slow-minded, dowdy.)*

smooth—*adj.* plain, flat, glossy, soft, unobstructed, oily, silken, suave, even, level, polished, sleek, unruffled, bland. *(rough, abrupt, unpolished, blunt, abrasive, uneven, rugged, precipitous, harsh.)*

smother—*v.* stifle, gag, suppress, strangle, swallow, asphyxiate, suffocate, repress, conceal, choke, allay. *(ventilate, cherish, vent, publish, divulge, excite, fan, foster, nurture, promulgate, spread, purify.)*

smug—*adj.* complacent, cocky, serene, placid, self-satisfied, triumphant, conceited. *(apologetic, hesitant, sheepish, modest, diffident.)*

snappy—*adj.* energetic, curt, keen, animated, crisp, quick, fashionable, stylish, smart. *(slow, threadbare, dowdy, languid, lazy, shabby, seedy.)*

sneer—*n.* gibe, taunt, contempt, superciliousness, grimace, disdain, scoff, jeer, disparagement, scorn. *(eulogy, deference, laudation, complement, commendation.)*

snub—*n.* check, reprimand, insult, rebuke.

snug—*adj.* housed, compact, sheltered, cozy, close, compressed, comfortable. *(loose, uncompact, bare, uncovered, shivering, exposed, disordered, uncomfortable.)*

sober—*adj.* unintoxicated, calm, dispassionate, sound,

serious, sedate, abstemious, rational, moderate, temperate, cool, reasonable, self-possessed, unexcited, grave, steady, deliberate, circumspect, lucid, staid, dignified, prim, severe, serious, somber. *(drunk, heated, extreme, impassioned, agitated, passionate, immoderate, erratic, befuddled, eccentric, intemperate, intoxicated, excited, unreasonable, furious, extravagant, exorbitant, flighty, besotted, crazed, gay, carefree, wanton, muddled.)*

society—*n.* polity, collection, fellowship, participation, sociality, intercourse, culture, sodality, community, company, association, companionship, connection, communion. *(personality, separation, unsociality, dissociation, privacy, individuality, segregation, solitariness, disconnection, seclusion.)*

soft—*adj.* pressible, smooth, fine, glossy, gentle, kind, flexible, sleek, luxurious, tender, undecided, mild, supple, yielding, impressible, delicate, balmy, feeling, effeminate, unmanly, irresolute. *(tough, unyielding, rigid, unimpressible, coarse, abrupt, rigorous, severe, unfeeling, austere, inflexible, self-denying, hard, determined, strident, stubborn, rough, harsh, ungentle, cutting, unkind, sharp, stern, ascetic, resolute.)*

soften—*v.* palliate, mitigate, dulcify, yield, humanize, compose, moderate, enervate, mollify, assuage, lenify, macerate, abate. *(indurate, excite, harden, infuriate, tough-*

en, aggravate, consolidate, intensify.)

solace—*v.* alleviate, calm, soothe, comfort, cheer, bolster, mitigate, console, reassure, ameliorate. *(depress, aggravate, irritate, undermine.)*

solemn—*adj.* formal, reverential, ceremonial, religious, serious, awesome, sacred, devotional, ritual, impressive, grave. *(undevotional, light, trivial, informal, frivolous, profane, secular, gay, unceremonial, unsolemn, flippant.)*

solid—*adj.* firm, resistant, strong, substantial, just, impenetrable, cubic, solidified, hard, compact, dense, weighty, valid, sound, stable. *(hollow, frail, flimsy, resilient, impressible, liquid, soft, light, weak, unsound, weakly, flexible, yielding, brittle, elastic, malleable, fluid, frivolous, trifling, invalid, fallacious.)*

solitude—*n.* remoteness, retirement, barrenness, privacy, withdrawal, loneliness, seclusion, isolation, desertion, wilderness. *(combination, continuity, conjunction, complication, union, mystification, integration, gregariousness, amalgamation, connection, entanglement, confusion.)*

somber—*adj.* funereal, grim, dark, melancholy, sepulchral, dreary, sad, doleful, gloomy. *(festive, cheerful, gay, bright, joyous.)*

sophisticated—*adj.* experienced, knowledgeable, aware, worldy, cosmopolitan, blase, intellectual, cultured. *(simple, naive, primitive, pro-*

vincial, unseasoned, ingenuous, sophomoric.)

sore—*adj.* irritated, excoriated, scarified, grievous, heavy, raw, abscessed, painful, susceptible, ulcerous, afflictive, burdensome, chafed. (sound, healthful, grateful, unbroken, light, unburdensome, untroublesome, delighted, painless, whole, healed, unsacrified, trivial, pleasant.)

sorry—*adj.* pained, afflicted, hurt, doleful, mortified, dejected, mean, shabby, apologetic, worthless, grieved, woe-be-gone, down-hearted, vexed, poor, vile. (rejoiced, pleased, fine, handsome, agreeable, glad, delighted, gratified, choice.)

sort—*n.* species, class, character, manner, condition, designation, category, genus, kind, nature, order, rank, quality, description. (solitariness, non-classification, heterogeneity, non-description, uniqueness, variegation.)

sound—*adj.* unbroken, perfect, well-grounded, unimpaired, firm, vigorous, solid, irrefutable, valid, correct, logical, substantial, entire, whole, unhurt, uninjured, healthy, strong, weighty, irrefragable, thorough, wholesome. (broken, impaired, frail, unsound, light, unfounded, weak, fallacious, unwholesome, risky, unsubstantial, partial, injured, unhealthy, fragile, trivial, hollow, imperfect, incorrect, invalid, feeble.)

sour—*adj.* rancid, turned, crusty, crabbed, morose, churlish, tart, acetous, peevish, fermented, coagulated, harsh, austere, pungent, acid, bitter, acrimonious. (wholesome, mellow, kindly, affable, sweet, genial, untainted.)

sovereign—*adj.* enthroned, imperial, sanctioned, ruling, authoritative, almighty, free, dominant, paramount. (dethroned, powerless, unauthorized, minor, subservient, secondary, petty.)

spacious—*adj.* extensive, vast, large, roomy, voluminous, broad, expansive, ample, capacious, wide. (restricted, narrow, cramped, inextensive, limited, uncomfortable, confined.)

spare—*v.* afford, reserve, husband, retain, grudge, omit, withhold, abstain, liberate, save, grant, do without, economize, store, discard, forbear, refrain. (squander, lavish, vent, expend, indulge, dissipate, spend, waste, scatter, pour.)

spare—*adj.* unplentiful, meagre, chary, frugal, restricted, niggardly, thin, superfluous, available, additional, minimal, scanty, inabundant, economical, stinted, parsimonious, disposable, lean. (plentiful, profuse, unrestricted, bountiful, ornate, unstinted, available, elaborate, ample, abundant, liberal, generous, unsparing, unbounded.)

spasmodic—*adj.* irregular, fitful, erratic, occasional, transient, sudden, convulsive, changeable, transitory. (continuous, lasting, regular, uninterrupted.)

special—*adj.* specific, appropriate, distinctive, especial, unique, exceptional, particular, peculiar, proper, extraordinary. *(universal, generic, typical, general, common.)*

speculation—*n.* consideration, view, weighing, theory, hypothesis, assumption, conjecture, contemplation, thought, scheme. *(proof, verification, certainty, substantiation, fact, realization.)*

speed—*v.* expedite, urge, hasten, press, plunge, dispatch, accelerate, hurry. *(delay, obstruct, loiter, linger, stay, dawdle, retard, postpone, drag, creep, lag.)*

speed—*n.* swiftness, haste, promptness, nimbleness, rush, rapidity, agility, quickness. *(sluggishness, inertia, laziness, slowness, delay.)*

spend—*v.* waste, squander, lay out, disburse, dissipate, lavish, bestow, exhaust, expend, consume. *(save, accumulate, economize, conserve, retain, hoard, husband.)*

spirit—*n.* breath, soul, essential, ego, quality, immateriality, disembodiment, apparition, energy, enthusiasm, earnestness, zeal, temper, motive, courage, distillation, air, life, vital force, essence, intelligence, spectre, ghost, ardor, activity, courage, disposition, principle. *(body, materiality, deadness, organization, embodiment, dejection, listlessness, lifelessness, flesh, torpor, sluggishness, timidity, substance, corporeity, frame, spiritlessness, soullessness,*

dejection, slowness.)

spirited—*adj.* lively, ardent, sprightly, enterprising, courageous, animated, vivacious, buoyant. *(dispirited, cowardly, inert, dull, depressed.)*

spiritual—*adj.* religious, ghostly, immaterial, intellectual, psychic, divine, holy, ethical, incorporeal. *(fleshly, gross, sensuous, secular, carnal, unspiritual, material.)*

spite—*n.* malevolence, pique, ill-will, rancor, bitterness, malice, spleen, grudge, hatred, vindictiveness. *(kindliness, benevolence, charity, good-will.)*

splendid—*adj.* showy, sumptuous, glorious, imposing, superb, heroic, signal, incredible, brilliant, magnificent, gorgeous, pompous, illustrious, famous, grand. *(obscure, somber, beggarly, ordinary, inglorious, dreadful, dull, tame, poor, unimposing, ineffective.)*

split—*v.* separate, cleave, rive, splinter, rend, disagree, divide, disunite, fragment, crack, burst, sunder, secede. *(unite, coalesce, agree, consolidate, integrate, cohere, amalgamate, conform, splice.)*

spoil—*v.* strip, devastate, denude, vitiate, deteriorate, damage, mar, plunder, rob, pillage, corrupt. *(enrich, replenish, improve, ameliorate, preserve, repair, invest, endow, renovate, better, rectify.)*

spontaneous—*adj.* self-generated, self-evolved, unbidden, extemporaneous, gratuitous, voluntary, self-originated, willing. *(imposed, unwilling, premeditated, involuntary, compulsionary, necessitated, calculated.)*

sporadic—*adj.* occasional, rare, spasmodic, unexpected, irregular, unscheduled, isolated, infrequent. *(regular, continuous, epidemic, extensive, frequent, general, unlimited.)*

sport—*n.* frolic, joke, fun, merriment, recreation, pastime, entertainment, play, wantonness, diversion, gaiety, amusement, game. *(seriousness, earnestness, work, toil, business.)*

spread—*v.* stretch, open, divulge, publish, diffuse, distribute, circulate, ramify, inflate, extend, expand, unfurl, propagate, disperse, overlay, scatter, disseminate. *(furl, fold, shut, suppress, restrict, hush, recall, stagnate, localize, close, condense, contract, gather, secrete, confine, repress, conceal, collect, concentrate.)*

spring—*v.* bound, start, issue, originate, emanate, burst, hurdle, flow, leap, jump, emerge, proceed, rise, germinate. *(alight, drop, issue, end, debouch, wither, disembogue, settle, land, arrive, eventuate, terminate.)*

squalid—*adj.* wretched, unkempt, dilapidated, shabby, dingy, filthy, untidy, poor, grimy, vulgar, disheveled, decayed. *(tidy, decent, neat, presentable, noble, well-kept, clean, respectable.)*

staid—*adj.* demure, sober, subdued, sedate, grave, steady, prudent, conservative.

(flighty, wanton, erratic, agitated, ruffled, capricious, unsteady, indiscreet, insedate, eccentric, discomposed.)

stammer—*v.* hesitate, falter, mumble, stutter. *(speak unhesitantly, speak clearly.)*

stamp—*n.* kind, make, impression, print, cast, character, signature, type, genus, description, mark, imprint, brand, mould. *(non-description, heterogeneity, formlessness, unevenness.)*

stand—*v.* remain, be, suffer, rest, depend, consist, continue, pause, tolerate, halt, stop, exist, insist, await, hold, endure. *(move, advance, fail, succumb, lie, fade, depart, oppose, progress, proceed, fall, yield, drop, vanish, run.)*

standard—*n.* gauge, test, exemplar, flag, model, plummet, pennant, measure, criterion, rule, banner, type, scale, emblem. *(misrule, non-criterion, miscomparison, misfit, confusion, incommensurateness, inconformity, mismeasurement, misadjustment.)*

state—*n.* condition, circumstance, predicament, province, position, situation, plight, case, emotion.

state—*v.* declare, aver, narrate, particularize, recite, utter, say, propound, set forth, specify, avow. *(repress, imply, retract, contradict, repudiate, suppress, suppose, deny.)*

stately—*adj.* imposing, elevated, proud, pompous, grand, lofty, awesome, dignified, lordly, majestic, magnificent. *(unimposing, mean,* *commonplace, squalid, undignified, unstately.)*

staunch—*adj.* resolute, firm, faithful, trustworthy, loyal, devoted, stalwart, reliable, true. *(questionable, unreliable, faithless, vacillating, ambivalent.)*

stay—*v.* stop, withhold, hinder, obstruct, rest, remain, dwell, halt, wait, confide, lean, hold, restrain, arrest, delay, support, repose, continue, await, abide, tarry, trust, linger. *(liberate, expedite, free, hasten, depress, fail, proceed, depart, mistrust, facilitate, loose, send, speed, accelerate, oppress, burden, fall, move, overthrow.)*

steady—*adj.* fixed, uniform, equable, undeviating, permanent, well-regulated, firm, constant, consistent, regular. *(variable, inconstant, wavering, sporadic, ill-regulated, infirm, unsteady, changeable.)*

step—*n.* pace, grade, degree, walk, progression, trace, proceeding, measure, stride, advance, space, gradation, track, vestige, gait, action. *(recession, station, nongraduation, stand-still, tracklessness, nonimpression, desistance, withdrawal, inaction, retreat, stop, halting, standing, nonprogression, untraceableness, desinence.)*

stern—*adj.* austere, harsh, rigorous, unyielding, stringent, forbidding, severe, rigid, strict, unrelenting. *(genial, easy, lenient, encouraging, compassionate, kindly, flexible.)*

stiff—*adj.* inflexible, unyielding, strong, obstinate, constrained, starched, ceremonious, firm, difficult, unbending, rigid, forceful, stubborn, pertinacious, affected, formal. *(flexible, yielding, easy, unaffected, affable, pliable, unceremonious, pliant, flaccid, genial.)*

still—*adj.* calm, hushed, pacific, motionless, peaceful, tranquil, inert, stationary, quiet, noiseless, silent, serene, stagnant, quiescent. *(disturbed, moved, resonant, moving, dynamic, transitional, unquiet, agitated, noisy, turbulent.)*

stingy—*adj.* avaricious, niggardly, hide-bound, sparing, penurious, miserly, close, mean, frugal, parsimonious, sordid. *(generous, handsome, bountiful, munificent, unsparing, liberal, large, lavish.)*

stop—*v.* obstruct, cork, seal, suspend, rest, hinder, delay, terminate, end, thwart, close, plug, bar, arrest, halt, suppress, cease. *(expedite, broach, promote, farther, proceed, hasten, initiate, open, clear, unseal, advance, continue, speed.)*

stout—*adj.* lusty, robust, brawny, resolute, valiant, pudgy, durable, strong, vigorous, sturdy, corpulent, brave. *(debile, thin, lean, feeble, timid, fragile, weak, frail, attenuated, slender, irresolute, cowardly.)*

straight—*adj.* rectilinear, linear, unswerving, nearest, direct, undeviating, right, horizontal. *(winding, tortuous, serpentine, waving, devious,* *crooked, indirect, incurved, sinuous, circuitous.)*

strange—*adj.* alien, unfamiliar, odd, abnormal, surprising, marvelous, uncommon, anomalous, peculiar, foreign, exotic, unusual, irregular, exceptional, wonderful, astonishing. *(domestic, usual, common, customary, unsurprising, general, indigenous, familiar, ordinary, regular, commonplace, universal.)*

strength—*n.* vigor, security, sinew, vehemence, hardness, nerve, vitality, force, power, validity, intensity, soundness, fibre. *(imbecility, insolidity, invalidity, delicacy, flimsiness, vulnerability, hollowness, weakness, feebleness, insecurity, frailty, softness.)*

strenuous—*adj.* resolute, earnest, ardent, energetic, arduous, strong, determined, vigorous, bold, vehement. *(irresolute, feeble, unearnest, effortless, emasculate, weak, undetermined, debile.)*

strict—*adj.* exact, rigorous, close, stringent, precise, meticulous, accurate, severe, nice. *(inexact, lenient, lax, indulgent, negligent, loose, inaccurate, mild.)*

striking—*adj.* affecting, wonderful, notable, surprising, impressive, admirable. *(indifferent, minor, mediocre, ineffectual, commonplace.)*

stringent—*adj.* exacting, hard, severe, stern, rigorous, relentless, firm, compelling, obedient, harsh. *(relaxed, equivocal, flexible, moderate, lenient, easy.)*

strong—*adj.* vigorous, secure, forcible, hale, brawny, sound, cogent, dynamic, zealous, pungent, hardy, tenacious, powerful, solid, fortified, hearty, impetuous, sinewy, robust, patent, influential, muscular, staunch. *(weak, insecure, feeble, calm, delicate, inefficacious, frail, unconvincing, vapid, unavailing, debile, nerveless, moderate, powerless, defenseless, mild, gentle, sickly, unsatisfactory, unimpressive, impotent, lukewarm, flaccid, tender, indifferent, fragile.)*

stubborn—*adj.* unbending, hard, intractable, stiff, inflexible, harsh, refractory, contumacious, dogmatic, tough, unyielding, obstinate, heady, obdurate, pig-headed, headstrong. *(tractable, pliant, malleable, indecisive, flexible, docile, manageable pliable.)*

studious—*adj.* diligent, attentive, thoughtful, reflective, erudite, literary, desirous, careful, assiduous. *(illiterate, indulgent, regardless, thoughtless, idle, uneducated, unliterary, careless, inattentive, indifferent, negligent.)*

stupid—*adj.* senseless, doltish, dull, insensate, prosy, dull-witted, vacuous, stolid, besotted, obtuse, asinine. *(sharp, sensible, quick, penetrating, brilliant, bright, clever, sagacious.)*

subdue—*v.* reduce, break, quell, overwhelm, subjugate, conquer, overpower, tame, vanquish, master, suppress. *(exalt, strengthen, liberate, capitulate, enfranchise, ag-*

grandize, fortify, empower.)

subject—*adj.* subservient, liable, disposed, amenable, dependent, subordinate, exposed, prone, obnoxious. *(independent, dominant, indisposed, unamenable, exempt, superior, unliable.)*

submissive—*adj.* compliant, docile, obsequious, passive, subservient, humble, obedient, yielding, modest, acquiescent. *(incompliant, recusant, inobsequious, refractory, resistant, domineering, disobedient, unyielding, recalcitrant, proud, renitent.)*

substantial—*adj.* real, true, stout, material, bulky, durable, solid, existing, corporeal, strong, massive, tangible, stable. *(unreal, fictitious, incorporeal, visionary, weak, airy, spiritual, fragile, ghostly, frail, imaginary, insubstantial, chimerical, supposititious, immaterial, disembodied.)*

subtle—*adj.* artful, insinuating, astute, discriminating, fine, sophistical, elusive, jesuitical, sly, cunning, wily, nice, crafty, shrewd. *(frank, artless, open, rough, undiscerning, simple, obtuse, honest, undiscriminating, blunt, unsophisticated.)*

success—*n.* luck, prosperity, good-fortune, attainment, victory, achievement, consummation. *(defeat, ruin, disgrace, failure, disaster.)*

succession—*n.* supervention, progression, sequence, series, continuity, suite, following, order, rotation, supply. *(anticipation, antecedence, disorder, solution, intermission, gap, incon-*

secutiveness, interim, precedence, prevention, irregularity, non-sequence, failure, break.)

succinct—*adj.* short, concise, crisp, laconic, condensed, compressed, compact, pithy, curt, clipped, abbreviated, terse. *(verbose, rambling, circuitous, wordy, loquacious, garrulous.)*

suffer—*v.* endure, undergo, grieve, permit, admit, experience, let, support, bear, sustain, allow, tolerate. *(repel, reject, repudiate, ignore, eliminate, resist, expel, disallow, forbid.)*

sufficient—*adj.* equal, satisfactory, qualified, suited, ample, fit, abundant, adequate, competent, adapted, enough. *(unequal, meagre, unqualified, insufficient, scanty, deficient, incomplete, inadequate, incompetent, short, unadapted, unsuited, bare.)*

suit—*v.* adapt, adjust, apportion, beseem, correspond, comport, serve, become, reconcile, accord, fit, match, harmonize, befit, tally, answer, please, agree. *(misadapt, misapportion, vary, disagree, dissatisfy, differ, miscomport, misfit, mismatch, unbeseem.)*

summary—*n.* tabulation, resume, digest, recapitulation, analysis, abridgment, compendium, epitome. *(dilution, expansion, dilatation, amplification.)*

superb—*adj.* magnificent, princely, showy, august, gorgeous, grand, exquisite, elegant, splendid, proud, stately. *(common, unimposing, infe-*

rior, shabby, mean, worth-less.)

supercilious—*adj.* contemptuous, arrogant, patronizing, insolent, haughty, disdainful. *(courteous, modest, humble, bashful, affable, respectful.)*

superficial—*adj.* slight, showy, flimsy, shallow, skin-deep, peripheral, light, imperfect, external, surface, smattering. *(profound, deep, recondite, exact, complex, abstruse, accurate, internal.)*

superior—*adj.* upper, preferable, loftier, remarkable, conspicuous, distinguished, higher, better, surpassing, excellent, eminent. *(lower, subordinate, common, average, mediocre, inferior, imperfect, worse, ordinary, mean, unremarkable.)*

supple—*adj.* bending, flexible, servile, cringing, sycophantic, limber, resilient, compliant, pliant, yielding, elastic, fawning, adulatory, lithe. *(unbending, stiff, inflexible, independent, rigid, supercilious, firm, unyielding, stubborn, inelastic, self-assertive.)*

supply—*v.* afford, accoutre, give, minister, contribute, replenish, furnish, provide, yield. *(use, waste, absorb, withhold, retain, deplete, expend, consume, exhaust, demand, withdraw.)*

support—*n.* stay, buttress, aid, influence, living, subsistence, food, prop, foundation, advocate, help, assistance, maintenance, patronage, livelihood.

support—*v.* uphold, underlie, help, assist, promote, suffer, foster, nourish, endorse, continue, stay, patronize, prop, sustain, bear, befriend, second, buttress, further, defend, nurture, cherish, maintain, countenance, subsidize, back, favor. *(betray, abandon, oppose, weaken, thwart, drop, disfavor, suppress, squelch, surrender, discontinue, discourage, exhaust, subvert.)*

suppose—*v.* presume, deem, fancy, regard, imagine, deduce, presuppose, guess, judge, consider, assume, believe, think, conceive, imply, conjecture, conclude. *(demonstrate, realize, conclude, deny, prove, substantiate, disbelieve.)*

sure—*adj.* secure, assured, stable, knowing, confident, unquestioning, unfailing, permanent, enduring, indisputable, absolute, fast, safe, certain, unmistakable, firm, strong, believing, trusting, positive, abiding, infallible. *(ignorant, doubtful, dubious, distrustful, vacillating, untrustworthy, insecure, transient, fallible, weak, loose, vulnerable, uncertain, hesitating, questioning, precarious, impermanent, evanescent, disputable.)*

surreptitious—*adj.* clandestine, covert, veiled, furtive, secret, stealthy, undercover, sneaky, concealed. *(exposed, candid, overt, public, open, straightforward.)*

susceptible—*adj.* impressible, sensitive, vulnerable, capable, tender. *(unimpressible, insusceptible, resistent, impassible, incapable, insensitive.)*

suspense—*n.* uncertainty, pause, solicitude, intermission, indecision, abeyance, indetermination, doubt, apprehension, protraction, cessation, waiting, discontinuance, stoppage. *(settlement, revival, continuance, finality, resolution, determination, execution, decision, uninterruption.)*

sway—*n.* influence, authority, supremacy, superiority, dominion, preponderance, ascendancy, force, jurisdiction, power, wield, rule, government, bias, control, domination, mastery, weight. *(inferiority, irresistance, subservience, weakness, debility, subjection, subordination, obedience.)*

sway—*v.* govern, bias, swing, teeter, wield, influence, rule, wave.

sweet—*adj.* luscious, dulcet, pure, harmonious, beautiful, wholesome, winning, fresh, amiable, genial, saccharine, fragrant, melodious, musical, lovely, pleasing, mild, agreeable, gentle. *(bitter, fetid, nauseous, stinking, inharmonious, unlovely, unwholesome, tainted, unamiable, repulsive, sour, unsweet, offensive, olid, nasty, discordant, repulsive, putrid, ungentle.)*

swell—*v.* extend, heighten, enhance, expand, augment, aggravate, dilate, distend, multiply, enlarge, heave, rise, increase, protuberate, amplify. *(curtail, diminish, shrivel, retrench, collapse, narrow, contract, concentrate, decrease, lessen, fold, reduce, condense.)*

sympathy—*n.* compassion, understanding, pity, tenderness, kindness, humanity, unselfishness. *(antagonism, animosity, pitilessness, compassionlessness, harshness, unkindliness, antipathy, incongeniality, mercilessness, unkindness.)*

system—*n.* scheme, regularity, arrangement, plan, organization, method, order, classification, rule. *(derangement, fortuity, medley, incongruity, non-classification, chaos, disorder, confusion, chance, haphazard, complication.)*

T

tact—*n.* delicacy, savoir faire, diplomacy, sensitivity, politeness, prudence, polish, subtlety, finesse. *(bluntness, grossness, crudeness, indiscretion, gaucherie, insensitivity, tactlessness.)*

take—*v.* grasp, capture, use, seize, pursue, follow, procure, catch, charm, engage, select, accept, admit, conduct, receive, apprehend, transfer, seige, obtain, employ, assume, captivate, interest, choose. *(reject, surrender, miss, release, repel, drop, abandon, lose.)*

tall—*adj.* lofty, elevated, high, towering, elongated. *(short, low, abbreviated.)*

tame—*adj.* reclaimed, subjugated, gentle, docile,

spiritless, dull, subdued, domesticated, tamed, flat, broken, mild, meek, tedious. *(unreclaimed, wild, unbroken, spirited, ferine, exciting, lively, disobedient, savage, undomesticated, untamed, fierce, animated, interesting, stirring.)*

tangible—*adj.* real, solid, actual, concrete, palpable, manifest, veritable, specific, factual, substantial. *(imaginary, flimsy, elusive, vague, ethereal.)*

task—*n.* function, job, business, drudgery, lesson, assignment, work, labor, operation, undertaking, toil. *(leisure, hobby, rest, relaxation, amusement.)*

taste—*n.* savor, sapidity, choice, perception, discernment, critique, predilection, elegancy, aroma, refinement, gustation, flavor, relish, judgment, nicety, sensibility, zest, delicacy. *(ill-savor, disrelish, indiscrimination, indelicacy, inelegancy, abhorrence, nongustation, insipidity, nonperception, indiscernment, coarseness.)*

tasteful—*adj.* relishing, agreeable, toothsome, elegant, artistic, refined, sapid, savory, tasty, palatable. *(unrelishing, unpalatable, inelegant, vapid, unrefined, vulgar, insipid, unsavory, nauseous, tasteless.)*

teach—*v.* tell, instruct, counsel, educate, enlighten, indoctrinate, edify, train, impart, direct, inform, admonish, inculcate, advise. *(misteach, misinstruct, misguide, learn, mislead, withhold, misdirect, misinform.)*

teacher—*n.* school-master, tutor, pedagogue, educator, school-mistress, scholar, instructor, preceptor, professor, educationist. *(scholar, learner, student, pupil, disciple.)*

tedious—*adj.* tiresome, dilatory, sluggish, dull, prolix, prosaic, monotonous, wearisome, dreary, irksome. *(exciting, charming, delightful, challenging, stirring, amusing, interesting, fascinating.)*

tell—*v.* number, count, utter, state, disclose, betray, explain, promulgate, teach, report, discern, discriminate, decide, narrate, describe, mention, enumerate, recount, recite, verbalize, publish, divulge, acquaint, inform, communicate, rehearse, judge, ascertain. *(suppress, misnarrate, misdeclare, misjudge, conceal, misdescribe, repress, misrecount, miscommunicate, misrecite.)*

temporary—*adj.* immediate, limited, impermanent, momentary, present, partial, transient. *(lasting, complete, perfect, entire, settled, perpetual, confirmed, final, permanent.)*

tenacious—*adj.* firm, cohesive, obstinate, resolute, persistent, iron, mulish, perseverant, willful, obdurate, adamant, stalwart. *(flexible, loose, yielding, wavering, irresolute, lax, tractable.)*

tendency—*n.* proneness, gravitation, scope, disposition, proclivity, bias, inclination, conduciveness, pen-

S
T

chant, course, vergency, drift, aim, predisposition, leaning, attraction. *(aversion, contravention, divergency, divarication, renitency, prevention, termination, hesitancy, disinclination, repulsive, deviation, tangency, opposition, reluctance, neutralization.)*

tender—*v.* proffer, bid, present, submit. *(withdraw, appropriate, withhold, retain, retract.)*

tender—*adj.* frail, susceptible, soft, weak, compassionate, careful, gentle, meek, merciful, sympathetic, pathetic, delicate, impressible, yielding, effeminate, feeble, jealous, affectionate, mild, pitiful. *(sturdy, robust, iron, unmerciful, hard-hearted, liberal, unchary, rough, coarse, unmoving, unimpressive, unimpressed, strong, insensitive, hardy, tough, pitiless, cruel, careless, lavish, ungentle, rude, unsentimental, unfeeling, unimpassioned.)*

tension—*n.* stretch, extension, rigidity, strain, tautness, worry, traction, anxiety, apprehension, stress. *(sag, calm, flexibility, serenity, tranquillity, looseness.)*

terminate—*v.* finish, stop, end, culminate, conclude, complete, expire, lapse, discontinue, cease. *(commence, initiate, pursue, begin, inaugurate, open, start.)*

terrible—*adj.* fearful, formidable, frightful, horrible, intimidating, shocking, awful, dreadful, terrific, tremendous. *(unastounding, unexcruci-*

ating, informidable, unstartling, unsevere.)

terror—*n.* dread, fright, horror, panic, dismay, fear, alarm, consternation. *(fearlessness, confidence, reassurance, security, boldness.)*

test—*n.* trial, proof, standard, touchstone, ordeal, probe, cupel, examination, criterion, experiment, experience. *(misproof, misindication, misjudgment, miscomputation.)*

testimony—*n.* evidence, affirmation, confirmation, affidavit, proof, witness, attestation, corroboration. *(contradiction, confutation, invalidation, denial, refutation, disproof, contravention.)*

theatrical—*adj.* scenic, showy, gesticulatory, meretricious, thespian, dramatic, melodramatic, ceremonious, pompous. *(genuine, unaffected, subdued, plain, retiring, chaste, simple, quiet, mannerless.)*

thick—*adj.* close, turbid, coagulated, dull, foggy, crowded, solid, deep, inarticulate, voluminous, dense, massive, compact, luteous, muddy, misty, vaporous, numerous, bulky, confused. *(fine, sparse, pure, limpid, scanty, slight, laminated, articulate, narrow, distinct, race, thin, strained, percolated, clear, crystalline, incompact, shallow.)*

thicken—*v.* befoul, bemire, increase, amalgamate, intermix, multiply, expand, broaden, intensify, solidify, obscure, becloud, coagulate, commingle, crowd, enlarge, extend, deepen, confuse, obstruct. *(dissipate, attenuate, purify, percolate, defecate, free, brighten, open, diminish, reduce, contract, unravel, loosen, dilute, rarify, refine, clear, strain, clarify, depurate, lighten, filtrate, separate, narrow, liberate, extricate, disentangle.)*

thin—*adj.* slender, attenuated, watery, unsubstantial, translucent, lean, slim, flimsy, diluted, meagre. *(opaque, corpulent, thick, obese, solid, wide, dense.)*

think—*v.* meditate, reflect, conceive, hold, believe, judge, opine, cogitate, reckon, ponder, consider, contemplate, imagine, fancy, regard, deem. *(act rashly, forget, be thoughtless, act unreasonably.)*

thought—*n.* reasoning, supposition, sentiment, conception, opinion, view, conceit, design, intention, care, calculation, provision, reflection, cogitation, meditation, idea, fancy, judgment, purpose, deliberation. *(incogitation, dream, aberration, incogitancy, vacuity, improvidence, inattention, thoughtlessness, hallucination, misconception, carelessness, unreflectiveness, distraction.)*

threatening—*adj.* intimidating, foreboding, imminent, ominous, impending, menacing, unpromising. *(promising, enticing, overpast, auspicious, withdrawn, encouraging, reassuring, passed.)*

thwart—*v.* balk, frustrate, baffle, prevent, circumvent, prevent, outwit, defeat, fail, obstruct, hinder. *(support, abet, help, facilitate, co-operate, aid, magnify, encourage, assist.)*

tide—*n.* course, rush, influx, movement, avalanche, flow, flood, current, inundation, stream. *(arrestation, cessation, subsidence, discontinuance, stagnation, stoppage, motionlessness.)*

tight—*adj.* compact, close, neat, natty, secure, firm, fast, tidy, smart, tense. *(incompact, flowing, large, lax, flexible, loose, open, loose-fitting, untidy, relaxed, insecure.)*

time—*n.* duration, interval, era, opportunity, term, span, cycle, spell, period, season, date, age, occasion, space. *(eternity, indetermination, neverness, indeterminableness, perpetuity, non- duration.)*

timid—*adj.* pusillanimous, shy, diffident, timorous, cowardly, inadventurous, apprehensive, coy, fearful, afraid, faint-hearted. *(confident, courageous, rash, spirited, bold, venturesome, overventuresome, audacious, aggressive.)*

tinsel—*adj.* tawdry, garish, cheap, superficial, trashy, gaudy, meretricious, glittering. *(genuine, conservative, previous, understated, low-key, tasteful.)*

tint—*n.* hue, dye, shade, color, complexion, tinge, stain, tincture. *(decoloration, achromatism, pallor, etiolation, sallowness, cadaverousness, paleness, exsanguineousness, ashenness, bleach-*

S
T

ing, colorlessness, wanness.)

tiresome—*adj.* wearisome, dull, monotonous, tedious, fatiguing, arduous, difficult, troublesome, exhausting, laborious. *(stimulating, restful, restorative, refreshing, exciting, delightful, fascinating.)*

title—*n.* heading, style, name, appellation, address, caption, inscription, denomination, designation, distinction, epithet. *(indistinction, namelessness, non-designation, nondescript, indenomination.)*

together—*adv.* conjointly, concertedly, coincidently, concurrently, unitedly, unanimously, contemporaneously, simultaneously, concomitantly. *(disconnectedly, variously, individually, separately, independently, incoincidently.)*

tolerable—*adj.* bearable, sufferable, permissible, passable, defensible, endurable, supportable, allowable, sufficient. (unbearable, insufferable, impermissible, intolerable, admissible, unendurable, insupportable, unallowable, insufficient.)

tolerate—*v.* permit, warrant, admit, indulge, authorize, sanction, concede, license, sustain, accord. *(forbid, ban, veto, prohibit, disapprove, repel, protest, refuse.)*

tongue—*n.* speech, dialect, articulation, idiom, discourse, language.

tool—*n.* implement, instrument, cat's-paw, appliance, hireling, utensil, machine, dupe.

topic—*n.* theme, subject-matter, thesis, question, subject.

torrid—*adj.* hot, fiery, suffocating, parched, scorching, tropical, fervent, amorous, erotic. *(cool, frigid, temperate, cold, arctic, indifferent.)*

tough—*adj.* stubborn, fibrous, refractory, unmanageable, firm, cohesive, strong, resistant, difficult, hard, tenacious. *(tender, soft, crumby, friable, yielding, fragile.)*

traditional—*adj.* usual, familiar, conventional, ritual, routine, prescriptive, normal, customary. *(unusual, rare, uncommon, unconventional, unfamiliar.)*

tragedy—*n.* calamity, adversity, grief, catastrophe, disaster, affliction, misfortune. *(delight, prosperity, fortune, joy, boon, comedy, merriment.)*

train—*n.* procession, cortege, series, appendage, suite, retinue, course.

train—*v.* rear, habituate, drill, practice, instruct, educate, familiarize with, lead, inure, accustom, exercise, discipline, bend. *(break, disaccustom, miseducate, misguide, disqualify, force, trail, dishabituate.)*

transfer—*v.* transport, sell, transplant, alienate, transmit, exchange, dispatch, convey, remove, assign, make over, give, translate, forward. *(withhold, retain, appropriate, keep, fix, retain.)*

transient—*adj.* fugitive, temporary, evanescent,

momentary, brief, migratory, fleeting, transitory, passing, ephemeral. *(permanent, persistent, enduring, resident, abiding, perpetual, lasting.)*

t r a n s p a r e n t — a d j . crystalline, limpid, obvious, indisputable, porous, self- evident, pellucid, translucent, diaphanous, clear. *(turbid, filmy, intransparent, dubious, thick, opaque, mysterious, questionable, complex.)*

travel—*n.* commuting, journey, progress, transportation, passage, expedition, cruising, tour, voyage. *(halt, cessation, pause, stay, rest.)*

treatise—*n.* essay, pamphlet, brochure, tractate, article, thesis, tract, paper, dissertation, monograph. *(notes, memoranda, ephemera, shedding, jottings, adversaria, effusion.)*

treaty—*n.* agreement, covenant, entente, negotiation, contract, convention, league, alliance. *(non-interference, non-agreement, indecision, non-convention, neutrality, non-alliance.)*

tremble—*v.* quake, tatter, shake, shudder, jar, pulsate, quiver, shiver, vibrate. *(steady, still, stand, compose, calm, settle.)*

tremendous—*adj.* dreadful, fearful, enormous, appalling, terrible, awful. *(unappalling, small, inconsiderable, little, unimposing.)*

tremulous—*adj.* quivery, spasmodic, throbbing, hesitant, palpitating, trembling, fearful, uncertain, flinching. *(motionless, brave, fixed, im-* mobile, heroic, still, phlegmatic.)*

trial—*n.* gauge, temptation, proof, affliction, burden, attempt, criterion, tribulation, scrutiny, verification, test, experiment, trouble, grief, suffering, endeavor, essay, ordeal. *(non-probation, miscalculation, trifle, alleviation, disburdenment, comfort, oversight, delight, non-trial, mismeasurement, misestimate, triviality, relief, refreshment, attempt.)*

trick—*n.* contrivance, guile, wile, cheat, antic, finesse, deception, delusion, subterfuge, legerdemain, artifice, machination, stratagem, fraud, juggle, vagary, slight, imposition. *(exposure, mishap, botch, fumbling, maladroitness, blunder, openhandedness, betrayal, artlessness, bungling, inexpertness, genuineness.)*

tribulation—*n.* ordeal, oppression, adversity, depression, suffering, curse, misery, affliction, pain. *(pleasure, joy, happiness, ease, blessing.)*

trifle—*n.* bagatelle, straw, triviality, joke, bubble, toy, kickshaw, plaything, bauble, trinket, nothing, levity, cipher, gewgaw. *(portent, crisis, weight, importance, seriousness, muddle, treasure, phenomenon, conjuncture, urgency, necessity.)*

triumph—*n.* success, achievement, exultation, conquest, trophy, victory, ovation, coup. *(discomfiture, unsuccess, baffling, fiasco, disappointment, defeat, failure, abortion.)*

S
T

trivial—*adj.* trite, unimportant, nugatory, inconsiderable, paltry, frivolous, trifling, common, useless. *(weighty, original, trifle, novel, important, critical.)*

trouble—*n.* disturbance, perplexity, vexation, calamity, uneasiness, disaster, misfortune, anxiety, sorrow, grief, difficulty, toil, agony, effort, affliction, annoyance, molestation, inconvenience, distress, tribulation, torment, adversity, embarrassment, misery, depression, labor. *(composure, appeasement, assuagement, gratification, blessing, joy, ease, luck, amusement, indifference, inertia, treat, pleasure, indiligence, alleviation, delight, happiness, boon, exultation, gladness, facility, recreation, carelessness, indolence.)*

trouble—*v.* vex, confuse, distress, harass, molest, mortify, irritate, oppress, disturb, agitate, perplex, annoy, tease, grieve. *(calm, appease, soothe, gratify, entertain, refresh, elate, compose, allay, please, delight, recreate, relieve.)*

troublesome—*adj.* irksome, tedious, laborious, importunate, agitated, vexatious, tiresome, difficult, arduous, grievous. *(pleasant, facile, unlaborious, agreeable, untroublesome, easy, amusing, light.)*

true—*adj.* veracious, precise, faithful, loyal, pure, literal, real, veritable, exact, accurate, actual, genuine. *(unreliable, untrustworthy, false, unfaithful, fickle, erroneous, perfidious, adulterated, inaccurate, fictitious, unhistorical, inveracious, faithless, treacherous, spurious, counterfeit.)*

trust—*n.* confidence, belief, faith, expectation, duty, charge, reliance, dependency, hope, credit, commission. *(suspicion, doubt, distrust, uncertainty.)*

trust—*v.* rely, believe, deposit, repose, depend, hope, confide, credit, charge, entrust. *(suspect, doubt, resume, despair, be wary of, distrust, discredit, disbelieve, withdraw.)*

try—*v.* endeavor, aim, test, gauge, fathom, venture, attempt, strive, examine, sound, probe. *(abandon, ignore, misexamine, neglect, misinvestigate, reject, discard.)*

turn—*n.* winding, deflection, deed, alternation, occasion, act, purpose, convenience, gift, character, crisis, cast, manner, fashion, rotation, change, bend, vicissitude, curve, opportunity, time, office, treatment, requirement, talent, tendency, exigence, form, shape, mold, cut, pirouette, revolution, recurrence, alteration. *(fixity, stationariness, uniformity, indeflection, oversight, untimeliness, non-requirement, shapelessness, sameness, stability, immobility, unchangeableness, rectilinearity, continuity, incognizance, independence, malformation.)*

turn—*v.* shape, adapt, reverse, alter, convert, revolve, hinge, deviate, mold, diverge, change, swivel, round, spin, deflect, transform, rotate, metamorphose, depend, incline, decline. *(misadapt, stabilitate, fix, continue, maintain, proceed, misshape, perpetuate, stereotype, arrest.)*

turncoat—*n.* deserter, renegade, trimmer, defector, apostate.

tutor—*n.* governor, teacher, professor, savant, coach, guardian, instructor, preceptor, master. *(pupil, student, learner, ward, tyro, scholar, disciple, neophyte.)*

twine—*v.* wind, entwine, wreath, unite, bend, coil, meander, twist, embrace. *(unwind, disunite, separate, unwreath, disentwine, straighten, untangle, untwist, detach, unravel, continue.)*

twist—*v.* convolve, pervert, wrest, wind, form, unite, braid, contort, complicate, distort, wreath, encircle, weave, insinuate, interpenetrate. *(untwist, verify, reflect, preserve, substantiate, unwind, disengage, disunite, disincorporate, attest, unravel, straighten, rectify, represent, render, express, unwreath, detach, separate, disentangle.)*

type—*n.* stamp, kind, sign, form, pattern, idea, likeness, cast, mark, fashion, species, emblem, model, character, symbol, archetype, image, expression, mold. *(nonclassification, misrepresentation, falsification, deviation, monstrosity, aberration, nondescription, inexpression, misindication, abnormity, caricature.)*

tyranny—*n.* autocracy, czarism, despotism, severity, sterness, coercion, terrorism, savagery, authoritarianism, oppression. *(relaxation, understanding, ease, mercy, humanity, benevolence, democracy.)*

tyro—*n.* amateur, neophyte, beginner, student, novice, apprentice, freshman, novitiate, greenhorn. *(master, pro, veteran, professional, expert.)*

U

ugly—*adj.* hideous, frightful, ill-favored, ill-looking, hateful, homely, repulsive, loathsome, uncouth, unsightly, plain, ungainly, deformed, monstrous. *(fair, shapely, handsome, comely, attractive, seemly, beautiful.)*

ultimate—*adj.* final, conclusive, farthest, maximum, last, extreme, remotest. *(intermediate, preliminary, prior, proximate, initial.)*

umbrage—*n.* displeasure, antipathy, indignation, offense, pique, resentment, animosity, rancor, anger. *(good will, sympathy, amity, cordiality, harmony.)*

unanimous—*adj.* unified, solid, of one mind, agreeing, undivided, harmonious. *(disagreeing, split, discordant, differing.)*

U
Z

unappetizing—*adj.* uninviting, stale, unpalatable, vapid, insipid, unpleasant, unappealing, unsavory. *(agreeable, pleasant, attractive, interesting, appealing.)*

unbelievable—*adj.* inconceivable, improbable, preposterous, incredible, untenable, irrational, suspicious, absurd. *(credible, persuasive, convincing, believable, obvious.)*

uncertain—*adj.* dubious, fitful, ambiguous, variable, problematic, fluctuating, doubtful, questionable, equivocal, indistinct. *(fixed, decided, definite, steady, reliable.)*

unconscious—*adj.* comatose, senseless, lethargic, asleep, numb, unaware, incognizant, narcotized, insensible. *(awake, aware, sensible, conscious, alert, cognizant, knowing.)*

undeniable—*adj.* indisputable, incontrovertible, irrefutable, incontestable, unquestionable. *(doubtful, debatable, deniable, untenable, controversial.)*

undergo—*v.* suffer, sustain, bear, tolerate, experience, endure. *(avoid, reject, miss, forego, refuse.)*

understand—*v.* comprehend, perceive, conceive, recognize, imply, appreciate, apprehend, know, discern, learn, interpret. *(miscomprehend, misinterpret, state, express, misapprehend, ignore, declare, enunciate, neglect.)*

understanding—*n.* discernment, construction, intellect, mind, conception, brains, cognizance, knowledge, interpretation, agreement, intelligence, sense, reason. *(misapprehension, misinterpretation, mindlessness, ignorance, misunderstanding, misconstruction, irrationality, antipathy.)*

unethical—*adj.* dishonorable, shady, improper, corrupt, unscrupulous, immoral, conniving, unfair, unworthy, suspect. *(moral, ethical, upright, scrupulous, worthy, honorable.)*

unfit—*adj.* unsuitable, untimely, ineffective, incompetent, improper, inconsistent. *(suitable, competent, eligible, adequate, equipped, hale, sound.)*

unfortunate—*adj.* ill-fated, wretched, miserable, catastrophic, calamitous, unlucky, unhappy. *(lucky, successful, fortunate, affluent, happy, auspicious.)*

uniform—*adj.* invariable, regular, homogeneous, equal, alike, equable, undiversified, unvarying, even, conformable, consistent, unvaried, symmetrical. *(variable, irregular, incongruous, heterogeneous, diverse, multifarious, polymorphic, varying, eccentric, different, inconformable, inconsistent, unsymmetrical, erratic, multigenous, bizarre.)*

union—*n.* coalition, agreement, conjunction, league, alliance, concord, consolidation, fusion, junction, combination, harmony, concert, connection, confederacy, confederation. *(separation, divorce, discord, secession,* multiplication, division, rupture, disjunction, severance, disagreement, disharmony, disruption, diversification.)

unit—n. item, individual, part, piece, ace. (aggregate, sum, total, mass, collection, composite.)

unite—v. combine, attach, associate, embody, fuse, connect, add, cohere, integrate, converge, join, link, amalgamate, coalesce, merge, conjoin, couple, incorporate with, concatenate, reconcile. (sever, separate, resolve, disintegrate, disrupt, multiply, sunder, segregate, diverge, disjoin, dissociate, disamalgamate, disunite, disconnect, divide, part.)

unity—n. singleness, concord, agreement, indivisibility, identity, oneness, individuality, conjunction, uniformity. (multitude, multiplicity, disjunction, severance, heterogeneity, incongruity, disharmony, divisibility, plurality, complexity, discord, separation, variety, diversity.)

universal—adj. unlimited, total, entire, ecumenical, prevalent, pandemic, worldwide, common, comprehensive. (unique, rare, limited, particular, exclusive.)

unlawful—adj. illegal, unlicensed, illicit, unconstitutional, forbidden, lawless. (licit, authorized, permitted, legal, legitimate.)

unreasonable—adj. silly, exorbitant, preposterous, ridiculous, foolish, extravagant, absurd, immoderate. (sane, rational, sensible, logical, wise, equitable.)

upright—adj. erect, honest, pure, conscientious, fair, ethical, just, equitable, vertical, perpendicular, honorable, principled. (inclined, dishonest, dishonorable, unprincipled, unethical, unconscientious, inverted, corrupt.)

urge—v. push, impel, force, press, solicit, incite, stimulate, good, expedite, dispatch, drive, propel, importune, animate, instigate, hasten, accelerate. (hold, inhibit, restrain, hinder, discourage, obstruct, caution, repress, retain, coerce, cohibit, retard, damp.)

urgent—adj. imperative, grave, importunate, strenuous, serious, indeferrible, pressing, immediate, forcible, momentous, demanding. (insignificant, trivial, frivolous, deferrible, unimportant, trifling.)

use—n. custom, practice, habit, utility, exercise, advantage, service.

use—v. exercise, practice, utilize, habituate, employ, inure, treat, accustom. (suspend, avoid, dishabituate, save, disinure, discard, ignore, disaccustom.)

useful—adj. profitable, serviceable, available, suited, utilitarian, conducive, advantageous, helpful, beneficial, adapted. (unprofitable, obstructive, retardative, antagonistic, ineffectual, combersome, unbeneficial, hostile, inconducive, fruitless, applicable, disadvantageous, preventative, useless, burdensome, unavailable.)

U
Z

usual—*adj.* customary, normal, habitual, accustomed, prevalent, common, ordinary, regular, wonted, general, frequent. *(rare, uncustomary, abnormal, unusual, sparse, uncommon, exceptional, extraordinary, irregular.)*

utmost—*adj.* maximum, greatest, sovereign, remotest, terminal, uppermost, maximal, extreme, major, cardinal, foremost. *(minimal, adjacent, nearest, smallest, minimum, next, neighboring.)*

utter—*v.* issue, express, speak, pronounce, emit, circulate, promulgate, articulate. *(suppress, hush, check, conceal, swallow, recall, repress, stifle.)*

utter—*adj.* perfect, unqualified, thorough, entire, pure, sheer, unmitigated, extreme, complete, absolute, consummate. *(impure, limited, incomplete, imperfect, reasonable.)*

utterly—*adv.* completely, quite, entirely, extremely, totally, wholly, altogether. *(somewhat, rather, tolerably, partly, moderately, passably.)*

V

vacancy—*n.* void, hollowness, gap, blankness, vacuousness, hole, emptiness, depletion. *(plenitude, profusion, fullness, occupancy, completeness.)*

vacant—*adj.* leisure, unencumbered, void, mindless, depleted, empty, exhausted, unemployed, unoccupied, unfilled. *(replenished, employed, occupied, thoughtful, intelligent, full, business, engaged, filled.)*

vague—*adj.* lax, undetermined, intangible, unsettled, pointless, casual, general, indefinite, popular, equivocal, uncertain, ill-defined. *(definite, limited, pointed, specified, strict, specific, determined, scientific, mysterious.)*

vain—*adj.* worthless, unsatisfying, idle, egotistic, unreal, arrogant, conceited, complacent, empty, fruitless, unavailing, ineffectual, showy. *(substantial, worthy, effectual, potent, modest, humble, real, solid, sound, efficient, cogent, unconceited.)*

valid—*adj.* powerful, weighty, substantial, efficient, operative, logical, conclusive, strong, cogent, sound, available, sufficient. *(invalid, unsound, unavailable, insufficient, obsolete, superseded, vague, illogical, weak, powerless, unsubstantial, inefficient, inoperative, effete.)*

value—*v.* compute, estimate, treasure, prize, evaluate, appreciate, rate, esteem, appraise. *(misestimate, disregard, underrate, underestimate, scorn, despise, condemn, vilify, miscompute, disesteem, vilipend, undervalue, cheapen.)*

vanity—*n.* unsubstantiality, conceit, falsity, self-sufficiency, pride, triviality, narcissism, emptiness, unreality, ostentation, worthlessness. *(solidity, reality, modesty, simplicity, humility, diffidence, substance, substantiality, truth, self-distrust, unostentatiousness.)*

vaporize—*v.* mist, fume, spray, atomize, humidify, steam, evaporate, volatilize. *(dry, dehydrate, dehumidify, desiccate.)*

variable—*adj.* mutable, capricious, unsteady, shifting, elastic, changeable, fickle, wavering, inconstant. *(unchangeable, constant, true, staunch, steady, invariable, predictable, firm, unchanging, immutable, fast, unwavering, unalterable.)*

variation—*n.* alteration, diversity, change, exception, transformation, discrepancy, deviation, mutation, departure, abnormity. *(fixity, exemplification, rule, harmony, regularity, law, agreement, continuance, indivergency, uniformity.)*

variety—*n.* diversity, miscellany, multiformity, heterogeneity, abnormity, difference, medley, multiplicity. *(species, specimen, sameness, uniformity, type.)*

various—*adj.* diverse, sundry, multitudinous, manifold, miscellaneous, diversified, different, multiform, several, uncertain. *(same, uniform, similar, equivalent, one, few, identical.)*

vast—*adj.* wild, extensive, huge, spacious, gigantic, boundless, enormous, colossal, far-reaching, substantial, desolate, widespread, wide, measureless, mighty, immense, prodigious. *(close, frequented, cultivated, tilled, bounded, moderate, paltry, narrow, confined, populated, tended, limited, circumscribed.)*

vassal—*n.* serf, underling, slave, hireling, subordinate, puppet, dependent, minion, yes-man. *(overlord, master, boss, ruler.)*

vegetate—*v.* deteriorate, stagnate, languish, waste away, idle, loaf, laze. *(develop, bloom, grow, participate, react, accomplish, bustle, respond.)*

vehement—*adj.* impetuous, urgent, burning, raging, passionate, eager, zealous, violent, ardent, fervent, furious, fervid, forcible. *(feeble, subdued, unimpassioned, cold, gentle, mitigated, timid, mild, inanimate, controlled, passionless, stoical, weak.)*

vengeance—*n.* retaliation, revenge, vindictiveness, retribution, fury. *(pardon, amnesty, remission, oblivion, reprieve, tolerance, forgiveness, condonation, grace, absolution, indulgence.)*

venom—*n.* spite, hate, rancor, malice, hostility, rage, truculence, animosity, resentment, enmity. *(charity, pity, mercy, benevolence, humanitarianism, kindness.)*

venture—*n.* risk, hazard, undertaking, experiment, wager, speculation, chance, stake, luck, gamble. *(caution, calculation, law, surveillance, method, non-speculation, reservation, certainty.)*

U
Z

veracity—*n.* truthfulness, truth, exactness, integrity, accuracy, credibility. *(dishonesty, lying, mendacity, deceitfulness, guile, error.)*

verdict—*n.* judgment, opinion, sentence, evaluation, finding, answer, decision. *(indecision, bias, misconception, indetermination, nondeclaration.)*

verge—*v.* bend, incline, tend, approximate, bear, gravitate, slope, approach. *(deviate, depart, return, retrocede, deflect, decline, revert, recede, back.)*

verify—*v.* confirm, authenticate, identify, test, demonstrate, corroborate, establish, fulfill, substantiate, realize, warrant. *(subvert, falsify, fail, misrepresent, disappoint, refute, disestablish, mistake, misstate, invalidate.)*

versed—*adj.* practiced, acquainted, indoctrinated, familiar, proficient, qualified, skilled, conversant, initiated, clever, accomplished. *(illversed, untaught, inconversant, uninitiated, awkward, unversed, incompetent, unskilled, unpracticed, unfamiliar, ignorant, strange.)*

vex—*v.* irritate, plague, worry, tantalize, trouble, afflict, annoy, tease, provoke, torment, bother, pester, disquiet, harass. *(appease, quiet, mollify, please, soothe, gratify.)*

vibrant—*adj.* pulsing, resonant, ringing, vibrating, throbbing, sonorous, energetic, animated, forceful. *(sluggish,* *weak, inactive, thin, feeble, dull, phlegmatic.)*

vice—*n.* fault, evil, immorality, badness, imperfection, defect, corruption, crime, sin. *(faultlessness, virtue, goodness, attainment, soundness, purity, perfection, immaculateness.)*

vicious—*adj.* faulty, bad, morbid, peccant, profligate, impure, immoral, depraved, corrupt, defective, debased, unruly. *(sound, virtuous, friendly, healthy, pure, perfect.)*

victory—*n.* triumph, success, domination, conquest, ovation. *(defeat, disappointment, miscarriage, downfall, non-success, failure, frustration, abortion.)*

view—*v.* examine, explore, consider, reconnoitre, regard, judge, glimpse, behold, inspect, survey, contemplate, observe, estimate. *(overlook, misconsider, misobserve, misjudge, ignore, disregard, misinspect, misestimate.)*

view—*n.* vision, examination, light, judgment, scene, apprehension, aim, conception, object, intention, sight, design, scrutiny, survey, estimate, inspection, representation, sentiment, opinion, purpose, end. *(occultation, darkness, deception, delusion, misrepresentation, aimlessness, error, non-intention, blindness, obscuration, misexamination, misjudgment, misconception.)*

vile—*adj.* worthless, low, mean, hateful, impure, abandoned, cheap, sinful, ignoble, villainous, base, wretched, profligate, valueless, despicable, bad, vicious, abject, sordid, wicked, degraded. *(rare, valuable, exalted, honorable, venerable, virtuous, costly, precious, high, noble, lofty.)*

villain—*n.* wretch, scoundrel, reprobate, ruffian. *(prince, idol, hero.)*

villainous—*adj.* knavish, infamous, detestable, base, depraved. *(heroic, moral, humane, virtuous, saintly, righteous.)*

vindicate—*v.* maintain, clear, defend, substantiate, establish, exonerate, assert, uphold, support, claim, justify. *(abandon, forego, disestablish, nullify, subvert, vitiate, pardon, waive, surrender, disprove, neutralize, destroy, annul.)*

violate—*v.* injure, disturb, rape, debauch, infringe, transgress, desecrate, disobey, ravish, abuse, hurt, outrage, break, profane. *(foster, regard, cherish, obey, esteem, respect, observe, preserve, protect.)*

violence—*n.* impetuosity, rape, rage, injustice, infringement, oppression, truculence, force, destructiveness, outrage, profanation, fury, fierceness. *(mildness, feebleness, respect, self-control, obedience, conservation, humaneness, lenity, protection, self-restraint, gentleness, forbearance, observance, preservation.)*

virtue—*n.* capacity, force, excellence, morality, uprightness, chastity, rectitude, power, strength, ef-

ficacy, value, goodness, purity, salubrity, honor. *(incapacity, inefficacy, corruption, immorality, dishonor, unchastity, malignancy, weakness, inability, badness, vice, impurity, virulence.)*

visible—*adj.* apparent, plain, conspicuous, discernible, clear, manifest, evident, detectable, perceptible, obvious, observable, palpable, distinguishable. *(non-apparent, hidden, impalpable, invisible, concealed, withdrawn, indistinguishable, imperceptible, inconspicuous, microscopic, unobservable, eclipsed, indiscernible.)*

visionary—*adj.* dreamy, baseless, imaginary, fabulous, idealized, romantic, fanciful, chimerical, shadowy, unreal. *(real, sound, veritable, palpable, sober, actual, truthful, substantial, unromantic.)*

vital—*adj.* palpable, animate, viable, functioning, essential, crucial, critical, decisive, fundamental, mortal. *(dead, weak, inanimate, irrelevant, phlegmatic, superficial.)*

vivid—*adj.* brilliant, resplendent, radiant, clear, animated, lively, striking, sunny, scintillant, dynamic, bright, luminous, lustrous, graphic, stirring, glowing. *(opaque, obscure, dim, lurid, non-reflecting, dusky, nebulous, wan, colorless, dull, non-luminous, rayless, somber, cloudy, pale, nondescript.)*

volume—*n.* body, dimensions, work, capacity, compass, magnitude, quantity, ag-

U
Z

gregate, size, bulk, book, extent. *(tenuity, diminutiveness, minuteness, smallness.)*

voluntary—*adj.* spontaneous, intentional, discretional, willing, deliberate, free, optional, unconstrained, chosen. *(coercive, forced, involuntary, compelled, compulsory, necessitated.)*

volunteer—*v.* proffer, originate, provide, offer, tend. *(suppress, withhold, withdraw, refuse.)*

voluptuous—*adj.* luxurious, licentious, highly pleasant, sensuous, hedonistic, sensual, self-indulgent. *(abstinent, sober, ascetic, monkish,* unsensual, self-denying.)

vulgar—*adj.* general, ordinary, vernacular, uncultivated, low, coarse, uncouth, underbred, popular, loose, public, plebian, unrefined, mean. *(scientific, restricted, accurate, select, cultivated, polite, stylish, elegant, aristocratic, strict, philosophical, technical, patrician, choice, refined, high-bred.)*

vulnerable—*adj.* unguarded, insecure, unprotected, weak, destructible, delicate, defenseless, easily wounded. *(protected, impervious, invincible, guarded.)*

W

wages—*n.* compensation, salary, payment, allowance, remuneration, stipend, hire. *(douceur, bonus, gift, premium, grace, gratuity.)*

wakeful—*adj.* vigilant, restless, alert, cautious, wary, awake. *(dozing, heedless, drowsy, somnolent, asleep.)*

wander—*v.* range, rove, roam, stray, err, straggle, navigate, travel, cruise, ramble, stroll, expatitate, deviate, depart, swerve, saunter, circumnavigate. *(stop, bivouac, lie, alight, moor, repose, remain, pause, settle, rest, perch, halt, anchor.)*

want—*n.* lack, insufficiency, shortage, neglect, absence, hunger, non-production, omission, deficiency, failure, shortness, scantiness. *(sufficiency, abundance, allowance, adequacy,* affluence, supply, provision, production, supplement.)

wanton—*adj.* roving, playful, loose, uncurbed, unrestrained, licentious, inconsiderate, heedless, gratuitous, malicious, wandering, sportive, frolicsome, unbridled, reckless, irregular, dissolute. *(unroving, unplayful, joyless, demure, discreet, self-controlled, formal, purposed, staid, cold-blooded, puritanical, determined, stationary, unsportive, unfrolicsome, thoughtful, sedate, well-regulated, austere, deliberate.)*

warlike—*n.* aggressive, militant, hostile, bellicose, belligerent, pugnacious, strategic. *(nonviolent, friendly, conciliatory, pacifistic, accommodating, peaceful.)*

warm—*adj.* thermal, irascible, ardent, fervid, glowing, zealous, excited, animated, tepid, genial, blood-warm. *(cold, starved, cool, passionless, chilly, frigid, unexcited, indifferent.)*

warmth—*n.* glow, zeal, excitement, earnestness, animation, vehemence, sincerity, irascibility, life, ardor, affability, emotion, fervor, heat, intensity, cordiality, eagerness, passion, geniality. *(frost, iciness, chill, calmness, indifference, insensitiveness, slowness, insincerity, good-temper, frigidity, congelation, coldness, coolness, torpidity, apathy, ungeniality, death, passionlessness.)*

waste—*v.* destroy, impair, pine, squander, throw away, lavish, attenuate, shrivel, wane, trifle, ruin, devastate, consume, decay, dissipate, diminish, desolate, dwindle, wither. *(repair, preserve, stint, protect, economize, hoard, augment, accumulate, flourish, multiply, develop, restore, conserve, perpetuate, husband, utilize, treasure, enrich, luxuriate.)*

watchful—*adj.* expectant, heedful, observant, circumspect, cautious, alert, vigilant, wakeful, careful, attentive, wary. *(invigilant, slumbrous, heedless, inobservant, uncircumspect, incautious, reckless, distracted, unwatchful, unwakeful, drowsy, careless, inattentive, unwary.)*

weak—*adj.* infirm, powerless, fragile, inadhesive, frail, tender, flabby, wishy-washy, watery, spirit-

less, injudicious, undecided, impressible, ductile, malleable, inconclusive, pointless, enervated, feeble, limp, debile, incompact, pliant, soft, vulnerable, flimsy, foolish, destructible, diluted, inefficient, unsound, unconfirmed, wavering, easy, unconvincing, vapid. *(vigorous, muscular, powerful, stout, sturdy, adhesive, fibrous, indestructible, intoxicating, spirited, wise, judicious, valid, determined, stubborn, inexorable, irresistible, telling, robust, strong, energetic, nervous, tough, lusty, compact, resistant, hard, potent, efficient, animated, sound, cogent, decided, unwavering, unyielding, conclusive, forcible.)*

weaken—*v.* enfeeble, dilute, paralyze, sap, emasculate, debilitate, enervate, impair, attenuate. *(invigorate, corroborate, develop, confirm, strengthen, empower.)*

wealth—*n.* riches, lucre, affluence, opulence, assets, influence, mammon, plenty, abundance. *(poverty, impecuniosity, destitution, indigence, scarcity.)*

wear—*v.* bear, sport, don, impair, channel, excavate, rub, diminish, manifest, carry, groove, exhibit, consume, waste, hollow. *(abandon, renovate, increase, augment, expand, doff, repair, renew, swell.)*

weary—*adj.* tired, worn, faint, debilitated, toil-worn, fatigued, dispirited, exhausted, jaded, spent. *(vigorous, renovated, bouncy,*

U
Z

hearty, fresh, recruited.)

weather—*v.* withstand, surmount, survive, resist, bear, endure, suffer. *(collapse, fail, succumb, fall.)*

weave—*v.* braid, intermix, complicate, spin, intersect, loop, interlace, intertwine, plait. *(untwist, disentangle, simplify, dissect, segregate, unravel, disunite, extricate, enucleate.)*

weight—*n.* ponderosity, pressure, importance, influence, tonnage, consequence, impressiveness, gravity, heaviness, burden, power, efficacy, moment. *(levity, alleviation, insignificance, inefficacy, triviality, unimportance, worthlessness, lightness, portableness, weakness, unimpressiveness.)*

weird—*adj.* mysterious, mystic, strange, odd, uncanny, bizarre, queer. *(normal, common, orthodox, familiar, mundane, natural.)*

well—*adj.* hale, vigorous, sound, hearty, robust, healthy, strong, chipper. *(sick, ill, weak.)*

white—*adj.* pure, unblemished, stainless, clear, snowy, colorless, alabaster, unspotted, innocent. *(impure, ebony, black, inky.)*

whole—*adj.* entire, well, sound, perfect, undiminished, undivided, gross, total, complete, healthy, unimpaired, integral. *(imperfect, unsound, impaired, fractional, sectional, lacking, partial, incomplete, sick, diminished, divided.)*

wholesome—*adj.* salubrious, salutiferous, nutritious, healthful, invigorating, healing, salutary, beneficial. *(unhealthful, insalutary, unwholesome, detrimental, harmful, morbific, unhealthy, insalubrious, prejudicial, deleterious.)*

wicked—*adj.* bad, sinful, iniquitous, unjust, irreligious, ungodly, sinful, atrocious, dark, unhallowed, evil, naughty, flagitious, corrupt, black, godless, immoral, criminal, unrighteous, profane, vicious, foul, nefarious, heinous, abandoned. *(virtuous, godly, religious, honest, honorable, good, sinless, immaculate, ethical, stainless, just, moral, upright, pure, incorrupt, spotless.)*

wide—*adj.* ample, spacious, remote, extended, broad, vast, immense, widespread. *(restricted, scant, small, narrow, limited.)*

wild—*adj.* undomesticated, uninhabited, savage, unrefined, ferocious, violent, loose, turbulent, inordinate, chimerical, incoherent, distracted, barbaric, haggard, untamed, uncultivated, uncivilized, rude, untrained, ferine, disorderly, ungoverned, disorderly, visionary, raving. *(domesticated, inhabited, populous, polite, reclaimed, tame, mild, regulated, rational, trim, coherent, sober, calm, tranquil, cultivated, frequented, civilized, refined, gentle, subdued, orderly, collected, sane, sensible.)*

willful—*adj.* deliberate, intentional, premeditated, wayward, stubborn, headstrong, contemplated, purposed, designed, preconcerted, refractory, self-willed. *(accidental, unpremeditated, obedient, manageable, considerate, amenable, thoughtful, undersigned, unintentional, docile, obdurate, deferential.)*

wisdom—*n.* erudition, enlightenment, information, judgment, prudence, intelligence, light, knowledge, learning, attainment, discernment, sagacity. *(illiterateness, indiscernment, folly, darkness, smattering, nonsense, ignorance, injudiciousness, imprudence, empiricism, inacquaintance, absurdity.)*

wit—*n.* intellect, reason, humor, imagination, levity, mind, sense, understanding, ingenuity. *(senselessness, dullness, stupidity, doltishness, vapidity, folly, mindlessness, irrationality, stolidity, inanity, platitude.)*

withdraw—*v.* go, retire, leave, retreat, depart, disappear, abdicate. *(arrive, appear, propose, reiterate, come, repeat.)*

withhold—*v.* keep, stay, restrain, detain, suppress, retain, inhibit, refuse, forbear. *(afford, provide, permit, incite, lavish, promote, grant, furnish, allow, encourage, concede.)*

withstand—*v.* resist, thwart, endure, face, oppose, confront. *(surrender, falter, acquiesce, support, aid, back, yield, submit, encourage, abet.)*

witness—*n.* testimony, corroboration, corroborator, spectator, testifier, beholder, attestation, evidence, cognizance, eye-witness, auditor, voucher. *(incognizance, ignorance, ignoramus, alien, illiterate, stranger, invalidation, refutation.)*

woeful—*adj.* unfortunate, grievous, distressing, disastrous, tragic, mournful, doleful, anguished, miserable, pitiful, inadequate, worthless. *(fortunate, auspicious, beneficial, carefree, contented, generous, prosperous, enviable, glad.)*

wonder—*n.* miracle, surprise, awe, puzzlement, fascination, phenomenon, admiration, marvel, sign, surprise, prodigy. *(calm, apathy, anticipation, triviality, composure, expectation, indifference.)*

wonderful—*adj.* miraculous, astonishing, wondrous, fabulous, spectacular, awe-inspiring, unusual, startling, portentous, prodigious, strange, admirable, amazing. *(banal, normal, wonted, nondescript, every-day, regular, customary, expected, anticipated, current, natural, usual, expected.)*

wooly—*adj.* fuzzy, blurred, vague, hazy, foggy, clouded, murky, unfocused. *(clear, definite, well-defined, sharp.)*

word—*n.* message, report, news, promise, engagement, signal, warrant, declaration, term. *(idea, conception).*

wordy—*adj.* verbose, prolix, longwinded, talkative, garrulous, inflated, redundant, periphrastic, rambling. *(con-*

U
Z

cise, succinct, brief, terse, trenchant, pithy.)

work—*n.* travail, labor, toil, drudgery, product, result, issue, composition, operation, profession, business, chore, undertaking, project, feat, achievement. *(play, leisure, rest, non-performance, idleness, sloth, stall, collapse, non-production, fruitlessness.)*

worldly—*adj.* earthly, secular, profane, materialistic, mundane, temporal, carnal, shrewd, practical, urbane, experienced. *(unearthly, spiritual, metaphysical, heavenly, simple, naive, artless.)*

worn—*adj.* frayed, damaged, tattered, used, dingy, exhausted, threadbare. *(undamaged, fresh, unused, new.)*

worry—*v.* fret, brood, pester, harass, molest, annoy, tease, torment, importune, harry, plague, disquiet, vex. *(comfort, pacify, calm, soothe, gratify, please, quiet, amuse, reassure.)*

worsen—*v.* deteriorate, spoil, aggravate, decay, degenerate, contaminate. *(better, brighten, recover, improve, mend.)*

worship—*v.* revere, glorify, honor, respect, idolize, cherish, treasure, admire, venerate. *(dishonor, mock, blaspheme, scoff at, dislike, despise, hate.)*

worth—*n.* estimation, holdings, rate, value, merit, price, expense, importance, significance, estate, property. *(insignificance, worth-*

lessness, inappreciableness, paltriness, triviality, demerit, uselessness.)

worthless—*adj.* purposeless, unproductive, useless, valueless, meaningless, empty, trivial, reprobate, vile, trashy. *(important, worthy, essential, precious, virtuous, noble, advantageous, honorable, rare, costly, excellent, useful, lucrative.)*

wrap—*v.* envelop, enfold, cover, package, wind, conceal, roll up, bundle. *(unfurl, open, unwrap, unfold.)*

wrath—*n.* rage, anger, fury, indignation, resentment, choler, exasperation, irritation, vexation. *(pleasure, forbearance, delight, gratification, equanimity.)*

wreck—*v.* destroy, ruin, spoil, shatter, devastate, ravage, demolish, blast, smash. *(preserve, guard, secure, conserve, protect.)*

wrench—*v.* contort, jerk, twist, strain, blow, wring, sprain.

wretched—*adj.* dejected, depressed, mournful, forlorn, woeful, unfortunate, worthless, inferior, hopeless, pitiful. *(happy, glad, euphoric, affluent, noble, virtuous, comfortable, worthy, admirable.)*

wrinkle—*v.* crease, crumple, purse, furrow, fold, crinkle. *(flatten, smooth, straighten, iron, level.)*

wrong—*adj.* mistaken, faulty, untrue, inaccurate, inequitable, improper, inethical, unjust, unsuitable, erroneous, awkward, imperfect. *(perfect, correct, suitable, good, stan-*

dard, ethical, fitting, right, fair, moral, beneficial, straight, appropriate.)

wry—adj. distorted, askew, crooked, twisted, contorted, deformed, awry. (straight, unbent, normal, supple, limber.)

Y Z

yearn—v. crave, want, desire, wish, hunger for, long, covet, thirst for. (revolt, shudder, recoil, loathe.)

yet—adv. still, besides, hitherto, ultimately, at last, now, thus far, however, eventually, at last.

yield—v. supply, furnish, render, pay, submit, consent, acquiesce, grant, accede, assent, comply, bear, afford, succumb, give in, engender, resign, relinquish, produce. (oppose, refute, resist, dissent, protest, retain, disallow, withhold, deny, claim, assert, vindicate, recalcitrate, strive, struggle.)

yielding—adj. conceding, producing, submissive, unresisting, soft, surrendering, acquiescent, timid, crouching, spongy. (nonproductive, waste, fallow, stiff, defiant, firm, unyielding, resisting, fierce, unbending.)

yoke—v. connect, link, hitch, splice, mate, enslave, couple, subjugate, unite. (release, dissever, divorce, liberate, enfranchise, manumit.)

yonder—adj. yon, distant, faraway, thither, remote, faroff. (near, close, nearby.)

youth—n. minor, adolescence, juvenility, childhood, beginnings, start, youngster, kid, stripling.

youthful—adj. childlike, adolescent, juvenile, fresh, puerile, immature, maiden, early, unripe, virginal. (elderly, aged, mature, antiquated, olden, time-worn, patriarchal, decrepit, ancient, decayed.)

zeal—n. zest, drive, enthusiasm, ardor, interest, ambition, earnestness, passion, heartiness, energy. (detachment, indifference, apathy, coolness, carelessness, aimlessness, sluggishness, incordiality.)

zenith—n. acme, crest, culmination, pinnacle, top, summit, maximum, climax, peak, height. (bottom, nadir, depths, minimum, lowest point.)

zest—n. enjoyment, relish, gusto, eagerness, delight, exhilaration, life, appetizer, flavor, sharpener, satisfaction. (apathy, boredom, distaste, detriment, ennui.)

zip—n. energy, vitality, animation, dash, zing, sparkle, punch, drive. (sloth, lethargy, apathy, laziness, debility.)

zoom—v. climb, soar, rise, ascend, escalate, mount. spiral, grow, increase. (drop descend, plummet, decrease fall.)

U
Z

NOTES

SPECIAL OFFER
REFERENCE LIBRARY

THE WEBSTER'S FRENCH-ENGLISH ENGLISH-FRENCH DICTIONARY — $5.95

THE WEBSTER'S DICTIONARY — $5.95

THE WEBSTER'S SPANISH-ENGLISH ENGLISH-SPANISH DICTIONARY — $5.95

THE WEBSTER'S CONCISE DICTIONARY — $7.95

ROGET'S THESAURUS — $5.95

THE WEBSTER'S CROSSWORD PUZZLE DICTIONARY — $5.95

Please send me the following books:

_____ **CONCISE DICTIONARY**
_____ **ROGET THESAURUS**
_____ **FRENCH/ENGLISH DICTIONARY**
_____ **SPANISH/ENGLISH DICTIONARY**
_____ **WEBSTER'S DICTIONARY**
_____ **CROSSWORD PUZZLE DICTIONARY**

Plus $1.50 for postage & handling for each book.

Name _____

Address _____

City _____ State _____ Zip _____

I have enclosed $ _____ for _____ books which includes all postage & handling costs. (No C.O.D.)

Send to: P.S.I. & Associates, Inc.
13322 S.W. 128th Street
Miami, Florida 33186

NOTES